Human Rights Watch defends the rights of people worldwide.

We scrupulously investigate abuses, expose facts widely, and pressure those with power to respect rights and secure justice.

Human Rights Watch is an independent, international organization that works as part of a vibrant movement to uphold human dignity and advance the cause of human rights for all.

Human Rights Watch began in 1978 with the founding of its Europe and Central Asia division (then known as Helsinki Watch). Today it also includes divisions covering Africa, the Americas, Asia, Europe and Central Asia, the Middle East and North Africa, and the United States. There are thematic divisions or programs on arms; business and human rights; children's rights; crisis and conflict; disability rights; the environment and human rights; international justice; lesbian, gay, bisexual, and transgender rights; refugee rights; and women's rights.

The organization maintains offices in Amman, Amsterdam, Beirut, Berlin, Bishkek, Brussels, Chicago, Geneva, Goma, Hong Kong, Johannesburg, Kiev, Kinshasa, London, Los Angeles, Miami, Moscow, Nairobi, New York, Paris, San Francisco, São Paulo, Seoul, Silicon Valley, Stockholm, Sydney, Tokyo, Toronto, Tunis, Washington DC, and Zurich, and field presences in more than 50 other locations globally.

Human Rights Watch is an independent, nongovernmental organization, supported by contributions from private individuals and foundations worldwide. It accepts no government funds, directly or indirectly.

Table of Contents

Biden's Challenge:
Redeeming a US Role for Human Rights

By Kenneth Roth, *Executive Director*

After four years of a president who was indifferent and often hostile to human rights, the November 2020 election of Joe Biden to the presidency of the United States provides an opportunity for a fundamental change of course.

Donald Trump was a disaster for human rights. At home, he flouted legal obligations that allow people fearing for their lives to seek refuge, ripped migrant children from their parents, empowered white supremacists, acted to undermine the democratic process, and fomented hatred against racial and religious minorities. He also closed his eyes to systemic racism in policing, removed legal protections for lesbian, gay, bisexual, and transgender (LGBT) people, revoked environmental protections for clean air and water, and sought to undermine the right to health, especially for sexual and reproductive health and older people. Abroad, he cozied up to one friendly autocrat after another at the expense of their abused populations, promoted the sale of weapons to governments implicated in war crimes, and attacked or withdrew from key international initiatives to defend human rights, promote international justice, advance public health, and forestall climate change.

This destructive combination eroded the credibility of the US government even when it did speak out against abuses. Condemnations of Venezuela, Cuba, or Iran rang hollow when parallel praise was bestowed on Russia, Egypt, Saudi Arabia, or Israel. Support for religious freedom abroad was undermined by Islamophobic policy at home. The Trump administration did impose targeted sanctions and other punishments on the Chinese government and corporate entities for their involvement in human rights violations, but its own weak record on human rights, its evident mixed motives in criticizing Beijing, and Trump's scapegoating of China for his own pandemic failings left these interventions anything but principled, making working with allies difficult.

Yet it would be naive to treat a Biden presidency as a panacea. In recent decades, the arrival of each new White House resident has brought wild oscillations in US human rights policy. George W. Bush's "global war on terror," with its systematic torture and Guantanamo detentions without charge, was an earlier nadir. Barack Obama rejected important parts of it, although he maintained and even expanded such elements as unlawful drone attacks, intrusive surveillance, and arms sales to unsavory autocrats. Policy reversals, both at home and abroad, have become regular features in Washington.

Global leaders seeking to uphold human rights understandably ask whether they can rely on the US government. Even if Biden substantially improves the US record, the deep political divisions in the United States mean there is little to prevent the election of another US president with Trump's disdain for human rights in four or eight years.

Yet that reality should be cause for resolve rather than despair. As the Trump administration largely abandoned the protection of human rights abroad, other governments stepped forward. Rather than surrender, they reinforced the ramparts. So even as powerful actors such as China, Russia, and Egypt sought to undermine the global human rights system, a series of broad coalitions came to its defense. Those coalitions included not only a range of Western countries but also a group of Latin American democracies and a growing number of Muslim-majority states.

As Biden assumes office, the US government should seek to join, not supplant, these collective efforts. US leadership can still be significant, but it should not substitute for or compromise the initiative shown by many others. The past four years have demonstrated that Washington is an important but not indispensable member of this broader team defending rights. Biden's aim in his foreign policy should be to lead not from in front or behind but together with this larger group of rights promoters.

For the benefit of people in the United States, and to be most effective in advancing human rights around the world, Biden should also set a positive example by strengthening the US government's commitment to human rights at home. As with US foreign policy, that commitment has swung wildly from administration to administration. This fluctuation has been most pronounced on reproductive freedom, the rights of LGBT people, the rights of asylum seekers and immigrants, voting rights, racial and economic inequities, the right to health, and the rights implicated by climate change. The challenge for Biden will be not simply to reverse the damage to human rights done by his predecessor, but also to make it more difficult for future presidents to retreat yet again.

One step would be to reinforce a commitment to human rights by legislation, which the narrow Democratic majorities in both Houses of Congress may make possible. Ideally, Biden could press for ratification of core human rights treaties that the US government has long neglected, but finding the necessary two-thirds support in the Senate will be difficult. Biden should certainly allow justice to pursue its course with respect to Trump to show that the president is not above the law, resisting the "look forward, not back" rationale that Obama used to ignore torture under Bush. Like some of his predecessors, Biden can make short-term improvements by executive action, but as in the past, that is vulnerable to being undone by a future US president with less regard for human rights.

Ultimately, the goal for Biden should be to change the narrative on human rights in a more fundamental way – on both US domestic and foreign policy. A simple return to the ways of Obama – a so-called third Obama term – will not be enough. The large protests for racial justice across the United States in 2020, and the hardships imposed by the Covid-19 pandemic, could provide a boost for such a reframing.

For inspiration, Biden could look to Jimmy Carter, who first introduced human rights as an element of US foreign policy. At the time, that was seen as a radical move, but it has endured through the decades. Every US president since Carter has sometimes downplayed human rights in favor of other priorities – indeed, Carter did as well – but none could entirely repudiate them.

Biden's task is to find a way, through policy and practice, to make upholding human rights more central to US government conduct in a way that has a better chance of surviving the radical changes in policy that have become a fixture of the US political landscape. That will require reshaping the public's understanding by speaking about issues at home more regularly in terms of rights while announcing human rights principles to guide US conduct abroad, and then adhering to them even when it is difficult.

A More Global Defense of Rights

Although the US government has never been a consistent global backer of human rights, it can be a powerful supporter. That the Trump administration overwhelmingly abandoned the promotion of human rights was disappointing but turned out also to be galvanizing. Fortunately, many global leaders recognized that the defense of human rights was too important to forsake just because Trump had done so. A series of governments, some new to the cause, typically acting in coalition, repeatedly mounted a strong and often effective defense of rights. The number of nations involved made the defense more robust, because it was more global and less dependent on Washington.

Latin America illustrates this trend. Traditionally, governments there rarely critiqued each other's human rights record, in part because that was seen as something Washington did. But to address the cycle of repression, corruption, and economic devastation under Nicolás Maduro in Venezuela, 11 Latin American democracies plus Canada came together in 2017 as the Lima Group. The move was unprecedented. Maduro would probably have liked nothing better than to have Trump as the principal critic of his misrule, enabling the Venezuelan government to pass off criticism as "Yankee imperialism," but the Lima Group acted independently of the United States. It made clear that its concerns involved principle, not politics.

The Lima Group ramped up pressure on Maduro. It persuaded the UN Human Rights Council to launch a formal investigation of his repression. Six Lima Group members asked the International Criminal Court prosecutor to investigate Venezuela's alleged crimes against humanity – the first such request from a country's neighbors. Maduro is still continuing his repressive rule, but he is far more isolated than he would have been had the US government continued its traditional, largely unilateral leadership on human rights in Venezuela. Some Lima Group members have now extended their focus to Nicaragua as well, persuading the UN Human Rights Council to authorize the UN high commissioner for human rights to report on repression under President Daniel Ortega.

Another striking example of this broader defense of human rights involved the Organization of Islamic Cooperation (OIC), a group of 56 mainly Muslim-majority states. In the past, the OIC rarely used the United Nations to condemn human rights abuses other than those committed by Israel, but that began to change following the Myanmar military's 2017 campaign of murder, rape, and arson against Rohingya Muslims in Myanmar's Rakhine State, which sent 730,000 Rohingya fleeing to neighboring Bangladesh.

In 2018, the OIC joined with the European Union to lead an initiative at the Human Rights Council to create the Independent Investigative Mechanism for Myanmar, to collect evidence for possible prosecution. In 2019, Gambia, an OIC member, brought a case before the International Court of Justice alleging violations of the Genocide Convention by Myanmar against the Rohingya – the first of its kind by a third-party state. As a provisional measure, the court ordered Myanmar to protect from genocide the 600,000 Rohingya who remain in Rakhine State. In addition, the International Criminal Court is investigating Myanmar officials for atrocities against the Rohingya during their forced deportation to Bangladesh.

Some of the global defense of human rights took place largely outside international institutions. The move that may have saved the most lives involved Syria's northwestern Idlib province, where three million civilians, half of them displaced from elsewhere in Syria, had been living under repeated aerial bombardment by Russian and Syrian aircraft. Often these attacks targeted hospitals, schools, markets, and residential areas. The German, French, and Turkish governments (the latter despite worsening repression at home under President Recep Tayyip Erdogan) put sufficient pressure on Russian President Vladimir Putin to secure a ceasefire ending these attacks beginning in March 2020 and largely continuing throughout the year.

With the Russian and Chinese governments having vetoed an effort at the UN Security Council to refer atrocities in Syria to the International Criminal Court, other governments have begun to fill the breach. Circumventing the Security Council, Liechtenstein and Qatar in December 2016 led a successful effort at the UN General Assembly to establish the International, Impartial and Independent Mechanism for Syria to collect evidence of war crimes and other atrocities for prosecution – the first such mechanism ever created. Several European governments – foremost Germany – have begun investigations and prosecutions in their own national courts, based on the legal principle of universal jurisdiction. The Netherlands has started a process to address systematic torture by the Syrian government, which could lead to a case before the International Court of Justice.

European governments have taken the lead on other important initiatives as well. As the increasingly authoritarian governments in Hungary and Poland undermined the checks and balances on executive power that are essential to democracy, the European Union pressed to condition its generous subsidies to those governments on their respect for the rule of law, although an end-of-year compromise ended up making this tool less powerful than many had hoped. When Belarusian President Aliaksandr Lukashenka made the highly controversial claim that he had won the August 2020 elections, and forces under his command proceeded to detain and torture protesters, the EU imposed targeted sanctions on 88 individuals whom it deemed responsible for the repression, including Lukashenka. Following the earlier US example, the EU also adopted a new regime of targeted sanctions involving travel bans and asset freezes for individuals and entities responsible for serious human rights abuses worldwide. The United Kingdom and Canada have set up similar regimes, and Australia seems poised to adopt one soon.

At the UN Human Rights Council, a core group consisting of the Netherlands, Belgium, Canada, Ireland, and Luxembourg secured and then strengthened an inquiry into war crimes in Yemen. Finland led a similar initiative for war crimes in Libya, as Iceland initially did for the thousands of summary executions of drug suspects instigated by Philippines President Rodrigo Duterte. Australia, Austria, Belgium, France, Germany, and the Netherlands took the lead in securing an investigation of repression in Eritrea. Australia and then Denmark orchestrated condemnatory statements about Saudi repression.

When Trump reinstated and then dramatically expanded the "global gag rule" – a policy that prohibits foreign organizations receiving US assistance from advocating or providing information, referrals, or services for legal abortion in their own countries – the Netherlands, Belgium, Denmark, and Sweden launched a global initiative in defense of sexual and reproductive health and rights, called SheDecides. African governments, led by South Africa, demanded an inquiry into systemic racism and police violence around the world, building a cross-regional coalition to stand up to the US government following the May 2020 police murder of George Floyd in Minneapolis. Costa Rica, Switzerland, and Germany led joint statements to repudiate Trump's efforts to undermine the independence of the Hague-based International Criminal Court. Belgium secured a similar statement from many UN Security Council members. And a broad collection of governments – notably India and South Africa – pressed for greater access to vaccines and treatment for Covid-19.

This more global defense of human rights did not always prevail. Abusive governments remain a potent threat. But the greater breadth of the defense intensified the pressure on leaders who would flout the rights of their people. That mounting pressure is an important bulwark against today's autocratic tendencies.

A renewed outpouring of popular support for human rights bolstered this governmental defense. In country after country, often at great risk, people took to the streets in large numbers to press abusive and corrupt governments to be more democratic and accountable. The causes varied, but the aspirations had remarkable commonality. In Egypt, protests were sparked by social-media posts from a former military contractor detailing outrageous corruption. In Thailand, student-led protests arose because a military-backed government resisted calls for democratic reform. In Belarus, demonstrations, often led by women, were in response to the widespread belief that President Lukashenka had stolen an election – and to his security forces' brutal crackdown on protesters. In Poland, protests challenged the virtual elimination of access to abortion imposed by a constitutional court whose membership had been manipulated by the ruling Law and Justice Party.

Throughout the United States, people took to the streets to demand an end to police brutality and systemic racism. In Russia, protesters objected to constitutional reforms that weakened human rights and allowed Putin to extend his term in office; protracted protests also erupted in Russia's far east in response to the Kremlin's removal of a popular governor. In Hong Kong, the trigger for protests was Beijing's threat to permit extradition to mainland China without legislative or public oversight – protests that proved intolerable to President Xi Jinping because they demonstrated that when people on Chinese territory are free to express themselves, they reject the dictatorship of the Chinese Communist Party. The global defense of human rights was greatly strengthened when these popular movements joined an expanding array of governmental actors.

7

China's Worsening Repression

The most powerful target of this increasingly global defense of human rights was China. Repression in China has deepened severely in recent years under Xi Jinping, with the detention of more than one million Uyghur and other Turkic Muslims in Xinjiang to pressure them to abandon Islam and their culture, the crushing of Hong Kong's freedoms, ongoing repression in Tibet and Inner Mongolia, and the crackdown on independent voices throughout the country. This has been the darkest period for human rights in China since the 1989 massacre that ended the Tiananmen Square democracy movement.

Yet governments have long been reluctant to criticize Beijing for fear of retaliation. Australia suffered economic reprisal in 2020 when the Chinese government imposed punitive tariffs on various Australian goods, because Canberra supported an independent investigation into the origins of the Covid-19 pandemic. Beijing most likely feared that the probe would spotlight its early, three-week denial of human-to-human transmission in late December 2019 and January 2020 as millions of people fled or traveled through Wuhan – an average of 3,500 a day traveling abroad – and the virus went global. The Wuhan lockdown began only on January 23.

In 2016, the US government had organized the first common statement of governments willing to criticize China on human rights, but only 11 other states joined it. When the Trump administration withdrew from the UN Human Rights Council in 2018, many assumed that criticism of the Chinese government's repression would end. In fact, it strengthened. Over the past two years, governments have grown more confident to criticize Beijing's repression by finding safety in numbers, reflecting Beijing's inability to retaliate against the entire world.

The first step took place at the Human Rights Council in 2019, when 25 governments banded together to condemn the extraordinary repression in Xinjiang. Yet fear of Beijing was still on display when, despite a tradition that joint statements are read out loud at the council, none of the 25 would do so.

Since then, the British government has taken responsibility for reading similar condemnations at the council and at the UN General Assembly. Most recently, in October 2020, the German government took the lead in organizing at the General Assembly a condemnation of repression in Xinjiang that attracted 39 countries. Turkey issued a similar parallel statement.

After each statement criticizing its repression, Beijing organized a counterstatement of other countries willing to praise its conduct. The pro-China statement was typically signed by many of the world's worst human rights abusers, and its numbers were large, given the economic leverage used to secure support. However, the most recent statement, delivered by Cuba in October 2020 to applaud the Chinese government's conduct in Xinjiang, attracted only 45 signatories – a drop from 54 the year before. That shift, approaching parity with the condemnatory statement, suggests the day may soon arrive when UN bodies can begin to adopt formal resolutions criticizing at least some aspects of Beijing's repression.

For much of the past two years, the OIC and Muslim-majority governments have tended to support China. In October, however, that, too, began to change. The number of OIC states supporting China's repression in Xinjiang dropped from 25 in 2019 to 19 in 2020, with the remaining 37 OIC members refusing to join. Albania and Turkey went further and added their voices to the joint condemnation of China's abuses in Xinjiang. These numbers suggest that the tables may be turning, as more Muslim-majority countries are rightfully outraged by the Chinese government's horrendous treatment of Muslims in Xinjiang.

The Chinese government in October also sought a seat on the UN Human Rights Council. The last time it ran, four years ago, it received the most votes of any country running from the Asia-Pacific region. This time, it received the fewest votes of any such government that secured a seat. Only Saudi Arabia received fewer votes and, in a positive result, was denied a seat.

This growing international willingness to condemn the Chinese government forced it to respond. For the first time, Beijing gave a number for the Uyghur and other Turkic Muslims directly affected by its conduct in Xinjiang – 1.3 million – although it claimed they were in not detention but "vocational training centers." It also claimed that many had "graduated," although this allusion to release must be tempered by the inability to verify independently the number remaining in detention and by the growing evidence that many who were released from custody were coerced into forced labor. Growing global efforts to ensure that supply chains in Xinjiang and other regions of China are not tainted by this forced labor could create a new source of pressure on Beijing to stop its persecution of Muslims.

All of these initiatives are noteworthy for how peripheral the US government has been. Often the Trump administration had nothing to do with the effort. When it did speak out – such as on China – the selectivity of its concern, as Trump embraced a multitude of friendly autocrats, meant the US voice lacked much credibility.

The lesson of recent years for other governments is that they can make a big difference even without Washington. Even under a more rights-friendly US administration, this broader collective defense of rights should be maintained. Even if Biden manages to overcome the swings and double standards that often plague US policy, the defense of human rights will be stronger if a wide range of governments continues to lead.

Lessons for Biden

Biden cannot guarantee that a new US administration in four or eight years will not again turn back the clock on human rights, but he can take steps to make that retrenchment more difficult. Those steps would make the US government a more reliable member of the global human rights system.

Obviously, the more a rights-respecting policy is enshrined in legislation, the harder it is to reverse, which a Democratic majority in the US Congress may make possible . Without two-thirds of the Senate, the prospect remains remote of the United States joining most of the rest of the world in ratifying the major human rights treaties that it has long neglected. For the most part, Biden will have to resort to executive orders and presidential policy to undo the damage of the Trump years. Such steps by Biden would in principle be reversible, but they can be done in a way that makes it harder for the next president to make a 180-degree turn.

To provide greater staying power to a renewed commitment to human rights, Biden needs to reframe how these rights are understood in the United States. As noted, Jimmy Carter accomplished such a reframing when he introduced human rights as an element of US foreign policy. Many of Carter's successors did not share his commitment to human rights, but none formally rejected it. It had struck a chord with the US public and met a global popular demand. So, for example, although Ronald Reagan broke with Carter's commitment in Central America and elsewhere, he still ended up institutionalizing the State Department's reporting on human rights and played an important role in pushing for democratic change in Chile and the Soviet bloc. Biden should aspire to a similar reconceptualization as Carter achieved.

The moment is ripe because the pandemic has laid bare gross disparities in access to health care, food, and other basic necessities, while the Black Lives Matter movement has spotlighted deep-seated racial injustice. Many people in the United States remain hostile to governmental efforts to remedy these human rights violations, which is part of why no administration has taken them on, but the extraordinary events of 2020 could provide a spur for action by having exposed the common interest in respect for everyone's rights. The challenge for Biden is to seize that opportunity and use it to entrench respect for human rights as a central element of US policy at home and abroad.

One way would be by more regularly framing social issues in terms of rights. Traditionally, the US government has been more focused on civil and political rights than on economic, social, and cultural rights. It has ratified the leading treaty on the former, which codifies rights such as freedom of speech, the right to a fair trial, and the right not to be tortured, but never the companion treaty on the latter, which addresses such rights as those concerning health, housing, and food. Yet the pandemic has shown how linked these concepts are – for example, how censorship about a government's response to the pandemic undermines people's ability to demand that resources be devoted to their health rather than the government's political interests. Indeed, both sets of rights often can be found in US law. Biden could begin to speak about human rights in the broader terms in which most people understand them.

With the pandemic still raging, an obvious place to begin would be with Biden's stated plan to bolster access to health care in the United States, which he should describe as a right. He should make clear that the issue is not simply reinforcing or expanding the Affordable Care Act (or Obamacare) but upholding everyone's right to see a doctor without bankrupting their family. Similarly, as he pushes for federal aid to workers left unemployed by the lockdown, he should make clear that everyone is entitled to an adequate standard of living – that the richest government in the world is supposed to help people put food on the table even if they have lost their jobs in tough times. As he addresses the closing of schools, he should speak about the right to education – that a family's ability to educate its children should not depend on whether it can afford a strong internet connection and a laptop. The more that people in the United

States recognize that human rights reflect fundamental values, the less they will allow each passing president to treat rights as mere policy preferences.

Facing his own extraordinary challenges, Franklin D. Roosevelt launched the New Deal and made the case for a "freedom from want" in his famous "Four Freedoms" speech. Biden should seize on this pivotal moment to enlarge upon that vision and make it a more permanent reality in the United States.

Even within the realm of civil and political rights, more regular reference to rights could help to reduce the major shifts in policy that have accompanied most changes of administration. For example, Biden has expressed a desire to curtail the risk of deportation and provide a path to legalization for the 11 million undocumented immigrants in the United States. Because some two-thirds have been in the United States for a decade or more, many with US-citizen children and spouses, Biden could speak of their right to live with their family without the constant fear of deportation.

On the issues of racial discrimination in education, housing, health, or the criminal justice system, or the right to choose whether, when, or how to form a family, Biden could note not only that these rights are upheld by US law but also that they are seen as fundamental in most countries around the world. And he should certainly repudiate the Commission on Unalienable Rights, the brainchild of Trump's secretary of state, Mike Pompeo, which was a thinly disguised effort to pick and choose among rights instead of recognizing them as a set of binding obligations. That ploy was music to the ears of the world's autocrats.

More regular invocation of rights will not alone be enough but it could help to shift the public conversation about the fundamental values involved. That might make it harder for the next president to do an about-face.

Adopting a Principled Foreign Policy

A similar shift would help to instill more consistency in US foreign policy. Biden should affirm that the promotion of human rights around the world is a core principle of US policy – and then abide by it. But to make such a statement meaningful, Biden would need to apply it even when it is politically difficult.

For example, Biden has indicated a determination to rejoin global efforts to fight climate change. He should do so by fulfilling his campaign pledge to drastically reduce US greenhouse gas emissions and encouraging other governments to do the same. He also said he would reverse Trump's planned departure from the World Health Organization. He should go further and work to increase global access to health care.

He should re-embrace the UN Human Rights Council and fully participate in it even though it regularly criticizes Israel's oppressive and discriminatory treatment of Palestinians in Occupied Palestinian Territory (OPT), and even when it scrutinizes human rights in the United States. He should resume US funding for the UN Relief and Works Agency for Palestine Refugees in the Near East and the UN Population Fund, which keep countless people, especially women and girls, healthy and alive. And he should void Trump's appalling sanctions on the International Criminal Court's work – an affront to the rule of law – regardless of the prosecutor's steps to investigate unprosecuted crimes that are sensitive to the US government, such as US torture in Afghanistan (and elsewhere) and Israeli war crimes in the OPT.

UN Secretary-General António Guterres's term concludes at the end of 2021, with a new election due before then. The Biden administration should condition support for any candidate – whether Guterres seeking a second term or anyone else – on a pledge not to repeat Guterres's lackluster performance on human rights over the past four years. That should include using the UN's powerful bully pulpit to call out repressive governments by name – something that Guterres has been loath to do – and fully implementing his February 2020 "Call to Action on Human Rights," which has yet to move from "call" to "action."

Biden should similarly announce and live by human rights principles as a major determinant of US relations with abusive countries. Biden can be expected to maintain less cozy relations than Trump with certain friendly autocrats such as Putin. But he should also insist that, absent improvement in their conduct, the US government will curb its military aid or (often subsidized) arms sales to highly abusive friendly governments such as Saudi Arabia, Egypt, the United Arab Emirates, and Israel. He should reject the fiction that mere "engagement" without serious pressure modifies rather than bolsters their repression. He should press for continued UN reporting on Sri Lanka and concrete steps toward accountability, now that many of the officials who were responsible for past war crimes have returned to power. He should be more outspoken about Indian Prime Minister

Narendra Modi's encouragement of discrimination and violence against Muslims, even if India is seen as an important ally against China.

To bolster the global defense of human rights, Biden plans to host a "Summit for Democracy." He should not repeat the mistake of Bill Clinton who invited allied authoritarian governments to his Community of Democracies in the hope that they might become democratic. That devalues the currency of the invitation. A standing meeting of democracies can provide an incentive to respect democratic standards only if adherence to those standards is the price of admission.

Biden's biggest foreign-policy challenge may be China, given Beijing's severe repression at home and its determination to undermine the global human rights system out of fear that the system will target its repression. Trump, after initially embracing Xi Jinping – going so far as to praise the possibility that he might serve as president for life and reportedly to endorse the mass detention of Uyghur and other Turkic Muslims – ultimately soured on Xi, particularly as Trump needed a "China virus" scapegoat for his administration's failure to contain the pandemic in the United States. Although parts of the US government did address Beijing's repression – the administration imposed targeted sanctions on individuals and entities responsible for the mass detention of Muslims in Xinjiang and the crushing of freedoms in Hong Kong – Trump took a more transactional approach, as if enough Chinese purchases of soybeans from his supporters in Iowa would alleviate any problems. The sense that Trump was using human rights to pursue other agendas, coupled with his "America First" unilateralism, discouraged other governments from joining his efforts.

To be effective, Biden will need to pursue a more principled, consistent, and multilateral approach. After years of global ridicule brought on by the Trump administration, significant portions of the US electorate would take pride in Washington speaking with a clear voice on human rights – and demonstrating on the world stage its difference from competing powers such as China, Russia, or India.

Biden should embrace broad coalitions of governments to condemn Beijing's repression – even if the locale of their statement is the UN Human Rights Council, where the Trump administration refused to join statements on China because of the council's criticism of Israel. US diplomacy could help to expand those coalitions to include governments that have not yet spoken out, especially in the

Global South, and reassure economically vulnerable countries that the US government will help them if they face retaliation from Beijing. Having spoken in strong terms about Chinese repression in Xinjiang, Biden should also press for an independent international investigation, as well as accountability for those responsible.

Biden could endorse a strong version of legislation being considered by the US Congress to force companies sourcing from Xinjiang – and China more broadly – to ensure that their supply chains are not tainted by the forced labor of Uyghur Muslims. And he should encourage other governments to do the same. He should impose targeted sanctions on companies that assist the Chinese government with its highly intrusive surveillance state – and encourage similar action by others. He should set a model for combatting Chinese Communist Party influence in the United States without resorting to bigotry against all Chinese people. And, again, he should adopt a more principled approach to human rights at home and abroad, so others cannot dismiss talk of Chinese repression as a tool of superpower competition but see it as reflecting genuine concern for the human rights of one-sixth of humanity that is matched by parallel attention to people wherever they face persecution.

Conclusion

It will not be enough for Biden to respond to Trump by simply turning the clock back four years, as if an abandonment of Trump's policies can reverse the devastation he caused. The world has changed, and so must the promotion of human rights. Many rights-respecting nations have responded to the void created by Trump's indifference and hostility to human rights by stepping forward and playing a more active leadership role. The Biden administration should join that enhanced defense of rights, not seek to replace it.

Meanwhile, Biden needs to recognize that Trump has magnified the traditional shifts in policy between US administrations into a crisis of credibility for Washington and a profound risk to the rights of people in the United States and around the world. Biden should seek to reframe the US public's appreciation of human rights so the US commitment becomes entrenched in a way that is not so easily reversed by his successors. The sustained role of the US government as a useful partner in defending human rights worldwide depends on Biden's success.

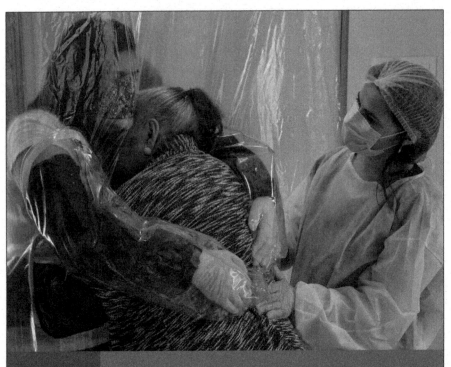

"Whoever Finds the Vaccine Must Share It"

Strengthening Human Rights and Transparency around Covid-19 Vaccines

HUMAN
RIGHTS
WATCH

WORLD REPORT
2021

COUNTRIES

HUMAN
RIGHTS
WATCH

"You Have No Right to Complain"
Education, Social Restrictions, and Justice in Taliban-Held Afghanistan

Afghanistan

2020 saw the first serious negotiations among all the parties to the Afghanistan conflict to end the war. However, fighting between Afghan government forces, the Taliban, and other armed groups continued, causing almost 6,000 civilian casualties in the first nine months of the year, a marked reduction over previous years. Urban attacks by the Taliban and airstrikes by US forces declined, but improvised explosive devices (IEDs) planted by the Taliban killed a large number of civilians, as did Afghan government airstrikes. Abductions and targeted killings of politicians, government employees, and other civilians, many by the Taliban, increased. On March 5, the Appeals Chamber of the International Criminal Court (ICC) reversed the Pre-Trial Chamber's 2019 decision and authorized the court's prosecutor to investigate possible war crimes and crimes against humanity by all parties in Afghanistan.

Human rights groups called for a broad representation of Afghans in the peace talks, including women, and for any settlement to preserve human rights protections, including constitutional guarantees on women's rights and freedom of expression.

The government failed to prosecute senior officials responsible for sexual assault, torture, and killing civilians. Although the government dropped a proposed law that would have imposed restrictions on media, threats to journalists by both the Taliban and government officials continued.

Violations of International Humanitarian Law

According to the United Nations Assistance Mission in Afghanistan (UNAMA), the Taliban were responsible for 45 percent of attacks that caused civilian deaths and injuries in the first nine months of 2020. Pro-government forces were responsible for 27 percent. Attacks by the Islamic State of Khorasan Province (ISKP), the Afghan branch of the Islamic State (ISIS), declined, but the group was responsible for several deadly bombings. Women and children comprised over 44 percent of all civilian casualties.

On May 12, gunmen attacked the Médecins Sans Frontières (MSF)-run maternity wing of the Dasht-e Barchi hospital in Kabul, killing at least 24 people, including five women in labor and 10 who had recently given birth, a healthcare worker, and three children, and injuring 14 others. Three weeks after the attack, MSF suspended its support for the hospital, citing a failure by the authorities to adequately investigate the incident. No group claimed responsibility for the attack; the predominantly Hazara Dasht-e Barchi neighborhood has been the site of numerous ISKP attacks. Also, on May 12, ISKP carried out a suicide attack at a police commander's funeral in Nangarhar, killing 24 and injuring 82.

Roadside and magnetic IEDs, mostly planted by the Taliban, caused at least 1,274 civilian casualties. The Taliban's widespread use of pressure-plate IEDs, which function as banned anti-personnel mines, killed and injured hundreds of civilians using public roads, a 43 percent increase over 2019.

On July 11, a vehicle carrying civilians hit a roadside IED in the Jaghato district of Ghazni, killing six members of one family and injuring eight. On May 23, three boys ages 5 to12 were killed when they triggered a pressure-plate IED in Badghis province. On June 8, seven boys ages 9 to 15 were injured when their donkey stepped on pressure-plate IED in Faryab province. The Taliban also continued to target civilians, including humanitarian workers, members of the judiciary, tribal elders, religious leaders, and civilian government employees.

Afghan government forces were responsible for killing and injuring civilians in indiscriminate mortar attacks and airstrikes. In one of the deadliest incidents, on June 29, the army fired three mortar rounds that landed in a busy marketplace in Sangin, Helmand, killing at least 19 civilians, including 6 children, and injuring 31. Civilian casualties from government airstrikes saw a 70 percent increase compared to the same time period in 2019; women and children comprised more than 60 percent of civilian deaths and injuries. On September 19, government airstrikes in Kunduz killed 15 civilians.

Although President Ashraf Ghani pledged to ban night raids in September 2019, such operations by special forces continued, including a December 2019 raid in which special forces killed a 15-year-old boy in Laghman. A January 7 operation by National Directorate of Security (NDS) forces killed a prominent politician, Amer Abdul Sattar, and five others at a house in Kabul. Government officials claimed to be investigating the killings of civilians in night raids by CIA-backed special forces, but no findings from these investigations were made public.

US military operations declined after the US-Taliban agreement was signed in February, but a number of US airstrikes in the beginning of the year caused apparently disproportionate civilian casualties, including an airstrike on February 17 in Kushk district, Herat, which destroyed a house, killing three women and five children.

Women's Rights and Violence against Women and Girls

The government-backed delegation to the intra-Afghan negotiations included four women among its 21 members. The Taliban team included no women.

Former governor and Afghan Football Federation president, Keramuddin Karim, remained at large in Panjshir province, despite having been indicted on multiple counts of rape, sexual assault, and harassment of female players dating to 2017. On August 23, Afghan government special forces launched an operation to apprehend Karim, but were thwarted by local militia forces in Panjshir protecting him.

In February, the Ministry of Women's Affairs reported a slight increase in registered cases of violence against women, including murder, assault, and rape. Such cases are seldom prosecuted due to pressure from family members, and there are very few services available to people seeking to escape violence. In the case of Lal Bibi, a 17-year-old girl in Faryab who had been beaten and burned by her father and husband, local strongmen exerted pressure to secure the release of the accused perpetrators.

In September, human rights organizations called for a total ban on so-called virginity tests, abusive procedures that are a routine part of criminal proceedings in Afghanistan even though they have no scientific validity. The Afghan penal code requires a court order and the consent of the woman for the tests, but these requirements are often ignored.

On September 3, the government approved a law allowing for the inclusion of the mother's name on national identity cards (tazkiras), a move Afghan women's rights groups had long demanded.

Sexual Orientation and Gender Identity

In February 2018, Afghanistan adopted a new penal code that explicitly criminalizes consensual same-sex relations. The penal code punishes musaheqeh (sexual relations between women) with up to one year in prison. It punishes sodomy, defined as "penetration of a male sexual organ into a female or a male anus," with up to two years in prison. Under the previous penal code, "pederasty," not further defined, was criminalized, as was all sex outside of marriage (zina).

Attacks on Media and Human Rights Defenders

Fatima Natasha Khalil and Ahmad Jawid Folad, both employees of the Afghanistan Independent Human Rights Commission (AIHRC), were killed when an IED attached to their car in Kabul detonated on June 27. The AIHRC vehicle had government plates.

In late November 2019, the NDS detained and threatened two staff members of a human rights group that reported the widespread abuse of hundreds of schoolboys in Logar province. In January, the attorney general's office arrested 18 people in connection with the reported abuse. However, none of the police or senior officials alleged to have been responsible were arrested.

In June, media organizations, human rights groups, and other civil society organizations denounced the government's proposed amendments to the Media Law that would have compelled journalists to reveal sources and allowed government censorship of news reports. In response to the outcry, President Ghani withdrew the amendments.

While media remained generally free, after Pajhwok Afghan News reported on June 22 that 32 ventilators meant for Covid-19 patients had been stolen and sold by government officials, Pajhwok's editor Danish Karokhel was summoned for questioning and accused of "acting against national security." On July 1, NDS officers detained a Pajhwok journalist whom they accused of criticizing President Ghani on Facebook. Also, on July 1, NDS officers detained a Reuters correspondent in Khost; the NDS later said his detention had been "a mistake."

On May 30, two employees of Khurshid TV were killed and six others were wounded in Kabul when an IED detonated on their van. ISKP claimed responsibility.

On May 9, protests broke out in Chaghcharan, the capital of Ghor province, over allegations of unfair bread distribution during a lockdown implemented between March and June to stop the spread of Covid-19. Ahmad Khan Navid, a correspondent for Ghor's local radio station, was fatally shot along with at least three protesters and two police officers. Police allege shots first came from the crowd; protesters claim police opened fire first. The results of a government investigation were not made public.

Covid-19

As of October 15, Afghanistan had officially registered more than 40,026 cases of Covid-19 and nearly 1,500 deaths. With only 115,968 tests conducted, the actual number of deaths was almost certainly significantly higher.

Afghanistan's healthcare system has long been underfunded and understaffed, with many rural districts and areas affected by the conflict lacking even basic healthcare services. According to a September UN report, hospitals and clinics had little capacity to maintain essential services while treating patients with Covid-19, causing a 30-40 percent decline in people accessing health care. The pandemic and the government's response to it had a disproportionately adverse impact on people with disabilities, particularly women and girls, who already lack access to adequate health care and social services due to widespread discrimination.

In June 2020, 200 medical staff at government hospitals in Herat, the city with the highest number of reported Covid-19 cases, protested the lack of personal protective equipment (PPE) and claimed they had not been paid since March. At least 76 healthcare workers across the country had died from Covid-19 as of mid-October.

Almost 10 million students were out of school from March through early September, even as the number of children studying was already falling in many provinces because of the escalating conflict and diminished donor funding. Options for distance education are low in Afghanistan, as only 14 percent of

HUMAN
RIGHTS
WATCH

"Disability Is Not Weakness"
Discrimination and Barriers Facing Women and Girls
with Disabilities in Afghanistan

Afghans have access to the internet. Many parents cannot help their children study as only about 30 percent of women and 55 percent of men are literate.

Because of insufficient PPE, the government suspended polio vaccinations of children between March and July; reported total polio cases reached 34. In June, the government vowed to investigate reports that ministers had embezzled funds provided by donors for the response to the pandemic, but had yet to make the results of any such investigation public at time of writing.

On March 26, the Afghan government announced that it would release up to 10,000 prisoners, including women, children, and older people, to reduce the risk of the virus spreading in prisons. A UN report noted that despite the releases, there were still "concerns related to overcrowding and the spread of Covid-19" among the remaining prison population. Detainees and prisoners in Afghanistan have extremely poor access to health care, and cramped and unsanitary conditions in prisons make Covid-19 prevention measures extremely difficult.

Partial lockdowns in major cities caused increased hardship for daily wage earners; in June, the United Nations estimated that 14 million people—nearly 40 percent of the population—needed urgent humanitarian assistance, a 50 percent increase since December 2019. Price rises led to food shortages in some areas, and the government established bread distribution centers.

Key International Actors

On February 29, 2020, a US negotiating team led by Ambassador Zalmay Khalilzad concluded an agreement with Taliban leaders in Doha, Qatar, outlining the terms for a withdrawal of US forces by May 2021.

Five countries have played a critical role supporting talks between the Taliban and a government-back delegation—Germany, Norway, Qatar, Indonesia, and Uzbekistan, collectively known as the "quint." Qatar, the seat of the Taliban's political office, hosted the first round of the intra-Afghan negotiations that began on September 12.

On May 29, the European Union affirmed that its political and financial support for Afghanistan would be contingent upon compliance with key principles, including "safeguarding democratic and human rights gains made since 2001."

As the intra-Afghan negotiations began, a number of Afghanistan's donors addressed the proceedings and called for human rights protections. EU High Representative Josep Borrell said the process "must preserve and build on the political, economic and social achievements ... since 2001, especially on women's rights." German Foreign Minister Heiko Maas said Afghans "want to see rule of law and human rights respected—not in theory, but in practice." He noted that "continued international support depends on the adherence to these fundamental rights and Afghanistan's constitutional order."

Norway's Minister of Foreign Affairs Ine Eriksen Søreide stated that "inclusion of women, victims, minorities and other stakeholders in the process" was important to ensure successful implementation of any agreement. The French government called on the negotiators "to ensure justice for the victims of the conflict," and said it would "pay close attention" to ensuring that the process was inclusive and included the effective participation of women."

On November 23-24, Afghanistan's donors and the World Bank met in Geneva to discuss renewed assistance, including conditions on women's rights, and a draft economic plan for post-settlement Afghanistan.

Despite allegations of war crimes by foreign forces since 2002, few cases have been investigated. One exception was on March 19, when Australia's Defence Department announced that it had identified and suspended from duty "Soldier C.," an Australian Special Air Service Regiment (SAS) member implicated in killing Afghan civilians and captured combatants in 2012, and that the matter had been referred to the Australian Federal Police. Since 2016, the inspector-general of the Australian Defence Force has been conducting an inquiry into violations of the laws of war in Afghanistan. In August, new evidence came to light that in 2012, a British military unit in Afghanistan had a "deliberate policy" of killing Afghans even when "they did not pose a threat." The UK government continued to pursue legislation that would make it difficult to prosecute alleged crimes committed by UK forces overseas.

In June, the US authorized sanctions that could be used against ICC officials and others assisting the court. The US has not held senior officials to account before its courts for authorizing or failing to punish torture and other grave crimes its personnel committed in relation to the conflict in Afghanistan.

On April 15, the Afghan government requested a deferral of the ICC investigation, claiming it was investigating 151 cases. However, none of these involved senior police, intelligence, or military personnel, and few were prosecuted. Some Taliban members accused of serious crimes were released as part of a prisoner exchange in which the Taliban released hundreds of captured government soldiers for 5,000 Taliban prisoners as a precondition for the talks.

Algeria

Algerian authorities continued repressing the "Hirak," a pro-reform protest movement that pushed President Abdelaziz Bouteflika to resign in April 2019. Abdelmadjid Tebboune, opposed by the Hirak, won a presidential election held in December 2019. Despite his promises of "dialogue," authorities continued to arrest and imprison protesters, activists, and journalists in an attempt to muzzle the Hirak. Under the president's auspices, a new constitution was approved that offers stronger language on women's rights, but also restricts freedom of speech and undermines judicial independence.

Presidential Election

On December 10, 2019, two days before the presidential election that the Hirak opposed peacefully, the police arrested Kadour Chouicha, vice president of the Algerian League for the Defense of Human Rights in Oran. A court convicted him the same day and sentenced him to one year in prison for "rebellion" and "compromising the integrity of the national territory." The accusation relied on Facebook posts Chouicha published in November opposing the presidential election, and his participation a week before the vote in a protest outside a hall where a presidential candidate had organized a rally.

Abdelmadjid Tebboune, a former prime minister under Bouteflika, won the election with a historically low turnout. In his inauguration speech, Tebboune stated he was "open to dialogue" with the Hirak and announced that his government would consolidate democracy, the rule of law, and respect for human rights.

On January 2, 2020, about 70 Hirak detainees were released the same day as Tebboune appointed a new government. The National Committee for the Liberation of Detainees, a group tracking the status of imprisoned Hirak protesters, estimated that the releases left about 80 protesters behind bars. Arrests of protesters resumed shortly afterwards, including of a group of 20 protesters on January 17.

On January 13, Anouar Rahmani, a novelist, was charged with "insulting the president of the Republic" over satirical comments about Tebboune that he posted on Facebook. He was granted provisional release and was sentenced on November 9 to a fine of about US$400.

Freedom of Assembly

Hundreds of Hirak protesters were arrested throughout the country during protests that occurred in early 2020. While a majority were released the same day, some were tried and sentenced to prison sentences on charges of "illegal gathering," "harming national unity," or "demoralizing the army."

On June 21, a tribunal in Cheraga, a city in the suburbs of Algiers, sentenced Amira Bouraoui, a gynecologist and noted Hirak figure, to a year in prison. She had been prosecuted for "participating in a non-armed gathering," "offending the president of the republic," "harming national unity," and "denigrating Islam." She was granted provisional freedom on July 2. Her appeals trial was scheduled to resume on November 12.

On September 15, an appeals court sentenced Samir Ben Larbi, a protest leader, and Slimane Hamitouche, the national coordinator of the Families of the Disappeared, to one year in prison, with eight months of the sentences suspended, over their participation in Hirak protests in March. They were released after serving their unsuspended four-month terms.

On March 17, the government banned all street demonstrations before establishing a nationwide lockdown, as a precaution to slow the spread of Covid-19. Hirak leaders themselves had called for a suspension of protests a couple days earlier to protect public health. The government went on to establish a general Covid-19-related lockdown on March 23, first in Algiers, then in the rest of the country. After gradually easing the lockdown starting in May, the police brutally dispersed attempts by Hirak activists to resume demonstrations. They arrested protesters, including in Algiers, Blida, Setif, and Tizi Ouzou in August 21, and in Annaba and Bejaia on September 24.

On April 1, President Tebboune signed a decree pardoning 5,037, apparently in an effort to reduce the prison population in response to the Covid-19 pandemic. The pardon did not include Hirak activists.

Freedom of Speech

On March 24, an appeals court in Algiers sentenced prominent politician and Hirak supporter, Karim Tabbou, to one year in prison. The national coordinator of the unrecognized Democratic and Socialist Union party, Tabbou was charged with "harming national defense," "harming national unity" and "undermining the morale of the army," because of peaceful comments he posted on social media. His trial was marred by due process violations, including refusal by the judge to wait for Tabbou's lawyers' arrival before starting an audience, even though he had not notified them of it. On July 2, Tabbou was released after spending more than nine months in detention.

On March 27, police arrested in Algiers prominent journalist Khaled Drareni, founder of the Casbah Tribune website, correspondent for French TV5 Monde and Reporters Without Borders. Drareni was accused of "calling for an illegal gathering" and "undermining national unity" for his regular coverage of the Hirak protests, including in his widely followed social media accounts, since they began in February 2019. Authorities had warned him several times before to curtail his coverage, during arrests and interrogations. On August 10, a court pronounced Drareni guilty of both charges and sentenced him to three years in prison, before an appeals court reduced the term to two years on September 15. He has been in prison since his arrest.

On April 27, Walid Kechida, founder and administrator of the satirical Facebook page, Hirak Memes, was arrested in Setif and charged with "contempt and offense to the president" and "undermining the precepts of religion." He was sentenced to three years in prison on January 4, 2021.

On August 24, Abdelkrim Zeghileche, director of web-based Radio Sarbacane, was sentenced to two years in prison for "harming national unity" and "insulting the head of State," for a post in which he called for the creation of a new political party. His defense appealed the verdict. Zeghileche has been in prison in Constantine since June 23.

On September 21, the Ministry of Communications banned French TV station M6 from operating in Algeria, one day after it aired a documentary film about the Hirak protests, arguing that the M6 crew had used a "forged filming authorization" to shoot images in Algeria. The ministry's communiqué announcing the ban added that M6 "harmed the reputation of Algeria (and attempted to) breach the indefectible trust between the Algerian people and their institutions."

On April 22, the parliament unanimously passed a reform of the penal code, including new laws criminalizing fake news and hate speech. Some offenses, such as "harming public security and the public order" and "harming the stability of State institutions," which carry sentences of up to three and seven years in prison, respectively, are so vaguely worded that they can be used to criminalize peaceful criticism.

Judicial Independence

On February 10, the Justice Ministry ordered the apparently punitive transfer of a prosecutor, Mohamed Sid Ahmed Belhadi, to El Oued, 600 kilometers south of Algiers, after Belhadi had urged an Algiers court to acquit 16 protesters, saying they had been prosecuted solely for exercising their right to freedom of assembly. The National Union of Algerian Magistrates labelled the transfer "political punishment and retaliation" for the prosecutor's remarks.

Constitutional Reform

On November 1, Algerians approved a new constitution with a 66 percent margin in a referendum that drew a historically low turnout of 23 percent.

Amnesty International noted that the constitution "introduces positive language on women's rights," including the mention that "the State protects women from all forms of violence in all places and circumstances, (and) guarantees the access of victims to shelters, care centers, appropriate means of redress and free legal assistance."

The president of the republic presides over the "Higher Judicial Council," a constitutional body that appoints judges and controls their careers through promotions and disciplinary measures, thus undermining its mission to "guarantee the independence of the judiciary."

Like the previous constitution, the new fundamental law guarantees the right to "receive and impart information," but subjects the exercise of that right to vague, speech-restricting conditions, such as not infringing on "the require-ments of national security."

Women's Rights and Sexual Orientation

Killings of women and girls continued in 2020. Two women, who launched a campaign to raise awareness of such killings, reported that there had been at least 36 femicides in 2020. While Algeria's 2015 law on domestic violence crimi-nalized some forms of domestic violence, it contained loopholes that allow con-victions to be dropped or sentences reduced if victims pardoned their perpetrators. The law also did not set out any further measures to prevent abuse or protect survivors, such as protection orders (restraining orders against abusers).

Article 326 of the penal code, a colonial-era relic, allows a person who abducts a minor to escape prosecution if he marries his victim.

Algeria's Family Code allows men to have a unilateral divorce without explana-tion but requires women to apply to courts for a divorce on specified grounds.

Same-sex relations are punishable under article 338 of the penal code by up to two years in prison.

Migrants and Asylum Seekers

Citing "the fight against illegal migration," Algerian authorities summarily rounded up and collectively expelled over 17,000, mostly Sub-Saharan African, migrants between January and October 10, including hundreds of women and children and some registered asylum seekers. The expulsions continued even after borders closed in March due to Covid-19. Security personnel separated some children from their families during mass arrests, stripped migrants of their belongings, failed to screen them individually for immigration or refugee status, and failed to allow them to challenge their removal. A little more than half

(8,900) were Nigeriens, forcibly repatriated in truck convoys and handed over to the Nigerien military per a 2014 bilateral oral agreement. The Algerian military left the others—over 8,100 migrants of at least 20 different nationalities—in the desert at the border, ordering them to walk to Niger. Some expelled migrants and aid workers assisting them in Niger alleged that Algerian authorities had carried out beatings and other abuses during the expulsions.

Angola

During 2020, Angolan authorities struggled to contain abuses by state security forces implicated in killings and excessive use of force against unarmed people who allegedly violated Covid-19 restrictions.

There was progress in respecting the rights to freedom of expression and peaceful assembly, allowing several protests and marches across the country. But the crackdown on peaceful protesters and activists in the oil-rich enclave of Cabinda continued. Angolan authorities continued forced evictions and demolitions without the necessary procedural guarantees or the provision of alternative adequate housing, even during the Covid-19 pandemic lockdown. The government approved the country's long-awaited human rights strategy, making human rights an issue of state security.

Covid-19

Authorities struggled to contain the rise of Covid-19 cases, despite declaring a partial lockdown in late March. Under the lockdown, people were only allowed out of their homes to buy medicine, food, water, and cooking gas, with a schedule put in place for markets to operate.

But many Angolans, especially street traders, broke the lockdown rules to try to earn some money. Government forces reacted with excessive use of force, which in some cases resulted in killings of innocent unarmed people. In May, after the end of a three-month state of emergency permitted by the constitution, the government introduced a state of calamity until further notice. This allows the government to keep some of the state of emergency measures to contain the spread of Covid-19, including restrictions on the movements and gatherings of people. State security forces were implicated by human rights groups and media in serious human rights abuses, including killings, harassment and arbitrary arrests, as they tried to enforce lockdown rules and restrictions.

In September, a medical doctor died in police custody after being detained for not wearing a face mask inside his car. His suspicious death sparked protests on social media and the streets of Luanda, the country's capital. In response, Angolan authorities opened an investigation into the circumstances surrounding the doctor's death. As of early December, the results of the investigation were not publicly known.

In September, Police Chief Paulo de Almeida condemned what he called "bad actions" of some officers," including excessive use of force, and asked the Angolan people not to lose trust in the police. Earlier in August, Amnesty International released a report showing that security forces tasked with implementing Covid-19 restrictions had killed at least seven boys and young men between May and July 2020.

In April, Angolan authorities released nearly 1,900 people in pretrial detention to help prevent the spread of the coronavirus in the nation's prisons. In April, Interior Minister Eugénio César Laborinho visited prisons across the country to assess their capability to prevent and treat Covid-19 cases. He expressed concerns over the prisons' inadequate capacity to quarantine newly arrived inmates. Nevertheless, Angola's police continued to detain and place hundreds of people in custody for low-level crimes, leading to a daily influx of new detainees. On May 1, police released data showing that almost 300 people had been detained in 24 hours for violating state of emergency rules. Despite recommendations by human rights groups such as Human Rights Watch, the Angolan government did not consider alternatives to jail time and avoid detaining people for nonviolent or minor offenses, including those who violate the state of emergency law.

Crackdown on Cabinda Activists

The crackdown on peaceful protesters and activists in the Cabinda enclave continued in 2020. In violation of the International Covenant on Civil and Political Rights, of which Angola is a state party, authorities refused all the requests by Cabinda pro-independence activists to peacefully assemble. Where protests and marches took place, police violently interrupted them, and illegally detained the participants. In January, state security forces rounded up activists from their homes after they attempted to hold a protest in December 2019, to demand independence from Angola.

In June, plainclothes police officers arbitrarily arrested the president of the separatist group Union for the Independence of Cabinda and his vice president after they displayed leaflets of the organization in the streets of the city of Cabinda.

According to their lawyers, the police officers physically assaulted the two during the arrest. They were charged with rebellion, outrage against the state, and criminal association. As of early December, the two men were still detained at Cabinda Province Civil Prison under concerningly inhumane conditions, despite calls for their release.

Forced Evictions and Illegal Demolitions

Angolan authorities continued to forcibly evict people and conduct demolitions without the necessary procedural guarantees or the provision of alternative adequate housing or adequate compensation for those evicted. This practice continued even during the Covid-19 pandemic and government-imposed restrictions on movement, exposing those evicted to increased risk of infection.

In June, authorities in Benguela province demolished over 70 homes, a health center, and a school at Salinas neighborhood, allegedly because its structures had been illegally built in an area reserved for state projects. As of early December, the evicted people were living in makeshift homes near the site of the demolition.

In July, authorities in Luanda demolished 24 houses in Viana area, without previously notifying the residents and without presenting a court order. Moreover, hundreds of families who were forcibly evicted from their houses from 2013 to 2019 continued to await resettlement, including the residents of an informal settlement of "Areia Branca" in Luanda, who were illegally evicted in 2013 by a company contracted by the office of Luanda's governor to modernize the city.

Human Trafficking

Angolan authorities began in 2020 to implement measures to fight human trafficking which according to government is reaching "alarming levels." Between February and July, dozens of officials from the defense, security, and judicial sectors received training on combating human trafficking, and identifying and protecting victims. In July, the Angolan state secretary for human rights revealed that the country had recorded over 100 cases of human trafficking between 2015 and 2020. According to the official, the border provinces of Cunene, Cabinda, Zaire and Luanda Norte, as well as the capital, Luanda, had registered most of the cases of human trafficking. Victims included children used as beggars, and women used for sexual exploitation.

Human Rights Strategy

The Angolan government adopted the country's first and long-awaited human rights strategy in February. The document, which was first drafted in 2017, establishes that the country's human rights situation is subject to a periodic evaluation by the state security council, the introduction of an award for human rights activists, and teaching of human rights as a subject in schools, among other things. In July, Angola's vice president, Bornito de Sousa, launched the first training of human rights for teachers as part of the human rights strategy.

Key International Actors

Angola continued its mediation efforts to bring peace and stability to the Great Lakes region. In February, the president of Uganda, Yoweri Museveni, and his Rwandan counterpart, Paul Kagame, met in Luanda to discuss a border dispute between the two countries, and review the August 2019 peace pact that they signed.

During a visit to Luanda in February, US Secretary of State Mike Pompeo praised President Joao Lourenco for his efforts in fighting corruption.

In September, the European Union and Angola agreed to launch a roadmap aimed to establish a partnership on security and defense. The initial focus will be on consolidating the global rules-based order in support of the United Nations and the African Union, on possible Angolan participation in EU Common Security and Defence Policy missions and operations, and on maritime security in the Gulf of Guinea.

Argentina

Longstanding human rights problems in Argentina include police abuse, poor prison conditions, and endemic violence against women. Restrictions on abortion and difficulty accessing reproductive health services remain serious concerns. Impunity for the 1994 bombing of the AMIA Jewish center in Buenos Aires and delays in appointing permanent judges are likewise concerns.

In December 2019, President Alberto Fernández took office. In March, he promised to send a bill to Congress to decriminalize abortion. The bill's introduction was delayed due to the Covid-19 pandemic and, as of October, had not been introduced.

As of October 2020, Argentina had reported more than 1,130,000 confirmed Covid-19 cases and over 30,000 deaths. In March, the government imposed a mandatory, nationwide lockdown. While many provinces progressively lifted the restrictions, the Buenos Aires metropolitan region continued under partial lockdown at time of writing.

Argentina continues to make significant progress protecting lesbian, gay, bisexual, and transgender (LGBT) rights and prosecuting officials for abuses committed during the country's last military dictatorship (1976-1983), although trials have experienced delays.

Confronting Past Abuses

Pardons and amnesty laws shielding officials implicated in the 1976-1983 dictatorship's crimes were annulled by the Supreme Court and federal judges in the early 2000s. As of September 2020, the Attorney General's Office reported 3,329 people charged, 997 convicted, and 162 acquitted. Of 597 investigations into crimes against humanity, judges had issued rulings in 246.

As of August 2020, 130 people illegally taken from their parents as children during the dictatorship had been identified and many had been reunited with their families, according to the Abuelas de Plaza de Mayo, a human rights group.

The large number of victims, suspects, and cases of alleged crimes of the dictatorship makes it difficult for prosecutors and judges with limited resources to bring those responsible to justice. Argentine law allows judges to order house arrest for people age 70 and older who are in pretrial detention or have been convicted. The Attorney General's Office reported in September 2020 that 659 pretrial detainees and convicted prisoners were under house arrest for alleged crimes of the dictatorship, including 37 who had been transferred in connection with the Covid-19 pandemic.

Prison Conditions and Abuses by Security Forces

A 2018 United Nations report found that prisons and jails were so crowded that some pretrial detainees were being held in police stations. Prison guards had taken "disobedient" detainees to isolation cells without following established procedures, and security forces had detained and abused children, the report found.

The National Penitentiary Office reported 421 alleged cases of torture or ill-treatment in federal prisons in 2019 and 87 from January through June 2020. Between January and September, the Attorney's General's Office reported nine violent deaths of people detained in federal prisons.

More than half of the 11,570 detainees in federal prisons have not been convicted of a crime but are awaiting trial, the government reports.

Between March and April, federal courts transferred 320 detainees in federal prisons to house arrest to reduce prison overcrowding and prevent the spread of Covid-19. Similarly, the judiciary in the province of Buenos Aires transferred 800 people in provincial prisons to house arrest between March and April. In September, the National Penitentiary System reported that 13 detainees had died due to Covid-19 in federal prisons.

Security forces occasionally employ excessive force. In December 2019, the federal Security Ministry revoked a resolution granting federal agents overly broad discretion to use firearms.

Between March, when a nationwide Covid-19 lockdown began, and August, the National Human Rights Secretary received 531 complaints of abuse by national and provincial agents enforcing measures to curb the spread of the virus, including 25 cases involving deaths.

In August, Facundo Astudillo Castro, 22, was found dead in Buenos Aires province. He had been missing since April, when police officers reportedly stopped him for violating the lockdown. In July, the press published a photo of Castro, handcuffed, standing next to a police car, before his disappearance. On September 3, media reported that the police found evidence that could belong to Castro inside a police car. In October, an autopsy revealed that Castro had died from "drowning," apparently without the intervention of third parties. As of October, prosecutors were investigating the case as an "enforced disappearance, followed by death."

Freedom of Expression

In June, the interim head of Argentina's Federal Intelligence Agency presented evidence to a federal court that the agency had compiled profiles of more than 400 local and international journalists seeking accreditation to cover international summits in Argentina in 2017 and 2018. Profiles were classified by "ideology and political profile," media reported, and journalists who did not meet "political criteria" were denied access to events. At time of writing, a court was investigating the role of a former director and deputy director of the intelligence agency in these alleged activities.

In 2015, former President Mauricio Macri adopted "temporary" decrees to modify a law adopted during the previous government to regulate media. Despite a stated commitment to adopt a new media law, one was never presented to Congress during the Macri administration. As of September 2020, the National Communications Entity (ENACOM), the agency charged with implementing these rules, was still reporting to the executive branch, compromising its ability to act independently.

In May and August, the government issued decrees establishing a price freeze on mobile data, fixed-line internet connection, and television services through the end of 2020, requiring ENACOM's approval for tariff increases in 2021, and declaring these services as "essential and strategic public services." The decree argued this measure is necessary to protect citizens' access to information, freedom of expression, and children's access to education during the pandemic.

A 2016 law created a national agency to ensure public access to government information and protect personal data. From 2017 to July 2020, individuals had filed 11,750 information requests. Authorities responded to most within a month, the legal deadline, but as of September 2020, citizens had filed 778 appeals, in most cases after authorities failed to respond by the deadline, according to official data.

Some provinces and municipalities lack freedom of information laws, undermining transparency.

Judicial Independence

In August 2020, the government initiated an overhaul of the country's judiciary. The government appointed a "council of experts" to propose reforms to the Magistrate's Council and Supreme Court, including increasing the number of Supreme Court magistrates. Some of the 11 experts have ties to officials under investigation. One of them is a lawyer for Vice President Cristina Fernández de Kirchner, who is facing multiple corruption charges but has immunity from arrest due to her position. The experts had not presented a reform proposal at time of writing.

As part of the overhaul, the government promoted legislation to create dozens of new criminal courts to be staffed by temporary judges until tenured judges are appointed—which often takes years. As of September, the bill was pending in the House of Representatives. The Senate had approved it.

For years, delays have left temporary judges, who lack security of tenure, in place. The Supreme Court ruled in 2015 that this undermines judicial independence. As of August 2020, 291 judgeships remained vacant.

In September, the pro-government majority in the Senate transferred three federal judges who had been working on cases investigating Vice President Fernández de Kirchner to posts they had previously held, in which they would no longer investigate those cases. The government argued that in 2018, former President Macri had unlawfully transferred these judges to these posts. In September, the Supreme Court suspended the Senate's decision to transfer them back, while it analyzes the measure's constitutionality. The case remained pending as of October.

HUMAN
RIGHTS
WATCH

A CASE FOR LEGAL ABORTION
The Human Cost of Barriers to Sexual and Reproductive Rights in Argentina

Impunity for the AMIA Bombing

Twenty-six years after the 1994 bombing, which Argentine prosecutors have alleged was carried out by Iranian suspects, of the Argentine Israelite Mutual Association (AMIA) in Buenos Aires that killed 85 people and injured more than 300, court battles continue and no one has been convicted. Alberto Nisman, the prosecutor charged with investigating the bombing, was found dead in January 2015 with a gunshot wound to the head and a pistol beside him after he accused then-president Cristina Fernández de Kirchner of covering up Iran's role in the attack. In June 2018, an appeals court held Nisman's death appeared to be a murder. As of September 2020, no one had been convicted of Nisman's murder.

In March 2018, an appeals court upheld a decision ordering the pretrial detention of now-Vice President Kirchner for allegedly conspiring with Iranian officials to undermine the bombing investigation during her previous presidency. She had immunity from arrest, first as a senator, and now as vice president. In December 2019, a federal court overturned the pretrial detention order.

In February 2019, former President Carlos Menem was acquitted of interference in the investigation into the AMIA bombing, while a former head of intelligence and a judge were convicted. In September 2020, a federal prosecutor appealed Menem's acquittal.

Indigenous Rights

Indigenous people face obstacles accessing justice, land, education, health care, and basic services. Argentina repeatedly fails to implement laws protecting indigenous peoples' right— guaranteed by international and regional law—to free, prior, and informed consent to government and business decisions that may affect their rights. Debates on a national law on indigenous communal ownership of traditional lands, which the Argentine Constitution protects, is continually postponed.

In November 2017, Congress approved a law extending the deadline for completing a survey of indigenous lands to 2021. The survey is being conducted, slowly.

In April 2020, the Inter-American Court of Human Rights issued a landmark ruling upholding the rights to a healthy environment, land, water, and cultural identity of 132 indigenous communities in Salta province—ordering Argentina to cede 4,000 square kilometers of land to the communities.

Children's Rights

For years, the Justice Ministry has published the personal data of children with open arrest warrants online—a practice that runs counter to children's rights. The Buenos Aires city government has loaded the images and identities of these children into a facial recognition system used at the city's train stations, despite significant errors in the national government's database and the technology's higher risk of false matches for children.

In October, in response to a letter from Human Rights Watch, the Ministry of Justice blocked access to the public national database, saying that it would conduct an "audit" of it.

Women's and Girls' Rights

Abortion is illegal in Argentina, except in cases of rape or when the life or health of the pregnant person is at risk. Even in such cases, pregnant people face obstacles to legal abortion and are sometimes subject to criminal prosecution. A bill to decriminalize abortion completely during the first 14 weeks of pregnancy and, after that period, to allow termination of pregnancies in specific circumstances was approved by the House of Representatives but rejected by the Senate in 2018.

Despite a 2009 law detailing comprehensive measures to prevent and prosecute violence against women, their unpunished killing remains a serious concern. The National Registry of Femicides, administered by the Supreme Court, reported 268 femicides—the murder of women based on their gender—but only 7 convictions, in 2019.

During the Covid-19 lockdown, reports of domestic and sexual violence to a government hotline increased by 24 percent between April and June compared to the same period the previous year, the government reported in August.

Sexual Orientation and Gender Identity

In 2010, Argentina became the first Latin American country to legalize same-sex marriage. The Civil Marriage Law allows same-sex couples to enter civil marriages and affords them the same marital protections as different-sex couples. Since 2010, more than 20,000 same-sex couples have married.

In 2012, Argentina passed a Gender Identity Law, respecting self-identification. It allows anyone to change their gender and name in their identity card and birth certificate through a simple administrative procedure.

In September 2020, President Alberto Fernández issued a decree establishing that at least one percent of employees in the federal government should be transgender people.

Key International Actors and Foreign Policy

In February 2020, the UN Committee on the Protection of the Rights of all Migrant Workers and Members of their Families voiced concern, in its concluding observations on Argentina, about a 2017 decree that is inconsistent with international standards, including through a process of summary expulsion of foreigners.

In August 2020, Argentina said that the rejection by the secretary general of the Organization of American States (OAS) of an executive secretary, whom the Inter-American Commission on Human Rights (IACHR) had unanimously selected, undermined the "legitimacy and effectiveness" of the regional human rights system.

Argentina remains a member of the Lima Group, a coalition of governments that monitors Venezuela's poor human rights record and has called for the release of political prisoners, but it did not sign the group's statements in 2020. In August, Argentina joined the International Contact Group on Venezuela, a coalition of European and Latin American governments seeking to achieve democratic elections in Venezuela.

The number of Venezuelans moving legally to Argentina has steadily increased since 2014, reaching more than 207,000 as of July 2020. Argentina has largely facilitated their legal stay in the country.

As a member of the UN Human Rights Council, Argentina has supported United Nations scrutiny of rights violations in Belarus, Syria, Iran, and Nicaragua. In October 2020, Argentina voted in favor of a UN Human Rights Council resolution that condemned human rights abuses in Venezuela, extended the mandate of a UN fact-finding mission that had reported crimes against humanity were committed in Venezuela, and required the UN High Commissioner for Human Rights to continue its periodic reporting on the human rights situation there, despite prior statements by Argentina's ambassador to the OAS criticizing the fact-finding mission's report.

Armenia

The Covid-19 pandemic and later renewed hostilities over Nagorno-Karabakh dominated events in Armenia. A Russia-brokered truce ended six weeks of fighting on November 10, with Armenia ceding control over several territories to Azerbaijan and without defining the political status of Nagorno-Karabakh. All parties to the conflict committed violations of international humanitarian law. Armenian forces carried out attacks using banned cluster munitions.

The military defeat prompted a sharp political crisis in Armenia with opposition to Prime Minister Nikol Pashinyan demanding snap elections.

In March, the government responded to the pandemic with a state of emergency that lasted for nearly six months and involved restrictions on privacy rights and freedom of movement and assembly. Domestic violence, discrimination against people with disabilities, and violence and discrimination based on sexual orientation and gender identity persisted.

Conflict over Nagorno-Karabakh

On September 27, Azerbaijan launched a military offensive that escalated fighting between Azerbaijan and Armenia and the de-facto authorities in Nagorno-Karabakh. Tens of thousands of people evacuated Nagorno-Karabakh mainly to Armenia in response to the fighting. Russia deployed peacekeeping forces to oversee the ceasefire it negotiated.

Warring parties committed violations of international humanitarian law (See the Azerbaijan chapter for violations by Azerbaijani forces), that unlawfully harmed civilians. During the fighting, Armenian forces carried out indiscriminate attacks, launching unguided artillery rockets, and firing heavy artillery shells and ballistic missiles on population centers, including in some places where there were no evident military targets, causing civilian deaths and injuries.

The Armenian military also used banned cluster munitions in populated areas, resulting in dozens of civilian casualties. Cluster munitions have been banned because of their widespread indiscriminate effect and long-lasting danger to civilians.

Covid-19

Armenia confirmed its first Covid-19 case on March 1. On March 16, the government declared a state of emergency and extended it five times, ending it on September 11. In March, parliament passed amendments requiring telecommunications companies to provide authorities with phone records for all of their customers in order to facilitate tracking of people exposed to the virus.

For months, authorities refused to reveal information on the group of people in charge of the tracking system, saying that it was developed by volunteer programmers, free of charge; their names were eventually revealed without information about their affiliations. Authorities suspended the data-tracking after the state of emergency ended.

In September, the government replaced the state of emergency with a special regime until January 11, which allows the national government to impose national or local lockdowns, and restrictions on gatherings and protests, without announcing a state of emergency.

Around 4 million children were impacted by school closures. A rapid analysis of 3,000 families by World Vision Armenia showed that nearly 14 percent of school-age children in those households did not attend online classes. Nearly 80 percent of children lacked equipment and an internet connection.

According to Armenian Helsinki Committee, which monitored around 30 protests and rallies during the state of emergency, the police response varied considerably. In some cases, police did not intervene; in other cases, police terminated assemblies with fewer than five participants, including single-person protests, even when the protest participants wore masks and observed social distancing.

Accountability for Law Enforcement Abuse

In April, the government approved a strategy and action plan for police reform for 2020-2022. The plan includes re-establishing an Interior Ministry and increasing parliamentary oversight over police. The reforms also envisage creation of a new patrol police and granting police investigative powers.

Meanwhile, investigations into past abuses by law enforcement remain incomplete. Investigations into police violence during the protests in 2016 resumed in 2019, but no charges were filed.

In January, authorities brought charges against one policeman involved in the violent dispersal of protests in 2015 and suspended investigations into the remainder of the incidents from the 2015 protests. In July, authorities also suspended the investigation into police conduct during the summer 2018 protests. In both cases, authorities claimed they were unable to identify alleged perpetrators.

Environment and Human Rights

Despite Covid-19-related restrictions, protests against plans to restart construction on the Amulsar gold mine continued throughout the year. Protesters are concerned with the mine's potential environmental and health impacts. Protests escalated towards the end of July, when private security personnel hired by the mining company removed makeshift cabins used by the protesters and replaced them with booths to be used by the security company. The escalation led to clashes with police. On August 4, police arrested more than 10 people, including protesters and security personnel. Several protesters accused the police of using excessive force in detaining protesters.

On August 6 and 10, protesters in Yerevan, observing social distancing, staged single person-pickets in support of the Amulsar protests. Police briefly detained them, citing Covid-19 restrictions. Among those detained were human rights defenders Nina Karapetyants, Zaruhi Hovhannisyan, and Ara Gharagyozyan. On August 6, authorities also banned a bicycle rally in support of the Amulsar protests, detaining several bikers. Police pressed misdemeanor disobedience charges and released all detainees within hours. Authorities did not interfere with further protests in support of Amulsar days later.

Violence against Women and Children

Media and civil society groups publicized several brutal cases of domestic violence, including a killing in March in Gyumri, when a man beat his female domestic partner to death. He also injured her 13-year-old daughter, who spent months in a hospital recovering from the assault. The man is awaiting trial on manslaughter and other charges. Domestic violence is neither a stand-alone felony nor an aggravating criminal circumstance in the criminal code.

According to official data, during the first half of 2020, authorities investigated 395 criminal domestic violence cases. They brought charges against 196 people and sent 62 cases to courts.

Coronavirus-related measures further jeopardized the security of domestic violence survivors. The Women's Support center, a nongovernmental organization, reported in June that calls to their hotline were 50 percent higher than during the same period last year. However, it also noted that many women experiencing abuse may not have been able to reach out for help during lockdowns.

Armenia has only two shelters for domestic violence survivors, run by the Women's Rights Center, with total capacity for 17 to 20 people. During the pandemic-related lockdown, the government did not take targeted measures to ensure victims of domestic violence could access shelters.

Reinforcement of traditional gender roles in some case put their health and life in danger during the pandemic. In one case, a 66-year-old woman died of complications from Covid-19 after doctors said her husband repeatedly refused testing and treatment for her.

Armenian law does not effectively protect survivors of domestic violence, jeopardizing their lives and well-being. The Council of Europe Convention on Preventing and Combating Violence against Women and Domestic Violence (Istanbul Convention) had not yet been sent to parliament for ratification. The government signed the convention in 2018.

Disability Rights

Authorities remained committed to ending institutionalization of children with disabilities. During the pandemic, they continued to transform some residential institutions for children into community centers and to support family-based care. Nevertheless, many children with disabilities remain segregated in specialized orphanages.

In April, the government approved the 2020-2023 Comprehensive Program and Action Plan on Fulfillment of the Right to Live in a Family and Harmonious Development of the Child. The program features an alternative care service network, including specialized services for children with disabilities.

Armenia plans to guarantee inclusive education by 2025, whereby children with and without disabilities study together in community schools. Due to the pandemic, schools shifted to remote education in March, but largely reopened in September. According to one survey, more than half of the children with disabilities in Armenia only partially participated in remote classes. For some children, remote education increased accessibility of classes. But for others, it created additional barriers, due in part to lack of guidelines on providing inclusive education through remote education, as well as lack of support—called reasonable accommodations—necessary for inclusion, including assistive devices, hearing aids, books in braille, or other adjustments.

For several months, due to strict lockdown measures, community support service centers were closed, cutting children with disabilities off from such services as rehabilitation and therapy. The services restored partially as the authorities eased lockdown rules. According to authorities, the state largely continued to provide social services and food assistance to children and people with disabilities throughout the lockdown.

Adults with psychosocial or intellectual disabilities can be deprived of legal capacity, or the right to make decisions, and Armenia lacks supported decision-making mechanisms. A bill on rights of people with disabilities, which is to replace the outdated 1993 law and contains significant improvements, has not yet been introduced in the parliament.

Authorities approved and introduced to parliament a bill to ratify the Optional Protocol to the Convention on Rights of Persons with Disabilities, which would allow victims in Armenia access to an individual complaint mechanism for alleged violations of the convention.

Sexual Orientation and Gender Identity (SOGI)

Lesbian, gay, bisexual, and transgender (LGBT) people continue to face harassment, discrimination, and violence. The criminal code does not recognize homophobia and transphobia as aggravating criminal circumstances in hate crimes. Public debate around the ratification of the Istanbul Convention descended into hateful and derogatory speech against LGBT people by some public officials, who suggested incorrectly that the convention aims to promote LGBT "propaganda" and to legitimize same-sex marriage.

PINK Armenia, an LGBT rights group, documented 12 incidents of physical attacks based on sexual orientation or gender identity from January through July 2020, and 10 cases of threats and calls for physical and psychological violence. Police dismissed five of the twelve attack reports filed by victims, claiming absence of a crime, and suspended three cases, due to reconciliation of the parties.

In August, the Court of Appeal ruled there had not been a proper investigation into a violent homophobic attack in 2018 against a group of LGBT activists, which left at least six activists injured. The court ordered a re-investigation.

Fear of discrimination and public disclosure of their sexual orientation and humiliation prevent many LGBT people from reporting crimes. Openly gay men fear for their physical security in the military, and some seek exemption from obligatory military service. In one case, after a young man disclosed his sexual orientation during the investigation into his alleged draft evasion, the information was passed to a local official, who outed him to his family, urging his brother to "restrain him" for bringing shame to the family.

Key International Actors

Armenia ratified the Council of Europe's Convention on Protection of Children against Sexual Exploitation and Sexual Abuse ("Lanzarote Convention"), which enters into force in January 2021.

In September, parliament also ratified the Optional Protocol to the International Covenant on Economic, Social and Cultural Rights allowing access to the individual complaint mechanism.

In January, the United Nations Human Rights Council held the Universal Periodic Review of Armenia. In the council's report, Armenia received numerous recommendations, including to ratify the Istanbul Convention without further delay;

strengthen anti-discrimination policies; and criminalize all forms of torture and ill-treatment.

In December 2019, the Council of Europe's Committee for the Prevention of Torture and Inhuman or Degrading Treatment or Punishment (CPT) carried out a periodic visit to a number of Armenia's police and penitentiary establishments, psychiatric facilities, and an institution for people with disabilities.

Australia

Australia is a vibrant multicultural democracy with robust institutions, but in 2020 the global Black Lives Matter movement refocused attention on the severe disadvantage suffered by First Nations people in Australia, particularly the over-representation of Aboriginal and Torres Strait Islander people in prison and high rate of deaths in custody.

While Australia largely contained the spread of Covid-19, a severe outbreak in Victoria after a mismanaged hotel quarantine scheme led to more than 700 deaths, mostly residents of aged care homes. Police efforts to enforce curfews and lockdowns during the pandemic raised concerns over freedom of expression and the misuse of police powers.

Asylum Seekers and Refugees

2020 marked seven years since the Australia government introduced offshore processing of asylum seekers. Approximately 290 refugees and asylum seekers remained in Papua New Guinea and Nauru at time of writing, with more than 870 resettled to the US under an Australia-US resettlement deal. Of those remaining offshore, all are adults, and most have been there since 2013.

Australia has rejected offers by New Zealand to take some of the refugees, with the government arguing that accepting the offer would encourage more boat arrivals as New Zealand is a "backdoor route" to Australia. At least 12 refugees and asylum seekers have died in Australia's offshore processing system since 2013, six of them suicides.

More than 1,200 refugees and asylum seekers transferred to Australia from Papua New Guinea and Nauru for medical or other reasons remain in limbo, with no permanent visas. Authorities placed more than 120 male asylum seekers and refugees in detention under guard in hotels for months, not allowed to go outside and with visitors banned during the pandemic. In April authorities forcibly removed a Kurdish asylum seeker who complained to the media about hotel conditions and placed him in immigration detention.

The government introduced a bill in May that would enable detention center staff to confiscate mobile phones in immigration detention. It would also grant detention facility officers new search and seize powers without the need of a warrant. The bill passed the lower house of parliament in September and was still pending at time of writing.

Indigenous Rights

Indigenous Australians are significantly over-represented in the criminal justice system, with Aboriginal and Torres Strait Islander people comprising 29 percent of Australia's adult prison population, but just 3 percent of the national population.

There were at least seven Indigenous deaths in custody in Australia in 2020— four in Western Australian prisons, two in Victoria, and one in a Brisbane police watch house.

In April, a Victorian coroner found the 2017 death of Aboriginal woman Tanya Day "clearly preventable" and that "unconscious bias" was a factor in her being reported to police and arrested. Day died when she sustained a head injury in a police cell. Despite the coroner ruling that police officers may have committed an indictable offense, Victoria Police decided not to bring charges.

In June, the Western Australian parliament passed laws to reduce the practice of jailing people for unpaid fines, which disproportionately impact Indigenous people and people with lower incomes.

Three young Indigenous men in Western Australia took the government to court in July, alleging they were held for more than 23 hours a day for up to eight weeks in solitary confinement in prison, prompting an official review of prison policy.

In August, the Queensland health ombudsman found that the health care delivered to a 6-year-old Australian boy who died from a sudden illness in 2017 was "likely inadequate" and that "Aboriginal and Torres Strait Islander peoples remain at a significant disadvantage compared to other Queenslanders across many health measures."

The chief executive of global mining giant Rio Tinto announced he would be stepping down following an outcry over the company's destruction of a 46,000-year-old Indigenous site in Western Australia in May.

Children's Rights

Incarceration disproportionately affects Indigenous children: they are 21 times more likely to be detained than non-Indigenous children.

Across Australia, about 600 children under the age of 14 are imprisoned each year. State and territory attorney generals had the opportunity to increase the age of criminal responsibility from 10 to 14 years, the recommended international minimum, after a major public campaign ahead of their annual summit, but they declined. In August, the Australian Capital Territory parliament committed to introducing their own legislation to raise the age of criminal responsibility.

A landmark report by the South Australian Guardian for Children and Young People revealed disturbing treatment inside Adelaide's Youth Detention Centre including invasive body searches.

A bill introduced to parliament in May would allow Australia's domestic spy agency, the Australian Security Intelligence Organisation (ASIO), to question children as young as 14. The bill raised concerns about the sufficiency of safeguards to protect children's rights.

The Queensland Human Rights Commission called for an independent prison inspector in the state after reports of prolonged lockdown and potential solitary confinement at Brisbane Youth Detention Centre during a Covid-19 outbreak in August.

Freedom of Expression

Pretrial proceedings in the case of former spy "Witness K" and his lawyer Bernard Collaery continued, with both charged with breaching secrecy laws for exposing wrongdoing by the Australian government to obtain an advantage in trade negotiations with Timor-Leste. The court ruled that it would hold parts of the trial in secret after the attorney general invoked powers under the National Security Information Act.

56

The University of New South Wales apologized in August after deleting a twitter post and temporarily removing an article about human rights in Hong Kong that pro-Beijing students had criticized. In response, the federal education minister announced an independent review into whether universities were meeting national free speech standards.

A Deakin University report in September found that more than half of environmental scientists working for the government said they had been "prohibited from communicating scientific information." Government workers said they had been restricted from speaking out on threatened species, climate change, and logging.

Following police raids in June 2019 on several Australian journalists, a parliamentary inquiry into press freedom recommended that journalists not be immune from secrecy prosecutions but be granted new defenses for "public interest" journalism. In April, the High Court ruled that a police warrant issued to raid the home of a NewsCorp journalist in 2019 was invalid because the warrant was "impossibly wide."

Disability Rights

Human Rights Watch research analyzing coroners' inquest reports between 2010 and 2020 found that about 60 percent of people who died in prisons in Western Australia had a disability. Of that group, 58 percent died as a result of lack of support provided by the prison, suicide, or violence.

Rights of Older People

The Covid-19 pandemic has had a devastating impact on people living in aged care facilities in Australia. At time of writing, in Victoria there had been 655 deaths in aged care homes, and many outbreaks were preventable, according to experts. The pandemic has shone a light on insufficient staffing and inadequate community-based models of care in such facilities.

Many aged care facilities across Australia routinely give dangerous drugs to residents with dementia to control their behavior, rather than providing them with the support they need.

Broome Regional Prison

HUMAN
RIGHTS
WATCH

"He's Never Coming Back"
People with Disabilities Dying in Western Australia's Prisons

Terrorism and Counterterrorism

Despite a continuing public campaign to change its approach, the Australian government was unwilling to repatriate Australian citizens held in northeast Syria for suspected involvement in the extremist armed group Islamic State and their family members. At time of writing, approximately 80 Australians, 47 of them children, remained trapped in harsh conditions in camps and prisons. The government had helped bring home eight children from northeast Syria in 2019.

A parliamentary committee approved a proposal that would authorize the home affairs minister to strip dual nationals of Australian citizenship if the minister is "satisfied their conduct demonstrates a repudiation of their allegiance to Australia and it is not in the public interest for the person to remain an Australian citizen."

Covid-19

A spate of cases of racial abuse and attacks against people of Asian descent were reported across the country after the Covid-19 outbreak began in February.

Victorian authorities subjected more than 3,000 people in public housing towers in Melbourne to a sudden, mandatory lockdown for 14 days in July after a rise in coronavirus cases among residents. The discriminatory approach included a heavy police presence outside the towers and reports that police and health officials blocked a mother from breastfeeding her ill baby in the hospital. Residents complained about lack of communication by authorities and difficulties accessing food, exercise, fresh air, and medical supplies. The state compensated those held under the lockdown with hardship payments of A$1,500 (US$1,080) to residents forced to miss work and A$750 (US$540) to those without employment.

The disruption caused to around 4 million students' schooling was compounded by inconsistent messaging from federal and state politicians. Pre-existing inequalities were reflected in differences in student access to internet-connected devices.

Early research suggests that rates of domestic violence increased during Covid-19 lockdowns. The government committed more than A$3 million (US$2.1 million) in additional funding to service providers and announced a new emergency accommodation program for victims.

In response to the threat of Covid-19, the government announced restrictions on visits to nursing homes. Some facilities banned visitors altogether, cutting off older people from important family and social connections.

In Queensland and Victoria, several prisons and youth detention centers endured long periods of lockdown and extreme isolation during Covid-19, with visitor bans and conditions reportedly akin to solitary confinement.

The Covid-19 pandemic resulted in restrictions on freedom of peaceful assembly. In June, Black Lives Matter protest leaders in Melbourne were fined for organizing a public rally that police claimed breached social distancing restrictions in place to stop the spread of Covid-19, while in July Sydney police won a Supreme Court case to prohibit a Black Lives Matter protest. Police then arrested and fined six attendees for not abiding by the ban. In September, police arrested and fined protesters at Sydney University despite protester measures to abide by health advice.

Metropolitan Melbourne was placed under a strict lockdown in August after a rise in Covid-19 cases, with a daily curfew from 8 p.m. to 5 a.m. and residents only allowed to leave their homes within a 5 kilometer radius for a limited time to buy food, provide care, or exercise while permits were required to attend approved work.

Victoria's police have used harsh measures during that lockdown that threaten basic rights. In September police were recorded arresting a pregnant woman on incitement charges for organizing an anti-lockdown protest on Facebook. The Victorian government introduced problematic new legislation that would give anyone designated an "authorized officer," such as a police or public security officer, the power to preemptively detain individuals who test positive for Covid-19 and are "likely to refuse or fail to comply with the direction." After public pressure, the government removed that provision.

Australia banned citizens from leaving the country as a public health measure during the coronavirus pandemic unless they met strict criteria. Restrictions on the number of passengers allowed into Australia left tens of thousands of Australians stranded overseas including 3,000 classified as vulnerable because they were experiencing health complications or financial troubles. This punitive approach to travel left thousands of Australian families separated from their loved ones.

Foreign Policy

In November, the government released a redacted report of a four-year military investigation into alleged war crimes by Australian forces in Afghanistan. The report found credible information about 23 incidents in which Special Forces unlawfully killed 39 civilians or captured combatants, none of which were "disputable decisions made under pressure in the heat of battle." The Morrison government responded by announcing the creation of an Office of the Special Investigator to gather evidence and refer cases to the prosecutors.

2020 marked Australia's third and final year on the United Nations Human Rights Council. At the council, Australia was on a core group on Eritrea, and supported joint statements calling for greater scrutiny of human rights violations in China, Saudi Arabia, and several other countries. However, Australia was weak on international accountability for "drug war" killings in the Philippines. Officials said they would instead pursue "constructive engagement," not appreciating that private advocacy without public pressure often only shields violators from international scrutiny. Australia was the only UN Human Rights Council member to vote against all resolutions seeking to address rights violations in the Occupied Palestinian Territories.

Tensions between the Australian and Chinese government grew in 2020 as Beijing retaliated with trade sanctions after Australia led calls for an independent international inquiry into the origins of the Covid-19 pandemic.

Beyond statements in Geneva, the Australian government rarely called out human rights violations in other Southeast Asian countries such as Indonesia, Cambodia and Vietnam. A meeting between Australia's ambassador to Myanmar and Myanmar's military commander-in-chief in January undercut international efforts to sideline the senior general for his role in serious abuses against ethnic Rohingya Muslims since 2017.

Australia has not endorsed the Safe Schools Declaration, an intergovernmental pledge now signed by 105 countries to protect education in times of conflict.

Australia exports military equipment to Saudi Arabia and the United Arab Emirates, despite grave concerns about alleged war crimes by the Saudi-led coalition in Yemen.

Azerbaijan

Hostilities over Nagorno-Karabakh renewed at the end of September, dominating events in Azerbaijan for the rest of 2020. All parties to the conflict committed violations of international humanitarian law. The Azerbaijani military carried out attacks using banned cluster munitions.

National solidarity during the war served to suspend an intensifying conflict between the government and political opposition, however the government remained hostile to dissenting voices. Authorities misused restrictions imposed to slow the spread of Covid-19 to target critics, particularly those affiliated with the opposition Azerbaijan Popular Front Party (APFP).

In five individual cases in 2020, the European Court of Human Rights (ECtHR) found that from 2014 to 2016, Azerbaijani authorities had wrongfully imprisoned government critics in retaliation for their activism.

Restrictive laws continue to prevent nongovernmental organizations (NGOs) from operating independently. Reports of torture and ill-treatment persisted throughout the year.

The snap parliamentary vote in February was marred by credible claims of election violations and resulted in continued dominance of the ruling party.

In April, the Supreme Court acquitted two former political prisoners, politician Ilgar Mammadov and human rights defender, Rasul Jafarov, years after judgments in their favor by the ECtHR.

Conflict over Nagorno-Karabakh

On September 27, Azerbaijan launched a military offensive that escalated hostilities between Azerbaijan and Armenia and the de-facto authorities in Nagorno-Karabakh. Tens of thousands of people fled Nagorno Karabakh in response to the fighting. A Russia-brokered truce ended six weeks of fighting on November 10, with Armenia ceding control over several territories to Azerbaijan and without defining the political status of Nagorno Karabakh. Russia deployed peacekeeping forces to oversee the ceasefire it negotiated.

The warring parties committed violations of international humanitarian law (See the Armenia chapter for violations by Armenian forces), that unlawfully harmed civilians.

During the fighting, Azerbaijani forces launched large air-dropped munitions and fired rockets that lacked the capacity to be targeted with precision, into populated areas. Attacks on dual purpose infrastructure such as power stations may have caused excessive harm to the civilian population and in addition to striking military targets, some attacks damaged schools, private residences and businesses, and hospitals, and interrupted regular supply of services such as power, gas, and water to civilians.

Azerbaijan's military also used banned cluster munitions in populated areas, resulting in civilian casualties. Cluster munitions have been banned because of their widespread indiscriminate effect and long-lasting danger to civilians.

In a serious violation of humanitarian law, Azerbaijani soldiers subjected Armenian prisoners of war to physical abuse and acts of humiliation, which were filmed and shared widely online.

Freedom of Expression, Freedom of Media

In its February decision, the ECtHR ruled that Azerbaijan had wrongfully imprisoned investigative journalist Khadija Ismayilova from 2014 to 2016 to silence and punish her.

In March, a Baku court unexpectedly ordered early release for investigative journalist Afgan Mukhtarli, and allowed him to join his family abroad. Mukhtarli had served half of his six-year sentence on bogus charges. In August, Fuad Ahmadli, a blogger and senior APFP activist was released after completing a four-year prison sentence on politically motivated charges.

At least three other journalists and bloggers who criticized the authorities are still in prison on politically motivated charges. In November 2020, Polad Aslanov was sentenced to 16 years on treason charges, and Araz Guliyev and Elchin Ismayilli continued to serve prison sentences. Others, including Ismayilova and Shahvalad Chobanoglu, continue to face arbitrary travel bans.

In September, the General Prosecutor's Office put a group of political exiles who criticize the country's authorities on an international wanted list, which included prominent bloggers Tural Sadigli and Ordukhan Babirli.

Under amendments to the Law on Information that parliament adopted in March in response to the Covid-19 pandemic, owners of internet information resources face up to three years in prison for failure to prevent the publication of information online that authorities deem false and could pose a threat to public health or safety. Human Rights Watch is aware of at least 10 cases in which the authorities invoked the law to compel website owners, bloggers, and Facebook users to delete online posts criticizing the government's response to the pandemic.

Covid-19

In his major speech about challenges posed by the Covid-19 pandemic, President Ilham Aliyev implied he would use measures introduced to slow the spread of the coronavirus to crack down on political opponents, whom he described as traitors, enemies, and a fifth column.

Days afterwards, authorities arrested dozens of activists and bloggers. Most had criticized conditions in government-run quarantine centers or the government's failure to provide adequate compensation to people struggling financially from the pandemic's fallout.

Courts sentenced most to between 10 and 30 days' detention on charges such as breaking Covid-19-related lockdown rules or disobeying police orders, which had not occurred. Among them was APFP member Niyameddin Ahmedov. Police allegedly beat Ahmedov in custody in an attempt to coerce him to falsely testify against the APFP leader. Days before his scheduled release, authorities pressed dubious charges against him for allegedly financing terrorism.

Prosecuting Political Opposition

In March, authorities arrested Tofig Yagublu, a leading politician of the opposition Musaval party, on bogus hooliganism charges. In September, he was convicted and sentenced to four years and three months in prison. Police falsely claimed Yagublu had physically attacked a motorist and his passenger after a car accident. Trial monitors noted numerous due process violations, including the court's refusal to grant a defense request to retrieve and introduce CCTV footage that would have corroborated Yagublu's defense. In September, a court ordered Yagublu transferred to house arrest after he needed hospitalization due to health complications arising from his hunger strike.

In May, a court sentenced Jalil Zabidov, an activist with an anti-corruption Facebook page, Korrupsiyaya-Yox-De ("Say-No-to-Corruption"), to five months in prison on bogus hooliganism charges. In February, Zabidov had filmed and posted evidence of alleged election fraud at a precinct. The next day, Zabidov said, a local election official attacked him, in response to which authorities charged Zabidov.

Authorities also continued to target both leading and rank-and-file members of the APFP with bogus or disproportionate charges and other harassment. In March, police detained Agil Humbatov, and forcibly placed him in a psychiatric clinic after he uploaded a video to Facebook criticizing the authorities' handling of the pandemic. Several days later, a court ordered his release. Police detained Humbatov a second time after he posted a video describing conditions in the clinic, and an appeals court ordered him, groundlessly, to be forcibly placed in a psychiatric hospital. He was released in July without any explanation or medical documentation.

In August, a court sentenced APFP member Pasha Umudov to four years and five months on bogus drug charges. Authorities had detained Umudov ahead of the unsanctioned rally in October 2019.

In mid-July, authorities arrested and filed criminal charges against 17 senior APFP members for public order, property destruction, and other offenses that stemmed from a July 14 pro-war protest related to Nagorno Karabakh and neighboring Armenia. During the rally, a group of people forcibly but briefly entered the parliament building, reportedly causing minor damage. After police removed them, violent confrontations between protesters and police ensued on the street.

Most of the 17 APFP members had not participated in the rally. Among those arrested were Asif Yusifli, Mammad Ibrahim, Fuad Gahramanli, Bakhtiyar Imanov, and Ayaz Maharramli, members of the party's leadership. Only Yusifli was at the rally but was not in the group that broke into parliament. In November, a court transferred 12 of the APFP members, including these five men, to house arrest.

Most of the 17 were refused access to a lawyer of their choosing; some, including Gahramanli, were held incommunicado for almost two weeks. Authorities did not present any material evidence to support accusations that they participated in any illegal actions.

In December, a court sentenced one of the detainees, Mahammad Imanli, to one year in prison on false criminal charges of spreading Covid-19. He remained in detention at time of writing.

In the weeks after the protest, police held at least 25 APFP members for up to 30 days on bogus charges of violating Covid-19 lockdown rules.

Freedom of Assembly

Azerbaijan effectively imposes a blanket ban on protests in the central areas of Baku.

In February, police detained over a hundred opposition supporters, including parliamentary candidates, as they were gathering to protest alleged violations during the parliamentary elections. Before the unauthorized protest was scheduled to start, police detained several activists at their homes. Police drove most of them to remote areas 200 to 300 kilometers from Baku and abandoned them there.

Torture and Ill-Treatment

Authorities routinely dismissed complaints of torture and other ill-treatment in custody, and the practice continued with impunity.

In an open letter posted on social media by his family, APFP member Alizamin Salayev, arrested in January and convicted in April on criminal defamation charges, alleged that police at the station knocked him to the ground and ordered him to film himself putting his head into the toilet. When he refused, police began to beat him. According to Salayev, while in police custody, he was twice taken to hospital. Both times, doctors recommended surgery for a ruptured hernia he said he had sustained as a result of the beatings. Police did not allow this. Salayev's lawyer was allowed access to him only nine days after his arrest and confirmed he saw Salayev's bruises. The trial court dismissed Salayev's torture complaint and authorities refused to investigate the allegations.

In June, riot police in Baku raided an apartment building and detained at least 11 people. The raid came one day after police detained one of the building's residents on suspicion of breaking Covid-19 lockdown regulations; a group of residents threw trash at the vehicle in which police detained the man. Police used excessive force to detain the 11; some were sentenced to fines, others to up to 15 days' detention. Among the latter was Karim Suleymanli, who in a video alleged that numerous police beat him for five hours. His bruises are visible in a video published after his release. Suleymanli's lawyer, Javad Javadov, filed the ill-treatment complaint, which authorities declined to investigate. Javadov received a warning from the Bar Association for raising concerns about his client's treatment.

Seymur Ahmadov, one of the APFP members detained in July, filed a complaint with the prosecutor's office describing severe beatings in custody. In a letter he wrote in remand prison, Ahmadov said a plainclothes officer beat him for an hour with a truncheon "so bad that I could no longer feel the pain." Authorities failed to conduct an effective investigation.

On 30 March, police arrested Agil Humbatov after he posted a video on social media criticizing the government. The next day, police officers took him to the Psychiatric Hospital №1, where he was confined as a patient purportedly suffering from paranoia.

Key International Actors

In January, the Parliamentary Assembly of the Council of Europe (PACE) adopted a resolution that deemed the problem of political prisoners in Azerbaijan as "systemic in nature," which needed to be solved once and for all. It cited findings by the ECtHR, which found a "troubling pattern" of politically motivated misuse of the criminal justice in Azerbaijan.

In February, PACE, the Organization for Security and Co-operation in Europe (OSCE) Office for Democratic Institutions and Human Rights (ODIHR), and other independent observers found that the parliamentary election failed to meet international standards for a free and fair vote.

In March, the during the annual bilateral meeting on human rights, democracy and justice, the European Union welcomed Azerbaijan's Presidential Decree on the Open Government Action Plan and addressed persisting challenges to freedoms of assembly, association, and expression, as well as developments related to gender equality and children's rights.

In May, the EU welcomed the acquittals of Ilgar Mammadov and Rasul Jafarov and urged Azerbaijan to continue to implement the remaining judgments of the ECtHR.

Yagublu's conviction and the government's relentless crackdown on opposition figures, which worsened during the Covid-19 pandemic, prompted statements from Azerbaijan's international partners.

In March, the PACE rapporteurs on Azerbaijan expressed outrage at the government "launching yet another round of concerted political repression," noting that the case against Yagublu had been "fabricated."

In September, US Embassy called on the government "to reverse the string of recent politically-motivated detentions, reevaluate Mr. Yagublu's case, and respect the fundamental freedoms of speech and association."

In a September statement, the spokesperson for the EU's Foreign Affairs and Security Policy said Yahublu's sentencing raised questions "about the authorities' commitment to protecting and enhancing political freedoms for all" and called for a re-examination the case.

Bahrain

The human rights situation in Bahrain did not improve in 2020. There are 27 individuals currently on death row, of whom 25 are at imminent risk of execution. The government has put six people to death since it ended a moratorium on executions in 2017.

Authorities arrested, prosecuted, and harassed human rights defenders, journalists, opposition leaders, and defense lawyers, including for their social media activity. All independent Bahraini media have been banned since 2017 from operating in the country and all opposition groups dissolved.

Nabeel Rajab, one of Bahrain's most prominent human rights defenders, was released from prison on June 9 to serve the rest of his five-year sentence under house arrest.

Health and hygiene conditions in Bahrain's overcrowded prisons remain extremely serious. Although Bahrain released 1,486 prisoners in March due to the health risk posed by Covid-19, the releases have excluded opposition leaders, activists, journalists, and human rights defenders—many of whom are older and/or suffer from underlying medical conditions.

Authorities failed to hold officials accountable for torture and ill-treatment. Oversight mechanisms are not independent of the government.

Bahrain continued to deny access to independent rights monitors and the UN special procedures, including the special rapporteur on torture.

Freedom of Expression, Association, and Peaceful Assembly

On June 9, 2020, authorities released from prison prominent human rights defender Nabeel Rajab to serve the rest of his five-year sentence on speech charges under house arrest. Rajab's conviction arose from his 2015 tweets alleging torture in Jau Prison and criticizing Bahrain's participation in the Saudi-led military campaign in Yemen. Rajab was released under a 2017 law that allows courts to impose "alternative" sentences after a detainee serves half of their sentence, which Rajab completed on November 1, 2019.

Thirteen prominent dissidents have been serving lengthy prison terms since their arrest in 2011 for their roles in pro-democracy demonstrations. They include Abdulhadi al-Khawaja, a founder of the Bahrain Center for Human Rights, as well as Abduljalil al-Singace, a leader in the unrecognized opposition group Al Haq, both serving life terms.

Shaikh Ali Salman, leader of Al-Wifaq, Bahrain's largest but now forcibly dissolved opposition political society, is also serving a life term after the Court of Cassation upheld his sentence in January 2019 on trumped-up charges of allegedly spying for Qatar.

In 2020, Bahrain escalated its suppression of online and social media activity and prosecuted several public figures solely for their posts on social media, including prominent lawyers Abdullah Al Shamlawi and Abdullah Hashim. In May 2019, the Interior Ministry declared that it will prosecute people who follow "inciting accounts" or share their posts on Twitter.

No independent media have operated in Bahrain since the Information Affairs Ministry suspended *Al Wasat,* the country's only independent newspaper, in 2017. Foreign journalists rarely have access to Bahrain, and Human Rights Watch and other rights groups are routinely denied access. International wire services, when they cover Bahrain, do so from Dubai or elsewhere outside the country. Six journalists are currently imprisoned.

Death Penalty

There are 27 individuals currently on death row, of whom 25 are at imminent risk of execution.

On July 13, the Court of Cassation upheld the death sentences on Mohamed Ramadan and Hussein Ali Moosa, despite unfair trials and credible evidence that their convictions were based on confessions coerced under torture.

The Special Investigation Unit's (SIU)'s investigation into Moosa and Ramadan's torture allegations found "suspicion of the crime of torture ... which was carried out with the intent of forcing them to confess to committing the crime they were charged with."

However, the investigation failed to comply with the Istanbul Protocol, the internationally recognized legal and professional standards for effective investigations of torture allegations.

Agnes Callamard, the United Nations special rapporteur on extrajudicial, summary or arbitrary executions, warned that Moosa and Ramadan's "conviction resulting in the death penalty would be arbitrary and a clear violation of their right to life."

In 2017, Bahrain ended a moratorium on the use of the death penalty. In July 2019, Bahrain executed three men, including Ali al-Arab and Ahmad al-Malali who had been sentenced to death in a mass trial marred by allegations of torture and serious due process violations.

Security Forces and Prisons

Bahrain released 1,486 prisoners in March due to the health risk posed by Covid-19, but the releases excluded opposition leaders, activists, journalists, and human rights defenders – many of whom are older and/or suffer from underlying medical conditions.

Overcrowded conditions in Bahrain's prisons compound the risk of Covid-19 spreading. The lack of adequate sanitation led to scabies outbreaks in Jau Prison—Bahrain's largest prison—and the Dry Dock Detention Center in December 2019 and January 2020.

Authorities continue to deny Bahraini prisoners adequate medical care, causing unnecessary suffering and endangering the health of some unjustly imprisoned persons with chronic medical conditions, such as Hassan Mushaima and Abdel Jalil al-Singace.

Authorities in 2020 failed to credibly investigate and prosecute officials and police officers who allegedly committed serious violations, including torture.

Arbitrary Citizenship Revocations

Almost 300 persons whom the authorities have stripped of their citizenship in recent years remain without Bahraini nationality, rendering most of them stateless.

In 2019, King Hamad reinstated the citizenship of 551 individuals and courts restored the nationality of another 147 individuals. Bahrain also amended its citizenship revocation laws, restricting the power to strip nationality to the cabinet. Under the amendments, the king and the judiciary no longer have the power to unilaterally strip Bahrainis of their citizenship for national security or terrorism crimes. All known citizenship revocations since 2012 have been handed down by the courts, or by royal decree, or by order of the Interior Ministry.

Human Rights Defenders

On March 5, authorities released Hajer Mansoor, the mother-in-law of prominent exiled human rights defender Sayed Ahmed al-Wadaei. Police arrested Hajer in March 2017 and a court convicted her in October 2017 on dubious terrorism charges that appear to have been filed in reprisal against al-Wadaei's human rights work. The judicial process was marred by due process violations and allegations of ill-treatment and coerced confessions. Two other members of al-Wadaei's family remain imprisoned.

Migrant Workers

Migrant workers faced a range of abuses that worsened during the Covid-19 pandemic. While the authorities attempted to ease overcrowding by offering migrants accommodation in schools, the authorities are also reported to have forced workers to leave the accommodation by cutting off electricity and water during the peak of the summer and without providing them alternative accommodation. The authorities paid salaries of 100,000 citizens working in the private sector between April and June but did not provide similar benefits to migrant workers who form the majority of Bahrain's workforce. Migrant workers reported facing dismissal, reduced pay or unpaid wages, and faced eviction from their accommodation by landlords.

In 2017, Bahrain introduced a unified standard contract for domestic workers, which requires detailing the nature of the job, work and rest hours, and weekly days off. But the standard contract does not limit working hours, set out the minimum wage or rest days to which workers are entitled, and lacks enforcement mechanisms to ensure the rights of domestic workers are respected. There is no law setting out more extended rights and decent working conditions for domestic workers. Migrant domestic workers faced further risks of abuse during Covid-19 lockdown restrictions.

Women's Rights, Gender Identity, and Sexual Orientation

Bahraini family laws discriminate against women's right to divorce, inherit, and transmit Bahraini nationality to their children on an equal basis to men, and deprive their children of the right to obtain citizenship on an equal basis with children of Bahraini men.

Article 353 of the penal code exempts perpetrators of rape from prosecution and punishment if they marry their victims. Bahrain's parliament proposed a full repeal of that article in 2016, but the cabinet rejected the proposal. Article 334 of the penal code reduces the penalties for perpetrators of so-called honor crimes.

Bahrain's penal code criminalizes adultery and sexual relations outside marriage, a violation of the right to privacy, which disproportionately harms women and migrant women. Although no law explicitly criminalizes same-sex relations, authorities have used vague penal code provisions against "indecency" and "immorality" to target sexual and gender minorities. There is no law that prohibits discrimination on the grounds of gender identity or sexual orientation.

In December 2018, Bahrain amended its labor law to ban discrimination based on sex, origin, language or creed, and sexual harassment in the workplace, but the law does not refer to sexual orientation or gender identity.

Key International Actors

Bahrain continued to participate in Yemen military operations as part of the Saudi Arabia-led coalition, which is responsible for serious laws of war violations. The coalition has failed to credibly investigate potential war crimes, and coalition members, including Bahrain, have provided insufficient or no information about their role in alleged unlawful attacks.

The US maintains a major naval base in Bahrain.

On September 15, Bahrain established formal diplomatic ties with Israel. The head of Israel's Mossad intelligence agency, Yossi Cohen, visited Bahrain at the end of September to meet Bahraini intelligence and security officials.

In June, the European Union welcomed the partial release of Nabeel Rajab. In July, the EU expressed concerns about the death sentences of Mohamad Ramadan and Hussein Ali Moosa and urged Bahrain to halt their executions and reintroduce a moratorium on executions as a step towards abolition. In September, the European Parliament reiterated its call to halt the export of equipment that can be used for internal repression to Bahrain.

Bahrain has not responded to a visit request by the special rapporteur on human rights defenders sent in 2012 or a reminder sent in 2015. Bahrain has also not responded to visit requests in recent years by the special rapporteurs on torture, freedom of expression, and freedom of assembly.

Bangladesh

Bangladesh's Awami League-led government doubled down on an authoritarian crackdown on free speech, arresting critics, and censoring media. Arrests under the abusive Digital Security Act (DSA) increased dramatically. Impunity for abuses by security forces, including enforced disappearances and extrajudicial killings, remained pervasive.

Host to nearly 1 million Rohingya refugees from neighboring Myanmar, Bangladesh kept its commitment under international law not to force returns and allowed ashore refugees stranded at sea who were pushed back by other governments. However, policies over the year violated refugee rights. Authorities arbitrarily detained over 300 refugees on Bhasan Char island, while refusing to allow a safety assessment or protection visit by United Nations experts.

The government took positive steps by restoring internet in the refugee camps, after a nearly year-long internet blackout, and promising to allow refugees to study under the formal Myanmar curriculum through secondary school.

A court ordered the first ever conviction under the 2013 Torture Act, which activists hoped would pave the way for investigations and accountability for the dozens of documented reports of torture by security forces.

Authorities released from detention nearly 3,000 people convicted of minor offenses and granted bail to over 20,000 people being held in pretrial detention in order to reduce crowding and protect against the spread of Covid-19 in prisons. However, those being held in detention for criticizing the ruling party were not included in these releases. Juvenile detention centers granted bail to nearly 500 children in the wake of the pandemic but, according to UNICEF, more than 1,000 children awaiting trial or sentenced for petty crimes remained in detention.

Freedom of Expression and Association

Authorities increasingly used the DSA to harass and indefinitely detain activists, journalists, and others critical of the government and its political leadership. Police even arrested a child under the act for "defaming" the prime minister in a Facebook post.

The international community, including the UN High Commissioner for Human Rights, UN independent experts, and European Union, as well as journalists in Bangladesh repeatedly criticized the DSA for stifling free speech and violating international law. In May, 311 members of Bangladesh civil society issued a joint statement calling for the government to release those held under the DSA.

Authorities also used the Covid-19 pandemic as pretext to censor free speech and the media and threaten academic freedom, arresting artists, students, doctors, political opposition members, and activists for speaking out about the government's handling of the pandemic.

The government silenced healthcare workers and cracked down on those who spoke out over a lack of personal protective equipment (PPE) and resources for treating Covid-19. In May, the government issued a circular banning all government employees from posting, "liking," sharing, or commenting on any content which might "tarnish the image of the state" or the government's "important persons."

The government censored media by blocking news sites and dropping the media from the list of emergency services that remained exempt from lockdown restrictions. In August, the Cabinet approved a draft amendment to the 2017 National Online Media Policy, requiring all media outlets to obtain government approval to run their online media portals.

The government increased surveillance, including by creating two units to identify Covid-19 "rumors"—one under the Information Ministry and another under the Rapid Action Battalion (RAB), the country's primary counterterrorism unit, notorious for abuse and flouting rule of law. In reality, these initiatives primarily led to the arbitrary arrest of individuals who spoke out against the government's response to the pandemic or were otherwise critical of the ruling party.

Disappearances and Extrajudicial Killings

The government continued to deny its unlawful practice of enforced disappearances and ignored concerns raised by the UN Working Group on Enforced or Involuntary Disappearances, the UN Committee against Torture, and the UN Human Rights Committee. Authorities continued to forcibly disappear critics and deny justice for victims and their families.

Shafiqul Islam Kajol, a journalist, was forcibly disappeared for 53 days before he was "found" in a field, blindfolded and tied. Rather than investigating his disappearance, authorities arrested him under three separate DSA cases.

Security forces continued to commit extrajudicial killings with near-complete impunity. However, when police killed a retired military officer, Maj. Sinha Rashed Khan, authorities were forced to take action and "crossfires"—a euphemism for extrajudicial killings in Bangladesh—dropped precipitously, indicating that authorities can bring these killings to an end whenever they choose.

Right to Health

Bangladesh's healthcare system was overwhelmed by the Covid-19 pandemic, shedding light on massive disparities in healthcare access. Many people with symptoms consistent with Covid-19 initially reported being turned away from hospitals. Healthcare workers reported that they did not have sufficient PPE to safely provide medical care.

Doctors told Human Rights Watch that they were overwhelmed and under pressure to reserve limited intensive care facilities for patients with clout or influence. Delivery of essential sexual and reproductive health services fell to the wayside, putting women and girls' health at increased risk.

Refugees

With Myanmar failing to create conditions for their safe and voluntary return, Bangladesh continued to host nearly 1 million Rohingya refugees. However, with their welcome wearing thin, the government's policies violated basic rights, including by building barbed wire fencing around the camps and shutting off internet access for nearly a year, which violated rights to freedom of expression and access to information and hampered aid workers' ability to coordinate emergency responses, conduct contact-tracing, and share critical information about Covid-19.

In August, the government reiterated a promise made in January to finally allow Rohingya children access to formal education under the Myanmar curriculum, but the initial "pilot" plan to reach 10,000 children, up to class 9, has yet to be implemented.

Bangladesh rescued two boats of Rohingya refugees in May after other governments pushed them back to sea for months. However, the government placed the refugees at risk by holding them on the remote silt island of Bhasan Char, initially saying that it was only a temporary quarantine to prevent the spread of Covid-19. However, over six months later, the government had refused to allow the refugees to return to their families in Cox's Bazar or for UN officials to conduct a protection visit.

Refugees on the island described being held without freedom of movement or adequate access to food or medical care; some alleged that they were beaten and ill-treated by Bangladesh authorities on the island. The government ignored calls from UN Secretary-General António Guterres and humanitarian experts to safely return the refugees to the camps in Cox's Bazar.

Labor Rights

Following massive order cancellations during the pandemic, more than 1 million garment workers—mostly women—were laid off, many of whom did not receive payment of owed wages. Retailers took advantage of the crisis by demanding discounts on producer prices, thus putting pressure on workers to return to work for lower wages, often without adequate PPE, reliable healthcare, or sick leave.

The government provided US$600 million in subsidized loans to companies to support payment of wages to workers in the garment sector. It is unclear, however, how the payments of back wages were made to workers, particularly women who may not have financial control or access.

Women and Girls' Rights

Women and girls faced widespread violence. According to Bangladesh human rights organization Ain O Salish Kendra, 975 women and girls were reportedly raped in the first nine months of 2020, and 235 women were murdered by their husband or his family. NGOs reported a marked increase in reports of domestic violence during the nationwide lockdown instituted to stop the spread of Covid-19.

HUMAN
RIGHTS
WATCH

"I Sleep in My Own Deathbed"
Violence against Women and Girls in Bangladesh:
Barriers to Legal Recourse and Support

Yet, survivors faced further reductions to already limited options for safe shelter or other protection measures as well as significant obstacles to legal recourse.

Despite promises, the government failed to pass a long overdue sexual harassment law or make amendments to the discriminatory rape law. Instead, the government hurriedly approved an amendment to allow for the death penalty for rape to quell protests that broke out after several gang-rape cases came to light.

Prime Minister Sheikh Hasina committed to end marriage for girls under 15 by 2021, but there was little meaningful progress during the year. Instead, a special provision remained in effect that allows for child marriage in "special cases," with permission of their parents and a court.

Sexual Orientation and Gender Identity

Section 377 of the Bangladeshi penal code punishes "carnal intercourse against the order of nature" by up to life imprisonment.

Though the government took an important step in recognizing hijras as a third gender, in practice, it remained difficult for hijras to access health care and other government services, a problem exacerbated during the Covid-19 pandemic. Lesbian, gay, bisexual, and transgender people and advocates in Bangladesh continued to face violence and threats of violence without adequate protection from the police.

In positive steps, the National Human Rights Commission formed a committee to address issues for marginalized groups, including transgender people, and the National Curriculum and Textbook Board of Bangladesh agreed to incorporate third gender issues into the secondary school curriculum.

Indigenous Rights

Activists continued to call for the full implementation of the Peace Accord in the Chittagong Hill Tracts.

Two years after the disappearance of Michael Chakma, an Indigenous rights activist, the government has ignored appeals from his family, as well as inquiries from the High Court, the National Human Rights Commission, and the United Nations Committee against Torture. In January, the police finally responded to an order from the High court by simply stating that they "could not find anybody named Michael Chakma in any prisons in Bangladesh."

Key International Actors

The European Union, which accounts for over 60 percent of Bangladesh's garment exports, warned of its readiness to withdraw important trade preferences if Bangladesh continued to flout human rights obligations, particularly labor rights. A European Commission ombudsman report in March decided against a complaint by labor unions calling for the EU to begin withdrawing trade preferences, but said that option "remains open." Citing the economic impact of the Covid-19 pandemic, Bangladesh applied for a continuance of the trade preferences beyond 2024, when it is expected to graduate from least developed country status and would lose zero duty benefits.

In March, the EU welcomed the release of opposition leader Begum Khaleda Zia, which the bloc had advocated for.

The Bangladesh government ignored or dismissed key recommendations by the United Nations and others, particularly with regard to its crackdown on free speech under the DSA and increasing cases of enforced disappearances and killings. Bangladesh failed to submit a requested follow-up report to the Committee against Torture's review of its practices.

India failed to speak up against human rights violations in Bangladesh, even when journalist Shafiqul Kajol was found at the border after being forcibly disappeared for nearly two months.

China blocked international efforts to hold the Myanmar military accountable for grave abuses against the Rohingya, and instead continued to push for repatriation and supported Bangladesh's initiatives to relocate refugees to Bhasan Char island. Bangladesh accused Myanmar of failing to create conditions that would enable the safe and voluntary return of Rohingya refugees.

The International Monetary Fund (IMF) approved emergency loans totaling US$732 million to Bangladesh to help address the impact of the Covid-19 pandemic. The government committed to the IMF to conduct an audit within 12 months of receiving the loan and to publish all Covid-19-related procurement contracts. The World Bank provided a fast track loan of $1 million for its Covid-19 Emergency Response and Pandemic Preparedness Project and approved another $1.05 billion for economic stimulus projects. The United States provided over $56 million and the EU provided over $388 million in aid to Bangladesh in response to the Covid-19 pandemic.

Belarus

An unprecedented wave of mass and largely peaceful protests swept Belarus following the August 9 contested re-election of Aliaksandr Lukashenka, who has been president since 1994. Belarusian security forces arbitrarily detained thousands of people and subjected hundreds to torture and other ill-treatment in an attempt to stifle the protests. However, the abuse only served to increase public outrage. Tens of thousands continued to demonstrate peacefully for fair elections and justice for abuses.

Authorities launched hundreds of politically motivated criminal cases against political opposition members, protesters, and their supporters. In many cases they detained, beat, fined, or deported journalists who covered the protests and stripped them of their accreditation. They temporarily blocked dozens of websites and, during several days, severely restricted access to the internet.

Free and Fair Elections

The presidential elections were marred by arrests of leading opposition candidates, groundless refusals to register certain opposition candidates for the ballot, and allegations of widespread fraud.

In May, the Central Electoral Commission (CEC) refused to register the nomination for Siarhei Tsikhanousky, a popular blogger who at the time was serving a sentence for the administrative offense of organizing an unauthorized protest, on the grounds that he had not signed the registration papers personally. Sviatlana Tsikhanouskaya, his spouse, advanced her candidacy instead. In mid-June, Tsikhanouskaya received an anonymous call threatening her children's safety unless she dropped out of the race. Tsikhanouskaya remained in the race but sent her children to a safe country.

On June 18, authorities arrested leading opposition candidate Viktar Babaryka and his son Eduard. Authorities later announced they had charged Babaryka with tax evasion, money laundering, and bribery. At time of writing, Babaryka, who said the charges were fabricated, remained in pretrial detention.

CEC barred from running another key opposition candidate, Valer Tsapkala, on dubious claims that over half of his nomination signatures were invalid.

The Organization for Security and Co-operation in Europe's Office for Democratic Institutions and Human Rights (OSCE ODIHR) did not monitor the election due to the lack of a timely invitation from Belarus.

A consortium of Belarusian human rights organizations sought to monitor the vote and reported that election officials did not let them observe ballot counting. The consortium alleged major irregularities in the officially reported vote count. In September, authorities arrested Maria Rabkova of Viasna, a leading human rights organization, as part of a criminal investigation into alleged "mass riots." Rabkova played an important role in the election monitoring effort.

Governmental Crackdown on Peaceful Protests

Officials and police violently dispersed protests on August 9-12 in Minsk and other large cities, using excessive force and resorting to rubber bullets, stun grenades, and tear gas. Riot police detained almost 7,000 protesters and by-standers in four days, subjecting hundreds to torture and other ill-treatment and holding them in inhuman and degrading conditions. At least three protesters died as a result of police actions.

Former detainees described beatings, prolonged stress positions, electric shocks, and in at least one case, rape. Some had serious injuries, including broken bones, skin wounds, electrical burns, or mild traumatic brain injuries. Detainees said that police, riot police, and special forces picked them up off the streets, in some cases using extreme violence, then beat them in dangerously confined spaces in vehicles where they struggled to breathe. Some detainees alleged riot police officers threatened them with rape, in most cases while they were in transit. At least one man was raped with a truncheon.

At precincts and other detention facilities, police beat detainees and forced them to hold stress positions for hours, then held them for days in overcrowded cells. Police often denied detainees food and water and denied their requests to go to the toilet. Police and guards at detention facilities confiscated detainees' medications, frequently ignored calls for medical care, and in some cases denied it altogether.

Detainees were denied access to a lawyer. Those taken before a judge said the proceedings lasted only a few minutes and ended with short custodial sentences for administrative offenses. Others were released early. Detainees' family members struggled, in many cases for days, to find out their relatives' fate or whereabouts.

On August 14, the deputy internal affairs minister denied that anyone had been beaten or tortured. On August 26, the Prosecutor's Office announced the creation of an inter-agency commission to gather facts about any criminal acts by law enforcement, both during arrests and in detention facilities. Dozens of former detainees lodged complaints. Although several preliminary inquiries were launched by the authorities, at time of writing they had not opened any criminal cases.

In early September, police again began to arrest large numbers of peaceful protesters, with the Interior Ministry reporting hundreds of arrests every weekend, and during two successive weekends in early November, they arrested more than 2,000.

By mid-November, authorities had detained a total of 25,000 since early August.

Many of the detainees were women. As women were at the forefront of the protests, authorities used misogynistic tactics against women in particular to undermine their participation in protests, such as threatening them with loss of custody of their children and labeling them "aggressive" and "unfeminine."

Arrest and Harassment of Opposition Members and Supporters

Starting in early summer, authorities launched more than 500 criminal cases against potential presidential candidates, their campaigns' team members, and peaceful protesters on false charges ranging from mass rioting to hooliganism. Authorities also launched criminal cases against businessmen and staff of companies that supported certain opposition presidential candidates and victims of police violence during the protests, including on charges of tax evasion and fraud. By November 15, at least 118 people remained in pretrial detention on these politically motivated charges.

Authorities arrested two members of the presidium of the opposition's Coordination Council, Maryia Kalesnikava and Maksim Znak, and Illia Salei, Kalesnikava's lawyer, and charged all three with "inciting actions aimed at harming [Belarus's] national security." Salei was released on bail in October. Tsikhanouskaya herself and the rest of the presidium's members were forced to leave the country under threats of personal safety or criminal prosecution.

Freedom of Expression and Attacks on Journalists

The Belarusian Association of Journalists (BAJ) documented more than 500 incidents of harassment, detention, fines and temporary arrests of journalists from January through mid-November 2020. BelSAT, a Poland-based broadcaster long targeted by Belarusian authorities, estimates it has already paid over US$100,000 in the first nine months of 2020, surpassing 2019's total fines by June, mostly for reporting without accreditation.

Authorities targeted journalists who covered and livestreamed protests, detaining and charging them with participating in unauthorized mass events and illegal distribution of media products.

During June protests over the arrest of Babaryka, police in Hantsevichi detained and beat journalists Aliaksandr Pazniak and Siarhei Bahrou. In July, police in Minsk detained RFE/RL correspondent Anton Trafimovich and broke his nose.

In June, authorities arrested RFE/RL consultant and blogger Ihar Losik, on charges of "organizing group actions disrupting the public order". If convicted, he faces up to three years in prison. Seven other popular Youtube bloggers and moderators of Telegram channels were arrested on similar charges in late June and early July and, like Losik, remain in pretrial detention at time of writing.

Persecution of journalists escalated after the election. BAJ reported 54 instances of police brutality against journalists from August through the end of September.

On August 9, Nasha Niva journalist Natalia Lubnevskaya was hospitalized with a rubber bullet leg wound in Minsk. When the newspaper's editorial office tried to claim insurance compensation, authorities informed them that they were liable for "untimely reporting of a work-related injury," although such charges were not brought. On the same day, NRC journalist Emilie van Outeren was wounded by stun grenade fragments.

Also on August 9, police detained Witold Dobrowolski and Kacper Sienicki, freelance journalists from Poland, in central Minsk. The journalists endured repeated beatings and threats during three days in detention.

Police violently detained TUT.by portal's reporter Nikita Bystryk on August 10 while he was filming the protests and beat him, causing kidney damage and rib fractures. After issuing four warnings to TUT.by for its protest coverage in August and September, the Information Ministry suspended its registration for three months and filed a lawsuit to revoke it altogether.

On August 10, police in Minsk detained and beat Maxim Solopov, a journalist with a prominent Russian-language portal Meduza. His whereabouts were unknown for over a day, until the Russian ambassador to Belarus intervened and secured his release. On the same day, riot police detained another Russian reporter, Nikita Telizhenko from Znak.com, who then alleged he was brutally beaten at the detention facility.

At the end of August, a governmental commission stripped at least 19 journalists working for foreign outlets, including Reuters, Associated Press, and the BBC, of their Foreign Ministry accreditation.

Authorities also brought criminal defamation charges against journalists covering the protests. In September, police detained Nasha Niva editor-in-chief, Yahor Martsinovich, and interrogated him for publishing an interview with a former detainee who claimed that a top Interior Ministry official had beaten him in custody. Police searched Martsinovich's apartment and seized his data-carrying devices. He was released on bail.

Freedom of Information

From August 9 to August 12, internet access in Belarus was severely restricted for 61 hours, leaving access only to 2G networks, permitting text messages and voice calls. Government officials blamed foreign cyber-attacks for the disruptions, but independent experts and an independent monitoring group have attributed them to government interference. Periodic internet access disruptions continued throughout August and September, in particular during weekend protest marches.

Authorities also blocked websites that covered the presidential election, subsequent nationwide protests, and police brutality. In August, Belarus blocked over 70 international and independent news websites, reportedly in response to their coverage of the August protests. In September, websites of three charities that raised funds to help victims of police violence were also blocked. The government also appeared to be blocking services that facilitate circumvention of online censorship such as virtual private networks (VPNs), used by millions in Belarus to access the blocked websites.

Death Penalty

Belarus remains the only country in Europe to carry out the death penalty. In the past year, Belarus is known to have executed one person, Aliaksandr Asipovich, who was sentenced to death in January 2019, and executed by firing squad on December 9, 2019.

There are currently four people on death row: Viktar Paulau, Viktar Syarhel, Stanislaw Kosteu, and Ilya Kosteu. The Supreme Court denied their appeals and they all are at risk of imminent execution.

In June, the Supreme Court vacated the death sentence of Viktar Skrundzik in light of evidence of a coerced confession and remanded the case to the Minsk regional court. Hearings began in September, but authorities suspended the hearings in October, citing the COVID-19 pandemic.

Covid-19

Since March, Belarus recorded over 70,000 cases and 632 deaths. At time of writing, Belarus has 1,208 reported cases per 100,000 people.

Throughout the pandemic, President Lukashenka dismissed the seriousness of Covid-19. Authorities did not introduce any lockdown measures despite high levels of community transmission. In November, authorities in Minsk and several other cities required mask-wearing in public.

Authorities attempted to silence medical professionals who spoke up about the danger of the pandemic. After Dr. Sergei Lazar gave an interview critical of the government's slow response, the government fired him from his position as chief of emergency medicine at Vitebsk hospital.

Key International Actors

The annual report by the United Nations special rapporteur on Belarus, Anaïs Marin, concluded that there were no significant improvements in the human rights situation. Belarus continued to refuse to recognize her mandate and failed to cooperate with her investigations. A thematic report by the special rapporteur documented serious concerns with the administration of justice in Belarus.

The European Union and the Parliamentary Assembly of the Council of Europe (PACE) condemned Belarus for handing down five new death sentences and carrying out at least one execution. Marin also condemned Belarus for prohibiting officials from releasing the date of the execution or burial location of those executed to their families.

The EU did not recognize the purported outcome of the presidential election, calling the election unfree and unfair, and imposed sanctions on 55 Belarusian officials, including Lukashenka, his son, and his national security advisor, involved in the post-election crackdown. The UN, the OSCE, and the Council of Europe (CoE) condemned Belarusian authorities for the violent response to protests. Many countries throughout Europe, including Germany, the Baltic States, Czechia, Poland, Slovakia, and the UK, declared the vote illegitimate and no longer recognize Lukashenka as president. The US also refused to recognized Lukashenka as president and condemned violence against protesters, detentions of opposition supporters, and internet shutdowns.

In September, 17 OSCE participating states led by the UK launched an independent expert investigation into torture and repression in Belarus. The independent expert, Professor Wolfgang Benedek, issued his report on November 5 and found "massive and systemic" human rights violations before and in the aftermath of the presidential election. Benedek called on Belarus to hold new elections, free all prisoners held for political reasons, and hold those responsible for torture and other abuses accountable.

Also in September, the UN Human Rights Council (UNHRC) held an urgent debate on Belarus and adopted a resolution that requests the UN High Commissioner for Human Rights (UNHCHR) to closely monitor the situation in Belarus in the context of the 2020 presidential elections and provide updates in 2020 and 2021. Marin and other UN human rights experts urged Belarus to stop torturing protesters and to free Kalesnikava, who remains in jail at time of writing. In November, they also criticized Belarus for persecuting women human rights defenders in the context of the mass protests.

Also in September, the UN Committee on the Elimination of Discrimination against Women (CEDAW) hailed the Women in White movement as key to advancing democracy Belarus.

In August, Estonia, Latvia, and Lithuania banned President Lukashenka and 29 other Belarusian officials from entering their countries due to the violent response to the protests. Later, this list was expanded to include a total of 128 officials. The UK and Canada also introduced visa bans and froze the assets of Lukashenka and several other top officials on human rights grounds. The US administration added eight Belarusian officials to its list of sanctioned Belarusian officials.

Bolivia

Luis Arce, from the Movement Toward Socialism (MAS, in Spanish), the party of former President Evo Morales, won the October 18 presidential election by wide margin. Arce received the presidential sash from Jeanine Áñez, who became interim president in November 2019, after president Morales resigned amid nationwide protests motivated by allegations of fraud—now disputed—in the October 2019 elections, and after the commander of the armed forces asked him to step down.

The Morales administration had created a hostile environment for human rights defenders and promoted changes to the judiciary that posed a serious threat to the rule of law. Instead of breaking with the past, interim President Áñez adopted measures that undermined fundamental human rights standards.

Her administration abused the justice system to persecute associates and supporters of Morales, and it failed to promote independent investigations into human rights abuses and election-related acts of violence in October and November 2019.

Interim President Áñez issued decrees that would have shielded military personnel from accountability for abuses during crowd-control operations and that threatened freedom of expression. Her government repealed both measures in response to criticism.

Covid-19

Bolivia had confirmed over 141,000 cases of Covid-19 and over 8,700 deaths as of November 2.

In March, the interim government closed the country's borders in response to the pandemic, leaving some 1,300 Bolivians, including older people, children, and pregnant women, stranded in camps in Chile. Weeks later the government let them enter, and they were quarantined.

The pandemic revealed structural weaknesses in the healthcare system. Bolivia had 490 intensive care beds in March, an intensive care doctors' association reported, and had only added 30 by August.

In May, the interim government bought 170 respirators—for use in ambulances, not hospitals—allegedly paying almost three times their real cost, prompting prosecutors to open a criminal investigation into possible corruption against government officials, including the then-health minister.

Medical personnel repeatedly protested lack of personal protective equipment and medical supplies. In June and July, several hospital directors said they were at full capacity, unable to admit additional cases.

Medical examiners reported finding the bodies of more than 3,000 people who had died of suspected or confirmed Covid-19 outside hospitals from April to mid-July. Some of the bodies were lying on the streets.

In August, demonstrators blocked roads to oppose the postponement of elections. The government accused protestors of keeping oxygen from reaching hospitals and, as a consequence, causing the death of about 40 Covid-19 patients. Hospitals had reported running out of oxygen even before the protests.

United Nations Women reported that the economic consequences of the pandemic disproportionately affected Bolivian women. Women earn 30 percent less than men on average; 70 percent of them work in the informal sector; and demands for their work as the primary caregivers for older people, children, and the sick rose during the pandemic. The interim government's Covid-19 aid programs did not adequately address women's needs, UN Women concluded, particularly in rural areas.

Government restrictions on movement in response to Covid-19 reduced many Indigenous communities' access to food, medicines, and markets for their products, the Ombudsperson's Office, a state agency tasked with protecting human rights, reported. Some indigenous people in remote areas had difficulty accessing government aid and some lacked identification documents needed to obtain aid.

Instead of working with schools to maintain lessons during the pandemic, the interim government in early August cancelled the remainder of the 2020 school year, through December, leaving almost 3 million children without education.

Overcrowded and unsanitary conditions in prisons were conducive to the spread of Covid-19. In January, 18,126 people were incarcerated in facilities operating at

212 percent capacity, the Ombudsperson's Office reported. Sixty-six percent of detainees were awaiting trial.

In April, the interim government issued a decree, which entered into effect in May, to release certain categories of people in detention, including pregnant people, some older inmates, and some inmates with chronic health conditions, "serious" disabilities, or caregiving responsibilities. In June, the government said as many as 3,500 detainees would be released, but only about 300 had been released a month later.

The government reported that 40 detainees had died of Covid-19 as of July. Detainees staged protests in several facilities, saying they lacked healthcare and protection from the virus. As of September, the Ombudsperson's Office was continuing to report a lack of cleaning and hygiene products in several prisons.

Judicial Independence

Evo Morales weakened judicial independence during his almost 14 years as president. The 2009 constitution made voters responsible for electing high court judges from lists created by the Plurinational Assembly, where Morales' party held a majority in both houses during most of his time in office. The party packed the lists with its supporters. In 2010, all judges appointed before 2009 were deemed "temporary." Scores of them were summarily removed.

During Morales' government, prosecutors filed what appeared to be politically motivated charges against several of his political rivals.

About 80 percent of judges and 90 percent of prosecutors remain "temporary," heightening the risk that they will issue decisions to please authorities in order to remain in their positions.

Instead of strengthening judicial independence, the Áñez government publicly pressured prosecutors and judges to further its interests. Prosecutors launched criminal investigations, many apparently politically motivated, of more than 150 people linked to the Morales government for sedition, terrorism, or membership in a criminal organization.

Human Rights Watch documented baseless charges, violations of free speech and due process, infringement on freedom of expression, and excessive and arbitrary use of pretrial detention.

Morales himself faced terrorism charges that appeared politically motivated. Prosecutors also charged Patricia Hermosa, Morales' attorney and former chief of staff, with terrorism, financing of terrorism, and sedition, based solely on her having telephone contact with Morales after he had resigned. She was held in pretrial detention for more than six months while pregnant, in violation of Bolivian law, and without access to medical care. She had a miscarriage in jail in March 2020.

The Áñez administration filed criminal complaints against at least four judges for granting house arrest to people linked to the Morales administration who had been awaiting trial in detention. Police initially detained one of the judges, but the judge was released the next day after another judge ruled the detention illegal.

In August 2020, the Plurinational Assembly, where Morales' party had a majority, passed a law that prohibits former officials from traveling outside Bolivia for three months after leaving office. The law arbitrarily infringes on outgoing officials' right to freedom of movement.

After winning the October 18, 2020 presidential election, Arce said the justice system should be independent from politics. In December 2020, he established a commission of experts to draft proposals to reform the justice system.

Protest-Related Violence and Abuses

Allegations of electoral fraud and the resignation of Morales sparked massive anti- and pro-Morales demonstrations in October and November 2019. While most protests were peaceful, some anti- and pro-Morales demonstrators allegedly abducted people identified as supporting the other side, burned homes and other buildings, and committed other acts of violence.

At least 37 people died in protest-related violence, and more than 800 were injured, the Ombudsperson's Office reported. Two anti-Morales protesters were killed in the town of Montero. Twenty people were killed in two massacres in

HUMAN
RIGHTS
WATCH

JUSTICE AS A WEAPON
Political Persecution in Bolivia

Sacaba and Senkata, in which scores of witnesses said state forces opened fire on pro-Morales demonstrators. Prosecutors told Human Rights Watch in February 2020 that the armed forces had refused to provide the names of soldiers who participated in those operations, let alone grant interviews with them. In September, the attorney general said the armed forces had not abided by a judicial order to provide prosecutors with the operation plans for those deployments.

The massacres occurred after Interim President Áñez issued a decree on November 15, 2019, that granted the military overly broad discretion in using force against protesters, sending a dangerous message that soldiers would not be held accountable for abuses. In response to criticism, President Áñez repealed the decree.

The Office of the United Nations High Commissioner for Human Rights and the Ombudsperson's Office documented scores of cases of arbitrary detentions and torture by police in the city of El Alto on November 11, 2019.

Authoritarian-Era Abuses

Bolivia has only prosecuted a few of the officials responsible for human rights violations committed under authoritarian governments between 1964 and 1982, partly because the armed forces have at times refused to share information about abuses.

A "Truth Commission" established in 2017 transferred 6,000 case files of victims of the dictatorships to the Plurinational Assembly in December 2019 and presented its final report in March 2020.

Freedom of Expression

The National Press Association, which represents the country's main print media, documented 87 instances of physical attacks against journalists in 2019, most of them by demonstrators; 14 attacks against the premises of media outlets; and 16 cases of authorities and politicians harassing and threatening the press. For instance, in November 2019 then Communication Minister Roxana Lizárraga said journalists who "commit sedition" would suffer "pertinent actions," including "deportation." Attacks against reporters, mostly by demonstrators, continued in 2020.

The interim government adopted policies threatening free speech, including an overly broad provision in a Covid-19 decree that would have allowed prosecution of government critics. In response to public outcry, the government revoked the provision in May 2020.

The interim government also established a "cyberpatrolling" unit to identify those who "misinform" the public about Covid-19, particularly political opponents. The "cyberpatrols" resulted, for instance, in charges of sedition and other crimes against Mauricio Jara, a Morales supporter, for calling the government "dictatorial" through a private messaging service, "misinforming," and urging protests. He was detained in April 2020 and, as of September, awaited trial behind bars.

Women's and Girls' Rights

Women and girls remain at high risk of violence, despite a 2013 law establishing comprehensive measures to prevent and prosecute gender-based violence. The law created the crime of "femicide": the killing of a woman under certain circumstances, including domestic violence.

The Attorney General's Office reported 117 femicides in 2019, and 86 between January and September 2020. It reported more than 20,000 cases of violence against women from January through August 2020.

Under Bolivian law, abortion is not a crime when a pregnancy results from rape or is necessary to protect the life or health of a pregnant woman or girl.

Sexual Orientation and Gender Identity

In July 2020, a court in La Paz ordered the national civil registry to register a same-sex couple's relationship as a "free union," ruling that the Bolivian Constitution and the country's international legal obligations require laws and administrative procedures to be interpreted in a manner consistent with equality and non-discrimination principles.

The civil registry appealed the ruling to the Constitutional Court.

Key International Actors

The interim government assented to a recommendation by the Inter-American Commission on Human Rights to establish an Interdisciplinary Group of Independent Experts to investigate acts of violence and human rights violations in Bolivia between September 1 and December 31, 2019., but the interim government backtracked on its commitment. The group started its work in November 2020, after Arce became president.

In August 2020, UN High Commissioner for Human Rights Michelle Bachelet said justice for those crimes was "essential" for victims and for the country. Her office called for investigations into threats and attacks against journalists, as well as human rights defenders working for the Ombudsperson's Office.

Bosnia and Herzegovina

There remained serious human rights concerns in Bosnia and Herzegovina (BiH) in 2020 over ethnic divisions, discrimination, and the rights of minorities and asylum seekers. Pressure on media professionals continued. A long-delayed strategy was adopted to clear the backlog of war crime case prosecution.

Discrimination and Intolerance

In June, an agreement was reached in Mostar between the main political parties to enable local elections to be held for the first time since 2008; they were scheduled for December 20, 2020. An October 2019 European Court of Human Rights (ECtHR) ruling had ordered Bosnia to amend the Election Act 2001 within six months to enable local elections to be held in Mostar. In 2010, the Bosnian Constitutional Court decided that Mostar's power-sharing structure was unconstitutional and discriminated against the residents of the city, but the government had never changed the law to allow elections to take place.

Eleven years since the Sejdić-Finci ruling by the ECtHR found that the Bosnian Constitution discriminates against ethnic and religious minorities by not allowing them to run for the presidency, the constitution still has not been amended.

The so-called two schools under one roof' system, referring to the segregation of children in schools based on their ethnicity, persisted in 2020.

The Organization for Security and Co-operation in Europe (OSCE) mission to BiH recorded 91 hate crimes between January and September 2020, the majority targeting victims based on their ethnicity or religion, six involving physical violence. At time of writing, eight trials against perpetrators were ongoing and two were convicted in 2020.

According to Vaša Prava BiH, a nongovernmental organization (NGO) providing free legal aid, the fallout from the Covid-19 pandemic disproportionally impacted marginalized populations, including Roma in BiH. Roma people, who are often employed in the informal sector, lost means of income and Roma children lacked access to online education, the organization said.

In April, the Constitutional Court in BiH examined the blanket ban on outdoor movement for older people and children put in place in response to Covid-19 and determined that the ban was disproportionate and violated the right to the liberty of movement.

In May, the Catholic church held a mass in Sarajevo commemorating the killings of Croatian Ustaša troops and civilians by Yugoslav partisans at the end of World War II. The event sparked protests in Sarajevo accusing the organizers of attempting to rehabilitate the Ustaša regime.

Accountability for War Crimes

In September, the Council of Ministers of BiH adopted the long-delayed Revised National War Crimes Processing Strategy submitted in May 2018. The strategy seeks to efficiently distribute war crime cases from the state to lower-level courts to clear the backlog in cases. The NGO TRIAL International voiced concerns that in 2020, 25 years since the Srebrenica genocide, war crimes and human rights violations are still denied or trivialized.

According to the OSCE, in August, 243 war crime cases against 483 defendants were in the post-indictment phase pending before all courts in BiH. Between January and July, BiH courts rendered first instance judgments in 11 cases, and 12 of the 19 defendants were convicted. During the same period, Bosnian courts rendered final judgments in six cases, five of nine defendants were convicted, and in two cases proceedings ended by the death of the accused.

In January, the United Nations mandated Residual Mechanism in The Hague rejected the plea for early release of Miroslav Bralo, convicted of war crimes and crimes against humanity against Bosniak civilians in 1993. In March, the UN Residual Mechanism denied Radoslav Brdjanin's request for early release from a 30-year sentence for war crimes and crimes against humanity committed in BiH.

In August, Ratko Mladić appeared before the mechanism to appeal his conviction for genocide against Bosnian Muslims of Srebrenica and other crimes committed during the 1992-1995 war. The prosecution also appealed the lower court's decision to acquit Mladić of committing genocide in six other Bosnian municipalities.

In August, the UN Committee on the Elimination of Discrimination against Women (CEDAW) said that BiH had failed to conduct effective and timely investigations into conflict-related sexual violence and that compensation and support for victims was insufficient.

According to information provided by the OSCE, in August 2020 there were 59 cases involving allegations of conflict-related sexual violence, against women and men, against 120 defendants in all courts of BiH. At time of writing, one first instance judgement which can still be appealed, and no final judgments were rendered; one proceeding ended by death of the accused.

Asylum Seekers and Migrants

The state Service for Foreigner's Affairs between January and August registered 11,292 irregular arrivals compared to 18,071 during the same period in 2019: 10,738 persons expressed the intention to apply for asylum, and 185 submitted an asylum application. According to the UN Refugee Agency (UNHCR), short application deadlines and limited state capacity to process claims hinder access to asylum procedures. As of August, 15 people were granted subsidiary protection. No one received refugee status.

Around 3,500 refugees and migrants in the northwestern Una-Sana Canton (USC) live outside official centers, many sleeping rough. A growing concern is the number of unaccompanied or separated children among them, left without access to adequate accommodation and child protection services. The UN special rapporteur on the human rights of migrants found in his May 2020 report following a 2019 visit to BiH that "many protection risks remain" for unaccompanied or separated children accommodated in regular reception facilities, due to the lack of appropriate alternatives.

In August, USC authorities severely restricted the movement of migrants and asylum seekers outside official reception centers, including prohibiting new arrivals to the Canton, leaving people stranded on the road without access to basic services.

Domestic and Other Gender-Based Violence

The lack of systematic data collection and analysis of gender-based and domestic violence continued in 2020. According to the women's rights organization United Women, domestic violence increased during the pandemic while services for victims were reduced.

In May, the revised Law on Protection from Domestic Violence entered into force in Republika Srpska, making domestic violence a criminal offense and introducing fines for failure to report domestic violence.

Sexual Orientation and Gender Identity

The second-ever Sarajevo Pride march took place in August. The Sarajevo Open Center (SOC), a lesbian, gay, bisexual, transgender, and intersex (LGBTI) and women's rights group, observed an increase in online threats against activists around the time of the march. The organization documented 13 hate incidents against LGBTI people, including cases of domestic violence, noting that due to restrictions imposed in response to the Covid-19 pandemic, LGBTI children were at higher risk of violence at home.

Freedom of Media

In 2020, journalists in BiH continued to face interference to their work, including defamation lawsuits, verbal threats, and physical attacks. From January until August 2020 the BiH journalists' association, BH Novinari, documented 51 violations of media freedom. Reporters without Borders in its 2020 World Press Freedom Index, stated that defamation suits are regularly used to obstruct journalists' work and silence critics.

Key International Actors

In July, UN Secretary-General Antonio Guterres stated that the peace in BiH is still fragile and urged regional leaders to counter hate speech and rhetorical division.

In July, Council of Europe Human Rights Commissioner Dunja Mijatović warned that many politicians continue to deny the truth about the Srebrenica genocide, deepening the suffering of the survivors and endangering peace.

OSCE Media Freedom Representative Harlem Desir expressed his concerns over attacks and threats against several journalists and attempts to restrict freedom of expression during the Covid-19 pandemic.

In October, the European Union Commission, in its Communication on EU enlargement policy, said that in BiH "[o]bstructions to justice reform from political actors and from within the judiciary, and the poor functioning of the judicial system continued to undermine citizens' enjoyment of rights" and that "Bosnia and Herzegovina needs to guarantee freedom of expression and of the media, and the protection of journalists, as well as an enabling environment for civil society, notably by upholding European standards on freedom of association and freedom of assembly."

Brazil

President Jair Bolsonaro tried to sabotage public health measures aimed at curbing the spread of Covid-19, but the Supreme Court, Congress, and governors upheld policies to protect Brazilians from the disease.

Bolsonaro's administration has weakened environmental law enforcement, effectively giving a green light to criminal networks that engage in illegal deforestation in the Amazon and use intimidation and violence against forest defenders.

President Bolsonaro accused Indigenous people and nongovernmental organizations (NGOs), without any proof, of being responsible for the destruction of the rainforest. He also harassed journalists.

In 2019, police killed 6,357 people, one of the highest rates of police killings in the world. Almost 80 percent of victims were Black. Police killings rose 6 percent in the first half of 2020.

Covid-19

President Bolsonaro downplayed Covid-19, which he called "a little flu;" refused to take measures to protect himself and the people around him; disseminated misleading information; and tried to block states from imposing social distancing rules. His administration attempted to withhold Covid-19 data from the public. He fired his health minister for defending World Health Organization recommendations, and the replacement health minister quit in opposition to the president's advocacy of an unproven drug to treat Covid-19.

Brazil had 5.4 million confirmed Covid-19 cases and 158,969 deaths as of October 29. Black Brazilians were more likely than other racial groups to report experiencing symptoms consistent with Covid-19, and more likely to die in the hospital. Among other factors, experts attributed the disparity to higher rates of informal employment among Black people, preventing many from working from home, and to higher prevalence of pre-existing conditions.

Poor access to health care and prevalence of respiratory or other chronic diseases made Indigenous people particularly vulnerable to complications from

Covid-19. The Articulation of Indigenous Peoples of Brazil, an NGO, had registered 38,124 cases and 866 deaths of Indigenous people in Brazil as of October 29.

In June, Congress passed a bill forcing the government to provide emergency healthcare and other assistance to help Indigenous people cope with the pandemic. President Bolsonaro partially vetoed it, but Congress overturned the veto. In July, the Supreme Court ordered the Bolsonaro administration to draft a plan to fight the spread of Covid-19 in Indigenous territories.

The cramped quarters, poor ventilation, and inadequate health care prevalent in Brazil's prisons and juvenile detention centers offered prime conditions for Covid-19 outbreaks.

As of December 2019, more than 755,000 adults were incarcerated, exceeding the maximum capacity of jails and prisons by about 70 percent, according to the Ministry of Justice. Prisons had one general doctor per 900 detainees and one gynecologist per 1,200 incarcerated women.

The Bolsonaro administration failed to address prison overcrowding, but the National Council of Justice (CNJ, in Portuguese), a body that regulates the functioning of the judicial system, asked judges to reduce pretrial detention during the pandemic and consider early release for certain detainees. As of September 16, judges ordered nearly 53,700 people transferred to house arrest in response to Covid-19, according to official data obtained by Human Rights Watch.

In July, President Bolsonaro vetoed legislation requiring the use masks in prisons and juvenile detention facilities, but the Supreme Court found the veto had violated procedural rules and ordered that the legislation be implemented. The Court also based its decision on the existence of "structural deficiencies" in health services in detention facilities.

About 46,210 detainees and detention facility staff had contracted Covid-19 and 205 had died as of October 26, according to CNJ.

The CNJ also asked judges to consider alternatives to detention for children in conflict with the law during the pandemic. Following that recommendation, the number of children and young adults in detention fell to about 14,600, according to judicial data obtained by Human Rights Watch. Yet, at least 38 juvenile detention facilities exceeded their maximum capacity by up to 90 percent during the pandemic.

In August, Brazil's Supreme Court ordered judges to end overcrowding in juvenile detention centers by applying alternatives to detention.

People with disabilities confined in institutions are at a greater risk of contracting Covid-19 due to overcrowded and often unhygienic conditions, although lack of centralized data makes it impossible to assess the impact of the virus. In May, the National Secretariat of Social Assistance called on local authorities to consider alternatives to institutionalization and adopt anti-Covid-19 measures in institutions.

Public Security and Police Conduct

In Rio de Janeiro, police killed 744 people from January through May 2020—the highest number for that period since at least 2003—even though crime levels were lower, as Covid-19 social distancing measures reduced the number of people on the streets.

In May, as volunteers outside a school in an impoverished Rio neighborhood handed out food to families left hungry by the economic fallout from Covid-19, police opened fire, killing a 19-year-old student. They said they were responding to gunfire from unidentified suspects. Shootings involving the police had already disrupted food distribution on at least four occasions in a month.

In June, the Supreme Court prohibited police from conducting raids in low-income neighborhoods in Rio de Janeiro during the pandemic, except in "exceptional cases." As a result, police killings dropped by 72 percent from June through September, compared to the same period in 2019.

In São Paulo, killings by on-duty officers were up 9 percent from January through September.

Nationwide, killings by police rose 6 percent in the first half of 2020, according to official data compiled by the nonprofit Brazilian Forum of Public Security. In 2019, police killed 6,357 people. Almost 80 percent of them were Black.

In August 2020, police launched an operation in Nova Olinda do Norte, in Amazonas state, after drug dealers allegedly shot at a boat fishing without a permit in an environmentally protected area, slightly wounding the state secretary for social development. At least seven people were killed during the operation, including two police officers, and three people were missing as of September 24, the Justice Ministry told Human Rights Watch. Residents reported that police committed extrajudicial executions and other abuses, including torturing a community leader.

While some police killings are in self-defense, many others are the result of excessive use of force. Police abuses contribute to a cycle of violence that undermines public security and endangers the lives of civilians and police officers alike. From January through June 2020, 110 police officers were killed, according to the Brazilian Forum of Public Security.

Homicides rose 7 percent in the first half of 2020, reversing two years of declining rates.

Children's Rights

Around 150 bills banning discussion of sexual orientation, gender identity, or political views in schools had passed or were pending before Congress and state and municipal legislatures as of September 2020, according to a website maintained by university professors. As of October, the Supreme Court had struck down eight laws against "political indoctrination" or the promotion of "gender ideology," finding that they violated academic freedom and the right to education.

In September, the education minister said gender should not be discussed in schools and that people "choose to be gay" and they often come from "misfit families."

A study by the Senate estimated that 18 percent of students in private primary, secondary, and tertiary schools and 40 percent of students in public schools had their classes cancelled due to the pandemic as of July. The rest had to access classes online, but 20 percent of those lacked internet connection at home.

Sexual Orientation and Gender Identity

In May 2020, the Supreme Court revoked a ban enacted by the federal government on men who had sexual relations with other men donating blood.

Between January and June 2020, the national Human Rights Ombudsman's Office received 1,134 complaints of violence, discrimination, and other abuses against lesbian, gay, bisexual, and transgender (LGBT) persons.

Women's and Girls' Rights

The adoption of the 2001 "Maria da Penha" law was an important step in fighting domestic violence, but implementation has lagged.

In 2019, one million cases of domestic violence and 5,100 cases of femicide—defined under Brazilian law as the killing of women "on account of being persons of the female sex"—were pending before the courts.

Police reports of violence against women dropped significantly amid the Covid-19 pandemic, while calls to a hotline to report violence against women increased 27 percent in March and April 2020 compared to the previous year, suggesting women may have difficulty going to police stations to report violence.

Abortion is legal in Brazil only in cases of rape, to save a woman's life, or when the fetus has anencephaly, a condition that makes it difficult for the fetus to survive.

In June, the Bolsonaro administration removed two public servants after they signed a technical note recommending that authorities maintain sexual and reproductive health services during the Covid-19 pandemic, including "safe abortion in the cases permitted by Brazilian law."

In August, the Bolsonaro administration erected new barriers to accessing legal abortion, including by ordering health professionals to report to police rape survivors who sought to terminate pregnancies.

Only 42 hospitals—in a country of 212 million people—were performing legal abortions during the Covid-19 pandemic, the NGO Article 19 and the news websites AzMina and Gênero e Número reported, compared to 76 during 2019. In August, a hospital in Espírito Santo state denied an abortion to a 10-year-old girl who was raped for years, saying it lacked authority to conduct it. After a judge's intervention, the girl obtained an abortion in another state.

Women and girls who have unsafe and illegal abortions not only risk injury and death but face up to three years in prison, while people convicted of performing illegal abortions face up to four years in prison.

An outbreak of the Zika virus in 2015-2016 caused particular harm to women and girls. When a pregnant woman is infected, Zika can cause complications in fetal development, including of the brain. In April 2020, the Supreme Court rejected on a technicality a petition that sought to legalize abortion for people infected with Zika during pregnancy and to increase state support for families affected by Zika.

In September 2020, Brazil's football association announced it would pay equal salaries to women and men on the country's national teams.

In 2018, several Supreme Court rulings and a new law mandated house arrest instead of pretrial detention for pregnant women, mothers of people with disabilities, and mothers of children under 12, except for those accused of violent crimes or crimes against their dependents. Official data show that judges granted house arrest to more than 3,380 women in 2019, but 5,111 women who should have benefited from the new rules awaited trial behind bars, the Ministry of Justice told Human Rights Watch. From January through July 2020, judges granted house arrest to at least an additional 938 women, but the ministry did not provide data on how many were awaiting a decision.

In October 2020, the Supreme Court decided that the rules for house arrest instead of pre-trial detention should apply to fathers who have sole responsibility for children under 12 or for people with disabilities, as well as to any other person who is "indispensable" for the care of children under 6 or people with disabilities.

Freedom of Expression

In March, President Bolsonaro suspended deadlines for government agencies to respond to public information requests during the Covid-19 emergency and prevented citizens from appealing declined requests. The Supreme Court overturned these orders.

Since taking office, President Bolsonaro, political allies, and government officials have lashed out at reporters more than 400 times, according to Article 19. The president threatened to punch one journalist in the face in August 2020. His supporters harassed reporters at demonstrations and outside the presidential palace, which made several outlets suspend coverage in May. The government asked the Federal Police to investigate alleged defamation by two journalists and a cartoonist who criticized the president.

The Justice Ministry prepared confidential reports on almost 600 police officers and three academics it identified as "antifascists." The Supreme Court ordered the ministry to stop collecting information about people exercising their rights to freedom of expression and association.

Brazil's Senate passed a "fake news" bill that threatens the right to privacy and free speech. It was pending in the Chamber of Deputies at time of writing.

Disability Rights

Thousands of adults and children with disabilities are needlessly confined in institutions where they may face neglect and abuse, sometimes for life.

In September 2020, the government issued a new national policy that appeared aimed at establishing segregated schools for certain people with disabilities, despite the right of all people with disabilities to an inclusive education.

Migrants, Refugees, and Asylum Seekers

Thousands of Venezuelans, including hundreds of unaccompanied children, have crossed the border into Brazil in recent years, fleeing hunger, lack of basic health care, or persecution. More than 262,000 Venezuelans lived in Brazil as of August 2020.

Brazil's June 2019 legal recognition of a "serious and widespread violation of human rights" in Venezuela speeds up the granting of asylum to Venezuelans. In August 2020, Brazil's federal refugee agency extended the policy for another year. From January through August, Brazil granted refugee status to 38,000 Venezuelans.

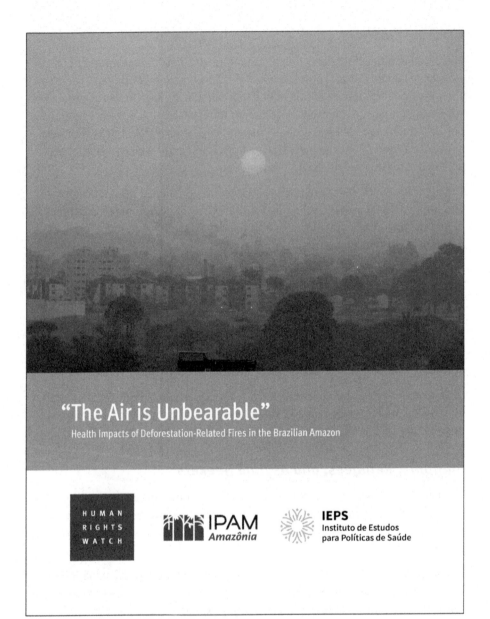

"The Air is Unbearable"
Health Impacts of Deforestation-Related Fires in the Brazilian Amazon

In March, in response to the Covid-19 pandemic, the federal government banned Venezuelans from entering Brazil through land, later adding other nationalities. By October, most foreign nationals except for permanent residents of Brazil were barred from entering the country through land or water. Permanent residents could return to Brazil unless they entered the country from Venezuela, in which case they were still banned. In addition, the federal government ordered the repatriation or deportation of those who managed to enter, even if they were asylum seekers.

Those measures violate Brazil's international obligations. Even in times of emergency, governments remain obliged not to return refugees to a threat of persecution, exposure to inhumane or degrading conditions, or threats to life and physical security, and they should not impose restrictions that are discriminatory.

Environment and Indigenous People's Rights

Criminal networks that are largely driving illegal deforestation in the Amazon continued to threaten and even kill Indigenous people, local residents, and public officials who defended the forest.

From 2015 to 2019, more than 200 people were killed in the context of conflicts over the use of land and resources in the Amazon—many of them by people allegedly involved in illegal deforestation—the non-profit organization Pastoral Land Commission reported. In the vast majority of these cases, the perpetrators have not been brought to justice.

Since taking office in January 2019, the Bolsonaro administration has weakened the enforcement of environmental laws. In April 2020, after a successful anti-illegal mining operation, the administration removed the three top enforcement agents at the country's main environmental agency.

In October 2019, the environment ministry implemented new procedures establishing that environmental fines do not need to be paid until they are reviewed at a "conciliation hearing." Environmental agents have issued thousands of fines since then, but the ministry had only held five hearings as of August 2020.

In May 2020, the government transferred responsibility for leading anti-deforestation efforts in the Amazon from environmental agencies to the armed forces, despite their lack of expertise and training.

Deforestation in the Amazon rose by 85 percent in 2019, according to preliminary data. From January through September 2020, deforestation fell 10 percent, but the number of fires reached the highest level in 10 years.

Fires had burned more than a quarter of Pantanal, the largest marshland in the world, as of October 2020, the greatest destruction in more than two decades. Federal Police and prosecutors believe large landowners illegally set fires to clear land for cattle.

Air pollution caused by forest fires takes a major toll on public health. A study by Human Rights Watch, the Institute for Health Policy Studies (IEPS), and the Amazon Environmental Research Institute (IPAM) found that millions of people were exposed to harmful levels of air pollution due to the fires in the Amazon in 2019, resulting in an estimated 2,195 hospitalizations.

President Bolsonaro called NGOs working in the Amazon a "cancer" that he "can't kill," and accused them, without any proof, of being responsible for the destruction of the rainforest. He also blamed Indigenous people and small farmers for Amazon fires.

In September 2020, the environment minister petitioned a federal court to order a leading environmental defender to explain comments criticizing the minister, a measure seemingly intended to intimidate the defender. In October, media reported that the Bolsonaro administration had deployed the country's secret service to spy on the Brazilian delegation, NGOs, and others at the December 2019 UN Climate Change Conference in Madrid.

In 2019, invasions of Indigenous territories to access their resources increased by 135 percent, according to the nonprofit Indigenist Missionary Council.

In February 2020, President Bolsonaro sent a bill to Congress to open Indigenous territories to mining, dams, and other projects with heavy environmental impacts. The bill was still pending at time of writing.

Military-Era Abuses

The perpetrators of human rights abuses during the 1964 to 1985 dictatorship are shielded from justice by a 1979 amnesty law that the Supreme Court upheld in 2010, a decision that the Inter-American Court of Human Rights ruled was in violation of Brazil's obligations under international law.

Since 2010, federal prosecutors have charged about 60 former agents of the dictatorship with killings, kidnappings, and other serious crimes. Lower courts have dismissed most of the cases, citing either the amnesty law or the statute of limitations.

In May 2020, a federal court dismissed charges against people involved in the torture and killing of journalist Vladimir Herzog in 1975. Prosecutors had reopened the investigation in compliance with a 2018 ruling by the Inter-American Court of Human Rights.

In September, German company Volkswagen admitted its representatives had cooperated with Brazil's dictatorship. Brazil's National Truth Commission had found in 2014 that company representatives had provided information about its workers to authorities, which might have resulted in illegal arrests, torture, and other abuses. As part of a settlement agreement with Brazilian prosecutors, Volkswagen agreed to pay 36 million reais (approximately US$6.5million) in compensation to victims and to fund efforts to identify the remains of victims and to educate the public about past abuses.

President Bolsonaro has repeatedly praised the dictatorship. In October his vice-president, a retired general, expressed his admiration for a late colonel identified as commander of a torture center.

Key International Actors

The United Nations High Commissioner for Human Rights has expressed concern over attacks against human rights defenders, the downplaying of Covid-19 by "political leaders," and increased involvement of the military in public affairs and law enforcement.

Five UN rapporteurs said President Bolsonaro has minimized human rights violations during the dictatorship and spread "misinformation" about the military regime.

Some European leaders, the European Parliament, and several national parliaments across Europe have expressed strong reservations about ratifying a pending trade agreement between the European Union and Mercosur. They have noted that Bolsonaro's environmental policies call into question Brazil's readiness to implement the deal's environmental commitments to fight deforestation and uphold the Paris Climate Agreement.

Brazil endorsed the World Health Organization's Solidarity Call to Action for the Covid-19 Technology Access Pool, an initiative to "realize equitable global access to COVID-19 health technologies through pooling of knowledge, intellectual property and data."

Foreign Policy

In 2019, Brazil ran for one of two vacant seats on the UN Human Rights Council along with Venezuela, with Costa Rica presenting its candidacy shortly before the election. Venezuela's narrow win was likely facilitated by Brazil lobbying Latin American countries against presenting a third candidate.

In 2020, Brazil's Foreign Ministry pressed for exclusion of references to "sexual and reproductive health" in UN resolutions, which it said could "give a positive connotation to abortion." For instance, by resisting a UN resolution—which nevertheless passed in July—Brazil opposed affirming the rights to universal access to "sexuality education," "safe abortion where not against national law," and "post-abortion care."

Burkina Faso

The human rights, security, and humanitarian situation in Burkina Faso was precarious amid ongoing violence and atrocities by Islamist armed groups, state security forces, and pro-government militias engaged in counterterrorism operations.

In 2020, the Burkinabé security forces allegedly executed hundreds of suspects, last seen in their custody, for their perceived support of Islamist groups. Armed Islamists allied to Al-Qaeda and the Islamist State in the Greater Sahara attacked civilians and summarily executed people, causing the death of over 160 people. Armed group attacks caused 450,000 people to flee their homes in 2020 alone, bringing the total number of internally displaced since the conflict started in 2016 to over one million.

A 2019 law criminalizing some aspects of reporting on security force operations had a chilling effect on freedom of the press and on journalists and human rights defenders, some of whom received threats after reporting on security forces abuses.

While the government opened several investigations into reported abuses, little progress was made toward providing justice for victims, including of large-scale atrocities by all sides. Rule-of-law institutions remained weak and hundreds of terrorism suspects remained in custody without trial, in part because of the lack of defense lawyers.

Burkina Faso's international partners including the United Nations, France, the European Union and the United States readily denounced violence by armed Islamist groups but were largely reluctant to denounce abuses by government forces.

Abuses by Islamist Armed Groups

Islamist armed groups attacked churches, mosques, aid convoys and schools. They sought to justify their attacks by linking victims to the government and allied militias, the West, or Christianity. Their attacks, including several massacres, largely targeted members of the Mossi and Foulse ethnic groups.

A December 24, 2019 attack in Arbinda killed at least 35 civilians, mostly women previously displaced by the violence. Attacks on Rofénèga, Nagraogo, and Silgadji villages between January 17 and 25 left over 90 civilians dead. On February 1, at least 20 civilians, including a nurse, were killed in Lamdamol village, and a February 16 attack on a church in Pansi village killed over 20 civilians, including the pastor.

In May 2020, Islamist armed groups were implicated in an attack on a convoy of traders in Lourom Province that killed at least four women, and another on a convoy transporting food aid near Barsalogho that killed five civilians. Both convoys were escorted by government troops, some of whom also died.

Islamist armed group attacks on villages have put women and girls at increased risk of physical and sexual violence.

Armed Islamists abducted several local government officials and prominent elders, later killing some of them. The village chief of Nassoumbou was abducted in July and released in September, and in August, the 73-year-old Grand Imam of Djibo, Sonibou Cisse, was executed several days after being taken off a public transport vehicle south of Djibo.

Numerous civilians, including children, were killed by improvised explosive devices (IEDs) believed to have been planted on roadways by armed Islamists, including 14 civilians, at least two of them children, in January, when their bus hit an explosive device in Boucle du Mouhoun region, and six shepherds, all children, in Tangaye village in August.

Islamist armed groups also imposed their version of Sharia (Islamic law) via courts that did not adhere to international fair trial standards.

Abuses by State Security Forces

Burkinabé security forces from the army and gendarmerie unlawfully executed suspects during counterterrorism operations in both Burkina Faso and Mali, during cross-border operations. Most of the victims were from the Peuhl ethnic group and were rounded up by security forces in marketplaces and taken from villages, watering holes, or off public transport vehicles.

The remains of 180 men were found around the northern town of Djibo between November 2019 and June 2020. The bodies were found in groups of up to 20 along major roadways, under bridges, and in fields and vacant lots, and the majority were buried in common graves. Many were found blindfolded and with bound hands.

In early March, security forces in Cisse village executed 23 people. On April 9, security forces executed 31 detainees just hours after being arrested, unarmed, during a counterterrorism operation in Djibo. On May 11, 12 men arrested by gendarmes in Tanwalbougou, Est Region, were found dead in their cells hours later. Witnesses said the men appeared to have been shot. According to the United Nations, Burkinabè forces were implicated in at least 50 extrajudicial killings committed during cross-border operations into Mali between May 26 and 28.

Some allegations involved security forces and civil defense forces working together, including on February 29 when at least 15 people were reportedly killed during a joint operation around Kelbo.

On May 2, security force members burst into the Mentao refugee camp, allegedly looking for armed Islamists, and physically abused over 30 Malian refugees.

Attacks by Self-Defense Groups

On January 21, the National Assembly passed a law institutionalizing government support for and training of self-defense groups, known as Volunteers for the Defense of the Homeland (VDH). The law's provisions on accountability are ambiguous. Some members of the Koglweogo, an anti-crime force largely composed of ethnic Mossi, and which has for years been implicated in serious abuses, including the 2019 Yirgou massacre of over 40 men, were subsumed into the VDH.

Self-defense groups were implicated in numerous grave crimes including the killing in February of 19 men taken off a public transport bus near Manja Hien village, attacks on three villages in Yatenga province on March 8 that killed 43 Peuhl villagers, and numerous other killings in villages in northern and eastern Burkina Faso.

Accountability for Abuses

Authorities opened investigations into several allegations involving the security forces and civil defense forces, including the May deaths of 12 men in gendarme custody in Tanwalbougou and the deaths of over 200 men in Djibo. However, there was no progress in the investigations opened into abuses in 2018 and 2019, and there was scant public information about the status of investigations. No charges were brought against armed Islamists.

The military justice directorate, mandated to investigate incidents involving the security forces, was seriously under resourced.

The high-security prison for terrorism-related offenses is overcrowded, mirroring the overcrowding in prisons nationwide. Hundreds of detainees accused of terrorism-related offenses have been held without trial, some for up to four years. Few had access to lawyers. In April, over 1,200 detainees were pardoned and released in a bid to decongest the prisons to slow the spread of Covid-19.

Access to Education and Attacks on Teachers, Students, and Schools

Islamist armed groups carried out over 45 attacks on education in 2020. In 21 documented attacks between January and March, armed men killed, abducted, beat, robbed, and threatened education professionals; intimidated students and parents; and burned and looted 15 schools. From April to August, at least 25 schools were burned, according to news reports. Most of these attacks took place in Est, Nord, and Boucle du Mouhoun regions. The Burkinabè military used at least three schools as bases.

Before the government closed all schools nationwide in response to the Covid-19 pandemic in March, 2,500 schools had already closed due to attacks or insecurity— depriving nearly 350,000 students of education—and schools hosting displaced students suffered from overcrowding, unable to accept all who sought to enroll.

The government responded to attacks by relocating teachers, increasing security patrols near some schools, reopening closed schools, and implementing programs to help students catch up or regain access to school. As part of its Covid-

19 education response, the government expanded distance-learning programs to national radio, television, and online platforms.

Key International Actors

The rapidly deteriorating security, humanitarian and human rights situation garnered significant attention from Burkina Faso's key international partners. They issued several statements denouncing abuses by Islamist armed groups, but for much of the year did not publicly denounce the security forces for serious abuses or publicly press the national authorities to investigate the allegations.

In December 2019, the European Parliament urged the Burkinabè government to end its abusive counter-insurgency strategy and investigate abuses committed by security forces. Following the July 2020 allegations of mass atrocities by security forces in Djibo, the United States said the killings could put US military aid at risk and the European Union and the United Kingdom urged Burkina Faso authorities to investigate the abuses.

The UN Office of the High Commissioner for Human Rights committed to strengthening its presence in Burkina Faso.

In June, France launched the International Coalition for the Sahel, to coordinate among the G5 Sahel countries (Burkina Faso, Chad, Mali, Mauritania, and Niger) and their international partners.

The United States trained more than 3,000 Burkinabè soldiers and gendarmes in 2020, and provided US$2 million in counter-IED training programs, as well as $5 million in anti-terrorism funding to develop the investigative capacities of law enforcement to handle complicated terrorism cases.

The European Union has mobilized €4.5 billion in budget support for the G5 Sahel joint counterterrorism force.

France provides military training to Burkinabè troops and supported security operations in the Sahel region through its 5,100-strong Operation Barkhane counterinsurgency operation.

In June, in response to the gravity and number of attacks on schools and the killing and maiming of children, the UN secretary-general added Burkina Faso as a situation of concern for the UN's monitoring and reporting mechanism on grave violations against children during armed conflict.

Burundi

Former President Pierre Nkurunziza, whose tenure was marked by widespread abuses, died in June, days after Évariste Ndayishimiye took power in Burundi following the May 2020 presidential elections. However, the serious human rights situation in the country remained largely unchanged.

The presidential, legislative, and communal elections in May and the senate and local elections in July took place in a highly repressive environment, marred by allegations of irregularities. The ruling National Council for the Defense of Democracy-Forces for the Defense of Democracy (Conseil national pour la défense de la démocratie-Forces de défense de la démocratie, CNDD-FDD) maintained its monopoly on power, with civil society groups reporting an escalation in killings and arbitrary arrests after the elections. A United Nations Human Rights Council-mandated Commission of Inquiry (COI) reported in September that serious human rights violations, which in some cases may amount to crimes against humanity, persisted in 2019 and 2020.

Burundians cast their ballot amid the Covid-19 pandemic, which the government initially downplayed, including by suppressing the real death toll.

Civil society and independent media are still unable to effectively function, and several human rights defenders and journalists remain in jail despite international calls for their release.

Abuses Related to the Elections and Security Incidents

The 2020 elections took place in the absence of any international observation mission and, on election day in May, authorities blocked access to social media and messaging apps throughout the country, restricting independent reporting and information sharing. Throughout the pre-election period, members of the ruling party youth league, administrative officials, and state security forces committed widespread abuses with near-total impunity. Killings, enforced disappearances, arbitrary arrests, beatings, extortion, and intimidation, especially against people perceived to be against the ruling party, persisted. The elections were funded in part by "contributions" forcibly collected from the population between 2017 and 2019.

Since the elections, Human Rights Watch has received credible reports of real or suspected opposition members being killed, disappeared, arbitrarily arrested, threatened, and beaten, particularly in rural areas. Local media have also reported arrests of opposition members, accused of threatening the security of the state.

Little information has been released about several major security incidents during 2020. In February, there were reports of skirmishes between security forces and alleged "criminals" in western Bujumbura Rural province, as photos and videos circulated online showing detained people and dead bodies surrounded by police and local residents. After the elections, local civil society groups and media reported several attacks in provinces bordering neighboring Rwanda and Democratic Republic of Congo by unidentified armed men, often leading to civilian casualties. Authorities did not release information about the incidents.

Reports of arrests of scores of Kinyarwanda-speaking Banyamulenge asylum seekers and refugees from eastern Congo appeared to escalate after the Burundian interior and public security ministry's spokesperson told the population in October to inform the authorities of anyone speaking Kinyarwanda.

Civil Society and Media

The January 30 conviction after a flawed trial of four Iwacu journalists who were arrested while going to report on fighting between security forces and the rebel group RED-Tabara in October 2019 underscored the dangers of investigating security incidents. Their conviction was upheld on appeal in June.

In February, the trial of human rights defenders and journalists in exile began in their absence and without the presence of their lawyer.

Media were heavily restricted in their coverage of the elections. The 2018 amended press law and a new Code of Conduct for Media and Journalists in the election period require journalists to provide "balanced" information or face criminal prosecution, and prevented them from publishing information about the elections that did not come from the national electoral commission.

The Appeal Court's confirmation of the 32-year sentence of human rights activist Germain Rukuki, a member of Action by Christians for the Abolition of Torture (ACAT), was overturned by the Supreme Court in June. Rukuki was convicted on trumped-up charges related to state security in April 2018. Nestor Nibitanga, an observer for the Association for the Protection of Human Rights and Detained Persons (APRODH), was sentenced to five years for "threatening state security" in August 2018.

The government continued exerting pressure on UN agencies and international nongovernmental organizations (NGOs) in Burundi to control their work and their ability to share information on the humanitarian situation in the country. Authorities passed several decrees creating recruitment committees and other mechanisms to enforce the application of ethnic quotas in the recruitment of local staff by foreign NGOs and ensure greater government oversight of their work.

Humanitarian Situation and Covid-19

The humanitarian situation in Burundi, one of the world's poorest countries, was dire, with around 1.7 million people facing food insecurity, according to the UN Office for the Coordination of Humanitarian Affairs (OCHA).

In August, the foreign affairs minister wrote to the UN resident coordinator, requesting he share a note-verbale with all UN agencies and international NGOs in Burundi which sought to restrict the kind of data that could be collected in the country. The minister called on them to share a "positive, real and evolutive image" of the country; otherwise, only authorized data collection would be allowed.

The government's response to the Covid-19 pandemic was marked by repression and misinformation. High-level government officials, including Nkurunziza and Ndayishimiye, downplayed the threat of the virus. Nkurunziza's government refused to follow the World Health Organization (WHO) guidelines to prevent the spread of the virus, claiming Burundi was protected by God, and declared the WHO's country director and three of its experts persona non grata on May 12. Medical workers and experts told Human Rights Watch they were concerned that suspected cases were not being transparently accounted for and that the public health authorities were failing to adequately respond to the pandemic.

On June 30, Ndayishimiye declared Covid-19 the country's "worst enemy," pledging to ramp up testing and lower the price of water and soap, marking a change in the government's approach to the disease. In September, the health minister declared the Covid-19 epidemic in Burundi over, without providing data to substantiate the claim.

Refugees

There are still over 300,000 Burundian refugees outside the country, many of whom fled in the aftermath of former president Nkurunziza's decision to run for a third term in 2015. During the campaigns and since his election, Ndayishimiye repeatedly promised that political exiles and refugees could safely return to the country. Between September 2017 and 2020, almost 100,000 refugees returned to Burundi under the UN refugee agency-backed assisted voluntary repatriation program, most of whom returned from Tanzania. After the May 2020 elections, the UN refugee agency began facilitating returns from Rwanda, Namibia, and Congo.

Human Rights Watch received credible reports alleging that Tanzanian police arbitrarily arrested and forcibly disappeared Burundian refugees in Tanzania, some of whom were forcibly returned to Burundi. There were concerns about the voluntary repatriation program, following reports of repatriated refugees being the targets of attacks upon their return, and threatening statements by authorities about political exiles.

Sexual Orientation and Gender Identity

Burundi punishes consensual same-sex sexual relations between adults with up to two years in prison under Article 567 of the penal code. Article 29 of the Constitution of Burundi explicitly bans same-sex marriage, and Ndayishimiye has made disparaging comments about abortion and same-sex relationships.

Accountability

During his inaugural speech, President Ndayishimiye promised to reform the judiciary and ensure that all government or other officials who commit offenses are held accountable. Since his election, there have been isolated cases of ar-

rests and trials of ruling party youth league members and security forces accused of committing crimes.

The appointments of Prime Minister Alain Guillaume Bunyoni and Minister for
the Interior, Community Development, and Public Security Gervais Ndirakobuca,
both under international sanctions for their alleged role in violence in 2015, cast
doubt over the new administration's commitment to accountability and raises
concerns about the possible interference with criminal investigations into past
abuses.

Key International Actors

The East African Community, whose election observation mission did not travel
to Burundi amid the Covid-19 pandemic, in a May 26 statement praised the
"peaceful and successful" elections process, saying that it was "domestically
driven through [the country's] own funding," despite the forcible collection of
funds to pay for the vote.

Burundi refused to cooperate with any international and regional human rights
mechanism. The COI on Burundi was not given access to the country, despite repeated requests.

The European Union's 2016 suspension of direct budgetary support to the government of Burundi under article 96 of the Cotonou Agreement remained in
place. In January, the European Parliament called for tougher European Union
measures and enhanced support to Burundian civil society and media given the
worsening crackdown in the country.

Following the election of President Ndayishimiye, the EU has attempted to improve relations with Burundi, which is currently under restrictive EU measures,
including sanctions against senior government officials and the suspension of
direct budgetary support to the government.

Despite some divisions among EU member states, and amid lack of concrete
human rights reforms on the ground, the EU eventually tabled a resolution at the
UN Human Rights Council to renew the COI's mandate for another year, which
was adopted by the Human Rights Council in October.

The UN Security Council has been divided over whether to maintain Burundi on its agenda. In September, Bintou Keita, assistant secretary-general for Africa, and Huang Xia, special envoy of the secretary-general for the Great Lakes region, carried out an assessment mission to Burundi. Michel Kafando, the UN special envoy to Burundi who resigned in October 2019, was not replaced.

The International Criminal Court (ICC) continued investigations into crimes committed in Burundi since 2015.

Cambodia

Prime Minister Hun Sen, whose 35-year rule makes him one of the world's longest serving leaders, used the Covid-19 pandemic as a pretext to further tighten his grip on power. During the year, the government repeatedly resorted to violence against peaceful protesters, and arrested human rights defenders, journalists, opposition party members, and ordinary citizens for peacefully expressing their opinions. At time of writing, Cambodia held over 60 political prisoners.

Amid the pandemic, the ruling Cambodian People's Party (CPP) used its 125-to-0 margin in the National Assembly to adopt new laws that further threaten civil and political rights. The government's response to the Covid-19 pandemic reinforced underlying discrimination against Cambodia's minority Muslim communities by mentioning their religion when reporting on persons who contracted Covid-19.

The government and micro-loan providers failed to protect borrowers from an already spiraling micro-loan debt crisis, undermining the right to an adequate standard of living. Authorities did not release persons who are at increased risk of contracting and suffering complications from Covid-19 being held in Cambodia's notoriously overcrowded prisons. Of the more than 3 million students who had their education disrupted since schools closed in March, children from poorer and rural families have had less access to alternative education.

Draconian New Laws

The government adopted repressive new laws that further curtail the rights to freedom of expression, peaceful assembly, and association.

In April, Hun Sen used the Covid-19 pandemic to enact a draconian state of emergency law that severely restricts fundamental liberties. The law grants extensive powers to the prime minister, allowing bans on the distribution of information, intrusive surveillance of telecommunications "by all means," and total control of media. It also empowers the government to restrict movement and demonstrations, and opens the way for unfettered governmental powers. The penalties and fines under the emergency measures are unlawfully disproportionate.

In June, the government considered a public order law that purports to achieve "a more civilized society." In reality, it is a highly intrusive, rights-violating law that polices ordinary actions of citizens and prohibits a vast array of public and private behavior, including regulating what people can wear. The law restricts Cambodians' right to free expression and peaceful assembly and incorporates provisions that violate the rights of women and persons with actual or perceived mental or developmental disabilities.

In July, the Ministry of Post and Telecommunications' proposed a sub-decree on a National Internet Gateway, which seeks to route all internet traffic through a regulatory body monitoring online activity, which will allow for the "blocking and disconnecting [of] all network connections that affect safety, national revenue, social order, dignity, culture, tradition and customs."

Attacks on Human Rights Defenders

Authorities banned protests organized by youth and environmental activists. Between August and October, authorities detained and charged 12 activists based on bogus allegations of "incitement to commit a felony" when organizing protests to call for the release of political prisoners, including detained union leader Rong Chhun. Peaceful protests by family members calling for the release of detained opposition activists were frequently met with excessive use of force by Phnom Penh district level security forces and plainclothes police officers.

Environmental activism continues to be dangerous in Cambodia. In March, authorities arrested four environmental activists, including activists of the Prey Lang Community Network and prominent environmentalist Ouch Leng, following their investigation into allegations of illegal logging in Kratie province by the company Think Biotech. The company held the activists incommunicado overnight and inflicted a bleeding head injury on one of them. The next day, they were handed over to police for questioning. Authorities released the activists after two days but said they would continue a criminal investigation against them. So far, no charges have been imposed.

Between January and April, authorities detained and interrogated at least 30 people, including a 14-year-old girl, for Facebook posts related to the Covid-19 pandemic. The government labelled their posts as "spreading fake news."

Twelve persons with affiliation to the opposition Cambodian National Rescue Party (CNRP) and four others were charged with criminal offenses; fourteen were held in pre-trial detention and two released on bail. Those released upon arrest had to sign "re-educating" pledges to refrain from similar posts in the future.

On July 31, authorities arrested prominent union leader Rong Chhun. The next day, the Phnom Penh municipal court charged him with incitement and sent him to pre-trial detention. The charges against Rong Chhun appear linked to his advocacy for aggrieved villagers facing land problems because of the demarcation of Cambodia's border with Vietnam.

In June, Thai pro-democracy activist Wachalearm Satsaksit was abducted in front of his Phnom Penh apartment. Witnesses and CCTV footage revealed unidentified armed men seizing him, pushing him into a black SUV, and driving away. Despite requests from the Thai government, Cambodian authorities had at time of writing failed to conduct an effective investigation into the incident, made no progress in determining his whereabouts, and did not respond to allegations of official knowledge or involvement in the abduction.

Arrest and Harassment of Opposition Members and Supporters

Hun Sen continued to threaten opposition activists. In June, he claimed that the Cambodia National Rescue Party (CNRP) was trying to use the pandemic to "cause chaos." He alluded to a statement by exiled former opposition leader Sam Rainsy that borrowers unable to repay their micro-loan debts should not have to sell their land or homes to pay back their debtors. Hun Sen threatened CNRP activists with arrest, repeating "If you act, I will arrest."

Over 30 opposition activists were imprisoned at time of writing. Another 78 opposition activists released on bail in November 2019 have charges pending against them and risk re-arrest at any time. The CNRP's leadership remains largely in exile because of fear of being arrested if they return to Cambodia.

The government released Kem Sokha, head of the CNRP, from *de facto* house arrest in November 2019. However, he continued to face trumped-up treason charges. In mid-May 2020, authorities said that his trial would be delayed indefinitely. On July 20, the Phnom Penh municipal court warned him to not violate the conditions of his bail, which prohibit, among others, any political activities.

Freedom of Media

The government significantly curtailed media freedom by targeting independent media outlets and critical journalists. In the first six months of 2020, the government revoked the licenses of independent media outlets TVFB, Rithysen radio station and online news site, and CKV TV Online. The license of *Cheat Khmer* newspaper was under review after the politically motivated arrest of its owner, Ros Sokhet in June.

Two Radio Free Asia journalists, Yeang Sothearin and Uon Chhin, faced a never-ending investigation on fabricated espionage charges, for which a judge ruled in October 2019 there was no evidence. However, inexplicably, the judge refused to dismiss the case. In January and October, Phnom Penh's appeal court and the Supreme Court, respectively, rejected an appeal to dismiss the case, allowing for continued investigations. While both journalists were released on bail after nearly one year in arbitrary pretrial detention, they are not allowed to leave the country.

In March, Interior Minister Sar Kheng warned that anyone who spread misinformation about Covid-19 "to stir chaos" would face legal action. In April, authorities arrested and detained reporter and director of online TVFB news site, Sovann Rithy, alleging he committed "incitement to commit a felony" by quoting sections of Hun Sen's speech regarding the economic impact of Covid-19. Authorities ordered his pre-trial detention and convicted him on October 5, sentencing him to 18 months in prison—deducting time served in pretrial detention and suspending the remainder. At time of writing, authorities detained a total of three journalists: Sok Oudom, Ros Sokhet, and Rath Rott Mony. Mony is currently serving a two-year prison sentence upon conviction for incitement.

Lack of Adequate Standard of Living

Covid-19 sparked an economic crisis in which hundreds of thousands of people were suspended from work with little or no pay, or laid off outright. Many Cambodians have taken out microloans, often using land titles as collateral, but without jobs or income, they cannot afford to repay the loans.

The Cambodian government and micro-loan providers did little to respond to this micro-loan debt crisis, leaving hundreds of thousands of borrowers facing serious financial burdens without debt relief or loan restructuring that could alleviate that burden. A lack of oversight and enforceable debt relief, exacerbated by micro-loan providers' unethical lending practices that intend to push borrowers into insurmountable debt, resulted in cases of coerced land sales by indebted borrowers.

Rather than heeding desperate appeals by poor communities urging the government to suspend micro-loan debt collection, government officials arrested protesters and threatened borrowers with confiscation of property if they acted on exiled CNRP leaders' calls to refuse to repay loans.

The government also failed to take adequate steps to halt human trafficking of "brides" to China, a trade driven by economic desperation.

Key International Actors

Cambodia distanced itself from the European Union and the United States economically, and strengthened economic ties with China by signing a Free Trade Agreement on October 12. In January 2020, China comprised 43 percent of Cambodia's foreign direct investment of a total of US$3.6 billion in 2019, making it Cambodia's largest foreign investor. Cambodia is one of China's "Belt and Road Initiative partners," with US$7.9 billion invested between 2016 and 2019.

In August, following 18 months of enhanced monitoring and dialogue with Cambodian authorities—and given Hun Sen's persistent refusal to take meaningful action to address the violations of civil and political rights, as well as land and labor rights identified by the European Union—the European Commission partially withdrew Cambodia's preferential access to the EU market in application of the "Everything But Arms" scheme.

In June, Sweden announced that it will phase out its bilateral aid for the Cambodian government by July 1, 2021, in response to Cambodia's severe restrictions on democratic space in recent years. While continuing to support civil society groups, Sweden will redirect its bilateral cooperation with the government to-wards "better support for change with regard to human rights, democracy and the rule of law."

In July, the US listed Cambodia's Banteay Meanchey Provincial Police Commis-sariat as a unit that would no longer receive US assistance under the US Leahy Law—prohibiting the US from funding foreign security forces that commit rights abuses with impunity—based on "credible information that such unit has com-mitted a gross violation of human rights."

Cameroon

Armed groups and government forces committed widespread human rights abuses, including extrajudicial or summary executions and mass killings across Cameroon's Anglophone regions throughout 2020.

The government continued restricting freedom of expression and association and has become increasingly intolerant of political dissent. Political space was limited as authorities cracked down on opponents of President Paul Biya and his ruling party. Hundreds of opposition party members and supporters were arrested in September following demonstrations calling for a peaceful resolution to the crisis in the Anglophone regions. In these regions, violence between government security forces and armed separatists intensified.

In February, Cameroonian soldiers and armed ethnic Fulani men massacred 21 civilians in Ngarbuh, a village in the North-West region. Separatists targeted aid workers, their premises, and property across the two English-speaking regions. They also attacked other civilians, posting some of the videos of such attacks on social media. Separatists have violently enforced a boycott on children's education since 2017, and on October 24, gunmen attacked a school in Kumba, South-West region, killing 7 children and injuring 13.

The Islamist armed group Boko Haram carried out attacks in the Far North region from January 2020, killing hundreds of civilians. Responding to these attacks, government forces forced civilians to perform local night guard duties to protect against Boko Haram attacks in March and April in at least one town.

The government took measures to curb the spread of the Covid-19 virus, including closing schools and banning mass gatherings at the onset of the pandemic. However, the pandemic was also used as a pretext to silence the opposition and quell dissent. There has been little government transparency with regards to its disbursement of funds collected to address the pandemic.

The Anglophone Crisis

Hundreds of civilians have been killed since January 2020 in the North-West and South-West regions, where violence has been acute since the crisis began in late

2016, as separatists seek independence for the country's minority Anglophone regions. Violence displaced tens of thousands of people in the past year, adding to the hundreds of thousands who have fled their homes since the start of the violence.

In March, the Southern Cameroons Defence Forces (SOCADEF), a separatist group, called for a ceasefire as the Covid-19 pandemic was declared. In June, government officials held peace talks in the capital, Yaoundé, with the leaders of the Ambazonia Interim Government, a major separatist group. Neither initiative led to an end to the violence.

Abuse by Government Forces

Security forces responded to separatist attacks with a heavy hand, often targeting civilians and killings hundreds of people across the North-West and South-West regions.

Between January 17 and 20, 2020, security forces conducted a military operation in Bali, North-West region, in retaliation for separatist attacks on polling centers, destroying over 50 homes and killing several civilians, including two men with intellectual disabilities.

On February 14, government forces and armed ethnic Fulani killed 21 civilians, including 13 children and 1 pregnant woman, in Ngarbuh in North-West region. Residents told Human Rights Watch the attack was to punish civilians suspected of harboring separatist fighters. The government initially denied soldiers were involved in the attack, but in March, following international pressure, President Biya established a commission of inquiry into the killings.

In April, the government admitted their security forces bear some responsibility for the killings and announced the arrest of two soldiers and a gendarme.

On June 10, a grenade was fired into the courtyard of the district hospital in Bali, North-West region, following clashes between government soldiers and separatists, leading to the death of one cardiac patient. At least four others were injured.

Security forces damaged a health facility in the North-West region on June 30 and arbitrarily arrested seven health workers, accused of collaborating with separatists, in the South-West region on July 6.

Soldiers from the 42nd Battalian in Mozogo, in the Far North, forced civilians to perform local night guard duty to protect the area against attacks by Boko Haram. From mid-March to late April, soldiers beat or threatened those who refused.

Denunciations by local nongovernmental organizations and the National Human Rights Commission in April stopped the beatings, but people in Mozogo continued to live in fear of beatings, and the forced labor and threats continued.

Abuse by Armed Separatists

Armed separatist groups have killed, tortured, assaulted and kidnapped hundreds of people. They also prevented humanitarian workers and teachers from doing their jobs, depriving children of access to education.

In the run up to the regional elections in February, armed separatists targeted those willing to participate, whether as candidates, election officials, activists, or citizens, kidnapping over 100 people and destroying property. Ransoms were paid for release. Voter participation was low in the Anglophone regions because of insecurity and fear of and threats of attacks.

On January 30, separatists kidnapped a 19-year-old secondary school student in Buea, South-West region, and chopped her finger off with a machete for going to school. The girl was released three days later following a ransom payment.

Separatists have killed at least six civilians since mid-May, including on May 17 a teacher working at the University of Bameda in the North-West region.

On July 6, separatists killed a community health staff working for Doctors Without Borders in the South-West region after accusing him of collaborating with the military.

In August, separatist fighters in Muyuka, South-West region, filmed the beating of a 35-year-old woman as she begged for her life. The video was shared on social media and the fighters killed the woman they accused of collaborating with the government.

Separatists continued to attack schools, students, and teachers across the Anglophone regions. According to the United Nations, 81 percent of children were out of school across the North-West and South-West regions during the 2019 to 2020 academic year.

Attacks in the Far North by Boko Haram

In 2020, attacks and raids by the Islamist armed group Boko Haram increased in the Far North Region, with almost daily killings, kidnappings, thefts, and destruction of property.

In April, Boko Haram fighters stormed Amchide, Far North region. Two teenage suicide bombers detonated their explosives in the center of the town, killing nine men and injuring 10 others. Another man was shot in a confrontation between Boko Haram fighters and the military.

An attack by apparent child suicide bombers, carried out overnight between August 1 and 2, in a displacement camp in the town of Nguetechewe, killed at least 17 civilians, including 5 children and 6 women, and wounded at least 16. There was no evident military objective in the vicinity.

Crackdown on Political Opposition

The government limited the ability of political opponents to function freely.

In August, authorities in Far North region and Littoral region, prohibited two private meetings planned by the opposition party, Cameroon Renaissance Movement (Mouvement pour la renaissance du Cameroun, MRC) citing concerns around Covid-19 and general public order.

In September, the government used anti-terror laws and limitations on movements due to Covid-19 as a pretext to restrict freedoms of association and expression, after opponents announced plans to protest the holding of regional elections set for December. The governors of the Littoral and Centre regions banned public meetings and demonstrations indefinitely.

The Territorial Administration Minister warned that law enforcement forces would break up unauthorized demonstrations and advised regional governors to arrest anyone organizing or leading demonstrations. The communication minister warned political parties that protests could be considered "insurrection" and that illegal demonstrations across the country would be punished under the anti-terror law.

Five hundred and six people were arrested for protests in September, 100 people were released while approximately 250 were brought before the courts. Some were charged with terrorism and rebellion, crimes that are heard in military court. The spokesmen and the treasurer of the MRC were held for over two weeks at the State Defense Secretariat (Secrétariat d'Etat à la défense, SED) a prison in Yaoundé.

In May, police arrested nine volunteers from the Survival Initiative, a fundraising initiative by the opposition leader Maurice Kamto, the president of the MRC, to respond to Covid-19, while they were handing out protective masks and sanitizing gel in Yaoundé. They were charged with rebellion, but then later released and the charges dropped.

Sexual Orientation and Gender Identity

Cameroon's penal code punishes "sexual relations between persons of the same sex" with up to five years in prison. Police and gendarmes continued to arrest and harass people they believe to be lesbian, gay, bisexual or transgender (LGBT).

Justice and Accountability

In March, following international pressure, President Biya agreed to establish a commission of inquiry into the killings in Ngarbuh. In an April report, the Cameroon government admitted their security forces bear some responsibility for the killings. In June, the government announced the arrest of two soldiers and a gendarme in connection with the massacre in Ngarbuh. On November 25, the Cameroonian army spokesperson announced that the trial of two soldiers and the gendarme will begin on December 17 in Yaoundé, Cameroon's capital, before a military court. The defendants are accused of murder, arson, destruction, violence against and disobeying orders.

In June, the French ambassador to Cameroon told media that President Biya had assured him that an investigation would be opened into the death in custody of journalist Samuel Wazizi. The declaration was made the same day that the military spokesman, announced that Wazizi had died of severe sepsis on August 17, 2019, at the military hospital in Yaoundé.

Having failed to release any information about Wazizi for 10 months, or the fact that he died in detention, at time of writing authorities had not said whether anyone will be prosecuted for his death. In September, a military court sentenced four soldiers to 10 years in prison and another to two years for the brutal 2015 killing of two women and two children in the village of Zelevet in Far North region. The killings were captured in a video that went viral in early July 2018. The trial was held behind closed doors.

In September, an appeal court in Yaoundé upheld a life sentence on 10 leaders of the separatist group "Ambazonia Interim Government" on charges including terrorism, rebellion, and secession, failing to address the violations of fair trial standards that occurred during their prosecution and conviction before a military court.

Key International Actors

In June, in response to the gravity and number of attacks on schools, the killing and maiming of children, and the recruitment and use of children, the UN secretary-general added Cameroon as a situation of concern for the UN's monitoring and reporting mechanism on grave violations against children during armed conflict.

Canada

The government of Prime Minister Justin Trudeau, re-elected in October 2019, has made efforts to advance human rights in Canada, but serious and longstanding challenges remain. Many of these relate to the rights of Indigenous peoples, including violations of their right to safe drinking water, violence against Indigenous women and girls, and violations of the right to food in these communities as a result of failures to mitigate the impact of climate change.

Canada also grapples with serious human rights issues abroad relating to abuses by Canadian mining companies and the government's failure to suspend arms sales to the Saudi-led coalition in Yemen despite calls by the United Nations to refrain from providing arms and military support to the parties to the conflict. The Trudeau government has also failed to take meaningful steps to repatriate dozens of Canadians, most of whom are children, unlawfully detained in life-threatening conditions for nearly two years in prisons and camps for Islamic State (ISIS) suspects and their families in northeast Syria.

Rights of Indigenous Peoples

Longstanding and systemic discrimination against Indigenous peoples persists across Canada. The water supplied to many First Nations communities on lands known as reserves is contaminated, hard to access, or at risk due to faulty treatment systems. The poor water and sanitation conditions have a disparate and negative impact on at-risk populations, including children. While the most severe public health concerns—water-borne illnesses and related deaths—have mostly been avoided through water advisories, the social costs and human rights impact of the water crisis are considerable.

Both the provincial government of Ontario and the federal government have consistently failed to address the health consequences of decades-old mercury contamination in the First Nation community of Grassy Narrows. While the federal government committed funds to support the building of a mercury care home in Grassy Narrows in April, it has yet to provide compensation to most of the affected community, who continue to live with the physical and mental health impacts of mercury exposure.

Climate change is also contributing to a growing problem of food poverty and related negative health impacts for Indigenous peoples in Canada. Warming temperatures and increasingly unpredictable weather are reducing the availability of Indigenous peoples' traditional food sources and increasing the difficulty and danger associated with harvesting food from the land. As a result, households must supplement their traditional diet with more purchased food. But healthy foods, such as fruits and vegetables, are cost-prohibitive in remote areas. With Canada warming at about twice the global average, the harmful impacts of climate change that Indigenous populations in Canada are experiencing point to more devastating impacts in the future.

Human Rights Watch research found that the Canadian government has failed to put in place adequate measures to support First Nations in adapting to current and anticipated impacts of climate change. Federal and provincial climate change policies have largely ignored the impacts of climate change on First Nations' right to food. Food subsidies and health resources that could help counter current and projected impacts are often not available, insufficient, or do not reach those most in need.

Violence against Indigenous Women and Girls

In June, the federal government promised to release a national action plan to mark the one-year anniversary of the National Inquiry into Missing and Murdered Indigenous Women and Girls. The National Inquiry made 231 recommendations to the government to address endemic levels of violence against Indigenous women and girls in Canada. While Prime Minister Trudeau vowed to "turn the inquiry's calls to justice into real, meaningful, Indigenous-led action," no action plan had been released at time of writing.

In May, more than 1,500 academics and activists sent a letter to Crown-Indigenous Relations Minister Carolyn Bennett demanding that she act on the National Inquiry's calls for justice. In June, the Native Women's Association of Canada issued a report that handed the federal government a failing grade for its response to the National Inquiry recommendations.

Immigration Detention

In recent years, Canada's federal government, the Canada Border Services Agency, and the Immigration Division of the Immigration and Refugee Board have embarked on policy developments to reform the immigration detention system. New regulations require decision-makers to consider children's best interests in decisions related to immigration detention.

It is in the best interests of children to be united with their families in community-based, non-custodial settings but, according to the most recently published 2019-2020 statistics, children are still being placed in detention to accompany their detained parents. It remains unclear how many children are separated from their detained parents.

At time of writing, the Canada Border Services Agency remained the only major law enforcement agency in the country without some form of independent civilian oversight.

Following the onset of the Covid-19 pandemic, in March 2020, immigration detainees in Quebec went on a hunger strike to protest the lack of protection from COVID-19 in detention facilities. Over the following weeks, the government released immigration detainees at unprecedented rates due to public health concerns.

Corporate Accountability

Despite being home to nearly half of the world's major mining companies, Canada has consistently failed to implement promised reforms to hold these corporations accountable for abuses committed abroad.

The Canadian Ombudsperson for Responsible Enterprise does not currently have the authority to independently investigate or publicly report on human rights abuses involving Canadian extractive companies and has limited capacity to hold responsible parties accountable. In May, a petition to the House of Commons called for the government to empower the ombudsperson with independence and restore the office's power to investigate allegations of human rights abuses by Canadian mining companies.

In February, the Supreme Court ruled that a case filed by three Eritreans who say they were victims of forced labor at a mine partly owned by Nevsun Resources could proceed in Canadian courts. In a 2013 investigation into this mine, Human Rights Watch found that an Eritrean construction firm, owned by the country's ruling party, which built part of the mine's infrastructure regularly exploited conscript workers assigned to it by the government. The Supreme Court's landmark decision could open the door for victims of corporate abuses overseas to sue companies in Canada for violations of international human rights law.

Counterterrorism

Human Rights Watch research in June found that Canada is failing to take adequate steps to assist and repatriate dozens of Canadians unlawfully detained in prisons and camps for ISIS suspects and their families in northeast Syria. In October, Canada repatriated a 5-year-old orphan from these camps but Prime Minister Trudeau said the government had no intention of bringing home the remaining Canadians detained for nearly two years in deeply degrading and often inhuman conditions. There are an estimated 46 Canadians still detained in northeast Syria including 8 men, 13 women, and 25 children. None of the Canadians has been charged with any crime or brought before a judge to review the legality and necessity of their detention.

The detainees are held in filthy, life-threatening conditions with inadequate hygiene and medical care. As of late September, one detainee had tested positive for Covid-19 and the World Health Organization warned of a "significant risk" of high transmission in the camps.

Freedom of Religion

In April, the Supreme Court of Canada refused to hear an appeal by civil rights groups seeking to prevent implementation of portions of Bill 21, a 2019 Quebec provincial law banning certain categories of civil servants from wearing religious symbols at work, pending a ruling on its constitutionality. The controversial law banning the wearing of religious symbols (including hijabs, kippahs, and turbans) by teachers, police officers, and judges among others also prohibits any-

HUMAN
RIGHTS
WATCH

"Bring Me Back to Canada"
Plight of Canadians Held in Northeast Syria for Alleged ISIS Links

one with religious face coverings from receiving government services, including healthcare and public transit.

The Quebec Court of Appeal had previously refused to pause implementation of key provisions of the law pending resolution of the legal challenges in part because, in enacting the law, Quebec had preemptively invoked the exceptional "notwithstanding" clause in Canada's constitution. The clause allows provincial or federal authorities to temporarily override some guarantees of the Charter of Rights and Freedoms. Supreme Court refusal to hear the appeal left the provincial court decision in effect.

Key International Actors

In May, six United Nations special rapporteurs and members of two UN working groups called on Canada to secure the urgent release and repatriation of a 5-year-old Canadian orphan detained in a camp for ISIS suspects and their families in northeast Syria. The UN experts noted that "Canada has primary responsibility for ensuring that she is treated with humanity and respect of her dignity and human rights" and urged the Trudeau government to "consolidate and deepen its efforts to enable her safe return."

In a report released in September, the UN special rapporteur on hazardous substances called on Canada to " ensure that the environmental standards on reserves are as strong as or stronger than the standards on neighboring provincial, territorial and federal lands, to ensure equal protection for Indigenous persons."

Foreign Policy

In September, Canada announced its intention to intervene, together with the Netherlands, in Gambia's case before the International Court of Justice alleging that Myanmar's atrocities against the Rohingya violated the Genocide Convention.

At the September session of the UN Human Rights Council, Canada joined 32 other governments in condemning Saudi Arabia's human rights record and calling for the release of all political dissidents and women's rights activists, accountability for past abuses, and an end to persistent discrimination against women. Canada has also supported joint statements condemning China's rights violations, and is a member of UN core groups addressing the rights situations in Yemen and Sri Lanka.

A report released in September from the UN Group of Eminent International and Regional Experts on Yemen named Canada for the first time as one of the countries helping to fuel the conflict through its arms transfers to Saudi Arabia and the United Arab Emirates. The report urged all states to refrain from providing arms and military support to the parties to the conflict.

Central African Republic

A 2019 peace deal between the government and 14 armed groups collapsed as a rebel coalition, created in December, launched attacks against major towns outside of Bangui. The coalition, called the Coalition of Patriots for Change (Coalition des patriotes pour le changement, CPC), created havoc in the run up to elections in December, preventing hundreds of thousands of people from voting.

Former President François Bozizé returned to the country, having fled the capital Bangui in 2013 as Seleka fighters advanced south. Bozizé's return was followed by the return of Michel Djotodia, the Seleka leader who took power from Bozizé and who served as president until January 2014. Djotodia is reported to have stayed in close contact with some Seleka factions. The return of both men came before general elections, scheduled for December. The United Nations Security Council imposed targeted sanctions on Bozizé in 2014, and the United States sanctioned both Bozizé and Djotodia in 2014.

Sidiki Abass, the leader of the rebel group 3R, suspended his participation in the peace deal. Abass resigned from a government position in 2019 after his fighters killed 46 civilians in coordinated attacks in Ouham-Pendé province.

Local courts prosecuted some members of armed groups implicated in serious crimes, but no prosecutions were brought against the leaders. Investigations were pending before the Special Criminal Court (SCC), a war crimes court based in Bangui staffed by national and international judges and prosecutors operating with substantial UN assistance. Five years on from its creation, funding for the court remained insecure. The International Criminal Court (ICC) in July announced the trial date of two suspects associated with anti-balaka militias.

Known cases of Covid-19 and deaths related to the coronavirus remained low across the country, but restrictions on travel and other activity, imposed to prevent spread of the virus, delayed the implementation of some programs tied to the 2019 peace deal. Due to the pandemic, schools were closed between April and September, affecting nearly one million school-going children and adolescents.

Attacks on Civilians by Armed Groups

Fighting escalated in the northeast as former Seleka groups continued to fracture along ethnic lines, particularly among the Rounga, Kara, and Gula groups. Fighting between factions of the Popular Front for the Rebirth of the Central African Republic (FPRC) in the towns of Bria in January and Ndele in April killed scores of civilians. Fighting between the FPRC and the Movement of Central African Liberators for Justice (MLCJ) in Birao in January, February, and March killed dozens of fighters, but also civilians.

Fighters from the Union for Peace in the Central African Republic (UPC) detained seven health workers, including a doctor, as they were traveling for a measles vaccination campaign near Obo, in Haut-Mbomou province. UPC had previously restricted road travel, seeking to consolidate control in the southeast of the country. UPC leaders claimed the health workers were detained for attempting to enter their zone without a permit from the UPC.

The United Nations reported that women and children were used as human shields by FPRC fighters in Ndele to prevent UN peacekeepers deploying in the town.

Violence erupted in the capital Bangui in late December 2019, and clashes between traders and self-defense groups in the PK5 neighborhood killed at least 30 civilians. The fighting was sparked by the increase in demands for taxes by armed groups in the neighborhood.

General Elections

On July 25, Bozizé announced his candidacy for the December 2020 presidential election on behalf of his Kwa Na Kwa party. Bozizé, who was president from 2003 to 2013, returned to the country in late December 2019. He was sanctioned in 2014 by the UN Security Council and the US for his role in providing support to anti-balaka militias. On December 3, the Constitutional Court ruled that Bozizé did not meet a morality requirement for candidates, citing the UN sanctions and an international arrest warrant, and barred his candidacy.

In August, Catherine Samba-Panza, the interim-president from 2014-2016, also announced her candidacy. While Samba-Panza oversaw a degree of stability across the country and supported the establishment of the UN peacekeeping mission, some state security officials, including officers from the Central Office for the Repression of Banditry (*Office Central de Répression du Banditisme*, OCRB), committed extrajudicial killings with impunity in Bangui during her tenure.

President Faustin-Archange Touadera, who was elected in 2016, announced in September that he will run again.

On December 3, the Constitutional Court ruled that Bozizé did not meet a morality requirement for candidates, citing the UN sanctions and an international arrest warrant, and barred his candidacy.

Refugees and Internally Displaced Persons

The total of displaced people remained alarmingly high, at over 1.2 million people, according to the UN. The total number of refugees in the region from the Central African Republic was 622,000. The total number of internally displaced people was 623,000. Conditions for IDPs and refugees, most of whom stay in camps, remained harsh and many had little to no access to humanitarian assistance.

About 2.6 million people, out of a population of 4.6 million, needed humanitarian assistance. The humanitarian response plan was underfunded, with a budget gap of around US$272 million in October.

Justice for War Crimes and Crimes Against Humanity

In February, the Bangui Court of Appeal sentenced 28 anti-balaka fighters for the killing of 75 civilians and 10 UN peacekeepers around Bangassou, in Mbomou province, in 2017. The sentences ranged from 10 years to life.

The SCC continued to take on more cases since its first session in 2018. At time of writing, four investigations were pending with the prosecutor's office and six were pending before the court's investigative judges. Victims have initiated additional cases before the court and three suspects are in pretrial detention. Additionally, in May, the court announced it had opened investigations into nine UPC fighters for crimes committed around Bambouti, Obo, and Zemio in the southeast. Also in May, the court announced it would launch investigations into the killings in Ndele in April.

In July, the ICC set February 9, 2021, as the opening of the trial for anti-balaka leaders Patrice-Edouard Ngaïssona and Alfred Yékatom. The charges against Ngaïssona and Yékatom include war crimes and crimes against humanity committed between December 2013 and December 2014. Ngaïssona was arrested in France and transferred to the ICC in December 2018. Yékatom was transferred to the ICC by Central African Republic authorities in November 2018. The ICC has not issued arrest warrants against any Seleka leaders, unless they are under seal.

In September, former presidential guard under Bozizé, Eric Danboy Bagale, was arrested in France for alleged war crimes and crimes against humanity for acts committed between 2007 and 2014, both as a head of the presidential guard and as a leader in the anti-balaka.

Key International Actors

The UN Security Council and the United States imposed sanctions on Sidiki Abass, the leader of 3R, in August. He was implicated in serious human rights abuses, including the killing of civilians.

In September, the US imposed targeted sanctions on two Central African mining businesses and three Russian employees who work in the country tied to Yevgeniy Prigozhin, a Russian oligarch said to be close to Russian President Vladimir Putin. Investigations into the 2018 murder of three Russian journalists has stalled. The men, found dead north of Sibut, Kemo province, were investigating Russia's increased role in the country and the possible role of Wagner, a mercenary outfit affiliated with Prigozhin.

The UN peacekeeping mission, MINUSCA, deployed 11,650 military peacekeepers and 2,080 police across many parts of the country.

Under Chapter VII of the UN Charter, the mission is authorized to take all necessary means to protect the civilian population from threat of physical violence and to "implement a mission-wide protection strategy." In November, the UN Security Council extended the mandate of the mission.

In October, the UN Human Rights Council continued the mandate of the Independent Expert on the Central African Republic for another year.

The European Union extended the mandate of its military assistance and training mission (EUTM CAR) until 2022 and established a civilian mission (EUAM RCA) to support security sector reform. The EU continued to support peace and accountability efforts in the country.

Chile

Chile's national police—the Carabineros—used excessive force in responding to massive demonstrations, some of them violent, in 2019. Thousands of people were injured or reported serious abuses in detention, including brutal beatings and sexual abuse. While initial steps have been taken to reform the police, structural changes to prevent police misconduct and strengthen oversight and accountability are still pending.

President Sebastián Piñera's administration established a state of emergency on March 18 to curb the spread of Covid-19, and extended it throughout the year.

On October 25, an overwhelming majority (78 percent) voted to establish a constituent assembly to rewrite the constitution.

Chile faces important human rights challenges related to prison conditions, accountability for past abuses, and protecting the rights of women; indigenous people; lesbian, gay, bisexual, and transgender people; migrants; and refugees.

Abuses by Security Forces

Massive, mostly peaceful, protests over public services and economic inequality erupted across Chile in October 2019. Some demonstrators threw rocks and Molotov cocktails at police and burned public and private property. Some people took advantage of the chaos to loot. Police responded using excessive force against demonstrators and bystanders, whether they were engaged in violence or not.

From October 18 to November 20, 2019, almost 11,000 people were injured, including 2,000 officers, and 26 people died. More than 15,000 people were detained, and some suffered ill-treatment. Several people suffered eye injuries, most hit by pellets that police fired from anti-riot shotguns.

Protests started again in Santiago in February, after police killed a 37-year-old in a hit and run after a soccer match. The same month, seven police officers were discharged and five were placed in pretrial detention for beating an 18-year-old protester. In October, the Prosecutor's Office opened a criminal investigation— ongoing at time of writing—and detained a police officer accused of causing the fall and injury of a 16-year-old protester from a bridge, as Carabineros were dispersing a demonstration.

In June, Carabineros said they had opened 1,228 administrative investigations into possible abuses against protesters. Of those, 173 resulted in disciplinary action, including the expulsion from the force of 14 officers. In September, the Comptroller's Office pressed charges in an administrative proceeding against seven police generals for not complying with use of force protocols.

The Prosecutor's Office told Human Rights Watch in October that 5,084 people were indicted for crimes related to lootings, arson, public disorder, and institutional violence related to the demonstrations and unrest that started in October 2019. Seventy-five state agents were indicted, mostly police officers. One police officer was convicted.

Chile has taken preliminary steps to reform the police, in response to abuses. A council convened in December 2019, by the Ministry of Interior and a Senate commission issued recommendations in the first months of 2020 to overhaul the institution, including by improving transparency, training, and accountability. At time of writing, a new unit for Carabineros reform under the Ministry of Interior had been tasked with implementing those recommendations.

In addition, there were at least four reform bills pending in Congress to modernize security forces. However, the bills do not go far enough in overhauling the Carabineros disciplinary system to ensure accountability for abuses.

Confronting Past Abuses

Chilean courts continue to prosecute former police and military officers responsible for human rights abuses during Augusto Pinochet's dictatorship from 1973 to 1990.

Chile maintains a 50-year secrecy order that seals from the public testimony provided by victims before the National Commission on Political Prison and Torture from November 2003 to May 2004. The testimony revealed places of detention and torture methods. Former President Michelle Bachelet's administration (2014-2018) submitted a bill to lift the secrecy order in 2017. At time of writing, the order had been set aside in approximately 15 cases, allowing access to files with testimonies, photographs, and press releases.

On March 6, a Chilean court convicted 31 former agents for their role in the 1974 disappearances of moviemakers Carmen Bueno Cifuentes and Jorge Muller Silva during the security forces' Operación Colombo, in which they forcibly disappeared 119 political prisoners. On September 9, another Chilean judge ordered reparations for a woman arbitrarily arrested and tortured by Carabineros in 1984.

Women's and Girls' Rights

Chile's 28-year total abortion ban ended in 2017 when the Constitutional Court upheld a law decriminalizing abortion under three circumstances: when a pregnancy results from rape, the life of a pregnant woman is at risk, or the fetus is unviable. The law, in its current form, allows doctors and private institutions to refuse to provide abortions for reasons of conscientious objection.

Significant barriers to access remain, even for legally permissible abortions. Measures to curb the spread of Covid-19, including a lockdown, have negatively impacted access to comprehensive sexual and reproductive health, including access to abortion, according to local groups.

In 2019, Chile outlawed sexual street harassment, including verbal assaults, groping, stalking, and indecency, which are now punishable by fines or prison time.

Between January and June, calls to the Carabineros' emergency number reporting gender-based violence more than doubled, although formal complaints dropped. Calls reporting rape more than doubled. Calls reporting sexual harassment more than tripled. Rape, sexual abuse, and other sex crimes reported to police rose to 17,950, the highest in a decade.

Indigenous Rights

Long-standing confrontations between the government and Mapuche land-rights activists continue. The Mapuche represent 87 percent of the Indigenous population of the country.

In June, Mapuche leader Alejandro Treuquil was shot to death by unidentified assailants. According to his family, the incident is related to threats he received from Carabineros and paramilitary groups.

In August, clashes broke out between Mapuches and anti-indigenous groups. Police in five municipalities intervened to clear local government buildings that Mapuches had occupied in support of a jailed leader's hunger strike.

In September, the Piñera administration created the Wallmapu Committee to discuss territorial, collective, and social development of native communities.

Indigenous communities see the pending revision of the constitution as an opportunity for recognition, including of land claims.

Sexual Orientation and Gender Identity

A gender identity law took effect in December 2019. It allows transgender people over 14 years old to change their name and gender in the civil registry without undergoing surgery. Married people, however, must divorce before exercising their right to legal gender recognition.

In January, the Senate voted to consider a 2017 bill to legalize same-sex marriage and allow same-sex couples to adopt children and pursue other reproductive options. In October 2020, a Committee in the Senate approved the majority of the articles in the bill. It remained pending at time of writing.

In June, the Constitutional Court denied a petition filed by a lesbian couple who were married in Spain and have a child to have their marriage recognized in Chile. The court held that that Chilean law, in its denial of marriage rights to same-sex couples, does not discriminate.

Refugees and Migrants' Rights

Immigration laws have not been updated since 1975. For several years, an immigration bill has been stalled in the Senate. The bill would establish long waiting periods to obtain social benefits, provide few avenues for challenging deportation orders, and prohibit changing legal status from within Chile. In April, the government announced that the stalled immigration bill was a high priority. At time of writing, it remained pending.

The government estimated that 1.5 million foreigners were living in Chile, as of March— more than a third (472,000) of them from Venezuela. Chile publicly welcomed Venezuelans, but rules for obtaining visas include requirements that make it hard for some to obtain legal status.

Children's Rights

The Piñera administration has taken several steps to overhaul the flawed National Service for Minors (SENAME). However, complaints against SENAME continued. In August, a SENAME residence worker in Valdivia was accused of mistreating children and suspended. In September, a judge in Valparaiso ordered pretrial detention of a man charged with six counts of prostitution, sexual harassment, and assaults against children in SENAME residences. In November, two children were wounded when police fired shots inside a SENAME center in Talcahuano, pushing the head of Carabineros, Mario Rozas, to resign.

At time of writing, two bills were pending in the legislature to strengthen children's rights protections. One seeks to replace SENAME.

In 2019, the statute of limitations on sex crimes against children was removed.

In March, schools closed to curb the spread of Covid-19, affecting the education of 3.5 million students. The Ministry of Education implemented an online platform for students to access educational content. According to the ministry, 89 percent of students in high-income households have access to online education, but only 27 percent in low-income households do. Despite an attempt to reopen classes in the metropolitan region at the beginning of October, some schools did not receive any students, and others no more than 11 pupils.

Disability Rights

Chile has failed to adopt a comprehensive legislative framework harmonized with international human rights law on disability rights. Its civil code continues to use derogatory language towards people with disabilities and still provides for full guardianship and other forms of stripping of legal capacity from people with disabilities.

Prison Conditions

Overcrowding and prison violence endanger Chile's detainee population of approximately 40,000 people. A 2019 report by the National Human Rights Institute showed 19 of 40 prisons above capacity in 2016 and 2017.

A bill presented by the government in 2018 to grant house arrest to individuals convicted for any crime, including human rights violations, who have a serious, lifelong, or terminal illness or are over 75 years old, and have served at least half of their sentence, is still pending before the senate.

Chile took steps to reduce prison overcrowding to curb the spread of the coronavirus. In April, Congress approved a bill introduced by the Piñera government allowing, at time of writing, 1,568 of 27,411 convicted prisoners to serve the remainder of their sentences under house arrest. Additionally, 1,778 of 14,546 pretrial detainees were placed under house arrest or other alternatives to detention—the most significant effort to reduce prison overcrowding in Latin America in response to Covid-19.

As of June, at least 493 prisoners and 631 officers had contracted Covid-19, and four people had died.

Freedom of Speech

In September, the House of Representatives passed a bill that would criminalize protected speech of people who "justify," "approve" of, or "deny" the human rights violations committed during the country's dictatorship, punishing them with up to three years in prison, if they "disturb the public order" or "illegitimately obstruct or limit" others' exercise of their rights. The Senate had yet to approve the bill at time of writing.

Key International Actors

In December 2020, Chile's term on the United Nations Human Rights Council expired.

As a member, Chile supported efforts in 2020 to scrutinize human rights violations in Nicaragua, Syria, Myanmar, Belarus, Eritrea, Iran, Burundi, Yemen and the Occupied Palestinian Territories.

In January, the Inter-American Commission on Human Rights (IACHR) visited Chile to observe first-hand the human rights situation following the October 2019 protests, and to assess the causes and consequences of the unrest. Among other reforms, the IACHR recommended that Chile take measures to end excessive use of force and ensure access to justice for people whose rights have been violated.

The IACHR submitted the free-speech case of lawyer and environmental activist Carlos Barona Bray to the Inter-American Court of Human Rights (IACtHR) in September. Barona Bray was found guilty in a criminal defamation lawsuit filed by a public official.

The IACtHR held a public hearing in January on Judge Daniel Urrutia Laubreaux's case. The judge brought his case to the commission in 2005, arguing that the Supreme Court violated his right to freedom of speech when it sanctioned him for criticizing in an academic paper the court's actions during the Chilean military regime.

Chile maintained a strong stance criticizing abuses by the Nicolás Maduro government in Venezuela. It participated in all Lima Group statements and welcomed the report issued in September by the United Nations Fact-Finding Mission on Venezuela.

Chile endorsed the World Health Organization's Solidarity Call to Action for the Covid-19 Technology Access Pool, an initiative to "realize equitable global access to Covid-19 health technologies through pooling of knowledge, intellectual property and data."

China

The Chinese government's authoritarianism was on full display in 2020 as it grappled with the deadly coronavirus outbreak first reported in Wuhan province. Authorities initially covered up news about the virus, then adopted harsh quarantine measures in Wuhan and other parts of China. The government has rejected international calls for independent, unfettered investigations into Chinese authorities' handling of the outbreak, and surveilled and harassed families of those who died of the virus.

Beijing's repression—insisting on political loyalty to the Chinese Communist Party—deepened across the country. In Hong Kong, following six months of large-scale protests in 2019, the Chinese government imposed a draconian "National Security Law" on June 30—its most aggressive assault on Hong Kong people's freedoms since the transfer of sovereignty in 1997. In Xinjiang, Turkic Muslims continue to be arbitrarily detained on the basis of their identity, while others are subjected to forced labor, mass surveillance, and political indoctrination. In Inner Mongolia, protests broke out in September when education authorities decided to replace Mongolian with Mandarin Chinese in a number of classes in the region's schools.

Chinese authorities' silencing of human rights defenders, journalists, and activists, and restrictions on the internet, also make it difficult to obtain accurate information about Chinese government policies and actions.

Despite these threats some prominent individuals publicly criticized President Xi Jinping. Entrepreneur Ren Zhiqiang wrote an essay calling Xi "a clown who desires power," while former Central Party school teacher Cai Xia called the Chinese Communist Party a "political zombie." Ren received an extraordinarily lengthy prison sentence—18 years—in September; Cai fled into exile.

Governments, civil society groups, and United Nations officials expressed growing concern over the Chinese government's human rights violations in 2020. In April, reports of Africans in China being targeted for Covid-19 testing led to complaints by African governments and civil society. In July, the US government sanctioned top Chinese officials responsible for Xinjiang abuses. In June, an unprecedented group of 50 UN Special Procedure mandate-holders issued a joint statement on China, calling for "renewed attention on the human rights situation in the country" as a matter of urgency, including through a special session of the UN Human Rights Council on China, and the creation of an international mechanism to address rights violations in the country.

Hong Kong

One million Hong Kong people marked the new year by marching peacefully for democracy, but in January 2020, the Chinese government replaced its top Hong Kong official with Luo Huining, who had no experience in Hong Kong but was known as a Communist Party enforcer.

In April, Beijing's representatives in Hong Kong threatened pro-democracy legislators with "serious consequences" over their delay in selecting a new chairperson for an internal committee in the semi-democratic Legislative Council (LegCo), again interfering with the territory's autonomy. The representatives then "reinterpreted" Hong Kong's constitution, the Basic Law, stating that they were not bound by the law's limitations on their powers. In May, with the help of dozens of security guards, pro-Beijing legislators removed at least 10 pro-democracy legislators from the LegCo internal committee through a dubious process. The leader of the pro-Beijing legislators, Starry Lee, asserted that she was now chair and had the power to oversee the proceedings. Lee's power grab gave mainland authorities greater control over LegCo, which in June passed a bill criminalizing "disrespect" of the Chinese national anthem.

Throughout the year, Hong Kong police arrested pro-democracy figures for peaceful activities. In February, Hong Kong police arrested pro-democracy media tycoon Jimmy Lai, and former lawmakers Lee Cheuk-yan and Yeung Sum, for their participation in the 2019 protests. In April, Hong Kong police arrested 15 prominent pro-democracy leaders, including 81-year-old barrister Martin Lee, for "organizing and participating in unlawful assemblies" during the 2019 protests.

On June 30, the Chinese government bypassed LegCo and imposed a new National Security Law (NSL) on Hong Kong. The law creates specialized secret security agencies, denies people fair trial rights, provides sweeping new powers to the police, increases restraints on civil society and the media, and weakens judicial oversight. Shortly before the law's enactment, a number of pro-democracy groups, including Demosisto, disbanded.

Hong Kong's education chief banned the protest anthem "Glory to Hong Kong" from schools. Public libraries pulled books by pro-democracy figures. Authorities deemed illegal the 2019 protest slogan, "Liberate Hong Kong, the revolution of our times."

Police used the NSL to arrest those who shouted or held placards with the slogan at protests, and against organizers of the pro-democracy movement. In late July, four associated with the political group Studentlocalism were arrested for NSL violations. In August, police raided the office of pro-democracy newspaper *Apple Daily*, arrested its owner Jimmy Lai, his two sons, and four executives for "collusion with foreign forces" and conspiracy to commit fraud. Two other democracy activists were also arrested.

In July, Hong Kong election authorities disqualified a dozen pro-democracy figures from the legislative election slated for September. That month, the Hong Kong government "postponed" the elections for a year, citing a rise in Covid-19 cases.

Also in July, the Hong Kong University governing council—dominated by members from outside the university and chaired by a pro-Beijing politician—sacked Professor Benny Tai, a leading figure in Hong Kong's pro-democracy movement.

Following the enactment of the NSL, some activists fled. A group of 12 protesters were intercepted by mainland authorities when attempting to reach Taiwan by sea. At time of writing they remained detained in China without access to lawyers.

No police officers alleged to have used excessive force during the 2019 protests have been held accountable. In some cases, the police obstructed efforts to press for accountability. In March, police arrested a pro-democracy official, Cheng Lai-king, for revealing on social media the identity of the officer who shot and blinded a journalist who covered the protests.

Press freedom continued to deteriorate. During a protest in May, police forced journalists to kneel down and pepper sprayed them. In June, public broadcaster Radio Television Hong Kong (RTHK) suspended its popular political satirical

HUMAN
RIGHTS
WATCH

CHINA'S "BILINGUAL EDUCATION"
POLICY IN TIBET
Tibetan-Medium Schooling Under Threat

show, the Headliner, following political pressure. In July and August, *New York Times* journalist Chris Buckley and incoming *Hong Kong Free Press* editor Aaron Mc Nicholas were denied visas to work in the city.

Xinjiang

The Chinese government's efforts to erase the unique identity of Uyghurs and other Turkic Muslims in the region persisted. In January, a CNN investigation examining satellite imagery concluded that over 100 traditional Uyghur cemeteries had been destroyed.

In August, another satellite imagery study by Buzzfeed revealed that Xinjiang authorities had built over 260 "massive" detention structures since 2017, providing more evidence to support earlier findings by rights groups and journalists that Chinese authorities are arbitrarily detaining Turkic Muslims en masse.

While the Chinese government appears to have shut down some political education camps and "released" detainees following global outrage, an untold number of Turkic Muslims remain in detention and imprisoned solely on the basis of their identities. A significant number of Uyghur diaspora continue to have no information concerning the whereabouts of their family members, more than five years after the launch of the government's "Strike Hard" campaign.

Some "released" Uyghur detainees are forced to work in factories and fields inside and outside Xinjiang under what the authorities describe as "poverty alleviation" efforts. In February, an Australian think tank revealed a list of 82 global brands that sourced from factories in China that used workers from Xinjiang under conditions that "strongly suggest" forced labor.

In July, a US-based mobile security firm, Lookout, reported that Chinese government-linked groups had used malicious hardware to hack into Uyghurs' phones inside and outside China on a large scale since 2013.

Tibet

Authorities in Tibetan areas continue to severely restrict religious freedom, speech, movement, and assembly, and fail to redress popular concerns about mining and land grabs by local officials, which often involve intimidation and un-lawful use of force by security forces.

Authorities' 13th Five-Year Plan for Tibet (2015-2020), which set ambitious state goals for rural transformation, includes the relocation of several hundred thou-sand more people. Official claims of "poverty alleviation" prompted fears of fur-ther marginalization and dispossession of Tibet's rural majority.

In May, regulations for the promotion of "Nationality Unity Model Areas" came into force, representing a new milestone for the coercive assimilationist policies of the current leadership. These policies encourage economic migration from other parts of China and phasing out Tibetan-medium instruction in primary schools. Intensified surveillance and intimidation in neighborhoods, work-places, and homes has prevented public protest, a goal emphasized repeatedly by leading officials.

At the 7th Forum on Tibet Work in August 2020, President Xi personally called for increasing political education in schools to ensure the loyalty of the next genera-tion, signaling central support for these policies.

In the Ngawa Tibetan region of Sichuan in November 2019, Yonten became the 156th Tibetan to set himself on fire in protest against the Chinese government since March 2009.

Covid-19

The Chinese government's response to the coronavirus outbreak was initially de-layed by withholding information from the public, under-reporting cases of infec-tion, downplaying the severity of the infection, and dismissing the likelihood of transmission between humans. Authorities also detained people for "rumor-mongering," censored online discussions of the outbreak, and curbed media re-porting.

In areas under lockdown, particularly in Wuhan in early 2020 and in Xinjiang in August, authorities failed to ensure appropriate access to medical care, food, and other necessities. In Xinjiang, authorities forced some residents to take tra-ditional Chinese medicine, sealed their apartment doors with iron bars, and chained those who violated lockdown measures to metal posts.

Authorities detained lawyer and citizen journalist Chen Qiushi, businessman Fang Bin, activist Zhang Zhan, and others for their independent reporting on the outbreak in Wuhan. In April, Beijing police detained Chen Mei and Cai Wei for archiving censored news articles, interviews, and personal accounts related to the outbreak.

In April, authorities in Guangzhou, home to China's largest African community, forcibly tested Africans for the coronavirus, and ordered them to self-isolate or to quarantine in designated hotels. Landlords evicted African residents, forcing many to sleep on the street, and hotels, shops, and restaurants refused to serve African customers.

Authorities across the country blocked family members of those who died of the virus from bringing allegations of negligence against the government, hospitals, and quarantine hotels.

Nationwide, more than 241 million pre-school to secondary school students were impacted by school closures, according to UN estimates. Pre-existing inequalities in education were reflected in students' lack of access to affordable internet and capable devices.

Beijing initially resisted a call for international investigation into the origin of the virus, punishing Australia, who initiated the call, by suspending a significant portion of beef imports from the country. After over 120 countries supported a resolution at the World Health Organization (WHO) supporting an independent investigation, Beijing allowed a WHO team to visit the country, but the experts' August visit did not include Wuhan.

Human Rights Defenders

Authorities continued to crack down on a once-growing community of human right defenders, and increasingly targeted family members of activists.

In December 2019, police across the country detained several participants at a gathering in Xiamen, Fujian province, where attendees had discussed human rights and China's political future. While others were later released, human rights lawyer Ding Jiaxi remained in detention on charge of "inciting subversion."

In the same month, a Sichuan court sentenced Wang Yi, a Christian pastor, to nine years in prison for "inciting subversion."

In February, authorities in Guangzhou apprehended prominent and previously imprisoned legal activist Xu Zhiyong, accusing him of "subversion." Police also placed Xu's girlfriend, Li Qiaochu, under secret detention for four months.

In March, Yunnan authorities forcibly disappeared artist and activist Wang Zang. Three months later, his wife, Wang Liqin, was also disappeared after calling for her husband's release on Twitter, leaving their four small children without their parents. The couple were later charged with "inciting subversion."

In April, after being wrongfully imprisoned for four-and-a-half years, human rights lawyer Wang Quanzhang was released from prison. Despite having tested negative repeatedly for Covid-19, authorities made him quarantine in his home-town before allowing him to return to Beijing and reunite—under guard— with his family.

In June, a court in Jiangsu province sentenced Yu Wensheng, a human rights lawyer detained since January 2018, to four years in prison after convicting him of "inciting subversion."

In September, Beijing police detained publisher and producer Geng Xiaonan and her husband, Qin Zhen, on suspicion of "illegal business operations." Geng is a long-time supporter of independent scholars and activists, and earlier spoke up publicly for her friend Xu Zhangrun, a prominent law professor who was detained for six days in July for publishing articles critical of President Xi.

Freedom of Expression

Authorities detained and prosecuted numerous netizens for online posts and private chat messages critical of the government, charging them with crimes such as "spreading rumors," "picking quarrels," and "insulting the country's leaders." The government continued to crack down on Chinese users of Twitter, which is already blocked in China. It was revealed in January that a mainland student at the University of Minnesota was sentenced to six months in prison in November 2019 for tweets critical of President Xi he posted when he was in the US.

Authorities expanded their internet censorship regime to suppress content not in line with "core socialist values." In March, the Cyberspace Administration implemented a set of new regulations to improve "online news eco-system governance." Including banning a wide and ever-expanding range of "negative" or illegal content. In August, authorities shut down Bainu, the only Mongolian-language social media site in China after Mongolian speakers posted complaints on the site about a policy that replaced Mongolian with Mandarin Chinese as the language of instruction in some classes.

In March, a court in Ningbo sentenced Swedish bookseller Gui Minhai to 10 years for allegedly "providing intelligence" to foreigners. This came five years after Gui, a publisher of books about China's political intrigues, was forcibly disappeared in Thailand in October 2015.

Freedom of Religion

The Chinese government's efforts to "Sinicize" religion—which aim to ensure that the Chinese Communist Party is the arbiter of people's spiritual life— continued in 2020.

Existing Chinese law already requires that people can only practice five officially recognized religions in officially approved premises, and that the authorities have control over their personnel appointments, publications, finances, and seminary applications. The Chinese government further tightened these restrictions on February 1, when it started to implement the new "Administrative Measures for Religious Groups." The measures declare the supremacy of the Chinese Communist Party in religious affairs, require religious organizations to publicize the Party's policies, put in the hands of officials the power to decide even the most minute of religious decisions, and prohibit religious groups from operating without authorization.

On April 2, Zhao Huaiguo, pastor of Bethel Church in Cili County, Hunan, was arrested for "inciting subversion."

Muslims reported increasing restrictions on Islam. Authorities scrubbed Arabic script from mosques and halal restaurants, and altered the architectural style of mosques and landmarks to make them look more "Chinese" across the country.

In July, hackers originating from China were found to be spying on the Vatican's computer networks. In October, the Vatican renewed a two-year unpublished agreement with the Chinese government that allows both parties a say in appointing bishops in China, despite heightened religious persecution in China.

Mass Surveillance

To combat Covid-19, Chinese tech giants developed an app known as the Health Code. Using unknown algorithms, the app generates one of three colors (green, yellow, or red) depending on a range of factors such as whether people have been to virus-hit areas. That color has a wide-ranging impact on people's lives, including their freedom of movement, as local authorities throughout the country require people to show their app when they move around.

In May, Canadian research group Citizen Lab found that Chinese social media service WeChat was monitoring the content of users outside China.

Apps, products, and tools developed by Chinese tech companies raise the threat of Chinese government interference and surveillance, leading some foreign governments to impose broad restrictions that themselves raise human rights concerns. The Indian government banned TikTok, WeChat, and other Chinese apps in June; the US government launched a vaguely worded "Clean Network" initiative to significantly curtail the use and sale of Chinese technology products and services in the United States, such as by removing major Chinese apps from US app stores.

Women's and Girls' Rights

According to women's rights activists, domestic violence cases surged in cities and towns under coronavirus lockdowns.

In June, the National People's Congress, China's rubberstamp parliament, introduced a civil code that, for the first time, defines sexual harassment and states that perpetrators can be held liable, though it is vague on what recourse is available to victims. The law also makes it harder to divorce by establishing a mandatory "cooling-off period" of 30 days for couples who apply for divorce-through-agreement. This provision will disproportionately harm women, as three-quarters of divorces are initiated by women, including potentially endangering women experiencing domestic violence.

Women's rights activists continued to face harassment from authorities. In March, authorities in Inner Mongolia forced Ye Haiyan—an activist who has advocated for the rights of sex workers and victims of sexual harassment—to demolish the yurts she and her partner had built as rentals for travelers, cutting off a main source of their income.

In September, feminists and netizens were disappointed when a high-profile #MeToo lawsuit ended with the top prosecutor clearing Bao Yuming, a lawyer and former executive at Chinese tech company ZTE, of charges of child rape by a woman who claimed to be his adopted daughter.

Sexual Orientation and Gender Identity

While China decriminalized homosexuality in 1997, it lacks laws protecting people from discrimination on the basis of sexual orientation or gender identity, and same-sex partnerships are not legal.

In January, a court in Beijing ruled that it was illegal for an e-commerce company to fire a woman when she took a leave of absence for gender-affirming surgery.

In June, a Zhejiang court accepted a case brought by a lesbian suing for custody and visitation rights of the children she had with her former partner whom she had married in the United States.

In August, organizers of the Shanghai Pride, one of China's largest LGBT festivals, announced that they would cancel all activities and events indefinitely, citing the need to "protect the safety of all involved."

Disability Rights

China ratified the Convention on the Rights of Persons with Disabilities in 2008. However, persons with disabilities continue to face discrimination in areas including education and employment.

Only five students were able to access the Braille version of China's university entrance exam, an exam taken by more than 10 million students in July.

Authorities across the country continued to harass and prosecute families with children who developed disabilities after receiving faulty vaccines. In January, authorities released He Fangmei, an activist for vaccine safety detained in March 2019.

In September, a Hunan court secretly tried Cheng Yuan, Liu Dazhi, and Wu Gejianxiong, staff members of the anti-discrimination and disability rights group Changsha Funeng, on "subversion" charges.

Refugees and Asylum Seekers

China continued to detain and forcibly return hundreds, and perhaps thousands, of North Korean refugees, thus violating its obligations as a party to the 1951 Refugee Convention. The government refused to consider fleeing North Koreans as refugees, even though those returned have long been persecuted. Human Rights Watch considers North Koreans in China as refugees sur place, meaning their arrival in China put them at risk if returned.

Key International Actors

An increasing number of governments expressed public concern about China's human rights violations in 2020, particularly in Hong Kong and Xinjiang, though relatively few took concrete action.

The US imposed some targeted sanctions on Chinese officials, agencies, and companies involved in abuses in those two regions, and the US Congress passed several new laws on a range of human rights concerns. The UK spearheaded a joint statement on China's rights violations at the Human Rights Council in June, and moved to offer safe haven to Hong Kongers with UK ties. Australia, Canada, New Zealand, the UK, and the US moved swiftly to suspend extradition treaties with Hong Kong and some to ease access for Hong Kong people to those countries in response to the National Security Law.

The European Union continued to condemn China's deteriorating human rights record, both bilaterally—including at the highest levels—and in international fora. However, despite sustained pressure from the European Parliament and civil society, divisions among EU member states have prevented the bloc from

adopting robust measures such as targeted sanctions against the Chinese officials responsible for the crackdown. Few governments in Muslim majority countries expressed concerns about abuses in Xinjiang.

The number of countries willing to publicly condemn the Chinese government for
its abuses in Xinjiang, Hong Kong, Tibet, and elsewhere continued to grow, while
the number of countries willing to praise Beijing declined. In October, Germany
delivered a joint statement condemning the Chinese government's violations to
the UN General Assembly's Third Committee with the backing of 39 countries,
and Turkey delivered a separate statement of concern. Similarly, over 400 civil
society organizations called for an international mechanism to monitor human
rights in China.

Another global coalition of 200 civil society groups launched a campaign to persuade companies at risk of complicity in Uyghur forced labor to leave Xinjiang. In
September, apparel company H&M said it would cut ties with an allegedly complicit supplier with which it had an indirect relationship, while five firms announced they would no longer conduct audits in that region due to restrictions.

Other global firms enabled Chinese authorities' repression. In June HSBC publicly expressed its support for the new Hong Kong National Security Law; in September Disney failed to respond to global outcry over its having cooperated with
abusive authorities in Xinjiang during its filming of Mulan.

Universities outside China continued to struggle to protect academic freedom in
the face of threats from pro-Chinese voices. The University of New South Wales in
Australia took down an article pro-Beijing voices found objectionable and then
reposted it, but failed to use the opportunity to robustly explain and defend academic freedom.

In October, China was elected to the UN Human Rights Council for a three-year
term beginning in January 2021—with the fewest votes of any elected member.

Foreign Policy

The "Belt and Road Initiative" (BRI), announced in 2013, is China's trillion-dollar
infrastructure and investment program stretching across some 70 countries.
Many BRI projects have been criticized for lack of transparency, disregard of

community concerns, and potential environmental degradation. Civil society groups in Cambodia, Laos, Myanmar, and Thailand have alleged BRI-backed hydroelectric dams have negatively impacted the Mekong River and caused water shortages. China is by far the world's largest emitter of greenhouse gases. It has done little to reduce its emissions that contribute significantly to global warming and climate change. It has continued to promote the development of heavily polluting coal both domestically and through BRI.

2020 marked rapid escalations in the Chinese government's mistreatment of foreign journalists. Beijing in February expelled three Wall Street Journal journalists. In March, authorities expelled at least 13 US nationals and dismissed seven Chinese nationals who worked for US news organizations. In September, authorities delayed visa renewals for a number of journalists with US outlets. That same month, authorities barred two Australian reporters from two Australian news organizations from leaving the country, citing the need to question them about the case of Cheng Lei, an Australian news anchor for the Chinese state broadcaster CGTN who was detained in August for unspecified reasons. The two Australian journalists fled China after the ban was lifted following negotiations between the two countries.

The effect of Chinese government censorship continues to reach beyond China's borders. In June, Zoom shut down a US-based Chinese dissident's account after he held a Tiananmen Massacre memorial that was joined by China-based activists and families of victims of the 1989 massacre. Chinese tech company ByteDance, which owns TikTok, censored content it considered as critical of the Chinese government on its news aggregator app in Indonesia from 2018 to mid-2020, according to a Reuters report.

At the June session of the Human Rights Council, China secured the passage of its resolution on "mutually beneficial cooperation," which ignores states' responsibility to protect human rights and minimizes the role of civil society. Support diminished considerably from China's previous "win-win" resolution, indicating diminishing enthusiasm for these initiatives.

Colombia

The peace accord in 2016 between the Revolutionary Armed Forces of Colombia (FARC) and the government ended a 52-year armed conflict and brought an initial decline in violence. But conflict-related violence has since taken new forms, and serious abuses continue. Violence associated with the conflicts has forcibly displaced more than 8.2 million Colombians since 1985.

In 2020, civilians in various parts of the country suffered serious abuses at the hands of National Liberation Army (ELN) guerrillas, FARC dissidents, and paramilitary successor groups. Human rights defenders, journalists, indigenous and Afro-Colombian leaders, and other community activists face pervasive death threats and violence. The government has taken insufficient steps to protect them.

As of October, the government had confirmed more than 860,000 cases of Covid-19 and 26,000 deaths. In March, the government established a nation-wide lockdown that lasted until September. The government closed schools in March, affecting an estimated 10 million students. While the government took some measures to ensure online teaching, many students were not able to attend. Some schools began reopening in September.

Impunity for past abuses, barriers to land restitution for displaced people, limits on reproductive rights, and the extreme poverty and isolation of indigenous communities remain important human rights concerns in Colombia.

Guerrillas and FARC Dissidents

In June 2017, the United Nations political mission in Colombia verified that FARC guerrillas who accepted the peace agreement with the government had handed over their weapons to the mission. The demobilized guerrilla group later announced it was forming a political party.

But a minority of dissident guerrilla fighters rejected the terms of the peace agreement, refused to disarm, and continue to commit abuses. Fighters of the guerrillas' former Eastern Bloc, which never demobilized, continue to operate in

HUMAN
RIGHTS
WATCH

"The Guerrillas Are the Police"

Social Control and Abuses by Armed Groups in Colombia's
Arauca Province and Venezuela's Apure State

several parts of the country under the leadership of Miguel Botache Santillana, known as Gentil Duarte.

Other FARC fighters disarmed initially but joined or created new groups, partly in reaction to inadequate reintegration programs and attacks against former fighters. As of August 2020, more than 300 former FARC fighters had been killed.

In August 2019, Luciano Marín Arango, known as Iván Márquez, the FARC's former second-in-command and top peace negotiator, announced he was taking up arms again. He and other former FARC commanders created the FARC Second Marquetalia, named after the area where the FARC were created in the 1960s.

In the southern state of Cauca, FARC dissident groups have committed serious abuses, including murder, child recruitment, and forced displacement. They also imposed their own measures to slow the spread of Covid-19, including lockdowns, and threatened, attacked, and killed some for allegedly not complying.

The ELN continued, in 2020, to commit war crimes and other serious abuses against civilians, including killings, forced displacement, and child recruitment.

In Chocó state, on the country's west coast, fighting continued between the ELN and the Gaitanist Self-Defense Forces of Colombia (AGC)—a group that emerged from right-wing paramilitaries. Fears of landmines, threats by armed groups, and the hazards of crossfire limited the ability of nearly 4,000 people in Chocó to leave their communities in August, a situation known as "confinement." In already poor communities, confinement often undermines access to food.

Paramilitaries and Successors

Between 2003 and 2006, right-wing paramilitary organizations with close ties to security forces and politicians underwent a deeply flawed government demobilization process during which many members remained active and reorganized into new groups. These successor groups, most notably the AGC, continue to commit violations of the laws of war and serious human rights abuses, including killings, disappearances, and rape.

Implementation of the Justice and Peace Law of 2005, which offers reduced sentences to demobilized paramilitary members who confess their crimes, has been slow. Of more than 30,000 paramilitary troops who officially demobilized, 4,000 have sought to exchange a confession for a reduced sentence. As of October 2020, 650 had been sentenced.

Santiago Uribe, brother of former President Alvaro Uribe, was on trial at time of writing, for charges of murder and conspiracy, for his alleged role in the paramilitary group "12 Apostles" in the 1990s.

In August, the Supreme Court called former President Uribe to testify about his alleged role in massacres when he was governor of Antioquia department and in the 1998 murder of Jesus María Valle, a human rights lawyer.

In March, Salvatore Mancuso, a former top paramilitary commander who was extradited to the US in 2008, completed his sentence there for drug trafficking. If returned to Colombia, Mancuso could help uncover the truth about hundreds of crimes. But Mancuso, who holds Colombian and Italian nationality, asked to be sent to Italy. After Colombian authorities made several flawed attempts to ensure his return, the US Department of Homeland Security finally ordered his deportation to Colombia in August. Mancuso has applied for asylum in the US, however, and as of October, his deportation remained pending.

Violations by Public Security Forces

From 2002 through 2008, army brigades across Colombia routinely executed civilians in what are known as "false positive" killings. Under pressure from superiors to show "positive" results and boost body counts in their war against guerrillas, soldiers and officers abducted victims or lured them to remote locations under false pretenses—such as promises of work—shot them dead, placed weapons on their bodies, and reported them as enemy combatants killed in action. The number of allegations of unlawful killings by security forces has fallen sharply since 2009, though credible reports of some new cases continue to emerge.

As of September 2020, the Attorney General's Office had opened over 2,000 investigations into alleged unlawful killings by army personnel from 2002 through 2008, and had achieved over 900 convictions in cases against more than 1,600 mid- and low-level soldiers, including convictions of the same individual in various cases. Over 250 members of the Armed Forces had testified about their roles in false positives before the Special Jurisdiction for Peace, a transitional justice mechanism created by the peace agreement with the FARC.

Authorities have largely failed, however, to prosecute senior army officers involved in the killings and instead have promoted many of them through the military ranks. As of September 2020, cases against at least 29 army generals under investigation for false-positive killings had made scant progress.

In 2019, the *New York Times*, *Semana* magazine, and Human Rights Watch published documents showing that the army had, that year, reinstated military policies resembling those that led to the false positives. In May 2019, President Iván Duque created a commission charged with reviewing army policies to ensure their consistency with international human rights and humanitarian law. The commission was asked to present a final report by November 2019, but had not issued findings as of October 2020.

In November 2019, the Colombian National Police committed multiple abuses against demonstrators who mobilized in the streets to protest issues ranging from tax reform proposals to the killing of human rights defenders. In several cases, the police engaged in arbitrary detentions and used excessive force, including beatings.

In December 2019, *Semana* magazine published evidence that army soldiers had, that year, unlawfully surveilled journalists, human rights defenders, and some government officials.

On March 21, 2020, 24 prisoners were killed and 76 injured as police guards repressed a riot in La Modelo jail in Bogotá. As of September, no one had been charged in connection with the injuries and deaths.

At least six civilians died between March and June, during police operations to eradicate crops of coca—the raw material of cocaine—in various parts of the country, media and local rights groups reported.

In September, Javier Ordoñez, a lawyer, died at the hands of police who repeatedly shocked him with a stun gun. The death prompted hundreds of Colombians to take to the streets in largely peaceful demonstrations. Police responded with force that often appeared excessive, leaving 13 dead and hundreds injured.

Also in September, the Supreme Court ordered that the government take action to avoid police abuses during protests, including by strengthening supervision over officers, reviewing protocols on the use of force, and suspending the use of 12-gauge shotguns.

Violence Against Community Activists

Threats and attacks against Indigenous, Afro-Colombian, and other community activists continue. As of October, the Office of the UN High Commissioner for Human Rights (OHCHR) had documented killings of 49 human rights defenders in 2020 and was verifying another 50 cases.

On June 8, Edison León Pérez, a community leader from Putumayo, was killed. Members of La Mafia, an armed group in the area, appear responsible: Days earlier, Léon Pérez had sent a letter to Putumayo authorities complaining that the group was forcing residents to organize checkpoints to question and screen people entering the area for symptoms of Covid-19.

As of September, the Attorney General's Office was investigating 397 cases of murder of human rights defenders since 2016 and had obtained convictions in 61 cases. Authorities have made much less progress in prosecuting people who ordered murders against human rights defenders.

Most such killings have occurred in areas where illegal economic activities, such as drug production and trafficking, are common. These include Putumayo, Cauca, Valle del Cauca and Nariño states in the south; the Catatumbo region, on the border with Venezuela; and the Bajo Cauca region.

The National Protection Unit has granted individual protection measures to hundreds of human rights defenders who have reported threats, providing cellphones, bulletproof vests, and bodyguards. But many murdered defenders had not reported threats or requested protection.

Collective protection programs created in 2018 for at-risk communities and rights groups had not been implemented at time of writing, and an action plan introduced in November 2018 to protect community leaders had produced no evident results.

Judicial Independence

In August, the Supreme Court ordered the pre-trial arrest of former president and senator Alvaro Uribe, mentor of current President Duque and leader of the governing party, the Democratic Center. Uribe was detained as part of an investigation into whether he bribed former paramilitary fighters to change their testimony about his alleged role in establishing paramilitary groups.

In reaction to the court's decision, President Duque and other Democratic Center leaders made statements that appeared designed to smear or intimidate the court and undermine the legitimacy of the decision. They proposed overhauling the entire court system and unifying the high courts into a single court—a move that could seriously undermine judicial independence in the country.

In late August, after Uribe resigned his seat in the Senate and the Supreme Court, which handles probes involving lawmakers, relinquished jurisdiction, sending the case to the Attorney General's Office. In October, the Supreme Court ruled that Uribe's resignation from the Senate meant that he should be investigated under a different law of procedure. On October 10, a judge ruled that Uribe could not be detained under the new law and ordered his release. The investigation continued at time of writing.

Peace Negotiations and Accountability

The peace agreement between the Colombian government and the FARC provided for the creation of a Special Jurisdiction for Peace.

At time of writing, Special Jurisdiction magistrates had prioritized seven situations for analysis: kidnappings by the FARC; false-positive killings; army and FARC abuses against Afro-Colombian and indigenous people in three municipalities in Nariño state; FARC and army abuses in the Urabá region; FARC and army abuses in the northern part of Cauca state; government abuses against members of the Patriotic Union, a political party created by the FARC in the 1980s; and FARC recruitment and use of children.

In July, the Special Jurisdiction concluded that demobilized FARC fighters were facing a "grave situation of human rights violations," and ordered government agencies to take action to protect them.

In August, the Special Jurisdiction began taking testimony from former FARC commanders about recruitment and use of children—a widespread practice that guerrilla fighters have often tried to whitewash.

Throughout 2020, the Special Jurisdiction issued precautionary measures to protect several cemeteries where the remains of people who went missing during the decades-long armed conflict are expected to be found.

Internal Displacement and Land Restitution

Conflict-related violence has displaced more than 8.2 million Colombians, out of a population of 49 million, since 1985, government figures reveal. More than 75,000 people were displaced in 2019.

Implementation of land restitution under the 2011 Victims' Law continues to move slowly. The law was enacted to restore millions of hectares left behind by or stolen from internally displaced Colombians during the conflict. As of August, the courts had issued rulings in only 11,300 of more than 125,000 claims filed.

The Covid-19 pandemic and its related restrictions hampered the work of humanitarian agencies helping displaced people in Colombia.

Migration from Venezuela

Colombia has received by far the largest number of Venezuelan exiles fleeing the human rights and humanitarian crisis in Venezuela. As of June 2020, more than 1.7 million Venezuelans lived in Colombia.

In July 2017, the Colombian government created a special permit allowing Venezuelans who enter the country legally but overstay visas to regularize their status and obtain work permits and access to basic public services. As of August 2020, over 600,000 Venezuelans had obtained the permit.

In November 2019, Colombian authorities expelled 60 Venezuelans accused of compromising public order and national security in the context of nationwide protests. Some expulsions appear to be arbitrary.

Between March and August, as the Covid-19 pandemic raged, more than 100,000 Venezuelans returned to their country.

Gender, Sexuality, and Gender-Based Violence

Gender-based violence, including by armed groups, is widespread. Lack of train-ing and poor implementation of treatment protocols impede timely access to medical services and create obstacles for women and girls seeking post-violence care and justice. Perpetrators of violent, gender-based crimes are rarely held ac-countable.

In the southwestern municipality of Tumaco, where sexual violence, including by armed groups, is pervasive, women face an array of obstacles to protection and justice.

In September 2019, a group of soldiers reportedly kidnapped and raped a 15-year-old indigenous Nukak Makú girl. In July 2020, Major General Eduardo Zap-ateiro, commander of the army, said authorities were investigating 118 soldiers for alleged cases of sexual abuse since 2016.

Abortion in Colombia is legal only when the life or health of the pregnant person is at risk, the pregnancy results from rape, or the fetus has conditions incompati-ble with life outside the womb. But women and girls seeking legal abortions face many barriers.

Despite Colombia's strong legal protections on the basis of sexual orientation and gender identity, the human rights ombudsperson has raised concerns about high levels of violence against lesbian, gay, bisexual, and transgender people.

In response to the Covid-19 pandemic, on April 8, 2020 the government of Bo-gotá established a gender-based quarantine. Despite transgender-sensitive pro-visions in the decree, there were reports of some cases of police abuse against transgender and non-binary people. Bogotá scrapped its gendered quarantine starting on May 11.

The government of Cartagena also implemented a gender-based quarantine on April 13 and lifted it on May 11.

Indigenous Rights

Indigenous people in Colombia endure disproportionate levels of poverty, im-peding their ability to exercise their social and economic rights. In 2019, at least

64 children under age five—the majority of them belonging to Wayuu indigenous communities—died in the state of La Guajira of causes associated with malnutrition and limited access to drinking safe drinking water. Inadequate government efforts and the Covid-19 lockdown have exacerbated the Wayuu malnutrition crisis.

Disability Rights

Colombia adopted Law 1996, which recognizes full legal capacity for people with disabilities. Legal capacity has been considered a threshold right because it is instrumental to enjoy other rights, like the right to marry, have a family, enter into financial transactions, and exercising political rights. In 2019, a law clinic and a private citizen challenged the constitutionality of Law 1996. A Constitutional Court ruling was pending at time of writing.

Key International Actors

The United States remains the most influential foreign actor in Colombia, and approved US$448 million in aid for Colombia for fiscal year 2020. A portion of US military aid is subject to human rights conditions, but the US Department of State has not rigorously enforced them.

In July, the US House of Representatives passed a bill requiring the US secretary of state to produce a report examining unlawful surveillance by Colombian security forces, possibly with US assistance, since 2002. The bill would also limit use of US funds for aerial fumigation of coca crops. As of September, the bill had yet to become law.

In August, the UN special rapporteur on the independence of judges and lawyers said he was following the situation in Colombia "closely," noting that judicial independence and separation of powers required respecting the Supreme Court's decision ordering Uribe's house arrest.

In July, the Inter-American Court of Human Rights concluded that Colombia's 2013 removal from office of then-mayor of Bogotá Gustavo Petro violated his political rights. The court ordered Colombia to modify legislation governing disciplinary proceedings against elected officials.

The Office of the Prosecutor of the International Criminal Court continues to monitor Colombian investigations of crimes that may fall within the court's jurisdiction.

In 2016, at the request of the government of then-President Juan Manuel Santos, the UN Security Council established a political mission in Colombia to monitor and verify implementation of the FARC peace accord. In September 2020, the Security Council extended the mission's mandate for another year, upon request of the Colombian government. But the government has yet to ask the council to expand the mission's mandate to include the verification of sanctions imposed by the Special Jurisdiction for Peace—one of the mission's tasks under the peace accord.

The UN Office of the High Commissioner for Human Rights continues to play a key role in defending and promoting human rights in Colombia.

In August, the UN offices in Colombia expressed concern about killings of former FARC fighters and human rights defenders, as well as a recent increase in massacres.

The Colombian government continues to support efforts to address the human rights crisis in Venezuela, leading initiatives by the Lima Group, a coalition of regional governments monitoring the crisis.

Cuba

The Cuban government represses and punishes dissent and public criticism. Tactics against critics include beatings, public shaming, travel restrictions, short-term detention, fines, online harassment, surveillance, and termination of employment.

In October 2019, Miguel Díaz-Canel was confirmed as president of Cuba, with nearly 97 percent of the votes of National Assembly members. His presidency has seen little change in the government's human rights policy. Arbitrary detention and harassment of critics continue. Under his government, Cuba has used Decree-Law 370/2018, which came into effect in July 2019 and severely limits free speech, to detain, fine, and harass critics.

Arbitrary Detention and Short-Term Imprisonment

The government continues to employ arbitrary detention to harass and intimidate critics, independent activists, political opponents, and others. From January through August 2020, there were 1,028 arbitrary detentions, according to the Cuban Human Rights Observatory, a Madrid-based human rights organization.

Security officers rarely present arrest warrants to justify detaining critics. In some cases, detainees are released after receiving official warnings, which prosecutors can use in subsequent criminal trials to show a pattern of "delinquent" behavior.

Detention or the threat of detention is often used to prevent people from participating in peaceful marches or meetings to discuss politics. Detainees are often beaten, threatened, and held incommunicado for hours or days. Police or state security agents routinely harass, rough up, and detain members of the Ladies in White (Damas de Blanco)—a group founded by the wives, mothers, and daughters of political prisoners—before or after they attend Sunday mass.

In May, activist and lawyer Enix Berrio Sardá was detained for violating Covid-19-related movement restrictions, when he was presenting a constitutional challenge to Decree-Law 370/2018.

In June, authorities detained or threatened to detain scores of people to prevent a demonstration against police violence in Havana. Police harassed at least 80 people, calling them or showing up at their homes to warn them not to attend the protest. In some cases, officers waited outside people's homes all day on the day of the protest to prevent them from leaving. At least 50 people were arrested while trying to head to protest sites and temporarily detained. Some were accused of "spreading the epidemic."

On September 8, authorities detained or threatened to detain scores of people across the country to suppress pro-democracy protests planned to coincide with an important religious festival. Journalists and pro-democracy activists reported police stationed outside their homes that morning, and opposition groups reported scores of people detained, including José Daniel Ferrer, founder and leader of the Cuban Patriotic Union, the main opposition party and largest and most active pro-democracy group on the island.

Freedom of Expression

The government controls virtually all media outlets in Cuba and restricts access to outside information. Cuba has the "most restricted climate for the press in the Americas" according to a 2019 Committee to Protect Journalists report.

A small number of independent journalists and bloggers manage to publish articles, videos, and news on websites and social media, such as Twitter and Facebook. The government routinely blocks access within Cuba to many news websites and blogs. In 2019, before a flawed referendum that endorsed a new constitution, it blocked several news sites seen as critical of the government, including 14ymedio, Tremenda Nota, Cibercuba, Diario de Cuba, and Cubanet. Since then, it has continued to block various news websites.

The high cost of—and limited access to—the internet prevents all but a small fraction of Cubans from reading independent websites and blogs. In 2017, Cuba announced it would gradually extend home internet services. In 2019, the government issued new regulations allowing importation of routers and other equipment and the creation of private wired and Wi-Fi internet networks in homes and businesses.

Independent journalists, bloggers, social media influencers, artists, and academics who publish information considered critical of the government are routinely subject to harassment, violence, smear campaigns, travel restrictions, internet cuts, online harassment, raids on their homes and offices, confiscation of working materials, and arbitrary arrests. They are regularly held incommunicado.

In July 2019, Decree-Law 370/2018, on the "informatization of society" took effect, prohibiting dissemination of information "contrary to the social interest, morals, good manners and integrity of people." Authorities have used the law to interrogate and fine journalists and critics and confiscate their working materials. In March, journalist Camila Acosta was fined in connection with three Facebook posts, including a meme of Fidel Castro.

Between February and September, Cuban authorities harassed Youtuber Ruhama Fernández, who has published videos critical of the government. Authorities repeatedly summoned her for police interrogation and denied her a passport. In April, after summoning Fernández to a police station, officials told her the harassment would cease if she stopped criticizing the government. In September, she received an anonymous phone call threatening to "finish" her off.

Between September 2019 and March 2020, the artist Luis Manuel Otero Alcantará was detained at least 10 times, often without charge, for performance art pieces in which he wore the Cuban flag while going about daily activities.

In March 2020, Law 128/2019, the National Symbols Law took effect, restricting use of the Cuban flag, seal, and national anthem.

Political Prisoners

The Cuban Center for Human Rights reported that as of August, Cuba was holding 75 people who met the definition of political prisoners, as well as 28 others who the group considered were being held for their political beliefs; another 33 who had been convicted for their political beliefs were under house arrest or on conditional release. The government denies independent human rights groups access to its prisons. Local groups believe the actual number of political prisoners is higher, but the restrictions limit their ability to document cases.

Cubans who criticize the government continue to risk criminal prosecution. They do not benefit from due process guarantees, such as the right to fair and public hearings by a competent and impartial tribunal. In practice, courts are subordinate to the executive and legislative branches.

In February, a judge in Santiago convicted José Daniel Ferrer, of the Cuban Patriotic Union, of assault and kidnapping in what activists say was an irregular trial. In April, after six months in pretrial detention, he was sentenced to four years of house arrest.

In April 2020, pro-democracy activist and opposition party member Maikel Herrera Bones was arrested after protesting power cuts in his neighborhood and arguing with a police officer. He was initially charged with disobeying orders, but a week after he was detained authorities increased the charge to "assault." In August, Herrera called a fellow activist from prison to report that officials were not providing him with proper treatment for HIV and that he was becoming ill. In September, Herrera told another activist that officials said they would provide proper medical treatment if he stopped complaining about abuses in the prison.

Travel Restrictions

Since reforms in 2013, many people who had previously been denied permission to travel have been able to do so, including human rights defenders and independent bloggers. The reforms, however, gave the government broad discretionary power to restrict the right to travel on grounds of "defense and national security" or "other reasons of public interest." Authorities have continued to deny exit selectively to people who express dissent.

The government restricts the movement of citizens within Cuba through a 1997 law, Decree 217, designed to limit migration from other provinces to Havana. The decree has been used to harass dissidents and prevent people from traveling to Havana to attend meetings.

In November 2019, authorities told journalist Camila Acosta that she was not allowed to leave the country. An immigration official stopped her when she was trying to board a plane for a human rights event in Argentina.

In August, Ruhama Fernández, the social media influencer, was denied a passport to travel to the United States to receive an award and visit her parents. An official told her she is "regulated" for "reasons of public interest."

Prison Conditions

Prisons are often overcrowded. Prisoners are forced to work 12-hour days and are punished if they do not meet production quotas, former political prisoners report. Detainees have no effective complaint mechanism to seek redress for abuses. Those who criticize the government or engage in hunger strikes and other forms of protest often endure extended solitary confinement, beatings, restriction of family visits, and denial of medical care.

While the government allowed select members of the foreign press on controlled visits to a handful of prisons in 2013, it continues to deny international human rights groups and independent Cuban organizations access to prisons.

In April, to reduce the risk of Covid-19 spreading in prisons, the government suspended family visits, restricted the type of food family members could send prisoners, and, in a welcome development, released more than 6,500 people. Independent media have reported cases of detainees being isolated with suspected Covid-19 cases in some prisons. However, as of October 2020, the Ministry of Health had not confirmed any cases of Covid-19 in prisons.

Labor Rights

Despite updating its Labor Code in 2014, Cuba continues to violate International Labour Organization standards it has ratified on freedom of association and collective bargaining. While Cuban law technically allows formation of independent unions, in practice, Cuba only permits one confederation of state-controlled unions, the Workers' Central Union of Cuba.

Cuba deploys tens of thousands of health workers abroad every year to help tackle short-term crises and natural disasters. The workers provide valuable services to many communities but under stringent norms that violate their rights, including to privacy, liberty, movement, and freedom of expression and association. In 2020, Cuba deployed around 4,000 doctors to help nearly 40 countries respond to the Covid-19 pandemic. They joined an estimated 28,000 Cuban health workers deployed prior to the pandemic.

Human Rights Defenders

The Cuban government still refuses to recognize human rights monitoring as a legitimate activity and denies legal status to local human rights groups. Government authorities have harassed, assaulted, and imprisoned human rights defenders who have attempted to document abuses. In March, two members of the Ladies in White were detained without charge for seven days after attending an International Women's Day event at the US Embassy in Havana. Authorities then "deported" them to their home city of Santiago, more than 460 miles away. Other members of the group had been detained to prevent them from attending the event.

Sexual Orientation and Gender Identity

The 2019 constitution explicitly prohibits discrimination on the basis of sexual orientation or gender identity. However, many lesbian, gay, bisexual, and transgender (LGBT) people suffer violence and discrimination, particularly in the country's interior. In its 2019 report on Cuba, the Inter-American Commission on Human Rights (IACHR) noted allegations that police often refuse to investigate anti-LGBT attacks and that LGBT people have been fired or excluded from university education due to their sexual orientation or gender identity.

Following public protest, the Cuban government removed language from the final draft of the constitution approved in February 2019 that would have redefined marriage to include same-sex couples. The government says that in March 2021, it will introduce a new version of the Family Code, which governs marriage, in the legislature for review, and then put the code to a vote in a referendum.

In May 2019, security forces cracked down on a protest in Havana promoting LGBT rights and detained several activists, media reported. The protest, which was not authorized, was organized after the government announced that it had canceled Cuba's 2019 Pride parade.

Sexual and Reproductive Rights

Abortion has been decriminalized for all reasons in Cuba since 1965. Cuba is one of the few Latin American countries to have adopted this policy. The procedure is available for free at public hospitals.

Covid-19

As of September 21, Cuba reported 6,305 cases of Covid-19 and 127 deaths. The government reacted quickly when the first Covid-19 cases were confirmed on the island in March, banning tourists, conducting widespread testing and contact tracing, and implementing mandatory facemask rules and stringent movement restrictions enforced with steep fines or even jail time. The resulting slump in tourism, plummeting foreign remittances, and acute supply shortages further stressed an already weak economy, jeopardizing some people's livelihoods and access to medicines and food.

The government closed schools from March to September. Primary and secondary education was provided through televised classes and an online homework correction service that required an email account from the state internet provider. Some classes were provided in sign language for deaf children. Activists and parents complained that classes were often difficult to follow, and that many people were not able to use the homework correction service given the high cost of and limited access to the internet.

In some cases, the government has used Covid-19 related movement restrictions as an excuse to suppress protests. In June, authorities suppressed a demonstration against police violence by harassing, threatening to detain, and detaining dozens of people.

Key International Actors

In April 2019, the US began allowing lawsuits against companies that benefited from the seizure, during the Cuban revolution, of property belonging to people who are now US citizens. This has led to lawsuits against European and international companies that operate hotel chains and cruise lines in Cuba. The European Union and Canada have denounced the policy.

Between June 2019 and August 2020, the US government imposed new restrictions on US citizens travelling to Cuba, banning cruise ship stops, educational trips, and most flights to the island, except for a limited number to Havana.

In a March 2020 report on the human rights situation in Cuba, the Interamerican Commission on Human Rights (IACHR) expressed concern regarding the criminalization and arbitrary detention of human rights defenders, absence of spaces for pluralistic political participation, and lack of judicial independence and free speech protections. The commission reiterated its call for the US to lift its embargo on Cuba, saying it has negatively impacted human rights.

In April, in a joint statement, various UN experts also called on the US to suspend the embargo, saying trade barriers could obstruct the humanitarian response to Covid-19.

In February, the European Union issued a statement on the case of José Daniel Ferrer calling on Cuba to release all those jailed for the exercise of fundamental rights.

In 2016, the EU signed a Political Dialogue and Cooperation Agreement with Cuba. The agreement has yet to be fully ratified because Lithuania has refused to approve it, citing human rights concerns. In March 2020, the Lithuanian legislature began to discuss ratifying the agreement, but the discussion was put on hold due to Covid-19.

In October, Cuba was elected to the UN Human Rights Council—its fifth term in the past 15 years. Given the country's disastrous human rights record, its election was widely criticized by human rights organizations.

Democratic Republic of Congo

Human rights in the Democratic Republic of Congo under President Felix Tshisekedi took a downturn in 2020, against the backdrop of the gains made during his first year in office. Congolese authorities cracked down on peaceful protesters, journalists, and politicians, while using state of emergency measures temporarily imposed due to the Covid-19 pandemic as a pretext to curb protests.

In July, Gen. John Numbi, who was implicated in the double murder of prominent human rights defender Floribert Chebeya and his driver Fidèle Bazana in 2010, was removed as inspector general of the army. While this was a positive step, Tshisekedi replaced Numbi with Gen. Gabriel Amisi, who has also long been involved in serious human rights abuses in eastern Congo. Other senior officers known for their involvement in serious abuses or under international sanctions have also been promoted, further undermining prospects of reform within the security apparatus, which is still firmly controlled by former President Joseph Kabila. Other reforms have been held back by infighting within the already troubled ruling coalition, formed by Tshisekedi and Kabila, whose political force controlled the parliament and most provinces. The collapse of the ruling coalition in December escalated the power struggle.

Allegations persisted over corruption within Tshisekedi's inner circle. On June 20, Vital Kamerhe, Tshisekedi's former chief of staff, was found guilty of embezzlement and corruption, becoming the most senior politician in Congo ever to be prosecuted on graft charges. He was sentenced to 20 years in prison. Many other senior figures implicated in corruption in recent years were not investigated, casting doubts over the real motives behind Kamerhe's prosecution.

In eastern Congo, numerous armed groups, and in some cases government security forces, attacked civilians, killing and wounding many. Some of the worst violence took place in Ituri, where ethnic Lendu-led militia have killed hundreds of mostly Hema villagers and forced hundreds of thousands out of their home. The humanitarian situation in the country remained alarming, with 5.5 million people internally displaced. Nearly 930,000 people from Congo were registered as refugees and asylum seekers in at least 20 countries as of November.

Freedom of Expression, Peaceful Assembly, and Media

Dozens of people who criticized government policies, including on social media, were intimidated and threatened, beaten, arrested, and in some cases prosecuted. Particularly targeted by authorities across the country, journalists faced threats and harassment, and some broadcast programs or outlets were shut down upon instructions from officials.

Between March and July, as large public gatherings were banned under the state of emergency aimed at stopping the spread of Covid-19, security forces used excessive and often lethal force to break up demonstrations.

On July 9, as mass protests took place in several cities against the appointment of a new president for the electoral commission, police killed at least one demonstrator in the capital, Kinshasa, and two in the southern city of Lubumbashi. Scores more were injured. In the following days, the bodies of four members of Tshisekedi's political party were found in Lubumbashi—three were floating in a river—in apparent murders.

Human rights defenders faced threats, intimidation, arbitrary arrest, and detention from both state authorities and armed groups. Nobel Laureate Dr. Denis Mukwege received death threats for his advocacy of justice for serious crimes.

Attacks on Civilians by Armed Groups and Government Forces

Non-state armed groups and government forces killed at least 1,300 civilians in separate conflicts between October 2019 and June 2020, according to the United Nations High Commissioner for Human Rights. Hundreds more were killed in the second half of the year. In many instances, armed assailants were responsible for sexual violence against women and girls.

More than 130 armed groups were active in eastern Congo's North Kivu, South Kivu, and Ituri provinces, attacking civilians. The groups included the mainly ethnic Lendu association of militia Cooperative for the Development of Congo (CODECO); the largely Ugandan Allied Democratic Forces (ADF); the Nduma Defense of Congo-Renové (NDC-R); the largely Rwandan Democratic Forces for the Liberation of Rwanda (FDLR) and allied Congolese Nyatura groups; the Mazembe and Yakutumba Mai Mai groups; and several Burundian armed groups. Many of their commanders have been implicated in war crimes, including ethnic massacres, rape, forced recruitment of children, and pillage.

The Congolese security forces conducted simultaneous operations against armed groups in eastern Congo, with mixed results and at times using militia as proxy forces against other groups.

According to the Kivu Security Tracker, which documents violence in eastern Congo, assailants, including state security forces, killed more than 1,250 civilians and kidnapped for ransom more than 450 others in North Kivu and South Kivu. Violence escalated in parts of Ituri province, where killings have been unrelenting. Beni territory, North Kivu province, also remained an epicenter of violence, with at least 520 civilians killed in more than 140 attacks by various groups, including the ADF.

Tension remained high in South Kivu's highlands, where fighting intensified among ethnic groups, killing at least 128 civilians between February 2019 and June 2020.

Armed violence also affected the Kasai and Tanganyika regions.

Several thousand fighters from various armed groups surrendered throughout the year, but many have returned to armed groups as the authorities failed to take them through an effective Disarmament, Demobilization, and Reintegration (DDR) program.

Between April 13 and 24, police used lethal force against the politico-religious movement Bundu dia Kongo in a crackdown across several towns of western Kongo Central province and Kinshasa. Law enforcement killed at least 55 people and injured scores more.

Justice and Accountability

Tshisekedi tasked his administration with delivering a proposal for transitional justice mechanisms but he has yet to fully commit to ending impunity for past and current serious crimes. Some of the military courts and other tribunals adjudicating cases of war crimes and crimes against humanity face serious shortcomings.

In November, a military court in Goma found Ntabo Ntaberi Sheka, the former leader of the Nduma Defense of Congo (NDC) armed group, guilty of seven counts of war crimes, including mass rape and sexual slavery, murder, pillage, and recruitment of child soldiers. He was sentenced to life in prison. Sheka was implicated in numerous atrocities in eastern Congo, and had been sought by Congolese authorities since 2011. He surrendered to the UN peacekeeping mission in Congo (MONUSCO) in July 2017.

In February, the administration suspended and opened an investigation into Gen. Delphin Kahimbi, then head of military intelligence with a long history of human rights abuses. But hours after a round of questioning, he died under mysterious circumstances in his home. His death is a missed opportunity for justice for his victims.

The trial for the murders of UN investigators Michael Sharp and Zaida Catalán, and the disappearance of the four Congolese who accompanied them in March 2017 in the central Kasai region, which started in June 2017 before a military court, was ongoing at time of writing, with no substantial progress made.

On March 28, Gédéon Kyungu, a notorious warlord responsible for atrocities in the southern region of Katanga, escaped from house arrest in Lubumbashi after dozens of his militiamen entered the city and other towns in the region. His whereabouts remain unknown.

Militia leader Guidon Shimiray Mwissa, wanted by Congolese authorities for participating in an insurrection, recruiting child soldiers, and committing crimes against humanity by raping girls and women remains active in North Kivu, commanding a faction of the Nduma Defense of Congo-Rénové (NDC-R). The group—which received some material support from Congolese army units—split in two in July, triggering an open conflict between both rival factions. Until then, the NDC-R controlled more ground than any other armed group in eastern Congo. In September, the Congolese army launched military operations against Guidon's wing.

A trial for the December 2018 Yumbi killings in the country's northwest—in which at least 535 people were killed—had yet to start at time of writing.

On September 3, police officer Christian Ngoy Kenga Kenga, implicated in the double murder of Chebeya and Bazana in 2010, was arrested in Lubumbashi and transferred to Kinshasa's military prison.

Covid-19

Congolese health officials confirmed more than 11,500 Covid-19 cases across 22 provinces as of November 7, 2020, with 315 deaths. However, the number of cases is likely higher given the limited testing capacity.

Between March 24 and August 15, the Congolese government imposed state of emergency measures to curb the spread of the virus. Borders were shut, large gatherings were banned, and schools, restaurants, bars, and places of worship were closed. School closures affected about 19 million children.

On March 30, the police killed at least 3 people and wounded 11 others, according to a UN source, when they fired live rounds at members of the Bundu dia Kongo politico-religious movement who were demonstrating in Kinshasa to "chase the spirit of the coronavirus."

On July 14, the Congolese government ordered copper and cobalt mining companies to stop confining workers on site as they restricted movements due to Covid-19. In many cases workers were given no choice but to either stay and work—confined on site 24 hours a day, seven days a week—or lose their jobs.

Key International Actors

On June 30, Belgium's King Philippe expressed his "deepest regrets" for the "past injuries" inflicted on the Congolese during 75 years of colonial rule. A parliamentary commission was set up to examine Belgium's colonial past.

In August, the United States resumed its military cooperation with Congo, suspended in 2018 as Congo's army was found to support armed groups known for child recruitment.

The EU renewed in December targeted financial and travel sanctions against 11 senior Congolese officials. Later that month, the UN Security Council adopted a resolution extending the mandate of MONUSCO for another year. However, the mission is working towards a transition program that would ensure its exit within the next few years.

Ecuador

Since taking office in 2017, President Lenín Moreno has implemented policy changes aimed at repairing the damage suffered by democratic institutions during former President Rafael Correa's decade in power. Reforms have restored the independence of key institutions, though implementation challenges remain.

Ecuador has been severely hit by Covid-19. A state of emergency with restrictions on movement, social gatherings, and travel that was declared to address it on March 16, 2020, was renewed through September 14, after which the Constitutional Court required a return to ordinary measures. Public health data suggest the number of Covid-related deaths is likely much higher than official counts. The pandemic has compounded existing economic difficulties; as a result, many are at risk of falling into poverty.

Ecuador continues to face significant human rights challenges, including with respect to judicial independence, excessive use of force by security forces, and protections for the right to privacy and the rights of indigenous people; women and children; lesbian, gay, bisexual and transgender (LGBT) people; and refugees.

Judicial Independence

Corruption, inefficiency, and political interference have plagued Ecuador's judiciary for years. During the Correa administration, high-level officials and Judiciary Council members interfered in cases affecting government interests, and in the appointment and removal of judges.

Under President Moreno, a transitional Council of Citizen Participation was tasked with evaluating the performance of key institutions and authorities, including the Judiciary Council, Constitutional Court, and Prosecutor's Office.

However, problems remained, including a flawed Judiciary Council process to select, evaluate, and appoint temporary National Court of Justice judges, allegations of improper pressure exerted by government officials on courts, and claims of lack of due process in high profile corruption cases.

HUMAN
RIGHTS
WATCH

"It's a Constant Fight"
School-Related Sexual Violence and Young Survivors' Struggle
for Justice in Ecuador

On March 17, 2020, the Judiciary Council responded to the Covid-19 pandemic by closing most of its offices, except for those handling "flagrant" criminal matters, domestic violence, traffic violations, and juvenile offenders. The council adopted measures, such as virtual hearings, after the Constitutional Court ordered the council to guarantee access to justice. However, challenges accessing justice remain.

On August 23, 2020, the Constitutional Court took a step toward dismantling the legal framework that allowed for interference in the judiciary. The court ruled that the Judiciary Council—which had generally been empowered to suspend or remove justice officials—cannot sanction a judge, prosecutor, or public defender without a prior judicial decision establishing justice officials had in fact acted with "criminal intent, evident negligence" or had committed an "inexcusable error."

Use of Force by Security Forces

After protests erupted on October 3, 2019, Ecuador's police used indiscriminate force, including firing teargas that damaged demonstrators' eyes and caused asphyxiation. Of the 11 people who died in the context of the protests, at least 4 appear to have been killed by security forces. Protesters committed serious crimes against police and vandalized public and private property. At time of writing, investigations were ongoing.

On May 14, 2020, police in Guayaquil used excessive force, beating and injuring peaceful demonstrators protesting the government's handling of the Covid-19 pandemic.

The Defense Ministry adopted a resolution on May 29, 2020, giving the military broad powers to use lethal force and to participate in security operations at demonstrations and meetings. The Constitutional Court held a public hearing on the measure on August 3, and at time of writing, was considering its constitutionality.

Prison Conditions

Overcrowding and other poor conditions, violence, and inadequate health care are longstanding problems in prisons. Media reported that prisons are severely understaffed, with only 1,447 guards for 53 detention centers holding 37,500 detainees. The Covid-19 outbreak exacerbated problems, infecting detainees in overcrowded cellblocks. Several reportedly died. On June 26, 2020, President Moreno decreed that prisoners from specific at-risk groups could serve time under house arrest. As of June, 26, 971 had left the prisons and most of them were under house arrest or conditional release.

On August 3, 2020, a prisoner uprising at the Litoral Prison in Guayaquil and the official response left at least 11 prisoners dead, according to official reports. Days later, a key witness in a corruption case was killed there, and two detainees died in a prison in Cotopaxi. President Moreno decreed a state of emergency in all prisons and sent the military to participate in law enforcement operations inside prisons.

Right to Privacy

To monitor compliance with Covid-19 quarantine measures, identify people who may have come into contact with an infected person, and pinpoint large gatherings, the Ecuadorean government rolled out a number of initiatives that used mobile location data and other personal data. The initiatives, which included satellite tracking of people suspected of having Covid-19, the development of a self-reporting application, and a database to analyze data from several sources, involve not only collection but aggregation, processing, and sharing, and could lead to the misuse of data and breaches of privacy.

In September 2019, President Moreno, moved by a major breach of citizens' personal data, sent a draft data protection law to the National Assembly. At time of writing, it had not been adopted.

Freedom of Expression

In 2018, legislators amended a 2013 communications law eliminating the Superintendency of Information and Communication (SUPERCOM), a regulatory body that had been used to harass and sanction independent media outlets. But the amended law includes problematic provisions, including treating "communications" as a "public service" and establishing an unrestricted right to a published correction and an opportunity to respond.

Rights of Indigenous Peoples

Constitutionally, indigenous peoples have a collective right to "free prior informed consultation" regarding nonrenewable resources on their lands and projects that could affect them environmentally or culturally. In July, 2020, the Constitutional Court ruled in favor of indigenous communities in the Amazon region that had complained about the imposition of a protected forest in their territory without prior consultation and the militarization of their communities.

Media reported an increase in confirmed Covid-19 cases in the Amazon region, but official data do not include specific information about impacts on ethnic groups and indigenous communities. On June 18, 2020, a judge ordered the Ministry of Health to send medical personnel and equipment to respond to an outbreak in Waorani indigenous communities.

Women's and Children's Rights

A 2019 government survey revealed high rates of gender-based violence, with 65 percent of women affected during their lifetimes. The 911 emergency number reported 38,288 calls linked to violence against women between March 12 and July 20, 2020, receiving 290 calls a day on average. From January through October 4, 2020, Ecuador reported 81 femicides—defined by the Criminal Code as murders of women based on their gender.

In December 2019, the United Nations special rapporteur on violence against women expressed concern about the high rates of rape and sexual violence against young girls and adolescents in educational settings and at home. From 2014 to May 2020, Ecuador's Ministry of Education received 3,607 complaints of school-related sexual violence, affecting 4,221 students enrolled in pre-school, primary, and secondary school.

The right to seek an abortion is limited to instances in which a pregnancy endangers the pregnant person's health or life, or results from the rape of someone with a psychosocial disability. Pregnant people face many barriers to accessing legal abortion and post abortion care, including criminal prosecution, stigmatization, and mistreatment. The National Assembly rejected a proposal in 2019 to decriminalize abortion in all cases of rape or severe fetal impairment. For illegal abortions, the maximum prison sentence is two years.

On August 25, 2020, the National Assembly approved a draft health code that prohibited delaying emergency health care for any reason, including healthcare workers' assertion of conscientious objection, and reiterated the duty of healthcare professionals to respect medical confidentiality, including in cases of an obstetric emergency. On September 25, 2020, President Moreno announced he had vetoed the bill in its entirety.

Disability Rights

A substitute decision-making model still prevails in civil legislation, failing to recognize the full legal capacity of people with disabilities. The health bill that President Moreno vetoed would have reinforced and expanded restrictions on the ability of people with disabilities to exercise their legal capacity in making health decisions.

Sexual Orientation, Gender Identity, and Sex Characteristics

In June 2019, the Constitutional Court ruled in favor of same-sex marriage, declaring the country's marriage legislation unconstitutional and citing international law and constitutional provisions against discrimination. In July 2019, the Civil Registry registered the first same-sex marriage.

The health bill that President Moreno vetoed would have reinforced a criminal code prohibition on conversion therapy, criminally sanctioning any attempt to change a person's sexual orientation or gender identity. It would have also protected intersex children, by prohibiting medical procedures that violate the personal integrity of those who have not reached puberty.

Refugees

In August 2019, the government began registering Venezuelans and issuing humanitarian visas to regularize their status. A March 2020 deadline for Venezuelans already in Ecuador to regularize their status was extended until August 13, due to the pandemic. The government granted 38,246 humanitarian visas during those 12 months.

As of August 2020, there were 362,862 Venezuelan migrants and refugees living in Ecuador. The pandemic has precipitated the departure from Ecuador of many Venezuelans who are returning to their country because they lack access to food and employment and often cannot afford to pay rent. Xenophobia against Venezuelans remains a serious concern.

Accountability for Past Abuses

In 2010, a truth commission created by the Correa administration to investigate government abuses from 1984 to 2008 documented gross human rights violations against 456 victims. To date, final rulings have been rendered in only two cases. Others appear to be stalled.

Key International Actors

President Moreno showed interest in rebuilding relations with human rights protection mechanisms. In September 2019, the UN special rapporteur on the right to health visited Ecuador, followed by a delegation of the Inter-American Commission on Human Rights (IACHR) and another of the UN Office of the High Commissioner on Human Rights (OHCHR). In November 2019, the UN special rapporteur on violence against women visited.

UN rapporteurs issued final reports in May 2020, after their visit, urging enhanced efforts to address gender-based violence and child and adolescent pregnancy.

The OHCHR and the IACHR reported, in November 2019 and January 2020, respectively, lootings and vandalism during the October 2019 protests, but concluded that security forces had used excessive force and called for independent

and impartial investigations. The government contested the IACHR report as partial and biased, but said it would implement "feasible" recommendations.

In March 2020, the IACHR held a public hearing on the case of 53 legislators who
claim they were arbitrarily removed from their congressional seats during the
Correa administration after they opposed the government's effort to draft a new
constitution in 2007. The legislators were suspended for a year and argued their
political rights were violated. At time of writing, a decision was pending.

In its first-ever case on school-related sexual violence—the Guzmán Albarracín
case—the Inter-American Court of Human Rights (IACtHR) ruled on June 24, 2020,
that Ecuador had failed in its obligation to protect children from sexual violence—especially violence perpetrated by government officials in state institutions. President Moreno committed to complying with the IACtHR's sentence and
to erradicating sexual violence in Ecuador's educational instititutions.

On November 25 and 26, 2019, the IACtHR held a public hearing on the disappearance of a patient from a public psychiatric hospital in Quito. A ruling was
pending at time of writing.

Ecuador endorsed the World Health Organization's Solidarity Call to Action for
the Covid-19 Technology Access Pool, an initiative to"realize equitable global access to COVID-19 health technologies through pooling of knowledge, intellectual
property and data."

The government ordered nation-wide school closures April 3, 2020, impacting
over 4.6 million students enrolled in pre-school through secondary education.
Six out of ten children lack access to internet connection and are excluded from
online remote learning.

Egypt

Egyptians in 2020 continued to live under the harsh authoritarian grip of President Abdel Fattah al-Sisi's government. Tens of thousands of government critics, including journalists and human rights defenders, remain imprisoned on politically motivated charges, many in lengthy pretrial detention. Authorities frequently used terrorism charges against peaceful activists and harassed and detained relatives of dissidents abroad.

Authorities used vague "morality" charges to prosecute female social media influencers for posts of themselves, as well as gang-rape witnesses following reporting of sexual assault cases online. Media close to the government smeared rape witnesses by publishing private photos and videos online without their consent.

The Covid-19 outbreak exacerbated dire detention conditions and dozens of persons detained on political grounds died in custody, including at least 14 who likely died of Covid-19 complications between March and July. Authorities arrested health workers who criticized the government's Covid-19 response.

Security forces continued to operate with impunity in war-torn North Sinai.

The government closed schools nationwide from mid-March until they reopened with a reduced schedule in mid-October, affecting the education of an estimated 20 million students.

Police and Security Forces Abuses

The Interior Ministry's security forces and National Security Agency (NSA) forcibly disappeared, arbitrarily arrested, and tortured dissidents, including children. In April, authorities disappeared for days Marwa Arafa and Kholoud Said, then detained the two women on unsubstantiated charges of joining a terrorist group and spreading false news. The NSA arrested at least 10 health workers for criticizing the government response to Covid-19 including the lack of protective equipment and testing. In late May authorities arrested and held incommunicado journalist Shaima' Samy for charges of "spreading false news."

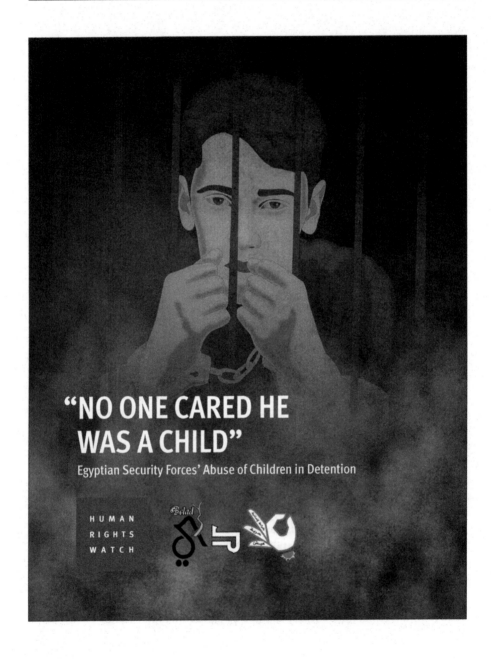

In June, the NSA arrested Sana' Saif when she tried to report being physically assaulted outside Tora Prison where her brother, jailed activist Alaa Abdel Fattah, was being held.

The Interior Ministry subjected the families of dissidents abroad to collective punishment, including arrests and prosecutions. In June, security forces arrested five cousins of Mohamed Soltan, an American-Egyptian rights defender. The raids were apparently in reprisal for Soltan filing suit in a US court in June under the Torture Victim Protection Act against former Prime Minister Hazem al-Beblawy, related to Soltan's 2013 arrest and torture during nearly two years of detention.

In North Sinai, armed conflict between government forces, particularly the military, and the local Islamic State affiliate Wilayat Sina' entered its eighth year. The army prohibited access to journalists and other observers and banned independent reporting. The army continued to demolish homes and forcibly displace thousands of residents, often without offering compensation or alternative housing.

Prison Conditions and Deaths in Custody

The Covid-19 outbreak, which began in Egypt in February, worsened already abysmal detention conditions. Authorities imposed a comprehensive information blackout on detention sites and ended visits, including by lawyers, from March 10 to late August, without offering alternatives such as video or phone calls. Since late August, families could pre-book visits by phone but were limited to one relative once per month, for 20 minutes.

According to credible human rights and media reports, dozens of prisoners in political cases died in detention in 2020 apparently due to inadequate medical care. In December 2019, Mariam Salem, 32, died in al-Qanater prison after authorities withheld live-saving medical treatment, including for a liver condition. On January 14, Mostafa Kassem, a 54-year-old Egyptian-American who was diabetic with a heart condition, died in Tora Leman Prison. He had been on hunger strike from early January to protest his 15-year sentence following an unfair mass trial of over 700 defendants. In May, Shadi Habash, a 24-year-old filmmaker imprisoned for directing a music video mocking al-Sisi, died in Tora Tahqiq Prison after he received no meaningful treatment for alcohol intoxication. In August, Essam al-Erian, 66, a senior Muslim Brotherhood leader, died in Tora's Scorpion Prison after spending seven years in near-total isolation. In the first week of September, five detainees died in different prisons, including Amr Abu Khalil and Ahmed Abdelnabi Mahmoud, after they spent many months in detention without trial. Authorities denied both access to adequate medical care.

According to the Committee for Justice, a Geneva-based human rights group, the number of detainees who died in custody between June 2013 and December 2019 could be as high as 958. Human Rights Watch documented several suspected Covid-19 outbreaks in Egyptian prisons and police stations between March and July. At least 14 prisoners during that time likely died of Covid-19 complications. Only nine had been transferred to hospitals, in some cases just hours before they died.

Egypt's overcrowded detention sites make social distancing impossible. Between March and late July, the government said it released about 19,615 prisoners. Those releases excluded people detained or prosecuted for political dissent and were insufficient to ease overcrowding.

Fair Trials, Due Process, and the Death Penalty

Judges and prosecutors kept thousands of people in pretrial detention, often solely for exercising their rights to peaceful assembly and free expression, and many beyond the two-year limit Egyptian law provides. Former presidential candidate Abd al-Moneim Abu al-Fotouh, arrested in February 2018 ahead of that year's presidential vote, was "recycled" into a new case just days before his detention would have reached the two-year limit in February 2020.

Between mid-March and mid-August, security and judicial authorities used the Covid-19 pandemic as a pretext to effectively preclude even a pretense of detention renewal hearings, in violation of Egyptian law, as well as regional African and international human rights treaties. Authorities have held hundreds, and most likely thousands, without even a pretense of judicial review. Prior to this, judges and prosecutors frequently deprived lawyers and detainees of a meaningful chance to present defense or review any purported evidence.

Egyptian courts continued to impose the death penalty for a wide range of crimes, including cases of alleged political violence and terrorism in which defendants' claims of forced disappearance and torture almost always went uninvestigated by judges. According to the Egyptian Front for Human Rights, an independent Czech-based group, during the first half of 2020 Egyptian military and civilian courts issued 171 death sentences and upheld the sentences of 10 others, including 7 in a political case. From January to late October, authorities executed at least 83 persons, 25 of whom were charged in cases involving political violence, according to numbers compiled by Human Rights Watch and the Egyptian Front for Human Rights.

Freedom of Association and Attacks on Human Rights Defenders

Authorities continued to severely curtail space for civil society groups and target human rights defenders.

At time of writing, the government has not issued implementing regulations for the draconian NGO law al-Sisi approved in August 2019 despite the requirement that it do so within six months of approving the law, and the stipulation in the new law that existing organizations must re-register within one year. The law prohibits a wide range of activities, such as "conduct opinion polls and publish or make their results available or conduct field research or disclose their results" without government approval. The law allows authorities to dissolve organizations for a wide range of "violations" and imposes fines of up to one million Egyptian pounds (US$60,000) for organizations that operate without a license or send or receive funds without government approval.

In December 2019, persons believed to be working under the direction of the National Security Agency physically assaulted human rights lawyer Gamal Eid for the second time in two months. Authorities failed to hold anyone accountable.

On February 7, Egyptian authorities detained Patrick George Zaki, a researcher with the Egyptian Initiative for Personal Rights (EIPR), and held him incommunicado for 24 hours, during which time he was allegedly tortured, including with electric shocks. Zaki has been in pretrial detention since then facing charges that include "calling for protests without permission," "spreading false news," and "incitement to commit violence and terrorist crimes."

Prosecutors and judges have regularly renewed the pretrial detention of Ibrahim Ezz el-Din, a housing rights researcher with the Egyptian Commission for Rights and Freedoms (ECRF), since November 2019. Security agencies had forcibly disappeared Ezz el-Din for over five months before the Supreme State Security Prosecution issued his official detention order. ECRF lawyers told Human Rights Watch that officers physically and psychologically tortured him, including with electric shocks, while questioning him about his activism.

In August, an Egyptian court sentenced veteran human rights defender Baheyeddin Hassan to 15 years in prison in absentia for tweets criticizing the government. A court had sentenced him in September 2019 to three years in prison in absentia for criticizing Egypt's prosecution office.

Authorities continued to arbitrarily detain without trial other human rights lawyers and defenders, including Mahinour al-Masry and Mohamed al-Baqer, whom security forces arrested in September 2019 when they were at the prosecutors' office in Cairo to defend other detainees.

In July, a Cairo criminal court rejected a request to lift the five-year-long travel bans imposed on 14 leading human rights defenders including Mohamed Zarea, Hossam Bahgat, and Mozn Hassan, 2020 winner of the Hrant Dink Award. The 14 are among more than 30 human rights defenders who remained banned from leaving the country, most in connection with the protracted Case 173 of 2011 investigation, known as the "foreign funding case" in which authorities also have frozen the assets of leading organizations and defenders.

Freedom of Assembly and Expression

The government continued to criminalize peaceful assembly and punish peaceful critics. In late September and early October, authorities arrested nearly 1,000 protesters and bystanders before and after scattered anti-government protests in towns and villages in 21 governorates, according to the Egyptian Commission for Rights and Freedoms. Arrests included at least 71 children, some as young as 13. In March, authorities arrested the academic and activist Laila Soueif, her sister, the novelist Ahdaf Soueif, her daughter, the prominent activist Mona Seif, and political scientist Rabab el-Mahdi for protesting peacefully for the release of unjustly detained prisoners over coronavirus fears.

Egypt continued to detain dozens of politicians and activists, including Ziad al-Elaimy and Hossam Mo'nis, for planning a new electoral coalition to contest the 2020 parliamentary elections. In late June, Interior Ministry forces besieged the doctors' syndicate building and forced its members to cancel a press conference to address government harassment of doctors in connection with Covid-19. Authorities arrested at least 10 healthcare professionals who challenged the official narrative on the pandemic or criticized the lack of equipment at work.

Authorities continued to silence journalists, bloggers, and critics on social media amid escalating use of the repressive 2018 cybercrimes law and have blocked hundreds of news and human rights websites without judicial authorization since 2017. Journalists Solafa Magdy, Hossam al-Sayed, and Mohamed Salah remain in pretrial detention on charges of "joining a terrorist group" and "spreading false news" since November 2019. According to international groups monitoring press freedoms, such as the Committee to Protect Journalists and the International Press Institute, the number of journalists behind bars in Egypt at a given time in 2020 was between 30 and 60, one of the highest in the world.

Freedom of Belief and Religion

On June 21, an appeals court in Alexandria upheld the three-year prison sentence of blogger and activist Anas Hassan and a fine of 300,000 EGP ($19,000) for "insulting religion" and "misusing social media." According to the EIPR, Hassan was prosecuted for managing a Facebook page called "The Egyptian Atheists" that authorities said published "atheistic ideas" and "criticism of the divinely revealed religions."

A week later, a State Security Misdemeanor Court in Sharqia Governorate sentenced two young men to a year in jail for promoting the Shi`a doctrine of Islam. State Security court decisions cannot be appealed.

Restrictions on church building remain largely in place. Four years after the issuance of Law 80 of 2016 on the construction of churches, the government has only conditionally legalized 1,638 churches that were operating without official permits, roughly 25 percent of church buildings that applied for legal status.

Women's Rights, Gender Identity, Sexual Orientation

Egyptian authorities carried out an extensive campaign of arrests and prosecutions against women social media influencers, in violation of their rights to privacy, freedom of expression, and non-discrimination. Between April and time of writing, authorities arrested at least 15 people, including 11 women and a 17-year-old girl, on vague charges of violating "public morals" and "undermining family values." Courts sentenced five of them to two and six years in jail. The prosecutions are based on videos and photos the women shared on social media apps showing themselves dancing and singing. Security forces arrested the 17-year-old girl after she published a video saying she was raped and assaulted by a group of men.

The National Security Agency in August 2020 arrested four witnesses to a high-profile 2014 gang rape case (known as the Fairmont case), and two of their acquaintances, weeks after independent women's rights activists exposed the case online. Three witnesses were shortly released but continued to face prosecution. Authorities had encouraged witnesses to the rape to come forward, but then accused them of consensual same-sex sexual conduct, "inciting debauchery," personal drug use, and "misuse of social media." According to sources, the authorities attempted to force the witnesses to change their testimonies and ill-treated them in detention. They also reportedly forced one woman to undergo a "virginity test" and two men arrested in the case to undergo anal examinations. These are cruel and degrading practices that can rise to the level of torture. Pro-government media subjected them to a coordinated smear campaign.

The Egyptian #MeToo movement became re-energized in 2020, as victims and survivors of sexual violence posted their accounts online, leading to a few arrests by authorities.

On September 5, al-Sisi approved amendments to the Criminal Procedural Code to ensure anonymity and protect the identities of victims. But lawyers voiced concerns that the amendments did not provide protection for witnesses. Serious gaps remain in Egypt's laws relating to sexual violence and treatment of survivors including a weak definition of rape and lack of a comprehensive violence against women law.

Egypt continued to arbitrarily arrest and detain people based on their sexual orientation or gender identity and subjected them to torture and ill-treatment in detention, including forced anal examinations.

In June, Sarah Hegazy, an LGBT rights and feminist activist, took her own life in exile in Canada. Hegazy left Egypt out of fear for her life after authorities detained and subjected her to ill-treatment in prison for three months in 2017.

In March, during its third Universal Periodic Review at the UN Human Rights Council, Egypt rejected recommendations by several states to end arrests and discrimination based on sexual orientation and gender identity. Egypt responded that it "does not recognize the terms mentioned in this recommendation."

For several months, Egyptians living with HIV, including gay men, faced obstacles to accessing HIV treatment as they feared retrieving their medication from fever hospitals, the only centers where people living with HIV can access lifesaving medications after the government designated them as treatment centers for Covid-19.

Key International Actors

Despite its disastrous record of human rights violations, Egypt's regional and international partners did not go beyond occasional, weak expressions of concern and largely failed to condition security assistance on accountability or improvement in the human rights situation.

In 2020, the US Congress again appropriated to Egypt $1.3 billion in foreign military financing. In May, the Defense Security Cooperation Agency notified the US Congress of an approved sale to Egypt of AH-64E Apache attack helicopters, worth $2.3 billion. Following the death of Egyptian-American citizen Mostafa Kassem in Egyptian custody in January, members of Congress sent multiple letters expressing concern regarding arbitrary detention, the targeting of American citizens or the families of US citizens, and increased risks of Covid-19 in overcrowded prisons.

The UK's relationship with Egypt privileged security, trade, environmental, and other cooperation over pressure on Cairo to tackle its grave record of human rights abuse.

Divisions among European Union member states prevented the bloc from adopting effective measures to address the human rights crisis in Egypt. The EU, France, and Italy prioritized cooperation with Egypt on issues including the Libya crisis and migration management, limiting their public criticism to improved statements at the UN Human Rights Council, which were stronger than previous years.

EU member states have continued to export arms and surveillance technology to Egypt, ignoring calls by the European Parliament and contravening the EU pledge in 2013, as well as in disregard for the EU common position on military exports. In June, Italy announced it was negotiating an €11 billion (around $13 billion) arms deal with Cairo—the largest arms transfer ever for both countries—despite lack of progress in the investigations for the brutal torture and murder in Cairo in 2016 of the Italian student Giulio Regeni, likely at the hand of Egypt's security forces.

The International Monetary Fund (IMF) approved two loans totaling $8 billion with weak governance conditions that do not address human rights and transparency concerns, such as the independence of Egypt's main anti-corruption entity, the Central Auditing Agency. The World Bank approved a $50 million Covid-19 health project that did not take into account reprisals against healthcare workers.

El Salvador

Since taking office, President Nayib Bukele has undermined basic democratic checks and balances. In February 2020, he entered the Legislative Assembly with armed soldiers in an apparent effort to intimidate legislators into approving a loan for security forces. He has publicly defied three rulings by the Constitutional Chamber of the Supreme Court prohibiting arrests for violations of a Covid-19-related lockdown Bukele had decreed.

In March, Bukele decreed a nationwide, mandatory lockdown in response to the Covid-19 pandemic, and ordered security forces to detain people breaking it. Thousands have since been detained in overcrowded and unsanitary centers called "containment centers."

Gangs exercise territorial control over neighborhoods and extort residents throughout the country. They forcibly recruit children and sexually abuse women, girls, and lesbian, gay, bisexual, and transgender (LGBT) people. Gangs kill, disappear, rape, or displace those who resist.

Historically, security forces have committed extrajudicial executions, sexual assaults, enforced disappearances, and torture. They remain largely ineffective in protecting the population from gang violence.

Girls and women accused of having abortions have been imprisoned for homicide and aggravated homicide. LGBT individuals face discrimination and police violence.

Abuses by Security Forces

President Bukele continued using the military in public security operations, despite a 1992 peace accord stipulation against it.

During the Covid-19 lockdown, which lasted from March 21 through June 14, he ordered law enforcement agents to detain violators and send them to containment centers, which became rapidly overcrowded and unsanitary. Authorities did not isolate people who tested positive for the coronavirus from other detainees. More than 16,000 people were sent to these facilities and some were detained for up to 40 days.

President Bukele has encouraged abusive lockdown enforcement measures, including excessive use of force. In April, he ordered the police and military to be "tougher with people violating the quarantine," and said he would not mind if the police "bent someone's wrist" during an arrest.

During the enforcement of lockdown measures, the Ombudsperson's Office reported more than 1,600 complaints of human rights violations, including over 620 of the right to freedom of movement.

After a spike in murders in April, Bukele announced he "authorized" the use of lethal force by security forces for "self-defense and to protect the lives of Salvadorans," even when not a measure of last resort, saying "the government will see to the legal defense of those who may be unjustly charged for defending the lives of honorable people."

Between 2014 and 2018, the police committed 116 extrajudicial killings, according to the Ombudsperson's Office. Only two cases resulted in convictions.

Prison and Police Barracks

The country's penal institutions held over 36,600 detainees in August, twice the official capacity, the World Prison Brief revealed, including approximately 23 percent in pretrial detention.

Overcrowding and poor sanitation endangered the health of prisoners. The risk of tuberculosis infection among people in prisons in El Salvador is 99 times higher than in the general population. These conditions risk further spreading Covid-19.

In April, President Bukele declared a "state of emergency" in maximum security prisons holding gang members, ordering 24-hour block confinement. While gangs are typically separated to avoid clashes, he mixed gangs in shared cells. Official photographs and videos showed thousands of mostly-naked detainees—few wearing face masks—jammed together on cellblock floors in contravention of public health guidance to slow the spread of Covid-19, while police searched cells, further exacerbating the already heightened risk of contagion.

Gangs and Violence

Approximately 60,000 gang members operate in El Salvador, according to media. They exert control over territory and extort and gather intelligence on residents and those passing through, particularly around public transit, schools, and markets.

Numerous security and elected officials have collaborated with gangs in criminal operations, media report, and all political parties have negotiated with them, including for electoral campaigns.

The National Police reported 706 homicides from January to July 2020, compared to more than 1,700 during the same period in 2019, a 59 percent drop. In September, *El Faro*, a digital outlet, reported that President Bukele's government had been negotiating with MS-13 over the past year, granting jail privileges to imprisoned members in exchange for MS-13 commitment to lower the homicide rate and to provide electoral support for the February 2021 elections. On September 4, Attorney General Raúl Melara said his office would investigate.

Disappearances

From January 2014 to October 2019, police registered over 11,900 disappearance victims (including more than 400 children)—which exceeds the estimated 8,000 to 10,000 disappeared during the civil war (1979-1992). The disappearances are committed by a range of actors, including gangs and the police. Few cases are investigated.

Government Accountability

Impunity for government abuses is the norm.

A trial of former military commanders accused for the 1981 El Mozote massacre started in 2016 and continued at time of writing. Soldiers committed mass rape and killed 978 civilians at El Mozote, including 553 children. In September 2020, soldiers refused to comply with a court order that allowed a judge to review military records about the massacre. President Bukele said he was the only one entitled to declassify military files and announced he would hand over to the judge "all of the existing military archives" on the massacre. In October, the court reported that it had received the military records. However, the information they contained was almost identical to the records the previous government had given to the courts, which also stated that the presidency had no additional information on the massacre.

Investigations have reached hearings in only 14 of 48 cases involving 116 extrajudicial killings committed from 2014 to 2018, the Salvadoran Ombudsperson for the Defense of Human Rights (PDDH) has reported. Two cases resulted in convictions.

In September 2020, a Spanish court found Inocente Montano, a former Salvadoran army colonel and former vice minister of public security, guilty of the 1989 murder of five Jesuit priests at the Central American University in San Salvador. He was sentenced to 133 years in prison.

Former President Antonio Saca (2004-2009) is serving a 12-year prison sentence on corruption charges for embezzling over US$300 million. Former President Mauricio Funes (2009-2014), who has been living in Nicaragua since 2016, faces multiples criminal charges, including corruption, embezzlement, and money laundering. Nicaraguan President Daniel Ortega granted him political asylum in 2019.

To address the Covid-19 crisis, the National Assembly authorized flexible purchasing rules for the executive branch during the emergency, including for "direct purchases" of medical supplies and services. At time of writing, the Attorney General's Office was investigating six government officials, including the current health minister, for corruption and improper purchases.

Women's Sexual and Reproductive Rights

Abortion is illegal under all circumstances. Providers face prison sentences of 6 months to 12 years.

According to the latest available statistics, over 150 girls and women, mostly from impoverished areas, were prosecuted between 2000 and 2011 for what lawyers and activists say were obstetric emergencies. In multiple cases, the courts accepted as evidence a questionable autopsy procedure known as the lung float test to support claims that a fetus was delivered alive.

As of September 2020, 19 women who said they had suffered obstetric emergencies remained imprisoned on charges of abortion, homicide, or aggravated homicide. At least 16 of them had been convicted of aggravated homicide.

Since 2009, 41 women who were being prosecuted by the Attorney General's Office have been found not guilty or have had their sentences commuted.

Evelyn Hernández stood trial for a second time in August 2019 on charges of aggravated homicide for a stillbirth in 2016, which followed her rape at age 17. Hernández was acquitted in July 2020.

Disability Rights

El Salvador continues to have a legislative framework inconsistent with international disability rights law, including restrictions on legal capacity for people with intellectual and psychosocial disabilities, as well as insufficient measures to improve physical and communication accessibility. Criminal gangs have attacked women and girls with disabilities with high levels of impunity.

LGBT Rights

LGBT individuals remain targets of homophobic and transphobic violence by police, gangs, and others. Salvadoran LGBT rights organizations report over 600 killed since 1993. Official statistics released in January 2020 showed 692 cases of violence against LGBT and intersex people from January 2015 to June 2019.

In May 2019, the Ombudsperson's Office documented 19 unsolved murders of LGBT people, primarily transgender women, between 2009 and 2016.

Between October 2019 and April 2020 alone, at least seven trans women and two gay men were murdered in El Salvador, with details in the cases suggesting the killers had been motivated by hatred based on the victims' gender identity or sexual orientation.

In July 2020, three police officers were found guilty in connection with the death of Camila Díaz Córdova, a transgender woman deported from the United States. They were given 20-year prison sentences. It was a landmark case, delivering El Salvador's first conviction for the killing of a transgender person.

HUMAN
RIGHTS
WATCH

"Every Day I Live in Fear"

Violence and Discrimination Against LGBT People in El Salvador,
Guatemala, and Honduras, and Obstacles to Asylum in the United States

In June 2019, President Bukele dissolved the Secretariat of Social Inclusion, within which the Directorate on Sexual Diversity was based, and subsumed the directorate into an existing Gender Unit in the Ministry of Culture, renamed the Gender and Diversity Unit. LGBT activists criticized the move, protesting that few of their grave concerns regarding safety and discrimination could be adequately addressed under the ambit of culture.

Attacks on Journalists

The Association of Journalists of El Salvador reported 61 press freedom violations from June 2019 to May 2020, including attacks, digital harassment, and restrictions on journalists' work and access to public information.

Since taking office, President Bukele has assaulted the credibility of independent media, particularly *El Faro*, *Revista Factum* and *Gato Encerrado*, accusing them of spreading "fake news," and used government-administered media to publish articles attacking them. In July 2020, a cyber-attack on *Gato Encerrado* resulted in the loss of everything published over the preceding six months. That same month, *Gato Encerrado* reporter Julia Gavarrete's computer was stolen from her home. The editor of *Revista Disruptiva* likewise suffered the theft of two computers at home. Human rights and press freedom groups suspect these robberies were related to their journalistic work, given their critical stance on government policies and the fact that no other valuable items were stolen in either case.

Displacement

According to the latest available statistics, 71,500 people were internally displaced from 2006 to 2016.

As of 2019, Salvadorans had over 136,000 asylum applications pending in other countries, the majority of them in the US.

From 2013 through 2019, 138 Salvadorans were killed after deportation from the US, and more than 70 were beaten, sexually assaulted, extorted, or tortured.

Key International Actors

For fiscal year 2020, the US appropriated over US$72 million in bilateral aid to El Salvador, particularly to reduce extreme violence and strengthen state institutions.

In March 2020, the United Nations Working Group on Arbitrary Detention, citing long periods of imprisonment of women who had suffered obstetric emergencies or miscarriages, urged El Salvador to adopt structural reforms to "end the arbitrary detention of women in vulnerable conditions."

After an in-country visit to El Salvador in December 2019, the Inter-American Commission on Human Rights expressed concern about high levels of violence, military participation in law enforcement operations, prison overcrowding and poor conditions, and violence against women, girls, and LGBT people.

Eritrea

Two years on from the peace deal with Ethiopia, Eritrea's leadership has increased its regional and international diplomatic engagement, but without improving the plight of Eritreans through critical human rights reforms.

Eritrea's government remains one of the world's most repressive, subjecting its population to widespread forced labor and conscription, imposing restrictions on freedom of expression, opinion, and faith, and restricting independent scrutiny by international monitors.

Eritrea remains a one-man dictatorship under President Isaias Afewerki, with no legislature, no independent civil society organizations or media outlets, and no independent judiciary. Elections have never been held in the country since it gained independence in 1993, and the government has never implemented the 1997 constitution guaranteeing civil rights and limiting executive power.

In response to Covid-19, Eritrean authorities increased pervasive controls and movement restrictions on its population. From March, the government prohibited citizens, except those engaged in "essential developmental and security" tasks, from leaving their homes, unless for procuring food and medical emergencies.

The coastal Danakali region, predominantly inhabited by Afar communities— cross-border pastoralists—was especially affected by border closures. Media reported that the government intercepted camel convoys bringing foodstuffs from Djibouti and Ethiopia, a key food supply for local Afar communities. The government has also confiscated Afari fishing boats, thereby preventing access to food and income.

In September, the government ignored its own restrictions on movement, its ban on public transport, and its school closures, by channeling thousands of school students to the infamous Sawa military camp where all secondary school students must complete their schooling and simultaneously undergo military training.

Positively, Eritrea took part in the Committee on the Elimination of Discrimination Against Women (CEDAW) review. Although a member of the United Nations

Human Rights Council (HRC), it refused to cooperate with or grant access to the UN special rapporteur on the situation of human rights in Eritrea and publicly attacked her mandate.

Unlawful, Abusive Detentions

Mass roundups and prolonged arbitrary arrests and detentions without trial or appeal remain common.

Many detainees, including government officials and journalists arrested in 2001 after they questioned Isaias's leadership, are held incommunicado. In June, a daughter of journalist Dawit Isaak told media he was alive, but without substantiating the assertion. Ciham Ali Abdu, daughter of a former information minister, has been held for seven years since her arrest age 15. Former finance minister and critic of the president, Berhane Abrehe, remains in incommunicado detention since September 2018.

Prisoners often do not know why they are being detained. Relatives are seldom informed of prisoners' whereabouts, sometimes learning of their fate only when a body is returned.

Authorities hold detainees in inhumane conditions. Facilities are overcrowded and unsanitary, made worse by Covid-19 restrictions that denied many detainees vital food parcels and sanitary products their families would have provided. For months, the government ignored calls by international rights actors to release those unlawfully detained to decongest detention facilities in response to Covid-19.

Eritrea has long criminalized consensual homosexual conduct; the 2015 penal code mandates imprisonment for five to seven years.

Indefinite Military Conscription and Forced Labor

The government took no steps to reform the country's national service system. It continued to conscript Eritreans, most men and unmarried women, indefinitely into military or civil service for low pay and with no say in their profession or work location. Conscripts are often subjected to inhuman and degrading punishment, including torture, without recourse. Conscientious objection is not recognized; it is punished. Discharge from national service is arbitrary and procedures opaque.

For secondary students, some under 18, conscription begins at Sawa. Students are under military command, are subjected to harsh military punishments and discipline, and female students have reported sexual harassment and exploitation. Dormitories are crowded and health facilities very limited.

The government continued to conscript youth, some perceived as seeking to evade conscription during mass round-ups.

No conscripts, including students, were released from Sawa during 2020, despite the risk of exposure to Covid-19. And, despite calls for reforms, including the separation of schooling from compulsory military training, in September the government again bused students to Sawa, forcibly channeling thousands of young people into national service.

The government assigns conscripts to military duties but many are assigned to civil service jobs or work on agricultural or construction projects. In February, the Supreme Court of Canada held that the Canadian mining company, Nevsun, accused of using conscript forced labor at its Bisha mine could be sued in Canada for human rights abuses in Eritrea. In October, the parties announced they had agreed to a settlement in the case but the terms remained confidential.

The government continued to rely on poorly trained national service teachers, which affects quality of primary and secondary education, and teacher retention. Conscripted teachers have no say about where they will be assigned, the subjects they will teach, or the length of their assignment.

Some conscript pay was increased but it remains inadequate to support a family.

Freedom of Religion

The government "recognized" only four religious denominations: Sunni Islam, Eritrean Orthodox, Roman Catholicism, and Evangelical (Lutheran) churches.

Eritreans affiliated with "unrecognized" faiths have faced imprisonment and have often been forced to renounce their religion, including by being tortured. In September and October, two nongovernmental organizations reported the release of as many as 69 "non-recognized" Christians, some detained for over a decade—possibly due to fears of Covid-19 infection—on condition they signed property deeds to hold them liable for future behavior. But the government still arrested people because of religious practices, including during wedding cele- brations.

None of the 52 Jehovah's Witnesses long incarcerated in Mai Serwa have been released, including three jailed since 1994 because of their conscientious objec- tions to military service.

Even "recognized" religions faced restrictions. A Catholic Church delegation led by the archbishop of Addis Ababa was refused entry at the Asmara airport and deported. The Orthodox patriarch deposed by the government in 2007 and ex- pelled from the church in 2019 because of "heresy" remained under house ar- rest.

In November 2019, 21 Muslims were reportedly arrested in Mendafera and Adi Quala, including a local imam; the whereabouts of many remains unknown. Media reported that peaceful demonstrators arrested in 2017 and early 2018 for protesting the government takeover of Al Diaa Islamic school were released in August; officials of the school remain incarcerated.

In January, Finn Church Aid, one of the very few nongovernmental organizations based in Eritrea, ended its activities after the government suddenly stopped its teacher training project, which aimed to recruit teachers outside the national service system.

Refugees

Eritrea's ongoing rights crisis continues to drive thousands of Eritreans into exile, with many children and youth escaping conscription.

In the first three months of 2020, 9,436 Eritreans fled to Ethiopia alone, a third of whom were children. In January, the Ethiopian government unofficially changed its asylum policy, which for years granted all Eritrean asylum seekers refugee status as a group, only registering some categories of new arrivals at the Eritrea border, excluding others, notably unaccompanied children.

Among those fleeing Eritrea were four football players participating in a tournament in Uganda in November 2019. Some footballers defected at tournaments in 2015 and 2009.

Israeli authorities continued to systematically deny the asylum claims of the roughly 32,000 Eritrean and Sudanese asylum seekers in the country. However, in April, Israel's Supreme Court struck down a law that permitted the confiscation of a portion of their salaries.

Key International Actors

More than two years after the Eritrea and Ethiopia declared peace, their border remains demarcated and Ethiopia has not withdrawn from Badme, the Eritrean village that triggered the 1998 war. In 2019, Eritrea unilaterally closed the border. In March 2020, Ethiopia shut the border because of pandemic-related fears.

After having been sued by a European human rights organization and criticized by the European Parliament for funding the procurement of material for the construction of a road in Eritrea that employs conscript forced labor, the European Union announced it would fund "no more roads." It also announced it would be conducting a review of its "dual-track" approach in Eritrea, which de-linked political and development policy with its development arm focused on job creation activities, and its political arm reportedly raising human rights issues. In contrast, a subsidiary of a state-owned Chinese company remains involved in building a 134-kilometer road.

In 2013, Human Rights Watch documented how a state-owned construction company, which regularly used forced conscript workers built part of the Bisha mine's infrastructure.

Two mining companies that provide 20 percent of the country's income are 60 percent owned by Chinese firms, and 40 percent by the government.

The development of a massive 50 percent Australian company-owned potash development project, the Colluli potash project in the Danakali region, moved ahead. In May, the special rapporteur on the human rights situation in Eritrea reported allegations that the military had been clearing local Afar communities off their land around Colluli since 2017.

The Global Partnership for Education, a global education donor, awarded a US$17.2 million grant to Eritrea, despite ongoing human rights abuses in the country's education sector.

Eswatini

In 2020, Eswatini remained an absolute monarchy ruled by King Mswati III, who has led the country since 1986. There are no legally recognized political parties in the country due to a ban by a 1973 decree. Despite the adoption of the 2005 constitution, which guarantees basic rights and the country's international human rights commitments, the government has not reviewed the decree or changed the law to allow the formation, registration, and participation of political parties in elections. In 2020, the government of Eswatini proposed a new omnibus cybercrime bill which threatens freedom of speech and media freedoms.

Freedom of Association and Assembly

Restrictions on freedom of association and assembly continued in 2020. On October 20, the Eswatini High Court heard a challenge from Eswatini Sexual and Gender Minorities (ESGM) against the Eswatini Registrar of Companies' refusal to register ESGM as a company. ESGM is a human rights community-based advocacy organization working to advance the protection of the rights of lesbian, gay, bisexual, transgender and intersex persons in the kingdom of Eswatini. The registrar argued that ESGM could not be registered as a company because "ESGM's objectives were unlawful because same-sex sexual acts are illegal in the country."

ESGM responded by arguing that Eswatini's constitutional rights apply to everyone, that everyone in the kingdom has a right to their dignity, and that freedom to associate should not be denied based on arbitrary grounds, including one's sexual orientation. At time of writing, the court had yet to issue its ruling.

Rule of Law and Media Freedoms

King Mswati III continues to hold supreme executive power over parliament and the judiciary due to a 1973 State of Emergency decree. The country's courts have upheld the legality of the decree despite the fact that the 2005 constitution provides for three separate organs of state—the executive, legislature and judiciary. The prime minister theoretically holds executive authority, but in reality, the king exercises supreme executive power and controls the judiciary. The 2005 constitution provides for equality before the law while simultaneously elevating the king above the law.

In 2020, Reporters Without Borders ranked Eswatini 141 out of 180 countries on media freedom, based partly on constraints that journalists face in working freely under the absolute monarchy, and because courts are not permitted to prosecute representatives of the monarchy.

In August, Eswatini authorities gazetted a new omnibus cybercrime bill. The bill has a number of disturbing elements, including serious criminal penalties for publishing so called fake news and for "cyber bullying." It provides that any person who publishes a statement or "fake news" through any medium, including social media, with the intention to deceive any other person or group of persons commits an offense, and if convicted is liable to a fine not exceeding £10 million (US$600,000) or imprisonment not exceeding 10 years, or both. The bill, if adopted, will further constrain independent journalism and critical speech.

Women and Girls' Rights

The under-representation of women in leadership and decision-making positions in both public and private sectors continued during 2020, with little effort to implement provisions of the 2018 Election of Women Act. The act is designed to ensure the fulfillment of the constitutional requirement of representation quotas for women and marginalized groups in parliament.

Eswatini has committed itself to some regional and international instruments to promote gender equality. These include the Convention for the Elimination of All Forms of Discrimination Against Women (CEDAW). Eswatini has ratified this convention without reservation and the Southern African Development Community (SADC) Declaration on Gender and Development. Article 20 of the Eswatini Constitution provides for equality before the law and non-discrimination on several protected grounds, but not including language, sexual orientation or gender identity. Eswatini's dual legal system where both the common law, which is based on Roman Dutch law and Eswatini unwritten customary law operate side by side. This has resulted in conflicts, resulting in numerous violations of women's rights over the years.

Workers' Rights

In June, the International Trade Union Confederation (ITUC) published results of an annual survey indicating that Eswatini has one of the worst workers' rights records in the world. Eswatini scored five on the Global Rights Index—five being worst on the scale—capturing its failure to respect workers' rights and the fact that Eswatini workers are exposed to repression and unfair labor practices. According to the ITUC, countries with the five rating provide no guarantees for rights and are among the worst countries in the world in which to work.

Covid-19

During 2020, Eswatini grappled with the coronavirus pandemic, which severely strained the health infrastructure and negatively impacted the economy and people's livelihoods. By mid November, Eswatini had 6,144 confirmed Covid-19 cases with 119 deaths. On March 17, King Mswati III declared a national emergency in response to the pandemic and closed schools, colleges, and universities. All public and private gatherings of 50 or more people including conferences, funerals, weddings, entertainment and sporting activities were suspended. The government partially re-opened schools for external examination classes only, while the rest of the classes are scheduled to resume in 2021, according to a statement issued by Eswatini Prime Minister Ambrose Mandvulo Dlamini.

Key International Actors

On September 25, despite a lack of progress on women and girls' rights, King Mswati III in his address to the 75th session of the United Nations General Assembly noted that 2020 marks the 25th anniversary of the Fourth World Conference on Women and the adoption of the Beijing Declaration and Platform for Action. He said 2020 was a significant year for the accelerated realization of gender equality and the empowerment of all women and girls. He called on all UN members to "recommit ourselves to our common goal of achieving gender equality and the empowerment of all women and girls and their enjoyment of human rights, everywhere."

In June, the Commonwealth secretariat issued a statement committing to continue its support to Eswatini to help ensure the country's Commission on Human Rights and Public Administration (CHRPA) meets international standards. The Commonwealth noted that since its inception the commission has not complied with the standards set out in the Paris Principles as it operates without any legislation to clearly define its operational parameters.

In a March 8 statement to mark International Women's Day, the UN resident coordinator for Eswatini, Nathalie Ndongo-Seh, noted that 48 percent of women and girls in the country experience some form of sexual violence in their lifetime. She nevertheless commended the government for working to ensure that women and girls are protected from sexual and gender-based violence. On behalf of the UN agencies in Eswatini, Ndongo-Seh pledged continued support to the government of Eswatini and civil society to design and implement educational programs that promote human rights and gender equality.

Ethiopia

The security and human rights situation in Ethiopia deteriorated as Prime Minister Abiy Ahmed struggled to maintain order amid growing unrest and political tensions. The rights landscape was defined by ongoing abuses by government security forces, attacks on civilians by armed groups, deadly violence along communal and ethnic lines, and a political crisis.

The government postponed national elections in March citing Covid-19-related health risks. Several opposition parties condemned the decision. National elections are now slated to be held sometime in 2021. Relations between the federal government and Tigray regional officials worsened after the region held elections in September in defiance of the federal government's directive. On November 4, Abiy ordered the military to take action against the ruling party in Tigray, in retaliation for what he described as an attack by Tigray regional forces on a federal military base, triggering significant clashes between regional and federal forces. The fighting raised concerns that the phone and internet communication blackout, as well restrictions on air and road access, threatened relief operations to communities at risk.

The June 29 assassination of popular Oromo singer Hachalu Hundessa triggered protests, a heavy-handed security force response, large-scale property destruction, and violence by civilian assailants that targeted minority communities in Oromia. The attacks heightened existing social and political tensions, which were further exacerbated by the arrest of dozens of members of opposition parties in July for their alleged connection with the violence.

In southern and western Oromia, government counterinsurgency campaigns against armed rebel groups resulted in serious human rights violations and abuses against local communities committed by all sides.

Schools were closed due to the pandemic until at least September 2020, affecting over 26 million children.

Little progress was made into ensuring justice for past and recent abuses, including investigations into the deadly October 2019 violence. The national human rights commission issued several critical statements and visited detainees in the capital and in Oromia. Institutional reforms, notably around the security sector, and truth, reconciliation, and accountability—key commitments made earlier in the Abiy administration and all of which are key to dealing with heightened political and ethnic tensions—were limited.

Conduct of Security Forces, Attacks by Armed Groups

Since January, government security forces, including Ethiopian National Defense and Oromia regional police forces, carried out abusive counterinsurgency operations in western and southern Oromia region. The fighting by all sides undermined the ability of humanitarian actors to operate in insecure areas.

Reports of extrajudicial killings, mass arrests and detentions, and violence against ethnic Oromo civilians, including medical professionals, accused of supporting or being sympathetic to the armed rebel group the Oromo Liberation Army (OLA), were widespread. On June 3, after coming under attack by unidentified groups, regional security forces stormed into Nekemte Specialized Hospital, threatened staff into treating two wounded regional police officers and temporarily interrupted health services.

Armed groups operating in the area also carried out attacks against officials, police, and civilians, including killings and lootings. The enforced disappearance of over a dozen Amhara university students, allegedly abducted by armed groups in western Oromia in December 2019, stoked anger at the government over its inaction and lack of transparency. On November 1, after federal forces left the area, unidentified armed groups attacked mainly ethnic Amhara residents in Guliso village in western Oromia, resulting in dozens killed and property damage.

In the aftermath of Hachalu's killing, security forces used excessive force against protesters and mourners gathered in different towns in Oromia and in Addis Ababa in June and July. A heavy security force presence established in many Oromia towns carried out abusive operations against Oromo communities. On August 17, protests broke out in eastern Oromia in response to the continued detention of prominent Oromo opposition leaders Jawar Mohammed and Bekele Gerba. In August, security forces arrested, beat, and used excessive force against scores of protesters, and allegedly killed over 40 people in eastern Oromia.

Following the arrest of local officials and activists, protests erupted on August 9-12 in Sodo, capital of Wolaita zone, in Southern Nations, Nationalities and Peoples' Region (SNNPR). In response, security forces beat and shot at crowds, and reportedly killed over 16 people.

Ethnic and Communal Violence

Longstanding grievances and increasing polarization over historical and complex questions about land, politics, and identity, led to deadly violence among ethnic communities in 2020.

Violence on 22 university campuses in 2019, mainly in the Oromia and Amhara regions, continued in the first half of the year, prompting an estimated 35,000 students to flee.

In January, conflict between Amhara and Oromo groups erupted in Harar over the use of the old national flag and decorations during the Orthodox Christian celebration Epiphany, resulting in an unknown number of casualties and the destruction of property.

Afar and Somali communities routinely clashed over border demarcations and access to land and resources, claiming civilian lives on both sides. Fighting since January reportedly resulted in 35,5000 displaced—half of the conflict-induced displacements recorded in the country between January and June 2020.

Hachalu's killing triggered one of the deadliest periods of unrest. Over 170 people were killed, some by security forces, others in attacks by civilian assailants who also looted and burned the businesses and homes of ethnic Amharas and other minority communities, causing significant property destruction and the displacement of over 9,000 people. In some cases, security forces failed to intervene in time to protect lives and property or participated in the looting.

Violence by armed groups, and among ethnic-Gumuz, Agew, Amhara, and other communities in the Metekel zone of the Benishangul-Gumuz region, intensified in April, causing residents to flee. Yet, authorities in Benishangul-Gumuz and Amhara region began returning thousands of internally displaced people within Metekel in April. Attacks by armed groups escalated in August and September, targeting security forces, officials, and residents, including ethnic Amharas, resulting in scores killed, kidnappings, property destruction, and renewed displacement.

Due Process Rights and Fair Trial Standards

On February 29, police arrested Abdi Regassa and eight other members of Oromo Liberation Front (OLF). Though the eight members were later released, Abdi Regassa's whereabouts remained unknown for several months. He continues to be detained on an unclear basis and without charge at time of writing.

On March 27, Oromia police and intelligence officials arrested journalist Yayesew Shimelis following his comments about the government's response to Covid-19. Police accused Yayesew of disseminating false information and refused to comply with two court bail orders for his release.

Following the late June violence, authorities arrested over 9,000 people, including government critics and journalists. In several high-profile cases, authorities appealed or seemed to ignore bail orders, requested more time to investigate, or transferred suspects between police authorities, some with overlapping jurisdictions, without informing relatives or counsel.

In September, authorities charged prominent opposition figures Jawar Mohammed, Bekele Gerba, and Eskinder Nega under the criminal code and under the newly enacted terrorism law for their suspected involvement in the unrest.

Freedom of Expression, Media, and Association

On January 3, the government shut down internet and phone connections for three months in western Oromia, significantly restricting freedom of expression and hampering the delivery of essential services, including amid a global health pandemic. Connectivity was restored on March 31.

On June 30, following Hachalu's killing, authorities imposed a nationwide three-week internet shutdown. The shutdown impacted the communication and coordination of humanitarian agencies and limited access to information and critical reporting. Officials also arrested over a dozen journalists and media workers and launched independent investigations into several media outlets. Similarly, on November 4, internet and phone connectivity was cut in the Tigray region after the federal government ordered troops to respond to an alleged attack by Tigray forces on a military base in the area.

In January, parliament approved a law on hate speech and disinformation, taking effect on March 23. Rights groups warned that the law contained overbroad and vague language that could have a chilling effect on free expression and access to information online. In May, journalist Yayesew Shimelis was the first person charged under it.

On April 8, Ethiopia declared a five-month state of emergency, giving authorities sweeping powers to respond to Covid-19. The regulations limited gatherings to four people, suspended suspects' right to appear before a judge within 48 hours, and broadly restricted media reporting on Covid-19 news if reporting could "cause terror and undue distress among the public."

Refugees

In January, the Ethiopian government unofficially changed its asylum policy, which for years granted all Eritrean asylum seekers refugee status as a group, and began only registering some categories of new arrivals at the Eritrea border, excluding others, particularly unaccompanied children. The fighting between federal government forces and Tigray regional forces sparked concerns by humanitarian actors of the risk to vulnerable groups in Tigray regional state, including 100,000 IDPs and 96,000 refugees.

Key International Actors

Ethiopia enjoyed support from international actors and most of its regional neighbors, due to its role as host of the African Union (AU), its contributions to United Nations peacekeeping and regional negotiations and counterterrorism efforts, and migration partnerships with Western countries.

The European Union has been trying to boost its relations with Ethiopia. EU Commission President Ursula von der Leyen visited Addis in December 2019, the first place she officially visited outside Europe.

In February, the EU high representative and several commissioners visited Ethiopia, reaffirmed EU support for Ethiopia's reform efforts, and promised to deploy an EU electoral observation mission for the March elections, which was later postponed. EU high officials visited the country again in October, reiterating their support for the country's reforms, though raising concerns over the "more complicated" situation.

In February, US Secretary of State Mike Pompeo visited Ethiopia, reiterated US support for Ethiopia's domestic reforms, and emphasized the importance of holding free and fair elections.

The United Arab Emirates (UAE) committed US$3 billion in investment and assistance and is financing large-scale infrastructure and development initiatives.

Two years after Ethiopia and Eritrea signed a peace agreement, issues around the agreement remain unsettled, and the borders remain heavily fortified.

Relations with Egypt remained rather tense due to Egypt's concerns that Ethiopia's Grand Renaissance Dam (GERD) would divert water from the Nile River. Although negotiations under AU auspices resolved some concerns of the parties, disagreements related to drought mitigation and dispute resolution remained unsolved. On September 2, the US said it would suspend around $100 million in aid to Ethiopia, reportedly over the lack of progress on the dam talks, in which the US had played an earlier role in mediating.

Then UN special rapporteur on freedom of expression, David Kaye, visited Ethiopia in December 2019, the first official mission by any mandate holder to the country since 2006. In a June report, the special rapporteur welcomed steps to reform previous laws restricting freedom of expression but remained concerned by significant penalties in the media law and vague provisions in the hate speech and disinformation law.

Following the late June unrest, UN special procedures, the EU and US Senate and House Representatives, issued statements of concern surrounding the violence and unrest. The UN called for a transparent and independent investigation into the singer's death, while the AU called for an independent investigation into the events, underscoring growing global concerns over Ethiopia's human rights situation.

Escalating tensions and clashes in the Tigray region prompted an urgent international response urging de-escalation and dialogue, including from the UN secretary-general, the German foreign minister, the UN high commissioner for human rights, the AU, and the regional body, the Intergovernmental Authority on Development (IGAD).

European Union

The Covid-19 pandemic altered the lives of everyone in the European Union in 2020, with some member states more affected than others by the public health emergency and socioeconomic consequences of lockdown measures. Despite some efforts at the EU and national levels to mitigate the worst impacts, the public health crisis had a disproportionate impact on certain groups—older people, people in poverty, marginalized groups including people with disabilities, Roma, and migrants—and deepened existing fault lines in EU societies and politics.

In March, the EU Commission proposed a European Climate Law to make obtaining climate neutrality—including by reducing greenhouse gas emissions—by 2050 a legally binding objective, building on commitments in its December 2019 European Green Deal. In October, the EU Council proposed that over a third of the funds of its latest pandemic recovery plan would contribute to climate action and environmental sustainability, pending approval from the European Parliament. The United Kingdom exited the EU in January.

Migration and Asylum

The European Commission released a wide-ranging New Pact on Migration and Asylum in September, capping off a year marked by border closures, pushbacks, and increased vulnerability of asylum seekers and undocumented migrants amid the Covid-19 pandemic. Though promoted as a "fresh start," the pact confirmed the focus on sealing borders and boosting returns, included proposals that could undermine safeguards and increase detention, and failed to present innovative proposals for rights-respecting migration management.

About 73,000 people arrived irregularly at EU's southern borders in the first 10 months of 2020—a decrease compared to the same period in 2019—while 726 died or went missing at sea.

Despite guidance from the European Commission in March and April on migration and asylum in the context of the Covid-19 pandemic, including the obligation to ensure access to asylum even amid border closures, some member states *de jure* or *de facto* suspended asylum procedures. Italy, Spain, and Portugal took measures to protect and in some cases extend access to public health care and other rights during the pandemic.

Nongovernmental and international organizations reported cases of pushbacks, often accompanied by violence, or denials of access to asylum at many EU land external borders, including in Greece, Croatia, Slovenia, Bulgaria, Hungary, and Poland. Greece used force in response to a spike in the number of migrants and asylum seekers arriving at its land border with Turkey in March and officially suspended its asylum procedure for one month. Malta, Cyprus, and Greece engaged in pushbacks at sea. In November, the Management Board of the European Border and Coast Guard Agency (Frontex) set up a working group to conduct inquiries into allegations of the agency's involvement in pushbacks in the Aegean Sea.

In April, Italy and Malta declared their ports "unsafe" because of the Covid-19 pandemic. Italy allowed nongovernmental rescue boats and merchant ships to disembark people, often after unnecessary delay, but then impounded ships and airplanes deployed by rescue groups. In September, the European Commission issued guidance to prevent criminalization of sea rescue, though the narrow interpretation seemed to allow for continued harassment of other humanitarian activities.

Substandard and crowded living conditions of asylum seekers and seasonal migrant workers, many of them undocumented, in countries across the EU put them at heightened health risk during the pandemic. National authorities in Spain, Italy, Germany, and Greece resorted to indiscriminate lockdowns of reception facilities. Malta detained hundreds of people on small tourist ferries for weeks without any clear social distancing or isolation protocols. Spain failed to ensure adequate conditions or access to information or asylum amid a significant increase in arrivals by sea to the Canary Islands.

A fire that destroyed the overcrowded Moria refugee camp on the Greek island of Lesbos, in September, leaving almost 13,000 people homeless, was a stark reminder of the humanitarian crises at the EU's external borders. A handful of countries pledged to relocate small numbers of persons disembarked in Italy and Malta following sea rescues, and in April, a group of 13 EU and other European countries started relocating at least 1,600 unaccompanied migrant children from Greece.

In April, the Court of Justice of the European Union (CJEU) ruled that Poland, Hungary, and the Czech Republic broke EU law by refusing to implement the 2015-2017 emergency relocation mechanism.

In its pact, the commission proposed new criteria for determining which EU country should examine asylum claims, including considering family ties, but left in place the general rule that the first country of entry into the EU is responsible. The commission also proposed a "responsibility-sharing approach" under which a country that refused to accept relocating asylum seekers would instead "sponsor" deportations.

The EU pursued its long-standing efforts to enlist third countries in migration control, notably in its support to the Libyan Coast Guard to facilitate interceptions. At least 8,247 people were disembarked in Libya in the first 9 months of the year, despite risks of arbitrary detention, torture, and other abuses in Libya.

Discrimination and Intolerance

The European Commission published in September an action plan against racism, the first high-level recognition of structural racism in the EU. The plan commits the commission to appointing an anti-racism coordinator and to mainstreaming an intersectional approach to countering discrimination throughout EU policymaking.

The Covid-19 pandemic triggered an increase in racist and xenophobic incidents against national or ethnic minorities, including verbal insults, harassment, physical attacks, and online hate speech. The EU's Fundamental Rights Agency (FRA) noted reports of racist incidents linked to the pandemic in most EU member states in February-March, particularly targeting people of or perceived to be of Asian origin, but also Roma, Muslims, Jews, asylum seekers, and people with disabilities. The FRA said in July that the pandemic is increasingly exploited as a pretext to attack minorities already subject to discrimination, hate speech, and hate crime, particularly on social media. There were reports of discriminatory police enforcement of Covid-19 related restrictions.

The FRA noted in September that antisemitism remains a problem in Europe and called on EU countries to do more to tackle under-reporting and gaps in data collection.

In April, the European Disability Forum said people with disabilities face obstacles in accessing community-based support and protective equipment during the pandemic. The Council of Europe (CoE) Human Rights Commissioner called on European countries to incorporate the views of people with disabilities in policymaking, prevent disruption of support services, and address additional risks in closed institutions, including by moving people out of these institutions as much as possible.

Roma continued to face discrimination in housing, employment, education, and healthcare. The Open Society Foundations noted in April that Bulgaria, Hungary, Italy, Romania, Slovakia, and Spain have not responded with proportionate attention to the much higher risk of death from Covid-19 in Roma communities. A 2019 FRA survey, published in September, found that Roma in five EU countries and the UK cannot afford basic items "such as healthy food or heating," and up to a fifth of their children go to bed hungry. In January, the CoE Committee of Ministers adopted a new action plan for Roma and Traveller inclusion, to combat "anti-Gypsyism" and discrimination and to support equality.

Following the killing of George Floyd in the United States in May, the FRA called on EU countries to fight discriminatory ethnic profiling, better support victims of racism, and properly prosecute perpetrators. In July, the European Commission against Racism and Intolerance (ECRI), a CoE monitoring body, warned against racial profiling in policing in Europe and called for the establishment of fully independent bodies to investigate incidents of alleged police abuse.

ECRI expressed concern about the lack of comprehensive and systematic data collection on hate crime in Austria, Belgium, and Germany in reports published in 2020.

Discrimination on the grounds of gender and sex remained widespread. The pandemic triggered a surge in domestic violence, especially violence targeting women, and deepened existing gender inequalities. In June, the European Committee of Social Rights said it found violations of the rights to equal pay and to equal opportunities in the workplace in 13 EU member states. At time of writing, six member states and the EU had yet to ratify the CoE Istanbul Convention on combatting and preventing violence against women, while Poland was threatening to pull out of the convention.

While France, England, Spain, and Germany, among other places, facilitated access to medical abortion in light of pandemic-related travel restrictions and the need to minimize hospital stays, women in countries including Italy, Romania, and Poland reported increased difficulty in accessing safe and legal abortion during lockdown measures.

The EU adopted in mid-November its first-ever five-year LGBTIQ Equality Strategy. A 2019 FRA survey published in May, found that physical or sexual attacks against sexual and gender minorities remain widespread, with victims of discrimination and abuse reluctant to report incidents to authorities. The survey found that one in five trans and intersex people across the EU were physically or sexually attacked, double that of lesbian, gay, and bisexual people.

Attacks in Austria, France, and Germany during the year, attributed to Islamist or far right extremists, claimed the lives of twenty-two people (including three attackers) and wounded dozens. There were concerns that legal and policy responses could further stigmatize Muslims. A joint statement in November by EU interior ministers on countering terrorism raised concerns about discrimination and freedom of expression and religion, despite their pledge to not compromise fundamental rights and freedoms.

Poverty and Inequality

The public health crisis caused by the Covid-19 pandemic, lockdown measures, and ensuing economic recession had a disproportionate impact on people living on low incomes or in poverty.

In April, the European Commission made European Social Fund (ESF) rules more flexible to allow member states to deploy resources to mitigate the socioeconomic effects of the pandemic, and by September had created a €100 billion ($117 billion) fund to lend states to help preserve employment.

Nevertheless, Eurostat data showed increasing unemployment across the EU from March through July, with women workers more affected than men and unemployment among people under 25 rising particularly sharply. Several governments quickly put in place additional temporary income and job support measures to mitigate the impact of widespread business closures, helping to shore up workers' living standards. At time of writing, a proposed EU-wide permanent unemployment benefit reinsurance scheme was still under development.

Reliance on emergency food aid—a key indicator of poverty—rose across the EU during the year. The European Food Bank Federation estimated that demand for food in June was up 50 percent higher than in the previous year. National food bank networks in Greece, Ireland, and Spain, and in regions of Italy reported increases of 50 percent or more throughout the pandemic. Emergency food providers expressed concern that certain groups including older people, undocumented migrants, single parent households (overwhelmingly women-led), as well as families with children deprived of school meals amid widespread school closures, were relying increasingly on food aid in many countries.

Around 58 million children were affected by school closures across European countries. The European Commission warned that educational inequalities would increase particularly among children who lacked resources and educational support. Children and young people with intellectual disabilities were generally excluded from online or remote learning.

In April and May, the European Commission increased resources and announced measures to allow the Fund for European Aid to the Most Deprived (FEAD)—an emergency fund allowing the distribution of food, clothing, and sanitary items and programs for economic reintegration—to respond faster to the crisis.

Unemployment and underemployment amid lockdowns and the economic recession also led to many people in EU countries falling behind on rent and mortgage payments, and worrying about continued access to housing. Several member states—including France, Germany, Ireland, Italy, the Netherlands, Poland, and Spain—announced or extended temporary bans on evictions. Housing rights advocates called on governments to extend evictions bans through 2021 to avoid a surge in homelessness.

The pandemic underscored the connection between housing and health inequalities. With an estimated 700,000 homeless people across the EU, governments took temporary measures to provide accommodation. But homeless people, whether sleeping rough or in crowded emergency shelters, as well as people living in poverty and in inadequate housing, faced increased health risks. Roma people in Europe—with an estimated 80 percent in overcrowded housing and 30 percent living with no running water—have been particularly exposed.

Rule of Law

Despite important rulings by the CJEU and some progress by the European Parliament and the European Commission in their scrutiny of attacks on the rule of law and democratic institutions in the EU, member states remained reluctant to pursue decisive action. In her first State of the Union speech, EU Commission President von der Leyen stressed that "the Commission attaches the highest importance to the rule of law" and that breaches "cannot be tolerated."

EU member states only made limited progress in their scrutiny of Hungary and Poland under Article 7—the mechanism set up by the EU treaty to address threats to EU values. European Affairs ministers held a debate on the situations in both countries in September but have not convened formal hearings under Article 7 on Poland since 2018 and on Hungary since 2019. In September, the European Parliament called on the council to broaden the scope of its scrutiny and step up action on Poland under Article 7.

In April, the CJEU ordered Poland to suspend the powers of the Disciplinary Chamber of the Supreme Court, in response to a request for interim measures filed by the European Commission in January. Also in April, the commission opened a new legal proceeding against Poland over the law that increases disciplinary sanctions against judges who issue rulings counter to government policy. Poland has yet to fully comply with June 2019 and November 2019 rulings by the CJEU on the laws on the Supreme Court and on ordinary courts.

The CJEU issued key rulings on Hungary in response to infringement proceedings brought by the European Commission. In June, it ruled that Hungary's 2017 restrictions on the financing of civil society groups were not in line with EU law. In October, it ruled that the law that forced the Central European University to leave Hungary was illegal. A case against Hungary's 2017 asylum law, known as the "Stop Soros" law, that allows for automatic detention of asylum seekers in transit zones and criminalizes legitimate activities in support of migrants, is pending before the court.

In response to concerns over Hungary's Covid-19 related state of emergency law that allowed the government to rule by decree, EU Commission President Ursula von der Leyen committed in March to monitor whether emergency measures comply with human rights; 20 member states expressed their concerns in April about the impact of certain emergency measures on human rights. Neither statement pointed at situations in specific countries.

In July, the European Commission withheld funding to six Polish cities for having established "LGBT-free zones" in contravention of EU values of tolerance and non-discrimination.

In November, EU member states and the European Parliament agreed on a proposition to tie central governments' access to certain EU funds to respect for the rule of law, but made it easier for states to block the commission's specific proposals to cut funds. Final negotiations were ongoing at time of writing.

In September, the European Commission released its first Rule of Law report, with comprehensive country chapters for each member state focused on national justice systems, anti-corruption, media, and other institutional checks and balances, including civic space. Member states peer-reviewed the records of Belgium, Bulgaria, Estonia, Czech Republic, and Denmark based on the commission's report. In October, the European Parliament adopted a stronger peer-review tool in its proposal for an EU mechanism on Democracy, the Rule of Law and Fundamental Rights.

In October, the European Parliament passed a resolution on the rule of law and fundamental rights in Bulgaria, regretting a significant deterioration and flagging concerns on the judiciary, media freedom, and the refusal to ratify the Istanbul Convention.

Malta's Prime Minister Joseph Muscat left office in January following a political crisis over allegations that he may have association with the murderers of investigative journalist Daphne Caruana Galizia in 2017. An independent public inquiry into Galizia's murder continued at time of writing, with media freedom groups alleging interference with its activities. In Slovakia, three people have been sentenced separately since December 2019 for the 2018 murder of investigative journalist Ján Kuciak and his fiancée, while the alleged mastermind was acquitted in September.

Foreign Policy

In response to the Covid-19 pandemic, the EU collectively mobilized dozens of billions of Euros in financial support to third countries. The EU Commission also joined the COVAX Facility, a global vaccine procurement mechanism to support access to any vaccine found to be safe and effective worldwide.

Although it encouraged cooperation at the global level on research and development for a vaccine, it also negotiated bilateral deals with companies to secure vaccine doses for priority use within the EU, a practice that risks undermining universal and equitable global access to the vaccine especially for low- and middle-income countries. The EU also opposed efforts at the World Trade Organization to temporarily waive some intellectual property rules that would facilitate the wide production of tests, treatments, and vaccines needed for the pandemic response.

In several instances, the EU's unanimity rule in its foreign policy prevented timely and more robust responses to international developments. The most notable example was Cyprus delaying the adoption of EU targeted sanctions against those responsible for the crackdown in Belarus; but on several different occasions, other individual member states, most often Hungary, either prevented the adoption of EU statements or made negotiations extremely difficult and muted the outcomes. In several such cases, the EU's high representative would eventually take action or issue a principled EU statement, which would then be amplified and endorsed by a large group of EU member states.

Over the year, the EU collectively and several of its member states played a leading role in UN fora to respond to human rights violations worldwide, supported efforts seeking accountability for violations, and defended multilateral institutions and mechanisms. The EU led resolutions at the UN Human Rights Council on important country situations, including Belarus, Burundi, Myanmar, and North Korea, and pressed for an urgent debate on Belarus following the brutal post-election crackdown. However, its member states took inconsistent positions on some other situations of concern, with not all EU members supporting joint statements on Saudi Arabia and China.

In September, the EU's high representative and several EU member states firmly condemned the US sanctions against International Criminal Court officials and reiterated their unwavering support for the ICC. In April, Estonia endorsed the Safe Schools Declaration, leaving endorsements from Hungary, Latvia, and Lithuania necessary for all member states to make universal commitments to protect students, teachers, schools, and universities during war.

In March, the European Commission and the EU High Representative for Foreign Affairs proposed to member states to adopt a new EU Action Plan on Human Rights and Democracy 2020-2024 and to implement it by qualified majority voting instead of unanimity. Regrettably, in November, member states only took note of the proposal and adopted the action plan keeping the unanimity rule for implementation.

In December, following more than a year of negotiations, the EU finally adopted a global human rights sanctions regime. The new system will allow the EU to impose targeted sanctions, such as travel bans and asset freezes against individuals responsible for human rights violations whatever their nationality and wherever the abuses occur, without having to adopt a country-specific legal framework each time.

Meanwhile, the EU renewed all existing arms embargoes and targeted sanctions for another year, and listed further individuals and entities from Nicaragua, Venezuela, Russia, Belarus, Ukraine, Libya, and Syria.

There were welcome shifts in the EU's narrative over the human rights crises unfolding in China—including in Hong Kong and Xinjiang—and in Egypt. But growing calls for targeted sanctions against officials responsible for serious rights violations and continued impunity for abuses remained unheeded.

Despite the EU and its member states being major humanitarian donors, and notably hosting or co-hosting international conferences to secure funding to support refugees displaced by the crises in Syria, in Venezuela and in Myanmar, they continued to engage cynically with transit and source countries to prevent and divert irregular cross-border movement of refugees, asylum seekers, and migrants, often under the fig leaf of providing protection in place.

Despite knowledge of inhuman and abusive conditions in migrant detention centers in Libya, the EU provided training and equipment to the abusive Libyan coast guard forces to capture and return people fleeing via sea. A new EU Pact on

Asylum and Migration, proposed by the commission in September, risks exacerbating the focus on externalization, deterrence, containment, and return.

In August, Cambodia lost part of its preferential access to the EU internal market pursuant to the EU's Everything But Arms (EBA) scheme due to Hun Sen's government's crackdown on human rights and democracy. The European Commission continued its enhanced engagement with Bangladesh and Myanmar, which remain at high risk of losing their EBA preferences due to their violations of human rights. Pressure also increased for taking similar steps with regards to the Philippines and Sri Lanka.

Meanwhile, progress towards the ratification of the EU-Mercosur free trade deal met growing resistance due to concerns by several European governments and parliaments over Brazil's disregard for its commitments under the Paris Climate Agreement and failure to curb illegal deforestation in the Amazon forest.

The European Parliament played an important role on a number of trade and human rights-related initiatives, including EU negotiations on new rules to curb exports of European surveillance technology to rights-abusing regimes ("dual use" recast), proposed legislation to halt and reverse EU-driven global deforestation, and worked on a legislative proposal to introduce mandatory human rights and environmental due diligence for companies operating in the EU. The parliament also formulated recommendations for the reform of the EU arms export framework, and through numerous debates, resolutions, and letters played a key role in EU foreign policy.

The parliament, however, failed to condition its consent to an EU-Vietnam trade deal on progress in the country's human rights record and the release of political prisoners. In October, the European Parliament announced its decision to award the 2020 Sakharov Prize to the Belarus democracy movement, celebrating the movement's courage while the regime's crackdown continued.

France

Announced changes in law enforcement and crowd control tactics fell short of addressing concerns of abusive and disproportionate use of force by the police, including during demonstrations. Discriminatory police identity checks targeting minority youth continued. Child protection authorities often failed to provide unaccompanied migrant children appropriate care and services. Migrants and asylum seekers faced inhuman and degrading living conditions, as well as police abuse and harassment. Instances of harassment and attacks remained high against minorities, including ethnic, religious, national, and lesbian, gay, bisexual, transgender (LGBT) minorities.

In its October rule of law report, the European Commission flagged that the efficiency of civil justice has deteriorated in recent years and that France adheres to media pluralism and independence, despite a surge of online and offline threats against journalists.

Covid-19

France's state of health emergency, declared in March in response to the Covid-19 pandemic, was criticized by rights groups, lawyers, magistrates, and the Human Rights Consultative Commission for giving excessive power to the executive branch to restrict freedoms. Lockdown was imposed from March 16 to May 11. The law lifting the state of emergency in July maintained some emergency powers. On October 17, the state of emergency was declared again. Parliament adopted a law extending the state of health emergency until February 16. Lockdown was imposed again on October 30, for at least four weeks.

In March, the government adopted a massive aid plan for companies, employees, and independent workers and ensured the right to parental leave for childcare. The nongovernmental organization (NGO) Secours Populaire estimated in September that one out of three people had lost income since the first lockdown and millions of people faced poverty. The unemployment insurance agency (Unedic) expected 420,000 additional unemployed persons in 2020 compared to 2019. The government extended the normal winter evictions ban until July 10.

Schools were closed for 14 weeks, during which the government organized on-line classes, but children have unequal access to computers and the internet. The United Nations Children's Fund (UNICEF) France and other groups pointed to the disproportionate impact of school closures on children in child protection structures and living in precarious situations. In April, the education minister said that 15 to 25 percent of children in overseas departments were falling behind in school during lockdown compared to 4 percent of students in metropolitan France.

In mid-April, the government extended the legal timeframe for medical abortion at home from seven to nine weeks to minimize hospital visits during the pandemic.

Law Enforcement and Police Abuse

In September, the Interior Ministry published a new National Scheme for Law Enforcement, following criticism of police crowd control and anti-riot tactics during demonstrations in 2018 and 2019. It replaces the controversial GLI-F4 tear gas grenade by a non-explosive grenade, called GM2L, which releases tear gas while having a deafening effect and has also been criticized by rights groups. The scheme fails to ban the use of other weapons, such as rubber bullet launchers, which have injured thousands of people, despite calls from the French ombudsperson and rights groups. Journalists and rights groups raised concerns about new rules that could hamper the ability to observe and report on demonstrations.

Discriminatory police identity checks continued, including during the enforcement of Covid-19 lockdown measures. Human Rights Watch found that police target minority youth, including children as young as 12, for the stops, which often involve invasive, humiliating body pat-downs and searches of personal belongings.

Following demonstrations against police abuse in France, President Emmanuel Macron said he wanted to generalize the wearing of body cameras by police officers by the end of his term in 2022. Rights groups and lawyers have long stressed that body cameras alone are not an effective means of combating ethnic profiling.

Unaccompanied Migrant Children's Rights

The French National Human Rights Consultative Commission (CNCDH) and the French Ombudsperson said authorities do not guarantee to unaccompanied migrant children access to basic rights and the care to which they are entitled. Child protection authorities in different regions of the country failed to provide shelter and other essential services even during the Covid-19 pandemic, putting them at further risk.

In April, a court ordered authorities in Marseille and Gap to provide unaccompanied children with shelter, more than a month after lockdown measures were implemented. On March 30, the European Court for Human Rights (ECtHR) ordered France to provide a Guinean boy "housing and food until the end of the [COVID-19] lockdown" after he ended up on the streets when authorities refused to recognize him as a child.

Unaccompanied children camped in a Paris park for a month in July before the authorities gave them shelter in a gymnasium and a few weeks later in a hotel. At time of writing, they were still awaiting placement in permanent accommodations.

In June, the ECtHR ruled against France for detaining and deporting in November 2013 two unaccompanied children, aged 3 and 5 at the time, from Mayotte, a French overseas department, to Comoros.

France committed in May to welcome 350 unaccompanied children from overcrowded and unsuitable refugee camps on the Greek Aegean islands by the end of the year. In late August, it relocated the first 49 children. After a fire destroyed the Moria camp on Lesbos in early September, France announced it will relocate up to 150 additional children. In November, it relocated 54 children.

Migrants and Asylum Seekers' Rights

In July, the ECtHR ruled that France violated the rights of three asylum seekers in depriving them material and financial support to which they were entitled, forcing them to live in the streets in "inhuman and degrading living conditions."

In Calais, NGOs providing assistance to migrants and asylum seekers reported continued harassment and abuse by police against migrants and aid workers. In

September, the interior minister prohibited food distribution by NGOs not authorized or contracted by the State through December 14. The French Ombudsperson said the measure constitutes "discrimination based on nationality."

France continued to detain people in immigration detention centers during the pandemic despite calls in March from the French Ombudsperson and the General Controller for Prisons for their closure given the risks of contracting Covid-19 and the fact that deportations could not be carried out in a reasonable timeframe due to travel restrictions. In September, the government announced it would use a detention center outside Paris for people who tested positive for the virus that causes Covid-19 while they awaited deportation.

Discrimination and Intolerance

In June, the CNCDH published data on bias crimes in 2019 from the Interior Ministry: racist acts increased by almost 57 percent compared to 2018, with anti-Semitic acts increasing by 27 percent, anti-Muslim acts by 54 percent, and "all other racist acts" by 131 percent. The ministry's statistics unit recorded 5,350 victims of offenses due to ethnicity, nationality, religion, or race in 2019, an increase of 11 percent over 2018.

In May, the ECtHR ruled that France breached the rights to private and family life and to an effective remedy of several Roma families when it dismantled the informal settlement where they lived outside Paris without offering alternative accommodation.

Sexual Orientation and Gender Identity

In June, SOS Homophobie, an NGO, said it received 26 percent more reports of physical and verbal abuse targeting lesbian, gay, bisexual, transgender, and intersex people for 2019 compared to 2018. The number of recorded physical attacks against transgender people increased by 130 percent.

In August, the National Assembly adopted a bill allowing lesbian couples and single women to access fertility treatments available currently only to heterosexual couples. The bill, under examination in the Senate at time of writing, excludes transgender persons from these treatments.

Women's Rights

Rights groups and feminist organizations, as well as a Senate report, point to the lack of resources allocated to implement government measures announced in 2019 against domestic violence. According to French authorities, reports of domestic violence rose by more than 30 percent during the first week of lockdown. Service providers and women's rights groups said the government response did not ensure adequate support for victims during the pandemic. By December, 90 women had been killed by a current or former intimate partner in 2020. In July, Parliament approved a law increasing sentences for perpetrators whose actions led to a victim's suicide or attempted suicide and permitting doctors to break patient confidentiality in cases where they believe there is immediate danger to a victim's life.

In April, the CNCDH called on France to ratify by the end of 2020 International Labour Organization C190 Convention concerning the elimination of violence and harassment in the world of work.

In October, the National Assembly adopted a bill, before the Senate at time of writing, extending the legal deadline for abortion on any grounds from 12 to 14 weeks.

Disability Rights

In July, the French Ombudsperson welcomed progress on implementation of the Convention on the Rights of Persons with Disabilities, such as guarantees of the rights to vote and marry for all adults living under some form of guardianship, while pointing at shortcomings, particularly in terms of accessibility of infrastructure open to the public, housing, public transport, and online public services. In 2019, 23 percent of the ombudsperson's cases concerned discrimination based on disability.

Prisons

In January, the ECtHR found that detention conditions amounted to cruel and degrading treatment in a joined case involving 32 inmates in 6 prisons. The court ordered France to take action to end overcrowding, improve general conditions, and establish an effective preventive remedy for inmates to seek redress.

In October, the Constitutional Court ruled that French legislators should pass a new law by March 2021 allowing people in pretrial detention to enforce their right that their conditions of incarceration do not violate human dignity.

Between mid-March and late May, during Covid-19 lockdown measures, around 7,000 detainees serving short sentences were released as part of measures to reduce crowding and prevent further spread of the disease.

Counterterrorism

In August, the Constitutional Court struck down a provision in a 2020 security law that imposed restrictions on freedom of movement and other security measures on persons convicted for terrorism offenses after they served their prison sentence.

In April, France repatriated a seriously ill 7-year-old French girl from a locked camp holding family members of Islamic State (ISIS) suspects in northeast Syria, followed in June by a group of 10 children.

Taking a case-by-case approach, French authorities have brought back a total of 28 French children since March 2019, leaving more than 250 French children and their mothers in indefinite and arbitrary detention in deeply degrading, and often inhuman and life-threatening conditions, despite calls by France's independent rights institutions and UN bodies for their repatriation. France continued to refuse to repatriate French men and boys detained without judicial review in northeast Syria for suspected ISIS links.

In September, the trial of 14 people for the January 2015 attacks against the satirical newspaper Charlie Hebdo and a kosher supermarket began in Paris. Later that month, a man stabbed two people outside the newspaper's former office. In October, a man beheaded a history teacher who had shown caricatures of the Prophet Muhammad in a class on freedom of expression. At the end of the month, three people were killed and several were injured in a knife attack inside a church in Nice. The government responded by announcing it would close some mosques and Muslim associations, and deport foreigners it deemed "radical-ized."

Environment and Human Rights

A group of 15 children lodged a United Nations complaint against France and four other countries for its lagging efforts to fight the global climate crisis. The government disputed that the complaint falls within the jurisdiction of the child rights treaty. France's independent High Council for the Climate reported that France is not on track to meet its emissions reductions target.

Foreign Policy

France claimed multilateralism, human rights, and international humanitarian law as key priorities for its diplomacy but the record is mixed.

France played an active role at the UN Security Council to try to secure access to humanitarian aid in Syria, and backed the efforts at the Organization for the Pro-hibition of Chemical Weapons to investigate chemical attacks by Syrian govern-ment forces. In June and September, it also defended the International Criminal Court against attacks by the Trump administration and firmly condemned un-precedented US sanctions against court officials.

In October, France was elected for a three-year membership term at the UN Human Rights Council. As an observer state for most of the year, France showed little leadership on addressing specific human rights situations and was some-times slow to endorse resolutions and joint statements proposed by others, such as on China, Libya, Saudi Arabia, and Yemen.

France increased its military presence in the Sahel amid continued attacks by armed Islamist groups against civilians, including French aid workers, and se-rious human rights abuses by security forces and affiliated militias in Burkina Faso, Mali, and Niger.

France continued to sell arms to Saudi Arabia and the United Arab Emirates de-spite risks they could be used against civilians in Yemen. It also provided uncon-ditional military and strategic support to the government of Egypt's President Abdel Fattah al-Sisi, despite its dismal human rights record.

France has slowly emerged from its silence over China's attacks on human rights but failed to take concrete measures. In July, France criticized the National Security Law in Hong Kong and in September, President Macron called for a UN mission to go to Xinjiang.

In August, Macron co-hosted with the UN a donors' conference to mobilize international aid for the Lebanese people after the explosion at Beirut's port and pressed Lebanese political leaders to commit to a roadmap of structural reforms, including to fight corruption.

President Macron took a strong stance against the flawed elections in Belarus in August and expressed support for the peaceful demonstrators. In September, France supported the triggering of inquiries into abuses committed in Belarus at the Organisation for Security and Cooperation in Europe and the UN Human Rights Council.

In August, France condemned the poisoning of Russian opposition leader Alexei Navalny and called on Russia to investigate.

In September, France reiterated its position against ratifying the European Union-Mercosur trade agreement until concerns regarding deforestation of the Brazilian Amazon were addressed.

Georgia

Political tensions rose in Georgia following the October 31 parliamentary elections. The ruling Georgian Dream (GD) party maintained a parliamentary majority amid allegations of fraud, prompting the opposition to boycott the new parliament. International observers, led by the Organization for Security and Co-operation in Europe (OSCE), concluded that the elections were held in a competitive environment, but marred by "widespread allegations of voter pressure."

Lack of accountability for law enforcement abuses persisted. Other areas of concern included threats to media freedom, disproportionately harsh drug policy, and discrimination against lesbian, gay, bisexual, and transgender (LGBT) people.

Parliament adopted much-needed labor reform, restoring some protections to labor rights.

Covid-19

Georgia went into lockdown shortly after announcing its first confirmed Covid-19 case at the end of February. It declared a state of emergency, closed borders and airports, restricted movement inside the country, and closed all educational institutions, affecting close to 600,000 school children. Authorities imposed a nationwide curfew, locked down the four largest cities, and managed to contain the virus at low levels in the initial months.

The pandemic had a devastating impact on the economy, which shrunk by over 16 percent in the second quarter, resulting in a spike in unemployment and poverty. To mitigate the fallout, the government enacted a US$1.5 billion anti-crisis plan in April, including a social assistance package for individuals, and tax relief and exemptions for businesses for at least six months. Three months before the October elections, the government announced additional anti-crisis measures of US$132 million, including a further social assistance package. Opposition and some civil society groups saw the steps as "manipulation to attract voters."

The state of emergency ended on May 23. But a day earlier, citing the ongoing Covid-19 pandemic, parliament granted the government the power to restrict certain rights, such as freedom of movement, freedom of assembly, as well as property, economic, and labor rights without declaring a state of emergency until July 15. The parliament later extended this through the end of 2020. Human rights groups in Georgia noted that the manner of this granting of extensive government power without parliamentary oversight was incompatible with the Constitution.

Parliamentary Elections

Although GD's electoral victory allowed it to maintain its parliamentary majority, opposition parties rejected the outcome, called for snap elections, and at time of writing, were boycotting their seats in the new parliament. The OSCE found that the vote respected fundamental freedoms but was marred by a "blurring of the border between the ruling party and the state." Local election-monitoring groups called it "the least democratic and free among elections" held under GD rule. They criticized election-day incidents such as verbal and physical confrontations against journalists and observers, numerous cases of breach of voting secrecy, and vote-buying. On November 8, police used water cannons, without warning, against dozens of peaceful protesters who had gathered outside the central election commission building to protest alleged election violations.

Parliament modified its mixed electoral system following months of protests that started in 2019, and lengthy negotiations between the GD and opposition parties. The reform decreased the number of single-mandate seats and increased proportional representation to 120 deputies in the 150-member legislature.

Gender quotas, introduced via election legislation amendments adopted in July, require women to make up at least 25 percent of candidates proposed by political parties or election blocs.

Lack of Accountability for Law Enforcement Abuses

The State Inspector's Office, an independent body created in 2018 to investigate abuses committed by law enforcement, became operational in November 2019. By August, the office received over 1,300 reports of alleged abuses by law enforcement and other officials and launched criminal investigations in 168 cases, mostly into abuse of authority, but also inhuman and degrading treatment. In the same period, the Ombudsman's Office received 68 complaints of ill-treatment by prison staff or police.

Lack of accountability for law enforcement abuses persisted, particularly with regard to incidents that took place before the State Inspector's Office became operational. The investigation into June 2019 events, when riot police fired rubber bullets and used tear gas against thousands of protesters outside the parliament building in Tbilisi, continued to be largely one-sided. According to the public defender, who was allowed to monitor the proceedings, the investigation "only focused on the offenses committed by rank-and-file police officers but failed to objectively or fully assess command responsibility."

Freedom of Media

In February, dozens of employees of Adjara TV and Radio company, a publicly funded broadcaster based in Batumi, held a silent protest in the channel's newsroom to protest the new management's alleged interference with the broadcaster's editorial policy. The ruling party members had openly expressed discontent with editorial policy under the previous management. In March, the new management dismissed one of the organizers of the silent protest, Teona Bakuridze, anchor of the broadcaster's main news program, allegedly for "gravely violating" the broadcaster's internal regulations. Reporters without Borders (RSF) condemned Bakuridze's dismissal and called on the Georgian authorities to "stop political pressure" on Adjara TV.

Later in May, Adjara TV's director Giorgi Kokhreidze fired Malkhaz Rekhviashvili, host of a talk show and head of the Alternative Trade Union of Adjara TV. Rekhviashvili said that he was dismissed for his Facebook posts that criticized disciplinary measures against his colleagues. Management claimed the posts discredited the TV channel. On July 30, the new management fired three more employees, including two active members of the Alternative Trade Union who also organized a protest four days earlier against its editorial policies. The employees were later reinstated after more than 280 Adjara TV employees signed a petition demanding they be allowed to return.

In July, the State Security Service initiated an investigation into an alleged act of sabotage in connection with a story aired by the pro-opposition Mtavari Arkhi. The story alleged that local officials had falsified Covid-19 data and were engaged in other misconduct. Local human rights groups regarded the investigation as a dangerous precedent for interference with freedom of expression, especially considering the authorities' negative attitude towards Mtavari Arkhi's editorial policies.

In July, parliament amended the Law on Electronic Communications, giving the Communications Commission, the broadcasting and communications regulatory body, the power to appoint a "special manager" to oversee any electronic communications company that fails to enforce the commission's decisions. The law authorizes such "special managers" to make any managerial decision, except those regarding selling the company's shares. The Media Advocacy Coalition, an alliance of local watchdog groups, and Reporters without Borders criticized the law for restricting broadcast media freedom. The Communications Commission said the bill only affects mobile and internet providers, not media or broadcasting.

Labor Rights

In September, the parliament adopted sweeping labor reforms, expanding the Labor Inspectorate's mandate to monitor all labor standards guaranteed under Georgian law. The amendments also introduced new regulations for work hours, overtime, night shifts, mandatory weekly rest, and breaks during shifts.

Workplace safety and decent labor conditions remain a persistent problem. According to the Georgian Trade Union Confederation, 22 workers died and 110 were injured in work-related accidents through September.

In June, several hundred coal workers in Tkibuli organized protests after 22 miners got stuck in a mine for several hours due to a malfunctioning elevator. Earlier in March, three miners from the same company were hospitalized because of gas poisoning in a mine.

Sexual Orientation and Gender Identity

Authorities continue to refuse to allow transgender people to obtain legal gender recognition, without sex-altering surgery. Lack of legal gender recognition represents a serious obstacle in the daily lives of transgender people in Georgia, including their ability to find jobs.

Several dire cases highlighted how the economic fallout from Covid-19 exacerbated poor living arrangements for transgender people, many of whom work in the informal sector. In April, transgender women held a protest asking for the government's assistance, as they lost their income and means to cover their rent. At the protest, a 19-year-old transgender woman attempted suicide by self-immolation in a desperate effort to draw attention to the lack of government social support for transgender people. Local human rights groups also criticized the government's Covid-19 related Anti-Crisis Economic Plan for failure to address the social needs of transgender women and queer people, many of whom lack alternative means of support due to family rejection and social opprobrium.

Drug Policy

Authorities maintained harsh drug laws that can be used to prosecute people for mere possession or consumption (except for marijuana) of drugs for personal use.

In June, the Constitutional Court ruled as unconstitutional, imprisonment for possession of drugs in quantities that are too small to cause intoxication. However, draft legislative reform that would have introduced public health approaches to drug use and largely overhaul punitive practices remained stalled in parliament.

Key International Actors

In March, OSCE Representative on Freedom of the Media Harlem Désir expressed concern about developments at Adjara TV, and "about reported management's interference in its editorial policy."

In a May joint statement, the United Nations, European Union, and Council of Europe (CoE) representatives in Georgia, together with the ambassadors of 21 countries, urged Georgian officials to address LGBT rights during the Covid-19 pandemic and beyond.

In July, the EU delegation in Georgia welcomed the adoption of the election reform package and expressed regret that Georgia did not use this opportunity to address other electoral shortcomings, such as voter intimidation, dispute resolution, and commission compositions.

In September, the EU and US ambassadors in Georgia also welcomed adoption of the labor reforms as a step towards delivering on EU commitments.

In September, the European Parliament adopted a report on the implementation of the EU's Association Agreement with Georgia, positively assessing Georgia's progress in adopting reforms and calling on the authorities to "refrain from pursuing politically-motivated cases" against opposition, to reform selection procedures for judges, and to investigate all incidents of excessive use of force by law enforcement.

In October, the EU expressed concerns over the adoption of legislative amendments on the selection process of Georgia's Supreme Court judges prior to the publication of the urgent Venice Commission Opinion on the legislation.

In November, US Secretary of State Michael Pompeo visited Georgia to discuss, among other things, Georgia's post-election political crisis, the state of its judiciary, and the US-Georgia partnership.

The International Criminal Court (ICC) continued its investigation into war crimes and crimes against humanity committed during the August 2008 Russia-Georgia war over South Ossetia.

Germany

Nine people were killed in February in a racist attack. Right-wing extremist structures are surfacing within the police and armed forces. Crimes committed based on far-right and anti-Semitic ideology remain a serious concern. Protests against the government's Covid-19 measures attracted people with neo-Nazi and antisemitic views. Vulnerable groups, such as migrant workers, asylum seekers, and homeless people were disproportionately affected by the Covid-19 pandemic. In its October rule of law report, the European Commission praised media freedom and pluralism in Germany but flagged some concerns about increasing attacks on journalists.

Discrimination and Intolerance

Racism, antisemitism, and Islamophobia, including violent hate crimes, remained a concern.

According to government data, in the first half of 2020, 9,305 "far-right politically motivated crimes" were reported, 390 of which involved violence, compared to 8,605 during the same period in 2019. According to the same data, as of July, 876 antisemitic crimes, including 21 violent attacks, had been reported. At time of writing, 469 suspects of antisemitic crimes had been investigated, with 4 arrests. In the first half of 2020, 463 anti-Islamic offenses were reported to police, injuring 21. Thirty-three attacks targeted mosques. No one had been convicted at time of writing.

In a March report, the European Commission against Racism and Intolerance (ECRI), a Council of Europe monitoring body, said the police do not sufficiently co-operate with civil society to detect and register hate crimes, resulting in under-reporting of such offenses.

A report by the Ministry of Interior in the same month recorded 1,620 attacks on refugees and 128 attacks on refugee camps in 2019.

In June, the trial began against two men accused of involvement in the killing of local politician Walter Lübcke in Hesse in June 2019. The prosecution relied on evidence indicating that the defendants were involved in neo-Nazi circles and targeted Lübcke because of his pro-refugee stance.

A lawyer, politicians, activists, and public figures received threats throughout the year. The threats, which started in August 2018, were sent by a secretive group calling itself "NSU 2.0," referring to the German neo-Nazi group that between 2000 and 2007 killed at least 10 people in Germany. Investigations initiated in 2018 revealed that personal information of victims was retrieved from police computers, intensifying the public debate over right-wing extremism within police forces. By mid-September, 25 investigations against 50 suspects, including police, were ongoing.

In October, the Federal Office for the Protection of the Constitution for the first time presented a report on right-wing extremism within the police, documenting 350 suspected cases between March 2017 and March 2020.

In September, 30 police officers were suspended and placed under disciplinary investigations for being part of a chat group where racist and extremist material was shared, including symbols banned under German law. In February, 7 police cadets were suspended for exchanging antisemitic and misogynistic content in chat groups, while in October, 26 cadets were found to be members of a racist chat group.

In January, the Military Counterintelligence Service said it was investigating 550 soldiers from the German Army for alleged right-wing extremism. In July, the German defense minister partially dissolved the elite unit, commando special forces (KSK) over concerns of right-wing extremism in its ranks.

In its March report, ECRI found that police authorities are unaware of or unwilling to acknowledge evidence of extensive use of racial profiling by the police and recommended the government commission a study on police racial profiling.

Becoming the first federal state to do so, Berlin adopted a law in June entitling victims to seek compensation for discrimination by public authorities, including police.

In August, the federal labor court upheld a 2018 court decision granting financial compensation to a woman who was not hired for a teaching position because she wore a headscarf.

International Justice

In April, the trial of two alleged former Syrian intelligence officials began in Koblenz in a landmark case, under Germany's universal jurisdiction laws, concerning torture in a Syrian prison.

Business and Human Rights

In August, the government stated that over 80 percent of German businesses were not meeting their due diligence obligations under the National Action Plan on Business and Human Rights. In the same month, the ministers of Labor and Development announced a law to make human rights due diligence throughout global supply chains mandatory. However, the minister of economy opposed key elements of the proposal, and no agreement had been found at time of writing.

Migrants and Asylum Seekers

In the first 8 months of 2020, 74,429 people applied for asylum in Germany, almost 35 percent less than in the same period in 2019. Most applicants came from Syria, Iraq, Afghanistan, and Turkey. By the end of August, 43,316 applications were pending.

By September 30, Germany had relocated 713 asylum seekers and refugees from Greece, as part of a commitment in March to accept children with health conditions and their close family members, or unaccompanied children below the age of 14. In September, Germany said it would also relocate 1,500 people from Greek islands, including from Moria's camp on the island of Lesbos that was ravaged by fires, who have already been granted protection.

Surveillance and Terrorism, Counterterrorism

In February, a German far-right gunman killed nine people from ethnic minority groups in attacks on two shisha bars in the city of Hanau before killing his mother and himself. The attacker had published an online manifesto containing xenophobic, racist, and misogynist views.

In July, the trial began for the gunman who in 2019 livestreamed his attacks on a synagogue and a restaurant in the city of Halle in which he killed two people.

The gunman had posted antisemitic and misogynist comments online. At time of writing, the trial was ongoing.

Also at time of writing, there were several constitutional complaints were pending against changes in laws in some states broadening police powers while failing to increase transparency and oversight. These measures include broad surveillance powers, such as the use of malware and extension of preventive custody.

In May, the German constitutional court ruled that the German Federal Intelligence Service's (BND) practice of monitoring worldwide internet traffic was unconstitutional and did not ensure the protection of media freedom. Reporters without Borders said reforms proposed in response to the ruling further widen BND powers.

In a September report, parliament's scientific service found that planned amendments to the Network Enforcement Act (NetzDG) are not in line with the German constitution. The planned changes, designed to combat hate crime, require internet companies to report suspected illegal content and some of the poster's personal information, including their IP address, to the Federal Criminal Police Office.

In November 2019, the government repatriated a German woman and her three children from a locked camp in northeast Syria for Islamic State (ISIS) suspects. More than 80 other German ISIS suspects and family members are still held in filthy, overcrowded, and life-threatening conditions in northeast Syria.

Covid-19

Germany took steps to mitigate the impact of the lockdown it implemented in response to Covid-19. The government introduced the largest financial aid package in its history to stabilize the economy and prevent unemployment.

Despite intense lobbying from the car industry, the government did not include subsidies for petrol and diesel-driven cars in its recovery package, opting to support less polluting electric cars. The government facilitated access to state social support and introduced temporary bans on termination of rental contracts between April and June if tenants were unable to pay rent. But the vulnerable situation of already-marginalized populations deteriorated.

Asylum seekers living in large-scale shared accommodation had a higher risk of contracting Covid-19, according to the German public health institute (RKI), and several camps faced large outbreaks among residents. In May, two-thirds of the roughly 600 people housed in a reception center in Bavaria, contracted Covid-19, highlighting the lack of sufficient space to practice social distancing in camps.

Large outbreaks of Covid-19 among meat plant workers, including in June among more than 2,000 employees at Tönnies, a meat processing company, highlighted the deplorable living and exploitative working conditions in the industry. Many employees were migrants from Romania and Bulgaria and worked for sub-contractors. In July, the government presented a bill to improve conditions in the meat processing industry, by banning the use of subcontractors and increasing companies' accountability for health and safety of workers.

According to the Federal Working Group on Homeless People, a nongovernmental group, the pandemic exacerbated the precarious situation of homeless people, further limiting their access to psychosocial and medical support, means of income, and state financial support.

In March, schools closed as a measure to reduce the spread of Covid-19 and lessons were held online for most children, although children of essential workers were able to access school. Children from low-income households, including refugee children, often lacked equipment and an internet connection to participate in online lessons. Evidence suggests that Germany is lagging in developing digital learning in schools.

Protests against government measures to tackle Covid-19, such as the obligation to wear masks in certain places, attracted people with antisemitic and neo-Nazi views. Following two mass rallies in Berlin in early and late August, the German Union of Journalists documented attacks against nine camera crews, twenty-two journalists, and threats against two editorial departments.

Women's Rights

In April, the government-supported national helpline for violence against women documented a 20 percent increase in requests for consultation related to domestic violence. This increase persisted in subsequent months, according to the helpline.

Data published in March by the Federal Statistics Authority showed that women in Germany still earn significantly less than men, with an average 20 percent gender pay gap.

Persistent barriers to accessing legal abortion remain due to a law prohibiting "advertising" of abortion, which significantly restricts sharing of information about abortion services, and lack of medical personnel trained to perform abortions.

Foreign Policy

The government considered the protection of human rights as one of the central pillars of its foreign policy, advocated for international human rights standards, and played an important role in the fight against impunity. But this approach was contested when other policy priorities were at stake.

During the year, Germany was a non-permanent member of the United Nations Security Council and elected to the UN Human Rights Council. In New York, the German mission successfully moved human rights high up on the Security Council's agenda: it invited the UN Human Rights Commissioner to New York, regularly organized meetings with civil society representatives, and addressed crisis situations. In the Human Rights Council, Germany engaged in getting a swift response to the Covid-19 pandemic but did not live up to expectations on specific country situations where it could have demonstrated leadership more often.

During Germany's European Union presidency in the second half of the year, the government identified the crisis of rule of law within the EU, the reform of European migration policy, and an EU-wide sanctions regime against human rights abusers as important areas for human rights protection. But during this period, EU institutions did not pursue more decisive action against rule of law declines in countries including Hungary and Poland.

In its bilateral relations, Germany addressed human rights violations with countries such as China and Russia. Foreign Minister Heiko Maas requested an independent UN investigation into the political education camps in Xinjiang and the withdrawal of the security law in Hong Kong, although a vocal stance on China by other ministers of the government was often missing. Germany offered protection and medical treatment for the Russian opposition politician, Alexei Navalny.

The German human rights commissioner in the Foreign Office, Bärbel Kofler, was a strong voice for human rights defenders and independent civil society worldwide. The Human Rights Committee in parliament was an important actor for the protection of international standards.

In early 2020, the government disputed the admissibility of a UN complaint filed last year by a group of 15 children against Germany and four other countries for its lagging efforts to fight the global climate crisis. The government argued that the complaint does not fall within the jurisdiction of the child rights treaty and that its obligations do not extend to the 14 children living outside Germany because emissions in one country do not foreseeably affect the realization of rights in other countries.

Greece

In October, the leadership and multiple members of the neo-Nazi Golden Dawn party were convicted of running a criminal organization. Greece continued to host large numbers of asylum seekers while failing to protect their rights. Thousands are confined to the islands in abysmal conditions amid the Covid-19 pandemic under discriminatory lockdowns. A new law limits asylum seekers' access to protection. Unaccompanied children are often held in police custody or detention. Civil society organizations face legislative restrictions, while nongovernmental organizations (NGOs) and aid workers working with refugees are smeared by government officials. A new protest law unduly restricts the right to freedom of peaceful assembly. Survivors of gender-based violence encounter obstacles in seeking protection and justice. Law enforcement abuse remains a widespread practice. Hate crimes and anti-immigrant sentiment remain an issue.

Covid-19

By mid-October, Greece had 25,802 confirmed Covid-19 cases and 520 deaths from the virus.

A nationwide lockdown implemented in March was eased in May for the general population, but the government maintained discriminatory restrictions on thousands of migrants and asylum seekers living in camps on the islands and mainland, and failed to take measures to alleviate overcrowding or improve sanitation in the camps.

Cases soared starting in August and continuing at time of writing, adding pressure on the already-strained public health sector, after a decade of economic crisis and austerity measures that included drastic budget cuts for public hospitals. Healthcare workers protested throughout the year against working conditions, and lack of staff, medicine, testing, and equipment in public hospitals.

School closures in Greece began in early March and students and teachers faced obstacles in distance learning due to lack of equipment and network problems. Before the pandemic, an estimated one in five students attending the poorest quartile of Greek schools did not have access to a computer they could use for schoolwork, while one in ten did not have access to the internet, according to an analysis by the United Nations Education, Scientific and Cultural Organization (UNESCO).

Schools reopened in mid-September amid student protests over unsafe conditions; within a week, dozens of schools closed again after staff or students contracted Covid-19. At time of writing, hundreds of schools across Greece were occupied by high school students demanding more teachers, smaller classrooms, permanent cleaning staff, and rejecting a government proposal to install cameras in schools for e-learning.

As of early October, children on the Greek mainland, living in migrant camps under lockdown due to Covid-19 cases in these facilities, were unable to attend schools, and only around 50 of more than 4,000 school-age migrant and refugee children on the Aegean islands of Lesbos and Samos were enrolled in schools, according to humanitarian agencies.

In May, according to the National Confederation of Disabled People Greece, authorities failed to ensure support for people with disabilities who were disproportionally affected by the prolonged confinement in their homes, in closed institutions or supported living structures.

Domestic violence spiked during the first month of lockdown, with the governmental emergency hotline receiving 1,760 calls about alleged acts of domestic violence in April compared to 325 in March. The government launched TV, online, and radio campaigns to encourage reporting of cases during the pandemic.

Inmates in prisons across the country protested Covid-19-related measures limiting leave and contact with relatives and demanded measures to tackle chronic overcrowding and improve conditions and care.

Migrants and Asylum Seekers

With limited exceptions, the government maintained its policy of blocking asylum seekers who arrive on the Aegean islands from moving to the mainland. The containment policy trapped thousands in overcrowded and abysmal conditions with limited access to protection, health care, adequate water, sanitation, and hygiene products to limit the spread of Covid-19. At time of writing, 19,929 asylum seekers were on the islands, including more than 16,000 in camps designed to host around 13,000.

Fires destroyed Europe's largest refugee camp, Moria camp, on Lesbos, in September, leaving thousands, including more than 4,000 children, homeless and without food and water until the majority were rehoused in a temporary tent camp.

According to aid groups, authorities failed to provide camp residents in the new camp with adequate and safe access to water, education, sanitation, supplies for menstrual hygiene management, and health care, or sufficient protection from the elements and from sexual and gender-based violence and harassment. Services for survivors and those at risk of violence remained insufficient, and access to pre- and post-natal care and support for people with newborns remained limited. At time of writing, there were 19 confirmed Covid-19 cases in the new camp, with a population of about 9,500. There were concerns about the risk of lead poisoning in the new camp due to its location on a former military shooting range.

A new asylum law that entered into force in January undermines access to protection and exposes asylum seekers to greater risks of deportation and longer periods of detention. In July, the United Nations Working Group on Arbitrary Detention (WGAD) said new provisions appear to introduce more restrictive procedures that may compromise the general legal principle that detention of asylum seekers should be exceptional.

Following Turkey's announcement in February that it would no longer stop asylum seekers and migrants from leaving Turkish territory to reach the European Union, thousands of people attempted to cross by sea and overland in March.

In response, Greece barred the lodging of asylum claims for anyone crossing the border irregularly during that month, prosecuted people for irregular entry, arbitrarily detained nearly 2,000 people in unacceptable conditions in two newly established detention sites on the mainland, under the pretext of Covid-19, and violently pushed back people attempting to enter Greece.

Since then, law enforcement officers have summarily returned thousands of people to Turkey, including people picked up by police hundreds of kilometers inside Greece. In June, Greece's Supreme Court Prosecutor opened a criminal investigation into the pushbacks that occurred in March in Evros, including into the alleged shooting and deaths of two people by Greek security forces. The UN WGAD urged authorities to promptly and fully investigate all allegations of pushbacks, including any acts of violence or ill-treatment, and to ensure that such practices do not occur in the future.

In June, the Greek government began evicting more than 11,000 recognized refugees from government-provided apartments, hotels, and camps, leaving hundreds of people— including families with children, pregnant and single women, as well as people with disabilities—on the streets. The government announced in September a two-month pilot plan to house recognized refugees leaving the islands until they find a more permanent home.

Unaccompanied Children

At time of writing, 176 unaccompanied children were still detained in abysmal conditions in police stations and detention centers across Greece, under the so-called protective custody regime, while hundreds more were in camps with adults or homeless due to authorities' failure to provide adequate shelter or foster care. In May, parliament decreased the time such children can be detained from 45 to 25 days.

At time of writing, 11 countries had agreed to relocate by the end of the year at least 1,600 unaccompanied children from overcrowded and dangerous camps on the Greek islands to other EU countries. By October 30, 362 unaccompanied children and 1,089 "vulnerable" people had been relocated from Greece to other EU countries, including 920 to Germany.

Attacks on Civil Society

News emerged in September that 33 members of nongovernmental groups, and two "third-country nationals," are facing criminal charges of espionage, violating state secrets, and belonging to a criminal organization for allegedly facilitating the irregular entry of foreign nationals from Turkey to Lesbos.

During the Greece-Turkey border crisis in March, a series of attacks against staff of international and nongovernmental organizations (NGOs), including UNHCR, aid workers and journalists, was reported after inflammatory comments were made by government officials targeting NGOs working with refugees. On Lesbos, angry mobs attacked NGO facilities and vehicles with bats. Some NGOs suspended operations and even evacuated volunteers back to Athens. Threats from right-wing sources and intimidation of aid workers and vandalism and arson directed against NGO properties continued at time of writing.

With legislative changes adopted in March, May, and September, the government introduced strict and intrusive registration and reporting requirements for nongovernmental groups and all their members, staff, and volunteers, working in the areas of asylum, migration, and social inclusion, raising concerns about disproportionate interference with the rights to privacy, data protection (it requires publication of personal data of donors and supporters), and freedom of association. In July, the Expert Council on NGO Law at the Council of Europe concluded that the new regulations should be substantially revised so that they are brought into line with European standards.

In its October rule of law report, the European Commission said that despite reforms, concerns remain over the efficiency and quality of the justice system. It also flagged concerns about attacks and threats against journalists and the narrowing space for civil society groups, particularly those working on the rights of migrants and asylum seekers.

In July, the government passed a highly controversial law regulating demonstrations that raised concerns about undue interference with the right to peaceful assembly. The law gives authorities broad discretion to disband assemblies that have not been notified, even though it allows for spontaneous protests, and provides that organizers can be held accountable for harm or damage caused by protesters under certain circumstances.

Racism and Intolerance

Far-right groups continued to campaign against asylum seekers on the islands, and there were reports of attacks across the country on persons perceived to be migrants or Muslims. Statistics for hate crimes by the nongovernmental Racist

Violence Recording Network for 2019, released in July, showed a marked increase in recorded attacks on lesbian, gay, bisexual and transgender (LGBT) individuals compared to the previous year.

In a landmark ruling in October, the leadership, former MPs, and multiple members of the neo-Nazi Golden Dawn party, were convicted for constituting and/or participating in a criminal organization that orchestrated or colluded in the murder of the 34-year-old anti-fascist activist and rapper Pavlos Fyssas, the murder of 27-year-old Pakistani national Shehzad Luqman, and numerous other brutal attacks against migrants and trade unionists.

The trial of six people, including four police officers, for causing fatal bodily harm in the 2018 killing of 33-year-old queer activist and human rights defender Zak Kostopoulos began in October. Kostopoulos was brutally beaten up by two men after entering a jewelry shop in central Athens, while footage showed police violently attempting to arrest Kostopoulos while he lay on the ground.

Women's Rights

The UN Working Group on discrimination against women and girls expressed concern in June that survivors of domestic and family violence in Greece are routinely encouraged to engage in mediation with their abusers, noting that this is contrary to international standards, and that perpetrators are rarely prosecuted or punished.

In May, the European Court of Human Rights ordered Greece to ensure adequate health care and living conditions for a pregnant woman living in the Pyli camp on Kos Island. Even before the Covid-19 pandemic, the Greek government was not meeting international standards for health care, nutrition, and bedding for migrant pregnant people and new mothers.

In its June report on Greece, the UN Working Group on discrimination against women and girls said migrant and asylum-seeking women who are survivors of gender-based violence lack access to support and safety, and that there are insufficient shelters and emergency accommodations and inconsistent coordination of services.

Disability Rights

In July, the UN WGAD criticized the procedure for involuntary admission of persons with psychosocial disabilities to psychiatric hospitals, including the fact that police officers are frequently required, by order of the Public Prosecutor, to arrest persons who have been reported by relatives or neighbors to have a psychosocial disability.

Law Enforcement Abuse

In April, the Council of Europe Committee for the Prevention of Torture (CPT), said that ill-treatment by the police, especially against migrants and Roma, remains frequent, particularly in police facilities, and noted that most cases of alleged police ill-treatment are not prosecuted and only very few result in criminal sentences or even disciplinary sanctions. The CPT concluded that the current system of investigations into allegations of ill-treatment is not effective.

Guatemala

Since former President Jimmy Morales declined to extend the mandate of the United Nations-backed International Commission against Impunity in Guatemala (CICIG) in 2018, investigations have slowed down, limiting accountability for large-scale government corruption and abuses of power. Current President Alejandro Giammattei, who took office in January 2020, supported ending the mandate.

President Giammatei and his government have shown a hostile attitude toward the press and have been accused of hiding information about Covid-19 cases.

There are significant delays in the appointment of judges and high court justices. The congressional appointment process has been marred by allegations of corruption. Congress has flouted Constitutional Court rulings to ensure suitable candidates are appointed, instead ordering prosecutors to pursue criminal charges against Constitutional Court magistrates for ruling on the matter.

The Human Rights Ombudsperson faces a congressional effort to remove him and a possible criminal investigation for promoting LGBT and sexual and reproductive rights.

Guatemala faces challenges in protecting the rights of asylum seekers, human rights defenders, women and girls, people with disabilities, and lesbian, gay, bisexual, and transgender (LGBT) people.

Public Security, Corruption, and Criminal Justice

Violence and extortion by powerful criminal organizations, which the government has often been unable or unwilling to control, remain serious problems in Guatemala. Gang-related violence is an important factor prompting people, including unaccompanied children and young adults, to leave the country.

In recent years, investigations by the CICIG and the Attorney General's Office have exposed more than 60 corruption schemes, implicating officials in all three branches of government, and prompting the resignation and arrest, in 2015, of the country's then-president and vice-president.

However, long delays impede accountability, as courts often fail to respect legally mandated timeframes and may take months to reschedule suspended hearings. Criminal proceedings against powerful actors often suffer unreasonably long delays due to the extensive use of motions by criminal defendants. Intimidation of judges and prosecutors and corruption in the justice system remain problems.

Separation of Powers and Judicial Independence

Under Guatemalan law, Congress selects and appoints judges and justices from lists presented by Nominating Commissions. The process lacks a consistent system for ranking candidates and is marred by arbitrary decisions and conflicts of interest.

Thirteen seats on the Supreme Court and 135 seats on the Courts of Appeals for the 2019-2024 period should have been filled by the end of October 2019. On February 26, 2020, in response to a petition by prosecutors, the Constitutional Court suspended the appointment process, citing a criminal investigation that uncovered evidence of possible influence-peddling in the selection of judges. On May 6, the Constitutional Court ordered Congress to move forward with appointments but required lawmakers to consider whether candidates met constitutional requirements and whether their names had surfaced in the criminal investigation. At time of writing, Congress had yet to select judges and justices.

However, on June 28, Congress requested the Attorney General's Office to investigate the Constitutional Court justices who ruled on the selection process for alleged malfeasance, violating the Constitution, and abuse of power. These crimes carry sanctions of up to 10 years of prison.

On August 7, the Attorney General's Office announced an investigation into alleged crimes by dozens of public officials with immunity, including 92 members of Congress, 13 alternate justices of the Supreme Court, 7 members of the Permanent Commission of Congress, and 6 magistrates of the Constitutional Court.

Accountability for Past Human Rights Violations

The limited progress that Guatemala had been making in recent years to adjudicate major crimes seems to have come to a standstill.

In March 2019, Congress passed the second of three required approvals for a bill that would provide amnesty for genocide and other atrocities, in clear violation of international human rights law. The same month, the Inter-American Court of Human Rights ordered Guatemala, in a binding ruling, to shelve the proposed legislation. In July 2019, Guatemala's Constitutional Court issued a similar ruling. At time of writing, the bill had not been shelved.

Freedom of Expression

President Giammattei's government has shown open hostility toward the press and has limited access to information regarding confirmed cases and measures to address Covid-19.

In 2020, officials attacked media and individual journalists through discrediting remarks, false accusations, and anti-press rhetoric. The Attorney General's Office for Crimes against Journalists had, as of July, registered over 60 complaints of threats and attacks on journalists by private individuals, security forces, and public officials. Complaints included cases of theft, abuse, and murder.

Unidentified gunmen shot journalist Bryan Guerra, a reporter at cable news channel TLCOM, on February 27, and he died on March 3. At time of writing, Guatemalan authorities had not announced any progress in the investigation or identified a potential motive, adding Guerra's name to the list of 17 Guatemalan journalists killed between 2000 and 2020.

In September, Miguel Martínez, director of the Presidential Commission of the Center of Government—a commission of the executive branch in charge of coordinating, supporting, and advising the ministries—filed a criminal complaint alleging online media outlet Plaza Pública had harassed, threatened, and attempted to extort him and his family. The complaint came after Plaza Pública published a report on alleged business links between Martínez and President Giammattei, through what the report claimed may be a shell company.

Human Rights Defenders

Attacks against human rights defenders and social leaders increased in early 2020, according to the nongovernmental organization Unidad de Protección a Defensoras y Defensores de Derechos Humanos de Guatemala (Udefegua). It reported that 651 human rights defenders were subject to various types of attacks or harassment from January 2019 through the first four months of 2020.

The Inter-American Commission on Human Rights (IACHR) said at least eight human rights defenders had been murdered between June and August 2020.

On August 10, Benoit María, representative of Agronomists and Veterinarians without Borders (AVSF), a French non-governmental organization (NGO), was assassinated by unknown individuals. His car was shot at least 17 times. AVSF suspended its work in Guatemala while the murder was being investigated.

In February 2020, members of Congress from the ruling party approved amendments to the law regulating NGOs, limiting their right to free association. The following month, the Constitutional Court temporarily suspended the changes, which would have allowed the government to shut down organizations for disturbing public order and to establish restrictions on their receiving international funds.

Sexual and Reproductive Rights

A "Life and Family Protection" bill that would expand the criminalization of abortion remains under consideration by Congress. Abortion is currently legal only when the life of a pregnant person is in danger. The bill could subject women who have miscarriages to prosecution. It would also raise the maximum sentence for abortion from 3 to 10 years.

The Supreme Court ruled on August 12, 2020, that Ombudsperson Jordán Rodas had failed to comply with a 2017 decision ordering his office to cease activities that support or promote abortion, present abortion as a right, or promote its legalization. The decision contravenes international human rights standards on sexual and reproductive rights. Several international bodies have called on Guatemala to decriminalize and legalize abortion and to ensure access to safe abortion services.

Guatemala's civil code limits the sexual and reproductive rights of women and girls with disabilities.

Sexual Orientation and Gender Identity

Guatemala has no comprehensive civil legislation protecting people from discrimination on the grounds of sexual orientation and gender identity. Employers, landlords, health care facilities, schools, and other public and private institutions face no penalty for discriminating. No law allows transgender people to change their name or gender marker on official documents.

The Life and Family Protection bill contains provisions that discriminate against LGBT people. It defines marriage as a union between a man and a woman and establishes that "freedom of conscience and expression" protects people from being "obliged to accept non-heterosexual conduct or practices as normal."

In June 2020, several lawmakers attempted to remove the ombudsperson from office for using a rainbow flag on social media to commemorate Pride month, and for releasing videos calling on the government to fulfill its international obligation to prevent anti-LGBT violence and discrimination. At time of writing, the attempt had not succeeded.

Asylum Seekers and Refugees

The US-Guatemala Asylum Cooperative Agreement (ACA) entered into force in November 2019, allowing rapid transfer ofnon-Guatemalan asylum seekers to Guatemala without their being able to lodge asylum claims in the United States. Between November 21, 2019, and March 16, 2020, the US transferred 939 Honduran and Salvadoran asylum seekers, the vast majority women and children, to Guatemala under the agreement.

President Giammattei has reaffirmed Guatemala's commitment to the ACA. Evidence shows that asylum seekers experience mistreatment, trauma, and stress at the US border. Guatemala has a nascent and cumbersome asylum system that is not capable of providing effective protection to asylum seekers forcibly transferred from the United States.

DEPORTATION WITH A LAYOVER
Failure of Protection under the US-Guatemala Asylum Cooperative Agreement

In mid-March, transfers under the ACA were temporarily suspended in response to the Covid-19 pandemic. In October, a large group of migrants from Honduras seeking to travel to the United States entered Guatemala. President Giammatei stated that 3,384 were returned to their country.

Key International Actors

From its start in 2007 until the government failed to extend its mandate in 2018, the UN-backed CICIG played a key role in assisting Guatemala's justice system in prosecuting corruption and violent crime. The CICIG worked with the Attorney General's Office, the police, and other government agencies to investigate, prosecute, and dismantle criminal organizations operating in Guatemala. It identified more than 60 criminal structures, presented more than 110 cases—in which over 680 people were involved—and presented 34 proposals for legal reforms to Congress. An opinion poll in April 2019 showed more than 70 percent of the population supporting the CICIG.

In January 2020, the UN High Commissioner for Human Rights issued a report on Guatemala, referring to a "challenging human rights context, with persisting high levels of inequality, discrimination, insecurity and impunity." The report cited "significant setbacks" in the advancement of human rights, the rule of law, and the fight against corruption and impunity.

In September 2020, the IACHR referred a case to the Inter-American Court related to the granting and establishment of a mining project in the territory of the Mayan Community. It noted that there is no legislation in Guatemala guaranteeing the Mayans' right to collective property and there is an absence of adequate and effective recourse for the protection of their rights. The same month, the commission also urged Guatemala to investigate, prosecute, and punish both the material and intellectual perpetrators of murders and attacks against human rights defenders.

Guinea

Guinea held presidential elections on October 18, the culmination of a year-long effort by incumbent President Alpha Condé to secure a third term in office. The post-election period was marred by violence, with the security forces killing at least 12 people, including 2 children in Conakry, between October 18 and October 23. On October 24, the election commission announced that Conde had won the election with 59.5 percent of the vote. The main opposition candidate, Cellou Dalein Diallo, on October 19 claimed victory, rejecting the official results on October 24. Alleging fraud, Diallo called for mass demonstrations.

On March 22, Guineans voted in a constitutional referendum and legislative elections that paved the way for a Condé third term, despite both the new constitution and the original 2010 text limiting presidents to two terms. The controversial poll triggered violence in Conakry and several other cities, with least 32 people killed in intercommunal clashes in Nzérékoré, southeastern Guinea. During the weekend of the March legislative elections and constitutional referendum, access to social media was severely limited.

In the lead up to the March elections and the October presidential poll, Guinean security forces frequently used excessive and at times lethal force to suppress sometimes violent demonstrations by those opposed to a new constitution, with at least 23 people allegedly killed by security forces. The government also arbitrarily arrested and detained scores of leaders and members of the National Front for the Defense of the Constitution (Front national pour la défense de la Constitution, FNDC), a coalition of civil society groups and opposition parties opposed to the new constitution.

Members of the security forces continued to enjoy almost total impunity for the excessive use of force and other human rights abuses, with the 2019 conviction of a police captain still the only known conviction of a member of the security forces for the dozens of protest deaths that have occurred since Condé came to power in 2010. The government also failed to meet a self-imposed June deadline for the organization of a trial for alleged perpetrators of the 2009 stadium massacre.

Covid-19

Guinea has seen relatively low numbers of confirmed Covid-19 cases—10,901 as of October 9 and 68 deaths—although given limited testing capacity, the number of infections is likely much higher.

In March, President Condé announced a state of emergency and a series of measures to curb the spread of the virus that causes Covid-19, including a curfew, a ban on large gatherings, and restrictions on movement outside of Conakry. On May 12, security forces allegedly killed seven people during sometimes-violent protests against roadblocks set up to control the spread of Covid-19 on the outskirts of Conakry and in Kamsar, western Guinea.

The government has frequently invoked the state of emergency to prohibit anti-constitution demonstrations. After an FNDC spokesperson announced renewed protests against the new constitution to mark the end of Ramadan on May 21, the Ministry of Security and Civilian Protection said that "no threat to public order will be tolerated," and that the demonstrations aimed to "provoke clashes with the security forces" and "spread Covid-19." Local authorities banned an FNDC march scheduled for July 8, citing the state of emergency, and then banned another march on July 20, citing public health reasons and a lack of request for government authorization. The government prohibited another FNDC demonstration on September 29, citing the beginning of the presidential election campaign.

Schools were closed due to the pandemic for at least three months, affecting about 2.7 million students.

Despite the risk of Covid-19 infections, authorities took no steps to reduce severe overcrowding in Guinean prisons, with Conakry's central prison, designed for 300 people, continuing to house around 1,500. Authorities said that there were 68 positive Covid-19 tests in Conakry's central prison in May, as well as 28 in the main prison in Kindia.

Security Force Abuses

The security forces frequently used excessive and at times lethal force when breaking up protests and in response to violence by demonstrators. During op-

**HUMAN
RIGHTS
WATCH**

"They Let People Kill Each Other"
Violence in Nzérékoré during Guinea's Constitutional Referendum
and Legislative Elections

position protests in January, social media videos verified by international journalists showed members of the security forces firing toward
demonstrators, beating an elderly man, and using a woman as a shield against
stones thrown by protesters.

Clashes between the security forces and opposition protesters, and between opposition and government supporters, escalated the weekend of the March 22
legislative elections and constitutional poll. Several polling stations were attacked by demonstrators, while human rights groups reported that security
forces shot dead 9 people. Two others were reportedly killed after collisions with
vehicles belonging to the security forces. In some cases, government supporters
also attacked opposition demonstrators and journalists.

Security forces deployed to Nzérékoré during the March elections failed to protect people from election-related and intercommunal violence and also committed human rights abuses, including illegal and arbitrary detention and excessive
use of force.

While the October elections were largely peaceful, Diallo's declaration of victory
and the subsequent announcement of preliminary results by the National Electoral Commission led to clashes between Condé supporters and opposition sympathizers in several neighborhoods in Conakry, as well as clashes between
protesters and security forces. Police and gendarmes frequently used excessive
and sometime lethal force against protesters, including firing live ammunition.
They killed at least 12 people in Conakry, including 2 children, between October
18 and October 23.

Intercommunal Violence

In Nzérékoré, Forest Guinea, election day tensions ignited longstanding intercommunal divisions, leading to violent clashes that left at least 32 people dead,
90 injured, and dozens of homes, shops and churches destroyed or damaged.

Violence often ran along ethnic lines with groups of armed Guerzé, an ethnic
group seen as sympathetic to the opposition, facing off with armed ethnic Koni-
anké and Malinké, largely considered ruling party supporters. Some of the victims were apparently targeted based on their ethnic identity. Many were shot,
hacked, or beaten to death, and at least one was burned alive.

The bodies of over two dozen people killed during the violence were removed from Nzérékoré's regional hospital and secretly buried in a mass grave.

Arbitrary Arrests and Detention

On February 11 and 12, in advance of and during planned FNDC demonstrations, security forces arbitrarily arrested 40 people in Conakry and took them to a military base in Soronkoni, in eastern Guinea. They were held incommunicado and without the authorities acknowledging their detention until March 28, when the authorities released 36 and transferred 4 others to Conakry central prison.

On March 6, security forces arbitrarily arrested FNDC leaders Sekou Koundouno and Ibrahima Diallo and held them for a week without access to their lawyers. They were released on bail on March 13, and the Court of Appeal in Conakry dismissed charges against them on July 15.

On April 17, police arrested Oumar Sylla, an FNDC leader, and held him without charge until April 24, when he was charged with spreading false information. He was released on August 27 after judges dismissed the charges against him, but he was re-arrested on September 29 after he called for demonstrations. On May 7, the FNDC legal director, Saïkou Yaya Diallo, was arrested in Conakry for his alleged role in the temporary detention of a government informer. At time of writing, he remained in detention, while his trial was ongoing.

During the March election violence in Nzérékoré, dozens of those arrested were illegally detained for several days at the Beyanzin military camp, where some were beaten, kept in inhuman conditions, and deprived of food and water. Forty-three were subsequently transferred to a prison in Kankan, almost 240 miles from Nzérékoré. Thirty-five were released on September 28, but 8 remained in detention at time of writing.

Accountability for Serious Abuses

The judiciary continued to face various shortcomings, including lack of adequate court rooms and other physical infrastructure, as well as insufficient personnel and resources to investigate and prosecute human rights violations and other crimes.

Although the government announced investigations into alleged security forces' abuses during demonstrations—including the establishment of a pool of judges to investigate the "serious provocations, abuses, and destruction" committed in Conakry during the March elections—lack of political will, limited investigative capacity, and witnesses' unwillingness to come forward meant that most investigations did not result in charges against members of the security forces. The trial of several police officers for using a woman as a human shield to protect themselves from protesters in January did open on March 18 but has not concluded.

Eleven years after security forces massacred over 150 peaceful opposition supporters and raped dozens of women at a stadium on September 28, 2009, those responsible have not been tried. Then-Justice Minister Mohammed Lamine Fofana stated in November 2019 that the trial would take place no later than June 2020, and on January 13 the government began construction of the courtroom designed to hold the trial.

The International Criminal Court, which has an ongoing preliminary examination of the 2009 massacre, praised the beginning of construction, and urged the government to meet the June deadline. Fofana was, however, replaced in June by a new minister, Mory Doumbouya, and the trial had yet to begin at time of writing. President Condé said on October 6 that the government was still constructing the building for the trial. Five people charged in the case have been in detention beyond the legal limit while they wait for the trial to start.

Natural Resources

Guinea's natural resources, notably bauxite and gold, remained central to the economy. The bauxite sector continued to expand rapidly in the Boké and Boffa regions, leading to thousands of farmers losing their land to mining, often for inadequate compensation, and damaging vital water sources in the area. The Guinean government on June 4 confirmed an agreement with a Chinese-backed consortium to develop half of the enormous Simandou iron ore deposit, in southeastern Guinea. The consortium, which is already Guinea's largest aluminum exporter, has in the past failed to respect international human rights and environmental standards.

HUMAN
RIGHTS
WATCH

"We're Leaving Everything Behind"
The Impact of Guinea's Souapiti Dam on Displaced Communities

The government began a second wave of resettlements of villages to make way for the Souapiti hydroelectric dam, which in total is expected to displace 16,000 people. More than 10,000 people displaced in 2019have yet to receive alternative farmland or support finding new livelihoods and are struggling to access adequate food and other essentials.

Key International Actors

On October 2, the Economic Community of West African States (ECOWAS), the African Union, and the United Nations called on the Guinean security forces to "avoid the excessive use of force" during the presidential election and urged the authorities to secure the election with "respect for human rights." The European Union and the United States condemned the violence and killings that occurred during the March elections and called for respect for freedom of assembly ahead of the presidential poll.

The prosecutor of the International Criminal Court on October 9 condemned "inflammatory rhetoric" contributing to "growing ethnic tensions" ahead of the presidential election. She also called for the swift organization of a trial for the September 2009 stadium massacre. The EU, US, and France also on September 25 called for Guinea to "hold a trial as soon as possible" for the massacre.

Haiti

Protracted political instability and gang violence in 2020—often with state ties—contributed to the Haitian government's inability to meet the basic needs of its people, resolve long-standing human rights problems, and address humanitarian crises.

Since the government's announcement in July 2018 that it would eliminate fuel subsidies, widespread civil unrest has effectively paralyzed Haiti. Demonstrations intensified in 2019, amid evidence of embezzlement of funds intended for infrastructure and healthcare under three successive governments, including that of President Jovenel Moïse. Police responded with excessive force. Impunity for gang and police violence continued.

The electoral council postponed legislative elections indefinitely in October 2019, and President Moïse has been ruling by decree since January 2020, when the legislature's mandate expired. Moïse blamed parliament for the postponement, for failing to approve an electoral law, while his opponents accused him of maneuvers to hijack the process.

The first cases of Covid-19 were confirmed in March, against a backdrop of increased gang violence. Relatively low case numbers may be due in part to underreporting, as stigmatization and targeted violence against those perceived to be infected represses care-seeking. The pandemic has exacerbated vulnerabilities among marginalized populations.

In June, President Moïse decreed a new penal code, distinct from a draft code submitted to parliament in 2017. It will become law 24 months after its publication.

Violence, Lawlessness, and Instability

Haiti is facing one of its worst outbreaks of violence since 1986. The United Nations Integrated Office in Haiti (BINUH) reported 944 intentional homicides, 124 abductions, and 78 cases of sexual and gender-based violence from January through August 31, with at least 159 people killed as a result of gang violence, including a four-month-old infant.

Alleged complicity between politicians and gangs have contributed to a climate of insecurity. The Inter-American Commission on Human Rights (IACHR) has reported charges against 98 people, including 2 senior government officials, for a 2018 gang-related massacre of 71 people and related abuses in the La Saline neighborhood of Port-au-Prince. Perpetrators operated with complicity of authorities, including policeman Jimmy Cherizier, who has since been fired and now leads a coalition of gangs. The UN has called for authorities to bring those responsible to justice.

In 2019, Cherizier and other National Police also aided in killing at least 3, wounding 6, and burning the houses of 30 families in the Bel-Air neighborhood, where residents were protesting a rise in fuel prices, BINUH reported. Cherizier is suspected of attacks in the Grande Ravine neighborhood in 2017 as well. To date, no criminal proceedings have been initiated against those implicated.

The Core Group has called on authorities to investigate the August 29 killing of Monferrier Dorval, head of the Port-au-Prince bar association, outside his home hours after he called for constitutional reform in a radio interview.

Police did not intervene on August 31, when gangs killed at least 20 people and set houses afire in the Bel-Air and Delmas neighborhoods of Port-au-Prince, forcing at least 1,221 residents to shelter in public squares and a soccer field.

Human rights organizations such as the National Human Rights Defense Network (RNDDH) and Fondasyon Je Klere (FJKL) have documented numerous other attacks carried out by armed gangs with the protection of government authorities.

Displacement

At least 12,000 people were reported displaced in 2020, the majority due to gang violence and a cyclone in July. Many more displaced people likely went uncounted.

Over 140,000 families displaced by Hurricane Matthew in 2016 still need decent shelter.

Since the 2010 earthquake, nearly 33,000 people still live in displacement camps and at least 300,000 live in an informal settlement without government oversight. Authorities have not provided assistance to return or resettle them, or to ensure their basic rights in the settlement.

Rights to Health, Water, and Food

The country's most vulnerable communities face environmental risks, including widespread deforestation, industrial pollution, and limited access to safe water and sanitation. According to international agencies, some 4.1 million Haitians—more than a third—live with food insecurity, and 2.1 percent of children suffer severe malnutrition. Low rainfall, exacerbated by rising temperatures due to climate change, chronically affects much of the country.

Since its introduction by UN peacekeepers in 2010, cholera has infected more than 819,000 people and claimed nearly 10,000 lives. Intensified control efforts—including an ambitious vaccination campaign—have achieved zero confirmed cases since the last week of January 2019. But over a third of the population lacks access to clean water and two-thirds has limited or no sanitation service, leaving Haiti vulnerable to a resurgence, and now to Covid-19.

Criminal Justice System

Haiti's prisons remain severely overcrowded, with many inmates living in inhumane conditions. Overcrowding is largely attributable to arbitrary arrests and pretrial detentions, a UN independent expert on Haiti reported in 2017.

As of September 2020, prisons housed nearly 11,000 detainees, 78 percent of whom were awaiting trial. A six-week suspension of judicial hearings at the peak of protests in 2019 increased numbers of people in pretrial detention.

Seven of the ten women raped by male prisoners during a riot at Gonaives detention facility in November 2019 were in prolonged pretrial detention.

At least 140 detainees in Haiti's prisons tested positive for Covid-19 between March and July. According to a September 25 United Nations report, authorities had released 1,042 detainees from all prisons, including 80 women and 25 juveniles, falling short of the 5,000 discharges deemed necessary to manage the spread of Covid-19 among detainees, the UN secretary-general warned. Several of those released were facing serious charges and were granted executive clemency without consultation from BINUH or human rights groups.

Illiteracy and Barriers to Education

Just under half of Haitians age 15 and older are illiterate. The quality of education is generally low, and 85 percent of schools are private, charging fees often too high for low-income families.

Unrest and the pandemic kept 70 percent of Haitian children from classes throughout the school year. From September through November 2019, instability kept an estimated 3 million children out of school, and in March, the pandemic closed schools for five months. Prior to the pandemic, Haiti already had 500,000 school-age children out of school.

Abuses by Security Forces

Police officers were responsible for three summary executions and 47 injuries resulting from excessive use of force during October 2018 demonstrations, the UN Mission for Justice Support in Haiti (MINUJUSTH) found. The following month, excessive use of force resulted in 6 deaths and 15 injuries.

In the first eight months of 2020, BINUH reported 184 cases of human rights violations and abuses by police, including indiscriminate use of tear gas.

At least eight journalists were injured during protests from September 16 through October 17, 2019, RNDDH reported. In October 2019, a radio journalist covering the protests was shot dead. The UN High Commissioner on Human Rights attributed at least 19 of 42 deaths at protests from September 15 to November 1, 2019 to security forces.

Accountability for Past Abuses

Six months after former President Jean-Claude Duvalier died in 2014, a Court of Appeal ruled that statutes of limitations are inapplicable to crimes against humanity, ordering investigations to continue for crimes committed during Duvalier's presidency (1971-1986). As of October, re-opened investigations into arbitrary detentions, torture, disappearances, summary executions, and forced exile remained pending.

On June 23, former Haitian death squad leader Emmanuel "Toto" Constant, was deported from the US and detained. While on the payroll of the US Central Intelligence Agency, Constant founded a paramilitary organization that was complicit in murdering at least 3,000 Haitians between 1991 and 1994. In 2000, he was convicted in absentia for involvement in a 1994 massacre in the Raboteau neighborhood of Gonaïves. Under Haitian law, Constant has the right to a new trial. Given the climate of impunity characterizing the Moïse regime, lawyers and human rights groups have voiced concerns that Constant will go free. UN High Commissioner for Human Rights Michelle Bachelet urged Haiti to hold him accountable.

Jean-Robert Gabriel was also convicted in 2000 of involvement in the Raboteau massacre through command responsibility. President Moïse named Gabriel assistant chief of staff of the reinstated Haitian armed forces in 2018.

Women's and Girls' Rights

Gender-based violence is common. The new penal code lists sexual harassment and gender-based violence as punishable offenses. Rape is punishable by up to life imprisonment.

Until it comes into force in June 2022, there is no specific legislation against domestic violence, sexual harassment, or other forms of violence targeted at women and girls. Rape was only explicitly criminalized in 2005, by ministerial decree.

The new penal code also will legalize abortion in all circumstances up to the twelfth week of pregnancy, in cases of rape or incest, or if the mental or physical health of the woman is in danger. Abortion was previously prohibited in all circumstances. The penal code also lowers the legal age for consensual sex to 15 while only allowing legal abortion starting at age 18.

In November, the International Federation of Football Association (FIFA) Ethics Committee sanctioned Haitian Football Federation (FHF) President Yves Jean-Bart with a lifetime ban, following their investigation into evidence of systematic sexual abuse of female players. Throughout the investigation, witnesses and sexual abuse survivors reported being followed or threatened to intimidate them from cooperating with judicial authorities. As of October, FIFA had suspended four additional senior FHF officials implicated in the abuses.

Disability Rights

Despite ratifying the Convention on the Rights of Persons with Disabilities, Haiti's legislative framework is not yet harmonized with its standards. People with disabilities, including women and girls, continue to experience discrimination. The country lacks a minimum institutional framework to implement disability rights. Many people in Haitian society believe disability to be a curse, which places people with disabilities at a higher risk of being victims of violence.

The new penal code includes provisions prohibiting violence or incitement against persons with disabilities.

Sexual Orientation and Gender Identity

Lesbian, gay, bisexual, and transgender (LGBT) people continue to suffer high levels of discrimination in Haiti, and there is no comprehensive civil law forbidding it.

The new penal code makes any crime motivated by its target's real or perceived sexual orientation an aggravated offense. The code also punishes with up to life imprisonment any murder motivated by a victim's sexual orientation, and with higher sentences for many other crimes when they are motivated by a victim's sexual orientation.

Two anti-LGBT bills passed by the Senate in 2017 remained under consideration by the Chamber of Deputies at time of writing. One adds homosexuality as a reason for denying a Certificat de Bonne Vie et Mœurs, a certificate of good standing required by many employers and universities as proof that a person has not committed a felony. The other bans same-sex marriage, establishing prison sentences of up to three years and a fine of about US$8,000 for "parties, co-parties and accomplices" to a same-sex marriage. It also bans any public support or advocacy for lesbian, gay, bisexual and transgender rights.

In November 2019, Charlot Jeudy, a gay man who founded Haiti's LGBTQ advocacy group Kouraj, was found dead at his home. As of October, circumstances surrounding his death and the results of an autopsy remain publicly unknown.

Deportation and Statelessness for Dominicans of Haitian Descent

The precarious status of Dominicans of Haitian descent and Haitian migrants in the Dominican Republic remains a serious concern.

In response to Covid-19, the Dominican Republic suspended temporary legal status for more than 150,000 Haitian workers. Over 50,000 returned to Haiti from March 17 to June 28, according to the International Organization of Migration.

At least 250,000 Haitians returned between 2015 and 2018, after Dominican officials began deportations pursuant to a controversial Plan for the Regularization of Foreigners. Many were swept up in arbitrary, summary deportations. Others left under pressure or threat of violence.

Mining and Access to Information

Haiti is one of the most densely populated countries in the Western Hemisphere, and environmental degradation is a concern. In the past decade, foreign investors have pursued development of the nascent mining sector. Resistance is widespread, as communities fear the industry could destroy their farmland and contaminate their water.

A 2017 draft law the government presented to parliament is silent on the rights of those displaced by mining activities, the Global Justice Clinic of New York University School of Law reports, and it grants insufficient time for environmental review. It contains provisions that could render company documents, including those about environmental and social impacts, confidential for 10 years, preventing meaningful consultation with communities. It remained under consideration as of October.

Key International Actors

The US government and the Organization of American States (OAS) have both called on Haiti to hold elections, though democracy activists have warned that current conditions are not conducive to free and fair elections. In September, against opposition from the Supreme Court, President Moïse appointed a nine-member Provisional Electoral Council tasked with organizing elections and preparing a constitutional referendum. Human rights advocates and others have said the presidential decree is illegal and unconstitutional.

In October, the UN special representative for Haiti stated that the country is "struggling to avert the precipice of instability" and warned of the risk of contested election outcomes and further violence.

In 2016, the UN secretary-general apologized for the UN's role in the cholera outbreak and announced establishment of a trust fund to raise $400 million to provide "material assistance" to those most affected. As of October 2020, only $20.7 million had been pledged. Advocates have criticized the UN for blocking victims' participation in designing assistance.

The United States continued deportations to Haiti throughout the pandemic. From March 18 to October 16, Haiti received 24 flights holding deportees, including several who tested positive for the virus upon arrival.

Honduras

Violent organized crime continues to disrupt Honduran society and push many people to leave the country. Journalists, environmental activists, lesbian, gay, bisexual, and transgender (LGBT) individuals, and people with disabilities are among the groups targeted for violence. The government relies heavily on the military for public security.

Efforts to reform public-security institutions have stalled. Marred by corruption and abuse, the judiciary and police remain largely ineffective. In June 2020, a new criminal code came into effect. It included provisions that appeared aimed at reducing penalties for politicians linked to organized crime, by lowering sentences for corruption and related offenses. The new code also includes alternatives to detention for low-level crimes, including partial prison sentences and penalties that allow for conditional release. Impunity for human rights abuses, violent crime, and corruption remains the norm, even as the prison population has mushroomed.

Security forces committed abuses while enforcing a nationwide Covid-19 lockdown that President Juan Orlando Hernández imposed in March. An audit of government purchases of medical supplies to fight Covid-19 revealed supplies worth tens of millions of dollars had gone missing. Prisons saw significant Covid-19 outbreaks.

Gangs

Gang violence is widespread in and around urban areas. Estimates of the number of active gang members range from 5,000 to 40,000.

Gangs exercise territorial control over neighborhoods and extort residents throughout the country. They forcibly recruit children and sexually abuse women, girls, and LGBT people. Gangs kill, disappear, rape, or displace those who resist.

Gangs, particularly the Mara Salvatrucha (MS-13) and the 18th Street Gang (Barrio 18), are considered to be largely responsible for Honduras' murder rate, and are infamous for extortion and drug peddling.

Historically, governments have responded with iron-fist security strategies to combat organized crime, enacting tougher legislation and increasing police presence and mass detentions. In 2018, the government created a special force to fight gangs (Fuerza Nacional Anti Maras y pandillas). Members include officers from the police, the military, and the Attorney's General Office.

Abuses by security forces, including alleged collusion with criminal organizations, and weak state institutions, have contributed to the persistence of gang violence.

Police Abuse

Excessive use of force by police and deployment of the military in public security operations continued in 2020.

The media and nongovernmental organizations (NGOs) reported several cases of abusive police enforcement of the Covid-19 lockdown. In April, Public Order Military Police (PMOP) officers severely beat three brothers and shot two of them—one fatally—for allegedly violating a curfew in El Paraíso in order to sell bread.

In June, police detained and beat bus drivers who were allegedly protesting not being able to work due to lockdown restrictions.

Criminal Justice System

The criminal justice system regularly fails to hold those responsible for homicides to account.

Judges continue to face interference, including political pressure, threats, and harassment, from the executive branch, private actors with connections to government, and organized crime. Prosecutors and whistleblowers have received death threats. The Supreme Court, particularly its president, exerts excessive control over the appointment and removal of judges, the Inter-American Commission on Human Rights reported in 2019, and career instability limits judges' independence.

In January 2020, the government shut down the Mission to Support the Fight against Corruption and Impunity in Honduras (MACCIH). Established in 2016 by the government and the Organization of American States (OAS), the MACCIH contributed to the prosecution of 133 people, including congresspeople and senior officials, 14 of whom faced criminal trials.

Freedom of Expression, Association, and Assembly

In March 2020, the government declared a state of emergency in response to the pandemic, imposing a lockdown and restricting movement and freedom of expression. Following domestic and international criticism, the government backtracked and a week later re-established constitutional free speech guarantees.

Individuals and state agents continue to threaten and attack journalists, press freedom groups report. At least 86 journalists were killed from 2001 through July 2020, the Honduran College of Journalists reported, and 92 percent of those killings remain unpunished.

In July, police arrested two men in connection to the 2020 killings of 45 TV reporter Germán Vallecillo Jr. and his cameraman, Jorge Posas, in La Ceiba. Investigations were underway at time of writing. In September, two men shot and killed journalist Luis Alonzo Almendares in Comayagua. Almendares had repeatedly received death threats since 2017 in relation to his reporting.

The new criminal code decriminalized defamation, but retains other "crimes of honor"—including insult and slander—which have been used to prosecute journalists in the past. The code also includes poorly constructed provisions that could lead to violations of the rights to assemble and protest and an overly broad definition of "association to engage in terrorism," which could be used to criminalize and disproportionately punish behaviors that fall far short of what most reasonable observers would consider terrorism.

Radio Globo director David Romero, convicted of defamation in 2016, died in prison from Covid-19 in July. The Supreme Court had upheld Romero's 10-year sentence in January 2020.

Attacks on Lawyers, Human Rights Defenders, and Environmental Activists

The UN special rapporteur on the situation of human rights defenders called Honduras one of the most dangerous countries for human rights defenders in

Latin America. Activists say the government's Mechanism for the Protection of Journalists, Human Rights Defenders and Operators of Justice, created in 2015, lacks uniform criteria and is ineffective.

Marvin Damián Castro Molina, who, as part of the Coordination of the Southern Social Environmental Movement for Life, fought mining, agro-industry, and hydroelectric projects, was abducted and found dead in Choluteca in July 2020. The government had granted him protective measures in January 2019.

Iris Argentina Álvarez of the Cerro Escondido peasant cooperative, which has been working to recover land currently owned by a sugar company, was killed and three people were injured during a violent and allegedly illegal eviction in Choluteca in April 2020. Police were allegedly in the area when private security forces opened fired against several families but did not help the victims, witnesses told the press. Two private security officers were charged.

In July 2020, gunmen in police uniforms abducted five indigenous Garifuna men in Triunfo de la Cruz, where communities are claiming ancestral land from drug traffickers and developers. The men remained missing at time of writing.

After irregularities and delays, the trial of David Castillo, one of the men accused of planning the 2016 killing of environmental activist Berta Cáceres, began in September 2020. In October, the Civic Council of Popular and Indigenous Organizations of Honduras (COPINH), of which Cáceres was president, complained of continued delays and a lack of transparency in the case.

Sexual Orientation and Gender Identity

LGBT people in Honduras are frequently the targets of violence and discrimination, according to Human Rights Watch research. They face violence from gangs, the national civil police and the military police, members of the public, and their own families, as well as extortion by gangs and discrimination in schools and in the workplace.

Violence against LGBT individuals forces many to leave their homes, fleeing internally or leaving the country to seek asylum. Although there is a law that provides higher penalties for bias-based crimes, including on the grounds of sexual orientation and gender identity, the Attorney General's office told Human Rights Watch in September 2020 that no one has been convicted under the law.

In November 2020, the Inter-American Court of Human Rights heard the case of Vicky Hernández, a trans woman allegedly extrajudicially executed in 2009. In December 2018, the Inter-American Commission on Human Rights found Honduras responsible for failing to investigate Hernández's death. It submitted the case to the court in April 2019 due to Honduras' lack of compliance with its recommendations, such as introducing comprehensive policies to map and prevent anti-LGBT violence and designing training programs on anti-LGBT violence for state security bodies.

A law prohibiting same-sex couples from adopting children took effect in 2019.

Sexual and Reproductive Rights, Violence Against Women

Women in Honduras face high levels of gender-based violence. The country has the second-highest rate of femicide—defined as the killing of a woman by a man because of her gender—in Latin America, the UN Economic Commission for Latin America and the Caribbean reports. In 2013, Honduras reformed the penal code to recognize femicide as a crime.

A woman is killed every 23 hours on average, the National Autonomous University of Honduras' Violence Observatory reports. In 2018, the last year for which statistics are available, 60 percent of perpetrators were domestic partners.

Abortion is illegal in Honduras in all circumstances. Women and girls who terminate pregnancies face prison sentences of up to six years. The law also sanctions abortion providers.

The government bans emergency contraception, known as the "morning after pill," which can prevent pregnancy after rape, unprotected sex, or contraceptive failure.

Children's Rights

The government neither comprehensively protects the rights of children, including adolescents, nor ensures that they have access to basic services such as education and healthcare, the IACHR reported in 2019. Despite recent educational advances, around a third of children aged 3-17 did not attend school in 2018, according to the most recent survey by the National Statistics Institute.

The Covid-19 pandemic has further limited access to education for many children. Schools were closed from March onward due to the Covid-19 pandemic. Classes were broadcast on television, radio, and online, in some cases with assignments sent via Whatsapp. Just 18 percent of Hondurans have internet access in their homes and a quarter of homes in rural areas don't have electricity. Most who can access the internet do so on their phones. A study published in April reported that nearly half of teachers in rural areas had not been able to contact the majority of their students.

A quarter of women and girls become pregnant before turning 18—the second-highest rate in Latin America. Half of underage pregnancies result from rape.

Between 2005 and 2019, 34 percent of women who were 20-24 years old had married when they were 15-19, the UN Population Fund reported in 2020.

Of 25,000 gang members in 2012, nearly a fifth were children, UNICEF estimated. Since 2012, the Honduran police have implemented a program sponsored by the US Department of State called Gang Resistance Education and Training (GREAT) which aims to discourage youth crime and gang recruitment. There is limited data on the effectiveness of the program in Honduras.

Disability Rights

Public buildings, transportation, and information and communication services open to the public are not fully accessible to people with disabilities. Some are deprived of full legal capacity and are institutionalized in different settings, including psychiatric hospitals. Often, people with disabilities are threatened and subjected to extortion by criminal gangs.

Prison Conditions

Honduras's prison population has doubled over the past decade, partly due to a 2013 reform that greatly expanded the use of mandatory pre-trial detention. As of August 2020, more than 21,000 people were detained in prisons with capacity for just under 11,000. More than half of detained men and two-thirds of detained women were in pretrial detention.

Overcrowding, inadequate nutrition, poor sanitation, beatings, intra-gang violence, and detainee killings are endemic in prisons.

After a 2019 wave of gang violence that killed 37 detainees, President Hernández declared a state of emergency and put prisons under military control. Between December 2019, when prisons were placed under military control, and September 2020, 54 people died in eight prison incidents, the IACHR and OHCHR report.

To reduce overcrowding in response to the pandemic, the legislature approved alternatives to pretrial detention in June and judges released more than 1,600 people. As of August, prisons had reported 1,700 confirmed Covid-19 cases and 38 deaths. In September, the OHCHR and IACHR expressed concern regarding the continued spread of the virus in prisons.

The new criminal code that came into effect in June 2020 includes new alternative sanctions to detention for some minor crimes that could help reduce the prison population.

Migrants, Refugees, and Internally Displaced People

Every year, more than 100,000 Hondurans are internally displaced, migrate, seek protection abroad, or are deported back to Honduras. The groups most likely to be internally displaced or leave the country are children subjected to forced gang recruitment, professionals and business owners who face extortion, domestic violence survivors, and LGBT people and members of ethnic minorities who face violence and discrimination.

Around 191,000 people were internally displaced between 2004 and 2018, the Honduran government reported, and more than 75,000 Hondurans sought asylum abroad in 2017. The government has set up roadblocks, deployed security forces, and used violence to prevent people from leaving the country.

Almost 110,000 Hondurans were returned in 2019, mostly from Mexico. Since 2017, the government has operated centers to support returned migrants. Support focuses primarily on reintegration into the labor market, rather than assistance for people who fled seeking international protection.

Key International Actors

Honduras and the US signed an "asylum cooperative agreement" in 2019, whereby Honduras agreed to receive non-Honduran asylum-seekers transferred by the US. As of September 2020, the US had yet to begin deporting any third country nationals to Honduras under the agreement.

The IACHR expressed concern in 2019 regarding the "critical levels of impunity and inadequate and insufficient attention to victims" of human rights violations. In February 2020, it called on El Salvador, Guatemala, Honduras, and Mexico to protect the rights of migrants and refugees to leave their country of origin, noting that asylum applications from Central America and Mexico grew 50-fold from 2012 to 2018. Also in February, the OAS special rapporteur on freedom of expression called on Honduras to decriminalize defamation and to properly investigate killings of journalists.

In January 2020, the OHCHR released a report saying that the armed forces and military police had used excessive—even lethal—force in response to the protests that followed the 2017 election. It also documented widespread mistreatment of people detained and arrested during the protests. In April, the office expressed concern regarding accusations of excesive use of force by state security agents enforcing the government's Covid-19 restrictions.

In June, the OHCHR and IACHR jointly expressed concern that the new penal code disproportionately restricts freedoms of speech, press, and association and fails to criminalize torture committed by third parties acting on behalf of state agents.

Honduras has endorsed the World Health Organization's Solidarity Call to Action for the Covid-19 Technology Access Pool, an initiative to "realize equitable global access to COVID-19 health technologies through pooling of knowledge, intellectual property and data."

Hungary

The government used the Covid-19 pandemic as a pretext to continue its attacks on rule of law and democratic institutions. The government declared a state of emergency in March, seizing unlimited power to rule by decree without parliamentary and judicial review. Before the state of emergency was revoked in mid-June, the government had issued hundreds of decrees, including on issues unrelated to public health. The government made access to asylum close to impossible, interfered with independent media and academia, launched an assault on members of the lesbian, gay, bisexual, and transgender (LGBT) community, and undermined women's rights. Hungary's Roma minority continue to face widespread and systemic discrimination.

In its Rule of Law report released in October, the European Union Commission raised concerns about the lack of independence of the judiciary, intimidation of independent media, and the impact of the weakening of independent institutions and pressures on civil society on democratic checks and balances.

Attacks on Rule of Law

In March, the government declared a state of emergency in response to the pandemic and the parliament, where the ruling party has a two-thirds majority, passed an Authorization Act giving the government unlimited power to rule by decree indefinitely and without parliamentary oversight. The law also included a new criminal offense for the publication of "fake" or "distorted facts" pertaining to the pandemic.

The government adopted hundreds of decrees before the Authorization Act and state of emergency were revoked in mid-June, including several unrelated to public health, such as decrees that stripped funds to municipalities, disproportionally affecting localities ruled by opposition parties. The ruling Fidesz party had suffered a major blow in the October 2019 local elections when the party lost 10 larger cities to the opposition, including the capital city, Budapest.

While the Authorization Act was revoked in mid-June, Parliament simultaneously adopted a new law enabling the government to declare future public health or medical emergencies during which it could order any and all measures it deems necessary without parliamentary approval, including suspending laws and curtailing fundamental rights such as freedom of movement and assembly for six months. These powers are renewable every six months with minimal or no parliamentary or judicial oversight.

Freedom of Media

The government continued its attacks on media and freedom of expression. Most media outlets are directly or indirectly controlled by the government, which has a chilling effect on independent journalism. Between March and June, daily online government coronavirus task force press briefings required media outlets to submit questions by email, with the government in most cases ignoring questions posed by critical outlets and journalists.

In March, the government amended the criminal code to make it a crime to spread "fake news" or engage in "fear mongering" during a pandemic punishable by up to five years' imprisonment. At the time, Harlem Desir, then media freedom representative for the Organization for Security and Co-operation in Europe (OSCE), called on the government to ensure that the Authorization Act should not impede the work of media in Hungary. By July, police had launched 134 criminal investigations concerning "fear mongering." A majority of cases concern people who expressed critical comments on social media regarding the government's handling of the pandemic. At time of writing, investigations were ongoing.

In July, Szabolcs Dull, the editor-in-chief of the largest online independent daily, Index, was fired as a result of a financial takeover of the company controlling Index's revenue streams. The new owner has close links to Prime Minister Viktor Orban and his government. Index's entire staff resigned in protest. In September, the Media Council, a regulatory body the members of which are appointed by the ruling party, revoked the frequency for Klubradio, an independent radio station in Budapest, entering into effect in February 2021. The Media Council justified its actions referring to Klubradio's repeated breaches of the media law. Klubradio denied the allegations.

Academic Freedom

In October, the Court of Justice of the European Union (CJEU) ruled that a 2017 law that effectively forced the George Soros funded Central European University to leave Budapest and relocate in Vienna, violated European Union law.

Nonetheless, the government's efforts to control academic institutions continued. A law adopted in June, which entered into effect in September, effectively abolished the autonomy of the University of Theatre and Film in Budapest, depriving its highest governing body of decision-making power over budgetary, organizational, and staffing issues. The Ministry of Technology and Innovation single-handedly appointed the members of the new board of trustees and the supervisory body—all closely linked to the government and with limited to no knowledge of the arts.

Right to Health

Long-standing neglect of the public health care system and deficiencies in Hungarian hospitals, including lack of basic items such as hand soap and sanitizer, may have contributed to the spread of Covid-19. According to the Chief Medical Officer, as of July 12, 1,062 patients had contracted Covid-19 in hospitals, of whom 260 died. That means that 25 percent of reported confirmed infections by mid-July were contracted in hospitals, and hospital-acquired Covid-19 infections led to almost 50 percent of reported deaths.

Medical staff reported difficulties accessing adequate amounts of personal protective equipment and confusing protocols for referring suspected Covid-19 patients for testing. By September, Hungary had the third lowest rate of testing for Covid-19 in the EU.

In April, a government order required all hospital directors to free up two-thirds of all hospital beds in public hospitals to make room for a possible surge of Covid-19 cases, resulting in an unknown number of patients, many needing around-the-clock care, to be sent home to care for themselves. In response to concerns about patients forcibly removed from hospitals raised by the UN special rapporteurs on health and on poverty, the government denied any wrongdoing, saying the rapporteurs were "wasting our time by attacking Hungary based on false allegations" and were "spreading fake news."

Gender, Sexual Orientation and Gender Identity

The government continued to undermine women's and LGBT rights. In May, the parliament blocked the ratification of the Council of Europe Convention on Combating Violence Against Women and Domestic Violence, known as the Istanbul Convention, saying it "promotes destructive gender ideologies" and "illegal migration."

Hungary signed the convention, which mandates government measures to prevent domestic and gender-based violence, protect survivors, and prosecute perpetrators, in 2014. Also, in May, a new law made it impossible for transgender or intersex people to legally change their gender—putting them at risk of harassment, discrimination, and even violence in daily situations when they need to use identity documents. Council of Europe Human Rights Commissioner Dunja Mijatovic, called the law "a blow to the human dignity of trans people" and said it contradicted the case law of the European Court of Human Rights.

Migration and Asylum

The country saw a significant decline in asylum applications in 2020 due to border closures and other restrictions. By July, 95 people had filed for asylum, down from 266 people in the first 7 months of 2019; authorities granted some form of international protection to 113 people. Pushbacks from Hungary to Serbia, sometimes violent, continued.

Following a May ruling from the CJEU that automatic and indefinite placement of asylum seekers in transit zones on the Hungary-Serbia border amounted to unlawful detention, the government dismantled the transit zones and transferred approximately 400 asylum seekers to the only two open reception centers in Hungary. Authorities had already suspended asylum seekers' access to the zones in March, using the pandemic as a pretext.

In June, the government rammed through a law abolishing the right to seek asylum on Hungarian territory and requiring asylum claims be lodged at specifically designated embassies in non-EU countries. If granted access to the territory, the asylum seeker, including children, will be placed in automatic detention for 30 days with no possibility to appeal their detention. According to the Hungarian Helsinki Committee, as of late July, only seven people—all members of the same family—had applied under the new restrictive system; their application was rejected.

In October, the EU Commission initiated legal action against Hungary on grounds that the new procedures breach EU asylum law.

As of September, the government re-introduced further border closures in response to rising Covid-19 infections, barring entry to most non-Hungarian citizens. Exceptions made for citizens from Czech Republic, Slovakia, and Poland were criticized by the European Commission as discriminatory and contravening the principle of free movement within the EU.

Discrimination

Roma continue to be discriminated in workplaces and schools and many live in abject poverty. In January, following a lower court decision ordering €275,000 (US$327,112) in damages to 60 Roma students who had been unlawfully segregated in primary school, Prime Minister Orban said the ruling was an affront to people's sense of justice when "members of an ethnically dominant ethnic group can receive a significant amount of money without doing any kind of work." In May, the Supreme Court upheld the lower court's decision.

Human Rights Defenders

The government and ruling party members continued their smear campaign against human rights defenders, frequently describing them as "Soros agents" or "national security risks" in government-friendly media.

In June, the CJEU ruled that a 2017 law requiring civil society organization receiving over €20,000 ($23,790) from outside of Hungary to formally register as foreign-funded, was contrary to EU law. At time of writing, the government had taken no action to implement the CJEU ruling and revoke the law.

Civil society organizations and lawyers continued to work on behalf of migrants and refugee rights despite a controversial 2017 law criminalizing aid and assistance to asylum seekers, refugees and migrants. At time of writing, nobody had been charged under the law.

India

The Bharatiya Janata Party (BJP)-led government increasingly harassed, arrested, and prosecuted rights defenders, activists, journalists, students, academics, and others critical of the government or its policies.

The government continued to impose harsh and discriminatory restrictions on Muslim-majority areas in Jammu and Kashmir since revoking the state's constitutional status in August 2019 and splitting it into two federally governed territories.

Attacks continued against minorities, especially Muslims, even as authorities failed to take action against BJP leaders who vilified Muslims and BJP supporters who engaged in violence.

The Covid-19 lockdown disproportionately hurt marginalized communities due to loss of livelihoods and lack of food, shelter, health care, and other basic needs.

Jammu and Kashmir

Hundreds of people remained detained without charge in Jammu and Kashmir under the draconian Public Safety Act, which permits detention without trial for up to two years.

In June, the government announced a new media policy in Jammu and Kashmir that empowers the authorities to decide what is "fake news, plagiarism and unethical or anti-national activities" and to take punitive action against media outlets, journalists, and editors. The policy contains vague and overbroad provisions that are open to abuse and could unnecessarily restrict and penalize legally protected speech. The government also clamped down on critics, journalists, and human rights activists.

The restrictions, including on access to communications networks, since August 2019 adversely affected livelihoods, particularly in the tourism-dependent Kashmir Valley. The Kashmir Chamber of Commerce and Industries estimated that the first three months of the lockdown to prevent protests since August 2019 cost the economy over US$2.4 billion, for which no redress was provided. Losses nearly doubled since the government imposed further restrictions to contain the spread of Covid-19 in March 2020.

The pandemic made access to the internet crucial for information, communication, education, and business. However, even after the Supreme Court said in January that access to the internet was a fundamental right, authorities permitted only slow-speed 2G mobile internet services, leading doctors to complain that the lack of internet was hurting the Covid-19 response.

The Armed Forces (Special Powers) Act continued to provide effective immunity from prosecution to security forces, even for serious human rights abuses. In July, security forces killed three people in Shopian district, claiming they were militants. However, in August, their families, who identified them from photographs of the killings circulated on social media, said they were laborers. In September, the army said that its inquiry had found prima facie evidence that its troops exceeded powers under the AFSPA and it would take disciplinary proceedings against those "answerable."

The security forces also continued to use shotguns firing metal pellets to disperse crowds, despite evidence that they are inherently inaccurate and cause injuries indiscriminately, including to bystanders, violating India's international obligations.

Impunity for Security Forces

In the early weeks of the nationwide lockdown announced in March to contain Covid-19, in several states, police beat people who violated the lockdown, including those trying to get essential supplies. In West Bengal, police allegedly beat a 32-year-old man to death after he stepped out of his home to get milk. A video from Uttar Pradesh showed police forcing migrant workers, who were trying to walk home, to hop on the street to humiliate them. Police in several states also arbitrarily punished people or publicly shamed them for breaking the lockdown.

New cases of torture in police custody and extrajudicial killings highlighted continued lack of accountability for police abuses and failure to enforce police reforms. For the first 10 months, until October, the National Human Rights Commission reported 77 deaths in police custody, 1,338 deaths in judicial custody, and 62 alleged extrajudicial killings.

In June, a father and son died in police custody in Tamil Nadu state after being detained for allegedly violating Covid-19 lockdown rules. In September, the Central Bureau of Investigation, which was asked to investigate the deaths following nationwide outrage, charged nine policemen with murder and destruction of evidence.

In July, Uttar Pradesh police killed a suspect Vikas Dubey, saying he was trying to escape police custody, making him the 119th person to be killed in an alleged extrajudicial killing since the BJP government in Uttar Pradesh led by Ajay Bisht, who uses the title Yogi Adityanath, took office in March 2017. In September, the Uttar Pradesh government announced it would set up a special police force that would be empowered to search and arrest without warrant, raising further concerns about police abuse.

Dalits, Tribal Groups, and Religious Minorities

At least 53 people were killed in communal violence that broke out in Delhi in February. Over 200 were injured, properties destroyed, and communities displaced in targeted attacks by Hindu mobs. While a policeman and some Hindus were also killed, the majority of victims were Muslim. The attacks came after weeks of peaceful protests against the Indian government's discriminatory citizenship policies.

Violence broke out soon after a local BJP politician, Kapil Mishra, demanded that the police clear the roads of protesters. Tensions had been building for weeks, with BJP leaders openly advocating violence against the protesters, whom some called "traitors" to be shot. Witness accounts and video evidence showed police complicity in the violence. A July report by the Delhi Minorities Commission said the violence in Delhi was "planned and targeted," and found that the police were filing cases against Muslim victims for the violence, but not taking action against the BJP leaders who incited it.

In Uttar Pradesh, authorities continued to use allegations of cow slaughter to target Muslims. By August, the Uttar Pradesh government had arrested 4,000 people over allegations of cow slaughter under the law preventing it, and also used the draconian National Security Act against 76 people accused of cow slaughter. The NSA allows for detention for up to a year without filing charges.

HUMAN
RIGHTS
WATCH

"Shoot the Traitors"
Discrimination Against Muslims under India's New Citizenship Policy

Anti-Muslim rhetoric surged following the outbreak of Covid-19. In March, after Indian authorities announced that they found a large number of Covid-19 positive cases among Muslims who had attended a mass religious congregation in Delhi, some BJP leaders called the meeting a "Talibani crime" and "CoronaTerrorism." Some pro-government media had screamed "CoronaJihad" and social media platforms were flooded by calls for social and economic boycotts of Muslims. There were also numerous physical attacks on Muslims, including volunteers distributing relief material, amid falsehoods accusing them of spreading the virus deliberately.

According to 2019 government data, crimes against Dalits increased by 7 percent. This, Dalit rights activists said, was in part as backlash by members of dominant castes against any efforts toward upward mobility or what they might perceive as a challenge to caste hierarchy. In August, 40 Dalit families in Odisha were socially boycotted when a 15-year-old girl plucked flowers from the backyard of a dominant caste family. In July, a Dalit man was stripped and beaten along with his family members in Karnataka for allegedly touching the motorcycle of a dominant caste man. In February, a Dalit man was beaten to death by members of dominant caste in Tamil Nadu for defecating in their field. In September, a Dalit lawyer was killed over his social media posts critical of Brahminism.

In August, several United Nations experts raised concerns over the government's proposed revision to the environmental impact assessment process that exempts several large industries and projects from public consultation and allows post-facto clearance for projects that began without obtaining the required permissions. Environmental activists worry that diluting the provisions for public consultation and allowing post-facto clearances would undermine the rights of tribal communities, already facing a violation of rights due to the illegalities in forest clearances.

Civil Society and Freedom of Association

Indian authorities brought politically motivated cases, including under draconian sedition and terrorism laws, against human rights defenders, student activists, academics, opposition leaders, and critics, blaming them for the communal violence in February in Delhi as well as caste-based violence in Bhima

Koregaon in Maharashtra state in January 2018. In both cases, BJP supporters were implicated in the violence. Police investigations in these cases were biased and aimed at silencing dissent and deterring future protests against government policies.

In September, the parliament passed amendments to the Foreign Contribution Regulation Act (FCRA), the foreign funding law already used to harass outspoken rights groups. The amendments added onerous governmental oversight, additional regulations and certification processes, and operational requirements, which would adversely affect civil society groups, and effectively restrict access to foreign funding for small nongovernmental organizations. In September, Amnesty International was forced to suspend its India operations after the government froze the organization's bank accounts, accusing it of violating laws related to foreign funding. Amnesty said it was a "reprisal" for its work and that the government's actions were the latest in "the incessant witch-hunt of human rights organizations."

Freedom of Expression and Privacy

Several journalists faced criminal cases, arrest, threat, or even physical assault by mobs or police for reporting on Covid-19. In many cases, they were independent journalists working in rural India, targeted for their criticism of the government's handling of the pandemic.

Meanwhile, authorities continued to use sedition and laws related to national security against journalists. In September, journalist Rajeev Sharma was arrested under the Official Secrets Act for allegedly selling sensitive information to Chinese officials. The Press Club of India condemned the arrest, pointing to the police's "dubious" past record of arresting journalists under the law without basis. In August, Uttar Pradesh authorities arrested journalist Prashant Kanojia over a post on Twitter, accusing him of disrupting communal harmony. Kanojia was also arrested last year over social media posts critical of the state's chief minister but was granted bail.

In August, the Supreme Court convicted prominent lawyer Prashant Bhushan for criminal contempt of court for two social media posts, prompting widespread condemnation from former judges, retired bureaucrats, and lawyers who called it a "disproportionate response" that would have a "chilling effect" on people expressing critical views of the judiciary.

India continued to lead with the largest number of internet shutdowns globally as authorities resorted to blanket shutdowns either to prevent social unrest or to respond to an ongoing law and order problem. By early November, there were 71 shutdowns, out of which 57 were in Jammu and Kashmir, according to Software Freedom Law Centre.

Women's Rights

Cases of domestic violence rose during the lockdown, as witnessed in many countries globally. In March, authorities executed the four men convicted for the gang-rape and murder of Jyoti Singh Pandey in 2012 in Delhi, even as there was a 7.9 percent increase in rape cases registered in 2019 over the previous year. Calls for the death penalty also failed to address systemic barriers to justice for survivors of sexual violence in India, including stigma, fear of retaliation, hostile or dismissive police response, and a lack of access to adequate legal and health support services.

In September, a 19-year-old Dalit woman died after being gang-raped and tortured allegedly by four men of dominant caste in a village in Uttar Pradesh. The authorities' response highlighted how women from marginalized communities face even greater institutional barriers. State authorities cremated the victim's body without the family's consent and denied the woman had been raped, despite her dying declaration—apparently to shield the accused belonging to a dominant caste. The state government claimed that protests against the rape and killing were part of an "international conspiracy" and arrested a journalist and three political activists under terrorism and sedition laws, and also filed cases against some protesters for alleged criminal conspiracy.

Sexual harassment at work remains an entrenched problem. The government has failed to properly implement the 2013 Sexual Harassment of Women at Workplace Law, including ensuring the creation and proper functioning of complaints committees for women in the informal sector.

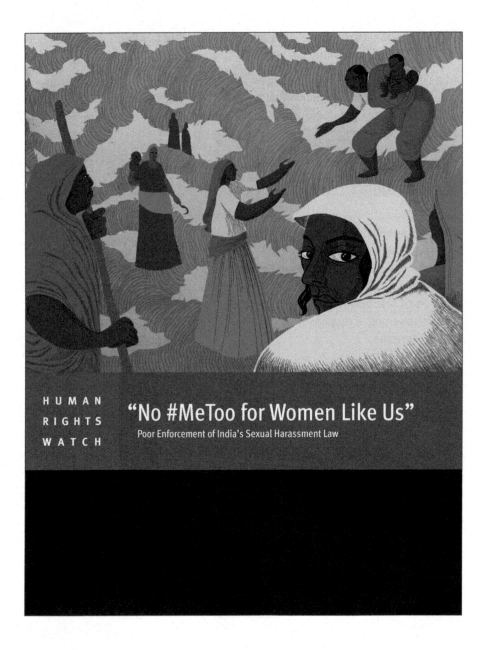

Children's Rights during Covid-19 Pandemic

Schools remained closed from March onwards and were still closed at time of writing in most of the country, affecting more than 280 million students and threatening to reverse the progress made in access to education for the poor, especially those who attended government schools. In most states, government schools did not deliver education during the lockdown, putting children from marginalized communities such as Dalit, tribal, and Muslims at greater risk of dropping out, and being pushed into child labor and early marriage. Girls were even more vulnerable.

While many private schools offered online classes, only 24 percent of Indian households had access to the internet because of a large urban-rural and gender divide, widening the learning gap across high, middle, and low-income families, according to an August UNICEF report.

Millions of children in India, particularly those from Dalit and tribal communities, were also at risk of malnutrition and illness during the pandemic because the government failed to adequately ensure the provision of meals, health care, and immunizations that many marginalized children rely on from the government schools and *anganwadi* centers, which were closed in order to stop the spread of Covid-19.

Disability Rights

For persons with disabilities, the Covid-19 lockdown brought particular challenges, including access to medical care and essential supplies, and exercising social distancing, especially for those who receive personal support for tasks of daily living.

In March, the central government introduced guidelines for protection and safety for persons with disabilities during Covid-19. These included ensuring access to information such as in braille, sign language, easy-to-read formats; exempting support people from lockdown restrictions; exempting employees with certain disabilities from essential services work; and training emergency service providers on disability rights and treating persons with disabilities. However, activists said the guidelines were poorly implemented by most state governments, remaining mostly on paper.

Sexual Orientation and Gender Identity

In September, a petition in the Delhi High Court sought the right of same-sex couples to get married under the Hindu Marriage Act. The matter was pending at time of writing.

In July, the government published the draft Transgender Persons (Protection of Rights) Rules, 2020, seeking comments from civil society. But rights groups called on the authorities to halt the process of finalizing rules for a law, passed last year, which failed to provide full protection and recognition to transgender people. The law is unclear on a transgender person's right to self-identify, which India's Supreme Court recognized in a landmark judgment in 2014. Its provisions are also contrary to international standards for legal gender recognition.

Key International Actors

The United States government said little about India's human rights record, including during President Donald Trump's visit to India in February, but several members of the US Congress continued to publicly voice concerns.

In September, following the Turkish president's critical remarks on Kashmir at the United Nations General Assembly, the Indian government called it "gross interference" in India's internal affairs and "completely unacceptable."

The European Union, working to strengthen ties with India and revamp negotiations for a bilateral free trade agreement, failed to publicly raise concerns on India's deteriorating human rights record. In July, the EU and India reiterated their commitment to human rights and pledged to reinstate their local human rights dialogue.

In February, the European Parliament negotiated and tabled an urgency resolution on India's Citizenship Amendment Act, but postponed its adoption indefinitely. In May and October, the chair of the European Parliament's Subcommittee on Human Rights raised concerns over "rule of law deterioration" in India, including arrest of human rights defenders, journalists, and peaceful critics.

In April, the Organisation of Islamic Cooperation criticized the "unrelenting vicious Islamophobic campaign in India maligning Muslims for spread of Covid-

19." The World Health Organization also cautioned against profiling Covid-19 cases "on the basis of racial, religious and ethnic lines."

The UN High Commissioner for Human Rights Michelle Bachelet voiced concerns over human rights violations in Jammu and Kashmir. In June, UN experts urged the Indian government to immediately release human rights defenders arrested for protesting against citizenship policies, saying the arrests seemed "clearly designed to send a chilling message to India's vibrant civil society that criticism of government policies will not be tolerated." In October, Bachelet also raised concerns over arrests of activists and use of vaguely defined laws to "punish NGOs for human rights reporting and advocacy that the authorities perceive as critical in nature."

Foreign Policy

Hostilities with China escalated with thousands of Indian and Chinese troops at a standoff in the Ladakh border region since May. In June, Indian army officials reported clashes that resulted in 20 deaths. In September, shots were fired in the air along the Line of Actual Control, making it the first acknowledged use of firearms between the two armies in over 40 years. Both countries accused each other's soldiers of being responsible. In response to escalating tensions, the Indian government banned over 200 Chinese-linked mobile applications, citing national security concerns.

In August, China called for a discussion on Kashmir at the UN Security Council. India and Pakistan traded allegations and counter allegations at the UN General Assembly in September over Kashmir and persecution of religious minorities.

India did not raise rights protections publicly during bilateral engagement with other neighbors including Bangladesh, Nepal, Sri Lanka, and Afghanistan. India's relations with Nepal strained over the year. In June, Nepal's parliament approved a revised map of the country, incorporating three areas disputed with India. Nepal's move came in response to India building a road through one the disputed areas and a revised map put out by India in November 2019, showing the disputed regions as belonging to India. In September, India and Sri Lanka held its first virtual bilateral summit after Prime Minister Mahinda Rajapaksa took office, and the Indian government pressed the Sri Lankan government to "address the aspirations of the Tamil people for equality, justice, peace and re-spect within a united Sri Lanka, including by carrying forward the process of rec-onciliation."

India was due to join the UN Security Council as a non-permanent member in Jan-uary 2021.

Indonesia

President Joko "Jokowi" Widodo announced the first Covid-19 cases in Indonesia on March 2, more than a month after China had imposed a lockdown in Wuhan. The virus has been devastating, killing 15,000 people, causing 2.6 million lost jobs, and an 3.49 percent decrease in GDP at time of writing.

The Jokowi government weakened Indonesia's Corruption Eradication Commission, nominating a controversial police general to head the anti-corruption body and prompting more than 30 employees to resign between January and September. His governing coalition passed a business-friendly bill in parliament that would dismantle environmental protections and labor rights.

In a victory for civil liberties, a draft criminal law was temporarily withdrawn in September 2019 after mass protests. The draft contained articles that would violate the rights of women, religious minorities, and lesbian, gay, bisexual, and transgender (LGBT) people, as well as restricting freedom of speech and association. The draft included a provision that would punish extramarital sex by up to one year in jail, effectively also criminalizing all same-sex conduct. But it is still on the list to be debated in parliament.

In a setback for justice and accountability, Defense Minister Prabowo Subianto, recruited by Jokowi to join his cabinet in 2019, appointed notorious senior military officers Dadang Hendrayudha and Yulius Selvanus to senior positions. Like Prabowo, the two were previously found guilty of kidnapping student activists in 1997-98.

LGBT rights continued to come under attack and became a worrisome rallying cry for social and political conservatives in many parts of the country.

Covid-19

Several provinces, including Jakarta, imposed lockdowns, but the government response was weak, with low testing and tracing rates and little transparency. With limited laboratories, Indonesia had tested 95,000 per week by August or around 36 percent of the World Health Organization's standard: one test per

1,000 population per week, ranking lowest among countries with 100,000 cases or more.

Jokowi deployed military, police, and intelligence bodies to conduct public health activities, including raids to enforce compliance with mask mandates. Indonesia's progress in reducing poverty over the last decade may be eliminated, with projections that the poverty rate will increase from 9.2 percent in September 2019 to 12.4 percent in September 2020.

In April, Minister of Law and Human Rights Yasonna Laoly instructed authorities to reduce the prison population by 50,000 and suspend prison visits. At the time, the prisons had almost 270,000 inmates, more than double their total official capacity

The government reacted to the pandemic by closing all public schools, 149,000 schools with over 60 million students, and moving to remote learning. This presented huge infrastructural and equity challenges, with the Internet Telecommunication Union estimating that only 48 percent of Indonesians use the internet. The Ministry of Education broadcast school materials over national television, simplified the curriculum to focus on essential numeracy and literacy skills, allowed schools to spend their budget on items such as laptops and mobile phones, and subsidized mobile data for students to improve their access to remote learning.

Freedom of Religion

Indonesian police arrested at least 38 individuals for blasphemy across 16 provinces in 2020. They included Doni Irawan, sentenced to three years for tearing a Quran inside a mosque in Deli Serdang. A Bogor court acquitted Suzethe Margareta, who has paranoid schizophrenia, for bringing her dog to a mosque. In August, Bandung police arrested Apollinaris Darmawan, a Catholic pensioner, who had written a book and posted a video on YouTube questioning the teachings of Islam.

The draft criminal code includes a provision expanding the blasphemy law from one to six articles to include offenses such as "persuading someone to be a nonbeliever."

Indonesian Christians in predominantly Muslim provinces continued to have difficulties opening new churches or keeping existing churches open in the face of opposition from conservative Muslim groups. In January, the Saint Joseph Catholic Church in Tanjung Balai, Karimun Island, had its building permit revoked after a local Muslim group protested its renovation. On September 7, a district head in Jonggol, West Java, ordered Rev. Donfri Polli, a Christian Pentecostal pastor, to stop conducting Sunday service, stating that he had no permit to operate a church. On September 21, a village head in Mojokerto, East Java, stopped Sumarmi, a Christian woman, from renovating and organizing prayers in her house unless she agreed "not to put a cross in her house."

In March, 15 Indonesians filed a lawsuit with the Supreme Court arguing that the government should stop shuttering thousands of houses of worship, mostly churches, under the discriminatory "religious harmony" regulation. In June, the Supreme Court rejected the petition, a decision that won praise from the Indonesian Ulama Council, the country's Islamic semi-governmental group, which has facilitated discrimination against religious minorities.

Freedom of Media

On January 31, American editor Philip Jacobson of the environmental news site Mongabay was deported from Indonesia after spending 45 days in detention in Palangkaraya, Central Kalimantan, over an alleged visa violation.

In June, intelligence officials pressured Lampung University to stop a webinar on racism against ethnic Papuans but the Teknokra student news website resisted. Shortly before the webinar, an editor of the Teknokra received anonymous threatening WhatsApp messages, while another editor alleged that her Gojek account (a transport, payment, and food delivery app) had been hacked.

Journalist Diananta Sumedi served three months in jail in Kotabaru, South Kalimantan, until August after writing stories about a land dispute between Dayak Indigenous people and the Jhonlin palm oil company.

In August, four news media organizations, including those that ran the websites Tempo and Tirto, were subject to hacking and other digital attacks after publishing critical stories on Indonesian military involvement in pushing a Covid-19 vaccine.

In September police arrested three student journalists after they joined fishermen on their boat to protest sand mining on Kodingareng Island, off Makassar. In October, at least 56 journalists were beaten, threatened, and arbitrarily arrested in Malang, Jakarta, and Surabaya, when covering protests against the new job creation law.

Women's Rights

Women's rights groups, including the National Commission on Violence Against Women and Legal Aid Foundation of the Indonesian Women's Association for Justice, reported domestic violence cases associated with pandemic-related lockdowns has doubled from the 2019 number. Women's rights groups campaigned for the parliament to take action on two long-awaited pieces of legislation: a sexual violence prevention bill and a domestic worker protection bill. The Sexual Violence Prevention bill, first proposed in 2016, was removed from the priority list in July. The Domestic Worker Protection Bill, under deliberation for 16 years, remains stuck in parliament.

Sexual Orientation and Gender Identity

In Jakarta, police arrested three men after a transgender woman was burned alive on April 7. On Madura Island, police arrested three male suspects after a transgender woman was robbed and killed in her salon on September 3.

Indonesian authorities continued their assault on the basic rights of LGBT people. On August 29, police forcibly broke up a party at a hotel, arresting nine men and charging them with the crime of "facilitating obscene acts" under the pornography law, which discriminates against LGBT people. East Java police arrested a police officer in Probolinggo who allegedly had a relationship with another man. In October, the Supreme Court announced that it had rejected appeals and dismissed at least 16 gay soldiers in several court cases including in Bandung, Jayapura, Medan, Semarang, and Surabaya.

Papua, West Papua, and the Moluccas Islands

Indonesian courts tried more than 70 Papuan activists in eight cities, including Jakarta, for participation in anti-racism rallies at which they unfurled the Papuan

Morning Star flag. The courts found them guilty of "treason" and sentenced them maximum to 11 months in prison, the amount of time already served.

On July 18 in Papua soldiers shot and killed father and son Elias and Selu Karunggu in an apparent extrajudicial execution after they pulled the son aside for interrogation as the two were waiting for a boat. On July 24, Indonesian soldiers from Raider 516/Caraka Yudha battalion allegedly assaulted and killed Papuan teenager Oktovianus Betera after he got into a verbal dispute with a shop owner who claimed he was trying to shoplift.

Rev. Yeremia Zanambani of the Gospel Tabernacle Church of Indonesia was shot dead when feeding his pigs near his house in Hitadipa village, Intan Jaya district, Papua, on September 19. Hostilities were ongoing in the area between Indonesian soldiers and a Free West Papua group during which two soldiers and two non-Papuan Indonesians were killed.

No one was arrested for the killing of at least 52 Papuans and migrants from other parts of Indonesia in Deiyai and Wamena during 2019 anti-racism protests. The precise number of deaths is unknown because the government continued to limit access to Papua in 2020.

In April in Ambon police arrested 23 activists, who participated in flag-raising ceremonies commemorating the 70th anniversary of the declaration of independence of the Republic of South Moluccas (Republik Maluku Selatan, RMS). The Ambon court found three of them guilty, sentencing two to two years and a third to three years in prison.

In Ternate, Khairun University dismissed four students for taking part in a protest against racism in Papua. The students filed a lawsuit in Ambon but the administrative court rejected their petition in September.

Indigenous Rights

Major Indonesian companies continued to cut old growth forests with impunity. Yet on May 19, a court sentenced Bongku of the Sakai Indigenous group in Riau to a year in jail for cutting down 20 trees in a forest that his tribe has claimed in a longstanding dispute with the Asia Pulp & Paper Group.

On April 26, Hermanus, a Dayak Indigenous farmer, died in a Sampit hospital while still facing trial for defending his land against Best Agro oil palm plantation. The land dispute began in 2003. On June 15, his colleagues, James Watt and Dilik, were sentenced respectively to 10 and 8 months in jail for "stealing" oil palm fruits from land the National Land Agency had declared in 2011 belonged to the village.

On August 18, police raided the Pubabu Indigenous community on Timor Island, displacing more than 600 people and destroying 47 homes in a long-lasting land dispute.

On August 26, the police arrested Effendi Buhing, the tribal chief of the Dayak Indigenous community in Kinipan forest, Central Kalimantan. Five of his colleagues had previously been detained for seizing chainsaws from the workers of PT Sawit Mandiri Lestari palm oil company in an attempt to stop them from clearing the forest.

Disability Rights

Despite government efforts, people with psychosocial disabilities (mental health conditions) are shackled—chained or locked in confined spaces—for weeks, months, or even years. According to government data, approximately 15,000 people are still living in chains.

The Indonesian Health Ministry rolled out a community outreach program to collect data, raise awareness, and provide services, including mental health services. As of September 2020, the program had reached 48 million—roughly 70 percent—of Indonesian households. However, Covid-19 has posed an extreme threat to people with psychosocial disabilities who are shackled in homes or overcrowded institutions without proper access to sanitation, running water, soap, or even basic health care. Covid-19 has disrupted services putting people with psychosocial disabilities at risk of being shackled or locked up in institutions.

Key International Actors

Indonesia, the largest country in Southeast Asia and a member of the Organisation of Islamic Cooperation, failed to press Myanmar on the atrocities against Rohingya Muslims or the nearly one million refugees in Bangladesh during the Association of Southeast Asian Nations (ASEAN) summit in Hanoi in July. Indonesia remained silent despite sympathetic public opinion and the continued arrival of Rohingya refugees to Sumatra.

Indonesia also was quiet on the plight of Uyghur and other Turkic Muslims in Xinjiang, China, instead inviting the Chinese Embassy to communicate directly with multiple Muslim groups in Indonesia.

In October, US Secretary of State Mike Pompeo visited Jakarta, urging Indonesians to focus on the treatment of Muslim Uighurs in China and describing it as the "gravest threat" to religious freedom in a speech to an Islamic group.

In his address to the United Nations General Assembly on September 23, President Jokowi called for greater international cooperation: "Our concern grew even deeper during the Covid-19 pandemic. At a time when we ought to unite and work together, what we see, instead, is a deep division and growing rivalries."

On September 25, Vanuatu asked Indonesia to fulfill President Jokowi's promise to have UN human rights monitors visit Papua and West Papua provinces.

In October 2019, the European Parliament adopted a resolution raising concerns about the draft criminal code and the overall human rights situation in Indonesia. The European Union also raised concerns about the draft criminal law a few weeks later during its bilateral human rights dialogue with Indonesia.

Iran

Iranian authorities continued to repress their own people. The country's security and intelligence apparatus, in partnership with Iran's judiciary, harshly cracked down on dissent, including through excessive and lethal force against protesters and reported abuse and torture in detention. President Rouhani and his administration have shown little inclination to curb or confront these serious rights violations perpetrated by Iran's security agencies, while Supreme Leader Ayatollah Khamenei continues to greenlight these rampant abuses. Broad United States sanctions also impacted the country's economy and Iranians' access to essential medicines and harmed their right to health.

Right to Peaceful Assembly and Expression

Over the past three years, Iranian authorities have responded to repeated widespread protests across the country with excessive and lethal force and the arbitrary arrests of thousands of protesters.

In one of the most brutal crackdowns, in November 2019, security forces used excessive and unlawful lethal force against massive protests across the country, particularly against protesters blocking roads, or in some cases throwing stones and attempting to take over public buildings.

During the crackdown, authorities ordered the near-total shutdown of the global internet across the country. According to Amnesty International, at least 304 people were killed during these protests. On June 1, Mojtaba Zonoor, the head of Iran's parliamentary national security committee, said that 230 people had been killed during the protests. He claimed 7 percent of those killed died in direct confrontation with law enforcement and 16 percent in attacks against military places. Authorities have not published any detailed investigations into, or held anyone accountable for, these abuses.

The judiciary and intelligence agencies continue to use several overly broad articles of the penal code, such as "propaganda against the state," "assembly and collusion to act against national security," "insulting the supreme leader," and "establishing or membership in a group to disrupt national security" to prosecute activists, dissidents, and human rights defenders.

Authorities have prosecuted at least 20 people who participated in protests against the Islamic Revolutionary Guard Corps' (IRGC) downing of a Ukrainian airliner on January 8 and the government's initial false denial of responsibility. The IRGC shot down the airliner amid heightened military tensions between Iran and the US, after the US killed the commander of the IRCG's elite Quds force, Qassim Suleimani, and several others in a drone strike in Baghdad on January 3. Among other cases, the court of first instance sentenced two prominent activists, Bahareh Hedayat and Mehdi Mahmoudian, to four years and eight months and five years in prison, respectively, for their participation in the protests and posting about it on their Twitter accounts.

On May 23, the media center of the judiciary reported that Ayatollah Khamanei had agreed to clemency or a reduction of prison sentences against several "national security convicts." According to lawyers and family members, those included: Ismael Bakhshi, Ali Nejati, and Mohamad Khanifar, labor rights activists who participated in the Hafttappeh Sugar cane company labor strike in 2018; Marzieh Amiri, Atefeh Rangriz, and Neda Naji, activists arrested during the 2019 May Day protests in front of parliament; and Leila Hosseinzadeh and Soheil Aghaei, student activists.

Other labor activists, however, still face imprisonment. On August 26, Keyvan Samimi, a veteran journalist, wrote in his Telegram channel that authorities had suspended the three-year prison sentence that he had received after his arrest during the 2019 May 1 ("May Day") protests on the charge of "assembly and collusion to act against national security." On June 21, authorities arrested Sepideh Gholian, another labor activist, who was sentenced to five years in prison on the charge of "assembly and collusion to act against national security," after she was arrested during the Haftappeh strike in November 2018. Gholian alleged that authorities tortured her and Bakhshi during their detention in November 2018.

On March 31, lawyer Mohammad Hossein Aghasi announced that his clients Hashem Khastar, Mohammad Nourizad, Mohammad Hossein Sepehri, and Fatemeh Sepehri—four civil society activists who signed a 2019 letter asking Ayatollah Khamenei to resign—had been sentenced to 16, 15, 6, and 3 years in prison, respectively. On September 6, authorities arrested Giti Fazel, a retired lawyer, and sentenced her to 3 years and 6 months' prison sentence for charges that stemmed from signing the letter requesting the resignation of Ayatollah Khamenei.

Death Penalty and Inhumane Treatment

Iran continues to be one of the leading implementers of the death penalty. According to rights groups, Iran had executed at least 233 people as of November 19. These include four people on vaguely defined national security crimes of *moharebeh* ("enmity against God"), *ifsad fil arz* ("sowing corruption on earth"), and *baghi* ("armed rebellion") and two people on espionage charges.

As of September 21, authorities executed two people who were convicted of allegedly killing security forces during the protests. Despite domestic and international outcry, on September 13 authorities in Shiraz executed Navid Afkari, a 27-year-old wrestler who was convicted of murdering a security guard. Authorities did not investigate the serious allegations of torture he had raised repeatedly throughout the court proceedings.

There are at least eight other people who have received the death penalty on vaguely defined national security charges in connection to their participation in widespread protests. After a popular social media campaign using the hashtag #Don'tExecute, on July 10, lawyers representing three defendants facing the death penalty announced that the judiciary had halted the executions of Amirhossein Moradi, Saeed Tamjidi, and Mohammad Rajabi. They had been convicted and sentenced to death for their role in the November 2019 protests on charges of "taking part in destruction and burning aimed at countering the Islamic Republic of Iran."

The judiciary also executed at least two individuals who were sentenced to death for crimes they allegedly committed as children. Under Iran's current penal code, judges can use their discretion not to sentence to death individuals who committed their alleged crime as children. However, several individuals who were retried under the penal code for crimes they allegedly committed as children have then been sentenced to death again.

Iranian law considers acts such as "insulting the prophet," "apostasy," same-sex relations, adultery, drinking alcohol, and certain non-violent drug-related offenses as crimes punishable by death. The law also prescribes the inhumane punishment of flogging for more than 100 offenses, including "disrupting public order," a charge that has been used to sentence individuals for their participation in protests.

According to the Norway-based NGO, Iran Human Rights, on July 8, authorities in Mashhad executed a man convicted of drinking alcohol repeatedly.

Human Rights Defenders and Civil Society Activists

Scores of human rights advocates, including Atena Daemi and Farhad Meysami, remain behind bars for their peaceful activism. On October 8, authorities released prominent human rights defender Narges Mohammadi after reducing her 10-year prison sentence to eight-and-a-half years.

Over the past two years, authorities have also prosecuted several lawyers, including Mohammad Najafi, Payam Derafshan, and Amirsalar Davoudi, for their human rights activism. On November 7, authorities temporarily released prominent human rights defender and lawyer Nasrin Sotoudeh who was currently serving a 12-year prison sentence in Evin prison.

In February, a court of appeal upheld prison sentences ranging from 4 to 10 years against 8 members of the Persian Wildlife Heritage Foundation, a local NGO focused on preserving biodiversity, on the charge of "collaborating with the hostile state of the US." Iranian authorities have failed to produce any evidence to support their charges nor have they investigated allegations of torture against them.

Due Process Rights, Fair Trial Standards, and Torture in Prison

Iranian courts, and particularly revolutionary courts, regularly fall far short of providing fair trials and use confessions likely obtained under torture as evidence in court. Authorities have failed to meaningfully investigate numerous allegations of torture against detainees. Authorities routinely restrict detainees' access to legal counsel, particularly during the initial investigation period.

The IRGC's Intelligence Organization continues to arrest Iranian dual and foreign nationals on vague charges, such as "cooperating with a hostile state." Over the past year, authorities have released: Michael White and Xiyua Wang, American citizens; Roland Marchal, a French academic; and two Australian bloggers in apparent prisoners' exchanges with their respective countries.

Several others, including Siamak Namazi, an Iranian-American dual national who was sentenced in unfair trials to 10 years in prison—remain behind bars. Baquer Namazi, Siamak's father, Nazanin Zaghari-Ratcliffe, an Iranian-British dual national, and Fariba Adelkhah, a French-Iranian academic, have been granted temporary releases but are not allowed to leave the country. On November 26, Iranian authorities released Kylie Moore-Gilbert, an Australian academic who was convicted to 10 years in prison, in exchange for three Iranian prisoners in Thailand, two of whom had been reportedly convicted in connection with the 2012 Bangkok bomb plot.

In April, after the country's first confirmed cases of Covid-19 in early March, Iran's judiciary announced that it had temporarily released or pardoned up to 100,000 prisoners and implemented measures to enable social distancing within prisons. Several human rights defenders, including Shahnaz Akmali, Masoud Kazemi, Abdolreza Kouhpayeh, and Mahmoud Beheshti Langroodi, were among those released under the judicial order. In many other cases, despite the health risks, authorities have refused to grant human rights defenders temporary releases.

Authorities also have opened new cases against human rights defenders who were serving time in prison. On May 28, Ismael Abdi, a prominent member of Iran's Teachers Union on a furlough from serving a 6-year sentence he received for his activism, was detained again after authorities reimposed another previously suspended 10-year prison sentence, without his prior knowledge.

Women's Rights, Children's Rights, Sexual Orientation, and Gender Identity

Iranian women face discrimination in personal status matters related to marriage, divorce, inheritance, and decisions relating to children. A married woman may not obtain a passport or travel outside the country without the written permission of her husband. Under the civil code, a husband is accorded the right to choose the place of living and can prevent his wife from having certain occupations if he deems them against "family values." Iranian law allows girls to marry at 13 and boys at age 15, as well as at younger ages if authorized by a judge.

Over the past two years, authorities have prosecuted several women's rights activists, including Yasaman Ariayi, Saba Kordafshari, Mojhgan Keshavarz, Monireh Arabshahi, and Farhad Meysami for their peaceful protests against compulsory hijab laws. On July 15, Saeed Dehghan, the lawyer of Alireza Alinejad, posted on Twitter that a revolutionary court has sentenced his client to eight years in prison on charges of assembly and collusion act against national security, insulting the supreme leader, and propaganda against the state. The sentencing appears to be a retaliatory act to silence Alinejad's sister, Massih Alinejad, a prominent political activist based abroad campaigning against compulsory hijab laws.

Iranian authorities and women's rights activists reported an increase in domestic violence during Covid-19 lockdown restrictions. Iran has no law on domestic violence to prevent abuse and provide protections to survivors. There was a national outrage following the gruesome beheading of 14-year-old Romina Ashrafi, allegedly by her father, on May 21, and several government officials called for expediting the approval of a bill to "support children and adolescents."

On June 7, 2020, the Guardian Council, the body responsible for ensuring the compatibility of the legislation passed by Iran's parliament with the constitution and Iranian authorities' interpretation of Sharia, approved this bill. It includes new penalties for certain acts that harm a child's safety and well-being, including physical harm and preventing access to education. The law also allows officials to relocate a child in situations that seriously threaten their safety. But the law fails to address some of the most serious threats against children in Iran, such as child marriage and imposition of the death penalty.

In early August, dozens of Iranian women took to social media in their own #MeToo moment to report their experiences of sexual harassment and assault. On August 25, the Tehran police chief announced they had arrested a man accused of rape by multiple women on social media. Women face barriers reporting sexual violence. Iranian law criminalizes consensual sexual relationships outside marriage, which are punishable by flogging, leaving women at risk of being prosecuted for reporting rape if the authorities do not believe her. Moreover, the criminal law has a limited and problematic definition of rape as "forced *zina*" (sex outside of wedlock), explicitly excludes marital rape, and the mandatory punishment for rape is the death penalty.

Authorities have long prosecuted hundreds of people for the vaguely defined acts against morality, as well as for consensual extramarital sex.

Under Iranian law, same-sex conduct is punishable by flogging and, for men, the death penalty. Although Iran permits and subsidizes sex reassignment surgery for transgender people, no law prohibits discrimination against them.

Iran closed schools and universities in early March due to the Covid-19 pandemic. The Education Ministry banned teachers from using foreign-made smartphone apps to teach classes and launched an online learning platform in April, as well as televised lessons. The disparity in quality of material produced by different schools across the country and levels of students' access to online education appear to vary across pre-existing socioeconomic disparities. For instance, more than 50 percent of families in some areas, like Sistan and Baluchistan, did not have internet access.

Treatment of Minorities

Iranian law denies freedom of religion to Baha'is and discriminates against them. Authorities continue to arrest and prosecute members of the Baha'i faith on vague national security charges and close down or suspend licenses for businesses owned by them. Iranian authorities also systematically refuse to allow Baha'is to register at public universities because of their faith. On June 30, a court in Bushehr convicted seven Christians who converted from Islam on the charge of propaganda against the state. According to the rights group Hrana, the charge stemmed from activities such as organizing "house churches" and being in contact with missionaries outside the country.

The government also discriminates against other religious minorities, including Sunni Muslims, and restricts cultural and political activities among the country's Azeri, Kurdish, Arab, and Baluch ethnic minorities.

Key International Actors

Following the United States withdrawal from the 2015 Joint Comprehensive Plan of Action (JCPOA) agreement on Iran's nuclear activities, the US has increasingly targeted Iran with broad economic sanctions. While the US government has built exemptions for humanitarian imports into its sanction regime, banking restrictions have drastically constrained the ability of Iranian entities to finance such humanitarian imports, including vital medicines and medical equipment, causing serious hardships for ordinary Iranians and harming their right to health, particularly as the Covid-19 pandemic has increased the burden on the healthcare system.

In January, the United States killed Qassem Soleimani, commander of Iran's IRGC Quds Force in a drone strike in Iraq. In response, Iranian forces carried out a ballistic missile attack against two US bases in Iraq. In the days following the strike, US President Donald Trump tweeted that the US had prepared targets of Iranian sites, including sites of cultural importance. Attacks during an armed conflict deliberately targeting sites of cultural importance are war crimes.

In September, following the United Nations Security Council's refusal to renew an arms embargo that had come to an end as part of the JCPOA, the US argued that it could trigger the "snapback" provision of the agreement to reimpose UN sanctions suspended as a result of the JCPOA. Other permanent members of the Security Council and parties to the JCPOA, as well as the UN secretary-general, refused to accept the US's position, arguing that the US cannot use the provision after already withdrawing from the agreement.

On numerous occasions, the head of the European Union External Action Service, as well as the European Parliament, condemned violations of human rights in Iran, including the crackdown against protests and use of the death penalty.

HUMAN
RIGHTS
WATCH

"We Might Call You in at Any Time"
Free Speech Under Threat in Iraq

Iraq

Arbitrary arrests, enforced disappearances, and extrajudicial killings of demonstrators by Iraqi security forces in late 2019 and into 2020 led to government resignations and the nomination of a new prime minister, Mustafa al-Kadhimi, in May 2020. Despite an initial seeming willingness to address some of Iraq's most serious human rights challenges, al-Kadhimi's government failed to end abuses against protesters.

Iraq's criminal justice system was riddled with the widespread use of torture and forced confessions and, despite serious due process violations, authorities carried out numerous judicial executions.

Iraqi law contained a range of defamation and incitement provisions that authorities used against critics, including journalists, activists, and protesters to silence dissent.

The Covid-19 pandemic had a particularly harmful impact on students kept out of school during nationwide school closures, many of whom were unable to access any remote learning.

Excessive Force against Protesters

In a wave of protests that began in October 2019 and continued into late 2020, clashes with security forces, including the Popular Mobilization Forces (PMF or *Hashad*, nominally under the control of the prime minister), left at least 560 protesters and security forces dead in Baghdad and Iraq's southern cities.

In July 2020, the government announced it would compensate the families of those killed during the protests and that it had arrested three low-level security forces officers. As far as Human Rights Watch is aware, no senior commanders have been prosecuted. After a spate of killings and attempted killings of protesters in Basra in August 2020, the government fired Basra's police chief and the governorate's director of national security but seemingly did not refer anyone for prosecution. In May 2020, when Prime Minister Mustafa al-Kadhimi took office, he formed a committee to investigate the killings of protesters. It had yet to announce any findings publicly as of late 2020.

In May, security forces in Iraq's Kurdistan Region arrested dozens of people planning to participate in protests against delayed government salaries, a persistent issue since 2015. At August 2020 protests by civil servants in the Kurdistan Region demanding unpaid wages, Kurdistan Regional Government (KRG) security forces beat and arbitrarily detained protesters and journalists.

Silencing Free Speech

Iraq's penal code, which dates back to 1969, enshrines numerous defamation "crimes," such as "insult[ing] the Arab community" or any government official, regardless of whether the statement is true. Although few individuals served prison time on defamation charges, the criminal process itself acted as a punishment. Reporting on corruption and abuses by the security forces was especially risky.

Authorities also invoked other laws and regulations to limit free speech. The Communications and Media Commission (CMC), a "financially and administratively independent institution" linked to parliament, in 2014 issued without legal basis "mandatory" guidelines to regulate media during "the war on terror"—a phrase it did not define. These guidelines were updated in May 2019 and renamed the "Media Broadcasting Rules." They restrict freedom of the press to the point of requiring pro-government coverage.

The CMC suspended Reuters's license under its broadcast media regulations powers for three months and fined it 25 million IQD (US$21,000) for an April 2, 2020 article alleging that the number of confirmed Covid-19 cases in the country was much higher than official statistics indicated. Authorities lifted the suspension on April 19.

The KRG used similar laws in force in the Kurdistan Region to curb free speech, including the penal code, the Press Law, and the Law to Prevent the Misuse of Telecommunications Equipment.

Arbitrary Detention

Iraqi forces arbitrarily detained Islamic State (also known as ISIS) suspects for months, and some for years. According to witnesses and family members, security forces regularly detained suspects without any court order or arrest warrant and often did not provide a reason for the arrest.

Iraqi authorities also arbitrarily detained protesters and released them later, some within hours or days and others within weeks, without charge.

Despite requests, the central government failed to disclose which security and military structures have a legal mandate to detain people, and in which facilities.

Fair Trial Violations

In January 2020, the UN Assistance Mission in Iraq (UNAMI) published a report assessing the criminal justice system, based on independent monitoring of 794 criminal court trials, 619 of them for men, women and children charged under Iraq's dangerously overbroad counterterrorism law. It supported Human Rights Watch findings that basic fair trial standards were not respected in terrorism-related trials.

Iraqi judges routinely prosecuted ISIS suspects solely on the overbroad charge of ISIS affiliation, rather than for the specific violent crimes they may have committed. Trials were generally rushed, based on a defendant's confession, and did not involve victim participation. Authorities systematically violated the due process rights of suspects, such as guarantees in Iraqi law that detainees see a judge within 24 hours and have access to a lawyer throughout interrogations, and that their families are notified and should be able to communicate with them during detention.

Detainees have shared graphic accounts of torture during interrogations in Mosul's prisons under the control of the Ministry of Interior, in some cases leading to their deaths. These allegations are consistent with reports of the widespread use of torture by Iraqi forces to extract confessions instead of carrying out robust criminal investigations.

Authorities can prosecute child suspects as young as 9 with alleged ISIS affiliation in Baghdad-controlled areas and 11 in the KRI, in violation of international standards, which recognize children recruited by armed groups primarily as victims who should be rehabilitated and reintegrated into society, and call for a minimum age of criminal responsibility of 14 years or older.

347

Conditions in Detention

Authorities detained criminal suspects in overcrowded and in some cases inhuman conditions. According to media reports, authorities released 20,000 prisoners in April as a preventive measure in response to the Covid-19 pandemic but did not share any information on the identities of those released and the criteria for selecting them. Authorities refused to respond when asked to share or make public the number of people in Iraqi prisons, making it impossible to assess whether the releases sufficiently reduced the acute overcrowding to enable social distancing. In July, there were 31 Covid-19 cases reported at a prison in Baghdad.

Death Penalty

Iraq had one of the highest rates of executions in the world, alongside China, Iran, and Saudi Arabia. The judiciary handed down death sentences to many of those convicted of ISIS affiliation under counterterrorism legislation and carried out executions without disclosing official numbers. In August 2019, authorities released Ministry of Justice data that showed 8,022 detainees were on death row and the state had executed over 100 between January and August 2019 but did not provide statistics for 2020.

The expedited nature of the trials of ISIS suspects contributed to concerns that courts were issuing death sentences despite serious due process shortcomings.

In the Kurdistan Region, the KRG has maintained a de facto moratorium on the death penalty since 2008, banning it "except in very few cases which were considered essential," according to a KRG spokesperson.

ISIS Crimes Against the Yezidi Community, including Sexual Violence

Despite ISIS's system of organized rape, sexual slavery, and forced marriage, and eeven where defendants admitted during prosecutions to subjecting Yezidi women to sexual slavery, prosecutors neglected to charge them with rape, which carries a sentence of up to 15 years. Instead, they charged them with ISIS membership, support, sympathy, or assistance under counterterrorism legislation.

On April 7, 2019, President Barham Salih submitted a draft Yezidi Female Survivors Law to parliament. The law aims to rehabilitate, reintegrate, and provide economic empowerment to Yezidi female survivors, and states it will provide "symbolic recognition of the genocide committed against Yezidis." However, the draft law has shortcomings, such as restricting the definition of survivors to Yezidi women and girls who were kidnapped by ISIS and then released. It did not include men and boys, as well as survivors and victims of ISIS from other communities.

Collective Punishment

Security forces denied security clearances required to obtain identity cards and other essential civil documentation to thousands of Iraqi families the authorities perceived to have ISIS affiliation, usually because of their family name, tribal affiliation, or area of origin. This denied them freedom of movement, their rights to education and work, and access to social benefits and birth and death certificates needed to inherit property or remarry.

Authorities prevented thousands of children without civil documentation from enrolling in state schools, including state schools inside camps for displaced people.

Some families were able to obtain a security clearance if they were willing to first open a criminal complaint disavowing any relative suspected of having joined ISIS. After individuals open the criminal complaint, the court issues them a document to present to security forces enabling them to obtain their security clearances.

At least 30,000 Iraqis who fled Iraq between 2014 and 2017, including some who followed ISIS as it retreated from Iraqi territory, have been held in and around al-Hol camp in northeast Syria. In 2019 the Iraqi government discussed plans to return, transfer, and detain these and other families with perceived ISIS affiliation in a mass internment scheme in Iraq, but has yet to agree on such a plan. As of late 2020, it had taken no further measures regarding Iraqis held in northeast Syria.

The Kurdistan Regional Government (KRG) has prevented thousands of Arabs from returning home to villages in the Rabia subdistrict and Hamdaniya district, areas where KRG forces had pushed ISIS out in 2014 and taken territorial control. At the same time, the KRG allowed Kurdish villagers to return to those areas.

Women's Rights, Gender Identity, Sexual Orientation, Morality Laws

Article 394 of Iraq's penal code makes it illegal to engage in extra-marital sex, a violation of the right to privacy that disproportionately harms lesbian, gay, bisexual, and transgender (LGBT) people, as well as women, as pregnancy can be deemed evidence of the violation. Women reporting rape can also find themselves subject to prosecution under this law. Iraq's criminal code does not explicitly prohibit same-sex sexual relations, but article 401 of the penal code holds that any person who commits an "immodest act" in public can be imprisoned for up to six months, a vague provision that could be used to target sexual and gender minorities, although such cases have not been documented.

Over the years authorities have not held accountable perpetrators, including security forces, of kidnappings, torture, and killings of people perceived as gay and transgender. A 2012 government committee established to address abuses against LGBT people took few tangible steps to protect them before disbanding.

Domestic violence continued to remain endemic in 2020, including the killings of women and girls by their families and husbands.

While Iraq's criminal code criminalizes physical assault, article 41(1) gives a husband a legal right to "punish" his wife and parents to discipline their children "within limits prescribed by law or custom." The penal code also provides for mitigated sentences for violent acts, including murder, for "honorable motives" or for catching one's wife or female relative in the act of adultery or sex outside of marriage. Iraqi parliamentary efforts to pass a draft law against domestic violence stalled throughout 2019 and 2020. The 2019 version of the draft anti-domestic violence law seen by Human Rights Watch includes provisions for services for domestic violence survivors, protection (restraining) orders, penalties for their breach, and the establishment of a cross-ministerial committee to combat domestic violence. However, the bill has several gaps and provisions that would undermine its effectiveness, including that it prioritizes reconciliation over protection and justice for victims.

Education

Schools were closed in March 2020 through the end of the school year in the Kurdistan Region, with schools in Baghdad-controlled territory closed from March through to at least November 2020, due to the Covid-19 pandemic. According to teachers, parents, and students, children living in poverty, and families displaced from their homes by earlier fighting between Iraqi forces and ISIS were most disadvantaged, as most lacked access to digital learning options. The loss of education during this period had a more dramatic impact on the many children who had lost three academic years before the pandemic when living under ISIS.

Key International Actors

Relations with the United States, a key partner in the fight against ISIS, came under strain. In 2019 and 2020, unnamed groups carried out multiple rocket attacks on US targets in Iraq. In response to one of those attacks, on January 3, 2020, a US drone strike killed Lt. Gen. Qassem Soleimani, the Quds Force commander of Iran's Islamic Revolutionary Guards Corps, at Baghdad airport. Two days later, Iraqi parliamentarians passed a non-binding resolution to expel US-led coalition troops from the country, which was not acted upon. In August, the Pentagon announced that it would be cutting the US force presence in Iraq by one third, to about 3,500 troops.

In the US Fiscal Year 2020, the US Congress allocated $451 million in military assistance to Iraq, including through Foreign Military Financing, International Military Education and Training, and other programs. The US Congress also appropriated $745 million in defense funding for Iraq programs under the Counter-ISIS Train and Equip Fund, and authorized another $30 million for the Office of Security Cooperation at the US Embassy in Baghdad, which helps administer training and support programs funded through foreign military sales and foreign military financing assistance.

In August 2020, the US State Department announced an increase in humanitarian assistance to Iraq, bringing the total to more than $706 million since October 2018, as well as an additional $49.5 million in Covid economic assistance and more than $22.7 million to assist Syrian refugees in Iraq.

Iran wields significant political influence in Iraq, largely through political parties and some armed groups within the PMF. Iraq also relies on Iran for natural gas, among other vital imports.

Turkish airstrikes throughout 2020, targeting the Iranian Kurdish Party for Free Life of Kurdistan (PJAK) and members of the Kurdistan Workers' Party (PKK) based in northern Iraq, killed over a dozen civilians in the region. Human Rights Watch was unaware of any investigations by the Turkish authorities into possible laws-of-war violations in northern Iraq or compensation of victims.

In 2017, the UN Security Council created an investigative team to document serious crimes committed by ISIS in Iraq. Given the deeply flawed Iraqi criminal proceedings against ISIS suspects and ongoing fair trial concerns in the country, it remained unclear to what extent the team could support the Iraqi judiciary in building case files in line with international standards.

Israel and Palestine

Israeli authorities in 2020 systematically repressed and discriminated against Palestinians in ways that far exceeded the security justifications they often provided.

For a 13th consecutive year, the government enforced a generalized travel ban on Palestinians in the occupied Gaza Strip and sharply restricted the entry and exit of goods. These restrictions, not based on an individualized assessment of security risk, robbed with rare exceptions the 2 million Palestinians living there of their right to freedom of movement, limited their access to electricity and water, and devastated the economy. Eighty percent of Gaza's residents depend on humanitarian aid.

Israeli authorities also facilitated the further transfer of Israeli citizens into settlements in the occupied West Bank, a war crime. The Israeli group Peace Now said that Israeli officials in 2020 advanced plans for more housing units in West Bank settlements, 12,159 as of October 15, more than in any other year since it began tracking these statistics in 2012.

According to the UN Office of Coordination for Humanitarian Affairs (OCHA), as of October 19, 2020, Israeli authorities demolished 568 Palestinian homes and other structures in the West Bank this year, including in East Jerusalem, displacing 759 people. Most buildings were demolished for lacking Israeli building permits, which are virtually impossible to obtain. As the Covid-19 pandemic spread between March and August, Israel averaged its highest home demolition rate in four years, OCHA found. On November 3, Israeli authorities razed the homes of most residents of the Palestinian community of Khirbet Humsah in the Jordan Valley for being in an area it designated as a "firing zone," displacing 73 people, 41 of them children.

The coalition agreement between the Likud and Blue and White parties that led to the formation of an Israeli government in May, after three rounds of elections in the preceding year, established a process to bring annexation of additional parts of the West Bank for approval. Prime Minister Benjamin Netanyahu said in August that Israel would delay the move following an agreement to normalize relations with the United Arab Emirates, but that "there is no change to my plan to extend sovereignty" over the West Bank. The Israeli Knesset dissolved in December, triggering new elections for March 2021.

Both the Fatah-dominated Palestinian Authority (PA) in the West Bank and Hamas authorities in Gaza detained opponents and critics for their peaceful expression and tortured some in their custody. The Palestinian statutory watchdog, Independent Commission for Human Rights (ICHR), received 269 complaints of arbitrary arrests, 147 against the PA and 122 by Hamas; 90 complaints of torture and ill-treatment, 40 against the PA and 50 against Hamas, and 62 complaints against the PA of detention without trial or charge pursuant to orders from a regional governor between January and September 2020. The number of complaints decreased compared to previous years, which the ICHR attributes primarily to the fewer prison visits it conducted amid the pandemic.

GAZA STRIP

Although fighting between Israel and Palestinian armed groups decreased compared to previous years, Israeli authorities maintained their closure of Gaza, alongside restrictions Egypt maintains on its border. Palestinian armed groups, as of October 21, fired 187 unguided rockets or mortar shells towards Israeli population centers in 2020, according to the Meir Amit Intelligence and Terrorism Information Center, inherently indiscriminate attacks that amount to war crimes.

Incendiary balloons launched into Israel by Palestinians in Gaza prompted Israeli authorities in August in retaliation to limit the entry into Gaza of goods, including food and medicine, to block access to Gaza's territorial waters for Palestinian fishermen and to slash fuel imports to Gaza's power plant, further reducing the already limited supply of electricity for almost three weeks. These measures, targeting Gaza's general civilian population, amount to unlawful collective punishment.

In August, Gaza recorded its first cases of community transmission of coronavirus. Hamas authorities, which since March had required returning residents to spend 21 days in quarantine at centers they oversee, imposed a 14-day lockdown and other restrictive measures. As of October 19, Gaza's Health Ministry had recorded 4,722 Covid-19 cases and 28 deaths, most of them since August.

Israeli Closure

Israel restricted the ability of most Gaza residents to travel through the Erez Crossing, the sole passenger crossing from Gaza into Israel through which Palestinians travel to the West Bank and abroad. A generalized travel ban applies to all Palestinians except those whom Israeli authorities deem as presenting "exceptional humanitarian circumstances," mostly those needing vital medical treatment and their companions, as well as prominent business people.

During January and February, an average of 778 Palestinians in Gaza exited via Erez each day, a fraction of the daily average of more than 24,000 before the beginning of the second Intifada in September 2000, according to the Israeli rights group, Gisha. After Israel tightened the closure amid the pandemic, that figure plummeted between April and September to about nine people per day.

In May, the PA suspended security and administrative coordination with Israel, including the issuance of travel permits, in response to Israel's annexation plans. This move left Gaza residents with no clear way to apply for permits, since Israeli authorities do not have a formal physical presence inside Gaza and did not create alternative mechanisms to accept applications directly. Several organizations in June began applying on behalf of Palestinians with scheduled appointments for urgent medical care outside Gaza and the World Health Organization (WHO) took on the coordination role in September. According to data received by the WHO, Israel denied or failed to respond in a timely manner to 54 percent of such applications in June. In November, the PA said that it would resume security and administrative coordination with Israel.

Gaza's exports between January and September, mostly destined for the West Bank and Israel, averaged 256 truckloads per month, compared to the monthly average of 1,064 truckloads prior to the June 2007 tightening of the closure, according to Gisha. Israel also sharply restricted and often prohibited the entry of what they deem "dual-use" materials, items that could be used for military purposes. The list included X-ray and communications equipment, construction materials, spare parts and batteries for assistive devices used by people with disabilities, and other vital civilian items.

Families in Gaza on average received slightly more than 12 hours of electricity a day during the first nine months of 2020, according to OCHA. Chronic prolonged power outages encumber everyday life, in particular for people with disabilities who rely on light to communicate using sign language or equipment powered by electricity, such as elevators or electric wheelchairs, to move. More than 96 percent of groundwater in Gaza is "unfit for human consumption," OCHA found. According to the WHO, 47 percent of what it deems to be "essential" medicines were at zero stock level (less than one month's supply) at Gaza's Central Drug Store at the end of September.

Egypt also sharply restricted the movement of people and goods at its Rafah crossing with Gaza, including restricting entry to those who do not have a Palestinian ID because Israel did not include them in the population registry they control. In the first nine months of 2020, an average of 4,767 Palestinians crossed monthly in both directions, less than the monthly average of 12,172 in 2019 and over 40,000 before the 2013 military coup in Egypt, according to Gisha.

Hamas and Palestinian Armed Groups in Gaza

Hamas authorities provided no information about two Israeli civilians with psychosocial disabilities, Avera Mangistu and Hisham al-Sayed, whom they have apparently held in violation of international law for more than five years after they entered Gaza.

In April, Hamas authorities detained seven activists for participating in a video chat where they answered questions from Israeli civilians about life in Gaza. Two were detained for more than six months and three were convicted under military law of "weakening the revolutionary spirit."

Hamas authorities carried out no executions in 2020; they had carried out 25, following trials marred with due process violations, since they took control in Gaza in June 2007. Courts in Gaza had, as of November 2, sentenced 145 people to death in that time, according to the Gaza-based Palestinian Center for Human Rights.

A British Mandate-era law still in force in Gaza punishes "unnatural intercourse" of a sexual nature, understood to include same-sex relationships, with up to 10 years in prison, although Human Rights Watch has not documented detentions for same-sex conduct.

WEST BANK

Israeli Use of Force & Detentions

In the West Bank, including East Jerusalem, Israeli security forces killed 20 Palestinians and wounded at least 2,001 as of October 5, according to OCHA, including those alleged to have attacked Israelis, but also those uninvolved in violence.

On May 30, Israeli border police in Jerusalem's Old City fatally shot an unarmed 32-year-old Palestinian man with autism, Eyad al-Hallaq, after he reportedly fled when they asked him to stop. According to what an officer on the scene reportedly told Israeli investigators, police shot him in a "closed space" where he did not "endanger" anyone. In October, authorities indicated that they will likely charge the officer who shot al-Hallaq with reckless homicide, pending a pretrial hearing.

On June 23, border police shot and killed, apparently unlawfully, 26-year-old Ahmed Erekat after his car crashed into a checkpoint and he exited the vehicle in circumstances where he did not appear to pose an imminent threat to life. Authorities characterized the incident as a car-ramming attack; his family said it was an accident.

Israeli authorities have rarely held accountable security forces who used excessive force or settlers who attacked Palestinians.

Settler violence against Palestinians during the first five months of 2020 remained at 2019 levels, a marked increase from prior years, OCHA found. Settlers killed one Palestinian civilian, wounded 103, and caused property damage in 136 incidents as of October 5, according to OCHA.

Palestinian attackers killed one Israeli soldier and wounded at least 28 Israeli soldiers and civilians in the West Bank, as of September 22.

Israeli authorities in September said they would continue withholding the bodies of Palestinians killed in what they consider security incidents primarily as leverage to secure Hamas's release of the bodies of two Israeli soldiers presumed killed in 2014 hostilities. Israel held, as of September, the bodies of 67 Palestinians killed since 2015, according to the Jerusalem Legal Aid and Human Rights Center.

In the East Jerusalem neighborhood of Issawiya, Israeli forces arrested 850 Palestinians between April 2019 and April 2020, according to the Israeli rights group, B'Tselem, as part of an "ongoing campaign of abuse" against its residents.

In April, Israeli police shut down a coronavirus testing center set up by residents in the East Jerusalem neighborhood of Silwan on the grounds that it operated with PA assistance.

Israeli authorities closely monitor online speech by Palestinians, in part relying on predictive algorithms to determine whom to target, and have detained Palestinians based on social media posts and other expressive activity.

As of August 31, according to Israeli Prison Services figures, Israel held 4,207 Palestinians in custody for "security" offenses, including 153 children, many for throwing stones, and 355 in administrative detention without formal charges or trial and based on secret evidence.

While applying Israeli civil law to settlers, Israeli authorities govern West Bank Palestinians, excluding Jerusalem residents, under harsh military law. In so doing, they deny them basic due process and try them in military courts with a near-100 percent conviction rate. Israel incarcerates many Palestinians from the OPT inside Israel, complicating family visits and violating international humanitarian law's prohibition against their transfer outside occupied territory.

Settlements & Home Demolitions

Israel allocated additional confiscated Palestinian land to unlawful settlements and provided security, infrastructure, and services for more than 647,000 settlers residing in the West Bank, including East Jerusalem.

In June, Israel's Supreme Court struck down a law allowing authorities to retroactively expropriate land on which settlements had been built but that Israel acknowledged to be privately owned by Palestinians. In its justification, however, the court cited "less harmful tools" that could have the same effect, including a military order that upholds land deals when authorities reasonably believed at the time of sale that the land was not privately owned, effectively approving the unlawful expropriations.

Jerusalem courts in several cases ordered the eviction of Palestinian families from homes in which they had lived for decades in the East Jerusalem neighborhood of Silwan largely based on discriminatory laws that favor claims that the land belonged to Jewish owners before 1948 or that allow the state to take over land as "absentee property."

The difficulty in obtaining Israeli building permits in East Jerusalem and the 60 percent of the West Bank under Israel's exclusive control (Area C) has driven Palestinians to construct housing, schools, and business structures that are at constant risk of demolition or confiscation for being unauthorized. OCHA considered, as of April 2020, 46 Palestinian West Bank communities to be at "high risk of forcible transfer" due to coercive Israeli policies. International law prohibits an occupying power from destroying property unless "absolutely necessary" for "military operations."

Freedom of Movement for Palestinians

Israel continued to enforce its permit regime requiring Palestinian ID holders with rare exceptions to apply for time-limited permits from the Israeli army to enter large parts of the West Bank, including East Jerusalem. B'Tselem describes this as "an arbitrary, entirely non-transparent bureaucratic system" where "many applications are denied without explanation, with no real avenue for appeal." Israeli authorities, as of June, maintained nearly 600 checkpoints and other permanent obstacles within the West Bank, in addition to nearly 1,500 ad-hoc "flying" checkpoints erected between April 2019 and March 2020, according to OCHA. Israeli forces routinely turn away or humiliate and delay Palestinians at checkpoints without explanation.

The separation barrier, which Israel said it built for security reasons but 85 percent of which falls within the West Bank rather than along the Green Line separating Israeli from Palestinian territory, cuts off thousands of Palestinians from their agricultural lands. It also isolates 11,000 Palestinians who live on the western side of the barrier but are not allowed to travel to Israel and whose ability to cross the barrier to access their property and basic services is highly restricted.

The Palestinian Authority in the West Bank

As of October 21, the PA reported 43,308 Covid-19 cases and 399 deaths since the outbreak began in the West Bank, not including East Jerusalem. While at times imposing restrictions across the parts of the West Bank where it manages affairs, it has largely relied on localized lockdowns of areas that experience a surge in cases.

Prime Minister Mohammad Shtayyeh pledged in July 2019 to end arbitrary arrests. In June, PA forces detained journalist Sami al-Sai for three weeks over suspicions that he administered a Facebook page that had posted information about PA corruption. PA forces in July arrested about 20 activists in Ramallah heading to a protest about PA corruption, detaining them for more than a week, and prosecuting them on charges of gathering illegally and violating restrictive Covid-19 measures.

PA personal status laws discriminated against women, including in relation to marriage, divorce, and decisions relating to custody of children and inheritance. Women's rights groups documented an increase in reports of domestic violence during Covid-19 lockdown restrictions. However, Palestine has no comprehensive domestic violence law. The PA is considering a draft family protection law, but women's rights groups have raised concern that it does not go far enough to prevent abuse and protect survivors.

ISRAEL

Israel had registered 306,649 Covid-19 cases and 2,278 deaths, including in East Jerusalem and West Bank settlements, as of October 21. Israel instituted lockdowns between late March and early May, and again between late September and mid-October. To track Covid-19, Israeli authorities authorized Shin Bet, Israel's internal security service, to collect from telecommunications providers, beginning in March, vast amounts of location-tracking data from the cellphones of ordinary Israelis without their consent. The Knesset in July authorized the surveillance for six months, following an Israeli Supreme Court ruling in April that the government must bring the program under legislation.

In June, the Knesset renewed a temporary order in place since 2003 that bars, with few exceptions, granting long-term legal status or residency inside Israel to

Palestinians from the West Bank and Gaza who marry Israeli citizens or residents, in many cases forcing the separation of families.

Thousands of Israelis participated in weekly demonstrations beginning in June, primarily against the government's handling of Covid-19 and corruption charges against Prime Minister Netanyahu. Israeli police forcibly dispersed several demonstrations and beat and arrested scores of protesters. The Israeli group Human Rights Defenders Fund said that between July 14 and 26 in Jerusalem alone it provided legal counsel to more than 150 demonstrators who had been detained.

Israeli authorities continued to systematically deny asylum claims of the roughly 32,000 Eritrean and Sudanese asylum seekers in the country. To pressure them to leave, the government tries to make their lives "miserable," in the words of Israel's interior minister in 2012, through restrictions on movement, work permits, and access to health care. The Supreme Court in April struck down a law that permitted confiscation of a portion of their salaries.

Key International Actors

The United States in January presented a plan that purports to offer a two-state solution but envisions permanent Israeli domination over large swaths of the West Bank and formal annexation of settlements, the Jordan Valley, and other parts of Area C, while setting conditions that would make the realization of a Palestinian state nearly impossible. In June, members of the US Congress raised concerns about annexation in letters to Prime Minister Netanyahu and US Secretary of State Michael Pompeo.

In response to the US plan, 27 European Union member states, including Germany and France, called for ensuring equal rights for Palestinians and Israelis. Over the year, the EU repeatedly urged Israel to abandon annexation plans and halt settlement construction, highlighting their illegality under international humanitarian law; however, strong divisions among EU member states have so far frustrated attempts to adopt punitive EU measures in response to Israel's persistent and serious violations of international humanitarian law.

In February, the Office of UN High Commissioner for Human Rights released the long-awaited database of businesses that have enabled or profited from settlements, listing 112 businesses.

The International Criminal Court (ICC) prosecutor's office concluded its preliminary examination of the Palestine situation in December 2019 and determined that all the necessary criteria to proceed with a formal investigation of alleged serious crimes by Israelis and Palestinians had been met. However, it requested guidance from the court's judges on the ICC's territorial jurisdiction before commencing a probe. At time of writing, a decision was pending.

Italy

Italy was the first country outside China to experience a major outbreak of Covid-19 and to declare a national state of emergency, and impose a strict lockdown, in early March 2020. The coalition government in power since September 2019 reversed some of the most problematic migration and asylum policies implemented by the previous government but continued to obstruct nongovernmental rescue organizations. Hate crimes remained a serious problem. Women faced obstacles to exercising reproductive rights and an increase in violence during lockdown. In its October rule of law report, the European Commission flagged concerns about efficiency of justice, political independence of media, and smear campaigns against some civil society groups, particularly those working on migration.

Covid-19

As of October 26, authorities had registered more than 542,789 cases and approximately 37,479 deaths. Between 8,000-12,000 older people are estimated to have died in nursing homes in March-April.

At least 31,100 healthcare workers were infected—over 11 percent of all cases—and at least 240 died, with many blaming shortages of personal protective equipment at the height of the crisis in March-April. By the end of August, a voluntary app to assist with contact tracing had been downloaded by only 14 percent of potential users amid privacy concerns. The number of new cases began increasing steadily in early August, and in October the government imposed new nationwide restrictions on certain businesses and activities in response to surging infection rates.

Beginning in mid-March with a massive aid package, the national government adopted a series of measures to protect some workers from being fired, provide cash infusions for freelance workers and poor families, support families with young children by ensuring the right to parental leave and providing child care vouchers, and increase food distribution to the needy. The UN special rapporteur on the right to food recommended in March that Italy adopt a comprehensive framework law to implement the right to food to eliminate hunger and food insecurity.

The government closed schools and universities across the country on March 4 and imposed distance learning for the remainder of the school year, affecting over 8.5 million students. An estimated 12 percent of 6 to 17 year olds do not have a computer at home; to date, there is no public evaluation of the use of 150 million euros (US$175 million) allocated by the Ministry of Education for the purchase of computers and other devices to facilitate online learning or alleviate the impact of distance learning on children with disabilities.

Schools reopened in September amid concerns over health and safety, a shortage of support teachers for students with disabilities, and a patchwork of solutions to address lack of space to ensure social distancing; in late October, the government ordered at least 75 percent online teaching for all secondary schools.

Prisoners rioted in over 40 prisons across the country from March 7-10 to protest rules implemented in response to Covid-19 that limited activities, work leave permits, and contact with relatives, as well as chronic overcrowding that put them at higher risk of contracting the disease. Thirteen inmates died and 69 inmates and over 100 guards were injured during the protests.

The government adopted a plan in mid-March to move detainees with less than 18 months left to serve on their sentences to house arrest, and expand the use of semi-liberty regimes; by the end of July, the national rate of prison overcrowding was 106 percent, down from 119 percent. As of the end of August, there were 290 confirmed cases of Covid-19 in prisons.

Dozens of people were released from migration detention pending deportation given the impossibility of returns amid Covid-19-related border closures, with numbers in detention dropping from 425 in mid-March to 178 in late May. Deportations resumed in early August, and numbers of detainees had increased to around 300 at time of writing.

A study conducted by the National Institute for Health, Migration and Poverty found that by mid-June there were 239 confirmed cases of Covid-19 in reception centers for asylum seekers, the majority in centers known as CAS, originally set up as emergency options due to lack of space in the permanent shelter system. In July, 133 residents in a large reception center in former military barracks in Veneto tested positive for the virus.

The government adopted some positive measures to protect migrants and asylum seekers amid the pandemic, such as extending the right to stay in reception centers until the end of the public health emergency for people who would otherwise have had to leave, including children who turned 18, and extending the validity of expired documents given the impossibility of renewal during lockdown.

Migrants and Asylum Seekers

During the adoption of the outcomes of its Universal Periodic Review before the United Nations Human Rights Council in March, Italy rejected a number of recommendations on the rights of migrants and asylum seekers, including ensuring compliance with prohibition of refoulement and collective expulsions.

In February, the Memorandum of Understanding with Libya on migration cooperation was renewed for another three years despite overwhelming evidence of brutality against migrants and the complete absence of an asylum system in Libya; at the time of writing Libya had not yet agreed to cosmetic amendments, while Italy, in July, commissioned six patrol boats to be donated to Libya for interceptions at sea.

In October, the government reversed some of the worst policies adopted under the previous government, reinstating humanitarian residency permits, guaranteeing asylum seekers access to specialized shelters, and removing obstacles to their access to rights. The new decree reduces but does not eliminate fines on ships that perform search-and-rescue at sea.

After declaring, in April, Italian ports "unsafe" because of the Covid-19 pandemic, authorities allowed, often with unjustified delay, nongovernmental rescue organizations to disembark rescued people but began impounding ships on technical or administrative grounds. In September, the government grounded an airplane deployed by Sea Watch, a rescue group, to spot boats in distress in the Mediterranean, and impounded the rescue ship the organization operates with Médécins Sans Frontières. In mid-September, Italy allowed Mediterranea Saving

Humans to disembark 25 people who had spent 38 days on an oil tanker as Malta (and Italy) refused to accept them.

The UN special rapporteur on the situation of human rights defenders called on Italy in early October to end the criminalization of humanitarian rescuers, highlighting the open cases against Carola Rackete, the captain of a Sea Watch ship, and 10 crew members of the Iuventa rescue ship.

Poor management of an increase in spontaneous arrivals led to severe overcrowding in the Lampedusa reception center. The government began in April to quarantine arriving migrants and asylum seekers on passenger ferries for 14 days; at time of writing 3 ferries were anchored off Lampedusa and Sicily, raising concerns about a normalization of offshore processing. In October, authorities began using at least one ship to isolate asylum seekers already accommodated in reception centers found to be positive for Covid-19.

According to government statistics, more than 25,900 people reached Italy by sea, including more than 3,190 unaccompanied children, by mid-October. According to the International Organization for Migration, 473 persons went dead or missing in the Central Mediterranean in the same period. Authorities reinforced border patrol guards at the land border with Slovenia citing increased arrivals, while rights organizations expressed concern over returns to Slovenia without procedural safeguards, leading to chain deportation to Croatia and then Bosnia.

Unaccompanied children who traveled on to France after spending a year or more in Italy, regularly told Human Rights Watch that lack of access to education and other poor reception conditions were factors in their decisions to leave.

A program to provide residency permits to undocumented migrants working in agriculture, domestic work, and home care was implemented in response to the Covid-19 but relied on employer participation. According to official statistics, 85 percent of the 207,542 applications received by the program's deadline came from domestic and home care workers and only 15 percent from farmworkers. Some 13,000 people applied under a more restrictive channel created in the same program for people whose residency permit had expired after October 31, 2019, and could prove they had previously been employed in the same 3 sectors. However, this was a missed opportunity to extend the program and secure rights for an estimated 600,000 people living in Italy without status.

Five Eritreans rescued at sea by the Italian Navy in July 2009 and subsequently returned unlawfully to Libya arrived in Italy in August. In a landmark ruling in November 2019, a court had ordered the government to allow them and nine others to come to Italy to apply for asylum.

The trial of former Interior Minister leader Matteo Salvini began in October on charges of abduction, unlawful detention, and abuse of power for refusing to allow 131 rescued people to disembark for 4 days from an Italian military ship in July 2019.

Racism and Intolerance

The brutal beating to death in September of 21-year-old Willy Monteiro Duarte, a Black Italian, in a disadvantaged town on the outskirts of Rome, provoked a nationwide debate about racism, social degradation, and violence. At time of writing, four men were in pretrial detention on charges of voluntary homicide, with prosecutors saying they will not prosecute as a bias crime.

Some elected officials in southern regions stoked rather than calmed unfounded fears linking migrants with Covid-19, and anti-immigrant candidates in regional elections engaged in xenophobic rhetoric.

Women's Rights

The Minister of Health announced in August new guidelines to allow medical abortion up to the ninth week of pregnancy. Previous rules allowed medical abortions only up to the seventh week and during a three-day hospitalization. The government did not ensure clear pathways to time-sensitive reproductive healthcare during the Covid-19 lockdown causing interruptions to abortion services and exacerbating long-standing barriers to people exercising the right to terminate a pregnancy during the legal timeframe of 90 days.

Calls and text messages to the national helpline for victims of domestic abuse more than doubled during lockdown, compared to March-June 2019. The government exempted women and children fleeing abuse from lockdown restrictions on movement and ordered local authorities to requisition vacant buildings to accommodate them if shelters were full.

367

Sexual Orientation and Gender Identity

A 20-year-old woman died in September when her brother rammed into the motorcycle she was riding on with her trans boyfriend. At time of writing, parliamentarians were examining a bill that would make incitement to violence or discrimination "based on sex, gender, sexual orientation or gender identity" a crime, and make such bias an aggravating factor in sentencing. The bill also increases funding for projects to prevent and counter violence based on sexual orientation and gender identity, as well as for victim support.

Japan

Japan is a liberal democracy with an active civil society. On September 16, Yoshi-hide Suga became Japan's prime minister after Prime Minister Shinzo Abe announced his resignation due to health concerns.

Japan has no law prohibiting racial, ethnic, or religious discrimination, or discrimination based on sexual orientation or gender identity. Japan does not have a national human rights institution.

Covid-19

As of November 5, there were 105,082 reported cases of people infected with Covid-19, and 1,808 deaths in Japan. The Japanese government declared a State of Emergency on April 7, which ended in June. The government has no legal authority to punish people should they leave their homes during the state of emergency.

In March, the Japanese government and the International Olympic Committee (IOC) agreed to delay the Tokyo 2020 Olympic and Paralympic Games until 2021 due to the Covid-19 pandemic.

Then-Prime Minister Abe requested that schools across the country close from the beginning of March to stop the spread of Covid-19, ending in-person classroom learning for about 13 million children for approximately two to three months.

The Ministry of Education, Culture, Sports, Science and Technology (MEXT) reported in April that only 5 percent of public schools provided live, interactive online education with teachers when the schools closed, causing many children to study by themselves at home using textbooks and other paper materials.

In April, Japan dramatically tightened re-entry restrictions on foreign nationals. With the narrow exception of special permanent residents who have ancestry related to Japan's former colonies of Korea or Taiwan, every foreign national (including permanent residents) who left Japan on and after April 3 in principle were denied return to Japan.

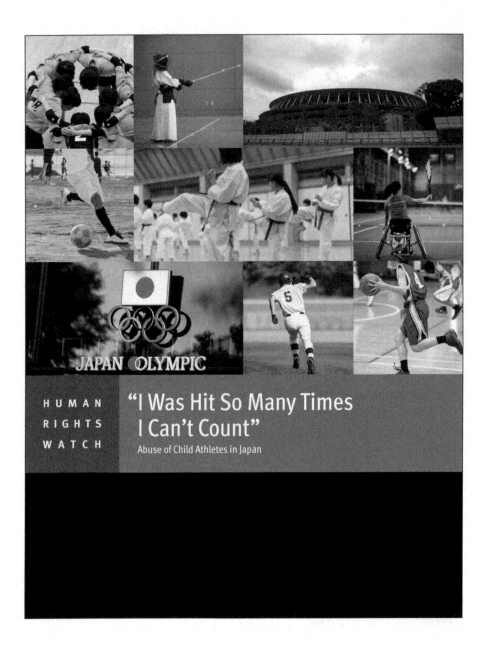

HUMAN RIGHTS WATCH

"I Was Hit So Many Times I Can't Count"

Abuse of Child Athletes in Japan

After widespread criticism that the ban violated rights, including of family reunification, Japan eased restrictions in September by allowing the re-entry of all foreign nationals with the status of residence under certain conditions.

Tokyo 2020 Olympic and Paralympic Games

A Human Rights Watch report in July found child athletes in Japan—at both the grassroots and elite levels—suffer physical, sexual, and verbal abuse when training in sport.

Following the report's release, IOC President Thomas Bach held a telephone conference with the Japanese Olympic Committee on possible measures to eradicate harassment and abuse in Japanese sport.

In October, Pride House Tokyo, a facility to build awareness and support of lesbian, gay, bisexual, and transgender (LGBT) rights, officially opened—the first Pride house to get official backing from the IOC.

Refugees

Japan's asylum and refugee determination system remains strongly oriented against granting refugee status. In 2019, the Justice Ministry received 10,375 applications for refugee status, largely from asylum seekers from Sri Lanka, Turkey, Cambodia, Nepal, and Pakistan. During the year, the ministry recognized only 44 people as refugees, and accepted another 37 persons in the category of needing humanitarian assistance, allowing them to stay in Japan.

In August, the UN Working Group on Arbitrary Detention adopted an opinion recognizing the detention of two asylum seekers by the Japanese immigration bureau as arbitrary and a contravention of international human rights law. The Working Group added that the two asylum seekers have the right under international law to receive compensation.

Criminal Justice

Former Nissan chairman Carlos Ghosn, who was arrested, charged with financial misconducts, and detained for 129 days, fled Japan while on bail and appeared in Lebanon in December 2019. Ghosn's defenders had alleged before his flight that the Japanese system abused his rights by using long pretrial detention and denial of bail to pressure him to confess, among other issues.

In response to the continued international criticism of Japan's hostage criminal justice system, then-Justice Minister Masako Mori tasked the new Reform Committee on Legal Affairs and Prosecutor's Practices to review current criminal justice procedures against international standards.

Death Penalty

In December 2019, Japan executed a Chinese national for killing a family of four during a robbery. There had been no executions in 2020 at time of writing. As of December 2019, 112 people were on death row. Concerns have long been raised about death row inmates including having inadequate access to legal counsel and being notified of their execution only on the day it takes place.

Women's Rights

Japan's rape law requires that prosecutors must prove that violence or intimidation was involved, or that the victim lost consciousness or was otherwise incapable of resistance. In June, a working group established by then-Justice Minister Mori began reviewing potential reforms to the rape law. The UN Committee on the Elimination of Discrimination against Women advises that the legal definition of sexual assault should be one that "is based on the lack of freely given consent and takes into account coercive circumstances."

In April, when Japan was under a state of emergency to stop the spread of Covid-19, calls to the government's national hotline regarding domestic violence increased by about 30 percent compared to the same time the previous year. Calls to national hotlines also increased in May and June.

Children's Rights

In November 2019, a group of 12 men and women filed a lawsuit against the state, claiming the Japanese civil code, which awards child custody to only one parent after a divorce, violates the constitution's guarantee of equality under law. In the same month, the Justice Ministry also started a review of the law, to see whether the current legal framework is desirable for the benefit of children. The lawsuit and the Justice Ministry's review came after the UN Committee on the Rights of the Child urged Japan in February 2019 to "revise the legislation ... to allow for shared custody of children when it is in the child's best interests."

In February 2020, the Ministry of Health, Labour and Welfare (MHLW) issued guidelines to implement 2019 amendments made to laws on children, finally ending all use of corporal punishments against children in Japan.

In March, MEXT published its first research on the educational status of foreign children. The study found that of more than 120,000 foreign school-age children, approximately 16 percent are possibly not receiving education. To date, the government interprets Article 26 of its constitution, which states that "all people shall be obligated to have all boys and girls ... receive ordinary education" as being only applicable to Japanese citizens, violating Japan's obligations under the Convention on the Rights of the Child.

Despite the Japanese government's call on local governments to uphold national goals on children in alternative care—including placing more than 75 percent of pre-school children needing alternative care into foster care within the next seven years—it was reported in March that more than 90 percent of local governments failed to incorporate the national government's goals into their 10-year plans submitted to MHLW. In response, the ministry issued a notice in April that said such failure cannot be overlooked and MHLW will contact and advise each local government. According to MHLW, Japan institutionalizes approximately 80 percent of children it keeps in alternative care.

Sexual Orientation and Gender Identity

In response to the national laws passed in May 2019 on workplace harassment, three ministries—MHLW, the Ministry of Internal Affairs and Communications, and MEXT—issued ministerial regulations and formal notices requiring for the first time that corporations, local governments, and schools take actions to prevent sexual orientation and gender identity harassment and publicly outing a person as LGBT.

LGBT groups in Japan launched a campaign for a national non-discrimination law in the lead up to the rescheduled Tokyo 2020 Olympics in 2021.

Academic Freedom

Prime Minister Suga received widespread criticism after he rejected the nomination of six scholars by the Science Council of Japan (SCJ) to become new members, the first time such a rejection was made public since the nomination system was introduced in 2004. The six scholars have been critical of the government's security and anti-conspiracy legislations. Under the Act on Science Council of Japan, the council nominates new members to the prime minister, who ultimately appoints them. SCJ is an independent council consisting of 210 council members that makes policy recommendations to the government.

Labor Rights

In October, the Supreme Court issued five different rulings related to equal pay for equal work as the population of non-regular workers —workers on a variety of fixed-term contracts—make up more than 30 percent of the work force in Japan. On October 13, the Supreme Court ruled in favor of employers in two different cases who did not pay bonus or severance pay to non-regular workers. Two days later, the same court ruled in favor of non-regular workers in three different lawsuits, saying it is unreasonable for the employer not to provide its fixed-term workers with the same allowances it pays to workers without fixed-term.

Foreign Policy

Japan's official policy is to "contribute to the improvement of the world's human rights environment" through methods including the "UN's primary human rights forums and bilateral talks."

However, Japan's diplomatic response to rights abuses in Asia often contradicted its commitment, primarily as it downplays concerns for human rights to compete for political and economic influence with China in countries such as Cambodia, Myanmar, the Philippines, Sri Lanka, Thailand, and Vietnam. In June, Japan abstained on a Myanmar resolution at the United Nations Human Rights

Council, perpetuating its stance since 2017 of abstaining on all UN resolutions addressing human rights issues in Myanmar.

Japan took a stronger stance on the Chinese government's human rights violations. It joined a G-7 statement urging the Chinese government to "reconsider" imposing national security legislation on Hong Kong, and a joint statement led by the UK raising concerns at the UN Human Rights Council about rights abuses in Hong Kong and Xinjiang. In October 2019, Japan also joined a joint statement at the UN General Assembly denouncing the Chinese government's human rights abuses.

Japan largely abandoned concerns about North Korean human rights in a failed diplomatic strategy to engage directly with Pyongyang, especially on the cases of abducted Japanese nationals. In March 2019, Tokyo walked away from over a decade as lead sponsor of annual UN Human Rights Council resolutions on human rights in North Korea and did not come back to the leadership in December 2019 at the UN General Assembly or in 2020.

Japan is among the world's top 10 emitters of greenhouse gases and its climate action has been highly insufficient. However, in October, the prime minister signaled new commitment on climate action by stating his government's ambition to move towards carbon neutrality by 2050.

Jordan

In March 2020, Jordan declared a state of emergency in response to the Covid-19 pandemic, granting the prime minister sweeping powers to rule by decree and curtail basic rights. Prime Minister Omar Razzaz pledged to carry it out to the "narrowest extent," but authorities later exploited the emergency measures to arbitrarily curtail fundamental rights, including freedom of speech and assembly.

In one such incident in late July, police raided the Teachers Syndicate headquarters in Amman and 11 of its branches across the country, shuttered them, and arrested all 13 syndicate board members on dubious legal grounds. Following the closure, authorities prevented or forcibly dispersed demonstrations across the country protesting the closure and arrested protesters and journalists covering the event.

In September, King Abdullah dissolved Jordan's lower house of parliament. New elections were planned for November 10.

Freedom of Expression

Jordanian law criminalizes speech deemed critical of the king, foreign countries, government officials and institutions, Islam and Christianity, and defamatory speech.

On August 26, police arrested Emad Hajjaj, 53, a prominent Jordanian cartoonist whose satirical cartoons have appeared in major Jordanian dailies for decades. The arrest stemmed from a cartoon he posted to his website and social media depicting a dove with an Israeli flag spitting in the face of the United Arab Emirates' de facto ruler, Mohammed bin Zayed. The cartoon referenced reports that the Israeli government had urged the United States not to sell F-35 warplanes to the UAE despite its agreement to normalize diplomatic relations with Israel. Authorities released Hajjaj on August 30 after State Security Court prosecutors declined to prosecute him on the charge of "disturbing [Jordan's] relations with a foreign state," an offense under Jordan's overly broad counterterrorism law.

In April, the government issued an emergency decree that criminalized sharing news that would "cause panic" about the pandemic in the media or online with a penalty of up to three years in prison. Between March and May, police detained two prominent media executives, a foreign journalist and a former member of parliament, apparently in response to their public criticism of Covid-19 policies, as well as three people for allegedly spreading "fake news." Among those arrested were the news director and general manager of Roya TV, a popular local media outlet. Authorities released them on April 12 but their case status was unclear at time of writing. Activists and commentators suggested that the arrests stemmed from a widely circulated Roya TV video where Jordanian day laborers expressed Covid-19 concerns.

Jordanian authorities further curtailed press freedom in 2020 by issuing arbitrary press gag orders prohibiting reporting on important local developments, including two bans in July. One prohibited publishing any news about the brutal killing of a woman by her father, and another prohibiting reporting on authorities' arbitrary closure of the teachers' syndicate and arrests of its leaders. Authorities arrested at least two journalists for their coverage of ongoing teachers' protests, one of whom security forces beat prior to his arrest. These restrictions reflected a broader degradation of press freedom in recent years.

Freedom of Association and Assembly

Following the closure of the teachers' syndicate in late July, authorities banned all public protests stemming from the closure citing health and safety rules tied to the country's state of emergency for the Covid-19 pandemic, which limits gatherings to a maximum of 20 people (though authorities did not enforce the limit with respect to places of worship and restaurants). Authorities prevented or forcibly dispersed protests in towns across the country in July and August and arrested numerous teachers and other protesters, holding some in detention. International human rights law allows authorities to limit public gatherings because of public health, but only when the restrictions are proportionate and on a case-by-case basis rather than a blanket ban.

In late December 2019, authorities announced changes to the country's pre-approval process for local nongovernmental organizations (NGOs) operating in Jordan to receive funding from foreign sources. Local NGO leaders complained that the pre-approval process remained onerous and lacked transparency. The changes did not generally apply to international NGOs operating in Jordan.

Under the Public Gatherings Law amended in March 2011, Jordan did not require government permission to hold public meetings or demonstrations, but organizations and venues continued to seek permission from the Interior Ministry or General Intelligence Department. In December 2019, Human Rights Watch was forced to postpone a press conference in Amman after authorities did not approve the event, but following press reporting of the cancellation authorities quickly granted permission for the event.

Refugees and Migrants

By late 2020, over 660,000 people from Syria had sought refuge in Jordan, according to the UN High Commissioner for Refugees (UNHCR). Over 85 percent of Syrians lived outside refugee camps in rented accommodation. Jordan continued its years-long policy of not permitting Syrians to enter the country to seek asylum.

According to the UNHCR, Jordan also hosted asylum seekers and refugees from other countries in 2020, including 66,800 Iraqis, 14,600 Yemenis, 6,100 Sudanese, 749 Somalis, and 1,600 from other countries. Authorities continued to enforce a January 2019 decision banning the UNHCR from registering as asylum seekers individuals who officially entered the country for the purposes of medical treatment, study, tourism, or work, effectively barring recognition of non-Syrians as refugees and leaving many without UNHCR documentation or access to services.

Authorities continued to implement the Jordan Compact, the 2016 agreement between the Jordanian government and donor countries, which aimed to improve the livelihoods of Syrian refugees by granting new legal work opportunities and improving the education sector. By the end of 2019, labor authorities had issued or renewed at least 176,920 work permits for Syrians since 2016, although many of these were renewals. Most professions remained closed to non-Jordanians, and many Syrians continued to work in the informal sector without labor protections.

The 233,000 school-age Syrian refugees in Jordan face multiple obstacles to education that are most acute for children ages 12 and older, including poverty-driven child labor and child marriage, lack of affordable school transportation, government policies that limit access to education, and lack of inclusive education and accommodation for children with disabilities.

Only a quarter of secondary-school-age Syrian refugee children in Jordan were enrolled in school. Non-Syrians refugees and asylum seekers were in many cases prevented from enrolling their children in school in 2020. The government used television and the internet to provide distance learning for students during Covid-related school closures. Around 70 percent of Jordanian children had internet access, but that figure dropped sharply for refugees and poorer and marginalized Jordanians, UNICEF reported. Even before the pandemic, only around a quarter of Syrian refugee students were able to continue their education as far as secondary school.

Authorities did not allow aid deliveries from Jordan to tens of thousands of Syrians at Rukban, an unofficial camp along Jordan's border with Syria. Authorities deported Syrians to Rukban in 2020 without permitting them to challenge their deportations.

Jordan hosted around 70,000 migrant domestic workers in 2020, mostly from the Philippines, Sri Lanka, and Indonesia. NGOs repeatedly referred domestic workers who had suffered multiple abuses to labor ministry investigators. Abuses included non-payment of wages, unsafe working conditions, long hours, document confiscation, and physical, verbal, and sexual abuse. Such risks of abuse were exacerbated during Covid-19 lockdown restrictions.

Women's and Girls' Rights

Jordan's personal status code remains discriminatory, despite a 2010 amendment that widened women's access to divorce and child custody. Women need the permission of a male guardian to marry, and marriages between Muslim women and non-Muslim men are not recognized. Women cannot travel abroad with their children, as men can, without the permission of their child's father or male guardian or a judge. While women can travel outside the country without needing permission, authorities sometimes comply with requests from male guardians to bar their unmarried adult daughters, wives, and children from leaving the country. Authorities also arrest women reported as "absent" for fleeing their home by their male guardians under the Crime Prevention Law.

Article 9 of Jordan's nationality law does not allow Jordanian women married to non-Jordanian spouses to pass on their nationality to their spouse and children. In 2014, authorities issued a cabinet decision purporting to ease restrictions on non-citizen children of Jordanian women's access to key economic and social rights, but the easing fell short of expectations. Non-citizen children of Jordanian women no longer require work permits for employment, but many professions in Jordan remained closed to non-Jordanians.

Women's rights and international groups reported an increase in domestic violence during Covid-19 lockdown restrictions.

In July, Jordanians circulated a video on social media outlets in which the screams of an unseen woman can be heard. The woman, identified as "Ahlam," was apparently killed by a relative. Article 98 of Jordan's penal code, amended in 2017, states that the "fit of fury" defense does not allow mitigated sentences for perpetrators of crimes "against women," but judges continued to impose mitigated sentences under article 99 if family members of victims did not support prosecutions of their male family members.

Criminal Justice System

As of November, authorities had not carried out any executions in 2020.

Local governors continued to use provisions of the Crime Prevention Law of 1954 to place individuals in administrative detention for up to one year, in circumvention of the Criminal Procedure Law.

Key International Actors

In 2020, the US Congress appropriated US$1.65 billion in Foreign Military Financing, Economic Support, and other aid to Jordan. This exceeded the amount requested by the Trump administration and outlined in the 2018 Memorandum of Understanding between the United States and Jordan. The US did not publicly

381

criticize human rights violations in Jordan in 2020 except within the State Department and other annual reports.

Jordan is a member of the Saudi/Emirati-led coalition fighting the Houthi forces in Yemen, which continues to commit violations of international human rights and humanitarian law in Yemen.

Kazakhstan

President Kasym-Jomart Tokaev's promises for reform did not bring about meaningful improvements in Kazakhstan's human rights record in 2020. Government critics faced harassment and prosecution, and free speech was suppressed, especially in the context of the Covid-19 pandemic. Although Kazakhstan adopted a new peaceful assemblies law, authorities with rare exception continued to detain peaceful protesters. Rights defender Max Bokaev remained unjustly jailed and authorities banned an opposition group. Kazakhstan adopted long-promised amendments to the Trade Union Law, but restrictions persist on independent organizing. On September 23, Kazakhstan joined the Second Optional Protocol to the International Covenant on Civil and Political Rights (ICCPR), paving the way for full ratification.

Freedom of Assembly

Although authorities hailed a new public assemblies law, which the president signed in May, as a reform, the law imposes onerous rules, bans spontaneous protests, and prohibits unregistered groups and some people with disabilities from organizing protests. Authorities allowed an opposition rally in mid-September and a rally for political reforms on October 31 to proceed, but hundreds of people who tried to exercise their right to peacefully protest on other occasions in 2020 were detained, fined, or sentenced to short-term custodial sentences for administrative offenses.

Civil Society

On August 12, an Almaty court convicted the activist Asya Tulesova of insulting the police and using violence against a police officer, fined her, and placed restrictions on her freedom of movement for 18 months. Tulesova had angrily confronted the police, knocking off an officer's hat, in response to police forcefully detaining dozens of people at a peaceful protest on June 6.

An Almaty court on June 22 convicted political activist Alnur Ilyashev of "disseminating knowingly false information" for social media posts criticizing the majority Nur Otan party. The court imposed restrictions on his freedom of movement and required him to serve 100 hours' community service annually for three years and banned him from civic activities for five years.

Police on February 24 announced the death in custody of Dulat Agadil, an outspoken government critic who had participated in numerous unsanctioned protests. Officials cited acute heart failure as the reason, but the suspicious circumstances of his death prompted protests and calls for an independent investigation, which authorities are obligated to conduct under human rights law.

An Almaty court on March 11 fined activists Arina Osinovskaya and Fariza Ospan on petty hooliganism charges for burning a funeral wreath in public. The symbolic act took place during a March 8 women's rights rally.

Authorities on March 3 paroled Mukhtar Dzhakishev, former head of the state-owned energy agency Kazatomprom. He had served nearly 11 years in prison on embezzlement and fraud charges. His allegations of torture were never investigated.

Freedom of Expression

Journalists in Kazakhstan face harassment, arrest, and prosecution for carrying out their work. Authorities retaliated against journalists and others who criticized the authorities' response to the Covid-19 pandemic. A judge in April sentenced a man to 10 days in detention for uploading a video to Facebook showing long lines of people waiting for social assistance during the pandemic.

According to Adilsoz, a local media watchdog, between January and July, seven journalists were physically attacked, and 21 journalists, bloggers, and activists were detained, seven of whom while reporting. Adilsoz reported that authorities brought 38 criminal cases against journalists for alleged crimes such as spreading false information, defamation, and incitement.

In June, Kazakhstan decriminalized defamation. The Organization for Security and Co-operation in Europe (OSCE) Representative on Freedom of the Media Harlem Désir welcomed the development and urged the authorities to also decriminalize "insult" and "disseminating knowingly false information."

An appeals court in January acquitted Amangeldy Batyrbekov, editor of Saryagash Info. In September 2019 Batyrbekov, who published articles critical of the head of a local education department, was sentenced to 27 months in prison for libel and insult.

Arrest and Harassment of Opposition Members

In February, authorities detained several activists to prevent them from taking part in the founding assembly of the Democratic Party of Kazakhstan (DPK). At time of writing, DPK was still unregistered.

Authorities continue to target perceived or actual supporters of the banned Democratic Choice of Kazakhstan (DVK). Police interrogated 52 people suspected of DVK membership in Shymkent in January, and opened a criminal case against 15 people in Almaty in March.

In May the opposition Koshe (Street) Party was banned by court order as "extremist." Dozens of Street Party activists were prosecuted for participating in unsanctioned peaceful protests. Others were threatened with sanctions for alleged membership in a banned extremist organization.

Labor Rights

In response to long-standing International Labour Organization (ILO) criticism of restrictions on trade union organizing and freedom of association, and of the restrictive 2014 Trade Union Law, Kazakhstan in May introduced amendments to the law, removing mandatory trade union affiliation requirements and simplifying registration requirements. Kazakhstan's largest independent trade union, the Congress of Free Trade Unions of Kazakhstan, remains unregistered. On March 20, Erlan Baltabay, a trade union leader, was released from prison upon completion of his 21-week sentence for failing to pay a court-ordered fine.

Counterterrorism and Extremism

Since 2018, Kazakhstan has repatriated a total of 609 citizens, mostly women and children, from Syria who are Islamic State (ISIS) suspects or relatives. According to media reports, of those repatriated, 31 men and 12 women have been convicted of participating in a terrorist organization.

In January, reporting on her May 2019 visit to Kazakhstan, the United Nations Special Rapporteur for Protecting Human Rights while Countering Terrorism Fionnuala Ní Aoláin noted she was "seriously concerned about the use of the term 'extremism' in national law and practice." She concluded that the broad formulations of "extremism" and "inciting discord" in national law "are used to unduly restrict freedoms of religion, expression, assembly and association."

An Almaty court in January jailed Zhuldyzbek Taurbekov for seven years on charges of "terrorism propaganda" and "inciting hatred" for discussing Islam on Whatsapp. Kazakhstan's Supreme Court in January sent for retrial the case against another defendant, Dadash Mazhenov, who was convicted in 2018 on "terrorism propaganda" charges for posting online talks on Islam. Mazhenov alleged he was tortured in a labor camp in 2019.

Violence against Women and Girls

Violence against women and girls persisted as a serious problem. Kazakhstan's judiciary and legislation do not provide sufficient protection to victims, while police and service providers lack sufficient training to identify, prevent, and adequately respond to domestic violence. Parliament in September passed in its first reading of a draft domestic violence law. The draft does not criminalize domestic violence as a standalone offense, nor include a comprehensive definition of "family members."

Sexual Orientation and Gender Identity

Kazakhstan's constitution does not prohibit discrimination on the basis of gender identity or sexual orientation, and there is no stand-alone anti-discrimination law. Parliament in June adopted discriminatory amendments to the new health code that regulate aspects of health care for transgender people. The process for changing gender identity in Kazakhstan remains invasive and humiliating.

Feminita's April Supreme Court appeal against the Justice Ministry's refusal to register their group, which focuses on the rights of lesbian, bisexual, and queer women, was still pending at the time of writing.

Poverty and Inequality

Hundreds of thousands of people in Kazakhstan are at risk of poverty due in part to the government's inadequate measures to counter the Covid-19-related economic downturn. Kazakhstan's weak social protection system and the limited financial and in-kind relief the government provided to people who had lost jobs during the pandemic were ineffective in preventing poverty and economic hardship. Financial relief was lower than a monthly living wage needed to cover basic expenses. Mothers with multiple children across Kazakhstan continued to intermittently protest calling for increased social and housing benefits.

Disability Rights

Progress on inclusive education remained slow. A mandatory medical and educational exam continued as the basis for determining a child's access to mainstream schools. Many children with disabilities remain isolated in segregated special schools or residential institutions, where they can face violence, neglect, physical restraint, and overmedication. Four children living in a residential institution in eastern Kazakhstan died in May and 16 others were hospitalized with measles and intestinal infections. Kazakhstan has no time-bound plan to close these institutions.

Torture

Torture and ill-treatment occur with impunity in Kazakhstan. The Coalition Against Torture, an anti-torture network of nongovernmental organizations and experts, reported they had received 140 complaints of torture between January and June. After an outbreak of ethnic violence on February 7 and 8, which left 10 Dungans and one Kazakh dead, the Dungan community in May issued a public appeal documenting the arbitrary arrests and torture of members of their community by law enforcement. The UN Committee on the Elimination of Racial Discrimination (CERD) issued a communication in August regarding Kazakhstan's Dungan minority under its early warning and urgent action procedure.

Between March and July, prison officials filed six defamation lawsuits against the Pavlodar-based human rights defender Elena Semenova. The officials alleged her reports of ill-treatment and torture of inmates were false and harmed their reputation. At time of writing, courts in two cases had found her guilty of defamation.

On December 27, 2019, the jailed businessman Iskander Erimbetov, who alleged in 2018 that he had been tortured in custody, was released on humanitarian grounds due to his ill-health. In a tweet, the US State Department welcomed his release and urged the Kazakh government to review other politically motivated cases of imprisonment.

Asylum Seekers and Refugees

A court in January sentenced ethnic Kazakhs Kaster Musakhanuly and Murager Alimuly to one year in prison for illegal border crossing but did not order their deportation to China. On October 17, Kazakhstan's migration agency granted them refugee status for one year.

Covid-19

Some measures that authorities implemented in response to the Covid-19 pandemic were arbitrary and disproportionate. Officials in Karaganda bolted shut entryways to entire residential buildings where Covid-19 cases were confirmed. Courts handed up to 15-day jail sentences to at least 1,626 people for violating state-imposed restrictions on movement. Others were criminally charged with spreading false information for criticizing the government's response to the pandemic. A Shymkent judge sentenced an activist to 35 days administrative arrest for allegedly violating emergency measures after he posted a video of himself passing through a police checkpoint.

The lockdown measures imposed in response to Covid-19 resulted in severe limitations on access to shelters or services for survivors of domestic violence. Authorities did not deem them as "essential services" to ensure they could continue operating during the lockdown.

The education of 4.5 million children was interrupted due to school closures. UN agencies estimate that 300,000 children in Kazakhstan lacked technical facilities to follow remote online learning, and children with disabilities were excluded from full participation.

Key International Actors

The United Nations Human Rights Council (UNHRC) in March adopted the outcome of Kazakhstan's third Universal Periodic Review. In November, member states had called on Kazakhstan to criminalize all forms of violence against women and girls, guarantee freedom of peaceful assembly, ensure inclusive education for all children with disabilities, and amend restrictive laws regulating the right to freedom of expression.

The European Union and Kazakhstan strengthened relations through the entry into force in March of a bilateral Enhanced Partnership and Co-operation Agreement. In September, the EU urged Kazakhstan to ensure that the new peaceful assemblies law is implemented in a rights-respecting way, and welcomed Kazakhstan's progress towards the full abolition of the death penalty.

Kenya

Although the March 2018 handshake between President Uhuru Kenyatta and main opposition leader, Raila Odinga, eased political tensions, authorities have not taken any significant steps to ensure electoral reforms. President Kenyatta and Odinga proposed a referendum to create the position of prime minister, presumably to accommodate Kenyatta who is term-barred from running again in 2022.

Extrajudicial killings, abusive evictions, and lack of accountability for serious abuses remain significant challenges. Arrest warrants remain pending before the International Criminal Court against three persons on allegations of witness tampering in cases relating to the 2007/2008 election violence.

Killings by police have remained largely unaddressed, with the Independent Policing Oversight Authority (IPOA), a civilian police accountability institution, unable, for various reasons, to investigate and prosecute most of the over 2,000 incidents of police killings currently on its files. IPOA has only managed six successful prosecutions since its establishment in 2011.

Abuses by Security Forces

Despite widely known and documented police abuses, Kenyan authorities have done little to end police brutality, rarely investigating these killings.

In February 2020, Human Rights Watch found that Kenyan police had, between December and February, shot dead at least eight people in Nairobi's Mathare, Kasarani, and Majengo settlements.

In April, Human Rights Watch found that police had killed at least six people within the first 10 days of Kenya's dusk-to-dawn curfew, imposed on March 27, to contain the spread of Covid-19. The police, without apparent justification, shot and beat people at markets or on the way home from work, even before the daily start of the curfew. Police also broke into homes and shops, extorted money from residents or looted food in locations across the country. In July, Kenyan organizations documented 15 cases of killings by police across Kenya while enforcing coronavirus control measures.

Covid-19

On March 25, President Kenyatta announced a nationwide dusk-to-dawn curfew starting March 27, 2020.

On April 3, authorities made mask wearing mandatory for everyone in public places and introduced mandatory quarantine for those who did not wear masks or breached curfew, but parliament rejected that requirement on April 21.

In joint research in May 2020, Human Rights Watch, Kenya Human Rights Commission, and Journalists for Justice found that Kenyan authorities could have been inadvertently facilitating transmission of the Covid-19 virus while forcefully quarantining tens of thousands of people in facilities that lacked proper sanitation, protective equipment, and food.

Authorities held crowds of people in the arrivals area at the Nairobi airport for more than four hours with no social distancing, sanitizers, or masks; ferried people in packed buses with little ventilation to quarantine facilities; and, at the quarantine facilities, did not enforce guidelines issued by the ministry of health. Such guidelines included wearing protective equipment to ensure that those quarantined do not become exposed to the virus. Interviewees described poor conditions at the quarantine facilities, including lack of bedding, water, food, and cleaning supplies, such as soaps and detergents.

On April 18, 2020, two human rights groups, the Nairobi-based Kenya Legal and Ethical Issues Network on HIV and Aids (KELIN) and the Mombasa-based Muslims for Human Rights (MUHURI) filed a petition seeking to compel government to cover all costs incurred by those quarantined. The petitioners alleged that government implemented quarantine measures in an abusive, degrading, and unconstitutional manner. At time of writing, the matter was still pending in court.

Environmental Rights

In June, a Kenyan court awarded $1.3 billion Ksh (US$12 million) to the 3,000 residents of Owino Uhuru, a suburb of Mombasa, for damages related to pollution from a nearby lead smelter that recycled lead-acid batteries. The court ruled that government agencies responsible for enforcing regulations at the plant must clean up the site within four months.

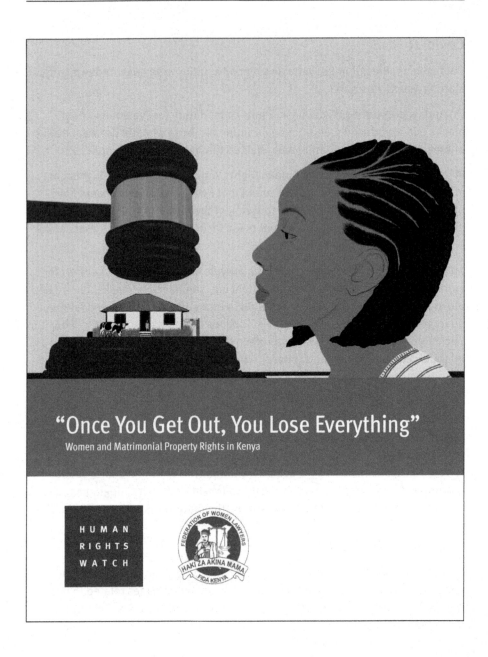

"Once You Get Out, You Lose Everything"
Women and Matrimonial Property Rights in Kenya

Forced Evictions

Human Rights Watch documented the forced eviction of more than 50,000 people from Mau Forest lands in an effort by authorities to conserve Mau Forest Complex, including more than 40,000 in July 2018 and around 10,000 between August and November 2019. Some of the evictees had been living on the land for over 30 years.

During each of the two phases of evictions authorities deployed a combined team of officers from Kenya Wildlife Service, Kenya Forest Service, Administration Police, regular police, and Narok county police, who used excessive force to evict people.

During the 2018 evictions, at least nine people, including two babies, died. Officials beat people, torched homes, and destroyed crops and people's livelihoods, leaving thousands of people homeless and stranded in the cold. In July 2020, Human Rights Watch found that, in the aftermath of the 2019 evictions, another seven people died, two directly due to police violence and the rest as a result of hostile camp conditions.

The government has not investigated the deaths, injuries, and other abuses. Authorities have not relocated, or compensated evictees as required under Kenyan law. Most of those evicted are living in harsh conditions in makeshift camps in Narok county.

In early May, authorities evicted more than 8,000 people in two of Nairobi's informal settlements, under the pretext of reclaiming government land, while in late June, the authorities evicted another 4,000 people from Mt. Elgon forest, western Kenya—all while Covid-19 was raging.

Women and Girls' Rights

In July 2020, President Kenyatta directed education officials and heads of schools to ensure that school girls receive ante-natal care, but authorities have not introduced measures to ensure that school heads do not expel pregnant girls from school. Kenya has made commitments to tackle exclusion in education, but the government's approach to teenage pregnancies threatens its promises for girls' education. Many adolescent mothers are out of school because they are blocked from returning or are not getting support to return.

Between May and July 2020, as a measure to combat the spread of Covid-19, the government ordered the closure of all schools across the country. These school closures exacerbated previously existing gender-based inequalities. Ministry of Health data reported by Kenyan media indicated an increase in teenage pregnancies in each of the 47 counties, whose numbers ran into several thousands, during the lockdown.

Kenyan media reported that government officials believed the pregnancies were as a result of defilement of teen girls, who would potentially drop out of school due to stigma. In April, the National Council on Administration of Justice reported "a significant spike in sexual violence" cases in many parts of the country in the first two weeks of the lockdown.

Sexual Orientation and Gender Identity

Kenya punishes consensual same-sex relations with up to 14 years in prison. Its High Court rejected a constitutional challenge to the ban in 2019. In April 2020, the court upheld a Kenya Film Classification Board ban on Rafiki, a love story about two young women. At time of writing, activists were appealing both rulings.

Intersex groups celebrated Kenya's November 2019 census results, the first in Africa to include data on intersex populations. Lack of awareness, stigma, and inconsistency in asking respondents' sex means data on intersex populations may not have been adequately captured.

Right to Property

In a June 2020 report, Human Rights Watch and FIDA-Kenya found that many women in Kenya lack support to claim their matrimonial property despite legal reform on equality and non-discrimination. The report found that ambiguous and antiquated laws on matrimonial property and inheritance remain on the books and that discriminatory practices make it difficult for married, divorced, separated, and widowed women to claim property the law entitles them to.

Despite a legal framework touted as being "gender-responsive" in Kenya, women encounter multiple social, legal, and judicial barriers in claiming their share of matrimonial property. The law requires that monetary and non-monetary contributions be considered in sharing property at the end of a marriage, but it does not clarify the proof of contribution required.

Key International Actors

Kenya continues to play a major role in the east and Horn of Africa region and has maintained close political and economic ties with the United States, China, and European nations.

In March 2020, tension between Kenya and Somalia appeared to escalate when clashes between Somali National government forces and Jubaland troops in Belet Hawa spilled across the border into Mandera, a Kenyan town bordering Somalia. Kenya warned Somalia against threatening its territorial integrity and sovereignty, but the tension appeared to ease after President Kenyatta and his Somali counterpart, Mohamed Abdullahi "Farmaajo," agreed to de-escalate the tensions.

Kenya received significant technical and financial support to address the Covid-19 crisis from the European Union, individual EU member countries, China, the United States, the World Bank, and the International Monetary Fund, even as Kenyan media and civil society groups have expressed concerns about the government's inability to investigate and prosecute those alleged to have misappropriated the COVID-19 response funds.

Kosovo

The first tranche of indictments issued by prosecutors attached to the Hague-based Specialist War Crimes court for Kosovo marked long-awaited progress towards justice for grave violations of international human rights and humanitarian law, as well as the laws of war. Journalists faced threats and intimidation, and prosecutions of crimes against journalists have been slow. Tensions between Serbs and Kosovo Albanians continued, particularly in the north. Roma, Ashkali, and Balkan Egyptian communities continued to face discrimination.

Accountability for War Crimes

In November, President Hashim Thaci was among four former senior members of the Kosovo Liberation Army (KLA) indicted for war crimes and crimes against humanity. The charges—which relate to the period during and just after the 1999 Kosovo war — were brought by the Hague-based Specialist Prosecutor's Office. Thaci resigned and all four were transferred to detention facilities in The Hague and had their first court appearances, pleading not guilty. The prosecution accusedThaci and the other defendants, Kadri Veseli, Rexhep Selimi and Jakup Krasniqi, of extensive witness intimidation and charged two men from the KLA's War Veterans Organization with leaking the names of witnesses. In September, another KLA commander, Salih Mustafa, was indicted and arrested for war crimes.

A Prizren court in June found a former Yugoslav police reserve officer guilty of war crimes against ethnic Albanians in the village of Mala Krusha in March 1999 and sentenced him to 22 years imprisonment.

Accountability of International Institutions

The United Nations human rights expert on Hazardous Waste in September called out the UN for repeatedly failing victims of lead poisoning in camps for displaced persons run by the UN Mission in Kosovo (UNMIK). The Human Rights Advisory Panel (HRAP), an independent international body set up to examine complaints of abuses by UNMIK, in 2016 found violations against members of displaced communities and recommended the UN pay individual compensation and apologize to victims—the UN has done neither. Since its establishment in 2017, only one state had contributed to the voluntary UN trust fund set up for community assistance projects not specifically targeted by lead poisoning. Victims are displaced members of the Roma, Ashkali, and Balkan Egyptian communities.

Treatment of Minorities

A comprehensive survey of Roma, Ashkali, and Balkan Egyptians in Kosovo published by the Organization for Security and Cooperation in January, concluded that the majority of members of these communities face high unemployment, poor housing, and experience discrimination, particularly women. It reported some improvement in access to education, which has traditionally been inadequate.

The trial against six defendants charged with the January 2018 murder of Kosovo-Serb politician Oliver Ivanovic started in February. Four defendants are accused of having been part of a criminal group that organized the murder of Ivanovic. Two defendants were Kosovo policemen. All entered not guilty pleas. Ivanovic was shot dead by unknown assailants outside his office in Mitrovica, northern Kosovo.

Women's Rights

Domestic violence remained a problem in Kosovo with an inadequate police response, few prosecutions, and continued failure by judges to issue restraining orders against abusive partners.

A 2018 mechanism set up to help provide financial compensation for the estimated 20,000 wartime survivors of sexual violence, continued to have limited reach. Between February 2018 and June 2020, around 1,239 survivors sought financial compensation, with 800 approved and 239 rejected, and the remaining pending at time of writing.

Asylum Seekers and Displaced Persons

During the first 9 months of the year, the United Nations High Commissioner for Refugees registered 245 voluntary returns of members of ethnic minorities to Kosovo from other countries, up from 115 during that period in 2019.

The Kosovo Ministry of Internal Affairs registered 304 deportations to Kosovo between January and September, most from Germany. The Ministry of Internal Affairs claimed to lack data on the ethnicity of those returned. Authorities provided returnees with limited assistance.

Human Rights Defenders

In June, 40 local civil society organizations condemned threats and smear campaigns against rights activist Shkelzen Gashi, fired as advisor to then-Prime Minister Albin Kurti after saying that individual members of the Kosovo Liberation Army had committed crimes during and after the war.

Sexual Orientation and Gender Identity

Hate speech on social media against lesbian, gay, bisexual and transgender (LGBT) rights activists continued. The Centre for Equality and Liberty of the LGBT Community in Kosovo (CEL) in October expressed concern about the frequency of homophobic comments and hate speech against LGBT people by high ranking politicians, particularly on social media.

Freedom of Media

Journalists continued to be targets of intimidation, threats on social media, and physical attacks. Investigations and prosecutions have been slow.

Between January and September, the Association of Journalists of Kosovo registered eighteen cases of threats and violence against journalists and media outlets, including five physical attacks on journalists and ten threats. Police were investigating four of the registered cases at time of writing.

In April, the director of TV Plus, Nenad Milenkovic, was physically attacked in North Mitrovica by four masked, unknown assailants, in what is believed to be actions linked to his reporting. Police were investigating at time of writing.

Key International Actors

The US and European governments consistently supported the EU-funded Kosovo special court but efforts by the US government to broker a stabilization agreement between Kosovo and Serbia did not address human rights concerns. Council of Europe Human Rights Commissioner, Dunja Mijatovic, called on states of former Yugoslavia to take the protection of war crimes' witnesses seriously and to ensure that no witness has to fear for their life when testifying in a war crimes case.

In July, the EULEX rule of law extended by one year due to the Covid-19 pandemic. In April, EULEX reinforced its commitment to establish the fate of over 1,640 persons who disappeared during the war and who are still unaccounted for.

EU Enlargement Commissioner Oliver Varhelyi told the new Kosovo government that reform efforts are needed to strengthen the rule of law and tackle corruption, but failed to raise other outstanding human rights concerns.

The European Commission October progress report stated that the judiciary remained vulnerable to political pressure and that witness protection mechanisms faced challenges as people have a low trust in authorities keeping them safe. The report raised concerns of continued threats and intimidation against LGBT people, and the inadequate measures to integrate Roma, Ashkali, and Balkan Egyptian communities.

Kuwait

Kuwaiti authorities continue to use provisions in the constitution, the national security law, and the country's cybercrime law to restrict free speech and prosecute dissidents, particularly focusing on comments made on social media.

Once a leading actor among its Gulf neighbors for the passing of the 2015 domestic workers law, Kuwait is now falling behind on reforming its *kafala* (sponsorship) system, which leaves migrant workers vulnerable to abuse and forced labor.

The Bidun, a community of stateless people who claim Kuwaiti nationality, remain in legal limbo while the government resorts to coercion and penalizes peaceful community activism.

While women continued to face violence in the family including killings, authorities passed a new law on domestic violence providing new protections from domestic violence for the first time and for the establishment of shelters for domestic violence, which Kuwait does not have.

Kuwait continues to allow Human Rights Watch access to the country, unlike many of its Gulf neighbors, and engaged in dialogue on a range of human rights issues.

Kuwait had over 100,000 confirmed cases of Covid-19 and 600 deaths by October 2020. The government imposed several restrictive measures, including a nationwide lockdown in March. The closure of schools affected the education of 800,000 students. Bidun children who are already socially marginalized, have reportedly a more difficult time accessing devices for online education.

Freedom of Expression and Assembly

Authorities prosecuted activists using penal code provisions and other laws that criminalize speech deemed insulting religion or the emir, or critical of neighboring countries. The 2015 Cybercrime Law expanded these restrictions to cover speech on social media platforms, particularly on Twitter.

In 2020, the Ministry of Interior's cybercrime department interrogated or arrested at least five activists and human rights defenders for comments on their

Twitter accounts, including journalist Abdulaziz al-Shaban, the blogger behind an account called the "Marxist Patron of People," and Hani Hussain, a human rights lawyer.

On July 20, the Court of Appeal sentenced Nasser al Duwailah, a former member of parliament, to six months in prison and a fine of 2,000 Kuwaiti Dinars (US$6,500) for insulting the United Arab Emirate on his Twitter account. A criminal court had previously acquitted him on charges stemming from a complaint filed by the UAE's attorney general.

On August 19, the parliament amended the media and publication law to lift the Ministry of Information's authority to decide whether a book could be imported.

Migrant Workers

Two-thirds of Kuwait's population is comprised of migrant workers, who remain vulnerable to abuse.

Human Rights Watch, during a visit to Kuwait in 2019, found that despite the protections provided under the 2015 domestic workers law, migrant domestic workers continued to face exploitation, forced confinement to their employers' houses, and physical and sexual abuse. Many domestic workers said they have not been able to claim their rights under the new law, in part because of the *kafala* (sponsorship) system under which they cannot leave or change employers without their employers' consent. Those who flee their employers can be arrested for "absconding."

As a result of the Covid-19 pandemic, many migrant workers found themselves dismissed without their wages, trapped in the country unable to leave due to travel restrictions and more expensive flight tickets, and increased risks of abuse by employers due to lockdown restrictions that left them confined to employers' homes.

Authorities issued an amnesty during April allowing migrant workers who overstayed their visas or were otherwise undocumented to leave the country without paying overstay fines and free to re-enter in the future. On July 7, al Qabas online newspaper reported that the Public Authority for Manpower had annulled all absconding cases lodged since the start of the pandemic. According to the paper, the decision came after the Public Authority's investigations revealed that many employers filed false absconding cases to sidestep their legal obligations to pay wages, or to provide food and accommodation.

Treatment of Minorities

The Bidun comprise between 88,000 to 106,000 stateless people who claim Kuwaiti nationality, dating back to the foundation of the Kuwaiti state in 1961.

Claiming that most of the Bidun moved to Kuwait from neighboring countries and hid their other nationalities to claim Kuwaiti citizenship, the government refers to them as "illegal residents," resulting in obstacles to them obtaining civil documentation, receiving social services, and impairing their rights to health, education, and work.

The Central System for the Remedy of Situations of Illegal Residents, the current administrative body in charge of Bidun affairs, has been issuing temporary ID cards since 2011. The process of determining applicants' eligibility for services and whether they hold another nationality remains opaque. The ID cards issued to Bidun in recent years often state that the cardholder possessed Iraqi, Saudi, Iranian, or other citizenship, but it was unclear how the agency determined the individual's alleged nationality and what due process procedures are available for Bidun to challenge the Central System's determination.

Article 12 of the 1979 Public Gatherings Law bars non-Kuwaitis from participating in public gatherings. On January 28, Kuwait's Fourth Circuit Criminal Court sentenced two Bidun activists to 10 years in prison and another in absentia to life in prison after they had organized a peaceful sit-in in the town of al-Jahra, near Kuwait City. Authorities arrested the two along with 12 other activists who were acquitted in July 2019. The charges included incitement to overthrow the government; publishing information on social media to incite violations of laws, and intentionally misusing means of communication.

Women's Rights, Sexual Orientation, and Gender Identity

Kuwait's personal status law applies to Sunni Muslims, who make up the majority of Kuwaitis, and discriminates against women in matters of marriage, divorce, and child custody, including a stipulation that women need male guardian permission to marry and should obey their husbands. A man can prohibit his wife from working if it is deemed to negatively affect the family's interests. The personal status rules that apply to Shia Muslims also discriminate against women. Kuwaiti women married to non-Kuwaitis, cannot pass citizenship to their children or spouses, unlike Kuwaiti men.

In 2019, Human Rights Watch spoke to women survivors of domestic violence who explained barriers to seeking protection from the authorities, including cases where police did not respond to their appeals or attempted to send them back to their abusers. The lack of a domestic violence shelter meant that many had nowhere to escape to from abusive homes. Discriminatory divorce laws mean that it can take years for women to obtain a divorce even when they have faced abuse. Kuwait, unusually, does not have any established shelters for adult victims of domestic violence in the country.

In September, there was outrage following the killing of Fatima al-Ajmi, a pregnant woman shot by her brother while she was in the hospital because he disapproved of her marriage—even though her father had approved it.

Women's rights activists complained that existing legal provisions that justify the murder of women encouraged such behavior. Under article 153 of the Kuwaiti penal code, a man who finds his mother, wife, sister, or daughter in the act of adultery (*zina*) and kills them is given a reduced sentence of either a small fine or a maximum three-year prison sentence. Under article 182, an abductor who uses force, threat, or deception with the intention to kill, harm, rape, prostitute, or extort a victim is spared any punishment if he marries the victim with her guardian's permission.

In September, Kuwait issued a Law on Protection from Domestic Violence, which provided measures to combat domestic violence and assistance for survivors for the first time. It has important provisions including the creation of a national committee for protection from domestic violence. It also establishes domestic violence shelters and a hotline to receive domestic violence complaints and provides for counseling and legal assistance for victims and emergency protection orders (restraining orders) to prevent abusers from contacting their victims. However, other than providing penalties, it does not explicitly criminalize domestic violence as a crime in itself. It also does not include people engaged in relationships outside of wedlock, including those engaged or in unofficial marriages or former partners.

The penal code criminalizes sexual relations outside marriage, and article 193 punishes consensual same-sex relations between men by up to seven years in prison. Transgender people can face one year in prison, a 1,000 Kuwaiti dinar fine ($3,293), or both, under a 2007 penal code provision that prohibits "imitating the opposite sex in any way." Transgender people have been subjected to arbitrary arrests, degrading treatment, and torture while in police custody. In July, a video of Maha al-Mutairi, a transgender woman who was summoned for "imitating women," caused a domestic and international outcry. According to her lawyer, during her detention, she was spat on, verbally abused, and sexually assaulted before authorities released her after three days without charge.

Key International Actors

Kuwait is a member of the Saudi and UAE-led coalition that intervened militarily in Yemen. Kuwait has not responded to Human Rights Watch inquiries regarding what role, if any, it has played in unlawful attacks in Yemen.

Kyrgyzstan

The death in custody of the wrongfully imprisoned human rights defender Azimjon Askarov in July was one of the low points of Kyrgyzstan's rights record during the year. Kyrgyzstan held parliamentary elections in October, which international observers found to be competitive but tainted by claims of vote buying. Protests and political turmoil followed the announcement of the results, leading to President Sooronbai Jeenbekov stepping down. Authorities misused lockdown measures imposed in response to Covid-19 to obstruct the work of journalists and lawyers. Measures put in place to protect women and girls have yet to end impunity for domestic violence, which is still the norm. Parliament advanced several problematic draft laws including an overly broad law penalizing manipulation of information. Thousands of children with disabilities live in institutions and have limited access to inclusive education.

Parliamentary Elections

The election monitoring mission of the Organization for Security and Co-operation in Europe's Office for Democratic Institutions and Human Rights (OSCE ODIHR) found that "fundamental rights and freedoms were overall respected" during October's parliamentary elections but that credible allegations of vote buying remain a serious concern." Opposition protests followed the outcome of the election. Kyrgyzstan's Central Election Committee on October 6 annulled the vote. New parliamentary elections were postponed until sometime in 2021.

Civil Society

On July 25, the human rights defender Azimjon Askarov died in custody, a violation of his right to life. Askarov had served 10 years of a life sentence imposed after an unfair trial on politically motivated charges. Kyrgyzstan blatantly ignored a 2016 United Nations Human Rights Committee (HRC) decision finding he was arbitrarily arrested, tortured, and which called for his release. His health, compromised from his long-term imprisonment, sharply deteriorated in the days before his death, but prison officials denied him adequate medical treatment.

At time of writing, authorities had yet to carry out an independent investigation into Askarov's wrongful imprisonment, denial of adequate medical care, or death in custody. UN Special Rapporteur on the Situation of Human Rights Defenders Mary Lawlor called Askarov's death "a stain on the human rights record of the Government of Kyrgyzstan." The European Union, which had called for Askarov's release, pressed the government of Kyrgyzstan to clarify the circumstances of Askarov's death.

Parliament advanced a widely-criticized bill on nongovernmental organizations (NGOs) that would impose additional burdensome financial reporting requirements on civil society groups. At a public hearing in May, representatives from the United Nations office and European Union delegation in Kyrgyzstan spoke out against adopting the bill.

Police on March 8 rounded up about 70 activists who had participated in a peaceful International Women's Day march in Bishkek. They were held without access to lawyers and were not informed of the grounds for their detention. A handful of activists later contested the legality of their detention. In June, a Bishkek court ruled against them, but Kyrgyzstan's Supreme Court in November overturned the court decision finding police actions lawful.

The State Committee on National Security (GKNB) on May 29 brought dubious forgery charges against the rights defender, Kamil Ruziev. Ruziev had filed a lawsuit against the GKNB and the prosecutor's office for failing to investigate how officials had threatened him, including at gunpoint. Ruziev's case was sent to court in September and is ongoing.

Access to Justice

Parliament adopted amendments to the Criminal Procedural Code removing a provision that obligates Kyrgyz courts to reconsider criminal cases in which an international human rights body, such as the HRC, has found a violation. The bill was sent to the president for signature after it passed a third reading in late June, but he returned the bill in early August for additional amendments.

June 10 marked 10 years since the outbreak of ethnic violence in southern Kyrgyzstan, in which 400 people were killed and nearly 2,000 homes destroyed. Authorities have failed to ensure accountability for crimes committed during the violence, or justice for the people arbitrarily arrested and convicted in trials marred by widespread allegations of ill-treatment and torture in the aftermath.

Freedom of Expression

In 2020, journalists were harassed by law enforcement, and in some cases threatened with criminal sanctions for critical reporting. Some journalists were attacked, including by police, during political unrest in October. Aibol Kozhomu- ratov, a social video producer at Current Time TV, tweeted a clip showing a law enforcement officer shooting a weapon at him while he was reporting on the un- rest. Other journalists were threatened and harassed by hostile individuals dur- ing and after protests.

On June 25, parliament adopted a vague and overly broad law on "manipulating information" that allows authorities, without judicial oversight, to order the re- moval of information officials consider "false" or "inaccurate" from internet plat- forms. The president returned the bill to parliament in July, where it was pending further review at time of writing.

Following the November 2019 exposeé on high-level corruption in Kyrgyzstan's customs agency, published jointly by the Organized Crime and Corruption Re- porting Project and local media agencies Kloop and Radio Azattyk, Raimbek Ma- traimov, a key figure in the report, filed multi-million some defamation lawsuits against several media outlets.

A court in mid-December 2019 approved freezing the media outlets' bank ac- counts but reversed its decision a day later following public outcry. In mid-De- cember, Organization for Security and Co-operation in Europe (OSCE) Representative on Freedom of the Media Harlem Désir said he was "highly con- cerned" about the defamation lawsuits, which are still pending court review.

On January 9, unknown assailants attacked the editor-in-chief of FactCheck.kg Bolot Temirov outside his office. Police opened an investigation and arrested four suspects, but the trial was delayed due to the pandemic.

Authorities in May dropped charges of interregional incitement against Aftandil Zhorobekov, a blogger who had written about corruption on social media. In February, authorities brought incitement charges against another blogger Elmirbek Sydymanov for speaking disparagingly about people from southern Kyrgyzstan.

Facial recognition technology provided by a Chinese state company and installed in Bishkek in November 2019 raised human rights, including privacy, concerns.

Labor Rights

Parliament in early November advanced in a second reading a restrictive trade union law after consideration of the bill had stalled for just over one year. The bill would grant the Federation of Trade Unions a monopoly over all federal-level union activity and require industrial and regional trade unions to affiliate with the federation. The bill undermines trade union pluralism and the right of trade unions to freely determine their structures and statutes. The International Labour Organization (ILO) and IndustriALL Global Union have criticized the proposed law, saying it would unjustifiably restrict freedom of association and the right to organize.

Terrorism and Counterterrorism

In the two years since Kyrgyzstan decriminalized possession of material the authorities label "extremist," dozens of persons have had their convictions overturned. Local human rights lawyers said that some judges ordered a prisoner's release upon review, but in other cases they rejected petitions and the detainees remained in prison. New cases suggest that authorities persist in targeting individuals under Kyrgyzstan's vague definition of extremism, which captures nonviolent behavior such as "affronts to national dignity" as well as acts that may not rise to the severity of a security threat such as "hooliganism" and "vandalism," and for the dissemination of extremist materials.

The government's plans to repatriate some of the hundreds of children of Islamic State (ISIS) suspects from Kyrgyzstan detained in Iraq stalled in 2020.

Violence against Women and Girls

Despite legislation, including amendments to the Criminal Procedural Code adopted in 2020, which provides better protections for victims of domestic violence, authorities do not fully enforce protective measures or hold perpetrators accountable. Impunity for domestic violence is still the norm. At a June meeting of the National Council for Women and Gender Development, a government advisory body, Vice Prime Minister Aida Ismailova noted a 65 percent rise in reported cases of domestic violence cases in the first quarter of 2020.

In June, after a video emerged on Kyrgyz social media showing a man forcing his wife to stand weighed down by tires while he slapped and doused her with water, police detained and charged him with "cruel treatment," though only after public outcry. A court convicted him, but only sentenced him to two years' probation instead of jail time.

Torture

Impunity for torture and ill-treatment remains the norm. As a part of Covid-19 related restrictions imposed in March, authorities denied lawyers and monitors from the National Center for the Prevention of Torture access to prisons and other places of detention. According to government statistics sent to the anti-torture group Voice of Freedom, 68 allegations of torture were registered in the first five months of 2020.

The Health Ministry in August proposed a draft decree establishing rules for conducting medical examinations in cases of violence, torture, and ill-treatment. The decree was pending adoption at time of writing.

Kyrgyz authorities on August 22 extradited the journalist Bobomurod Abdullaev from Kyrgyzstan to Uzbekistan despite the risk of torture he faced there. Abdullaev alleged he had been ill-treated by GKNB officials.

Children with Disabilities

Although the government has acknowledged the importance of ending segregation and discrimination against people with disabilities, an estimated 3,000 children with disabilities live in state institutions, where they face abuse and ne-

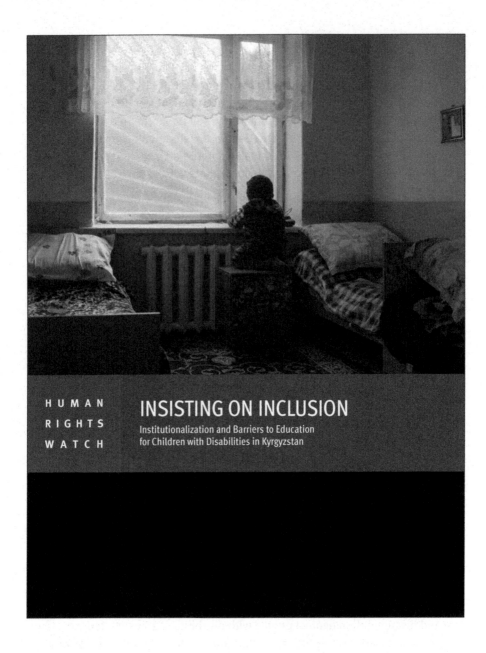

HUMAN
RIGHTS
WATCH

INSISTING ON INCLUSION

Institutionalization and Barriers to Education
for Children with Disabilities in Kyrgyzstan

glect. The government has not done enough to ensure children with disabilities receive a quality, inclusive education in mainstream schools in their communities, with reasonable supports as necessary.

Covid-19

Kyrgyzstan declared a state of emergency in March in response to the Covid-19 pandemic. While restrictions were in place, neither independent media outlets nor lawyers were granted permits to pass police checkpoints, interfering with their ability to work. Peaceful assemblies were banned in several cities in Kyrgyzstan. Authorities threatened criminal sanctions or opened investigations for spreading "false information" about the virus against doctors and others who voiced concerned about inadequate protective equipment. According to data published in mid-July, medical workers made up approximately 16 percent of the total number of infections in Kyrgyzstan.

During the Covid-19 related lockdown, the government did not classify domestic violence services as "essential" to ensure services remained operational, and shelters, crisis centers, and other services were closed to newcomers. Around 2.4 million children and young people are affected by educational facility closures, and had to continue education by remote learning where possible. In August, the World Bank cautioned that the Covid-19 pandemic could have a detrimental and long-lasting impact on education and human capital, and economic and social development in Kyrgyzstan.

Key International Actors

In December 2019, UN Special Rapporteur on Minority Issues Fernand de Varennes visited Kyrgyzstan and found that ethnic relations "remain fragile" and that factors including "underrepresentation of minorities" and "unfair treatment by law enforcement" could "bring the level of inter-ethnic tension to a breaking point."

In September, the UNHRC adopted the outcome of Kyrgyzstan's third Universal Periodic Review. In January, delegations had urged Kyrgyzstan to release Azimjon Askarov, adopt anti-discrimination legislation, and effectively combat domestic violence, amongst other recommendations.

The European Union and Kyrgyzstan had not signed their Enhanced Partnership and Cooperation Agreement by year's end, although negotiations had formally concluded in 2019. At the EU-Kyrgyzstan human rights dialogue in September, the EU raised Askarov's case and noted concern over controversial draft laws, restrictions on peaceful assembly and information, and the high increase in cases of domestic and gender-based violence during the pandemic.

Lebanon

In 2020, Lebanon endured multiple crises, including a massive explosion in Beirut's port, an economic collapse, rising political instability, and the Covid-19 global pandemic, all of which endangered residents' basic rights. The Lebanese political class failed to adequately address any of these crises, some of which were of their own making.

The Lebanese Pound has lost 80 percent of its value since October 2019, eroding people's ability to access basic goods, including food, shelter, and healthcare. The Covid-19 pandemic compounded poverty and economic hardship.

The economic crisis and the Covid-19 pandemic severely affected the medical sector, endangering the ability of hospitals to provide life-saving care. Electricity blackouts became widespread, lasting up to 22 hours per day in the summer.

On August 4, a massive blast in Beirut's seaport devastated the city killing almost 200 people, injuring more than 6,000, and leaving 300,000 people without shelter. Prime Minister Hassan Diab's government resigned shortly thereafter. Saad Hariri was nominated to be the country's prime minister on October 22, nearly one year after he resigned from the post amid popular protests.

Lebanese security forces, including army personnel, internal security forces, and the parliament police, have used excessive force on several occasions against demonstrators, especially following the country's October 17, 2019 uprising—often with impunity. Lebanese authorities continued to investigate and prosecute individuals for peaceful speech and refer civilians to military courts.

Women and children still face discrimination under the religion-based personal status laws, and child marriage and marital rape remain legal. Unlike men, Lebanese women cannot pass their citizenship to their children and foreign spouses.

There are approximately 1.5 million Syrian refugees in Lebanon, of whom about 78 percent lack legal status, an increase from the previous year. The situation of migrant domestic workers, who are subject to the restrictive *kafala* (sponsorship) system and are excluded from labor law protections, has worsened amid the economic crisis and Covid-19 pandemic.

Beirut Port Explosion

On August 4, a huge explosion at the Beirut seaport devastated the city. The explosion impacted Lebanon's food supply, as Lebanon imports 85 percent of its food, and the port previously handled around 70 percent of the country's imports. The explosion affected 163 public and private schools and rendered half of Beirut's healthcare centers nonfunctional.

President Michel Aoun and then-Prime Minister Hassan Diab said the explosion was caused by 2,750 tons of ammonium nitrate that had been stored in a warehouse in the Beirut port for over six years without appropriate safety precautions. The circumstances that led to the detonation of the material are not yet clear. Media reports claimed that many high-level officials were aware of the existence of the ammonium nitrate but failed to act.

President Aoun has promised a transparent investigation into the causes of the explosion. However, rights groups, including Human Rights Watch, have raised serious concerns about the credibility and independence of the investigation. Human Rights Watch, other civil society organizations, and victims groups have called for an international and independent investigation into the blast.

Financial and Economic Crisis

Lebanon's economy has long depended on a regular in-flow of US dollars, and the Central Bank has pegged the Lebanese pound to the US dollar at an official exchange rate of 1,507.5 Lebanese pounds since 1997. Over the last 10 years, as economic growth slowed and remittances from the Lebanese diaspora have decreased, the quantity of dollars in circulation has declined. An increasing lack of confidence in the stability of the Lebanese pound in 2019 and concerns about the stability of the banking sector led depositors to withdraw from dollar accounts, making dollars increasingly scarce and causing the unofficial exchange rate to hit 8,000 Lebanese pounds in September.

In November 2019, months before the threat of Covid-19 became apparent, the World Bank predicted that the portion of Lebanon's population below the poverty line would rise from 30 to 50 percent in 2020. Some Lebanese economists estimate that this figure has drastically increased.

As the Lebanese pound depreciates, the price of basic goods, most of which are imported, is rapidly increasing, eroding people's ability to afford food, shelter, and healthcare. The Covid-19 pandemic compounded the poverty and economic hardship many faced, and disproportionately affected marginalized groups, including low-income families, people with disabilities, migrants, refugees, and lesbian, gay, bisexual, and transgender (LGBTQ) people. The government did not develop a timely, robust, or coordinated plan to help.

The financial crisis has thrown Lebanon's healthcare sector into crisis. Hospitals are struggling to provide patients with urgent and necessary life-saving medical care due to the government's failure to provide private and public hospitals with the funds it owes them. In addition, a dollar shortage has restricted the import of vital medical equipment and led banks to curtail credit lines. Medical supplies, including gloves and masks, are scarce, compromising Lebanon's ability to deal with the coronavirus pandemic.

In May, the Lebanese government began formal negotiations with the International Monetary Fund (IMF) to discuss a plan to rescue the economy and request around US$10 billion dollars in aid. However, the negotiations stalled when politicians failed to agree on the size of the country's financial losses.

Freedom of Assembly and Expression

Anti-government protests, which began on October 17, 2019, against the political establishment's corruption and incompetence, continued in 2020.

Security forces—including the army, anti-riot police, and parliamentary police—used excessive and at times lethal force against mostly peaceful protesters. The Lebanese Armed Forces (LAF) unjustifiably used excessive force against protesters in Tripoli on April 27, killing one protester and injuring scores more.

Tens of thousands of protesters gathered in downtown Beirut on August 8 to express their outrage over the Beirut blast and demand accountability. Security forces fired live ammunition, metal pellets, and kinetic impact projectiles such as rubber balls, including at health workers, and police deployed excessive quantities of tear gas, including at first aid stations. Several teargas cartridges were fired directly at protesters, striking some in the head and neck. Security forces also threw stones at protesters and beat them: 728 people were injured.

Attacks on free speech escalated in the wake of the October 17, 2019, nationwide protests, and authorities continued to use Lebanon's criminal defamation laws to detain and charge individuals for speech critical of government officials, especially in relation to corruption allegations. Fourteen local and international organizations, including Human Rights Watch, announced on July 13 the formation of a "Coalition to Defend Freedom of Expression" to oppose the Lebanese authorities' attempts to stifle free speech in the country.

Environment and Health

Despite the passage of a solid waste management law in 2018 banning the open burning of waste, municipalities still engage in the practice, posing health risks to nearby residents, especially children and older persons.

The two major landfills servicing Beirut are set to reach capacity this year, but the government has not put in place a plan to tackle the looming trash crisis.

Since the 2015 trash crisis, during which garbage built up on the streets of Beirut, the government has been relying on stopgap measures and temporary fixes that do not solve Lebanon's underlying waste management problems, incurring huge environmental and public health costs.

Women's Rights

Women continue to face discrimination under 15 distinct religion-based personal status laws. Discrimination includes inequality in access to divorce, child custody, and inheritance and property rights. Unlike men, Lebanese women also cannot pass on their nationality to foreign husbands and children.

Lebanon has no minimum age for marriage, and some religious courts allow girls younger than 15 to marry. In 2017, Lebanon's parliament repealed article 522, which had allowed rapists to escape prosecution by marrying the victim, but left a loophole regarding offenses relating to sex with children aged 15-17 and sex with virgin girls with promises of marriage. Marital rape is still not criminalized.

Women's rights groups reported a significant increase in the number of calls about domestic violence during Covid-19 lockdown restrictions compared to the previous year.

Sexual Orientation and Gender Identity

LGBT people participated prominently in the nationwide protests that began on October 17, 2019. By taking their struggle to the streets, through chants, graffiti, and public discussions, LGBT people have moved demands of their rights from the margins to mainstream discourse.

However, article 534 of the penal code punishes "any sexual intercourse contrary to the order of nature" with up to one year in prison. Transgender women in Lebanon face systemic violence and discrimination in accessing basic services, including employment, health care, and housing. The economic crisis, compounded by Covid-19 lockdown measures, disproportionately affected LGBT people.

Education

More than half of school-age refugee children are out of school.

The Covid-19 pandemic and the transition to remote learning has exacerbated inequalities and increased the risk that some children, particularly the most vulnerable, will not come back once schools reopen. The government's distance learning strategy was not implemented consistently in "second shift" classes, attended by Syrian children, leaving the majority "completely out of learning," a group of international humanitarian organizations reported in June.

Children with disabilities are often denied admission to schools and for those who manage to enroll, most schools do not take reasonable steps to provide them with a quality education. Lebanon's Covid-19 response has overlooked children with disabilities, who cannot access remote education on an equal basis with others.

Migrant Workers

An estimated 250,000 migrant domestic workers, primarily from Ethiopia, the Philippines, Bangladesh, and Sri Lanka, are excluded from Lebanon's labor law protections, and their status in the country is regulated by the restrictive *kafala* (sponsorship) system, which ties migrant workers' legal residency to their employer.

Human Rights Watch and many other organizations have documented for years how the *kafala* system gives employers excessive control over workers' lives, leading to an array of abuses, including non-payment of wages, forced confinement, excessive working hours, and verbal, physical, and sexual abuse. During the economic crisis, many employers abandoned their workers, without pay or return flight tickets home, in front of consulates and embassies, and workers reported facing discrimination in receiving aid after the Beirut blast.

On September 4, the Labor Ministry adopted a new standard unified contract for migrant domestic workers that allows workers to terminate their contract without the consent of their employer, and provides key labor guarantees already afforded to other workers such as a 48-hour work week, a weekly rest day, overtime pay, sick pay, annual leave, and the national minimum wage, with some permissible deductions for housing and food. If implemented, the contract could improve the lives of migrant domestic workers in Lebanon. However, the contract does not include provisions to allow workers to join and form unions, and the authorities have yet to roll out oversight and enforcement mechanisms or extend labor law protections to domestic workers.

Refugees

Nearly one million Syrian refugees are registered with the United Nations High Commissioner for Refugees (UNHCR) in Lebanon. Lebanon's residency policy for refugees makes it difficult for Syrians to maintain legal status, heightening risks of exploitation and abuse and restricting refugees' access to work, education, and healthcare. Seventy-eight percent of Syrians in Lebanon now lack legal residency and risk detention and deportation for unlawful presence in the country.

At least 21 Lebanese municipalities introduced discriminatory restrictions on Syrian refugees that do not apply to Lebanese residents as part of their efforts to combat Covid-19.

According to the Lebanese Palestinian Dialogue Committee, there are approximately 174,000 Palestinian refugees living in Lebanon, where they continue to face restrictions, including on their right to work and own property. In addition, approximately 30,000 Palestinians from Syria have sought refuge in Lebanon.

Legacy of Past Conflicts and Wars

An estimated 17,000 Lebanese were kidnapped or "disappeared" during the 1975-1990 civil war. On November 12, 2018, parliament passed a landmark law creating an independent national commission to investigate the fate of the disappeared, and in June, the cabinet approved the members of the commission.

In August, judges at the Special Tribunal for Lebanon convicted a member of Hezbollah for his role in the killing of former Lebanese Prime Minister Rafik Hariri in a 2005 car bomb. The court acquitted the three other defendants in the case.

Key International Actors

Syria, Iran, and Saudi Arabia maintain a strong influence on Lebanese politics through local allies.

Tensions between Hezbollah and Israel remain high. The Israeli military said it thwarted a Hezbollah raid at the border on July 27, but Hezbollah denied carrying out an operation. Israel violated Lebanese airspace frequently.

Lebanon and Israel began talks over their disputed maritime border on October 14.

The international community has given Lebanon extensive, albeit insufficient, support to help it cope with the Syrian refugee crisis and to bolster security amid spillover violence.

Thirty-six countries pledged €253 million (around $300 million) for emergency support to Lebanon after the explosion during a donor conference co-led by France and the United Nations on August 9. A second conference was planned for November. French President Emmanuel Macron is pushing Lebanese leaders to implement reforms.

Lebanese armed forces and police receive assistance from a range of international donors, including the United States, European Union, United Kingdom, France, and Saudi Arabia.

Libya

Since April 2019, the United Nations-recognized and Tripoli-based Government of National Accord (GNA), supported by armed groups in western Libya nominally under its control, has been embroiled in an armed conflict with the rival Interim Government based in eastern Libya, which is affiliated with the armed group Libyan Arab Armed Forces (LAAF) under the command of General Khalifa Hiftar. On October 23, conflict parties signed a country-wide ceasefire agreement in Geneva.

The conflict hampered the provision of basic services including health and electricity. Armed groups on all sides continued to kill unlawfully and shell indiscriminately, killing civilians and destroying vital infrastructure.

In August, GNA affiliated armed groups in Tripoli used heavy weapons to disperse street protests against corruption and poor living conditions. In September, people in the eastern cities of Benghazi, Tobruk, and Al-Marj took to the streets to protest deteriorating living conditions. LAAF-affiliated armed groups and forces linked with the Interim Government quelled some of the protests using live fire.

Migrants, asylum seekers, and refugees in Libya—including thousands intercepted at sea while trying to reach Europe and returned by the European Union-supported Libyan Coast Guard—faced arbitrary detention, during which many experienced ill-treatment, sexual assault, forced labor, and extortion by groups under the GNA Interior Ministry, members of armed groups, smugglers, and traffickers.

Armed Conflict and War Crimes

On October 23, representatives of the GNA and LAAF—the two main Libyan conflict parties—signed in Geneva a permanent and country-wide ceasefire brokered by the United Nations. The agreement stipulated the departure of all foreign fighters and trainers from the country for a minimum of three months, the re-opening of land and air routes that had been practically shut for many months, and the exchange of prisoners between the parties.

The armed conflict in Tripoli and the surrounding area that had started on April 4, 2019, ended on June 4 when GNA-linked armed groups and their foreign backers, mainly Turkey, pushed the LAAF and its affiliates toward the central city of Sirte and to Jufrah in the south. The conflict resulted in at least 1,043 civilian casualties as of July and over 220,000 internally displaced people, according to the UN.

General Hiftar's main backers—the United Arab Emirates (UAE), Jordan, Egypt, and Russia—provided drones, fighter jets, and foreign fighters from Sudan and Syria. Private military companies, including the Kremlin-linked Wagner Group, also provided support. The GNA had substantial foreign fighter support from Sudan and Syria. In August, the GNA, Turkey and Qatar signed a three-way agreement in which Turkey and Qatar committed to sending military advisers and training Libyan cadets.

Internal and external conflict parties largely ignored an arms embargo ordered by the UN Security Council in 2011 and renewed multiple times. A report by the Security Council's Libya Panel of Experts that was leaked to the press in September stated that Turkey and the United Arab Emirates "were in repeated non-compliance" with the embargo, and named 11 companies as violating the embargo. No entity had been held to account over violations of the Libya arms embargo since 2011.

Between April 2019 and June 2020, the LAAF and its affiliates conducted indiscriminate artillery, air, and drone strikes that killed and wounded hundreds of civilians and destroyed civilian infrastructure. The LAAF and affiliated foreign forces used internationally banned cluster munitions and laid landmines and boobytraps in Tripoli's southern suburbs, which killed and wounded at least 116 civilians between May and September. Videos posted on social media in May showed LAAF-affiliated fighters torturing opposing fighters and desecrating corpses after apparent summary executions.

GNA authorities said they found between June and mid-November at least 115 unidentified bodies in 26 mass grave sites in Tarhouna, a town southeast of Tripoli that had been under the control of Al-Kani militia, the LAAF's main western ally. GNA authorities said they also found 29 bodies in 18 other locations in the southern suburbs of Tripoli. The GNA also said it discovered at least 106 bodies in the general hospital of Tarhouna after the withdrawal of Al Kani militias, who had controlled Tarhouna since 2013.

GNA-affiliated armed groups were responsible for indiscriminate shelling and air and drone strikes, and often failed to ensure that no civilians were near targeted military facilities, which resulted in civilian casualties. Reports of looting and destruction of private property by GNA-affiliated armed groups followed the GNA takeover of Tarhouna in early June.

A January 5 attack on a military cadets training facility, apparently carried out by a UAE-supplied drone in support of the LAAF, killed 26 cadets and wounded dozens. The same type of drone had been used by the UAE in support of the LAAF in a November 2019 attack on a biscuit factory in Tripoli outskirts, an apparent violation of the laws of war that resulted in the killing of eight civilians and wounding of 27 more.

Judicial System and Detainees

The criminal justice system remained dysfunctional due to impunity, insecurity, and armed conflicts. Judges and prosecutors were subject to harassment, threats, assaults, abductions, and even killings. Where civilian and military courts conducted trials, mostly in Tripoli and Benghazi, there were serious due process concerns. Prison authorities continued to hold thousands of detainees in long-term arbitrary detention without charge. Detainees included those held on security-related charges because of their participation in a conflict, terrorism suspects, and others held for common crimes such as murder or theft. Justice, interior, defense, and intelligence ministries linked with the respective governments in Libya all run detention facilities. Prisons nominally run by authorities but often controlled by armed groups are marked by overcrowding, poor living conditions, and ill treatment.

In January, Tunisia repatriated six orphaned children of ISIS suspects. GNA-linked Special Deterrence Force and the Justice Ministry have continued to hold dozens of other foreign women and children who are related to ISIS suspects in prisons in Tripoli and in Misrata since their capture in 2016. Prospects for their release remained dim because of the reluctance of their governments to repatriate them. They are held in facilities not adapted for children's needs, such as pediatric medical care and education.

International Justice and the ICC

Saif al-Islam Gaddafi, a son of Muammar Gaddafi who was sentenced to death in absentia by a Libyan court in 2015, is wanted by the International Criminal Court (ICC) for his alleged role in attacks on civilians, including peaceful demonstrators, during the country's 2011 uprising. Gaddafi's whereabouts remained unknown.

Two other Libyans continued to be subject to ICC arrest warrants: Al-Tuhamy Khaled, former head of the Internal Security Agency under Muammar Gaddafi, for war crimes and crimes against humanity committed between February and August 2011, and LAAF commander, Mahmoud El-Werfalli, for the war crime of murder related to several incidents in and around Benghazi between June 2016 and January 2018. Both men remained fugitives.

In September, two families brought lawsuits in the United States against Khalifa Hiftar, accusing his forces of atrocities during the months-long siege of Ganfouda in Benghazi in 2017 in which their relatives were killed. Previously, two families brought similar lawsuits against Hiftar for extrajudicial killings and torture of their relatives in eastern Libya by his forces.

Death Penalty

The death penalty is stipulated in over 30 articles in Libya's penal code, including for acts of speech and association. No death sentences have been carried out since 2010, although both military and civilian courts continued to impose them.

Internally Displaced Persons

As of October, the International Organization for Migration (IOM) estimated there were 392,241 internally displaced people in Libya, including 229,295 people displaced since the beginning of the April 2019 conflict in Tripoli and surrounding areas.

The displaced include many of the 48,000 former residents of the town of Tawergha, who in 2011 were driven out by armed groups predominantly from Misrata because of their support for the former Gaddafi government. Despite reconciliation agreements with Misrata authorities, they have been deterred by returning

by the massive and deliberate destruction of the town and its infrastructure between 2011 and 2017, predominantly by militias from Misrata, and the scarcity of
public services by the GNA.

Freedom of Speech and Expression

Armed groups in Tripoli linked with the GNA used lethal force to disperse largely
peaceful anti-corruption protests between August 23 and 29 and arbitrarily detained, tortured, and disappeared people in the capital before releasing them.
They used machine guns and vehicle-mounted anti-aircraft weapons to disperse
protesters, wounding some and killing one. One of those arrested and released
was Sami al-Sharif, director of the Tripoli-based Al-Jawhara Radio Station. Libya
al-Ahrar TV, a Libyan satellite TV station, announced that protesters harassed
and attacked a TV crew covering the protests. The armed groups included the
GNA-linked groups Special Deterrence Force, the Al-Nawasi Brigade and the General Security Force.

Armed groups affiliated with the LAAF and Interim Government in September violently suppressed anti-corruption protests in the eastern towns of Al-Marj and
Benghazi, reportedly killing one protester and arresting an unknown number of
people.

In Benghazi, unidentified masked gunmen shot dead on November 10 Hanan Al-
Barassi, an outspoken critic of violations by armed groups in eastern Libya. Al-
Barassi, who spoke up against alleged widespread corruption and abuse of
power by officials and members of armed groups in eastern Libya that included
direct family members of Hiftar, also alleged sexual assault and harassment
against women. In the days leading up to her killing, she said that she had received numerous death threats.

After a secret trial, a Benghazi military court in May sentenced freelance photo-
journalist Ismail Abuzreiba Al-Zway, who had been arrested in December 2018,
to 15 years in prison on terrorism charges for "communicating with a TV station
that supports terrorism," in reference to his previous work with a private Libyan
satellite television channel, Alnabaa.

On December 14, 2019, Al-Nawasi Brigade, a GNA-linked armed group, abducted
journalist Reda Fhelboom upon his arrival at Mitiga Airport in Tripoli and held

him for 12 days in two different facilities where he says he was interrogated and ill-treated, including by suspending him by his wrists for long periods and keeping him blindfolded in a forced position for hours on end.

Al-Nawasi initially accused Fhelboom of illegally establishing a nongovernmental organization (NGO) and targeted him for an article he wrote in 2015 on lesbian, gay, bisexual, and transgender (LGBT) issues, for which he won an award in 2016. The general prosecutor finally charged him in January for "practicing journalism without a license and communicating with an international organization without state permission." At time of writing, the case against him remained ongoing.

Women's Rights and Sexual Orientation

Libyan law does not specifically criminalize domestic violence. Personal status laws discriminate against women with respect to marriage, divorce, and inheritance. The penal code allows for a reduced sentence for a man who kills or injures his wife or another female relative because he suspects her of extramarital sexual relations. Under the penal code, rapists can escape prosecution if they marry their victim.

The penal code prohibits all sexual acts outside marriage, including consensual same-sex relations, and punishes them with flogging and up to five years in prison.

Migrants, Refugees, and Asylum Seekers

Over 25,738 migrants and asylum seekers arrived in Italy and Malta from January to mid-September, 11,295 of whom had departed from Libya, according to the IOM. The organization recorded 471 deaths in the central Mediterranean in the same reporting period.

The IOM identified 584,509 migrants in Libya as of October. According to the UN refugee agency UNHCR, 46,247 were registered asylum seekers and refugees. Due to conflict and Covid-19 disruptions, the IOM conducted fewer voluntary humanitarian returns of stranded migrants from Libya to their home countries—

1,466 during the first quarter of 2020— compared with 9,800 in the same period in 2019.

The European Union continued to collaborate with abusive Libyan Coast Guard forces by providing them with speedboats, training, and other support to intercept and return thousands of people to Libya. As of October, 9,448 people were disembarked in Libya after the LCG intercepted them, according to IOM, who said thousands then went missing after they were taken to undisclosed locations.

Migrants, asylum seekers and refugees were arbitrarily detained in inhumane conditions in facilities run by the GNA's Interior Ministry and in "warehouses" run by smugglers and traffickers, where they were subjected to forced labor, torture and other ill-treatment, extortion, and sexual assault. At least 2,467 were held in official detention centers in Libya as of September, according to UNHCR.

In May, unidentified gunmen killed 24 migrants from Bangladesh and six African migrants held in a trafficker's safehouse in the southern town of Mizdah after a group of migrants had killed their Libyan captor. At the time, Mizdah was under the control of LAAF forces. At time of writing, no one had been arrested in relation to the killings. In July, Libyan authorities shot and killed three Sudanese migrants who tried to flee upon disembarkation in Libya after their interception at sea.

In October, GNA-linked forces said they arrested Abd Al Rahman Al-Milad, also known as Bija, a member of the Coast Guard, in the western town of Al-Zawiya for his alleged role in human trafficking. In June 2018, the UN Security Council designated Al-Milad sanctions for his role in human trafficking and smuggling and violations against migrants.

Covid-19

In March, the LAAF's Chief of Staff banned medical doctors from voicing any criticism of the authorities' handling of Covid-19 and called anyone who did so "traitors." LAAF-linked military police arrested in March a medical doctor in Benghazi who had criticized conditions in hospitals in Benghazi in relation to the Covid-19 response, and subsequently released him.

In March, the GNA Justice Ministry said it released 466 pretrial detainees—who represent only a fraction of people held in pretrial detention—as well as detainees who met the rules for conditional release from prisons in Tripoli in order to reduce overcrowding and mitigate a Covid-19 outbreak.

The GNA Presidential Council imposed a four-day curfew and two weeks of partial curfews in August, during anti-corruption protests in Tripoli, citing a spread of Covid-19. Some protesters said this was an attempt to prevent them from demonstrating. The GNA had imposed partial curfews since March to reduce Covid-19 transmissions.

Key International Actors

The United States in September accused Russia of operating over 12 fighter jets in support of the LAAF with the help of the Wagner Group, a private military company believed to be linked with the Kremlin.

Tukey signed a memorandum of understanding in December 2019 with the GNA to demarcate maritime zones in the region, and a security agreement for cooperation on military matters including trainings and military materials.

The UN Human Rights Council on June 22 established a fact-finding mission to investigate violations of international human rights law and international humanitarian law by all parties to the Libya conflict since the beginning of 2016.

The European Union in March launched Operation EUNAVFOR MED IRINI to enforce the UN Libya arms embargo through aerial, satellite and maritime assets in accordance with UNSC Resolution 2292 (2016). EU governments agreed that IRINI patrol boats would avoid monitoring areas of the Mediterranean where they might have to respond to boats carrying migrants in distress. The EU continued its policy of cooperation and support to Libyan authorities to stop departures and ensuring that those intercepted at sea were returned to abusive and inhumane conditions in Libya. In September, the EU added to its sanctions list two persons responsible for human rights abuses in Libya and three entities involved in violating the UN arms embargo.

Malaysia

Malaysia's faltering reform movement was halted in March when the Pakatan Harapan coalition collapsed and was replaced by a new coalition comprised of the United Malays National Organization (UMNO), the Malaysian Islamic Parti (PAS), and defectors from the Pakatan Harapan coalition. The new government, headed by Prime Minister Muhyiddin Yassin, aggressively cracked down on critical speech and protest, backed away from creating a truly independent police complaints commission, and took a hard line on the treatment of refugees and undocumented migrants.

Freedom of Expression

Freedom of expression came under attack immediately after the change in government, when authorities opened a sedition investigation into activist Fadiah Nadwa Fikri for organizing a protest against the method by which the new government came to power. Since then, authorities have opened investigations into numerous activists and opposition politicians for speech critical of the government. The police had opened 262 investigations into the spread of "false and seditious news" as of May 11, and 264 investigations into "false news" on Covid-19.

Freedom of the press has also come under attack. On April 11, Defense Minister Ismail Saabri announced that the government would take "stern action" against online media that "misreport" the news. Journalist Tashny Sukumaran was questioned over her report on a round-up of migrant workers, and in June, police opened an investigation of Boo Su-Lyn, editor of the health news portal Code-Blue, under the Official Official Secrets Act and the penal code for a series of articles about the findings of an independent investigation into an October 2016 hospital fire that killed six patients. The investigation remained open at time of writing.

In July, after Al Jazeera aired a documentary about Malaysia's treatment of migrant workers during the Covid-19 pandemic, the police announced that they were investigating Al Jazeera for sedition, defamation, and violation of the Communications and Multimedia Act (CMA). The police questioned six Al Jazeera staff members and raided the organization's offices in Kuala Lumpur. In August, Malaysia refused to renew the visas of two Al Jazeera journalists based in the country.

The Immigration Department announced that it had revoked the work permit of Mohammed Rayhan Kabir, a migrant worker from Bangladesh who featured in the documentary. He was arrested on July 24 and remanded for investigation. Malaysia deported him back to Bangladesh on August 21.

The government also sought to hold online news portals responsible for comments posted by their readers. On June 15, the Attorney General filed an application to initiate contempt proceedings against online news portal Malaysiakini for five reader comments. On July 13, the Federal Court announced that it would be taking time to deliberate before issuing a decision.

In July, the home minister banned *Rebirth: Reformasi, Resistance and Hope in New Malaysia* under the Printing Presses and Publications Act after claims that the book's cover resembled the country's coat of arms. The book contains a collection of writings about the 2018 general election and subsequent events compiled by editor Kean Wong. Police raided the publishing company and questioned journalist Tashny Sukumaran and seven Malaysiakini journalists who had authored chapters.

Police Abuse and Impunity

Police abuse of suspects in custody continues to be a serious problem, as does a lack of accountability for such offenses. In August, the government withdrew a bill submitted by the prior administration to create an Independent Police Complaints and Misconduct Commission "because the police objected to it." The government instead introduced a bill to create a toothless Independent Police Conduct Commission that lacks both key investigative powers and the authority to punish wrongdoing. The proposed commission would not even be able to visit lock-ups without giving advance notice, and is precluded from even investigating any act covered by the standing orders issued by the police inspector general.

The standard of care for those in detention is also problematic, with detainees dying of treatable illnesses. The government reported that 23 people, including two children, died while in immigration detention during the first six months of 2020. During the same period, three people died while in police lock-ups, and 188 prison inmates died.

Refugees, Asylum Seekers, and Trafficking Victims

Malaysia has not ratified the 1951 Refugee Convention. Over 175,000 refugees and asylum seekers, most of whom come from Myanmar, are registered with the United Nations High Commission for Refugees (UNHCR) office but have no legal status and remain unable to work or enroll in government schools.

The new government has taken a hard line on refugees, with the home minister stating that they have "no status, rights, or basis to present any demands to the government." The authorities pushed boatloads of desperate Rohingya refugees who were trying to reach Malaysia's shores back out to sea, claiming that they were doing so to prevent the spread of Covid-19. Those that have been permitted to land have been detained as "illegal migrants," with some prosecuted for immigration violations. Even children have been detained in "shelters" and threatened with prosecution. Malaysia did little to stop a vicious online hate speech campaign against Rohingya refugees in the country in April.

The government confirmed in September 2020 that Malaysia will not entertain requests from China to extradite Uyghur refugees and will allow them safe passage to third countries.

The government has yet to release the findings of the Royal Commission of Inquiry (RCI) set up in 2019 to investigate mass graves found in remote jungle camps on the Thai-Malaysian border in 2015. To date, no Malaysians have been held responsible for their role in the deaths of over 100 ethnic Rohingya trafficking victims whose bodies were found in the camps. The 12 police officers initially charged in the case were released in March 2017.

Covid-19

Malaysia's efforts to contain the spread of Covid-19, while generally successful, had a disproportionate impact on marginalized communities. While authorities initially stated that they would not take action against undocumented migrants who came forward for testing, on April 29, the defense minister announced that all "illegal immigrants" found in areas under enhanced movement control orders would be sent to detention centers when those orders ended. On May 1, hours after the easing of some restrictions, authorities raided one such area and rounded up hundreds of migrants.

The authorities ultimately conducted multiple raids, ensnaring thousands of migrants and detaining them in overcrowded and unsanitary immigration detention centers to await deportation. Several UN experts expressed concern that the crackdown was "severely undermining efforts to fight the pandemic" and immigration detention centers subsequently reported an increase in confirmed cases of Covid-19.

Migrants and refugees who lost their jobs due to the pandemic were excluded from government aid programs, and many were left unable to feed their families. At least 17 migrants from Myanmar committed suicide between March and September.

In Malaysia, over 6.6 million students enrolled in pre-school through to secondary school were impacted by school closures, according to UN estimates. Pre-existing inequalities in education were exacerbated by students' unequal access to the internet, with rural and indigenous communities particularly affected.

Freedom of Religion

Malaysia restricts the rights of followers of any branches of Islam other than Sunni, with those following Shia or other branches subject to arrest for deviancy. In August, the Court of Appeal partially set aside a High Court ruling that Ahmadiyya adherents were not subject to Sharia (Islamic law) in Malaysia because the Islamic authorities there do not consider them as Muslims. The Court of Appeal ruled that if the Ahmadiyya were proven to have converted from Islam, then the religious authorities would have authority over them, and sent the case back to the High Court for a determination of the original faith of the 39 plaintiffs.

In January, the High Court granted Sisters in Islam, a civil society group working to promote the rights of Muslim women, a stay on the enforcement of a fatwa issued against it in 2014. The stay was issued pending appeal of a High Court ruling dismissing a challenge to the fatwa for lack of jurisdiction. The broadly worded fatwa declares that Sisters in Islam and "any individuals, organizations and institutions holding on to liberalism and religious pluralism" are deviant from Islamic teachings.

In April, the United States Commission on International Freedom of Religion recommended that Malaysia be placed on a special watch list for violations of religious freedom.

Criminal Justice

Malaysia permits the death penalty for various crimes and makes the sentence mandatory for 11 offenses. In August 2020, the Federal Court upheld the constitutionality of the mandatory death penalty. A special committee set up to consider alternative sentences to mandatory death penalty submitted its report to the government in July 2020. At time of writing, the government had not made public the report or taken steps to end the mandatory penalty.

Malaysia continues to detain individuals without trial under restrictive laws. SOSMA allows for preventive detention of up to 28 days with no judicial review for a broadly defined range of "security offenses." Both the 1959 Prevention of Crime Act and the 2015 Prevention of Terrorism Act give government-appointed boards the authority to impose detention without trial for up to two years, renewable indefinitely, to order electronic monitoring, and to impose other significant restrictions on freedom of movement and association. No judicial review is permitted for these measures.

Sexual Orientation and Gender Identity

Discrimination against lesbian, gay, bisexual, and transgender (LGBT) people remains pervasive in Malaysia. Federal law punishes "carnal knowledge against the order of nature" with up to 20 years in prison and mandatory whipping. Numerous state Sharia laws prohibit both same-sex relations and non-normative gender expression, resulting in frequent arrests of transgender people. Activists have filed two court cases, in the High Court and the Federal Court, challenging the existence and use of these laws in Selangor. In July, the minister in charge of religious affairs gave "full licence" to the religious authorities to take action against transgender people, both through arrests and religious education to "return" them to the "right path." In August, after activist Nicole Fong responded to his statement by posting a series of infographics online critical of the official "mukhayyam" program—which aims in part to influence LGBT people to renounce their non-normative gender identity or sexual orientation—religious authorities lodged a police report against her.

Child Marriage

Malaysia continues to permit child marriage under both civil and Islamic law, in violation of its obligations under international law. Girls age 16 and older can marry with permission of their state's chief minister. For Muslims, most state Islamic laws set a minimum age of 16 for girls and 18 for boys, but permit marriages below those ages, with no apparent minimum, with the permission of a Sharia court. Widespread school closures due to Covid-19 may also increase risks of child marriage, as research shows that leaving education is highly correlated with girls being married off.

Key International Actors

The Malaysian government has called for the Association of Southeast Asian Nations (ASEAN) to find effective solutions to the Rohingya crisis, declaring itself unable to take any more Rohingya refugees. Although China is Malaysia's largest trading partner, in July 2020 Malaysia "rejected in its entirety" China's claims to rights in the South China Sea encompassed by the nine-dash line. Malaysia has also joined the World Health Organization's Solidarity Call to Action, calling for a Covid-19 Technology Access Pool to "realize equitable global access to Covid-19 health technologies through pooling of knowledge, intellectual property and data."

Maldives

Upon taking office in 2018, President Ibrahim Mohamed Solih vowed to restore the fundamental rights eroded by longstanding authoritarian rule. However, his administration has failed to confront deep-rooted corruption and the continuing influence of extremist Islamist groups, including in the government, police, and courts.

The economic and social impact of the Covid-19 pandemic has compounded threats to vulnerable groups, particularly migrant workers. The government failed to curb threats of violence and investigate extremist Islamist groups for targeting social justice activists. Online intimidation of human rights groups continued to have a chilling effect on civil society in 2020.

Despite facing grave threats from climate change, the Maldives authorities have not adequately consulted local communities or implemented sufficient measures to mitigate or adapt to the growing risk of floods, erosion, and other natural disasters.

The government took action to address some issues facing migrant workers, including regularizing undocumented migrants and advancing the National Taskforce on Issues related to Migrant Workers.

Covid-19

Heavily dependent on tourism, the Maldives economy was badly hit by the Covid-19 pandemic. The ensuing socioeconomic crisis exacerbated existing inequalities and abuses, disproportionately affecting the livelihoods and wellbeing of migrant workers and women.

Covid-19 also underscored weaknesses in the government's capacity to provide essential needs and services. The emergency procurement of healthcare supplies and equipment raised concerns about corruption. In August, a government audit called for an investigation into "significant irregularities" it found in the Ministry of Health's procurement of ventilators.

Schools were closed down for three months during the pandemic, with no formal learning provided to 91,000 children.

Migrant Workers

The Maldives has the largest proportion of foreign migrant laborers in South Asia, roughly one-third of the resident population, at least 60,000 of whom are undocumented. The vast majority work in the construction and tourism industries.

Authorities cracked down on foreign workers protesting the wage abuses that had escalated during the pandemic. In July alone, police detained more than 80 migrants during protests. More than 8,000 were deported from July to September, some without receiving their owed wages.

Covid-19 also spotlighted longstanding abuses, including wage theft, passport confiscation, and unsafe living and working conditions. Agents use deceptive or fraudulent practices to recruit migrants to work in the Maldives, leaving them at risk of debt-based coercion and trafficking.

In August, the government published new migrant worker rules to regulate employer responsibility for arranging migrants' arrival in the Maldives, accommodations, registration, and repatriation.

The Maldives, not a party to the 1951 Refugee Convention, lacks an asylum system and refugee protection mechanism, leaving people who fear persecution in their home countries with no opportunity to seek protection.

The government has failed to implement adequate measures to identify and support trafficking victims or investigate and prosecute abusers.

Freedoms of Expression, Association, Assembly, Religion

The Solih administration has not effectively confronted threats to activists and civil society organizations, instead often capitulating to the demands of extremist Islamist groups. In December 2019, the government arbitrarily dissolved the Maldivian Democracy Network (MDN), the country's leading human rights organization, following claims that the group had insulted Islam in a 2016 report. The police investigated the authors of the report for alleged blasphemy. In January 2020, the government seized MDN's funds after freezing its bank accounts without notice.

In June, extremist groups initiated a social media campaign demanding that the government ban the women's rights organization Uthema for being anti-Islam after the group published a report on the government's adherence to its obligations under the Convention on the Elimination of All Forms of Discrimination against Women (CEDAW).

In March, the government established a Whistleblower Protection Unit to investigate allegations of corruption, human rights violations, obstruction of justice, and serious environmental harm, and to provide protection to whistleblowers.

In July, in response to various protests held across the country, the Home Affairs Ministry invoked a dormant 2016 law prohibiting street demonstrations except in one closed-off location in the capital, Malé, and only after obtaining prior police approval.

In her February report following her 2019 visit to the Maldives, the UN special rapporteur in the field of cultural rights raised serious concerns about the lack of protection for freedom of religion or belief. In its reply, the Maldives rejected the recommendation that it recognize freedom of religion in the constitution.

Lack of Accountability

A government-appointed commission investigating deaths and enforced disappearances found that groups affiliated with Al-Qaeda were responsible for the murder of several prominent activists and politicians, including journalist Ahmed Rilwan in 2014 and blogger Yameen Rasheed in 2017. The commission also recommended that the police charge former Vice President Ahmed Adeeb for intervening to release two suspects. After accusing the justice system of shielding suspects from prosecution, the commission announced in June that it was unable to proceed further with its investigations. No convictions have been made.

The Maldives is ranked 130 out of 180 countries in Transparency International's Corruption Perceptions Index, and holds the lowest score in the financial secrecy index owing to a lack of transparency and weak regulation.

A transitional justice bill has been submitted to parliament, but no justice mechanism for investigating past incidence of torture and other abuses is in place.

Environmental Harm

The Maldives is one of the most vulnerable countries to increased environmental impacts from climate change, yet the Solih government has failed to adequately enforce environmental protection laws governing development projects. Developers routinely gain approval for projects without adherence to environmental regulations or carrying out approved mitigation measures, causing long-term harm to communities from increased flooding, loss of livelihoods, and destruction of vital ecosystems.

The government has yet to fulfill its pledge to give the Environmental Protection Agency (EPA) increased independence. Environmental impact assessments for new projects often lack independence and genuine consultations with communities. Proposed mitigation measures are rarely implemented. In May, the EPA approved a dredging and land reclamation project in Gulhifalhu despite ongoing concerns of local citizen-led campaigns about potential irreversible environmental harms, and resulting loss of livelihood to communities. Despite a parliamentary inquiry into the potential damage and an anti-corruption investigation into irregularities in the awarding of the project, the reclamation went ahead.

Government ministers have bypassed environmental impact assessment requirements in pursuit of infrastructure projects. In January, the environment minister approved a project to expand the Maafaru airport, overriding the EPA, which had rejected the project because of erosion risks and harm to coral reefs.

In February, the parliament passed a resolution declaring a climate emergency, underscoring the devastating impacts that climate change will likely have in the Maldives.

Torture and Ill-Treatment

While hundreds of complaints of torture and ill-treatment have been filed with government commissions since the Anti-Torture Act was passed in 2013, none have led to the prosecution of officials or redress for victims. Cases of police violence are regularly dismissed for alleged lack of evidence. Following a visit to the Maldives in November 2019, the UN special rapporteur on torture found that this widespread impunity has caused a "profound erosion of public confidence in the integrity and reliability of the police and the judiciary."

Despite government promises in 2019 to address mistreatment in prisons, conditions remained deplorable, with extreme overcrowding, some at almost double capacity. Prisoner releases in response to Covid-19 were minimal. In late August, 11 detainees in Hulhumalé prison tested positive, five of whom were foreign workers being held for deportation.

In August, Yasir Yahya, a Yemeni national who was detained in 2017, died after undertaking a hunger strike while in custody in the immigration detention center in Hulhumalé. Yahya was detained for alleged ties to terrorist groups, but was never formally charged during his three years in detention.

Women's and Girls' Rights

Gender-based violence is endemic in the Maldives. Rising Islamist extremism has led to increased harassment and attacks against women on social media and in public, much of which goes unreported due to the overlying violence and threats. Marginalized women and girls are disproportionately targeted for penalties under Islamic law.

The nongovernmental organization Uthema reported that most victims of domestic violence decline to press charges, while complaints are withdrawn in almost 70 percent of cases. The United Nations noted reports of increased domestic violence during the Maldives' Covid-19 lockdown, while government support services remained under-resourced and understaffed.

Sexual Orientation and Gender Identity

The Maldivian penal code criminalizes adult, consensual same-sex sexual conduct; punishment can include imprisonment of up to eight years and 100 lashes, and applies equally to men and women. Same-sex marriage is outlawed and punishable by up to a year in prison. Extremist groups in the Maldives use social media to harass and threaten those who promote the rights of lesbian, gay, bisexual, and transgender (LGBT) people.

Key International Actors

President Solih has criticized the scale of Chinese-government debt incurred by the previous administration, but the countries remain closely linked. Chinese loans account for about 45 percent of the national debt. At the same time, the Maldives government continued its pivot toward India over the course of 2020. As part of its effort to counter Chinese influence, India pledged US$500 million to fund what will be the Maldives' largest infrastructure project.

In September, the Maldives signed a defense agreement with the United States to strengthen engagement "in support of maintaining peace and security in the Indian Ocean," with India's support. During an October visit, the US secretary of state announced the US would establish an embassy and resident ambassador in the Maldives for the first time.

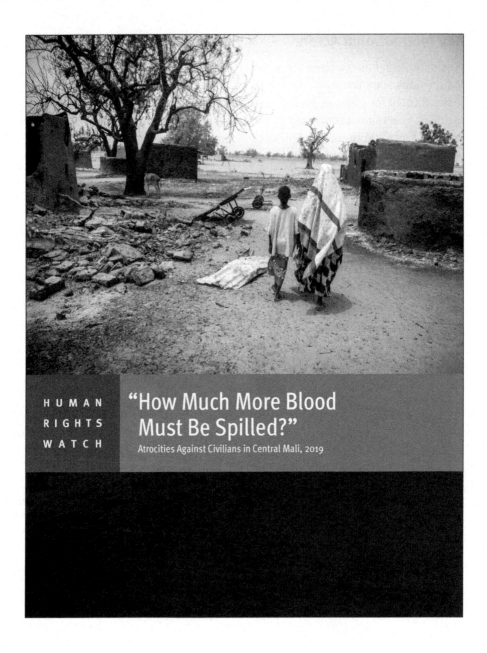

HUMAN
RIGHTS
WATCH

"How Much More Blood
Must Be Spilled?"
Atrocities Against Civilians in Central Mali, 2019

Mali

Mali's human rights situation deteriorated in 2020 amid ongoing abuses by armed Islamist groups, ethnic militias, and government security forces. A political crisis resulted in the August toppling of the government in a military coup.

Armed Islamist groups attacks on civilians, as well as soldiers and international forces, continued in northern Mali, intensified in the center, and spread into southern parts of the country. Ethnic self-defense groups, formed to protect villages from attacks, killed hundreds, leading to widespread displacement and hunger. The Malian security forces summarily executed scores of suspects for their perceived support of armed Islamist groups, and used excessive force when responding to political protests, resulting in at least 14 deaths.

The worsening security situation, perceived government corruption, and controversial parliamentary elections that were marred by violence and irregularities, provoked massive demonstrations in the capital, Bamako, and elsewhere.

The peace process envisioned to end the 2012-2013 crisis in the north made minimal progress, including on disarmament and the restoration of state authority. Over 40,000 civilians fled their homes as a result of violence in 2020. Attacks by armed groups on humanitarian agencies undermined their ability to deliver aid. Rampant banditry continued to undermine livelihoods. Attacks on children also continued. The United Nations reported that at least 185 children were killed due to communal violence, crossfire, or improvised explosive devices (IEDs). Armed groups and forces continued to recruit children as soldiers, and armed groups were responsible for at least 55 attacks on schools in 2019.

Little progress was made toward providing justice for victims of abuses, including several large-scale atrocities, and rule-of-law institutions remained weak.

Mali's international partners, notably the UN, France, Germany, Canada, the European Union, the African Union (AU), the Economic Community of West African States (ECOWAS), and the United States were more willing to denounce atrocities by the army than in past years but were inconsistent in their calls for accountability.

Political Crisis, Violent Protests

The March 29 and April 19 parliamentary elections were marred by violence and irregularities. Controversial constitutional court rulings on 30 contested seats gave the ruling party a parliamentary majority and sparked massive protests during June and July. The protests, underscored by frustrations over government corruption and slow progress on addressing the security crisis, were led by a coalition of opposition political parties, religious leaders, and civil society organizations under the umbrella of The June 5 - Rally of Patriotic Forces Movement (Mouvement du 5 juin Rassemblement des Forces Patriotiques or M5-RFP).

In May, three opposition leaders including Clement Dembele, also an anti-corruption campaigner, were arrested for disrupting public order. Two of them were released within days, but Dembele was held for two weeks without due process. Charges against him were later dropped.

During demonstrations on July 10-12, protesters erected barricades; threw stones and used slingshots; occupied, burned, and looted parts of government buildings; and threatened a judge's home. Security forces arrested, but released on July 13 at least five opposition leaders, ransacked the M5-RFP headquarters, and used teargas and live rounds to disperse protesters. Authorities blocked social media and messaging services in the country for several days during the unrest.

On August 18, military officers overthrew the government in a coup, and detained the president, prime minister, several cabinet members, and generals. The coup leaders, called the National Committee for the Salvation of the People and led by Col. Assimi Goîta, appointed Bah Ndaw, a former colonel and defense minister, as interim president on September 21. Ndaw promised a civilian government would be elected within18 months.

Communal Violence

During 2020, at least 400 villagers were killed in numerous incidents of communal violence, mostly in the Mopti region. The violence pitted ethnic Dogon self-defense groups against those of Peuhl, or Fulani, who sometimes had the support of armed Islamist groups. Most of those killed in 2020 were ethnic

Dogon. The attacks targeted people in their villages, farms, or markets, and provoked widespread displacement and a hunger crisis.

During attacks in March, Peuhl militiamen were implicated in the killing of 48 Dogon civilians in several villages in the Bankass administrative area, and at least 27 others on May 26 and 27, near Tillé village. In August, at least six Dogon were killed in Timiniri Administrative area near Bandiagara.

Dogon militiamen were implicated in several attacks: in January on Siba village, killing 14; the March 14 massacre of 35 Peuhl villagers in Ogossagou village, site of the 2019 massacre of 150 civilians; the March 22 killing of at least 20 Peuhl in Baye commune, and the May 5 killing of 18 near Djenne.

Abuses by Armed Islamist Groups

Armed Islamist groups allied to Al-Qaeda and the Islamic State in the Greater Sahara killed scores of mostly-Dogon civilians, as well as at least 5 peacekeepers and several hundred government security force members. In July, 32 Dogon were killed in attacks on Djimindo, Gouari and Fangadougou villages in Mopti region.

Armed Islamist groups disrupted the parliamentary elections by ransacking polling stations, intimidating voters, and attacking soldiers escorting election materials. They killed numerous civilians with improvised explosive devices planted on roadways, including nine people in a public transport vehicle on March 29 in Timbuktu region, and seven people on June 7, in Mopti region. They also kidnapped scores of civilians, including aid workers, local government officials and political leaders, including an opposition presidential candidate, Soumaïla *Cissé*.

Armed Islamists continued to threaten, and sometimes kill local leaders deemed government collaborators and beat those engaged in cultural practices they had forbidden. They also imposed their version of Sharia (Islamic law) via courts that did not adhere to fair trial standards.

Abuses by State Security Forces

Malian security forces were implicated in over 250 unlawful killings of suspects and civilians, and several enforced disappearances from December 2019

through August 2020. Most killings took place during counterterrorism operations in Mopti and Segou regions and targeted ethnic Peuhl. The UN also reported that soldiers from Burkina Faso were implicated in some 50 extrajudicial
killings perpetrated during cross-border operations from May 26 to 28.

On December 19, 2019, Malian soldiers allegedly detained and executed at least
26 traders and then threw their bodies into a well in Ndoukala, Segou region. In
June, soldiers were implicated in the killing of 14 people in Niangassadou village
and 29 civilians in Binidama. In February, they allegedly executed 19 people in
Ouro-Diam village.

Malian security forces also used lethal force in responding to protests in Bamako
in July, resulting in at least 14 deaths. Over 300 people, including demonstrators, bystanders, and security force members were wounded.

On October 22, Malian forces were accused of killing two dozen Peuhl villagers
in Libé, in the Bankass administrative area.

Numerous men accused of terrorism-related offenses were detained by the national intelligence agency in unauthorized detention facilities and without respect for due process.

Accountability for Abuses

There was little progress on delivering justice for war crimes and other atrocities
committed since 2012. The government appeared to favor short-term reconciliation efforts envisioned to mitigate communal tension.

The judiciary remained plagued by neglect and mismanagement, with many
abandoned posts in northern and central Mali due to insecurity. Hundreds of detainees were held in extended detention awaiting court trials. Over 1,600 prisoners were either pardoned or released to reduce the risk of the spread of Covid-19
in overcrowded prisons.

The Specialized Judicial Unit against Terrorism and Transnational Organized
Crime (SJU), the investigations mandate of which was expanded in 2019 to include international human rights crimes, made progress on terrorism cases, and
some progress on two 2019 atrocity investigations.

In late 2019, a court in the Mopti region tried and convicted some 45 people for several smaller incidents of communal violence, although magistrates had yet to question powerful militia leaders implicated in the worst atrocities. Security force members failed to respond to judicial summonses or help gendarmes arrest high-level suspects, hindering progress on these cases.

Military authorities opened investigations into four alleged atrocities by security force members in 2019 and 2020, but these and previous investigations into the killing of over 50 suspects in 2018, have yet to result in trials or prosecutions.

Transitional Justice Mechanisms and Human Rights Commission

The International Commission of Inquiry, established under the 2015 peace accord to investigate serious violations between 2012 and January 2018, submitted its report to the UN secretary-general on June 16. At time of writing the report remained confidential.

Public hearings scheduled for 2020 by the Truth, Justice and Reconciliation Commission, established in 2014 to investigate crimes and root causes of violence since 1960, were delayed because of the Covid-19 pandemic.

The National Commission for Human Rights investigated some abuses and issued numerous communiques but appeared reluctant to investigate abuses by the security forces.

Key International Actors

France and the United States led on military matters, the European Union on training and security sector reform, and the United Nations on rule of law and political stability. In the wake of the August coup, ECOWAS and the AU suspended Mali from their decision-making bodies; the US suspended military aid; and the EU suspended its military and police training programs.

In June, France launched the International Coalition for the Sahel, to coordinate between the G5 Sahel countries (Mali, Mauritania, Burkina Faso, Niger, and Chad) and their international partners.

Operation Barkhane, the 5,000-member French regional counterterrorism force, conducted numerous operations in Mali. Until the coup, the EU Training Mission in Mali (EUTM) and EU Capacity Building Mission (EUCAP) continued to train and advise Mali's security forces.

In June, the EU's high representative expressed outrage at the killing of over 40 civilians with the likely involvement of Mali's armed forces. He urged accountability for the crimes committed and stressed that the EU's engagement is conditional to the respect of international human rights and humanitarian law. In September, the European Parliament echoed those concerns, urged the EU to support Mali's democratic transition, and called for a comprehensive reform of the EUTM in order to ensure better selection, training and scrutiny of the armed forces and of their operations.

The UN Security Council renewed for one year the mandates of the UN Multidimensional Integrated Stabilization Mission in Mali, MINUSMA, and the Mali Sanctions Committee Panel of Experts which, in August issued a report implicating high-level Malian officials in obstructing the 2015 peace process and failing to prevent the 2020 Ogossagou massacre. In June, the UN Human Rights Council renewed the mandate of the UN independent expert on Mali for another year.

MINUSMA supported government atrocity investigations, justice sector reform, and increased patrols in areas vulnerable to attack. However, its ability to fulfill its civilian protection mandate was challenged due to lack of equipment, notably air assets. The human rights section significantly increased public reporting on abuses by all sides.

In July, the International Criminal Court (ICC) opened a trial against Al Hassan Ag Abdoul Aziz Ag Mohamed Ag Mahmoud, a former leader of the Islamist armed group Ansar Dine, on charges of war crimes and crimes against humanity, including rape and sexual slavery committed in 2012-2013. It is the ICC's second trial in the Mali situation, and the court's first trial of gender-based persecution.

Mauritania

In his first year in office, President Mohamed Ould Ghezouani did not progress in overhauling existing repressive laws on criminal defamation, spreading "false information," cybercrime, and blasphemy that authorities use to prosecute and jail human rights defenders, activists, journalists and bloggers.

Parliament adopted an overly broad Law on Combatting Manipulation of Information that stipulates fines and harsh prison sentences for publication of "false news" and the creation of fake digital identities.

Slavery in certain forms has not been eliminated despite multiple laws banning it and specialized courts to prosecute those who subject people to slavery.

Parliament has yet to pass a draft law on violence against women and girls introduced in 2016.

Freedom of Expression

Prosecutors use repressive legislation that includes criminal defamation and broad definitions of terrorism and "inciting racial hatred" to censor and prosecute critics for nonviolent speech.

Article 348 of the criminal code provides for punishment of six months to five years in prison for defamation. An anti-discrimination law adopted in 2017 states in article 10, "Whoever encourages an incendiary discourse against the official rite of the Islamic Republic of Mauritania shall be punished by one to five years in prison."

Parliament adopted on June 24 the Law on Combatting Manipulation of Information that states as its objective to prevent manipulation of information, publication of false news, and the creation of fake digital identities. Adopted as authorities were battling surging Covid-19 cases, the law also seeks to suppress manipulation of information "especially during periods of elections and during health crises." Penalties for violations range from three months to five years in prison, and fines from 50,000 to 200,000 Ouguiya (US$1,325-5,300).

On April 13, authorities arrested Mariem Cheikh, an activist and member of anti-slavery campaign group Initiative for the Resurgence of the Abolitionist Movement (IRA), for her criticism of continued slavery and racial discrimination in Mauritania. The public prosecutor in Nouakchott charged her for "racist comments through social media." Authorities released her on April 21.

On June 3, authorities arrested Eby Ould Zeidane, a journalist and member of the Advertising Regulatory Authority, over a Facebook post calling for the Muslim holy month of Ramadan to be observed on fixed dates according to the Gregorian calendar, contrary to Muslim tradition. Authorities on June 8 charged him with blasphemy under penal code article 306, which carries the death sentence, and for "publishing leaflets that undermine the values of Islam" under article 21 of the Cybercrime Law. Zeidane was released on June 8, and on July 2 publicly repented his remarks after meetings with religious scholars and the Minister of Islamic Affairs.

Freedom of Association

The restrictive 1964 Law of Associations requires associations to obtain formal permission to operate legally and gives the Ministry of Interior far-reaching powers to refuse such permission on vague grounds such as "anti-national propaganda" or exercising "an unwelcome influence on the minds of the people."

The ministry has withheld recognition from several associations that campaign on controversial issues, such as the Initiative for the Resurgence of the Abolitionist Movement (IRA). Members of the IRA, including its leader Biram Dah Abeid, have been subject to arrests and harassment.

Authorities in February arrested 14 people who were present during an inaugural meeting of the newly founded Alliance for the Refoundation of the Mauritanian State (AREM) after they held a meeting, in Nouakchott. AREM calls for reforming the Mauritania's public administration and health systems and rejects the country's caste system. Authorities soon after released all but five of them, who remained in provisional detention from February 26 until their trial on October 20.

The Nouakchott West Criminal Court on October 20 found all five detained men guilty of "violating the sanctity of God" based on article 306 of Mauritania's penal code and sentenced them to between six and eight month prison terms, and fines of 2,000 Ouguiya ($53) and 15,000 (about $400). Ahmed Ould Heida and Mohamed Fal Ishaq, who were sentenced to six months, were released due to time already served, and Ahmed Mohamed Al-Moctar, Mohamed Abdelrahman Haddad, and Othman Mohamed Lahbib were sentenced to eight months and were released on October 26. The court sentenced in absentia the remaining three men to prison terms of six months and one year and ordered them to pay fines.

Those arrested and released in February included journalist Eby Ould Zeidane and Aminetou Mint El Moctar, who heads a women's rights organization.

Slavery

Mauritania abolished slavery in 1981—the world's last country to do so—and criminalized it in 2007. The Global Slavery Index, which measures forced labor and forced marriage, estimates that in 2018 there are 90,000 people living in "modern slavery" in Mauritania, or 2.4 percent of the population, while 62 percent are "vulnerable" to modern slavery.

Three special courts that prosecute slavery-related crimes have tried a handful of cases since their creation under a 2015 law.

According to the 2020 US State Department Trafficking in Persons Report, Mauritania investigated one case, prosecuted three alleged traffickers, and convicted five traffickers. According to the same report, no slave owners or traffickers were held in prison, and ten appeals cases remained pending at the three anti-slavery courts. The government did not report any prosecutions or convictions of government officials who were accused of corruption in relation to human trafficking and hereditary slavery offenses.

Adults and children from traditional slave castes in the Black Moor (Haratine) and Afro-Mauritanian communities remain exposed to hereditary slavery practices such as forced labor without pay as domestic servants or farm laborers.

Death Penalty

Mauritania imposes the death penalty for a range of offenses, including, under certain conditions, blasphemy, adultery, and homosexuality. A de facto moratorium remains in effect on capital punishment since 1987 as well as on corporal punishments that are inspired by Islamic Sharia law and found in the penal code.

Women's Rights

The 2017 law on reproductive health recognizes reproductive health, including family planning, as a universal fundamental right, but Mauritania continues to outlaw abortion per article 22 of the law and article 293 of the penal code. The country's General Code on Children's Protection, also adopted in 2017, criminalizes female genital mutilation, but it remains prevalent in some communities.

Mauritanian law does not adequately define the crime of rape and other forms of sexual assault, although a draft law on violence against women and girls with more specific definitions was pending before parliament. Moreover, women and girls who report rape risk being prosecuted for having sexual relations outside of wedlock if the authorities do not believe them.

Mauritania's laws on divorce, child custody, and inheritance discriminate against women.

Sexual Orientation

Article 308 prohibits homosexual conduct between Muslim adults and punishes it with death for males by public stoning. If between two women, then the law prescribes imprisonment for three months to two years and a possible fine. There were no publicly known cases of persons sentenced to death in 2020 or in recent years for homosexual conduct.

The Court of Appeal in Nouakchott on March 4 confirmed the conviction of eight men for "committing indecent acts" and "inciting debauchery," but reduced their sentences to six months in prison. Authorities arrested the eight after a video appeared online in January of them celebrating a birthday at a restaurant. Police described the men in the report they submitted to court as "imitating women" and "sodomizers," based on their appearance and behavior. The appeals court gave seven of the defendants suspended sentences and the eighth man two months in prison, which he served. One woman received a one-year suspended sentence for participating in "inciting debauchery" by being present at the event.

Covid-19

On May 3, authorities arrested blogger and journalist for the news site Alakhbar.info, Mommeu Ould Bouzouma, over a tweet in which he characterized the authorities' enforcement of the government-mandated Covid-19 lockdown in the district of Tiris Zemmour as "erratic." Authorities released Bouzouma on May 15 after the governor of the region dropped the complaint against him.

Authorities on June 2 arrested Salma Mint Tolba over a series of audio recordings accusing the government of inflating Covid-19 infection rates to receive foreign funding. Authorities also arrested two men suspected of disseminating the audio recordings on social media. Authorities on June 11 released all three without charge.

Key International Actors

Mauritania is a member of the G5 Sahel, an alliance of five countries headquartered in Nouakchott that cooperate on security, including counterterrorism.

In February, Mauritania assumed the rotating presidency of the G5 Sahel. In April, the European Commission pledged €194 million in additional support for "security, stability and resilience in the Sahel" that included strengthening "the security and defence capabilities of the G5 Sahel countries, while ensuring respect for human rights and international humanitarian law."

Mexico

Human rights violations—including torture, enforced disappearances, abuses against migrants, extrajudicial killings, and attacks on independent journalists and human rights defenders—have continued under President Andrés Manuel López Obrador, who took office in December 2018. Impunity remains the norm. Reforms enacted in 2017 and 2018 have been slow and until now ineffective in addressing torture and impunity.

President López Obrador has greatly expanded the scope of the armed forces' activities, deploying them for law enforcement and customs enforcement, and to control irregular immigration, run social programs, and build and operate megaprojects.

The head of the National Search Commission (CNB) has increased transparency about the number of "disappeared" persons, but prosecutors continue to make little effort to investigate forced disappearances or identify those responsible.

In November 2019, the Senate named Rosario Piedra Ibarra as the new head of the National Human Rights Commission (CNDH). Many human rights defenders called her appointment unconstitutional, saying that Piedra Ibarra, a former senior member of the president's party, is too close to the administration to be autonomous and apolitical.

In September 2020, President López Obrador asked Congress to approve holding a referendum on whether every president since 1988—five in total—should be put on trial for "crimes" including electoral fraud, corruption, and loss of lives to neoliberalism.

The government has failed to provide adequate support or protection for the estimated 66,000 people seeking asylum in the US who have been placed in the "Remain in Mexico" program, including people at high risk of marginalization, like those with disabilities and chronic health conditions, older persons, and children. Many have taken refuge in makeshift camps or crowded shelters along the Mexican-US border.

Criminal Justice System

The criminal justice system routinely fails to provide justice to victims of violent crimes and human rights violations. Only 1.3 percent of crimes committed in Mexico are solved, the nongovernmental group Impunity Zero reports. Causes of failure include corruption, inadequate training and resources, and complicity of prosecutors and public defenders with criminals and other abusive officials. A 2018 reform intended to give prosecutors increased independence has not been properly implemented, local human rights and rule-of-law groups report.

In January, the attorney general proposed extremely regressive justice system reforms that would have made it easier for prosecutors to use evidence obtained through torture, eliminated judicial review of pre-trial detention, and expanded the use of arraigo detention, which allows prosecutors to seek judicial authorization to detain a person for up to 40 days without charge while they continue their investigation.

Military Abuses

Mexico has relied heavily on the military for drug control and to fight organized crime, leading to widespread human rights violations. From 2014 through 2019, the CNDH received nearly 3,000 complaints regarding alleged military abuses.

President López Obrador has doubled down on use of the military for public security, vastly expanding the scope of its activities and supplanting civilian law enforcement. In 2019, he created the National Guard, a military force, to replace the Federal Police as the government's principal law enforcement body. The National Guard is led by military officers, trained by the military, and composed largely of military troops. In May 2020, the president formally deployed the military to assist the National Guard in civilian law enforcement. The military is now legally permitted to detain civilians, take charge of crime scenes, and preserve evidence; under past governments, charging the military with these tasks has contributed to serious cover-ups of human rights abuses.

In 2014, Congress reformed the Code of Military Justice to require that abuses committed by members of the military against civilians be prosecuted in civilian, not military, courts. However, pursuit of justice remains elusive.

In July 2020, 12 civilians were killed in a shootout with soldiers in Tamaulipas state. A video leaked to the press in August showed a soldier giving the order to kill a civilian. In September, the Secretary of Defense announced that only military police—no civilian prosecutors—were investigating.

Torture

Torture is widely practiced in Mexico to obtain confessions and extract information. It is most frequently applied during the time between when victims are detained, often arbitrarily, and when they are handed to civilian prosecutors—a period when they are often held incommunicado at military bases or illegal detention sites. A 2017 law made it illegal to use confessions obtained through torture as evidence at criminal trials. However, authorities often fail to investigate allegations of torture.

The number of investigations into cases of torture by state and federal prosecutors has risen in recent years, from just 13 in 2006 to over 7,000 in 2019, according to a report by the Mexican Commission for the Defense and Promotion of Human Rights. In its 2019 review of Mexico, the UN Committee Against Torture expressed concern that few of these cases result in an arrest and trial.

In 2016—the last year for which data is available—Mexico's national statistics office surveyed more than 64,000 people incarcerated in 338 prisons. Almost two-thirds (64 percent) reported physical violence at the time of arrest, including electric shocks, choking, and smothering.

In its 2019 review of Mexico, the UN Committee Against Torture reported that of 3,214 torture complaints in 2016, only eight resulted in an arrest and trial. The committee expressed concern at reports that courts routinely fail to investigate torture allegations.

Disappearances

Since 2006, enforced disappearances by security forces have been a widespread problem. Criminal organizations have also been responsible for many disappearances. The government reported more than 75,000 people disappeared, as of November 2020—the vast majority from 2006 onwards.

The López Obrador administration has taken steps to determine and publish the true number of people disappeared. In 2019 a well-respected human rights defender was appointed to head the National Search Commission (CNB). Since then, the government has created an online platform to allow people to report disappearances anonymously and to show real-time statistics on the number of people disappeared, excluding personally identifying information.

However, prosecutors and police neglect to take even basic investigative steps to identify those responsible for enforced disappearances, often telling families of the missing to investigate on their own. The CNB reported that over 7,000 people disappeared in 2019. That year, the Attorney General's Office opened only 351 investigations into disappearances and prosecuted only 2.

Officials have conceded that more than 26,000 bodies remain unidentified. In 2019, the National Search Commissioner created a national forensic assessment to address obstacles to identifying and storing bodies. Following demands by families, the government also created an Extraordinary Mechanism of Forensic Identification to identify bodies.

In August 2020, the government recognized the jurisdiction of the UN Committee on Enforced Disappearances to consider cases in Mexico, as recommended by a number of UN member-states during its 2018 Universal Periodic Review. Families of victims will be able to submit cases to the committee once they have exhausted their legal options domestically.

Extrajudicial Killings

In November 2019, the UN Human Rights Committee expressed concern about reports of extrajudicial killings by the military and police, and impunity for such cases. Although the Defense Ministry said it stopped registering numbers of civilians the military killed, as of 2014, civil society organizations said in 2019 that declarations by the minister indicate the information exists.

In 2020, high-profile incidents of civilians dying in police custody prompted protests. In one incident, in the state of Jalisco, a man died after police detained him for not wearing a face mask in accordance with Covid-19 response measures.

Attacks on Journalists and Human Rights Defenders

Journalists and human rights defenders—particularly those who criticize public officials or expose the work of criminal cartels—often face attacks, harassment, and surveillance by government authorities and criminal groups.

There is evidence that digital surveillance is being deployed in public spaces without legal frameworks or oversight in ways that can have a chilling effect on freedom of assembly and the work of human rights defenders and journalists.

Mexico is one of the most dangerous countries in the world for journalists, on par with war zones like Syria and Afghanistan in terms of number of journalists killed, the Committee to Protect Journalists and Reporters Without Borders say. The CNDH reports 24 journalists killed since President López Obrador took office. In 2019, journalists registered 609 threats, attacks, or other forms of aggression—reportedly the highest year on record.

Authorities routinely fail to investigate crimes against journalists adequately, often preemptively ruling out their profession as a motive. Since its creation in 2010, the federal Special Prosecutor's Office to investigate crimes against journalists has opened more than 1,000 investigations, brought 217 charges for crimes, and obtained 14 convictions. In the face of uninvestigated violence, many journalists self-censor.

Mexico is also one of the most dangerous countries in the world for human rights defenders. In 2019, the Mexico Office of the UN High Commissioner for Human Rights reported 20 human rights defenders killed in Mexico. As with journalists, violence against human rights defenders is rarely investigated or prosecuted.

In 2012, the federal government established the Protection Mechanism for Human Rights Defenders and Journalists, which provides bodyguards, armored cars, and panic buttons, and helps journalists temporarily relocate in response to serious threats. A 2019 study by the Office of the United Nations High Commissioner for Human Rights documented the Mechanism's problems in coordinating protective measures, providing resources, and establishing clear procedures. Six journalists have been killed under the program's protection, four since President López Obrador took office. In October 2020, the government eliminated the public trust that paid for protection measures, putting the mechanism in a precarious financial situation.

Women's and Girls' Rights

In 2018, the UN Committee on the Elimination of All Forms of Discrimination Against Women expressed concern over persistent patterns of "general" violence against women, including sexual violence. Mexican laws do not adequately protect women and girls against gender-based and sexual violence. Some provisions, including those that peg the severity of punishments for sexual offenses to the "chastity" of the victim, contradict international standards.

Abortion is available on request for anyone, up to 12 weeks of pregnancy, in Mexico City and, since October 2019, in Oaxaca state. It is severely restricted elsewhere. In 2019, the Supreme Court ruled that rape victims need not file a criminal complaint to access abortion services and that health providers need not verify that a crime was committed to perform an abortion.

Women and girls continue to face alarming rates of gender-based violence. In 2019, the government reported more than 1,000 femicides—killings of women because of their gender—about a quarter of all women murdered. Women's rights groups say femicide is likely under-reported.

Migrants and Asylum Seekers

Criminal cartels, common criminals, and sometimes police and migration officials regularly target people migrating through Mexico to rob, kidnap, extort, rape, or kill them. Criminal cartels often do so with the "tolerance or even involvement of certain public officials," the Interamerican Commission on Human Rights reported in 2013. These crimes are rarely reported, investigated, or punished. In 2019, the CNDH received 606 complaints of abuses against migrants, and the attorney general opened 72 investigations of crimes against migrants.

From January 2019 to March 2020, the administration of US President Donald Trump—with the cooperation of the López Obrador administration—sent an estimated 66,000 non-Mexicans who were seeking asylum in the US to await the outcome of their claims in Mexico under the "Remain in Mexico" program. As of November 2020, many people were still waiting under the program, forced to live in precarious, unsanitary, and dangerous conditions with inadequate support from the Mexican government.

In March 2020, the US government stopped accepting most asylum applications made at the US-Mexican border, using the Covid-19 pandemic as a pretext to begin summarily expelling most people arriving at the US border or transferring them to Mexican officials who usually deport them to Central America.

In 2019, President López Obrador deployed the National Guard—a branch of the military—for migration enforcement. The government says soldiers only support migration officials. However, in a leaked audio recording from 2019, a senior migration official told her team they were now "under the instruction and supervision of the National Guard." In January 2020, National Guard troops clashed violently with a caravan of migrants in Chiapas state.

Before being deported to their countries of origin, most people detained by the National Guard are sent to immigration detention centers, where people have complained of crowded and unsanitary conditions.

In April, a Salvadoran man died of Covid-19 in a Mexico City hospital after spending more than a month in migration detention. In August, the CNDH stated the National Migration Institute (INM) was responsible for the man's death for failing to implement procedures to prevent Covid-19 infections in detention centers and for failing to provide the man with adequate medical attention.

In August 2020, a judge ruled that the INM had ignored a previous court ruling ordering it to release any migrants with conditions that would put them at increased risk due to the Covid-19 pandemic and to implement procedures to prevent infections in detention centers.

Mexico's asylum system is severely overstretched. Since 2013, the number of applications received has nearly doubled every year, and the capacity of the asylum agency has not kept pace. As of October 2019, there was a backlog of more than 63,000 people with pending asylum claims, and 44 percent of people who applied in 2018 were still waiting, according to the refugee rights group Asylum Access.

Sexual Orientation and Gender Identity

Twenty of 32 states have legalized same-sex marriage. Elsewhere, same-sex couples must petition for an injunction (amparo) to be allowed to marry. In 2019, the Supreme Court ruled that a same-sex couple from Aguascalientes state should be allowed to register their child, to protect the best interest of the child and uphold principles of equality and non-discrimination.

Twelve states allow transgender people to change their names and gender markers on birth certificates through a simple administrative process before the state Civil Registry.

Disability Rights

Under the López Obrador administration, serious gaps remain in protecting the rights of people with disabilities, including in access to justice, legal standing, legal capacity, informed consent in health decisions; access to buildings, transportation, and public spaces; violence against women; and education.

In many states, people with disabilities have no choice but to depend on their families for assistance or to live in institutions, which is inconsistent with their right to live independently and be included in the community. People with disabilities receive little government protection or support and are at a higher risk of abuse and neglect by their families.

Since President López Obrador took office and through time of writing, the National Council on People with Disabilities, the principal government body coordinating efforts to implement disability rights, has been effectively non-operational.

Covid-19

The López Obrador administration has failed to take many of the basic steps recommended by global health authorities to limit the spread of Covid-19. The official leading Mexico's response has called massive testing "useless" and "a waste of time," despite the World Health Organization's insistence on the importance of testing. As a result, Mexico has one of the lowest rates of Covid-19 testing—and highest rates of positive test results—in the world. Officials and experts

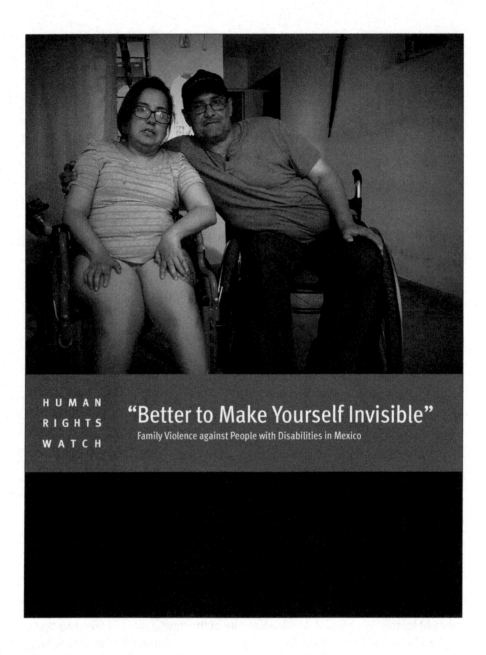

HUMAN
RIGHTS
WATCH

"Better to Make Yourself Invisible"
Family Violence against People with Disabilities in Mexico

agree that the real number of Covid-19 infections and deaths is likely many times higher than the official count, which was among the world's highest at time of writing.

People living in poor or indigenous areas are 50 percent more likely than others to die of Covid-19. The vast majority of Covid-19 patients who die have never received intensive care.

Amnesty International reported that Mexico has the highest known number of healthcare worker deaths from Covid-19 in the world. Healthcare workers have faced attacks and discrimination, and some healthcare workers say they were fired for protesting a lack of protective equipment at public hospitals.

The CNDH reported 2,234 confirmed cases of Covid-19 and 198 deaths, as of September 1, in prisons, which are notoriously overcrowded and unhygienic. Most states suspended family visits in response to the pandemic, which left many detained people without access to basic hygiene supplies such as soap.

In some parts of the country, criminal cartels provided food assistance to struggling residents and threatened to enforce pandemic curfews violently.

Schools closed in Mexico in March 2020, and the 2020-2021 school year is being conducted remotely, with classes broadcast on television and radio. Although 94 percent of Mexican households have television, a lack of affordable internet access leaves many children, especially those in low-income households and children with disabilities, without access to education. Some people in rural, often indigenous areas have been unable to participate at all.

Key International Actors and Foreign Policy

In June 2020, Mexico was elected as a non-permanent member of the UN Security Council for the period of 2021-2022. Mexico's foreign policy with regard to human rights under the López Obrador administration has been based on the principle of "non-intervention." Mexico highlighted that one of its priorities on the council would be the protection of children, although, unlike the majority of Security Council members, Mexico has yet to endorse the Safe Schools Declaration.

In October 2020, Mexico was re-elected to the UN Human Rights Council. In July 2019, Mexico supported a resolution condemning extrajudicial killings and forced disappearances in the Philippines.

In July 2020, President López Obrador took his first and only international trip to meet with President Donald Trump in Washington, DC. Mexico has cooperated with the Trump administration's attempts to curtail the right to asylum.

Since 2008, the US has allocated more than US$3.1 billion in aid via the Mérida Initiative to help Mexico combat organized crime and drug trafficking. President López Obrador said in May 2019 that his government would reject the initiative and re-orient US-Mexican cooperation to target the drivers of migration to the US by reducing poverty in Central America and southeastern Mexico. However, in 2019 and 2020, Mexico continued to receive nearly $150 million a year through the initiative—mostly for counter-narcotics efforts. It also diverted $4 million away from its own development programs for Central America to spend on migrant detention and removal.

In June, the European Union and Mexico held their ninth bilateral high-level dialogue on human rights. The EU has repeatedly denounced killings of journalists, activists, politicians and judges in Mexico, and urged Mexico to ensure thorough investigations and accountability for the crimes committed.

Mexico endorsed the World Health Organization's Solidarity Call to Action for the Covid-19 Technology Access Pool, an initiative to "realize equitable global access to COVID-19 health technologies through pooling of knowledge, intellectual property and data."

Morocco

Morocco cracked down harder on social media commentators, artists, and journalists critical of the monarchy. Despite a press code devoid of prison sentences as punishment, authorities continue to resort to penal code articles to imprison critics. Before authorities prohibited protests and public meetings to contain the spread of the Covid-19 virus, authorities had already banned several public meetings of opposition groups and continued to impede the activities of some human rights groups. Laws restricting individual freedoms remained in effect.

Criminal Justice System

The Code of Penal Procedure gives a defendant the right to contact a lawyer after 24 hours in police custody, extendable to 36 hours. But detainees do not have the right to have a lawyer present when police interrogate or present them with their statements for signature. Police agents often coerce or otherwise pressure detainees to sign self-incriminating statements, which judges later rely on to convict.

In prisons, some high-profile detainees were kept in isolation 23 hours per day and deprived of contact with other inmates, a cruel form of treatment that violates international standards. Abdelqader Belliraj, a dual Moroccan and Belgian citizen, sentenced to life in prison in 2009 after an unfair trial for terrorist plotting, had been held in such conditions for three years, until August 2020, according to his relatives.

Freedom of Association and Assembly

Authorities continued to impede the work of the Moroccan Association for Human Rights (AMDH), the country's largest human rights group. The AMDH said that, as of September 2020, 79 of its 99 local branches faced a situation where authorities had declined to process their administrative formalities, impeding their ability to carry out functions like opening new bank accounts or renting space.

According to the AMDH, authorities banned at least 13 public meetings, public protests and other public events called for by opposition groups or parties across the country, in January and February.

In March, authorities banned public protests as part of a package of measures to contain the spread of the Covid-19 virus.

Freedom of Expression

Morocco has in recent years arrested, prosecuted, and imprisoned several activists and independent journalists on questionable charges, including sex outside of wedlock. Some of these trials appeared to be politically motivated or failed to guarantee due process for all parties.

On July 29, noted journalist and human rights activist Omar Radi, whose smartphone was previously infected by a spyware that only governments have access to, was arrested under a string of accusations including espionage, harming external and internal state security, public drunkenness, and tax evasion. The two first charges, which stem from his work as a journalist and researcher, appear to be based on slim evidence. The same judicial case against him also includes a rape charge following an accusation brought by a female colleague against Radi. He denies the accusation and says the sexual encounter was consensual. His accuser, who has stepped forward publicly, has a right to be heard and respected, and, like Radi, a right to fair judicial proceedings. A judge rejected Radi's request for pretrial release. At time of writing, he was still imprisoned, and subjected to a judicial investigation that could last up to a year.

On July 16, a collective of 110 Moroccan journalists denounced a handful of news websites that they called "slander media" because of their incessant and seemingly coordinated attacks against Moroccan journalists, activists, and artists critical of the authorities. Known for their proximity to security services, these websites have published in the past years hundreds of articles including private information on targeted individuals.

The information included banking and property records, screenshots of private electronic conversations, allegations about sexual relationships (or threats to expose them), identities of roommates, and biographical details, sometimes as far back as their childhood, complete with information on the parents of the targeted individuals.

Between September 2019 and January 2020, authorities arrested and prosecuted at least 10 activists, artists, students, or other citizens in different cities
for their nonviolent, critical commentary on authorities via Facebook posts,
YouTube videos, and rap songs. They were sentenced to prison on such charges
as showing a "lack of due respect for the king," "defaming state institutions,"
and "offending public officials."

Authorities prosecuted all of these speech offenses, not under the Press and
Publications Code, but under the penal code. The penal code, unlike the Press
and Publications Code, punishes nonviolent speech offenses, including "causing harm" to Islam or the monarchy, and "inciting against" Morocco's "territorial
integrity," a reference to its claim to Western Sahara, with prison terms.

On February 18, an appeals court in Settat, south of Rabat, confirmed the four-
year sentence pronounced by a first instance court against Mohamed Sekkaki,
30, a popular YouTube commentator also known as "Moul Kaskita" ("The Man
with the Sports Cap"). Because he posted a video criticizing King Mohammed VI,
he was accused of "offending institutions of the State" and "lacking due respect
to the king."

On July 15, an appeals court in Khemisset, east of Rabat, confirmed the three-
year sentence pronounced by a first instance court against Mohamed Ben
Boudouh, a Facebook commentator also known as "Moul Hanout" ("The Shop
Owner") and Youssef Moujahid, a bank employee, who created a YouTube channel that publishes commentary videos on Moroccan affairs. Both men were accused of "insulting constitutional institutions [and] public officials," Ben
Boudouh because he published a video on Facebook criticizing King Mohammed
VI's lavish lifestyle, and Moujahid for publishing excerpts of that video on his
channel.

On September 10, an appeals court in Tetouan confirmed the two-year sentence
pronounced by a first instance court against Said Chakour, 23, a day worker, for
"insulting public officials." A month earlier, because he received what he believed was insufficient attention and medical care in a public hospital after he
was involved in a traffic accident, Chakour appeared in a YouTube video, insult-

ing hospital personnel and Moroccan officials at large, including King Mohammed VI.

Western Sahara

The United Nations-sponsored process of negotiations between Morocco and the Polisario Front, the liberation movement that seeks self-determination for Western Sahara, most of which is under de facto Moroccan control, remained stalled after the resignation in May 2019 of Horst Kohler, the envoy of the UN secretary-general. Kohler had not been replaced at time of writing. Morocco proposes for Western Sahara a measure of autonomy under Moroccan rule but rejects a referendum on independence, which the conflict parties agreed upon in the context of a UN-brokered ceasefire in 1991.

Moroccan authorities systematically prevent gatherings in the Western Sahara supporting Sahrawi self-determination, obstruct the work of some local human rights nongovernmental organizations, including by blocking their legal registration, and on occasion beat activists and journalists in their custody and on the streets.

On September 29, in response to the creation of the "Sahrawi Organ against Moroccan Occupation," a new pro-independence group by well-known activist Aminatou Haidar and others, a prosecutor in El-Ayun published a communique announcing the opening of a judicial investigation for "activities (aiming at) harming the kingdom's territorial integrity." The same day, police surrounded the house of five members of the new group, including Haidar. One of them told Human Rights Watch on October 5 that police cars had been following them whenever one of them left their home and prevented guests from visiting.

Walid El Batal, a pro self-determination Sahrawi activist, remained in prison after an appeals court in El-Ayoun, Western Sahara's largest city, sentenced him in October 2019 to two years for "rebellion" and insulting police officers. On February 25, authorities told Human Rights Watch that they opened an investigation following the publication on YouTube, nine months earlier, of a video showing police agents severely beating El Batal and two other persons upon arrest. The content of that investigation was not made public at time of writing, even though authorities told Human Rights Watch that tribunals in Smara and El-Ayun have prosecuted or investigated six police agents for illegal use of violence, in relation to El Batal's arrest. Human Rights Watch was not able to verify that information independently.

In 2020, 19 Sahrawi men remained in prison after they were convicted in unfair trials in 2013 and 2017 for the killing of 11 security force members, during clashes that erupted after authorities forcibly dismantled a large protest en-campment in Gdeim Izik, Western Sahara, in 2010. Both courts relied almost en-tirely on their confessions to police to convict them, without seriously investigating claims that the defendants had signed their confessions under tor-ture. The Cassation court, Morocco's highest judicial instance, was expected to rule on the fairness of the 2017 verdict on November 25.

Women's and Girls' Rights

The Family Code discriminates against women with regard to inheritance and procedures to obtain divorce. The code sets 18 as a minimum age of marriage but allows judges to grant "exemptions" to marry girls aged 15 to 18 at the re-quest of their family. In 2018, 40,000 such exemptions were granted, amounting to almost 20 percent of marriages recorded during the year, in what then-Justice Minister Mohamed Aujjar called "an alarming increase."

While Morocco's 2018 Violence against Women law criminalized some forms of domestic violence, established prevention measures, and provided new protec-tions for survivors, it required survivors to file for criminal prosecution in order to obtain protection, which few can do. It also did not set out the duties of police, prosecutors, and investigative judges in domestic violence cases, or fund women's shelters. Women's rights groups warned of risks of heightened domes-tic violence cases during Covid-19 lockdown restrictions and called for an urgent plan from the authorities to respond effectively to it. They reported an increase in domestic violence during lockdown months, while the authorities noted that the number of complaints to the authorities and prosecutions decreased during lockdown restrictions.

Women in Morocco revived their #MeToo movement. The Masaktach ("I will not be silent") collective published dozens of anonymized testimonies of women re-porting sexual violence and connected women to each other when they accused the same assailant. Morocco's law does not explicitly criminalize marital rape, and women who report rape can find themselves prosecuted instead for engaging in sexual intercourse outside marriage if authorities do not believe her.

Another online movement, the Diha F'Rassek ("Mind Your Own Business") movement was also launched to fight back against dozens of "revenge porn" accounts that appeared online during the country's coronavirus lockdown. They reported that 300 women and girls had contacted them about online abuse.

Domestic Workers

A law that took effect in 2018 provides domestic workers with labor protections, including mandatory labor contracts, mandatory days off, minimum age, minimum wage, and maximum working hours guarantees. It imposes fines on employers who violate the law, and prison sentences for some repeat offenders. However, the government did not engage in any noticeable communication efforts to make sure the general public, including domestic workers and employers, are aware of the existence of the law. During the Covid-19-related lockdown, some domestic workers were trapped at their employers' homes, overworked, and unable to get back to their families, according to media reports.

Right to Private Life and Sexual Orientation

Consensual sex between adults who are not married to one another is punishable by up to one year in prison. Moroccan law also criminalizes what it refers to as acts of "sexual deviancy" between members of the same sex, a term that authorities use to refer to homosexuality more generally, and punishes them with prison terms of up to three years.

In April, multiple individuals conducted a campaign of online harassment of presumed gay and bisexual men. Moroccan LGBT activists told Human Rights Watch that the "outing" campaign had led to some families expelling suspected homosexuals from their homes. It caused panic among people who sought to protect their privacy due to the social stigma toward homosexuality and the legal prohibition of same-sex relations.

In a memorandum published in October 2019, the National Human Rights Council, a state-appointed body, recommended decriminalizing consensual sex between non-married adults. More than 25 nongovernmental organizations expressed support for the recommendation. The Moroccan government did not act upon it.

Refugees and Asylum Seekers

The government has yet to approve a draft of Morocco's first law on the right to asylum, introduced in 2013. As of August 2020, the Ministry of Foreign Affairs had granted, or started the administrative process for granting, refugee cards, along with special residency permits and work authorizations to 812 persons, most of them sub-Saharan Africans, whom the UN High Commissioner for Refugees (UNHCR) had recognized. All of the 7,561 refugees recognized by UNHCR since 2007 have access to public education and health services, but only about half of them have regular residency permits and work authorizations, according to the UNHCR.

Mozambique

The human rights situation in Mozambique deteriorated in 2020 largely as a result of the ongoing conflict in the north of the country. The humanitarian situation in the northern province of Cabo Delgado worsened due to insecurity and violence, leaving over 250,000 people displaced. An Islamist armed group, locally known as Al-Sunna wa Jama'a, continued to attack villages, killing civilians, kidnapping women and children, and burning and destroying properties. State security forces were implicated in serious abuses, including arbitrary arrests, abductions, torture, use of excessive force against unarmed civilians, intimidation, and extrajudicial executions. In central Mozambique, armed men believed to be part of another insurgent campaign by dissident militants from the opposition Renamo party attacked private and public vehicles, killing dozens of people in August and September 2020.

Humanitarian Crisis in Cabo Delgado

The humanitarian situation in the northern province of Cabo Delgado continued to deteriorate due to insecurity and violence caused by fighting between state security forces and an Islamist armed group locally known as both Al-Shabab and Al-Sunna wa Jama'a (ASWJ). As of September 2020, the United Nations estimated that over 250,000 people had been displaced, forcing the authorities to set up camps for internally displaced people across the province.

In September, the UN's World Food Program warned that tens of thousands of people had been deprived of humanitarian aid in northern Mozambique as fighting intensified. Humanitarian access in Cabo Delgado decreased in June, after the International Committee of the Red Cross and Doctors Without Borders suspended operations in Macomia, Mocimboa da Praia, and Quissanga districts because of insecurity. In September, the UN estimated that about 1 million people in critical need were isolated due to violence.

Abuses by State Security Forces

State security forces were implicated in grave human rights violations during counterterrorism operations in northern, gas-rich Cabo Delgado province including arbitrary arrests, abductions, torture of detainees, excessive force against unarmed civilians, intimidation and extrajudicial executions. The government did not take any publicly known step to investigate those abuses or punish those implicated.

In May, the Catholic Bishop of Pemba, Luiz Lisboa, warned that security forces were using excessive force against displaced people who sought refuge in Pemba city after their villages were attacked by ASWJ. In April, 17 civil society groups wrote a letter to Mozambican President Filipe Jacinto Nyusi expressing concern about the deteriorating human rights situation in Cabo Delgado province.

In September, videos and pictures emerged showing torture and other ill-treatment of prisoners by Mozambican soldiers in Cabo Delgado. Also in September, a video showed men in army uniform summarily executing a naked woman near Mocimboa da Praia whom they called a "Shabab." The Mozambican Armed Defense Forces (FADM) released a statement calling the video footage "shocking and horrifying." But soon after, Mozambican Defense Minister Jaime Neto said that the video was created by Islamist armed extremists to tarnish the reputation of the Mozambican army.

Abuses by Islamist Armed Groups

Attacks by ASWJ continued in Cabo Delgado province. The group is implicated in the killing of civilians, attacks on public and private transport, and the burning and destruction of buildings, including homes, schools and hospitals. In January, the group torched a teacher training college run by a local charity and an institute of agriculture in Bilibiza, Quissanga district. In April, the group reportedly killed at least 52 civilians in Muidumbe district, after they refused to join the group. ASWJ insurgents have also been accused of kidnapping women. In May, two girls who said they escaped from a camp under ASWJ's control told police that their captors made them sleep naked to deter any plan of escaping. Earlier in February, local media had reported that ASWJ kidnapped two women during an attack on a village in Muidumbe district. In July, the Islamist insurgents attacked a private gas company vehicle in Mocimboa da Praia, killing eight workers. In August, they captured a strategic port in Mocimboa da Praia. Residents described panic as the insurgents burned houses and forced people out of the village to seek refuge in the bush.

Violence in Central Provinces

Attacks continued against private and public vehicles moving around in Manica and Sofala provinces, near Gorongosa in central Mozambique, by armed men believed to be part of a dissident group of Renamo guerrillas who rejected the August 2019 peace agreement. The leader of the group, Mariano Chongo, assumed responsibility for some of the attacks, claiming they were retaliation for what he called "excesses" perpetrated by the state security forces in rural areas. Local media reported that the armed attacks have killed at least 24 people since August 2019. In July, residents of Gondola district, who sought refuge in camps set up by the local authorities in Manica province, accused the armed men of burning, destroying and looting their properties.

Attacks against Journalists

Journalists continued to be harassed, intimidated, and arbitrarily detained by state security forces, and authorities failed to seriously investigate those abuses against press freedom. In April, Ibrahimo Mbaruco, a journalist and newscaster at Palma Community Radio Station in Cabo Delgado province, was forcibly disappeared on his way home from work, after sending a text message to a colleague saying that soldiers were harassing him.

Also in April, police officers detained Hizidine Acha, a journalist for SOICO, the largest Mozambican private media group, for two hours and forced him to delete images on his phone and camera. The images allegedly showed the officers beating people. In July, a court in Maputo convicted Omardine Omar, a reporter for the private news website Carta de Moçambique, on charges of civil disobedience, after he was detained while investigating a complaint about police harassment and extortion of street vendors. In August, unidentified people broke into the office of independent newspaper *CanalMoz*, and set the newsroom ablaze. In September, Luciano da Conceição, a Deutsche Welle correspondent in Inhambane province, was kidnapped by unknown individuals who beat him, before abandoning him seriously injured on a local beach. Also, in September,

Leonardo Gimo, a journalist of a local TV station in Nampula city, was attacked by three men who seized his equipment.

Disability Rights

There is little official data on the exact number of persons with albinism in Mozambique, but civil society organizations estimate that there are between 20,000 and 30,000 people with albinism across the country. Discrimination and violence against people with albinism continued. In Mozambique and neighboring countries like Malawi, people with albinism have been hunted for their body parts, which are used for witchcraft.

People with real or perceived mental health conditions risk being shackled—chained or locked in confined spaces—in homes as well as in traditional or religious healing centers where they often receive involuntary treatment. One man in Maputo described to Human Rights Watch the inhumanity of being shackled multiple times throughout his life: "This is a punishment, not a treatment. [They] are treating us as animals who are the property of their owners. No human should be treated like this."

Key International Actors

Although violence had been escalating for more than a year in Cabo Delgado, the African Union only noted for the first time, in February, the "unprecedented level of violence against civilians."

The special envoy for Mozambique of the UN secretary-general, Mirko Manzoni, expressed confidence in the process of disarmament and reintegration of former fighters of the opposition group Renamo, which started in July 2020.

In August, the SADC Heads of State summit pledged support, without specifying what type of support, to Mozambique in "fighting terrorism," although the final summit communique did not address the issue. During the summit, President Nyusi took over as chair of SADC.

In April, EU foreign ministers reiterated their support for the Peace and National Reconciliation Agreement and urged all parties to deliver on their commitments. They also raised concerns about the deteriorating situation in Cabo Delgado and urged authorities to take effective action to protect citizens, carry out investigations to bring perpetrators to justice, and identify the role of violent extremist organizations and their potential international links.

In September, the European Parliament expressed concern that the Islamist insurgency in Mozambique was gaining increasing support among regional and international armed extremist organizations. The EP also called on Mozambique to launch an independent and impartial investigation into torture and other grave violations allegedly committed by its security forces in Cabo Delgado.

Myanmar

The overall human rights situation in Myanmar deteriorated in 2020, including heightened restrictions on freedom of expression and peaceful assembly. Fighting between Myanmar's military and several ethnic armed groups continued, with government forces committing increased abuses against ethnic Kachin, Karen, Rakhine, Rohingya, and Shan minority populations. Military and police abuses were amplified with arbitrary arrests, detention, torture, and killings in custody.

August 25 marked three years since the security forces carried out a campaign of ethnic cleansing and crimes against humanity against the ethnic Rohingya population in Rakhine State, displacing several hundred thousand Rohingya within Myanmar and another 740,000 people fleeing to neighboring Bangladesh. Myanmar has made no significant progress in resolving the crisis, or providing accountability and justice for the victims. The court-martial conviction of three military personnel for crimes against Rohingya reflects ongoing government efforts to evade meaningful accountability, scapegoating a few low-level soldiers rather than seriously investigating the military leadership who directed and oversaw the atrocity crimes.

Aung San Suu Kyi's National League for Democracy (NLD) party was returned to power for another five years in general elections in November. During the year, the ruling NLD failed to expand democratic space or reform rights-abusing laws frequently used to punish persons exercising their basic rights. Instead, freedom of expression was further diminished, with rights defenders and community activists facing charges for criticizing the government and military. The government also effectively criminalized holding public protests without permission, despite the law only requiring notification.

International pressure increased on the government to cooperate meaningfully with UN rights investigators, including UN Special Rapporteur Thomas Andrews and the Independent Investigative Mechanism for Myanmar (IIMM), in pursuing accountability for grave rights violations against ethnic minority groups. The International Court of Justice unanimously ordered Myanmar to take provisional measures to protect the Rohingya from genocide as Gambia's case against Myanmar for violations of the Genocide Convention moves ahead. The court also

HUMAN
RIGHTS
WATCH

"An Open Prison without End"
Myanmar's Mass Detention of Rohingya in Rakhine State

mandated regular reports from Gambia and Myanmar on Myanmar's compliance, although the reports remain confidential.

Flawed 2020 Elections

Myanmar's constitution reserves 25 percent of seats in both upper and lower houses for military appointees. Any party not affiliated with the military must win over two-thirds of the remaining seats to form a majority in the parliament, while military-affiliated parties need to win just over one-third of the seats to obtain an effective majority.

Electoral problems in 2020 included discriminatory citizenship that barred most Rohingya voters and candidates; criminal prosecutions of government critics; unequal party access to government media; and a lack of an independent and transparent election commission and complaints resolution mechanism.

The Union Election Commission (UEC) authorized parties to deliver one 15-minute campaign message on state-owned television and radio stations during the two-month period leading up to the election. However, all political broadcasts were subject to pre-approval by the UEC, which applied overly broad and vague restrictions on what they could say, in violation of international standards for protection of freedom of speech. Six parties cancelled their broadcasts altogether after the UEC censored parts of their speeches, and ten participated under protest.

The UEC cancelled voting in parts of Chin, Kachin, Karen, Mon, Rakhine, and Shan States because of fighting, but provided no detailed explanations as to why specific areas were affected. No voting took place in Wa State, an autonomous region.

Rohingya Detention Camps

Approximately 130,000 Rohingya have been confined to open-air detention camps in Myanmar's central Rakhine State since being displaced by ethnic cleansing in 2012. For eight years, the Myanmar government has maintained the Rohingya's internment and segregation, violating their fundamental right to return home. They are denied freedom of movement in what amounts to arbitrary and discriminatory deprivation of liberty. Severe restrictions on humanitarian relief, including food and medicine, as well as little education; decrepit housing; restrictions on livelihoods; and highly restricted access to emergency health procedures have been responsible for increased morbidity and mortality in the camps. The squalid and oppressive conditions imposed on the Rohingya amount to the crimes against humanity of persecution, apartheid, and severe deprivation of liberty.

Myanmar has used Covid-19 response measures as a pretext to harass and extort Rohingya in the detention camps in central Rakhine State.

Rohingya in the camps have consistently asked to return to their places of origin, which the Myanmar government has long denied. The government has initiated measures to "close" the camps, but its plans entail constructing permanent structures in current camp locations, further entrenching the Rohingya's status as permanent detainees. In 2020, the government began "closing" Kyauk Ta Lone camp in Kyaukpyu, constructing shelters on isolated and flood-prone land, again rejecting the requests of Rohingya and Kaman displaced people to return home.

Freedom of Expression

Myanmar authorities continue to use overly broad and vaguely worded laws to arrest, detain, and prosecute human rights defenders, activists, journalists, and ordinary people for criticizing the government or military or engaging in peaceful protest.

Media reporting on events in Rakhine State have been a particular target for government action. In March, authorities charged Nay Myo Lin, editor-in-chief of the Mandalay-based Voice of Myanmar, under Myanmar's overly broad counterterrorism law for interviewing an official from the non-state armed group Arakan Army, on March 23. The charges against Nay Myo Lin were later dropped.

Aung Marm Oo, chief editor of Development Media Group (DMG), faces charges under the Unlawful Associations Act. While he has not seen the written charge sheet, he believes that it relates to the outlet's reporting on the conflict with the Arakan Army. The government also failed to act on DMG's application to renew the publishing license for its bimonthly print journal, which has been forced to cease publication.

The government used the broadly worded Telecommunications Law to order the blocking of numerous websites, including the websites of DMG and Narinjara News, the only two ethnic Rakhine media outlets. Government officials justified the blocking directives by referring to "fake news" and national security concerns. On August 27, the government ordered internet service providers to block the website of Justice for Myanmar, a group of activists working to expose corruption and rights abuses by the military.

The government, political parties, military, and private citizens continue to use Myanmar's many criminal defamation provisions to censor speech. While the government amended the Law Protecting the Privacy and Security of Citizens to preclude complaints by third parties, that law, the criminal defamation provisions in the Telecommunications Law, and the penal code continue to be wielded against critics.

Penal code section 505(b), which prohibits speech that may cause "fear or alarm in the public" and "upset public tranquility" is being used against critics of the government and military. From September, at least 58 students around the country were charged or faced arrest after joining protests, conducting public sticker campaigns critical of the authorities, or criticizing the mobile internet shutdown in Rakhine and Chin States. Students were charged under a combination of section 505(b), the Peaceful Procession and Peaceful Assembly law, and the Natural Disaster Management law, with 17 facing trial while detained.

Other activists have also been targeted using the Peaceful Assembly and Peaceful Procession Law. In January 2020, activist Naw Ohn Hla and three of her colleagues were sentenced to one month in jail for protesting the destruction of villagers' homes. A court convicted and fined the activist poet Maung Saungkha for hanging a banner reading, "Is the internet being shut down to hide war crimes and killing people?" from an overpass in downtown Yangon. In July, a court sentenced two student leaders, Myat Hein Tun and Kyaw Lin, to one month each in prison for holding anti-war protests without giving prior notice.

Escalating Conflict in Ethnic Areas

Civilians have suffered most in the escalating fighting between the ethnic Arakan Army and the Myanmar military in Rakhine and Chin States. OHCHR reported that approximately 500 civilians were killed in 2020 in the conflict. The United Nations Office for the Coordination of Humanitarian Affairs (OCHA) estimated in July, up to 81, 637 people were displaced by conflict. But local humanitarians estimated as many as 220,000 mainly ethnic Rakhine have been displaced due to the fighting. Civilians have been harmed in indiscriminate attacks and some have been deliberately targeted, including through enforced disappearances and extrajudicial killings, according to UN High Commissioner for Human Rights Michelle Bachelet. At least 200 villages in Chin State faced serious food shortages due to the conflict.

In September, two children were killed by indiscriminate artillery fire in Myebon township, Rakhine State. According to verified data from the UN Country Task Force of Monitoring and Reporting, 43 children were killed and 103 maimed between January and June 2020. This is more than the total casualties of 2019 or 2018.

Many residents in northern Shan and Kachin States face a humanitarian crisis. A group of NGOs said at least 48 civilians were killed between February and August due to the fighting in northern Shan State. In September, Myanmar troops clashed with the Kachin Independence Army in Muse, causing internally displaced peoples to flee multiple times. In October, Myanmar troops also clashed with the Shan State Army in southern Shan State, displacing approximately 4,500 people.

Trafficking of women and girls also remains a serious problem in both states, where conflict and economic desperation has made them vulnerable to being lured to China under false promises and sold as "brides." Of the 94 cases of trafficking involving 140 victims, the Myanmar Anti-Human Trafficking Police Force reported between January and September, 68 were cases of trafficking into China for forced marriage.

Although authorities are right to make public the number of cases, many more likely go unrecorded because the Myanmar government is still not taking sufficient steps to prevent trafficking, recover victims, bring perpetrators to justice, or assist survivors. The Prevention of Violence Against Woman Law—criticized for falling well short of international standards—was still awaiting parliamentary adoption at time of writing.

Unlawful Internet Shutdowns

The government maintained a second year of internet restrictions in Rakhine and Chin States in 2020, with the Myanmar military announcing it had no intention of lifting restrictions despite heightened fighting and displacement and need for better public health communication amid the Covid-19 outbreak. The government ordered a mobile internet shutdown on June 21, 2019, across eight townships in Rakhine State—Mrauk U, Buthidaung, Rathedaung, Ponnangyun, Myebon, Maungdaw, Minbya, Kyauktaw—and Paletwa township in Chin State.

Since that time, people in the affected areas have had difficulty reporting on conditions they are facing, including humanitarian needs, attacks on civilians, and rights abuses, including arbitrary detention, torture, and deaths in military and police custody. The mobile internet restrictions were removed in Maungdaw township on May 2, 2020.

Although the Communications Ministry announced in June that internet restrictions were provisionally extended only through August 1, the block on 3G and 4G services remained in place, with only 2G networks restored in early August. While 2G data can allow some basic communication and services, the speed is drastically slower than 3G and does not allow services such as video calls, access to webpages with pictures, or videos.

Labor Rights

The frequency of worker unrest and strikes around Yangon's industrial zones increased significantly in 2020, and the looming crisis in the industrial zones has further deepened during the Covid-19 pandemic as workers faced en masse dismissals and union busting tactics by their employers.

Myanmar's labor laws and associated dispute resolution systems do not adequately protect worker rights. Violations of freedom of association, the right to collectively bargain, and other labor rights are widespread. A combination of aggressive tactics against union members by employers, poor government enforcement and labor inspections, and lack of job security facilitates the exploitation and control of workers. Recent amendments to the Settlement of Labor Dispute Law 2012 failed to safeguard freedom of association or support processes to enshrine collective bargaining agreements in law.

Child labor also remains a serious problem but the government has failed both to issue a comprehensive list of what constitutes hazardous child labor as well as instructions on preventing hazardous child labor in up to 20 industries, as called for under Myanmar's child rights law. The Myanmar government should ensure that further labor law reform efforts result in statutes that align with the International Labour Organization's core conventions.

Sexual Orientation and Gender Identity

Myanmar's penal code punishes "carnal intercourse against the order of nature" with up to 10 years in prison and a fine.

Key International Actors

Bold steps were taken to hold Myanmar and senior military officials accountable for human rights crimes against the Rohingya. In 2019, Gambia brought a case against Myanmar before the International Court of Justice, alleging violations of the Genocide Convention. In January 2020, the court unanimously ordered Myanmar to prevent genocide against the Rohingya and to preserve evidence of atrocities as Gambia's case proceeds. The court also mandated regular reports from Gambia and Myanmar on Myanmar's compliance, although the reports remain confidential.

Two Myanmar Army soldiers who confessed their involvement in massacres, rape, and other crimes against Rohingya in 2017 were reported to be in The Hague in connection with the International Criminal Court's investigation into crimes against humanity against the Rohingya where at least one element took place in Bangladesh, including deportation and other inhumane acts.

Tensions between Bangladesh and Myanmar grew over border issues and Myanmar's failure to provide safe conditions for returning Rohingya refugees. In September, Bangladesh summoned the Myanmar ambassador after a sudden increase of Myanmar troops near the border, and later responded by beefing up its own troop numbers near the border in Cox's Bazar.

After a UN Security Council briefing in September, nine council members issued a joint statement calling on Myanmar "to create conditions conducive to the safe, voluntary, sustainable, and dignified return" of Rohingya refugees.

The European Union considered triggering a six-month review process on whether to strip Myanmar of its "Everything But Arms" designation due to grave crimes committed against the Rohingya. However, the EU human rights monitoring mission was stalled due to Covid-19.

At the Human Rights Council in September, the OIC and EU jointly called for Myanmar to ensure accountability, comply with the ruling of the International Court of Justice on the prevention of genocide, allow full and safe access to UN agencies, and mandate holders and human rights mechanisms.

Covid-19

Humanitarian organizations were severely hindered in reaching displaced people and others in need of assistance in Chin, Kachin, Karen, Rakhine, and Shan States, due to travel restrictions in place to stop the spread of Covid-19. While the Myanmar government has the right to implement restrictions in the interest of protecting public health, vital humanitarian operations carried out by the UN and other aid agencies should not suffer as a result of these measures. The Danish Refugee Council reported that aid was available but a nationwide curfew kept humanitarian workers from reaching people in need.

Between September 22 and October 2, just six UN agencies and NGOs had obtained travel authorizations to distribute life-saving aid in Rakhine State. Elsewhere in the country, daily reported Covid-19 cases and deaths rapidly increased from August onwards.

Myanmar released over 20,000 prisoners in a presidential amnesty amid Covid-19, the largest mass pardon in a decade, however, many political prisoners were not included in the release. The Assistance Association for Political Prisoners in

September estimated there were 180 political prisoners awaiting trial from prison, with 32 political prisoners incarcerated.

The government did not recognize journalists and newspapers as essential workers or services during the Covid-19 pandemic. Media professionals were denied permission to work outside their homes during lockdowns. Newspapers and magazines were forced to cancel printing, limiting information flow during a national health crisis and impeding press freedom.

In April 2020, a video showed police beating a man in Mandalay for violating curfew orders during the Covid-19 pandemic. Political protesters and labor rights activists were arrested under the auspices of breaking Covid-19 regulations and charged under various laws, including the Natural Disaster Management Law. Prosecuting and imposing prison sentences on quarantine violators is particularly harsh in the context of the Covid-19 pandemic, when overcrowded and unsanitary prison conditions could facilitate its transmission.

Nepal

The government of Prime Minister K.P. Oli proposed new laws curtailing free expression, while stalling on promises to implement transitional justice for abuses committed during the civil conflict that ended in 2006.

The government continued to favor impunity for perpetrators—both security forces and members of the ruling Nepal Communist Party—over justice for victims. Authorities also failed to effectively investigate ongoing cases of alleged extrajudicial killings by the security forces and deaths in custody, allegedly as a result of torture. Members of marginalized castes and ethnic communities were at greatest risk of abuse.

Several bills before parliament severely curtail freedom of expression by imposing draconian penalties for broadly defined new offenses regulating media and online speech. Other draft laws give unlimited search and surveillance powers to the intelligence service, and reduce the autonomy of the National Human Rights Commission. A draft citizenship bill retained provisions which limit women's rights to transmit citizenship to their children or their spouse. However, the draft law did benefit some people currently at risk of statelessness, such as orphans whose parents have not been identified.

Women and girls from the Dalit community were particularly at risk of sexual violence, which is frequently committed with impunity.

Despite a two-thirds' parliamentary majority, the Oli government made little progress in implementing the federal structure created under the 2015 constitution, including devolving some powers over justice and policing.

Accountability and Justice

On April 27, the Supreme Court rejected a government petition seeking to overturn a landmark 2015 ruling, which required the government to remove amnesty provisions from the 2014 Transitional Justice Act to bring it in line with international human rights law. The government failed to amend the law.

Two transitional justice bodies, the Truth and Reconciliation Commission (TRC) and the Commission of Investigation on Enforced Disappeared Persons (CIEDP),

NO LAW, NO JUSTICE, NO STATE FOR VICTIMS
The Culture of Impunity in Post-Conflict Nepal

have received over 60,000 complaints but neither completed any cases. The government failed to address concerns that both commissions lacked independence. In January, new commissioners were appointed to both bodies following a process that was rejected by victims' groups after authorities failed to hold meaningful consultations.

The government also failed to comply with numerous court orders relating to conflict-era police investigations and prosecutions. More than 14 years since the Comprehensive Peace Agreement of November 2006 promised justice to victims, hardly any perpetrator had been held accountable for conflict-era crimes.

Torture became a crime under Nepali law for the first time in 2018, however the practice remains widespread in police custody, and there have been no successful prosecutions. In cases of alleged abuses by police, the police often refused to register a First Information Report (FIR), the document used to initiate a criminal investigation.

The government routinely ignored recommendations by the National Human Rights Commission (NHRC), and in the case of Kumar Paudel, who was killed by the police on June 20, 2019, the Home Ministry asked the NHRC to revise its finding that his death was an extrajudicial killing. In 2019, the government introduced legislation that six United Nations special procedures mandates warned risks "severely undermining the NHRC's authority, effectiveness and independence."

On October 15, 2020, the National Human Rights Commission (NHRC) published 20 years of data, naming 286 people, mostly police officials, military personnel, and former Maoist insurgents, as suspects in serious crimes including torture, enforced disappearance, and extrajudicial killings. Investigators concluded the evidence warrants investigations and prosecutions, but in most cases the government had not taken any action at time of writing.

Treatment of Minorities

Scores of incidents of caste-based discrimination or violence were recorded, but Dalit activists said the vast majority of cases go unreported, and very few result in official action.

On May 23, the body of a 12-year-old Dalit girl, Angira Pasi, was found hanging from a tree, a day after community leaders in Rupandehi district ordered a 25-year-old man of a different caste who had raped her to marry her. It was one of numerous cases in which Dalit women and girls were allegedly raped and murdered. On the same day, five men were killed in Rukum West district, after a young Dalit man arrived to marry his girlfriend from another caste. Both incidents involved allegations against elected local government representatives.

In July and August, after two men died in separate incidents, independent activists and the NHRC called for investigations into allegations that they died after being abused in the custody of security forces. Both men—Raj Kumar Chepang, 24, who was detained by the army, and Bijay Mahara, 19, who was detained by police— were members of marginalized communities.

In July, rangers guarding the Chitwan National Park were accused of destroying houses belonging to members of the Chepang indigenous community. In June, park authorities at Bardia National Park attempted to forcibly evict members of the Tharu indigenous community.

UN High Commissioner for Human Rights Michelle Bachelet said, "Despite constitutional guarantees, impunity for caste-based discrimination and violence remains high in Nepal."

Nepal's 2015 constitution established separate commissions to protect the rights of Dalits, Tharus, Muslims, Madhesis, and indigenous people, and to promote inclusion, but the government left them largely vacant and non-functional.

Freedom of Expression

Numerous pieces of legislation before parliament proposed to severely curtail freedom of expression.

A new Special Service Bill, endorsed by the Upper House in May, provided Nepal's intelligence agency, the National Investigation Department (NID), with sweeping new powers to intercept communications and search properties without judicial oversight. Other bills currently before parliament, including the Media Council Bill, the Information Technology Bill, and the Mass Communications Bill, contain numerous draconian measures seeking to control the media and limiting freedom of expression for journalists and social media users, threatening custodial sentences for those who violate broad and vague prohibitions especially for online speech.

Covid-19

In 2020, the Nepal government repeatedly imposed national and local lockdown measures in an attempt to control the Covid-19 pandemic. The government has a duty to protect public health, but poor design and implementation of policies led to disproportionate impacts, especially on the most marginalized.

After decades of progress on maternal and infant health, research found that the number of births in health facilities fell by more than half during a four-month national lockdown which began in March. The rate of neo-natal deaths increased. Marginalized ethnic groups, such as Madhesis, suffered greater declines in access to clinical services. The government has an international legal obligation to ensure access to healthcare during lockdowns.

Daily wage laborers and farmers suffered disproportionate harm to their livelihoods and economic rights. Thousands of internal migrants were forced to walk hundreds of kilometers home after losing their jobs, while workers who had traveled abroad were stranded at the borders after entry points were closed. School closures disrupted the education of more than 8 million children, who remained out of school at time of writing.

Women's and Girls' Rights

Nepal's 2006 Citizenship Act, as well as the 2015 constitution, contain provisions that discriminate against women. A draft citizenship bill, which passed the parliamentary committee stage in June, retained several discriminatory provisions. In September, three UN human rights experts wrote to the government raising concerns that "the bill would continue to discriminate systematically against women, regarding their ability to transmit citizenship through marriage and to their children."

Legal gaps and lack of political will continued to mar accountability for sexual violence, especially for victims from minority communities. A statute of limitations of one year on rape and sexual violence allegations prevents many cases from being brought to justice.

The law was strengthened to increase penalties for perpetrators of acid attacks and to regulate the sale of acid.

Despite laws and policies to eradicate child marriage the practice remained widespread, with 7 percent of girls married by age 15 and 40 percent married by age 18. Ten percent of boys are married by age 18.

Sexual Orientation and Gender-Identity

The 2015 constitution recognizes a third gender and protects "gender and sexual minorities" in clauses related to equality before the law and social justice. The Supreme Court legally recognized a third gender category based solely on self-identification, but under the draft citizenship law, selection of the "other" gender category would require the presentation of a medical certificate. In 2007, the Supreme Court mandated a study on equal marriage rights for same-sex couples, but the 2018 criminal code only recognizes marriages between men and women.

Key International Actors

Relations with key neighbor India deteriorated, particularly after the two countries reopened a longstanding territorial dispute at Nepal's north-western border with India.

Nepal turned to China as a partner of increasing importance, strengthening investment and trading ties, including participation in China's "Belt and Road" Initiative. As a result, restrictions on free assembly and expression rights of the Tibetan community continued, under political pressure from China. Following a visit to Kathmandu by President Xi in October 2019, the two countries negotiated a series of new agreements, including an extradition treaty, which would place activists or Tibetan refugees at risk.

The Nepal government remains dependant for much of its expenditure on international development aid. Several of Nepal's donors have funded programs for many years intended to support respect for human rights, police reform, access to justice, and respect for the rule of law, but have not pressed the government to end the impunity of the security forces.

In its successful bid to be elected to the UN Human Rights Council in 2018, Nepal claimed, in 2017, to respect the authority and independence of the NHRC and the judiciary, and said it would pursue a credible transitional justice process. Despite failing to live up to these commitments, Nepal was re-elected for a second term from 2021-23.

Nicaragua

Since taking office in 2007, the government of President Daniel Ortega has dismantled nearly all institutional checks on presidential power. The Electoral Council, stacked with his supporters, has barred opposition political parties and removed opposition lawmakers. The Supreme Court of Justice has upheld Electoral Council decisions undermining political rights and allowing Ortega to circumvent a constitutional prohibition on re-election and run for a second term.

In October, Congress passed two bills, proposed by President Ortega, that could seriously undermine freedom of association and free speech.

The government's response to Covid-19 included denying its impact and failing to implement measures recommended by global health experts. Initially, the government encouraged large-scale public events. It has not closed schools or ordered lockdowns or social distancing. In April, Ortega said he was against public campaigns that urged people to stay at home.

A brutal crackdown by the National Police and armed pro-government groups left over 300 dead and 2,000 injured in 2018, and resulted in hundreds of arbitrary arrests and prosecutions. The Ortega government has continued to bring criminal cases against protesters and critics. Impunity for human rights abuses by the police continues.

Persistent problems include severe restrictions on freedom of expression and association, political discrimination against state workers who support the opposition, and stringent abortion laws that leave no options for rape victims.

Covid-19

Denial, inaction, and opacity have characterized the government's response to the Covid-19 pandemic. The government took no emergency measures in response to the pandemic and has kept schools open. Initially, Vice President Rosario Murillo encouraged people to attend massive events, including a government-organized march through Managua in April.

While the government reported over 5,000 cases and more than 140 deaths, as of September, the nongovernmental organization Covid-19 Citizen Observatory

(Observatorio Ciudadano Covid-19) registered twice as many suspected cases and 2,700—nearly 20 times as many—suspected deaths. Authorities have covered up suspected Covid-19 deaths, according to media, describing them as "atypical pneumonia" and sending health officials and police to conduct "express burials" of victims.

The government has refused to provide information on the number of Covid-19 tests performed.

Up to August 2020, the government fired at least 31 doctors from public hospitals in apparent retaliation for participation in protests or expression of disagreement with management of the Covid-19 response. During the 2018 crackdown, at least 405 doctors, nurses, and other health workers were fired from public hospitals, seemingly for providing care to protesters or criticizing the government.

Crackdown on Dissent

In April 2018, massive anti-government protests broke out countrywide. Police, in coordination with armed pro-government groups, brutally repressed protesters, which left a death toll of 328 people and almost 2,000 people injured, and led to hundreds of detentions. As the crackdown intensified, some individuals responded violently. Authorities reported that 21 police officers allegedly died in the context of demonstrations between April and September.

Hundreds of protesters were arbitrarily arrested and detained, many for months. Many were subjected to torture and ill-treatment including electric shocks, severe beatings, fingernail removal, asphyxiation, and rape. Serious violations of due process and other rights marred prosecutions.

Police abuses continued in 2020. In March, police attacked and detained demonstrators requesting release of political prisoners, media reported, and police and unidentified assailants attacked journalists.

In March 2020, Melvin Alberto Urbina Saavedra died after police beat him in detention, his family reported to the Nicaraguan Human Rights Center (CENIDH), an NGO. In April, police arrested at least nine and injured two demonstrators commemorating the 2018 protests in Esquipulas, Moyogalpa. In August, police summoned Francisco Aguirre Sacasa, a government critic and former foreign minister, to a police station. When Sacasa arrived, police arrested him without informing him of the charges against him and without allowing him access to a lawyer. He was also presented to the press surrounded by highly armed police officers. Sacasa was released a few hours later but remains subject to criminal prosecution for allegedly purchasing stolen goods for his antiques collection.

In 2019, the Ortega administration released 492 people detained in the context of the 2018 protests, mostly under restrictions such as house arrest. A broad amnesty followed, lifting the restrictions, Office of the United Nations High Commissioner for Human Rights (OHCHR) reported. As of September 2020, OHCHR estimated that 94 perceived critics remained incarcerated.

Owing in part to the amnesty, no investigations or criminal proceedings were underway, at time of writing, to identify and convict those responsible for human rights violations related to the 2018 crackdown. In 2019, President Ortega promoted top officials implicated in abuses.

Attacks on Human Rights Defenders and Independent Media

Human rights defenders and other critics are targets of death threats, intimidation, online defamation campaigns, harassment, surveillance, and assault. Some human rights defenders have suffered arbitrary prosecutions marred with due process violations. The government continues to employ unnecessary and disproportionate surveillance, harassment and selective attacks, and threats against human rights defenders and anyone identified with the opposition, according to the Inter American Commission on Human Rights (IACHR).

In October 2020, Congress passed a "foreign agents" bill, proposed by Ortega, that could be used to further suppress dissent. The law requires many people and groups that receive direct or indirect funding from abroad to register as "foreign agents" and bars them from intervening in "matters of internal politics." The law could impact journalists, nongovernmental organizations (NGOs), and political opponents. The law additionally prevents anyone registered as a "foreign agent" in the past year from running for public office. Also in October, Congress adopted a cybercrime bill that criminalizes a wide range of online communications, including by punishing with sentences of up to 4 years in prison the "publication" or "dissemination" of "false" or "distorted" information on the internet "likely to spread anxiety, anguish or fear."

In addition, Ortega said he would propose a constitutional amendment to allow life sentences for "hate crimes," in September. These bills could further undermine the political opposition's efforts to compete fairly in November 2021 presidential elections.

In September 2019, Army Commander-in-Chief Julio César Avilés Castillo accused NGOs of being "coup-plotters." As of June 2020, Congress had stripped 10 NGOs of legal registration, forcing them to close.

The Ortega administration restricts freedom of expression for journalists and media outlets through threats, insults, physical attacks, detentions, arbitrary financial investigations, and forced closures.

In March 2020, police stood by while people shouting pro-Ortega slogans attacked and robbed at least three journalists from independent news outlets covering a funeral in Managua. Also in March, Emiliano Chamorro, director of digital outlet El Portavoz Ciudadano, reported experiencing police surveillance and harassment. In July, Gerall Chávez, the co-founder of digital outlet Nicaragua Actual—who went into exile in 2018 after threats and harassment by government supporters—received threats on Facebook, including an animation that depicted him being killed.

In August, three employees of the El Rama mayor's office filed a criminal defamation complaint against Kalúa Salazar, a journalist at radio station La Costeñísima, after she reported on corruption. At time of writing, Salazar awaited trial. In October, a pro-government group attacked and gravely injured journalist Verónica Chávez, from the news outlet "100% Noticias," in Masaya as she was leaving a meeting with the opposition.

Between April 2018 and April 2020, over 90 journalists have fled Nicaragua, IACHR estimates.

Nicaraguan Asylum Seekers

As of April 2020, more than 103,000 citizens had fled Nicaragua since April 2018, IACHR reports. In March, the United Nations High Commissioner for

Refugees reported neighboring Costa Rica hosting some 77,000 Nicaraguan refugees and asylum seekers.

While most fleeing Nicaraguans have gone to Costa Rica, thousands have gone to Mexico, Panama, Europe, and the United States.

Women and Girls' Sexual and Reproductive Rights

Nicaragua has, since 2006, prohibited abortion under all circumstances, even if a pregnancy is life-threatening or the result of rape or incest. Women and girls who have abortions face prison terms as long as two years. Medical professionals who perform abortions face one to six years. The ban forces women and girls confronting unwanted pregnancies to seek illegal and unsafe abortions, risking their health and lives.

Key International Actors

Continuing human rights abuses have elicited strong regional and international condemnation.

In June, the United Nations Human Rights Council (HRC), with cross-regional support, renewed and strengthened the mandate of the Office of the United Nations High Commissioner for Human Rights (OHCHR) to monitor and report on Nicaragua. The HRC condemned abuses and urged the government to resume co-operation with international human rights bodies.

In September 2019, OHCHR released a comprehensive report on Nicaragua's human rights record from August 2018 to July 2019, urging the government to guarantee civil society freedoms; reinstate shuttered NGOs and media outlets; investigate and prosecute rights abuses in the context of protests; and end arbitrary arrests, among other measures.

As of September 2020, most recommendations had not been implemented, OHCHR reported, contributing to new violations and continued impunity. The OHCHR noted persistent restrictions on civic space, particularly the government's targeting of journalists and human rights defenders, and that the 2019 Amnesty Law had furthered impunity for serious human rights abuses.

In 2018, the government expelled the IACHR Special Monitoring Mechanism for Nicaragua (MESENI), the IACHR-appointed Interdisciplinary Group of Independent Experts (GIEI), and the OHCHR. The IACHR has continued to monitor the situation in Nicaragua, including by reporting on bans on social protest; the government's attack on freedom of expression; the lack of reliable information regarding the impacts of the Covid-19 pandemic; and the stigmatization and persecution of journalists and human rights defenders; among other topics. No other international monitoring bodies have been allowed since the 2018 expulsions.

In June 2019, the Organization of American States General Assembly passed a resolution that opens the door to evaluation of Nicaragua's compliance with the 2001 Inter-American Democratic Charter, which enables the OAS secretary general, or any member country, to convene a Permanent Council meeting to address situations where there has been an "unconstitutional alteration of the constitutional regime that seriously impairs the democratic order in a member state." The resolution urged the government to take steps toward resumption of negotiations with the opposition and restoration of access for international rights-monitoring mechanisms. It called for a commission to undertake diplomatic efforts. In September 2020, the government barred the commission from entering Nicaragua.

As of September 2020, the US Treasury Department had imposed targeted sanctions against 17 Nicaraguan officials responsible for abuses or corruption. Fourteen were sanctioned pursuant to Executive Order 13851 and three pursuant the Global Magnitsky Act of 2016, which allows for sanctions against human rights violators. Of the 14, 5 were also sanctioned pursuant to the Nicaraguan Human Rights and Corruption Act of December 2018.

In June 2019, Canada imposed targeted sanctions against nine senior Nicaraguan officials implicated in human rights violations.

In May 2020, the European Union and United Kingdom imposed sanctions against six Ortega administration officials, including travel bans and asset freezes against top officials responsible for abuse. In June, Switzerland also imposed financial and travel sanctions on six government officials. In October, the European Parliament adopted a resolution condemning Nicaragua's deteriorating human rights record and urging a tougher EU approach in the absence of any progress. EU member states renewed the sanctions against the regime until October 2021.

In October 2020, the Organization of American States General Assembly passed a resolution setting May 2021 as the deadline for the Ortega government to implement electoral reforms necessary to guarantee free, fair, and transparent elections in November 2021.

Nigeria

Nationwide protests calling on authorities to end police brutality and abolish an abusive police unit known as the Special Anti-Robbery Squad (SARS) received global attention and led to the dissolution of the unit. Authorities also took some action toward justice and accountability for police abuses. Protesters were however harassed and attacked by security forces and armed thugs in Abuja, the Federal Capital Territory, and some states. On October 20, social media footage showing men identified as military officers shooting at peaceful protesters in Lagos sparked global outrage. Several people were reportedly killed but the death toll remains uncertain.

The Covid-19 pandemic rattled Nigeria's socio-economic landscape and high-lighted serious gaps in the country's social protection system. Covid-19 also ex-acerbated challenges in the humanitarian response in Nigeria's northeast region, where the government's armed conflict with the Islamist extremist armed group Boko Haram, now in its 11th year, has left over 7.5 million people in need of humanitarian assistance.

Insecurity in the region persisted as Boko Haram and its splinter faction, Islamic State West Africa Province (ISWAP), continued to launch attacks against civilian, humanitarian, and military targets. At least 363 civilians were killed by the Is-lamist insurgents between January and September.

In August, authorities in Borno State in the northeast announced plans to send 1,860,000 Internally Displaced Persons (IDPs) and refugees back to their com-munities despite ongoing safety concerns. Sixteen days after IDPs were returned to Kukawa Local Government Area on August 18, Boko Haram insurgents at-tacked the community and abducted at least 100 people. The government con-tinued to participate in forced returns of Nigerian refugees from Cameroon.

In the northwest and parts of the south, intercommunal violence continued as herder-allied armed groups, vigilantes, and criminal gangs killed hundreds of civilians, kidnapped people for ransom, and raided cattle.

Widespread sexual violence against women and girls, including an attack that led to the death of a student in May, spurred a national outcry and prompted the authorities to declare a national emergency over rape and sexual violence.

Thousands of people with mental health conditions remain chained and locked up in various facilities, including state hospitals, rehabilitation centers, traditional healing centers, and both Christian and Islamic faith-based facilities. In February, the Senate Committee on Health held a public hearing on a draft mental health bill.

Covid-19

Since Nigeria recorded its first case of Covid-19 in February, authorities have taken various steps to curb the spread of the virus, including "lockdowns" in most states, requiring residents to stay indoors and for businesses to close, except certain essential services. By August, Nigeria's economy had shrunk by 6 percent.

The economic assistance announced in response to the pandemic failed to adequately target and provide for those left struggling to afford food and other basic necessities. Before the Covid-19 pandemic, over 90 million Nigerians lived in extreme poverty on less than $1.90 a day; the World Bank projected in June that the economic shock from Covid-19 will push 5 million more into poverty. The pandemic also brought into focus the country's inadequate healthcare infrastructure, which created inequitable access to Covid-19 testing and treatment for the poor and vulnerable.

The lockdown in Lagos State had a devastating and disproportionate impact on the livelihoods of the poor, many of whom rely on daily wages for subsistence and did not receive any economic relief from the government. Barriers to access to testing and treatment and inadequate Covid-19 education campaigns targeting those living in poor communities have also denied them equal access to healthcare.

Security forces used excessive force when enforcing stay at home orders, killing at least 18 people between March 30 and April 13, according to the National Human Rights Commission.

Schools were closed for at least six months due to the pandemic, affecting about 37 million children. In September, the Independent Corrupt Practices and Other Related Offences Commission (ICPC) announced that it had uncovered payments totaling 2.67 billion naira (about US$6.9 million) made to federal colleges for school meals during the lockdown, when children were not in school, which ended up in personal accounts.

Abuses by Boko Haram

Boko Haram and its splinter faction ISWAP continued attacks against civilians and humanitarian workers in the northeast.

In one of its deadliest attacks, Boko Haram reportedly killed about 81 people, injured 10 and abducted seven others in Gubio Local Government Area of Borno State in June. Days later, Boko Haram staged additional attacks in Gubio, Ngazai and Mongonu LGAs, killing at least 40 people and damaging a major humanitarian facility.

In January, ISWAP released a video of a boy it depicted as a member executing a man identified as a Christian hostage. Also in January, Boko Haram insurgents abducted and executed Reverend Lawan Andimi, chairman of the Christian Association of Nigeria, in Adamawa State.

In the same month, suspected Boko Haram insurgents attacked a United Nations facility housing several aid groups in Ngala, Borno State. At least 20 IDPs awaiting assistance at the facility were killed, according to media reports. In July, five men including three humanitarian workers were executed by the Islamist insurgents, who circulated a video of the execution on social media.

Boko Haram also launched a deadly attack against Borno State Governor Babagana Zulum's convoy on September 27, as he was returning to the state capital, Maiduguri, from Baga. At least 18 people, including four civilians were killed. The attack came two days after the governor survived another attack while traveling to an area near Lake Chad. His convoy was also ambushed earlier in July by insurgents.

Restrictions on Humanitarian Access in the Northeast

Military authorities continued to impose undue restrictions and requirements on humanitarian agencies in the northeast, which impede their ability to deliver timely and effective aid and run contrary to the humanitarian principle of independence.

Humanitarian agencies were restricted from operating outside government-controlled areas and must undergo lengthy processes to obtain compulsory authorization for moving personnel, cash, and cargo carrying relief materials in the northeast region, among other restrictions.

Intercommunal Violence

Intercommunal violence continued in many parts of the country. In April, armed bandits killed at least 47 people in a coordinated attack on several villages in Katsina State in the northwest. According to the UN refugee agency, at least 1,126 people died between January and June in the northwest region, 210,000 people were internally displaced and over 70,000 fled to seek refuge in Niger as at August due to the insecurity in the region.

In the southern Kaduna State, media reported that gunmen killed at least 43 people between July 21 to 24, and that 178 people were killed between January and July across southern Kaduna communities.

In April, at least 19 people were killed and about 100 houses burned in fighting between members of different ethnic groups in the northeastern Taraba State who were disputing fishing rights.

Accountability for Serious Crimes

In September, a military court dismissed and sentenced an army officer to a prison term of five years for "assaulting and defiling" a 13-year-old girl in 2018 while serving in Borno State. Beyond this, there was little progress on accountability for security force abuses within the context of the northeast conflict. The report of the Presidential Judicial Panel set up in August 2017 to investigate the military's compliance with human rights obligations, allegations of war crimes, and other abuses has still not been made public despite repeated calls from civil society and international actors.

Trials for hundreds of suspected Boko Haram insurgents slated for February in Maiduguri were postponed until further notice, following previous delays in January and in December 2019. Boko Haram suspects last faced trials in July 2018. Most of the more than 200 defendants in the July 2018 trials faced charges of material and non-violent support for Boko Haram, and some had been detained since 2009. The trials were fraught with irregularities including lack of interpreters, inadequate legal defense, lack of prosecutable evidence or witnesses, and non-participation of victims.

Nigeria's military released at least 333 children who were detained in the northeast for up to five years on suspicion of being Boko Haram members.

The Office of the Prosecutor of the International Criminal Court (ICC) continued its preliminary examination of the situation in Nigeria, which focuses on alleged crimes against humanity or war crimes committed in the Niger Delta, the Middle-Belt states, and the conflict between Boko Haram and Nigerian security forces.

Freedom of Expression, Media, and Association

The police continued to arrest, detain, and use excessive force against peaceful protesters. In March, security forces fired live ammunition and teargas to disperse members of the Shia Islamic Movement of Nigeria (IMN), who took to the streets in Abuja to protest the detention of their leader, Sheik El Zakzaky, since 2015. Two people sustained gunshot injuries, and at least 10 people were arrested and detained.

Authorities continued to clamp down on nationwide "Revolution Now" protests against insecurity and corruption, arresting and briefly detaining over 60 people during protests in Abuja in August.

Blasphemy-related cases in the north gained widespread attention and condemnation. Nigerian law criminalizes insult to religion. Sharia (Islamic law) applicable in the country's 12 northern states with a significant or majority Muslim population, including Kano, also criminalize blasphemy. Nigeria's constitution, however, protects freedom of thought, conscience, and religion, and guarantees the right to freedom of expression.

In April, police in Kaduna State arrested Bala Mubarak, president of the Nigerian Humanist Association, a nongovernmental organization, following a complaint by lawyers who accused him of publicly insulting the Prophet Muhammad on his Facebook page. Police transferred him to Kano State where he was being held incommunicado at time of writing.

In August, a Sharia Court in Kano sentenced a musician, Yahaya Sharif- Aminu, to death for blasphemy against the Prophet Muhammed in a song circulated via WhatsApp. Also, in August, a 13-year-old boy was sentenced by a Sharia court to 10 years in prison for making "profane remarks" about God during an argument with a friend in northern Kano State.

Civil society groups raised concerns over a new Corporate and Allied Matters Act, signed into law in August, being potentially used as a tool to restrict civic space and limit basic freedoms. The law empowers Nigeria's Corporate Affairs Commission to suspend the trustees of any registered association for reasons including fraud, misconduct, mismanagement or public interest and to appoint interim managers.

Sexual Orientation and Gender Identity

Charges against 47 men for crimes under the Same Sex Marriage Prohibition Act (SSMPA) of 2014 were struck out in October after the court found that the prosecution had failed to diligently prosecute the case and provide evidence. The trial, which began on December 2019, is the first to be brought under the SSMPA, which criminalizes same-sex conduct as well as public displays of same-sex amorous relationships, same-sex marriages, and the registration of gay clubs, societies, and organizations.

Key International Actors

Nigeria received significant loans from the International Monetary Fund, the African Development Bank, and the World Bank to support the country's health care sector and to shield jobs and businesses from the shock of the Covid-19 pandemic.

In June, the Nigerian Humanitarian Fund managed by the UN Office for the Coordination of Humanitarian Affairs announced that it had received a US$22.4 million funding allocation to address the increased vulnerability of people affected by both the Covid-19 pandemic and the humanitarian crisis in the northeast.

The United States, the European Union, and the United Kingdom continued to provide Nigeria with humanitarian and development aid.

They also repeatedly expressed concerns over terrorist attacks in the country, including attacks against civilians and humanitarian workers.

In January, the European Parliament adopted a resolution deploring the attacks, urging the government to respect human rights in its counterterrorism response and to end the military detention of children.

Foreign Policy

Nigeria supported the efforts of the Economic Community of West African States (ECOWAS), the African Union, and the United Nations in pressing for a swift return to civilian government after the military takeover in Mali in August, which President Muhammadu Buhari described as a setback to regional diplomacy.

Tijjani Muhammad-Bande, Nigeria's permanent representative to the United Nations, completed his term as the 74th president of the UN General Assembly. During his presidency, he advanced issues around education, poverty, and inclusion, including a landmark political commitment on universal health coverage.

Nigeria, which currently sits on the UN Human Rights Council, abstained from voting on some key resolutions, including those on the conflicts in Syria and Yemen, and on human rights in Venezuela, Nicaragua, Burundi, Eritrea, and Iran. Nigeria voted in favor of other resolutions to advance rights protections, including on accountability for violations of international law in the Occupied Palestinian Territories, and on human rights in Myanmar.

North Korea

North Korea in 2020 remained one of the most repressive countries in the world. Under the rule of Kim Jong Un, the third leader of the nearly 75-year Kim dynasty, the totalitarian government deepened repression and maintained fearful obedience using threats of execution, imprisonment, enforced disappearance, and forced labor. Due to the border closures and travel restrictions put in place to stop the spread of Covid-19, the country became more isolated than ever, with authorities intensifying already tight restrictions on communication with the outside world.

The government continued to sharply curtail all basic liberties, including freedom of expression, religion and conscience, assembly, and association, and ban political opposition, independent media, civil society, and trade unions.

Authorities in North Korea routinely send perceived opponents of the government to secretive prison camps where they face torture, starvation rations, and forced labor. Fear of collective punishment is used to silence dissent. The government systematically extracts forced, unpaid labor from its citizens to build infrastructure and public works projects. The government also fails to protect the rights of children and marginalized groups including women and people with disabilities.

North Korea's failures to promote economic rights resulted in increased harms to the population in 2020. On January 1, at a major party meeting, Kim Jong Un stated that North Koreas would need to "tighten our belts" and find ways to become self-reliant. However, the government continued its prioritization of strategic weapons development, leading the UN Security Council to maintain severe economic sanctions.

The economic impact of those sanctions, which was intensified by the Covid-19 lockdown—as well as severe floods that hit the country between June and September and destroyed crops, roads, and bridges—undermined the country's agricultural production plan. The government continued to rebuff international diplomatic engagement and repeatedly rejected offers for international aid.

HUMAN
RIGHTS
WATCH

"Worth Less Than an Animal"
Abuses and Due Process Violations in Pretrial Detention in North Korea

Freedom of Movement and Information

Moving from one province to another or abroad without prior approval remains illegal in North Korea. North Korea continued jamming Chinese mobile phone services at the border and arresting persons caught communicating with people outside the country, a violation of the right to information and free expression.

Networks that facilitate North Koreans' escape to safe third countries reported extreme difficulties due to Covid-19 health measures and checkpoints on top of surveillance and other existing obstacles to movement in countries through which people transit. Many North Koreans in China reportedly had to stay hidden in safe houses for months, with the Chinese government continuing to catch North Korean refugees and trying to return them, violating China's obligation to protect them under the Refugee Convention.

Despite the Covid-19 health measures, the Chinese government reportedly forcibly returned North Koreans until March. South Korean media with contacts in North Korea reported instances of the North Korean government rejecting Chinese proposals to return North Korean refugees in February and October.

The Ministry of Social Security considers defection to be a crime of "treachery against the nation." North Koreans fleeing to China are protected under international law as *refugees sur place*, since those forcibly returned by China face violations that a 2014 UN Commission of Inquiry (COI) on human rights in North Korea has condemned as crimes against humanity. While several thousand people escaped North Korea annually earlier this decade, the numbers have decreased in recent years. Just over one thousand North Koreans fled to the south in 2019, but only 195 did so between January and September of 2020.

Forced Labor

The North Korean government routinely and systematically requires forced, uncompensated labor from most of its population—including women and children through the Women's Union or schools; workers at state-owned enterprises or deployed abroad; detainees in hard labor detention centers (*rodong dallyeondae*); and prisoners at ordinary prison camps (*kyohwaso*) and political prison camps (*kwanliso*)—to control its people and sustain its economy. A significant number of North Koreans must perform unpaid labor, often called "portrayals of loyalty," at some point in their lives.

The government routinely compels many North Koreans, who are not free to choose their own job, to join paramilitary labor brigades (*dolgyeokdae*) that the ruling party controls and operates, working primarily on buildings and infrastructure projects. In theory, they are entitled to a salary, but in many cases, the *dolyeokdae* do not compensate them.

North Korea remained in 2020 one of only seven UN member states that has not joined the International Labour Organization (ILO).

Pretrial Detention, Due Process Violations, and Torture

The North Korean government's pretrial detention and criminal investigation system remained arbitrary, violent, cruel, and degrading. Ordinary citizens have no access to North Korea's laws, which are vaguely worded and lack definitions. Law enforcement agencies and courts are controlled by the Workers' Party of Korea, and connections and money are important determinants of whether one is detained or receives better treatment or shorter sentences. People in pretrial detention are subjected to beatings, torture, dangerous and unhygienic conditions, and other mistreatment in interrogation facilities (kuryujang), with women and girls particularly targeted for sexual violence.

Marginalized Groups

The North Korean government uses songbun, a socio-economic political classification system created at the country's founding that groups people into varying classes including "loyal," "wavering," or "hostile," discriminating against lower classed persons in areas including employment, residence, and schooling. Pervasive corruption allows some maneuvering around the strictures of the songbun system, with government officials accepting bribes to allow exceptions to songbun rules, expedite or provide permissions, provide access to certain market activities, or avoid possible punishments.

Women and girls in North Korea suffer widespread gender discrimination, high levels of sexual violence and harassment, and constant exposure to government-endorsed stereotyped gender roles, in addition to the abuses suffered by the population in general.

Human traffickers and brokers, often linked to government officials, subject women to forced labor, sexual exploitation, and sexual slavery in China, including through forced marriage. On July 28, 2020, the Office of the UN High Commissioner for Human Rights (OHCHR) published a report that said women forcibly repatriated from China to North Korea were imprisoned without due process or a fair trial and then subjected to egregious human rights abuses. While in detention, the women experienced food deprivation, sexual violence, infanticide, and forced labor and were held in overcrowded prisons with dangerous conditions.

Covid-19

In 2020, the North Korean government imposed various restrictions in response to the Covid-19 pandemic. While some measures that limited rights were justified by public health exigencies, others were not necessary or not proportionate and permitted grave abuses under the pretext of protecting against the spread of Covid-19.

For instance, the government intensified enforcement of a ban on "illegal" travel to China, including by executing persons caught while attempting to escape. In August, the government created buffer zones one to two kilometers from the northern border, with guards ordered to "unconditionally shoot" on sight anyone entering without permission. Also under the pretext of Covid-19 prevention, on September 22, the North Korean navy shot and killed a 47-year-old South Korean fisheries official on a boat near North Korea's western sea border.

The government also implemented drastic quarantines for anybody arriving from overseas at border cities, ports, and airports. North Koreans reentering the country through northern border cities did not have the option to quarantine at home and reportedly were quarantined in government-designated facilities with little food (three meals a day consisting of a bowl of boiled rice and crushed corn and some soup), inadequate medical treatment, and lack of basic needs products like electricity, some for up to 40 or 50 days.

North Korea maintains there are no Covid-19 cases in the country, but South Korean media with sources inside North Korea reported several deaths featuring coronavirus-like symptoms. According to the World Health Organization (WHO), as of October 29, North Korea had tested 12,072 people for Covid-19, with all resulting "negative" for the virus, and as of August 20, a total of 30,965 people had been placed under quarantine and as of October 29, 32,182 released.

The government also strengthened restrictions on travel domestically, issuing fewer official travel permits, imposing new temporary road checkpoints, and enhancing enforcement to prevent "illegal" travel. These measures, though justified on public health grounds, severely reduced people's ability to access food, medicine, and other basic goods. Schools delayed their scheduled start from March until June.

On June 9, Tomás Ojea-Quintana, special rapporteur on human rights in North Korea, recommended that the North Korean government seek more international assistance to prevent the spread of the virus, and make all public health data publicly available, allow citizens free access to electronic communication and global news, and permit international humanitarian organizations access to the country. The government did not respond.

Key International Actors

North Korea has ratified five human rights treaties, but it has ignored its obligations under all of them. A 2014 UN Commission of Inquiry on human rights in North Korea found that the government committed gross, systematic, and widespread rights abuses, including extermination, murder, enslavement, torture, imprisonment, rape, forced abortions, and other sexual violence. It recommended the UN Security Council refer the situation to the International Criminal Court (ICC). The North Korean government has repeatedly denied the commission's findings and refused to cooperate with the Office of the UN High Commissioner for Human Rights in Seoul or the UN special rapporteur on the situation of human rights in North Korea.

On June 22, 2020, the UN Human Rights Council adopted without a vote a resolution emphasizing the advancement of accountability efforts and mechanisms. As recommended by the Commission of Inquiry and mandated by subsequent council resolutions, the UN high commissioner for human rights continued to gather evidence of human rights abuses and crimes against humanity committed by the government. In November 2020, the UN General Assembly's third committee passed without a vote a resolution condemning human rights in North Korea.

Although the US-led efforts to place North Korea's human rights violations on the UN Security Council agenda as a threat to international peace and security between 2014 and 2017, since 2018 its mission to the UN failed to do so, and there was no formal council discussion of North Korea's record in 2020. However, the US government continued to impose human rights-related sanctions on North Korean government entities, as well as on Kim Jong Un and on several other top officials. The US also continued to fund organizations promoting human rights in North Korea.

Despite North Korea's rejection of any diplomatic engagement, South Korean President Moon Jae-in's administration attempted to develop better relations with Pyongyang in 2020, apparently to placate North Korea. The South Korean government has not adopted a clear policy on North Korean human rights issues and in 2020 it did not co-sponsor key resolutions on North Korea's human rights record at the UN Human Rights Council and the UN General Assembly.

On 6 July, the UK introduced new human rights sanctions, including against two North Korean entities in charge of the forced labor, torture, and murder that takes place in the country's political prison camps (*kwanliso*) and ordinary prison camps (*kyohwaso*).

Oman

Sultan Qaboos bin Said Al Said, the longest-serving ruler in the Arab World, died in January at age 79 after ruling since 1970. Qaboos recommended Haitham bin Tariq, the former culture minister, as his successor and the choice was quicky ratified by the ruling family. Sultan Haitham previously served as head of Oman's "Vision 2040" committee, the government's 20-year roadmap for social and economic reform.

Omani authorities continued to block local independent newspapers and magazines critical of the government, harass activists, and arrest individuals for their real or perceived gender identity and sexual orientation. Migrant workers in Oman were offered little protection amid the Covid-19 pandemic.

Freedom of Expression

Under Sultan Haitham bin Tariq, freedom of expression remained squeezed. Security agencies, particularly the Internal Security Service, continued to target activists and citizens, often for views they expressed on social media platforms like Facebook and Twitter. In one case, activist and blogger Awadh al-Sawafi was arrested in June for tweets that were critical of government institutions. On June 16, the court sentenced al-Sawafi to a suspended one-year prison sentence and a ban on using social media for one year for violating the Cyber Crime Law by publishing information harming public order. Similarly, on June 10, the Court of First Instance in Muscat sentenced former Shura Council member Salem al-Awfi and journalist Adel al-Kasbi to one year in prison each for "using information technology to spread harm to public order" under the Cyber Crime Law. Their charges relate to tweets that criticized government figures and the Shura Council.

Civil society and advocacy organizations were similarly targeted for social media posts. Notably, the women behind the "Nasawiyat Omaniyat" (Omani Feminists) Twitter account were reportedly summoned for questioning by authorities and forced to suspend their activity on the account, seemingly in retaliation for their work on women's rights.

The trial of writer and civil society activist Musallam Al-Ma'ashani was postponed indefinitely due to Covid-19. Al-Ma'ashani was arrested in November 2019 as he was crossing the border from Yemen. Authorities previously arrested Al-Ma'ashani in 2013 in retaliation for his literary work.

A United Arab Emirates (UAE) court sentenced Abdullah al-Shaamsi, an Omani man living in the UAE, to life in prison in May 2020 for allegedly spying for Qatar, in addition to other charges that were not made public, following a trial marred with due process violations. The evidence presented against al-Shaamsi included tweets he denied making and online competitions he participated in at age 17.

In response to the spread of Covid-19, the Omani government decided to "exceptionally" and temporarily ease some restrictions on some Voice Over IP (VoIP) apps and platforms, including Microsoft Teams, Skype for Business, Google Hangouts, and Zoom. WhatsApp, Skype, and FaceTime remained blocked, reducing the ability of Omanis and migrant workers to connect and communicate with their families and communities abroad amid the public health crisis and associated movement restrictions.

In July 2020, Sultan Haitham offered an amnesty to several high-profile political dissidents living outside Oman. Several Omani activists rejected the offer, however, as it required writing an apology and thank you letter to the sultan, according to activists who spoke to Human Rights Watch.

Authorities censored 51 literary works from the 25th annual Muscat International Book Fair, either due to the authors' political activities or the content of their work. Books by Omani authors Saeed al-Hashimi, Suleiman al-Maamari, Nabhan al-Hanashi, Hamoud Saud, Mohammed al-Fazari, and Zaher al-Mahrouqi have been repeatedly banned.

Women's Rights, LGBT People, and Gender Expression

Oman continued to discriminate against women with respect to marriage, divorce, inheritance, nationality, and responsibility for children in its Personal Status Laws. Women's representation in public office or senior legal positions remains disproportionately low. To date, no woman has ever acted as a judge in the country.

Oman's revised 2018 penal code increased penalties for consensual intercourse outside marriage. Article 259 punishes consensual intercourse outside marriage, between men and women, with six months to three years' imprisonment (previously three months to one year in prison), and at least two years if either person is married (previously one to three years' imprisonment). For a prosecution to proceed, the spouse or the guardian of the accused must file an official complaint, or if there is no guardian found, a prosecutor can still file a case.

The revised penal code also now criminalizes non-normative gender expression, making Oman one of the few countries in the world that directly criminalizes gender expression. Article 266 provides for a prison sentence of one month to one year, a fine of 100 to 300 rial (US$260-780), or both for any man who "appears dressed in women's clothing."

Additionally, while the previous penal code punished same-sex relations only if they led to a "public scandal," article 261 of the new penal code punishes consensual sexual intercourse between men with six months to three years in prison. Article 262 more closely echoes the language of the previous penal code, providing for six months to three years in prison for other sexual acts between people of the same sex if a spouse or guardian files a complaint.

In September 2018, two men were reportedly sentenced to four years in prison and a fine for crossdressing and posting photos on Snapchat.

Migrant Workers

Oman reported hosting over 287,000 migrant domestic workers in February, the vast majority of whom come from South and South-East Asia and East Africa. The government has done little to protect migrant domestic workers rights despite previously committing to review its *kafala* (sponsorship) system, which ties migrant workers' visas to their employers and prohibits them from leaving or changing jobs without their employer's consent. Human Rights Watch has previously documented how the *kafala* system facilitates multiple forms of abuse and exploitation that many migrant workers face in Oman. Migrant workers are often not paid their full wages, forced to work excessively long hours, and denied adequate food and living conditions. Physical and sexual abuse against migrant workers is also rampant. Their passports are frequently confiscated by their employers. During Covid-19 lockdown restrictions, migrant domestic workers faced increased risks of such abuse, and some were trapped from being able to leave the country due to travel restrictions.

Workers have few avenues for redress and risk imprisonment and deportation for "absconding," even when fleeing exploitation or abuse. The Omani labor dispute-resolution mechanism at the Ministry of Manpower has no power to force employers or agents to attend dispute-resolution sessions.

Low-paid migrant workers in Oman are acutely vulnerable to human rights abuses that increase their risk of infection from the coronavirus. These abuses include crowded labor accommodations and inequitable access to medical care and health insurance and immigration detention centers and prisons that have often been found to hold detainees in cramped, dismal, and unhygienic conditions.

The strain the Covid-19 pandemic has placed on the economy has in turn threatened the job security of migrant workers as Omani companies seek to cut their operations costs. In April, the state-owned Oman News Agency reported the Finance Ministry's directive to state companies to replace foreign workers with Omani nationals. Companies were also urged to ask non-Omani employees to "leave permanently," and were prohibited from firing Omani nationals. Hundreds of non-Omani employees have been laid off since April. Over 1.6 million expatriates live in Oman, comprising almost 40 percent of the total population.

Key International Actors

Under Sultan Haitham, Oman's relations with the United States and the United Kingdom remained strong. Both countries provide Oman with significant economic and military aid, including billions of dollars in automobiles and military aircraft. The US credits Oman with enforcing US sanctions on Iran and blocking the shipment of weapons to Yemen across its borders. The Covid-19 pandemic has caused further economic strain for the Sultanate, which has billions of dollars in outstanding loan payments to China, among others.

Oman's allies in Europe, North America, and the Middle East offered muted, if any, criticism of its human rights abuses in 2020.

Pakistan

In 2020, the Pakistan government harassed and at times prosecuted human rights defenders, lawyers, and journalists for criticizing government officials and policies.

Authorities used draconian sedition and counterterrorism laws to stifle dissent, and strictly regulated civil society groups and organizations critical of government actions or policies.

Women, religious minorities, and transgender people continued to face violence, discrimination, and persecution, with authorities often failing to provide adequate protection or hold perpetrators to account. The government failed to hold law enforcement agencies accountable for serious abuses even as new allegations of torture and extrajudicial killings emerged. Attacks by Islamist militants targeting law enforcement officials and religious minorities killed dozens of people.

Pakistani authorities cracked down on members and supporters of opposition political parties. Several opposition leaders, including former heads of state and cabinet ministers, continued to face prosecution on politically motivated corruption charges.

Freedom of Expression, Attacks on Civil Society Groups

A climate of fear continues to impede media coverage of abuses by both government security forces and militant groups. Journalists who face threats and attacks have increasingly resorted to self-censorship. Media outlets have come under pressure from authorities not to criticize government institutions or the judiciary. In several cases in 2020, government regulatory agencies blocked cable operators and television channels that had aired critical programs.

In late September, the Federal Investigation Agency (FIA) began investigating at least 12 journalists and activists for violations of the Electronic Crimes Act. Journalists also faced charges for statements made on social media. On September 11, Bilal Farooqi, a news editor at the *Express Tribune,* was arrested on charges of sedition and detained in Karachi for several hours before being released on bail.

On September 9, Absar Alam, a senior journalist in Jhelum, Punjab province, was charged with sedition and "high treason" for using "derogatory language" about the government on social media. On September 15, Asad Ali Toor, a journalist at Samaa television in Rawalpindi, was charged with sedition for comments made on Twitter.

Government officials continued to use the National Accountability Bureau (NAB), an anti-corruption agency, to target critics. On March 12, NAB agents in Lahore arrested Mir Shakil-ur-Rehman, editor-in-chief of the Jang group, the largest media group in Pakistan, on charges relating to a 34-year-old property transaction. He has remained detained ever since.

In July, the Pakistan Electronic Media Regulatory Authority (PEMRA) ordered 24NewsHD, a television news channel, off the air indefinitely for the alleged "illegal transmission of news and current affairs content." Journalists and opposition activists claimed that it was being punished for airing criticism of the government. On July 21, journalist Matiullah Jan was abducted by unidentified assailants in Islamabad the day before he was to appear before the Supreme Court for allegedly "using derogatory/contemptuous language and maligning the institution of judiciary." Jan was released after a few hours. He claimed the abduction was an attempt to intimidate him.

In August, a group of leading women journalists issued a statement condemning a "well-defined and coordinated campaign" of social media attacks, including death and rape threats against women journalists and commentators whose reporting has been critical of the government.

Nongovernmental organizations (NGOs) reported intimidation, harassment, and surveillance of various by government authorities. The government used the "Regulation of INGOs in Pakistan" policy to impede the registration and functioning of international humanitarian and human rights groups.

Freedom of Religion and Belief

The Pakistani government did not amend or repeal blasphemy law provisions that have provided a pretext for violence against religious minorities and have left them vulnerable to arbitrary arrest and prosecution. The death penalty is mandatory for blasphemy, and 40 people remained on death row as of late

2020. In September, Asif Pervaiz, a Christian man accused of sending a blasphemous text, was sentenced to death by a Lahore trial court.

In July, Tahir Naseem Ahmad, an Ahmadi man charged with blasphemy and imprisoned in 2018, was fatally shot by an assailant who smuggled a gun inside a high-security courtroom in Peshawar. Although the assailant was arrested, no government officials condemned the attack.

Members of the Ahmadiyya religious community continue to be a major target for prosecutions under blasphemy laws, as well as specific anti-Ahmadi laws. Militant groups and the Islamist political party Tehreek-e-Labbaik (TLP) accuse Ahmadis of "posing as Muslims." The Pakistan penal code also treats "posing as Muslims" as a criminal offense. In May, the government excluded Ahmadis from being part of a National Commission for Minorities, a new commission tasked with safeguarding the rights of the country's minorities.

Abuses against Women and Girls

Violence against women and girls—including rape, murder, acid attacks, domestic violence, and forced marriage—remains a serious problem throughout Pakistan. Human rights defenders estimate that roughly 1,000 women are killed in so-called honor killings every year. Data from domestic violence helplines across Pakistan indicated that cases of domestic violence increased 200 percent from January-March 2020, and further worsened during the Covid-19 lockdowns after March.

In September, nationwide protests took place to demand police reform after the Lahore Police chief made a public statement suggesting that a woman who had been gang-raped on a highway in Punjab was herself at fault because she should not have been traveling "without her husband's permission" on a motorway late at night.

In August, a Human Rights Ministry report found that women in prison receive inadequate medical care and live in poor conditions. According to the report, Pakistan's prison laws did not meet international standards and officials routinely ignored laws meant to protect women prisoners. The report also found that children who accompany their mothers in prison face additional risks of poor nutrition and lack of education.

Child marriage remains a serious problem in Pakistan, with 21 percent of girls marrying before age 18, and 3 percent marrying before 15. Women from religious minority communities remain particularly vulnerable to forced marriage. The government has done little to stop such forced marriages.

Children's Rights

Even before the Covid-19 pandemic, over 5 million primary school-age children in Pakistan were out of school, most of them girls. Human Rights Watch research found girls miss school for reasons including lack of schools, costs associated with studying, child marriage, harmful child labor, and gender discrimination. School closures to protect against the spread of Covid-19 affected almost 45 million students; Pakistan's poor internet connectivity hampered online learning.

Child sexual abuse remains common. The children's rights organization Sahil reported an average of over six cases daily of child sexual abuse across Pakistan from January through June 2020.

In September, the government released a judicial commission report on the 2014 Army Public School attack in Peshawar in which 145 people, mostly children, were killed. The report accused the school's administration of serious security lapses. Pakistan has yet to endorse the Safe Schools Declaration.

Attacks on the Political Opposition

In late September, the government intensified its crackdown on opposition leaders following the formation of an opposition alliance. On September 29, Shahbaz Sharif, a senior opposition leader, was arrested in Lahore and former President Asif Ali Zardari indicted in Islamabad, both on politically motivated money laundering charges. On October 5, former Prime Minister Nawaz Sharif was charged with sedition.

The National Accountability Bureau, Pakistan's anti-corruption agency, continued to intimidate, harass, and detain political opponents and critics of the government. In February, the European Commission criticized the NAB for political bias, noting that "very few cases of the ruling party ministers and politicians have been pursued since the 2018 elections, which is considered to be a reflection of NAB's partiality." In July, Pakistan's Supreme Court ruled that the NAB had violated the rights to fair trial and due process in the arrest of two opposition politicians, Khawaja Saad Rafique and Khawaja Salman Rafique, whom the NAB detained for 15 months without credible charge.

In February, the Supreme Court Bar Association and the Pakistan Bar Council, the top elected bodies of lawyers in the country, condemned the summons issued to an opposition leader, Bilawal Bhutto, calling it an "act of political victimization."

Terrorism, Counterterrorism and Law Enforcement Abuses

The Tehrik-Taliban Pakistan (TTP), Al-Qaeda, and their affiliates carried out suicide bombings and other indiscriminate attacks against security personnel that caused hundreds of civilian deaths and injuries during the year. At least 109 people were killed in 67 attacks between January and July, twice the number in 2019, according to the FATA Research Centre. Balochistan Liberation Army (BLA) militants targeted security personnel and civilians. In June, four BLA gunmen attacked the Pakistani stock exchange in Karachi killing two guards and a policeman and wounding seven others.

Pakistani law enforcement agencies were responsible for human rights violations, including detention without charge and extrajudicial killings. Pakistan failed to enact a law criminalizing torture despite Pakistan's obligation to do so under the Convention against Torture.

Pakistan has more than 4,600 prisoners on death row, one of the world's largest populations facing execution. At least 511 individuals have been executed since Pakistan lifted the moratorium on death penalty in December 2014. Those on death row are often from the most marginalized sections of society.

Sexual Orientation and Gender Identity

Pakistan's penal code continued to criminalize same-sex sexual conduct, placing men who have sex with men and transgender people at risk of police abuse, and other violence and discrimination. According to local human rights groups, at least 65 transgender women have been killed in Khyber Pakhtunkhwa province since 2015. In April, Musa, a 15-year-old transgender boy was gang-raped and killed in Faisalabad district, Punjab. In July, unidentified gunman in Rawalpindi district, Punjab, killed Kangna, a transgender woman. An unidentified assailant fatally shot Gul Panra, a transgender woman activist in Peshawar, in September. The murder prompted widespread condemnation on social media.

As Karachi, Pakistan's largest city, went into a Covid-19 lockdown in March, its commissioner, Iftikhar Shalwani, promised to ensure that the transgender community received health care and other social services without discrimination.

Disability Rights

In July, the Supreme Court of Pakistan directed the federal and provincial governments to take steps to fully realize equality of people with disabilities, as required by the Convention on the Rights of Persons with Disabilities , which Pakistan ratified in 2011. Pakistani law requires that 2 percent of people employed by an establishment be people with disabilities. In the absence of reliable data, estimates of the number of people with disabilities in Pakistan range from 3.3 million to 27 million.

Covid-19

Pakistan had at least 300,000 confirmed cases of Covid-19, with at least 6,400 deaths at time of writing. With little testing available, the numbers were likely much higher. From March through August, the federal and provincial governments announced partial or complete lockdowns. However, despite rising infection numbers, the Supreme Court justified reopening shopping malls in May, claiming that Pakistan was not "seriously affected" by Covid-19.

According to Pakistan Workers' Federation, in March at least half-a-million textile and garment industry workers were dismissed in Punjab province alone. These economic shutdowns had a disproportionate effect on women, especially home-based workers and domestic workers. The Sindh provincial government issued directives prohibiting employers from laying off workers during the lockdown period, ensuring payment of salaries, and establishing an emergency fund to address the negative economic consequences of Covid-19. The Sindh government also set up a tripartite mechanism with representatives of employers, workers, and government to deal with salary complaints. The federal and Punjab governments disbursed payments to workers who lost jobs, but at significantly lower rates than the minimum wage in any province.

The risk of contagion was particularly serious in Pakistani prisons, which are severely overcrowded. Pakistani authorities took some steps to mitigate the impact of the infection in the prison population. In March, the Sindh provincial government began screening inmates and prison staff for Covid-19. The Sindh and Khyber-Pakhtunkhwa government implemented a policy of early releases for many prisoners.

Key International Actors

Pakistan's volatile relationship with United States, the country's largest development and military donor, showed signs of improvement in 2020. The US acknowledged Pakistan's significant role as one of the stakeholders facilitating the intra-Afghan dialogue. In August, US Secretary of State Mike Pompeo said that US looked forward to strengthening US-Pakistan ties by "expanding US-Pakistan trade and working together to protect fundamental freedoms." In September, US Ambassador-designate William Todd, in his testimony before the Senate Committee on Foreign Relations, said that his "first goal will be advancing human rights, particularly freedom of religion and expression."

Pakistan is a beneficiary of the European Union's GSP+ scheme, which grants preferential access to the EU market conditional to the ratification and implementation of several human rights treaties. In its February 2020 biennial report, the EU noted lack of progress on enforced disappearances, labor rights, and torture, as well as shrinking space for civil society and growing repression of dissent.

Pakistan and China deepened extensive economic and political ties in 2019, and work continued on the China-Pakistan Economic Corridor, a project consisting of construction of roads, railways, and energy pipelines. In June, the government held talks with Chinese energy companies in an effort to renegotiate its debt, which it said was based on inflated costs. Pakistan continued to maintain its silence on the ongoing repression of ethnic Uyghurs and other Turkic Muslims in Xinjiang.

Historically tense relations between Pakistan and India deteriorated further. Following the Indian government's September 2019 decision to revoke the constitutional autonomy of Jammu and Kashmir state, Pakistan downgraded its diplomatic relations, expelled the Indian high commissioner , and in 2020 continued to seek international intervention on Kashmir with the United Nations, the EU, and the Organisation of Islamic Cooperation.

Papua New Guinea

Although a resource-rich country, almost 40 percent of Papua New Guinea's (PNG) population lives in poverty. The outbreak of Covid-19 in the country highlighted ongoing challenges with government corruption, economic mismanagement, and a fragile health care system. Lack of accountability for police violence persisted in PNG, and weak enforcement of laws criminalizing corruption and violence against women and children continue to foster a culture of impunity and lawlessness. Prime Minister James Marape committed to reforms and promised a crackdown on corruption in the country, but real progress has yet to be seen.

Women's and Girls' Rights

PNG remains one of the most dangerous places to be a woman or girl, where violence against women and children is rampant. More than two-thirds of the women in PNG are victims of domestic violence. In June alone, there were 647 cases of domestic violence reported in Port Moresby. A 2020 academic study found that over a 19-month period, a specialist police unit set up to receive complaints of sexual violence in Boroko, Port Moresby, averaged 27 complainants per month, 90 percent of whom were female, and 74 percent of whom were under age 18.

PNG has laws in place to protect women and children, including the Lukautim Pikinini (Child Welfare) Act 2015 and the Family Protection Act 2013, but they are rarely enforced. Initiatives such as Family Sexual and Violence Units within the police force remain limited, with police themselves targeting children and adults for sexual violence. Lack of services for victims requiring assistance compounds the problem.

In 2020, several instances of domestic violence sparked outrage in PNG. In June, boxer Debbie Kaoref released a video of her partner brutally beating her with an iron in front of her children. After footage of the assault was shared widely on social media, police arrested her partner and charged him with grievous bodily harm. In July, the partner of 19-year-old Jenelyn Kennedy reportedly killed her after six days of chaining her up, beating, and torturing her. Her partner has been charged with wilful murder.

Sorcery-related violence continued unabated. In November, in East Sepik province, according to the Guardian, police said five people were killed after being accused of sorcery. Police charged three people with the wilful murders of a woman, a teenage student and a 13-year-old-boy, all accused of sorcery. A man and his son were also killed that week for the same reasons.

PNG has one of the highest maternal mortality rates in the Pacific region and failure to implement measures to ensure women and girls can safely access healthcare facilities amid the Covid-19 pandemic has made pregnancy even more unsafe. Lack of Covid-19 testing equipment has resulted in hospital authorities turning pregnant women away from hospitals. Some do not feel able to seek care during pregnancy due to fear of contracting Covid-19, domestic travel shutdowns, and the economic impact of lockdowns, increasing risks to themselves and their babies.

Children's Rights

One in 13 children die each year of preventable disease and tuberculosis is endemic. Covid-19 has put child health outcomes at risk as closures related to PNG's pandemic response have interrupted vaccination and other health programs.

In April, schools closed down temporarily disrupting the education of 2.4 million students due to the Covid-19 pandemic, and the government, with international assistance, was still trying to return children to classes late in the year. Before the shutdown, net enrolment stood comparatively low at 74 percent in primary education and 32 percent in secondary.

Police Abuse

In September, Police Minister Bryan Kramer acknowledged that the police force has a "rampant culture of police ill-discipline and brutality." Kramer said the government is taking steps to reform the police force "from the top down," without elaborating on those steps or how they would be funded.

The PNG police force is chronically underfunded with a severe shortage of police: a ratio of one officer to every 1,145 people. The United Nations recommends a ratio of one officer for every 450 people. Police lack resources, such as uniforms and vehicles.

Children continue to experience brutal beatings, rape, and torture at the hands of police and other law enforcement officials.

In January, prison officers shot and killed a prison escapee at Buimo prison in Lae during a mass break out. A corrective services officer was also killed. In August, prison officers shot and killed 11 prison escapees at Buimo prison. Corrective Services promised investigations into the deaths, but at time of writing it was unclear whether any investigation had commenced.

Corruption

In May, police arrested and charged former Prime Minister Peter O'Neill with misappropriation, corruption, and abuse of office. The charges relate to the 2013 purchase of two generators from Israel for 50 million kina (US$14.1 million) while O'Neill was prime minister. The police complaint about the transaction was initially lodged by the PNG opposition in 2014. It is alleged that O'Neill directed the payments for purchase without parliament approval, without due consideration for procurement processes, and without a tender process.

Asylum Seekers and Refugees

At time of writing, about 145 refugees and asylum seekers remained in Papua New Guinea, transferred there by the Australian government since 2013. They are mostly in Port Moresby. Refugees and asylum seekers in PNG endure violence, threats, and harassment from locals, with little protection from authorities. The former detention center on Manus is now the site of a proposed new joint Australian-American naval base.

Medical facilities in Papua New Guinea are woefully inadequate and have proven unable to cope with the complex medical needs of asylum seekers and refugees, particularly their mental health needs.

The Guardian reported that around 30 asylum seekers, mostly Iranians, had signed agreements to "voluntarily" return to their country of origin in order to be released from the Australian-funded Bomana Immigration Centre. In January

2020, Papua New Guinea authorities released the last 18 failed asylum seekers detained in Bomana.

Land Rights

In September, 156 Bougainville residents petitioned the Australian government to investigate Rio Tinto's involvement in human rights abuses after inadequate reclamation following the closure of its Panguna mine in Bougainville left people with contaminated water. Petitioners said that polluted water from the mine pit flowed into rivers polluting fields. Many villages do not have access to clean drinking water and have reported serious health impacts, including sores and skin diseases, diarrhea, respiratory problems, and pregnancy complications. Rio Tinto did not accept the claims in the complaint, but acknowledged that there were environmental and human rights considerations.

In April, PNG refused an application by joint venture partners Canadian company Barrick Gold and Chinese company Zijin Mining Group to extend their mining lease for the Porgera gold mine, with Marape citing long standing environmental and resettlement issues. In August, Marape granted a lease to a state-owned company. Barrick Gold disputes the government's decision as a violation of the terms of its existing lease. At time of writing, Barrick Gold was appealing to the Supreme Court a lower court's decision upholding the lease rejection and referring the decision to the World Bank's International Centre for Settlement of Investment Disputes. In October, Marape and Barrick Gold commenced negotiations to reopen the Porgera gold mine under new partnership arrangements.

In October, 10 United Nation experts raised human rights concerns with the governments of PNG, Australia, Canada, and China about a proposed gold, copper, and silver mine to be built on the Frieda river. The mine, if approved and built, would be the largest in PNG's history. PanAust, the majority shareholder in the project, has not responded publicly to the UN special rapporteurs' concerns.

Disability Rights

Despite the existence of a national disability policy, PNG has yet to pass comprehensive disability legislation. People with disabilities are often unable to participate in community life, attend school, or work because of lack of accessibility, stigma, and other barriers. Access to mental health services is limited, and many people with psychosocial disabilities and their families often consider traditional healers to be their only option. Covid-19 has disproportionately affected people with disabilities who are left out of government Covid-19 policies and communications.

Sexual Orientation and Gender Identity

Same-sex relations are punishable by up to 14 years' imprisonment in PNG's criminal code. In May, on the International Day Against Homophobia, Biphobia, Interphobia and Transphobia, Australia's high commissioner to PNG, Jon Philp, faced a backlash after his Facebook post called for an end to homophobia in the country.

Covid-19

As of October 25, there were 588 confirmed cases of Covid-19 in PNG and seven deaths reported. PNG officials have said that they have limited capacity to test people, raising concerns that the actual number of cases is higher.

The fragile health system in PNG is underfunded and overwhelmed, with high rates of malaria, tuberculosis, and diabetes among its population of more than 8 million. Access to hospitals is extremely limited, with 80 percent of the population living outside urban centers.

In March, the Ministry of Health reported on Covid-19 preparedness detailing chronic deficiencies, as well as inadequate training on use of personal protective equipment and infection prevention and control. In March, PNG declared a state of emergency and a national lockdown, and some doctors told the Guardian they were forbidden from speaking with media under state of emergency powers. Nurses across the country threatened to strike over the lack of basic medical supplies. Police Commissioner David Manning warned anyone spreading "false" or "unsanctioned" information during the state of emergency would be prosecuted.

In June, the state of emergency was replaced by the National Pandemic Act 2020, raising concerns about the lack of parliamentary oversight over the operations of government and key emergency personnel. The opposition is challenging the law in the Supreme Court.

Key International Actors

In December 2019, the autonomous region of Bougainville voted overwhelmingly in favour of independence from PNG. The referendum is non-binding, but Marape has acknowledged the wish of Bougainvilleans to separate.

In 2020, the Chinese government provided multimillion dollar capital injections to fund airport runway expansions, seafood export deals, Covid-19 medical aid, and construction of the national courthouse. In August, Australian Prime Minister Scott Morrison signed a new Comprehensive Strategic and Economic Partnership with Marape and committed AUD$45 million (US$32 million) to fund technical and vocational training to Papua New Guineans living outside of Port Moresby and an additional AUD$6.5 million (US$4.6 million) towards the bilateral defence cooperation program as Australia seeks to strengthen security cooperation and boost bilateral trade and investment opportunities.

In August, Japanese Foreign Minister Toshimitsu Motegi visited PNG but failed to publicly raise human rights concerns with the PNG government.

Peru

Criminal investigations into grave abuses committed during the 20-year internal armed conflict that ended in 2000 remain slow and limited. Violence against women, abuses by security forces, and threats to freedom of expression are also major concerns.

Covid-19 had devastating effects in Peru. As of September, the country had confirmed over 800,000 cases and 30,000 deaths. In late August, it had the highest number of deaths per inhabitants in the world. The government established a strict lockdown to respond to the pandemic and, on March 15, declared a state of emergency, suspending some rights, particularly freedom of movement. Starting in June, authorities began easing lockdown restrictions by region and by risk category, the latter including age.

In November 9, Congress ousted then-President Martín Vizcarra citing an obscure constitutional provision allowing it to declare that the presidency has been "vacated" if the president faces "moral incapacity." Manuel Merino, the head of Congress, took office on November 10, but resigned five days later amid massive protests and reports that the police used excessive force in response. On November 17, Congress appointed Francisco Sagasti as the new interim president.

Confronting Past Abuses

Efforts to prosecute grave abuses committed during the armed conflict have had mixed results.

Almost 70,000 people were killed or subject to enforced disappearance by the Shining Path, other armed groups, or state agents during the armed conflict between 1980 and 2000, Peru's Truth and Reconciliation Commission estimated. The vast majority of those killed were low-income peasants; most spoke indigenous languages.

Authorities have made slow progress in prosecuting abuses committed by government forces during the conflict. As of September 2019, courts had issued rulings, including 46 convictions in 88 cases, Peruvian human rights groups reported.

Former President Alberto Fujimori was sentenced in 2009 to 25 years in prison for killings, kidnappings, and various corruption-related offenses. In 2017, then-President Pedro Pablo Kuczynski granted Fujimori a "humanitarian pardon," citing health reasons. In 2018, a Supreme Court judge overturned the pardon. Fujimori returned to prison in January 2019, and the following month, the Supreme Court's Special Criminal Chamber upheld the judge's decision to overturn the pardon.

An investigation into Fujimori's role in forced sterilizations of mostly poor and indigenous women during his presidency was still ongoing at time of writing. As of November 2019, 5,247 people had registered as victims of forced sterilizations committed between 1995 and 2001, the Ministry of Justice reported.

Courts have made little progress in addressing abuses, including extrajudicial killings, enforced disappearances, and torture, committed by security forces during the earlier administrations of Fernando Belaúnde (1980-1985) and Alan García (1985-1990). In 2019, the Supreme Court ordered a new trial of Gen. Daniel Urresti for the 1988 murder of journalist Hugo Bustíos, overturning the National Criminal Chamber's 2018 not-guilty finding, arguing the chamber had not properly evaluated the evidence. In January 2020, Urresti was elected to a seat in Congress.

At time of writing, criminal investigations continued into the role of former President Ollanta Humala (2011-2016) in killings and other atrocities committed in 1992 at the Madre Mía military base, in the Alto Huallaga region, and in their cover-up.

In 2018, then-President Martín Vizcarra established a genetic profile bank to help search for those disappeared during the armed conflict.

Police Abuse

Police used excessive force in Lima against demonstrators protesting the removal of President Vizcarra in November. While demonstrations were largely peaceful, some protesters became violent, including by throwing stones at the police.

Police officers arbitrarily dispersed peaceful demonstrations and used excessive force, including tear gas and other "less-lethal weapons," against peaceful protesters and journalists. Police officers, including in plain clothes, also engaged in some arbitrary detentions. Over 200 people were people were injured and two protesters died.

Security forces have also used excessive force when responding to largely peaceful protests that sometimes turned violent over mining and other large-scale development projects, the Ombudsman's Office and local rights groups have reported. Three civilians died in the context of protests between June 2019 and June 2020. In August, three protesters were killed and 17 people, including 6 police officers, were wounded during protests by indigenous people against an oil company in the Amazonian region of Loreto.

Decree 1186, issued by then-President Humala in 2015, limits the use of force by police. However, Law 30151, passed in 2014, granting immunity to police who kill in "fulfilment of their duty," may make it impossible to hold accountable police officers who use excessive force resulting in death.

In March 2020, Congress approved a so-called Police Protection Law, which could seriously aggravate the risk of police abuse. The law revokes the provision in Decree 1186 requiring that any use of force be proportionate to the gravity of the threat. It also limits judges' authority to order pretrial detention for police officers accused of excessive use of force.

Some cases of abuse by police and soldiers in enforcing the Covid-19 lockdown have surfaced in local media reports. In one, an Army captain was caught on video slapping a teenager in the face for violating lockdown restrictions.

In August, the police raided a clandestine nightclub, operating against Covid-19 regulations, resulting in the deaths of 13 people in a stampede. Video footage appears to show police closing a door, the only escape route. The Ministry of Interior stated that police denials that they closed the door were "false information."

Freedom of Expression

Threats to freedom of expression continue to be a concern in Peru, with some journalists facing criminal prosecution for their work, including under Peru's overbroad anti-defamation laws.

In late 2018, the archbishop of the northern region of Piura filed a criminal defamation complaint against journalists Paola Ugaz and Pedro Salinas, for a series of stories on sexual abuse by members of Sodalitium Christianae Vitae, a Catholic society. In April 2019, Salinas received a one-year suspended prison sentence, 120 days of community service, and a fine of approximately US$24,000. By August 2019, the archbishop had withdrawn his complaints, the cases were closed, and Salinas's conviction was revoked. But by then, a former manager of a real estate company mentioned in the stories had filed a new complaint against Ugaz. It remained pending at time of writing.

Throughout 2020, Ugaz was named in seven more criminal cases, including three allegations of defamation arising from her stories on sexual abuse. They all remained pending at time of writing.

In September, Salinas said unknown people in a neighborhood where he and Ugaz own houses were asking about them and their personal schedules.

Women's and Girls' Rights

Gender-based violence is a significant problem in Peru. The Ministry of Women reported 166 "femicides"—defined as the killing of a woman in certain contexts, including domestic violence—in 2019, and 111 from January through October 2020.

During the Covid-19 lockdown (March-June), the ministry reported 28 femicides, 32 attempted femicides, and 226 cases of sexual abuse against girls.

Women and girls can legally access abortions only in cases of risk to their health or life.

In 2014 the Ministry of Health adopted national technical guidelines for such legal therapeutic abortions that have since been challenged in two separate court filings by anti-abortion groups. Both cases were dismissed but appeals remained pending at time of writing.

Many women and girls face barriers to access legal abortion. In October 2020, "Camila," an indigenous girl, presented a petition before the United Nations Committee on the Rights of the Child, claiming that authorities denied her an abortion even though she was raped and the pregnancy put her life at risk.

In 2019, a Lima judge declared that a 2009 Constitutional Court ruling that had banned free distribution of emergency contraception pills was no longer applicable. In late October, however, an appeals court revoked the Lima judge's ruling on procedural grounds.

In July 2020, Congress amended the Organic Law on Elections to establish gender parity in congressional elections, requiring that 40 percent of candidates be female by 2021, 45 percent by 2026, and 50 percent by 2031.

Disability Rights

Peru has a legal framework recognizing full legal capacity for people with disabilities, but electoral authorities (RENIEC) have failed to take action to include in the electoral register people with disabilities who were previously under guardianship, depriving them of their right to vote. At time of writing, the Peruvian executive branch had not issued enabling legislation to fully implement legal capacity for people with disabilities.

Sexual Orientation and Gender Identity

Same-sex couples in Peru are not allowed to marry or enter into civil unions. In recent years, courts have begun recognizing same sex-marriages contracted by Peruvians abroad. In November, the Constitutional Tribunal denied recognition to a same sex-marriage contracted abroad.

In April, the government decreed a gender-based Covid-19 lockdown, allowing men and women to leave home on separate days. The rules did not account for transgender people, and media reported several cases of police abuse against them. The government reversed the measure shortly over a week after passing it, noting that most shopping was happening only on women's days.

In August, the Ministry of Justice issued a resolution allowing same-sex partners of public health workers to access state benefits in the event of Covid-19-related deaths.

Also in August, a judge ordered the civil registry to allow transgender Peruvians to change their name and sexual identification on national identity documents. The registry's appeal of the ruling remained pending at time of writing.

In March 2020, the Inter-American Court of Human Rights found Peru responsible for the arbitrary detention and rape of a transgender woman at the hands of police, marking the first time it has ruled on a complaint of torture related to a victims' gender identity or sexual orientation.

Human Rights Defenders and Community Leaders

Human rights defenders and environmental activists, as well as other community leaders, have been threatened and killed in recent years. In April 2019, the Ministry of Justice established measures to protect at-risk human rights defenders and their relatives.

In April 2020, Arbildo Meléndez Grandes, an indigenous leader and environmental defender, was killed in the central Andes region of Huánuco. In May, Gonzalo Pío Flores, an indigenous leader and environmental defender, was killed in the central region of Junín.

Refugees, Asylum Seekers, and Migrants

More than 480,000 Venezuelans were seeking asylum in Peru at time of writing, the largest number of registered Venezuelan asylum seekers in any country. This is in part because temporary residence permits are no longer available in Peru. Since 2019, applying for asylum has become the most straightforward way to regularize status.

More than 800,000 Venezuelans live in Peru. More than 486,000 received temporary work permits before the government stopped issuing them in 2019. The permits allowed them to work, enroll their children in school, and access health care.

The government has see-sawed on whether to require Venezuelans to show passports to enter the country. The requirement would close the door to many, as obtaining a passport in Venezuela is extremely difficult. In October 2018, a judge annulled a passport requirement that had been established that August. But in June 2019, the government passed a resolution requiring all Venezuelan migrants to apply for a humanitarian visa at a Peruvian consulate before entering. A lawsuit against the resolution by a coalition of non-governmental organizations was pending at time of writing.

In May 2020, lawmakers introduced a bill that would annul all previously issued temporary residence permits and criminalize undocumented immigration with up to five years in jail.

Key International Actors

In May, the Inter-American Commission on Human Rights (IACHR) expressed concern about the critical health situation of indigenous communities in Peru, in the context of the Covid-19 pandemic.

In August, UN experts on business and human rights urged Peru to ratify the Escazú Agreement, a treaty that seeks to strengthen transparency, political participation, and access to justice mechanisms in environmental matters. In October, Congress voted not to approve the treaty.

Peru is an active member of the Lima Group, a coalition of states seeking to address the human rights crisis in Venezuela.

In September 2018, Peru and five other countries referred the situation in Venezuela to the International Criminal Court prosecutor to determine whether a formal investigation by the court is warranted.

As a member of the UN Human Rights Council, Peru has supported resolutions spotlighting human rights abuses, including in Belarus, Eritrea, Iran, Syria, Myanmar, Nicaragua, and the Occupied Palestinian Territories.

Covid-19

Covid-19 had devastating effects in Peru. As of September, the country had confirmed over 800,000 cases and 30,000 deaths. In August, it had the highest number of deaths per inhabitant in the world. The government established a strict lockdown to respond to the pandemic and, on March 15, declared a state of emergency, suspending some rights, particularly freedom of movement. Starting in June, authorities began easing lockdown restrictions by region and by risk category, the latter including age.

The government closed schools in March. While the government took some measures to ensure remote teaching, many students have not been able to attend. The Ministry of Education said in September that 230,000 students had dropped out of school and 200,000 others were not attending classes, despite being enrolled. The ministry announced schools would reopen in 2021.

Some cases of abuse by police and soldiers in enforcing the Covid-19 lockdown have surfaced in local media reports. In one, an Army captain was caught on video slapping a young man in the face for violating lockdown restrictions.

In August, the police raided a clandestine nightclub, operating against COVID-19 regulations, resulting in the deaths of 13 people in a stampede. Video footage appears to show police closing a door, the only escape route. The Ministry of Interior stated that police denials that they closed the door were "false information."

In April, the government decreed a gender-based Covid-19 lockdown, allowing men and women to leave home on separate days. The rules did not account for transgender people, and media reported several cases of police abuse against them. The government reversed the measure shortly over a week after passing it, citing that most shopping was happening only on women's days.

In May, the Inter-American Commission on Human Rights expressed concern about the critical health situation of indigenous communities in Peru, in the context of the Covid-19 pandemic.

Peru endorsed the World Health Organization's Solidarity Call to Action for the Covid-19 Technology Access Pool, an initiative to "realize equitable global access to COVID-19 health technologies through pooling of knowledge, intellectual property and data."

HUMAN
RIGHTS
WATCH

"Our Happy Family Is Gone"
Impact of the "War on Drugs" on Children in the Philippines

Philippines

The human rights situation in the Philippines deteriorated in 2020. President Rodrigo Duterte's murderous "war on drugs," ongoing since he took office in June 2016, continued to target mostly impoverished Filipinos in urban areas. The police and unidentified gunmen linked to the police have committed thousands of extrajudicial executions. The killings increased dramatically during the Covid-19 lockdown, rising by over 50 percent during April to July 2020 compared to the previous four months. There has been almost total impunity for these killings.

In June 2020, the United Nations Office of the High Commissioner for Human Rights (OHCHR) published a highly critical report on the human rights situation in the Philippines. In October, the UN Human Rights Council passed a resolution continuing scrutiny of the situation in the country for another two years, but without creating an international investigation.

Threats and attacks, including killings, against left-wing political activists, environmental activists, community leaders, Indigenous peoples' leaders, journalists, lawyers, and others rose in the past year. The government harassed journalists and media companies, including through politically motivated prosecutions and other legal action; a court convicted journalist Maria Ressa of cyber libel in June, while the government shut down the country' largest television network the following month.

In March, the government placed the country under lockdown, restricting people's movement to limit the spread of Covid-19, using the military, as well as the police and local officials, to enforce the lockdown. Tens of thousands of people were arrested and often detained in crowded jails and holding centers where they were at increased risk of contracting the virus. Police and local officials targeted vulnerable populations, including lesbian, gay, bisexual, and transgender (LGBT) people and children, and in some cases using public humiliation and cruel treatment.

Unending "Drug War"

According to official government figures, members of the Philippine National Police and the Philippine Drug Enforcement Agency killed 5,903 individuals during anti-drug operations from July 1, 2016 to September 30, 2020. This number did not include the deaths of those killed by unidentified gunmen whom Human Rights Watch and other rights monitors believe operate in cooperation with local police and officials. Other sources, such as the UN Office of the High Commissioner for Human Rights, put the death toll at 8,663, although domestic human rights groups, including the government's Commission on Human Rights, believe the real figure could be triple the number reported in the OHCHR report.

Based on statistics released by the government through its #RealNumbersPH, "drug war" killings increased by over 50 percent during the lockdown months from April to July. Among those severely affected by the "drug war" violence are children left behind by the victims. These children are often driven deeper into poverty, suffer deep psychological distress, often drop out of school for financial and other reasons, and suffer bullying in their schools or communities.

The vast majority of "drug war" killings have not been seriously investigated by the authorities. Only a handful of cases are in varying stages of investigation by prosecutors. Only one case—the video recorded murder of 17-year-old Kian delos Santos in August 2017—has resulted in the 2018 conviction of several police officers.

The creation of a committee to investigate cases of police involvement in killings, originally pledged by the secretary of justice to the UN Human Rights Council, is of doubtful utility given the prominent role of key agencies responsible for killings in the committee's leadership.

President Duterte continues to encourage the killings, ordering customs officials in September to kill alleged drug smugglers. He also regularly denounced and dismissed groups that criticize the "war on drugs," accusing them of "weaponizing human rights."

Political Killings, Threats, Harassment

On June 4, OHCHR published a report that found "numerous systematic human rights violations" in the Philippines, among them the killing of 208 human rights defenders and activists since 2015.

Leftist activists and human rights defenders were key targets of physical and on-line attacks. On August 17, unidentified gunmen shot dead Zara Alvarez, a legal worker for the human rights group Karapatan, in Bacolod City in the central Philippines. Alvarez's killing came a week after peasant leader Randall Echanis was found dead, apparently tortured, in his home in Quezon City. Alvarez was the 13th Karapatan member killed during the Duterte administration.

The attacks against activists occurred in the context of the government's campaign against the communist New People's Army insurgency. Government and military officials have accused Karapatan and the other groups in its network of being supporters of the insurgents in a "red-tagging" campaign that puts them at heightened risk of attack. The military, national security agencies, and the police have actively used social media to convey threats that have resulted in tens of red-tagged people being killed in the past year.

In September, Facebook took down for "coordinated inauthentic behavior" dozens of what it called "fake accounts" being used by state forces to spread government and military propaganda. The accounts included posts that demo-nized activists, accusing them of being communists or communist sympathizers, and, in several cases, "terrorists."

In July, Duterte signed a new Anti-Terrorism Law. The law contains overbroad and vague provisions that the government can use to unjustly target critics. Among its provisions is the creation of a government-appointed Anti-Terrorism Council that can designate a person or a group as a terrorist, making them immediately liable to be arrested without warrant or charges and be detained for up to 24 days.

Freedom of Media

In June, a court in Manila convicted CEO Maria Ressa of the news website Rap-pler of cyber libel, along with Reynaldo Santos Jr., a former Rappler researcher. The case involved the retroactive application of the new law to an article that had been published years earlier.

The case is one of several that Ressa and Rappler face as part of the govern-ment's campaign of retaliation campaign of retaliation against media organiza-tions for their reporting on "drug war" killings and the Duterte presidency. Since

2016, the president and his supporters on social media have subject Ressa and Rappler to threats and harassment, including misogynistic attacks online.

In July, the Philippine Congress, in which Duterte controls a large majority, voted not to extend the franchise of ABS-CBN, the country's largest television network. The vote led to the shutdown of ABS-CBN. ABS-CBN earned the ire of Duterte and his officials who accused the network, which often criticized the government's "war on drugs," of bias.

The killing of journalists also continued with the murder of radio broadcaster and online commentator Jobert Bercasio on September 14. Bercasio was the 17th journalist killed during Duterte's term in office and the 189th since democracy was restored in the Philippines in 1986. In December 2019, a Manila court convicted two of the masterminds and several dozen accomplices for the 2009 Maguindanao Massacre in which a local ruling family murdered 58 people, including 32 media workers covering a political campaign. However, nearly 80 suspects remain at large, with little prospect of them being apprehended.

Death Penalty

The Philippine government began in 2020 to seriously consider legislation to reinstate the death penalty. The move in Congress came a week after President Duterte used his State of the Nation Address in July to call for capital punishment by lethal injection for drug offenders.

Reinstating the death penalty would violate the Second Optional Protocol to the International Covenant on Civil and Political Rights (ICCPR), which the Philippines ratified in 2007.

Covid-19

At time of writing, the Philippines had one of the highest recorded numbers of confirmed Covid-19 cases in Southeast Asia, with 400,000 cases as of mid-November. The Duterte administration's response to the Covid-19 pandemic has been led by former military officers, using police supported by the military, which has resulted in serious human rights abuses.

Since March 16, the government has imposed varying types of quarantines and lockdowns to contain the spread of the virus. Abuses reported include local officials putting curfew violators in dog cages or exposing them to hours sitting in the summer sun as a form of punishment. Two children who were arrested after curfew were put inside a coffin by local officials. In April, three LGBT people were accosted by authorities for violating curfew. Officials humiliated them by forcing them to dance and kiss each other in public. Many people arrested for violating Covid-19 regulations were thrown into overcrowded detention facilities where social distancing is impossible, increasing their risk of contracting the virus.

The C-19 law that President Duterte signed on March 24 criminalizes the spreading of "false information" with up to two months in prison and a 1 million peso (US$19,600) fine. This law has been used to censor free speech in cases filed against social media users, among them journalists, who criticized or even poked fun at the government's response.

Reports of domestic violence have risen during lockdown restrictions. Groups such as UNICEF and Save the Children have raised alarm about the impact the pandemic and lockdown have on the welfare of children, particularly concerning child sexual and physical abuse.

Key International Actors

In October, the UN Human Rights Council passed a resolution that called for the Philippines to "ensure accountability for human rights violations and abuses, and in this regard to conduct independent, full, and transparent investigations and to prosecute all those who have perpetrated serious crimes, including violations and abuses of human rights."

However, instead of establishing an independent international investigation into the human rights situation in the Philippines, the resolution granted the government's request for technical assistance for a joint UN-Philippines technical assistance program on human rights to supposedly address the killings. Human Rights Watch and dozens of other domestic and international groups view the request, as well as the government's compromised committee to review the deaths in the "drug war," as an attempt to evade UN scrutiny.

In September, the European Parliament overwhelmingly voted to adopt a resolution denouncing the "rapidly deteriorating human rights situation" in the Philippines and called on the Philippines to abide by its human rights commitment under the European Union's General Systems of Preference Plus program that allows the country to export 6,200 products to EU states without tariff. The resolution also called for dropping the cases against journalist Maria Ressa and Senator Leila de Lima, a longtime critic of Duterte who has been in pretrial detention for more than three years on bogus drug charges.

The International Criminal Court (ICC) continued its preliminary examination into alleged crimes against humanity related to the "drug war" killings. The Philippines withdrew from the court effective March 17, 2019, but the Office of the Prosecutor has indicated the court could still pursue crimes committed before that date, and it will continue to pursue its examination. UN human rights experts, among them Special Rapporteur on Extrajudicial Killings Agnès Callamard, have urged the ICC to prioritize completion of its examination.

In September, members of the US Congress introduced the Philippine Human Rights Act, which seeks to suspend US defense and security assistance to the Philippines for human rights abuses until the government undertakes significant reform. In order to lift the suspension, the US secretary of state would have to certify that the government had adequately investigated and successfully prosecuted members of the military and police forces who violated human rights; withdrawn the military from domestic policing activity; and established effective protection of trade unionists, journalists, human rights defenders, and government critics.

Poland

Presidential elections scheduled for March were postponed to July due to concerns over unfair campaigning as a result of movement restrictions due to the Covid-19 pandemic. Initial proposals by the ruling party to hold the elections in May via a hastily created mail-in voting system or to extend the incumbent president's term by two years raised concerns about free and fair elections. Observers from regional organizations concluded that the campaign was marred by cases of misuse of state resources, xenophobic, homophobic, and antisemitic rhetoric, and reporting by state-owned and pro-government media in favor of sitting president Andrzej Duda, a close ally of the ruling Law and Justice party. Duda won by a slim margin.

The conservative nationalist government continued to strengthen its grasp on the judiciary and to smear journalists critical of the ruling party. Attacks and harassment against lesbian, gay, bisexual, and transgender (LGBT) people increased, and several LGBT activists were arrested during the year and faced spurious charges.

Judicial Independence

The government continued its attacks on members of the judiciary. Judges and prosecutors are subject to arbitrary disciplinary proceedings for standing up for the rule of law and speaking up against problematic judicial reforms—an interference with their judicial independence.

In January, parliament adopted a law that could allow the firing of judges who carry out court rulings counter to the government's policies.

A Disciplinary Office, established in September 2018, by late June had brought 152 disciplinary proceedings against judges, of which 16 were pending before courts at time of writing. In October, the Disciplinary Chamber revoked the immunity of judge Beata Morawiec, suspended her from her official duties and halved her salary for alleged bribery. The judge, who denied all allegations and who is the head of a national judges' association, is known for being critical of the government's legal reforms and for defending the independence of the judiciary. In April, the Court of Justice of the European Union (CJEU) in an interim decision ordered the suspension of a 2017 law establishing the new disciplinary regime. A final judgment was due in the second half of 2020.

In its October Rule of Law report, the EU Commission raised concerns that the increasing influence of the executive over the justice system has put judicial independence at risk. It also flagged that civil society and other stakeholders were rarely consulted in the law-making process, instead subject to hostile statements by high-ranking ruling party officials.

In August, over 1,200 judges were under investigation for having signed a letter addressed to the Organisation for Security and Cooperation in Europe (OSCE) asking it to monitor the presidential elections in Poland.

In February, the Council of Europe Parliamentary Assembly voted to bring Poland under its monitoring mechanism, the first time in two decades that such steps have been taken against an EU member state. In August, a Dutch court suspended all extraditions to Poland due to concerns over lack of judicial independence, requesting the CJEU for guidance on the matter.

In January, the Council of Europe's Commissioner for Human Rights urged the Senate, the upper house in Poland's parliament, to reject the controversial bill curtailing the independence of judges and prosecutors and their freedom of expression.

Adam Bodnar's five-year term as Poland's commissioner for human rights ended in September. Bodnar was a frequent critic of the government's rule of law abuses and attacks on the LGBT community and women's rights and was often targeted due to his work. At time of writing, a battle between civil society and ruling party members for Bodnar's successor was underway. The Council of Europe's Venice Commission, Europe's top constitutional law expert body, in October expressed concerns about the "risk of paralysis" of the ombudsman's institution.

Freedom of Media, Pluralism

The government strengthened control over the press and continued its smear attacks on media outlets and journalists critical of the government and ruling party. In the lead up to June elections, Reporters Without Borders reported that the public service broadcaster in 97 percent of cases, portrayed President Duda in a positive light, while the opposition candidate in 87 percent of cases was portrayed in a negative light. In July, President Duda accused a German-owned broadcaster of interfering in the Polish elections due to an article criticizing the president for pardoning a convicted child abuser.

Following waves of dismissals in 2019 at the state-owned public broadcaster, in January, in what appeared to be a political move, the broadcaster fired two experienced independent journalists without providing reasons for their dismissals. Similarly, in May, a journalist working for the public broadcaster for 20 years was dismissed without reason.

Sexual Orientation and Gender Identity

The government ramped up its attacks on women's and LGBT rights, part of the government's increasing hostile rhetoric against what it refers to as "gender ideology."

In August, on the basis of an overly broad blasphemy law, police arrested several LGBT activists for placing rainbow flags on prominent public monuments. Polish police confirmed that they were investigating three activists for "insulting religious feelings and insulting Warsaw monuments." One activist, who was also arrested for defacing a truck carrying anti-LGBT slogans in June, spent three weeks in pretrial detention before being released following international pressure. The Council of Europe Commissioner for Human Rights, Council of Europe SOGI (Sexual Orientation and Gender Identity) Unit, and the European Parliament LGBTI Intergroup called on Polish authorities to release the activist immediately. Charges against the activist were pending at time of writing.

Elżbieta Podleśna, LGBT activist and artist, was arrested in May 2019 for possessing posters depicting the Virgin Mary with a rainbow halo, and faced criminal charges for "insulting religious feelings."

During his election campaign in early 2020, President Duda frequently made homophobic statements. In June, he stated that LGBT rights were an "ideology" more dangerous than communism and signed a "Family Charter" pledging to "defend children from LGBT ideology." In July, Duda stated that he would submit a bill for a constitutional amendment prohibiting the adoption of children by same-sex couples.

Authorities in one-third of Poland's cities have identified their localities as "LGBT Ideology Free Zones" although courts attempted in 2019 to curtail the anti-rights campaign. On August 6, an administrative court in Lublin annulled the anti-LGBT resolution of the Serniki Commune. In July, the European Commission announced that it would withhold development funding for six Polish municipalities in reaction to their insistence of retaining the label of an "LGBT-Free Zone." In March 2020, Polish authorities indicated they were planning to sue a group of LGBT rights activists who had created an "Atlas of Hate," which mapped anti-LGBT provisions that had been instituted across the country.

In a September statement, the UN human rights commissioner expressed her concerns about the continuing repression of LGBT people and activists.

Migration and Asylum

The European Court of Human Rights in July ruled that Poland had unlawfully refused entry to asylum seekers at the Poland-Belarus border. In March, Poland closed its border with Belarus in response to the Covid-19 pandemic, effectively making it impossible for people to access Polish territory to seek asylum.

Women's and Children's Rights

In July, the Minister of Justice declared that Poland would withdraw from the Council of Europe Convention on Preventing and Combating Violence against Women and Domestic Violence, claiming the Convention is "harmful" as it requires educators to teach children about gender. Earlier in the year, service providers reported that calls from domestic violence victims increased dramatically during the Covid-19 pandemic lockdown but that the government did not take measures to support prevention or ensure availability of services and appropriate police response.

Two controversial bills, "Stop Pedophilia," which would criminalize activities, educators and organizations providing sexuality education to children or information on sexual and reproductive health and rights, and "Stop Abortion," which would eliminate legal access to abortion in cases of severe or fatal fetal anomaly—further limiting what is already one of Europe's most restrictive abortion laws—were debated in parliament in April and subsequently sent to a committee for "further work." Both remained pending before parliament at time of writing. The bills sparked large street protests.

The Constitutional Tribunal, criticized for its lack of independence and legitimacy, ruled in October that access to abortion on the ground of "severe and irreversible fetal defect or incurable illness that threatens the fetus' life" was unconstitutional, making it virtually impossible for women to access legal abortion in Poland. The ruling triggered nationwide protests.

In February, in a submission to the Council of Europe Committee of Ministers responsible for monitoring implementation of European Court of Human Rights judgments, the Council of Europe's commissioner for human rights called on Poland to ensure women's access to lawful abortion.

In April, the commissioner urged the Polish parliament to reject bills restricting women's sexual and reproductive rights and children's right to comprehensive sexuality education.

HUMAN
RIGHTS
WATCH

"How Can We Work Without Wages?"
Salary Abuses Facing Migrant Workers Ahead of Qatar's FIFA World Cup 2022

Qatar

In September, Qatar introduced significant labor reforms allowing migrant workers to change jobs without employer permission and setting a higher and non-discriminatory minimum wage. Earlier, in January, Qatar extended the right to leave the country without employer permission to workers not covered by the labor law. However, certain elements of the kafala (sponsorship) system remain in place, facilitating abuse and exploitation of the country's large migrant workforce, and Qatari authorities' efforts to protect migrant workers' right to accurate and timely wages have largely proven unsuccessful. The Covid-19 pandemic further exposed and amplified the ways in which migrant workers' rights are violated.

In January, Qatar amended its penal code to further restrict the already-narrow space for free expression by setting criminal penalties for spreading "fake news" online. In that same month, Qatar issued a decision to lift the rule that Qatari women must have their guardian's permission to obtain a driving license. However, other male guardianship policies and discriminatory laws against women continue, including the policy requiring unmarried women under 25 to have male guardian permission before they travel abroad. In 2020, some women who had such permission or were over 25 were still asked to call their male guardian to confirm they had approval before they travelled. Lesbian, gay, bisexual, and transgender (LGBT) individuals continue to face discrimination.

Migrant Workers

Qatar has a migrant labor force of over 2 million people, who comprise approximately 95 percent of its total labor force. Approximately 1 million workers are employed in construction, while around 100,000 are domestic workers.

In March and April, Human Rights Watch and other international human rights organizations highlighted the unique risks Covid-19 poses to already-vulnerable migrant worker populations in Qatar and the Gulf, calling on governments to take several steps to adequately protect migrant workers from the spread of the virus, including in immigration detention, prison conditions, and labor accommodations.

In January, Qatar extended the right to leave the country without their employer's permission to migrant workers not covered by the labor law. The government had previously provided this right to most migrant workers in 2018, but not to those in government, oil and gas, agriculture, or domestic workers. However, employers can still apply for exceptions, and domestic workers are required to inform employers that they wish to leave at least 72 hours in advance.

In August, Qatar introduced legislation that allows all migrant workers to change jobs before the end of their contracts without first obtaining their employer's consent, one of the key aspects of the *kafala* (sponsorship) system that can give rise to forced labor. Qatar also amended certain provisions of the labor law to allow migrant workers to terminate their employment contracts at will, both during the probation period and after, as long as they notify their employers in writing within a prescribed notice period. In addition, Qatar passed a new law establishing a higher and non-discriminatory basic minimum wage and a national minimum wage commission to periodically review the amount taking into account economic factors, including economic growth, competitiveness, and productivity, as well as the needs of the workers and their families.

While positive, other abusive elements of the *kafala* system remain, namely that a migrant worker's legal status in Qatar remains tied to a specific employer, where an employer can apply, renew or cancel a worker's residency permit, and that "absconding," or leaving an employer without permission, remains a crime. Workers, especially low-paid laborers and domestic workers, often depend on the employer not just for their jobs, but for housing and food. Passport confiscations, high recruitment fees, and deceptive recruitment practices remain largely unpunished. Workers are banned from joining trade unions or striking. These remaining aspects of the *kafala* system continue to drive abuse, exploitation, and forced labor practices.

While the minimum wage and increase in penalties for wage abuse are important, this does not go far enough to tackle wage abuse. In August, a Human Rights Watch report found that employers frequently violated workers' right to wages and that mechanisms like the Wage Protection System did little to protect workers from wage abuse. These abuses only worsened during the Covid-19 pandemic.

Qatar continued to enforce a demonstrably rudimentary midday summer working hours ban. The heat stress guidelines are not comprehensive or obligatory for employers, and have no enforcement mechanisms. Moreover, for seven years, Qatar has not made public meaningful data on migrant worker deaths that would allow an assessment of the extent to which heat stress is a factor. Medical research published in July 2019 concluded that heatstroke is a likely cause of cardiovascular fatalities among migrant workers in Qatar.

Women's Rights

In January, the General Department on Traffic issued a decision in a letter to the Department of Licensing Affairs to stop requiring guardian permission for women to obtain driving licenses. While the authorities repealed this requirement in the traffic law in 2007, it continued to be imposed in practice. Some women have been able to obtain licenses without such permission, however some have expressed concern that it could easily be brought back as there is a lack of transparency due to unpublished rules.

The concept of male guardianship, which is incorporated into Qatari law, regulations and practices, undermines women's right to make autonomous decisions about their lives. Single Qatari women under 25 years of age must obtain their guardian's permission to travel outside Qatar. While married women at any age can travel abroad without permission, men can petition a court to prohibit their wives' travel. Qatari women are also prohibited from events and bars that serve alcohol, and unmarried Qatari women under 30 years old are not allowed to check into a hotel. Qatari women are also required to have guardian permission in order to work for some government ministries and institutions, and women who attend Qatar University face restrictions on their movements. Women cannot marry without their male guardian's permission regardless of age, while men can marry up to four wives without needing even their current wife's permission.

Qatar's personal status law also discriminates against women in marriage, divorce, child custody, and inheritance. Women are required to obey their husbands and can lose their husband's financial support if they work or travel against their wishes. Men have a unilateral right to divorce while women must apply to the courts for divorce on limited grounds. Under inheritance provisions, female siblings receive half the amount their brothers get.

While the family law forbids husbands from hurting their wives physically or morally, and there are general criminal code provisions on assault, Qatar has no law on domestic violence to help prevent domestic violence, measures to protect survivors and prosecute their abusers.

Qatar allows men to pass citizenship to their spouses and children, whereas children of Qatari women and non-citizen men can only apply for citizenship under narrow conditions. This discriminates against Qatari women married to foreigners, and their children and spouses. In 2018, Qatar passed a permanent residency law that permits children of Qatari women married to non-Qatari men, among others, to apply for permanent residency, allowing them to receive government health and educational services, invest in the economy, and own real estate. However, some have complained that they have not received a response to their application. The law falls short of granting women equal rights to men in conferring nationality to their children and spouses.

Freedom of Expression

In January, Qatar introduced an amendment to its penal code that imposes up to five years in prison for spreading rumors or false news with ill-intent. The new text does not define who determines what is a rumor or "fake news," how to make such a determination, or what standards are to be used in doing so. It also fails to require that the information in question causes real harm to a legitimate interest.

Qatar's penal code criminalizes criticizing the emir, insulting Qatar's flag, defaming religion, including blasphemy, and inciting "to overthrow the regime." Qatar's 2014 cybercrimes law already criminalizes spreading "false news" on the internet (a term that is not defined) and also provides for a maximum of three years in prison for anyone convicted of posting online content that "violates social values or principles," or "insults or slanders others."

Statelessness

Qatar's decision to arbitrarily strip families from the Ghufran clan of their citizenship starting in 1996 has left some members still stateless 20 years later and deprived them of key human rights. In 2020, Qatar made no commitments to rectify their status.

Stateless members of the Ghufran clan are deprived of their rights to work, access to health care, education, marriage and starting a family, owning property, and freedom of movement. Without valid identity documents, they face restrictions accessing basic services, including opening bank accounts and acquiring drivers' licenses, and are at risk of arbitrary detention. Those living in Qatar are also denied a range of government benefits afforded to Qatari citizens, including state jobs, food and energy subsidies, and free basic healthcare.

Sexual Orientation and Morality Laws

Qatar's penal code criminalizes sodomy, punishing same-sex relations with imprisonment between one to three years. Individuals convicted of *zina* (sex outside of marriage) can be sentenced to prison. In addition to imprisonment, Muslims can be sentenced to flogging (if unmarried) or the death penalty (if married) for zina. These laws disproportionately impact women, as pregnancy serves as evidence of extramarital sex and women who report rape can find themselves prosecuted for consensual sex.

Under article 296 of the penal code, "[l]eading, instigating or seducing a male in any manner for sodomy or dissipation" and "[i]nducing or seducing a male or a female in any manner to commit illegal or immoral actions" is punishable by up to three years. The law does not penalize the person who is "instigated" or "enticed." It is unclear whether this law is intended to prohibit all same-sex acts between men, and whether only one partner is considered legally liable.

Journalists and printers operate under section 47 of the 1979 Press and Publications Law, which bans publication of "any printed matter that is deemed contrary to the ethics, violates the morals or harms the dignity of the people or their personal freedoms." In 2018, private publishing partners in Qatar, including the partner of the *New York Times*, censored numerous articles that touched on LGBT topics.

Key International Actors

Throughout 2020, the diplomatic crisis persisted between Qatar on one side and Saudi Arabia, Bahrain, Egypt, and the United Arab Emirates on the other, over Qatar's alleged support of terrorism and ties with Iran.

Qatar hosted talks between the United States and the Taliban in Afghanistan that led to the February 29 peace agreement between the two adversaries aimed at ending the nearly 19-year-old Afghan war.

On September 1, the European Union issued a statement welcoming Qatar's re-cent labor reforms and calling for further improvements of the legal framework covering workers' rights in Qatar.

Russia

The Covid-19 pandemic provided a pretext for Russian authorities to restrict human rights in many areas, and to introduce new restrictions, especially over privacy rights.

Constitutional reform was a key development in 2020. Several abusive laws found further legal entrenchment in constitutional amendments. Following a controversial plebiscite on the reform in summer 2020, authorities launched a crackdown on dissenting voices, with new, politically motivated prosecutions and raids on the homes and offices of political and civic activists and organizations. Towards the end of the year, the government submitted a series of new bills expanding on Russia's "foreign agent law" and shrinking an already scarce space left for civic activism.

The poisoning of Russian political opposition leader Alexey Navalny in August led to a further deterioration in Russia's relations with the European Union.

Covid-19

In April, new harsher penalties were introduced for spreading information, including about the epidemic, deemed to be false, ranging from fines to three years' imprisonment. Within three months, according to one estimate, authorities opened at least 170 administrative and 42 criminal cases for allegedly spreading false information online about Covid-19.

Healthcare workers faced shortages of personal protective equipment, particularly in the first months of the pandemic. By June, at least 400 medical workers had died of Covid-19. In some cases, those who spoke out about the shortages faced retaliation, losing their jobs and/or facing charges of spreading false information.

Many regions introduced a pass system that required people to obtain permission online or through SMS to leave the immediate vicinity of their houses. Moscow city authorities also introduced an app to track the whereabouts of people exposed to or infected with Covid-19 or displaying symptoms of respiratory disease. The app automatically issued fines that in many cases were wrong. After protracted public outcry, several improvements were introduced. For example, the app no longer issues push notifications at night demanding an immediate selfie as proof of compliance with self-isolation. Authorities also used the city's vast network of surveillance cameras with facial recognition technology to identify and punish people for violating lockdown restrictions.

Authorities failed to publish regular and transparent information on Covid-19 outbreaks in nursing homes or institutions for people with disabilities.

Many Moscow hospitals suspended provision of legal abortion during the pandemic, even though it is an essential time-sensitive medical procedure that cannot be delayed.

Covid-19 related measures affected Russia's 16.5 million schoolchildren. More than one-third of schoolchildren reported experiencing depression due to self-isolation and distance learning, according to an official survey of primary and secondary school students.

Russian authorities coordinated at least one repatriation flight for detained migrants, but about 8,000 migrants remained stuck in detention centers at the start of the pandemic, since their deportations were not possible due to travel restrictions.

Freedom of Expression

In several cases, authorities resorted to wrongful prosecutions against journalists on terrorism and treason-related charges and other tactics aimed at interfering with their journalistic work.

In July, journalist Svetlana Prokopyeva was sentenced to a hefty fine on bogus terrorism charges for arguing that Russia's repressive policies on speech and assembly radicalized youth. Due to the verdict, she remains on the government's list of "terrorists and extremists" and is barred from foreign travel.

Ivan Safronov was arrested on dubious treason charges relating to the time when he worked as a journalist. Amended in 2012, the treason clause in the criminal code is vague and overly broad.

Authorities refused to investigate an incident in which police broke the arm of journalist David Frenkel, who was reporting from a voting precinct during the constitutional plebiscite. Instead, Frenkel was fined on three different counts over the same incident.

In July and September police searched the offices of MBKh Media, an opposition media outlet, allegedly in connection with the 2003 Yukos case, confiscating computers and other devices.

Dozens of journalists were detained while covering peaceful protests in Moscow and other cities, even when they wore press badges and other identification.

Authorities also targeted artists whose work touched on sensitive issues. In June, theater director and dissident, Kirill Serebrennikov, received a hefty fine and conditional prison sentence on dubious embezzlement charges. In January, a stand-up comedian fled the country after authorities opened an investigation into his comedy, following a complaint that it offended religious feelings.

In August, a court sentenced Alexander Shabarchin to two years' imprisonment on hooliganism charges for placing, in a public square, a life-sized doll with President Vladimir Putin's face and signs reading "Liar" and "War Criminal." At time of writing, Karim Yamadayev was on trial on charges of insult and "justification of terrorism" over a web video of a mock trial against Putin and other officials.

By March 2020, 12 months after a law banning "disrespect to authorities" was adopted, an independent group found that the overwhelming majority of such charges involved alleged insults against Putin.

In July, a court fined Ivan Zhdanov, head of the Anti-Corruption Fund (FBK), associated with opposition politician Alexey Navalny, for failure to comply with a court order to take down a video from YouTube alleging corruption by Dmitry Medvedev during the time he was prime minister.

Freedom of Assembly

Using Covid-19 as a pretext, authorities banned all mass gatherings. Police interfered with single-person protests, which do not require approval, in some cases referring to the social distancing and mandatory mask regime even when protesters wore masks. Authorities prosecuted single-person picketers, alleging they were part of a "mass protest." While other restrictions were gradually eased through the summer and authorities permitted officially sponsored mass outdoor festivals, peaceful protests remained effectively outlawed. In June, July, and August, police detained dozens of peaceful protesters.

In August, police opened a criminal case against Yuliya Galyamina, a Moscow municipal assembly member, on charges of repeatedly participating in unsanctioned but peaceful protests. At time of writing, a trial in her case was ongoing. Konstantin Kotov, sentenced in 2019 on such charges to four years' imprisonment, remained behind bars.

Mass protests started in Khabarovsk in July and were continuing at time of writing, sparked by the dismissal and arrest of the region's governor. Initially, authorities did not attempt to disperse the protests albeit police occasionally detaining some activists involved in these protests, as well as their supporters in other cities, and courts fined or sentenced them to short-term detention on charges of violating public assembly regulations.

However, in October, police beat and arbitrarily detained over 20 peaceful protesters. One of them faces charges of repeatedly participating in unsanctioned but peaceful protests. At least three others were under investigation for alleged low-grade violence against police, which can lead to sentences of up to five years in prison. Other protesters were charged with administrative offenses for taking part in an "unsanctioned gathering."

In June, the Constitutional Court ruled that the list of venues where protests are prohibited is overly broad and unconstitutional.

In November, two news bills concerning peaceful assemblies were introduced to parliament. One proposes to further restrict venues where assemblies can be held and to deem single-person pickets, if held in sequence, a mass event, thus requiring prior authorization. The other proposes restricting sources of donations and placing onerous requirements and obligations on organizers.

Human Rights Defenders

In July, police indicted human rights lawyer Semyon Simonov, holding him personally accountable for an unpaid fine issued against his human rights organization over alleged non-compliance with Russia's abusive "foreign agents" law.

Also in July, a court sentenced human rights historian, Yuri Dmitriev, to three-and-a-half years' imprisonment on apparently spurious and politically motivated charges of sexual abuse of a child. In September, an appeals court increased his sentence to 13 years.

In September, Svetlana Anokhina, who runs Daptar, an online women's rights platform in the Northern Caucasus, was forced to leave Russia because of death threats, which the authorities failed to investigate.

In December, authorities informed Vanessa Kogan, the director of Stichting Justice Initiative, a human rights litigation organization, that her residence permit was revoked. They gave her two weeks to leave Russia, where she had lived for 11 years with her family, who are Russian nationals.

Freedom of Association

Russian authorities raided the offices of independent groups under various pretexts and targeted their staff and affiliates, including under the "foreign agents" and "undesirable foreign organizations" laws.

Courts found Maxim Vernikov and Yana Antonova guilty of involvement with an "undesirable organization" and sentenced them to several hundred hours of mandatory labor over their association with Open Russia Civic Movement. The trial against Anastasiya Shevchenko on similar charges resumed in fall. Shevchenko has been under house arrest since January 2019. In July and September, police raided the offices of Open Russia and the apartments of several staff members. Two new cases were opened for alleged involvement with Open Russia against Mikhail Iosilevich, in October, and Leonid Malyavin, in November.

Two prominent Russian rights organizations were fined under the "foreign agents" law. The combined amount of fines against Memorial by mid-2020 was 5.3 million rubles (approximately US$69,000). Public Verdict, which documents police abuse, accumulated over one million rubles (US$15,000)

In November, at least five new bills were submitted to parliament that further expand the scope of organizations and individuals that can be designated a "foreign agent." They also restrict the rights of such organizations and impose on them additional reporting obligations and requirements on displaying the label "foreign agent".

Chechnya

Chechnya's leadership continued its onslaught against all forms of dissent and criticism.

In February, a group of thugs violently attacked human rights lawyer Marina Dubrovina and investigative journalist Elena Milashina shortly after a court hearing against Dubrovina's client, a blogger who had criticized the opulent lifestyle of Chechnya's governor, Ramzan Kadyrov. The women documented their injuries and filed a police report, describing the attacks as work-related. There was no effective investigation.

In September, a video circulated on social media showing 19-year-old Salman Tepsurkayev being forced to penetrate himself anally with a glass bottle in retaliation for "spread[ing] lies" about Chechen authorities. Tepsurkayev moderated the Telegram channel 1ADAT, which routinely features Chechen dissident voices, including those critical of Kadyrov. At time of writing, he remains disappeared and authorities have not opened an investigation.

A prominent Chechen separatist politician in exile, Akhmed Zakaev, made a statement condemning the torture and expressing support of 1Adat. Chechen authorities immediately forced Zakaev's relatives to publicly renounce him.

In June, 1ADAT extensively covered the suspicious death of Madina Umaeva, a victim of domestic violence, and published a video of Kadyrov forcing Umaeva's mother to apologize on camera for seeking justice for her daughter's killing. Authorities refused to open a criminal investigation into Umaeva's death.

Counterterrorism

Courts issued guilty verdicts in several terrorism or extremism cases marred by allegations of torture, dubious expert analysis, and reliance on secret witnesses.

In December 2019, 11 people were sentenced to prison terms ranging from 19 years to life over the 2017 St. Petersburg metro bombing. Russian authorities never investigated credible complaints of torture and fabricated evidence.

In February and June, in two separate trials, courts issued guilty verdicts, with prison terms ranging from five to 18 years, against nine defendants for alleged involvement in "Network," which prosecutors claimed was a terrorist organization. Most defendants insisted that no such organization existed. Authorities dismissed without proper investigation defendants' torture complaints. The judges accepted testimonies by secret witnesses and allegedly rigged evidence.

In August, seven defendants were convicted for establishing an "extremist organization," New Greatness. Sentences ranged from four years' probation to seven years in prison. The defendants complained security officials had entrapped them. The prosecution relied on secret witnesses' testimony. Torture complaints by one of the defendants were dismissed without a full investigation.

In June, three 14-year old boys were detained and later charged with creating a terrorist organization and planning to blow up an FSB building in the computer game, Minecraft. One of them refused to plead guilty and has been in pretrial detention since summer.

Russian authorities continued to prosecute people over alleged involvement in Hizb-ut-Tahrir (HuT), a pan-Islamist movement that seeks to establish a caliphate but denounces violence to achieve that goal. Russia banned HuT as a terrorist organization in 2003.

In February, 11 defendants in two separate military trials received prison sentences ranging from 11 to 23 years. In September, in a separate case, the Supreme Court upheld sentences ranging from 10 to 24 years for 21 men. At least one of the convicted alleged he had been tortured to extract a confession. Five more men were detained over alleged involvement in HuT in November in Tatarstan.

In August, a military court sentenced opposition writer Airat Dilmukhametov to nine years' imprisonment on extremism, separatism, and justification of terrorism charges for a legitimate speech. He appealed the verdict.

Neither the charges against Dilmukhametov nor against the 32 HuT defendants related to planning, carrying out or abetting any act of violence for political or ideological aims.

Authorities continued to prosecute people over affiliation with religious groups designated extremist under Russia's overly broad counter-extremism law.

In 2020, courts handed guilty verdicts to dozens of people for their religious activity as Jehovah's Witnesses banned as extremist in Russia. At least eight people are currently serving prison terms of up to six years, while 417 remain under criminal investigation, and 35 are in pretrial detention. These figures include people arrested in Russia-occupied Crimea.

Authorities arrested at least four people for supposed affiliation with Nurdzhular, a group of followers of the late Turkish theologian Said Nursi, banned as extremist in 2008, even though it has no history of incitement or violence. Experts repeatedly questioned the existence of such an organization in Russia and stated that the works of Said Nursi do not contain any extremist views. At least seven Nursi followers remain on Russia's "List of Terrorists and Extremists," their assets frozen, and travel restricted.

Yevgeniy Kim, stripped of his Russian citizenship in 2019 following his prison sentence on charges of alleged involvement with Nurdzhular, remained in deportation custody. Authorities stripped two Jehovah's Witnesses currently serving sentences on extremism charges of their citizenship in 2020. All three are now stateless.

Right to Asylum, Prohibition of Refoulement

In July and September, authorities forcibly removed at least four asylum seekers to Tajikistan and Uzbekistan despite the risk of torture, pending appeals of their rejected asylum claims, and injunctions against their removal issued by the European Court on Human Rights (ECtHR).

At time of writing, at least 39 current or rejected asylum seekers remained in what amounts to indefinite detention in Russia. The ECtHR enjoined their removal due to torture or inhuman treatment if returned to their home countries, and Russia has suspended removal pending the ECtHR judgment but is also not considering alternatives to detention.

Environment and Human Rights

In May, a subsidiary of Russian mining giant Nornickel spilled over 20,000 tons of diesel fuel in Russia's Arctic, contaminating 180,000 square meters of land before reaching nearby rivers. Two days after the incident, Nornickel publicly acknowledged the spill.

Rosprirodnadzor, the government's natural resource management agency, sued Nornickel for 148 billion rubles (US$2 billion) for environmental damage. National security and police attempted to suppress a journalist's investigation into the spill. A whistleblower from Rosprirodnadzor stated that Nornickel's security tried to prevent him from accessing the site and intimidated him. An official representative of the indigenous peoples of the North expressed concern that the spill could affect access to food for local indigenous peoples who rely on fishing and hunting.

In July, authorities adopted a new law that exempts contractors from carrying out environmental impact assessments for all "transportation infrastructure modernization projects." The new law and relevant bylaws could affect Lake Baikal, a UNESCO World Heritage site and other protected areas.

In January, after more than a year of continued protests against the construction of a waste dumping site in Shiyes, in Arkhangelsk region, a court ruled the construction illegal.

The contracting company lost an appeal against the ruling in October, but even before the verdict had announced it would cancel the project and restore the land by the end of the year. However, authorities did not drop charges against local activists who had been beaten, detained, prosecuted, and fined for protesting the illegal construction.

After weeks of protests in Bashkortostan against what local activists said was destructive limestone mining, authorities granted the area protected status and construction stopped. Authorities did not drop charges against peaceful protesters who suffered police brutality, detention, fines, and prosecution.

Nondiscrimination, National Minorities, Xenophobia

The Black Lives Matter protests in the US following the police killing of George Floyd sparked debate in the Russian press and social media about racism and discrimination in the country. A biracial Russian vlogger who discussed racism and racist violence in Russia faced threats and online bullying. Authorities responded by cautioning her against "spreading extremist materials."

According to a watchdog organization, the first eight months of 2020 saw at least 23 hate crimes, with one fatality, and at least 17 episodes of hate-motivated vandalism.

Migrants continued to encounter racial profiling, mass arbitrary detentions, police brutality, and xenophobia. Some Russian officials falsely claimed that crime by migrants had risen in the wake of the economic downturn caused by the pandemic. Authorities used this as a pretext to propose a mandatory, intrusive tracking app for migrants and tying migrant workers' visas to their employers.

Sexual Orientation and Gender Identity

The government continued its trajectory of homophobic discrimination and used the "gay propaganda" ban to justify a criminal prosecution.

Lesbian, gay, bisexual, and transgender (LGBT) activist Yulia Tsvetkova faces six years in prison on pornography charges for posting body-positive drawings of nude women on social media. In December 2019, a court fined Tsvetkova 50,000 rubles (US$665) for violating the "gay propaganda" law over LGBT-friendly and feminist posts in two social media groups which she administered.

As a result of the 2020 constitutional reform, the definition of marriage as a union between a man and a woman was incorporated into the constitution. A bill submitted to parliament includes a ban on same-sex marriage and changes that will negatively affect transgender people's rights, including to marry and raise children.

Gender-Based Violence

Serious gaps continued in the official response to widespread domestic violence, including lack of sufficient protection and recourse for survivors.

The draft law on domestic violence, introduced in December 2019, fell short of providing a comprehensive definition of domestic violence. It also failed to address several issues crucial to ensuring effective protection for survivors. In early 2020, parliament deprioritized the draft law's review, and it remained pending.

Several politicians and experts advocating for a robust domestic violence law reported threats against them and their families, including by those claiming to promote "traditional" or "family" values.

Russia's ombudsperson noted that domestic violence spiked during the Covid-19 pandemic, with reported cases more than doubling during the spring lockdown.

Digital Rights, Right to Privacy

In 2020, Russia tightened control over internet infrastructure and online content, expanding the capacity of authorities to filter and block online content in violation of the rights to freedom of expression and access to information.

These restrictions built on other internet censorship measures, such as legislative amendments in December 2019 required manufacturers to pre-install Russian apps, including browsers, messengers and maps on smartphones, computers, and Smart TVs sold in Russia.

In June 2020, a new law created a national digital repository of personal data, including employment and foreign residency information, of Russia's residents, accessible to law enforcement, tax and other government agencies. The creation of a centralized repository of personal data raises concern that it would be vulnerable to data leaks and breaches and other violations of the right to privacy. It is to become fully functional by 2025.

In November, a new bill was submitted to the parliament that would give authorities power to block websites that have censored Russian state media content; among the websites mentioned are Twitter, Facebook and YouTube.

Right to Health

In March, people with cystic fibrosis and their supporters protested a new government policy substituting original drugs with generic analogues, despite warnings from doctors about questionable effectiveness and reported severe side effects from the generic drugs.

In several 2020 cases concerning Russian children, the ECtHR issued urgent in-junctions, under Rule 39 of the European Convention on Human Rights (ECHR), instructing authorities to provide access to a life-saving drug meant to halt the progression of spinal muscular atrophy. In August, the Russian Ministry of Health included the drug in the federal list of vital medicines.

Russia and Crimea (see also Ukraine chapter)

Russian authorities continued to conscript males in occupied Crimea to serve in Russian armed forces, in violation of international humanitarian law, and im-posed criminal penalties against those who refused to serve.

Authorities continued to bring unfounded, politically motivated terrorism charges against Crimean Tatars. In September, a Russian military court sen-tenced seven Crimean Tatar activists to prison terms ranging from 13 to 19 years for alleged association with HuT. The organization is legal in Ukraine. One man was acquitted.

Russia and Syria (see also Syria chapter)

The Syrian-Russian military alliance continued to deliberately and indiscrimi-nately attack civilian infrastructure, including schools, hospitals, markets, homes, and shelters, through what has become trademark tactics over the years, including the use of internationally banned weapons.

Human Rights Watch documented 18 unlawful attacks in Idlib between January and March 2020, before a ceasefire was put into place. These 18 attacks dam-aged and destroyed six schools, one kindergarten, four healthcare facilities, three housing areas, two industrial sites, one market, one prison, and three camps for the displaced. The attacks killed at least 112 people and wounded at least another 359. Cluster munitions were used in two of the attacks, which were on one primary school and one secondary school in Idlib City in February 2020. At least three of the attacks were carried out by the Russian military. The attacks constituted apparent war crimes and may amount to crimes against humanity.

In 2019, Russia cast its 14th veto on Syria to block cross-border aid to northeast Syria, an area that is under the control of Kurdish-led groups. It also attempted to block funding for United Nations (UN) investigations into grave abuses in

Syria. Russia also tried to block funding for a unit at the Organisation for the Pro-hibition of Chemical Weapons tasked with identifying those responsible for chemical weapons attacks in Syria.

In February, Russia repatriated 25 orphans held as family members of Islamic State (ISIS) suspects in northeast Syria. In August-September, another 41 chil-dren were repatriated.

Key International Actors

The EU strongly condemned the poisoning of Navalny as an assassination at-tempt. The foreign ministries of France and Germany issued a joint communique that condemned the poisoning and noted this was not an isolated incident of the use of Novichok nerve agent. The UN High Commissioner for Human Rights (UNHCR) called for an independent and impartial investigation.

In June, the Council of Europe's (CoE) Venice Commission issued an opinion on the then-draft constitutional amendments. The commission reiterated its opin-ion that giving the Constitutional Court the power to declare a judgment of ECtHR non-executable, a position enshrined in the amendments, contradicts Russia's obligations under the ECHR.

The EU called on Russian authorities to condemn and investigate threats by Chechen authorities against Milashina, and to ensure her safety. The EU also called for criminal charges against Prokopyeva to be dropped and urged Russian authorities to "ensure that journalists can work in a safe environment without fear of reprisal."

In July, UN special rapporteur for human rights defenders and the CoE Human Rights Commissioner expressed concern over the criminal prosecution of Si-monov.

The EU condemned listing the European Endowment for Democracy (EED) as an "undesirable organization" and urged the Russian authorities to bring its legisla-tion in line with European and international human rights law.

In July, the EU called for the release of historian Yuri Dmitriev immediately and unconditionally, on humanitarian grounds, taking into account his age and state of health in the light of the coronavirus pandemic.

Rwanda

The ruling Rwandan Patriotic Front (RPF) continued to target those perceived as a threat to the government during 2020. Several high-profile government critics were arrested or threatened. Authorities failed to conduct credible investigations into the suspicious death in police custody of well-known singer and activist, Kizito Mihigo, in February.

Arbitrary detention, ill-treatment, and torture in official and unofficial detention facilities continued. Fair trial standards were routinely flouted in many sensitive political cases, in which security-related charges are often used to prosecute prominent government critics.

Rwanda continued to host tens of thousands of refugees, mainly from neighboring countries, as well as several hundred asylum seekers transferred from Libya. In August, the government began implementing, with the United Nations refugee agency, the first organized voluntary repatriation of refugees from Rwanda to Burundi.

Political Space and Freedom of Expression

The arrest and detention of Paul Rusesabagina, a prominent critic of the RPF, which started as an enforced disappearance, raised grave concerns over his ability to receive a fair trial in Rwanda. Rusesabagina, who fled to Belgium in 1996 and is now a Belgian citizen, was living in the United States when he traveled from the US to Dubai, United Arab Emirates, on August 27. He was forcibly disappeared on or about the evening of August 27 until the Rwanda Investigation Bureau (RIB) announced it had Rusesabagina in custody in Kigali, Rwanda, on August 31. Rusesabagina's family members were not able to speak with him until September 8, and it is disputed whether he was able to hire lawyers of his choosing. His trial was ongoing at time of writing.

On February 17, police announced that Kizito Mihigo had been found dead in his cell at the Remera Police Station in Kigali in an alleged suicide, four days after his arrest near the border with Burundi. Shortly before his death, he told Human Rights Watch that he was being threatened and told to provide false testimony against political opponents, and that he wanted to flee the country because he feared for his safety. Rwandan authorities issued a statement on February 26 concluding that Mihigo died by strangulation in a probable suicide, but failed to make details of the investigation public or meet standards expected for an investigation into a death in custody. In 2015, Mihigo had been sentenced to 10 years in prison on allegations including the formation of a criminal gang, conspiracy to murder, and conspiracy against the established government or the president, but was released in September 2018 after a presidential pardon.

On December 27, 2019, the Rwandan Court of Appeal upheld the conviction of two former military officials, although the court reduced their sentences to 15 years each. Col. Tom Byabagamba and retired Brig. Gen. Frank Rusagara were sentenced to 21 and 20 years in prison respectively by the Military High Court of Kanombe in 2016, on charges including inciting insurrection and tarnishing the government's image.

Prosecutors accused them of criticizing the government. The Court of Appeal failed to investigate allegations of torture and witness tampering made during the trial. After Byabagamba and Rusagara's lawyers filed an application with the East African Court of Justice, new charges were brought against Byabagamba, who was then accused of attempting to bribe his way out of prison. Between April 15 and 17, 2020, three people connected to Byabagamba were arrested and accused of helping him escape. Two were released in April, and the third was released in July.

Throughout the year, the RIB carried out house searches, seized property, including electronic equipment, and repeatedly called in for questioning Victoire Ingabire, the former president of the FDU-Inkingi opposition party who formed a new party, the Dalfa-Umurinzi, in November 2019. In a trial concluded on January 23, 2020, seven members of Ingabire's party were convicted of charges including complicity in forming or joining an irregular armed force, and handed sentences ranging from seven to ten years' imprisonment.

Three others—Théophile Ntirutwa, Venant Abayisenga, and Léonille Gasengayire—were acquitted of all charges and released. After their release, they gave video interviews to local YouTube channels detailing their pretrial detention and alleging ill-treatment and torture, including in Kwa Gacinya, an unofficial deten-

HUMAN
RIGHTS
WATCH

"As Long as We Live on the Streets,
They Will Beat Us"
Rwanda's Abusive Detention of Children

tion facility in the Gikondo neighborhood of Kigali, and in Mageragere and Nyanza prisons.

Abayisenga was reported missing in June, and is feared forcibly disappeared, after going out to buy phone credit. Ntirutwa was rearrested following an attack at his shop in Rwamagana District on May 11. On May 18, Ntirutwa and three others at his shop at the time of the attack were charged with offenses including murder, theft, and "spreading false information with intent to create a hostile international opinion against the Rwandan State." At time of writing, they were awaiting trial.

Freedom of Media

State interference and intimidation have forced many civil society actors and journalists to stop working on sensitive political or human rights issues. Most print and broadcast media continued to be heavily dominated by pro-government views. Independent civil society organizations are very weak, and few document and expose human rights violations by state agents.

In March, four bloggers who reported on alleged rapes by security forces and negative impacts of government directives to counter the spread of Covid-19 on vulnerable populations were arrested in circumstances that appeared retaliatory. In the months prior to their arrest, they also shared testimonies about a long-standing dispute with authorities over land evictions in Bannyahe, a poor neighborhood of Kigali.

On April 8, RIB and police agents arrested Valentin Muhirwa and David Byiringiro, two bloggers with Afrimax TV, in Kangondo II, a neighborhood of Kigali. Two residents said the bloggers had requested permission from the local leader to distribute food and goods after hearing about the population's struggles, but RIB and police agents arrested the men, accusing them of violating government directives and organizing an unauthorized distribution.

On April 12, RIB tweeted confirmation of the arrest of Théoneste Nsengimana, the owner of Umubavu TV, for alleged fraud. RIB accused him of promising 20,000 Rwandan Francs (US$21) to people to say they were receiving assistance from abroad.

The Rwanda Media Commission said in a statement on April 13 that none of the detained bloggers were arrested in retaliation for their work and that online bloggers, such as those using YouTube, are not journalists and are "not authorized to interview the population." Muhirwa and Byiringiro were released in April. Nsengimana, released in May, was awaiting trial at time of writing.

On April 15, Dieudonné Niyonsenga, also known as Cyuma Hassan, the owner of Ishema TV, was arrested with his driver, Fidèle Komezusenge. RIB accused Niyonsenga of violating the lockdown measures and giving Komezusenge an unauthorized press pass. According to the Committee to Protect Journalists, they were charged with forgery and claiming to be journalists. Their trial was ongoing at time of writing.

Arbitrary Detention of Street Children

Transit centers in Rwanda are governed by a 2017 law establishing the National Rehabilitation Service, which states that anyone exhibiting "deviant behaviors" can be held for up to two months, without any other further legal justification or oversight. In January 2020, Human Rights Watch found that the new legislation provides cover for the police to continue to round up and arbitrarily detain children in deplorable and degrading conditions at Gikondo Transit Center. In February, the UN Committee on the Rights of the Child called for a halt to arbitrary detention of children in transit centers in Rwanda, for investigations into allegations of ill-treatment—including beatings—and for amendments to the legal framework that regularizes this abuse.

Covid-19

Rwandan authorities reacted swiftly and aggressively to the threat of the global Covid-19 pandemic. Police arrested over 70,000 people for infractions related to the measures introduced in March to prevent the spread of Covid-19, including a curfew, the closure of bars of restaurants, and restrictions on movement. Authorities accused people of violating the measures and detained people in stadiums without due process or legal authority. Schools were closed for at least six months, starting in March, due to the pandemic, affecting about 3.4 million children.

International Justice

The arrest of Félicien Kabuga, one of the alleged masterminds of the Rwandan genocide, in France in May marked a major step toward justice for genocide victims and survivors. Kabuga is charged by an international war crimes court with genocide and related crimes during the 1994 genocide, and was living in France under a false identity at the time of his arrest.

Kabuga had evaded arrest since 1997, when he was first indicted by prosecutors with the International Criminal Tribunal for Rwanda (ICTR). On September 30, 2020, a French court ordered Kabuga's transfer to the International Residual Mechanism for Criminal Tribunals (IRMCT), which was established to handle the outstanding functions of the ICTR and the International Criminal Tribunal for the Former Yugoslavia as those tribunals closed. The mechanism has branches in Arusha, Tanzania, and The Hague, the Netherlands.

In May, the IRMCT announced that the remains of another high profile genocide suspect— Augustin Bizimana, the minister of defense at the time of the killings— were identified in a grave in Pointe-Noire, Republic of Congo. He is thought to have died around August 2000. In 1998, the ICTR indicted Bizimana on 13 counts of genocide and other related crimes.

In August 2020, Rwandan judicial authorities issued an international arrest warrant against Aloys Ntiwiragabo, the former head of military intelligence during the genocide, after media revealed in July that he was hiding in France. France opened a probe into alleged crimes against humanity by Ntiwiragabo after his whereabouts were revealed. Ntiwiragabo had previously been the subject of arrest warrants, including by the ICTR.

Saudi Arabia

Saudi Arabia held the presidency of the G20 in 2020 despite the country's long-standing human rights abuses, but the Covid-19 pandemic forced authorities to turn G20 events, including the leaders' summit, into virtual forums.

Authorities failed to hold high level officials accountable for suspected involvement in the murder of Saudi journalist Jamal Khashoggi in 2018. Instead, a Saudi court sentenced eight lower level operatives found responsible for the murder to prison terms of 7-20 years in a trial that lacked transparency. The court originally sentenced five of the eight men to death in December 2019, but the penalties were later reduced.

In August, former Saudi intelligence official Saad al-Jabri filed a lawsuit against Saudi Crown Prince Mohammed bin Salman in a United States court alleging that the crown prince sent a hit squad to murder him in Canada in 2018. Saudi authorities detained two of al-Jabri's adult children in March and held them incommunicado in an apparent effort to coerce al-Jabri to return to Saudi Arabia.

Through 2020, the Saudi-led coalition continued a military campaign against the Houthi rebel group in Yemen that has included scores of unlawful airstrikes that have killed and wounded thousands of civilians.

Freedom of Expression, Association, and Belief

Saudi authorities in 2020 continued to repress dissidents, human rights activists, and independent clerics. Prominent women's rights activists detained in 2018 remained in detention while on trial for their women's rights advocacy, including Loujain al-Hathloul, Mayaa al-Zahrani, Samar Badawi, Nouf Abdulaziz, and Nassima al-Sadah.

Capital trials continued against detainees on charges that related to nothing more than peaceful activism and dissent. By November, those on trial facing the death penalty included prominent cleric Salman al-Awda, whose charges were connected to his alleged ties with the Muslim Brotherhood and public support for imprisoned dissidents, as well as Hassan Farhan al-Maliki on vague charges relating to the expression of his peaceful religious ideas.

Authorities detained prominent royal family members in 2020, including former Crown Prince Mohammed bin Nayef and former Saudi Red Crescent head Faisal bin Abdullah, and held them incommunicado. Their legal status remained unclear at the time of writing.

In March, Saudi Arabia opened a mass trial of 68 Jordanians and Palestinians detained beginning in 2018 on vague allegations of links with a "terrorist organization." Family members of defendants described a range of abuses by Saudi authorities following the arrests, including enforced disappearances, long-term solitary confinement, and torture.

Over a dozen prominent activists convicted on charges arising from their peaceful activities were serving long prison sentences. Prominent activist Waleed Abu al-Khair continued to serve a 15-year sentence that the Specialized Criminal Court imposed on him after convicting him in 2014 on charges stemming solely from his peaceful criticism in media interviews and on social media of human rights abuses.

With few exceptions, Saudi Arabia does not tolerate public worship by adherents of religions other than Islam and systematically discriminates against Muslim religious minorities, notably Twelver Shia and Ismailis, including in public education, the justice system, religious freedom, and employment.

Saudi Arabia has no written laws concerning sexual orientation or gender identity, but judges use principles of uncodified Islamic law to sanction people suspected of committing sexual relations outside marriage, including adultery, extramarital, and homosexual sex. If individuals are engaging in such relationships online, judges and prosecutors utilize vague provisions of the country's anti-cybercrime law that criminalize online activity impinging on "public order, religious values, public morals, and privacy."

In July, a Saudi court sentenced a Yemeni blogger to 10 months in prison, a fine of 10,000 Saudi Riyals ($2,700), and deportation to Yemen for posting a video on social media calling for equal rights, including for gay people. He had fled Yemen in June 2019 after Yemeni armed groups threatened to kill him and has since been living in Saudi Arabia as an undocumented migrant.

Yemen Airstrikes and Blockade

As the leader of the coalition that began military operations against Houthi forces in Yemen on March 26, 2015, Saudi Arabia has committed numerous violations of international humanitarian law. As of June, at least 7,825 civilians had been killed in the conflict, including 2,138 children, and 12,416 wounded since 2015, according to the Office of the United Nations High Commissioner for Human Rights (OHCHR), although the actual civilian casualty count is likely much higher. Most of these casualties were a result of coalition airstrikes. The Armed Conflict and Event Data Project estimates that 112,000 people have died from the hostilities, including 12,000 civilians.

Since March 2015, Human Rights Watch has documented numerous unlawful attacks by the coalition that have hit homes, markets, hospitals, schools, and mosques. Some of these attacks may amount to war crimes. Saudi commanders face possible criminal liability for war crimes as a matter of command responsibility. Human Rights Watch reported in March that Saudi military forces and Saudi-backed Yemeni forces carried out serious abuses against Yemenis since mid-2019 in al-Mahrah, Yemen's far eastern governorate, including arbitrary arrests, torture, enforced disappearances, and illegal transfer of detainees to Saudi Arabia.

In September, the UN Group of Eminent International and Regional Experts on Yemen stated that it had "reasonable grounds" to believe that Saudi Arabia, the United Arab Emirates, and the Government of Yemen were responsible for human rights violations in Yemen, and recommended that the UN Security Council refer the situation in Yemen to the International Criminal Court.

The conflict exacerbated an existing humanitarian crisis. The Saudi-led coalition has imposed an aerial and naval blockade since March 2015 and restricted the flow of life-saving goods and the ability for Yemenis to travel into and out of the country to varying degrees throughout the war. (See also Yemen chapter).

Criminal Justice

Saudi Arabia applies Sharia (Islamic law) as its national law. There is no formal penal code, but the government has passed some laws and regulations that subject certain broadly defined offenses to criminal penalties. In the absence of a written penal code or narrowly worded regulations, however, judges and prose-cutors can convict people on a wide range of offenses under broad, catch-all charges such as "breaking allegiance with the ruler" or "trying to distort the rep-utation of the kingdom." Detainees, including children, commonly face system-atic violations of due process and fair trial rights, including arbitrary arrest.

Judges routinely sentence defendants to floggings of hundreds of lashes. Chil-dren can be tried for capital crimes and sentenced as adults if they show physi-cal signs of puberty. In 2020, judges based some capital convictions primarily on confessions that the defendants retracted in court and said had been coerced under torture, allegations the courts did not investigate.

In April, Saudi authorities announced criminal justice changes ending flogging as a punishment for some crimes and re-stating a 2018 legal change halting the death penalty for alleged child offenders for certain crimes. In August, the Saudi Human Rights Commission announced the judiciary would review three death sentences in accordance with the legal reforms. Ali al-Nimr, Dawoud al-Marhoun, and Abdullah al-Zaher were sentenced to death for allegedly commit-ting crimes when they were children.

Saudi Arabia dramatically reduced use of capital punishment in 2020. According to Interior Ministry statements, Saudi Arabia executed only 15 persons between January and November, down from 184 executions in 2019. Of the 15 executions, nine were for murder, five for non-violent drug crimes, and one for terrorism. Exe-cutions are carried out by firing squad or beheading, sometimes in public.

Women's and Girls' Rights

Despite major women's right reforms in recent years, including an end to travel restrictions (for example, women over 21, like men, can now obtain passports and travel abroad without a guardian's permission), Saudi women still must ob-tain a male guardian's approval to get married, leave prison, or obtain certain healthcare. Women also continue to face discrimination in relation to marriage, family, divorce, and decisions relating to children, including child custody. Men can still file cases against daughters, wives, or female relatives under their guardianship for "disobedience," which can lead to forcible return to their male guardian's home or imprisonment. Women's rights activists remain in jail or on trial for their peaceful advocacy.

In April, Saudi women took to Twitter, using pseudonyms, to share their experiences of sexual harassment, the reasons behind their hesitance to report these abuses to the authorities, and demands for the abolition of the discriminatory male guardianship system.

Migrant Workers

Millions of migrant workers fill mostly manual, clerical, and service jobs in Saudi Arabia. Government efforts attempts to increase citizen employment by nationalizing the workforce, imposing a monthly tax on foreign workers' dependents in mid-2017, increasing exclusions of migrants from certain employment sectors, and the economic effects of the Covid-19 pandemic in which vast numbers of migrant workers were dismissed from jobs, led to an exodus of migrant workers from Saudi Arabia.

Jadwa Investment, a Riyadh closed joint stock company headed by a son of King Salman, estimated in July that 1.2 million migrant workers would leave Saudi Arabia in 2020. The Saudi Arabian Monetary Authority (SAMA) annual statistics for 2019 reflected that 47,000 foreigners worked in the public sector and 6.5 million in the private sector, down from 70,000 and 8.4 million in 2015.

Migrant workers continued to report abuse and exploitation, sometimes amounting to forced labor. The kafala (visa sponsorship) system ties migrant workers' residency permits to "sponsoring" employers, whose written consent is required for workers to change employers or leave the country. Some employers confiscate passports, withhold wages, and force migrants to work against their will. Saudi Arabia also imposes an exit visa requirement, forcing migrant workers to obtain permission from their employer to leave the country. Workers who leave their employer without their consent can be charged with "absconding" and face imprisonment and deportation.

The Covid-19 pandemic has further exposed and amplified the ways in which migrant workers' rights are violated. In March and April, Human Rights Watch and other international human rights organizations called on governments to take several steps to adequately protect migrant workers from the spread of the virus, including in immigration detention and labor accommodations. Many migrant workers faced dismissals and unpaid wages, and were unable to return home due to expensive tickets and travel restrictions.

In November 2017, Saudi Arabia launched a campaign to detain foreigners found to be in violation of existing labor, residency, or border security laws, including those without valid residency or work permits, or those found working for an employer other than their legal sponsor. By December 2019, authorities announced that the campaign had totaled over 4.4 million arrests, including for over 3.4 million residency law violations and over 675,000 labor law violations. Authorities did not publish updates in 2020.

In April, Saudi border guards fired on Ethiopian migrants who were forced into the Saudi-Yemen border area by Houthi forces, killing dozens, while hundreds of survivors escaped to a mountainous border area. Saudi officials allowed hundreds, if not thousands, to enter the country, but then arbitrarily detained them in unsanitary and abusive facilities without the ability to legally challenge their detention or eventual deportation to Ethiopia. Following media reports highlighting the poor and unhygienic conditions, Saudi Arabia said it would investigate these detention centers.

Saudi Arabia is not party to the 1951 Refugee Convention and does not have an asylum system under which people fearing persecution in their home country can seek protection, leading to a real risk of deporting them to harm.

Migrant domestic workers, predominantly women, faced a range of abuses exacerbated by Covid-19 lockdown restrictions including overwork, forced confinement, non-payment of wages, food deprivation, and psychological, physical, and sexual abuse, for which there was little redress. Domestic workers found it difficult to access help, particularly from their own embassies, due to difficulties in providing shelter during Covid-19 lockdown restrictions.

Key International Actors

As a party to the armed conflict in Yemen, the US provided logistical and intelligence support to Saudi-led coalition forces. A US State Department Inspector General report issued in August found that "the department did not fully assess risks and implement mitigation measures to reduce civilian casualties and legal concerns associated with the transfer" of weapons to Saudi Arabia and the United Arab Emirates, raising concerns about potential US liability for war crimes.

In July, the United Kingdom imposed human rights sanctions on Saudi officials, including the deputy intelligence chief, in connection with Jamal Khashoggi's killing. The following day the UK announced it would resume approving arms sales to Saudi Arabia after authorities claimed they developed a "revised methodology" to support the conclusion that previous coalition violations in Yemen were "isolated" incidents despite repeated attacks that hit civilians or civilian infrastructure. A landmark court ruling in 2019 forced the UK government to pause sales until it could show that it had properly evaluated the risk that weapons sold to Saudi Arabia could be used in laws of war violations.

In March, the European Union raised concerns on Saudi Arabia at the UN Human Rights Council, including over the detention of human rights defenders, the death penalty, and the Khashoggi case. In October, the European Parliament adopted a resolution strongly condemning Saudi Arabia's treatment of Ethiopian migrants and the country's overall human rights record.

At the UN Human Rights Council in September, Denmark delivered a joint statement on Saudi human rights abuses on behalf of 33 countries, calling on Saudi Arabia to all political dissidents and women's rights activists, provide accountability for past abuses, and end persistent discrimination against women.

In June, the UN secretary-general removed the Saudi-led coalition from his latest "list of shame" of parties responsible for grave violations against children during conflict, even though his report concluded that the coalition was responsible for 222 child casualties and 4 attacks on schools and hospitals in Yemen in 2019.

Saudi Arabia's Public Investment Fund (PIF), the country's sovereign wealth funded headed by Mohammed bin Salman, attempted to acquire the Newcastle United F.C. Premier League club in 2020, but the bid was eventually withdrawn following protests.

Serbia

There was limited improvement in protections of human rights in Serbia in 2020. Journalists faced threats, violence, and intimidation, and those responsible are rarely held to account. Efforts to prosecute war crimes continued to focus on low-level perpetrators. People with disabilities continued to be placed and reside long term in institutions. Attacks and threats against lesbian, gay, bisexual and transgender (LGBT) people continued.

Freedom of Media

Attacks and threats against journalists remained a concern and were met by inadequate response from Serbian authorities.

Between January and late August, the Independent Journalists' Association of Serbia (NUNS) registered 28 physical attacks and 33 threats or intimidation against journalists.

In September, the Appeals Court in Belgrade overturned the 2019 convictions of four defendants accused of the 1999 murder of prominent journalist and editor, Slavko Curuvija.

While reporting on a protest against Covid-19 restrictions in July, BETA news agency journalist Zikica Stevanovic was beaten by several police officers, including by baton to the head despite him showing his journalist ID, according to NUNS. Stevanovic's beating was under investigation at time of writing. NUNS also reported that while covering the same protest, journalist Igor Stanojevic was beaten by police and arrested despite showing his journalist ID. He was charged with allegedly throwing stones at police and resisting arrest.

Accountability for War Crimes

Between January and August, the War Crimes Prosecutor Office launched two new investigations and issued two indictments against a total of four individuals. An appeals court in Belgrade convicted one low ranking official of war crimes. The first instance court in Belgrade convicted three people for war crimes in the same time period. As of August, 34 cases against 188 individuals were under investigation and 14 cases against 36 defendants were pending before Serbian courts.

In September, a Belgrade court issued an arrest warrant for a bailed former soldier Rajko Kozlina, after he failed to surrender in June for his 15-year prison sentence for killing civilians during the 1998-1999 Kosovo war. His conviction and sentence in December 2019 were upheld on appeal in June.

In March, the Belgrade Appeals Court upheld the conviction of Nikola Vida Lujic, a former member of Serbia's Red Berets special forces unit, sentencing him to eight years for a wartime rape of a woman in the village of Brcko in Bosnia in 1992.

A Belgrade court in July sentenced a former soldier to four years in prison for one murder and two attempted killings of civilians in Bosanski Petrovac, Bosnia, 1992. In the same month, the same court convicted an ex-Bosnian Serb Army soldier to two years in prison for beating and mistreating Bosniak civilians in Kljuc municipality in 1992.

The first trial in Serbia for war crimes in Srebrenica was marred by further delays, because the defendants, who are not being held in custody during the proceedings, failed to show up in court. Eight Bosnian Serb former police officers resident in Serbia are charged with the killing of more than 1,300 Bosniak civilians in July 1995. The trial has been postponed 18 times since it began in December 2016 because the accused claim to have poor health.

Following a meeting with Kosovo Prime Minister Avdullah Hoti in July, Serbian President Aleksandar Vucic offered to cooperate with Kosovo's government to identify the location of missing persons from the 1998-1999 war in Kosovo.

Migrants, including Asylum Seekers, Long-Term Displaced Persons, Refugees

Between January and August, Serbia registered 2,084 asylum seekers, significantly down from 6,156 asylum seekers during the same period in 2019. Afghans comprised the largest national group in 2020. UNHCR estimates of the numbers of asylum seekers and migrants in government centers were also down to 4,050 in August from 5,420 the previous year.

The asylum system continued to be flawed, with difficulties for asylum seekers accessing procedures, low recognition rates compared to EU averages, and long delays before decisions are made. Between January and August, Serbia registered 56 asylum applications, granting refugee status to 9 and subsidiary protection to 7. Over the past decade, Serbia has granted refugee status to a total of only 78 people and subsidiary protection to 96. In mid-October, 6 out of 16 government-run camps were overcrowded.

By end of July, 37 unaccompanied children were registered with Serbian authorities, the majority from Afghanistan, compared to 437 during the same period in 2019. Serbia still lacks formal age assessment procedures for unaccompanied children, putting older children at risk of being treated as adults instead of receiving special protection.

There was little progress towards durable solutions for refugees and internally displaced persons from the Balkan wars living in Serbia, with the number of people registered as refugees and internally displaced persons from those conflicts in 2020 barely changed from the previous year.

Sexual Orientation and Gender Identity

Attacks, threats, and smear campaigns against LGBT people and activists continued. Between January and September, Serbian LGBT rights organization DA SE ZNA! recorded 17 hate incidents against LGBT people, including 8 physical attacks, and 9 threats.

Women's Rights

In its first report on Serbia, the group of experts responsible for monitoring implementation of the Istanbul Convention on Preventing and Combating Violence Against Women and Domestic Violence noted ongoing gaps in services and obstacles to accessing help for survivors of violence against women and girls, particularly for rape and sexual assault, and called on the government to take urgent action to address gender stereotypes and promote equality.

Disability Rights

Thousands of adults and children with disabilities remained in institutions across Serbia. The government failed to adopt a deinstitutionalization plan to move people with disabilities out of institutions and into community-based living arrangements. The government failed to release data on how many people with disabilities in residential institutions died of complications from Covid-19. Remote education and online learning put in place when schools closed in March, were not accessible to many children with disabilities.

Key International Actors

In July, Serbia and Kosovo resumed the European Union-brokered dialogue on improving relations, stalled since November 2018, but failed to make specific commitments on strengthening protection of human rights.

Council of Europe Human Rights Commissioner Dunja Mijatovic in July called on Serbian authorities to investigate police violence against protesters during the July demonstrations in Belgrade against government Covid-19 restrictions.

After an April intervention by OSCE Representative on Freedom of the Media Harlem Désir, the Serbian government promptly withdrew a March decision to limit media access to information during the Covid-19 pandemic.

The October EU Commission progress report said Serbia should ensure the independence of its human rights institutions. The report noted serious concerns regarding intimidation, threats, and violence against journalists and the LGBT community and called on authorities to promptly investigate and penalize perpetrators.

Singapore

Singapore held elections in July, with the ruling People's Action Party taking 83 out of 93 seats, with 61.2 percent of the popular vote. The opposition Workers' Party won 10 seats—a record high for the opposition. The government continued to use harsh and overly broad laws restricting speech and assembly to prosecute critical speech, or to label it as "fake news," and order social media platforms to block content. The city-state's initial success in controlling the spread of Covid-19 was undermined by a failure to ensure that migrant workers could adequately protect themselves from the disease, leading to a surge in cases among migrants living in cramped workers' dormitories.

Violation of Freedoms of Peaceful Assembly and Expression

The Protection from Online Falsehoods and Manipulation Act (POFMA), which came into effect in October 2019, allows a minister to declare that online content is "false" and order a "correction notice" to be placed on the relevant social media pages. Failure to comply with a correction order can be punished with the shutdown of social media pages in Singapore, up to 12 months in prison, and a S$20,000 (US$14,670) fine. While those receiving a correction notice can appeal to the minister and then to the Singapore High Court, one High Court judge has ruled that the burden is on the appellant to prove that the statement is true, while another high court judge has ruled that the burden of proof falls on the government, as international law requires.

As of July 1, 2020, the government invoked POFMA more than 50 times, primarily against content critical of the government or its policies. Correction notices were issued to independent online media, such as *The Online Citizen* and *New Naratif*, opposition politicians, and activists. Ministers issued several correction notices to opposition politicians or political parties during the nine-day election campaign in July.

In January 2020, the minister for home affairs issued a correction notice to the Malaysian non-governmental group Lawyers for Liberty (LFL), asserting that its press statement outlining execution methods in Singapore was false. LFL declined to comply with the order, and on January 23, the Singapore authorities ordered the NGO's website blocked in Singapore.

Singapore's Administration of Justice (Protection) Act contains overly broad and vague powers to punish for contempt, with penalties of three years in prison or a fine of S$50,000 (US$36,658). In March, the Court of Appeal upheld the conviction of activist Jolovan Wham under that law for stating on Facebook that "Malaysia's judges are more independent than Singapore's for cases with political implications."

The court also upheld the conviction of John Tan, vice-chairman of the opposition Singapore Democratic Party, for posting on social media that Wham's prosecution "only confirms that what [Wham] said is true." Wham chose to serve seven days in jail in lieu of paying a fine of S$5,000 (US$3,666).

On July 28, Prime Minister Lee Hsien Loong's nephew, Li Shengwu, was found guilty of contempt and fined S$15,000 (US$10,997) for a 2017 private Facebook post in which he said the Singapore government is "very litigious and has a pliant court system."

Authorities also commenced investigations of lawyer M. Ravi, Terry Xu, editor of The Online Citizen, and two others for contempt of court following the publication of articles on The Online Citizen's website related to M. Ravi's client, Mohan Rajangam, a Singaporean who challenged the legality of his extradition from Malaysia in 2015.

During the nine-day election campaign period, the police announced the opening of an investigation into the Workers' Party candidate, Raeesah Khan, under section 298A of the criminal code, which criminalizes speech "promoting enmity" between different groups. The investigation centered on posts from February 2018 and May 2020 questioning whether law enforcement authorities treated all groups equally.

The government maintains strict restrictions on the right to peaceful assembly through the Public Order Act, requiring a police permit for any "cause-related" assembly if it is held in a public place, or in a private venue if members of the general public are invited. The definition of what is treated as an assembly is extremely broad and those who fail to obtain the required permits face criminal charges. On

August 20, 2020, the Court of Appeal upheld the constitutionality of the Public Order Act's licensing requirement for a permit to hold public assemblies in a challenge filed by activist Jolovan Wham.

After his constitutional challenge was rejected, Wham chose to serve 10 days in jail in lieu of paying a fine for "organizing a public assembly without a permit." He was convicted of permitting Hong Kong activist Joshua Wong to call in from abroad at an indoor event without obtaining a permit for a foreigner to speak. Wham is also facing charges under the Public Order Act for holding a vigil outside Changi Prison in July 2019 for a death row inmate, and for co-organizing a silent protest on the Singapore subway to commemorate the 30th anniversary of the arrest and detention of 22 activists and volunteers under the Internal Security Act 1987.

Even solo protests are treated as assemblies under the Public Order Act. In November, Wham was charged with holding an unlawful assembly for holding up a cardboard sign with only a smiley face on it near a police station. In April, the police investigated two students who held solo "climate protests" without seeking police permission. In each case, the student simply posed for a photograph holding a sign as part of the global "Fridays for Future" movement, and posted the images on social media.

Criminal Justice System

Singapore retains the death penalty, which is mandated for many drug offenses and certain other crimes. However, under provisions introduced in 2012, judges have some discretion to bypass the mandatory penalty and sentence low-level offenders to life in prison and caning. There is little transparency on the timing of executions, which often take place with short notice. After a halt in executions due to Covid-19, in September 2020 authorities began notifying death row inmates of scheduled execution dates.

Lawyers representing defendants in death penalty cases often face government harassment. On August 13, 2020, the Court of Appeal opined that a statement made by the Attorney-General's Chambers against a lawyer representing two Malaysian inmates on death row could have been "reasonably construed as intimidating." In September 2020, the Court of Appeal reversed its earlier decision and acquitted a Nigerian man of drug trafficking five years after it overturned a lower court acquittal and sentenced him to death.

Use of corporal punishment is common in Singapore. For medically fit males ages 16 to 50, caning is mandatory as an additional punishment for a range of crimes, including drug trafficking, violent crimes (such as armed robbery), and even some immigration offenses. The caning, which constitutes torture under international law, is alleged to leave some of those caned with permanent injuries.

Sexual Orientation and Gender Identity

The rights of lesbian, gay, bisexual, and transgender (LGBT) people in Singapore are severely restricted. On March 30, 2020, the High Court rejected three constitutional challenges to criminal code section 377A, which makes sexual relations between two male persons a criminal offense. There are no legal protections against discrimination on the basis of sexual orientation or gender identity. Singapore law precludes LGBT groups from registering and operating legally.

Migrant Workers and Labor Exploitation

Foreign migrant workers are subject to labor rights abuses and exploitation through debts owed to recruitment agents, non-payment of wages, restrictions on movement, confiscation of passports, and sometimes physical and sexual abuse. Foreign women employed as domestic workers are particularly vulnerable to abuse.

In September 2020, an Indonesian maid was acquitted of stealing from the family of the Changi Airport Group chairman, four years after her employment was terminated and the family brought charges against her, with the court finding that the employer acted with the improper motive of preventing her from filing a complaint with the Ministry of Manpower.

Work permits of migrant workers in Singapore are tied to a particular employer, leaving them extremely vulnerable to exploitation. Foreign domestic workers, which are covered by the Employment of Foreign Manpower Act rather than the Employment Act, are effectively excluded from many key labor protections, such as limits on daily work hours and mandatory days off. Labor laws also discriminate against foreign workers by barring them from organizing and registering a union or serving as union leaders without explicit government permission.

Many migrant workers in Singapore are housed in crowded and unsanitary dormitories, with up to 20 people sharing a room, and communal bathrooms, in conditions that increased the risk of spreading Covid-19. While Singapore had initial success in controlling Covid-19 infections in the country, a surge of cases among migrant workers in early April led the government to put all dormitories on lockdown, restricting the movements of almost 300,000 foreign workers. While some "essential" workers were moved, the bulk of the migrants were confined to hot, overcrowded rooms with little ventilation, leaving them at risk of infection. As of August 13, 52,516 dormitory residents had tested positive for the coronavirus, making up more than 90 percent of all reported cases in Singapore.

Covid-19

Singapore had initial success, using aggressive contact tracing, in controlling Covid-19 infections. However, in early April a surge of cases among migrant workers, most of whom live in crowded dormitories provided by their employers and commute to work on crowded buses, led the government to put all dormitories on lockdown, restricting the movements of almost 300,000 foreign workers. While some "essential" workers were moved, the bulk of the migrants were confined to hot, overcrowded rooms with little ventilation, leaving them at risk of infection.

As of August 13, 52,516 dormitory residents had tested positive for the coronavirus, making up more than 90 percent of all cases in Singapore. After authorities ordered schools closed in early April, the Ministry of Education loaned laptops to more than 12,000 students who did not have the electronic devices needed for home-based learning. Schools reopened in early June.

Key International Actors

Singapore is a regional hub for international business and maintains good political and economic relations with both the United States, which considers it a key security ally, and China. Most governments focused their priorities on trade and business, and did not publicly criticize Singapore's poor human rights record.

Somalia

Somalia's federal government received international praise for its planned economic reforms, including its national development plan, but it made little progress with security and judicial reforms while conflict-related abuses, insecurity, and the humanitarian crisis took a heavy toll on civilians.

All parties to the conflict committed violations of international humanitarian law, some amounting to war crimes. The militant group Al-Shabab conducted indiscriminate and targeted attacks on civilians and forcibly recruited children. Inter-clan and intra-security force violence killed, injured and displaced civilians, as did sporadic military operations against Al-Shabab by Somali government forces, African Union Mission in Somalia (AMISOM) troops, and other foreign forces.

Severe weather, locust infestations, and Covid-19 worsened the humanitarian crisis, with over 620,000 new displacements due to flooding, adding to the country's 2.6 million internally displaced.

Somali authorities restricted media freedoms and the federal and Somaliland parliaments considered problematic sexual offenses bills. The Somali government did not hand over Al-Shabab cases from military to civilian courts. Authorities throughout the country carried out executions, many following military court proceedings that violated international fair trial standards. The government did not establish a National Human Rights Commission, nor did it move forward with the planned review of the outdated criminal code, pending since the previous administration.

Relations between the federal government and member states deteriorated, leading to a stalemate over federal election modalities, and fighting on occasion caused civilian casualties, notably in the Gedo region. An agreement was reached in September on the electoral framework paving the way for another restricted electoral process in late 2020 and early 2021.

Attacks on Civilians

The United Nations Assistance Mission in Somalia (UNSOM) recorded at least 596 civilian casualties, including 296 killings, by early August. The majority were due to Al-Shabab targeted and indiscriminate attacks using improvised explosive devices (IEDs), suicide bombings, and shelling, as well as targeted assassinations. Al-Shabab continued to execute after unfair trials individuals it accused of working or spying for the government and foreign forces.

In the first quarter, the UN recorded an increase in civilian casualties due to clan conflict, including revenge killings. In April, civilians were killed, and thousands displaced during inter-clan clashes in Wanlaweyn, with media reporting that a man was burned to death.

On January 28, 2020, Jubaland's security minister, Abdirashid Hassan Abdinur "Janan," implicated in serious crimes in the Gedo region, escaped detention in Mogadishu. In March, forces loyal to Abdirashid Janan fought with federal government forces in Gedo. According to the UN, the clashes killed five civilians and displaced 56,000. The presence of federal forces in Gedo continued to create tensions between the government in Mogadishu and Kismayo.

The US increased its military activity; in the first three months of 2020, it conducted twice as many airstrikes as in the same period of 2019. Some US actions killed and injured civilians. A February 2 strike in Jilib town, Middle Juba, killed a young woman and injured her two sisters, both children, and her grandmother. A March 10 attack on a minibus near the town of Janaale, Lower Shabelle, killed five men and a child.

On May 27, five masked gunmen, four in government uniforms, abducted seven health workers and a pharmacist, in the village of Gololey in Balcad District. Their bodies were found bullet ridden. At time of writing, the outcomes of federal and regional investigations were unknown.

Sexual Violence

The UN documented over 100 cases of conflict-related sexual violence, mostly against girls. The UN Security Council Panel of Experts on Somalia found that on

April 6 two Somali National Army officers raped a woman and a girl during the takeover of Janaale town.

In August, the speaker of parliament in Mogadishu tabled a new Sexual Intercourse Related Crimes Bill that violates Somalia's international and regional human rights obligations. The bill would allow for child marriage by defining a child around physical maturity instead of age, reduce penalties for forced marriage, exclude a broad range of sexual offenses, and include weak procedural protections for survivors. The current status of the bill is unclear.

The Somali criminal code classifies sexual violence as an "offense against modesty and sexual honor" rather than a violation of bodily integrity; it also punishes same-sex relations.

Abuses against Children

All Somali parties to the conflict committed serious abuses against children, including killings, maiming, the recruitment and use of child soldiers, and attacks on schools.

Al-Shabab continued its aggressive child recruitment campaign with retaliation against communities, refusing to hand over children. National and regional forces recruited and used children, according to the UN.

Somali federal and regional security forces unlawfully detained children for alleged ties with armed groups, undermining government commitments to treat children primarily as victims. The government failed to put in place child rights compliant justice measures.

Freedom of Expression and Association

Federal and regional authorities repeatedly harassed, intimidated, and attacked journalists. Arbitrary arrests and detentions, sometimes followed by prosecutions on baseless charges under the criminal code, were common.

On February 16, journalist Abdiwali Ali Hassan was shot dead by unknown attackers in the town of Afgooye. Media groups reported that he had received journalism-related threats. While Somali authorities seldom investigate attacks on journalists, in September, the attorney general established a special prosecutor to investigate crimes against journalists.

On May 3, Somalia's president, Mohamed Abdullahi Mohamed "Farmajo," committed to reforming criminal code provisions that restrict media freedoms and to ending the use of criminal law against journalists. Mid-year, he signed into law a new media law, which while providing for key rights of free expression, contains overly broad content restrictions.

On March 7, National Intelligence and Security Agency (NISA) officials in Mogadishu arrested journalist Mohamed Abdiwahab Nur "Abuja" and held him incommunicado for three months. On August 5, the military court acquitted him of alleged charges of Al-Shabab membership and murder and ordered his release.

On July 29, the Benadir regional court sentenced Abdiaziz Ahmed Gurbiye, the chief editor of Goobjoog Media Group, to six months' imprisonment and a fine on baseless charges of having insulted a government body and for publishing "fake news" related to the government's Covid-19 response. His prison sentence was commuted.

Displacement, Access to Humanitarian Assistance

A combination of Covid-19 and natural events, increasing in intensity and frequency by climate change, such as flooding and desert locust swarms, exacerbated communities' existing vulnerabilities.

Between March 16, when the first Covid-19 case was confirmed, and November 20, there were 3,890 reported cases and 99 deaths; at least 133 health workers were infected. Flooding contributed to an uptake in acute watery diarrhoea and cholera and a deterioration in food insecurity. As of September, 3.8 million people faced acute food insecurity.

The United Nations and Norwegian Refugee Council (NRC) reported 1,092,000 people had been displaced as of late November, mainly due to flooding and conflict. The displaced communities faced sexual violence, cycles of forced evictions, dire living conditions and limited access to basic services. Restrictions imposed by the government to limit the spread of the pandemic, including restrictions on movement and measures to ease congestion, along with price hikes and reduced remittance flows, further limited access to livelihoods and health care for displaced communities.

Authorities in Baidoa announced a moratorium on forced evictions in order to mitigate the impact of Covid-19. As of September, 65,677 displaced were evicted in Mogadishu alone, two thirds of the total number recorded in the country.

Humanitarian agencies face serious access challenges due to insecurity, targeted attacks on aid workers, generalized violence, and restrictions imposed by parties to the conflict. Al-Shabab imposed blockades on a number of government-controlled towns and occasionally attacked civilians who broke them. According to the UN, between January and August, 11 humanitarian workers were killed.

Somaliland

The Somaliland government severely restricted reporting and free expression of journalists and perceived critics on issues deemed controversial or overly critical of the authorities. In January, Somaliland executed six prisoners.

In late August, Somaliland's lower house approved the Rape and Fornication Bill, which allows for child and forced marriage, criminalizes witchcraft and "false" reporting of rape, provides for the death penalty for same-sex sexual relations, and includes an unacceptable definition of rape that excludes the possibility of rape within marriage and does not take into account consent. At time of writing, the bill was pending for upper house review.

Key International Actors

International support focused on building Somalia's security sector, improving relations between federal and state authorities including the stalemate around the electoral process.

In September, the European Parliament called on the European Union Training Mission (EUTM) in Somalia to ensure better human rights monitoring and follow-up of the Somali government forces it trains. At the UN Human Rights Council, the European Union raised serious concerns over rights violations.

US military strikes increased in the first five months of the year. In April, the US military command in Africa (AFRICOM) released its first quarterly report on civilian casualty assessments, acknowledging killing two civilians and injuring three in February 2019. In July, it acknowledged that the February 2 Jilib strike (see above) had killed and injured civilians. It established an online reporting portal, but many Somalis do not have access to the internet to use it. In June, AFRICOM stated that it had not paid any compensation in Somalia for civilian casualties it had acknowledged since 2017.

In March, the International Monetary Fund and World Bank declared Somalia eligible for debt relief under the Heavily Indebted Poor Countries Initiative, after Somalia cleared its arrears with international support.

Competition among Gulf states over political and economic dominance in Somalia continued to exacerbate intra-Somalia tensions.

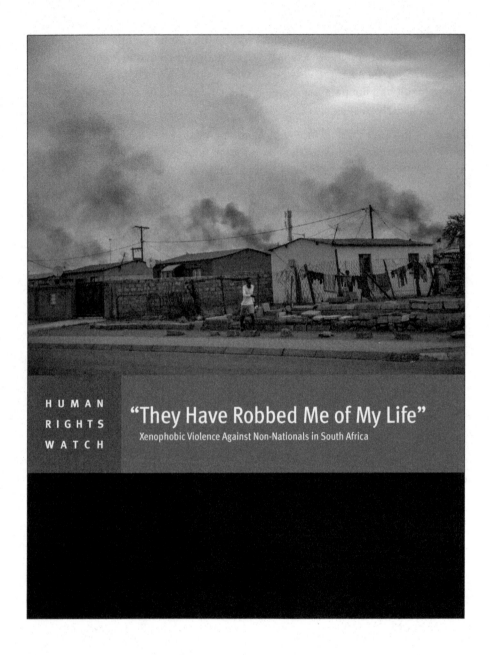

H U M A N
R I G H T S
W A T C H

"They Have Robbed Me of My Life"
Xenophobic Violence Against Non-Nationals in South Africa

South Africa

During 2020, South Africa continued to experience incidents of xenophobic violence and discrimination against non-nationals despite the government's launch of the National Action Plan to Combat Racism, Racial Discrimination, Xenophobia and Related Intolerance (NAP) in 2019. Law enforcement officials often responded with indifference or provided inadequate remedies to xenophobic attacks. Refugees and asylum seekers faced barriers to protection. This included a newly enacted law restricting access to asylum and a huge government backlog in processing claims and appeals. The government's Covid-19 aid programs, including food parcels during national lockdown, overlooked people with disabilities, refugees and asylum seekers and many lesbian, gay, bisexual, and transgender (LGBT) people. President Cyril Ramaphosa appointed two special envoys to help resolve the political crisis in Zimbabwe and South Africa joined 66 other states in reaffirming support for the International Criminal Court.

Xenophobic Attacks on Foreign Nationals

South Africa continued to be plagued by widespread incidents of xenophobic harassment and attacks against foreigners by mobs during 2020.The attacks and harassment were also committed by government and law enforcement officials. Non-nationals have also been harassed verbally and physically by South Africans for being foreign and not using local languages in their daily interactions. A common and hurtful insult thrown at foreigners is the label "kwerekwere," a derogatory slang used by Black South Africans to mean "foreigner."

Government and law enforcement officials throughout the country not only largely failed to ensure justice for xenophobic violence, but also operated in discriminatory and abusive ways against non-nationals. Some officials exacerbated xenophobia through inciteful rhetoric, while the South African Police Service (SAPS) and Metro Police used counterfeit goods raids as a cover to target foreign-owned shops and businesses. During the raids, police officers beat foreign shop owners and fired tear gas and rubber bullets at them. Ransacking and destroying their shops. Victims in the Johannesburg Central Business District and Diepsloot alleged that the police then resold confiscated goods back to them.

In coordination with the Department of Home Affairs (DHA), police conducted abusive "documentation raids" in areas where many non-nationals reside, including by entering foreigners' homes to verify documents and legal status while administering beatings.

While the 2019 National Action Plan to combat xenophobia, racism, and discrimination marked an important step toward recognizing and addressing these abuses, it has not ensured accountability for xenophobic crimes.

Women's Rights

South Africa is facing a crisis of gender-based violence (GBV). In April, Police Minister Bheki Cele noted that police registered over 2,300 complaints of gender-based violence between March 27 to March 31, 2020, during the lockdown implemented to reduce the spread of the coronavirus.

In June 2020, following protests against the murder of Tshegofatso Pule, a 28-year-old woman whose body was found dumped in Soweto, Johannesburg, President Ramaphosa acknowledged that South Africa had among the highest levels of intimate partner violence in the world. As much as 51 percent of South African women have experienced violence at the hands of someone with whom they were in an intimate relationship. He described violence against girls and women as South Africa's "second pandemic," after the coronavirus, and called on residents to end the culture of silence around gender-based violence and report perpetrators to the SAPS.

In September, Ramaphosa said three bills to amend the Criminal Law (Sexual Offences and Related Matters), Criminal and Related Matters Act, and the Domestic Violence Act had been introduced in parliament to "fill the gaps that allow perpetrators of these crimes to evade justice and to give full effect to the rights of our country's women and children." He said that a public register of sex offenders with all relevant details would also be introduced. Civil society organizations have expressed concerns that GBV victims faced worsening violence and the inability to access help under the lockdown

South Africa continues to criminalize sex work and prohibit other aspects of sex work. This includes criminalizing running or owning a brothel, living off of the earnings of "prostitution," and enticing a woman into "prostitution." Criminalization has undermined sex workers' access to justice for crimes committed against them and exposed them to unchecked abuse and exploitation by law enforcement officials, including police officers. Although the Department of Health's National Strategic Plan on HIV for Sex Workers is grounded in respect for the human rights of sex workers, criminalization hinders sex workers' efforts to access health care, including HIV prevention, treatment, care and support.

In October 2020, South Africa's Department of Social Development said it has failed sex workers by not providing them with services such as counselling, safety and security and giving them other options to opt-out of sex work when they wish to do so. Deputy Minister of Social Development Hendrietta Bogopane-Zulu committed to elevating sex workers' issues. Some government departments expressed support for the decriminalization of sex work to assist sex workers to access all government services and reduce their victimization and exposure to violence.

Children's Rights

Due to the Covid-19 pandemic, more than 13 million children across South Africa were affected by school closures. The closures lasted about six months, exacerbating existing inequalities. Children who were already at risk of being excluded from accessing quality education have been most affected.

The South African government's responses to the Covid-19 pandemic worsened the plight of children across South Africa in 2020. This included the closure of the National School Nutrition Programme (NSNP) without contingency plans to feed 9 million economically vulnerable children during the national lockdown.

The government also closed schools and Early Childhood Development (ECD) centers with inadequate plans to keep children learning during lockdown. The government also neglected to ensure that learning platforms were inclusive for learners with disabilities. There has been a failure to prepare for the timeous re-opening of ECDs, and a lack of provisions and resources to protect children from violence.

The case of *Centre for Child Law and Others v. Minister of Basic Education and Others,* decided by the High Court of South Africa in December 2019, on behalf of 37 children without birth certificates who were barred from enrolling in Eastern

Cape schools, revealed that many children born in South Africa, whether to citizens or foreigners, were not given birth certificates.

The court ordered Eastern Cape public schools to accept alternative proof of identity for the 37 undocumented children and declared that the Immigration Act 13 of 2002 did not "prohibit the admission of illegal foreign children into schools." Moreover, the minister of education was prohibited from removing or excluding already-admitted students because they lacked or could not produce specific identification documents.

Covid-19

As of mid-November, South Africa had 757,144 confirmed Covid-19 cases with 20,556 deaths, one of the highest figures across Africa. The government's Covid-19 aid programs, including food parcels, overlooked refugees and asylum seekers. Many lesbian, gay, bisexual, and transgender (LGBT) African asylum seekers and undocumented migrants were also overlooked. Sex worker rights groups also noted that this vulnerable population had been left out of relief planning. The government did not sufficiently consult with people with disabilities in its Covid-19 policies, leaving many at serious risk of Covid-19 infection, hunger, and other harms.

Authorities failed to take urgent steps to facilitate support, including from donors, for refugees and asylum seekers whose access to food and other basic necessities were limited during the nationwide lockdown. On May 12, the rapporteur for South Africa at the African Commission on Human and Peoples' Rights, Solomon Ayele Dersso, sent an urgent appeal to the government to protect the rights of vulnerable groups, including refugees, asylum seekers and migrants in the context of the lockdown to combat the coronavirus.

Foreign Policy

In February 2020, South Africa became the chair of the African Union (AU) for a year. In keeping with the summit theme of Silencing the Guns, President Ramaphosa, as AU chairperson, spoke in Addis Ababa of an Africa "that is prosperous and at peace with itself." Other leaders pledged that the 55-member bloc will play a greater role in resolving protracted conflicts and will work to unlock the continent's economic potential.

On March 24, the African Commission on Human and Peoples' Rights in a letter to President Ramaphosa expressed concern about the vulnerability of refugees and asylum seekers under South Africa's Covid-19 regulations. The commission urged the South African government to adequately address human rights issues in its responses to Covid-19, including ensuring that undocumented refugees and asylum seekers in South Africa have access to basic services.

In 2020, South Africa served its second year as a non-permanent member of the United Nations Security Council. On September 22, in his address to the 75th UN General Assembly, President Ramaphosa reaffirmed South Africa's commitment to the ideals and spirit of the UN Charter and to sparing no effort to bring about a more just, peaceful and equitable world.

In September, South Africa dispatched a high-level delegation to Zimbabwe to help find a solution to the country's escalating economic and political crisis. The team, led by the secretary-general of the governing African National Congress (ANC) party, Ace Magashule, met officials from Zimbabwe's ruling African National Union-Patriotic Front (ZANU-PF) party and raised concern about the country's deteriorating human rights situation.

In June 2020, South Africa jointly issued a statement with 66 other member states of the International Criminal Court (ICC) reaffirming unwavering support for the court as an independent and impartial judicial institution. They said the ICC is an integral part of this order and a central institution in the fight against impunity and the pursuit of justice, which are essential components of sustainable peace, security, and reconciliation. This followed the release of the United States executive order with travel restrictions and economic sanctions, such as freezing assets of certain persons associated with the ICC.

South Korea

The South Korean government, a democracy, largely respects most political, civil, and socio-economic rights but significant human rights concerns remain. Discrimination against women is pervasive, as is discrimination against lesbian, gay, bisexual, and transgender (LGBT) people, and racial and ethnic minorities. The government has also maintained or imposed several excessive restrictions on freedom of expression, association, and peaceful assembly. In 2020, South Korea implemented important public health measures to protect against the spread of Covid-19, but aspects of its response raised serious privacy rights concerns.

Covid-19

In March, the government managed to lessen the impact of the Covid-19 pandemic in South Korea by adopting massive testing, data-intensive contact tracing, and promotion of social distancing. The government used cell phone location data, CCTV cameras, and tracking of debit, ATM, and credit cards to identify Covid-19 cases, and created a publicly available map for people to check whether they may have crossed paths with people with the virus. However, some of these measures infringed upon the right to privacy.

Health authorities sent out cell phone notifications to large numbers of people containing detailed information on confirmed Covid-19 cases, including age, gender, and places visited before being quarantined. The extensive personal information made public to assist in tracing also allowed people to identify infected persons, which led to public harassment and "doxing."

In March, the National Human Rights Commission of Korea criticized authorities for these practices. In June and October, the Center for Disease Control and Prevention issued guidance not to publish patient age, sex, nationality, workplace, travel history, or home residency location, although some local governments still disclose some individual travel histories despite being directed against it. Concerns related to the collection and processing of sensitive personal information, which can reveal intimate information like a person's sexual orientation and private relations, remained.

In 2020, over 6 million students enrolled in pre-school, primary, and secondary schools were impacted by school closures, according to United Nations estimates. The Ministry of Education minimized learning disruptions by relying on the country's IT infrastructure and providers to deliver distance learning at scale and delayed the start of the school year by five weeks to minimize the loss of instruction time.

The public's reaction to the Covid-19 pandemic at times stigmatized LGBT persons, foreigners, and members of some religious groups, laying bare deep-seated discriminatory attitudes.

Sexual Orientation and Gender Identity

The LGBT rights movement in South Korean grew but hostility and severe discrimination persisted, especially in the armed forces. On January 22, 2020, the South Korean military discharged Byeon Hee-su, a transgender soldier who had undergone gender affirming surgery but wanted to continue to serve. The Constitutional Court is also currently reviewing the 1962 Military Criminal Act, which punishes sexual acts among soldiers with up to two years in prison under a "disgraceful conduct" clause, regardless of consent.

In early May, as bars and other venues reopened following a decline in Covid-19 cases, dozens of new cases appeared, linked to nightclubs in Seoul. Some media described the nightclubs as gay clubs, setting off a firestorm of online harassment and intimidation against LGBT people.

Women's Rights

Discrimination against women is widespread in South Korea. Relatively few women occupy decision-making positions. There is a 35 percent wage gap between men and women. The *Economist* magazine's "Glass Ceiling Index," which evaluates women's higher education attainment and numbers of women in managerial positions and in parliament, gives South Korea the lowest rank among countries that belong to the Organization for Economic Co-operation and Development (OECD).

On April 11, 2019, South Korea's Constitutional Court ordered the National Assembly to rewrite laws governing abortion, which are punitive and harmful to women and girls, and decriminalize the procedure by the end of 2020. On October 7, 2020, the South Korean government announced new draft legislation that would permit abortion up until 14 weeks and, in some circumstances, up to 24 weeks, but would continue to criminalize abortion outside these exceptions.

South Korea's #MeToo movement continued to gain ground in 2020 with several high-level local officials exposed for sexual violence, including former Seoul Mayor Park Won-soon, known as a women's rights champion, who died by suicide on April 7, two days after his former secretary had filed a police report saying he sexually harassed her for four years.

The government continued to struggle to address rampant problems with online gender-based violence, including non-consensually shared intimate images and *molka*—secretly filmed video or images of a sexualized nature posted online. On July 2, 2020, an appeal court imposed a one year jail term on Choi Jong-bum, the former boyfriend of Goo Hara, a Korean pop star whom he had blackmailed with sex videos and who died by suicide in 2019.

In March 2020, Korean police zeroed in on a network of chat rooms on the messaging app Telegram, where users were viewing, sharing, and trading non-consensual images of dozens of women and girls, including of acts of sexual violence, obtained through coercion and blackmail, and prosecuted several chat room operators. Within a month, 2.7 million people signed a petition demanding authorities release the identities of the chat room operators and all participants.

As of August 31, around 1,000 suspects were under investigation in the Telegram scandal, mostly men under 40. The exact scale of these alleged crimes is unknown, but according to the Korea Cyber Sexual Violence Response Center, there were 260,000 users of 56 chat rooms on Telegram in which abusive content was shared.

On April 29, as part of measures to establish a "zero-tolerance" policy, the National Assembly passed bills to make digital sex crimes easier to prosecute. Under the new law, those who possess, buy, store, or watch illegally filmed sexual content can be sentenced to three years in prison. Before the new legislation was enacted, it was not illegal to possess such content.

Policy on Human Rights in North Korea

President Moon Jae-in's administration weakened the South Korean government's criticism of North Korea's human rights record. South Korea had co-sponsored annual resolutions at the UN condemning North Korea's human rights abuses since 2008, but in December 2019 and December 2020 declined to do so at the UN General Assembly, and in 2019 and again in June 2020 declined to do so at the UN Human Rights Council.

In 2020, tensions between the South Korean government and human rights activists working on rights issues in North Korea sharpened significantly. On June 4, a few days after a human rights group sent 500,000 information leaflets into North Korea by balloon, Kim Yo Jong, the sister of North Korean leader Kim Jong Un, issued a statement demanding that South Korea "make a law" to ban the sending of leaflets and made threats of retaliation. For decades, the government had allowed groups to send leaflets with messages, considering the acts allowable freedom of expression and signals of support to North Koreans. But hours after Kim's statement, the South Korean government announced plans to prohibit leafleting, saying they can "raise tension in the border area."

On June 11, the South Korean government announced that authorities had initiated processes to revoke the registration of two groups that regularly sent leaflets and food into North Korea by balloon or by plastic bottles put to sea. In July, the government canceled the operation permits of the two groups, and announced that the 25 groups working on North Korea human rights issues or assisting defectors, registered as businesses with the Unification Ministry, would have to undergo "office inspections."

Authorities also sent notice of an administrative review of the registration status of 64 groups registered with the ministry as "non-profit private organizations" working in similar sectors. On July 22, a coalition of 25 organizations working on North Korean human rights and supporting North Koreans living in South Korea issued a joint statement rejecting office inspections. The coalition called the government's actions discriminatory, lacking in transparency, and intended to provoke fear and self-censorship among the human rights community working on North Korea.

Worker's Rights

South Korea joined the International Labour Organization (ILO) in 1991 but has only ratified four of the ILO's eight core conventions. On July 7, the cabinet approved the Labor Ministry's motion for parliamentary ratification of three ILO conventions on freedom of association, the right to organize and collectively bargain, and the prohibition of forced labor.

On September 3, the Supreme Court overturned a problematic 2013 decision outlawing the Korean Teachers and Education Workers' Union, and restored the union's legal status.

South Sudan

The year 2020 was marked by conflict, security forces' violations, entrenched impunity, and a lack of respect for rule of law, all of which were enhanced by the impact of the Covid-19 pandemic.

In February 2020, the parties to the 2018 peace deal formed a transitional government of national unity led by President Salva Kiir, with Riek Machar as first vice president, and four other vice presidents from opposition groups. The parties did not implement major provisions of the peace deal including security arrangements or establishing accountability mechanisms. The requirement that at least 35 percent at all levels of governance should be women was also ignored.

The government, the Sudan People's Liberation Movement/Army in Opposition (SPLA/IO), the National Democratic Front and non-signatory groups to the 2018 peace deal, recommitted to a ceasefire in January 2020. This ceasefire broke down in April, when fighting resumed in Yei, Lobonok, Mundri, Maridi, and other parts of the Equatoria region. Peace talks restarted in October.

All armed groups committed abuses against civilians including unlawful killings, abductions, and sexual violence. The army, as well as armed groups SPLM/A-IO and National Salvation Front (NAS) recruited and used children.

Leaders from all parties to the conflict failed to prevent abuses by their forces or hold perpetrators to account, with few exceptions. Eight leaders and commanders representing both government forces and rebel groups are subject to United Nations individual sanctions for war crimes and other roles they played in the conflict.

Intercommunal fighting, cattle raiding, and revenge attacks between armed youth groups in Central Equatoria, Jonglei, the Greater Pibor Administrative Area (GPAA), Lakes, Unity, Western Bahr el-Ghazal and Warrap states resulted in hundreds of deaths and injuries, displaced hundreds of thousands, and led to the suspension of humanitarian services in some areas.

Authorities continued to arbitrarily detain critics, including members of civil society and journalists, often holding them for extended periods without charge or trial.

The Covid-19 pandemic slowed implementation of the peace deal and the delivery of aid to populations in need. While enforcing curfews and other restrictions, security forces beat, arrested, and detained civilians.

Health care facilities were poorly staffed and ill-equipped, Covid-19 testing and access to information was inadequate. Schools were closed for six months due to Covid-19, forcing 2.2 million children out of school.

Attacks on Civilians and Aid Workers

In April and May, sporadic fighting between government army, joined by the SPLM/A-IO, and the NAS and allied groups displaced more than 19,000 people in Yei, Lainya and surrounding areas. Armed forces killed, tortured, abducted, and sexually abused civilians. In August, fighting spread to Lobonok, Mundri, Wonduruba and parts of Eastern Equatoria with similar abuses.

In June, security forces killed four civilians during a land dispute and one other person while responding to peaceful protests in Sherikat neighborhood in Juba.

Following a dispute over a government disarmament operation in August, at least 127 people including 82 civilians were killed and thousands more displaced in clashes between soldiers and armed civilians in Tonj town, Warrap state.

Armed groups attacked UN and humanitarian actors and restricted their movement.

In June, armed youth from Jonglei declared a no-fly zone over the Greater Pibor Administrative Area (GPAA) threatening to shoot down a United Nations Mission in South Sudan (UNMISS) aircraft. In July, army and National Security Service (NSS) officers blocked an UNMISS force that was mobilized to rescue two aid workers ambushed by unknown gunmen in the outskirts of Wau, Western Bar el Ghazal.

In July, two South Sudanese aid workers and four civilians were killed in Duk county, Jonglei state, by an unknown armed group. At least 14 aid workers were killed in 2020.

In August two humanitarian vehicles, including an ambulance carrying four patients, were ambushed by an unknown armed group on the Yei-Lobonok road.

Intercommunal Violence

In Jonglei and GPAA, attacks and counterattacks between the Lou Nuer, Gawaar Nuer, Dinka Bor and Murle communities intensified since late February. Hundreds of people were killed, injured, and abducted, and over 150,000 displaced.

In May, at least 287 people were killed during an attack by armed Murle youth groups against Lou Nuer villages in Pieri, Jonglei state.

In June, President Kiir formed a committee led by Vice President James Wani Igga, to resolve the violence involving the three communities.

In March, inter-clan fighting, triggered by the killing of two older men by unknown gunmen in Lakes states, killed 41 people and injured at least 60.

Sexual Violence

In May, the Ceasefire and Transitional Security Arrangements Monitoring Mechanism (CTSAMM) to the peace deal reported that government forces had raped three women and a 14-year old girl in Rubeke village, Central Equatoria during attacks on rebels on February 13. In September, CTSAMM also reported that four SPLA/IO soldiers gang-raped two girls in August in Mundri, Western Equatoria.

Between June and September, UNMISS said it had documented at least 21 cases of rape, gang-rape, forced marriage, forced nudity, sexual slavery, and attempted rape. The victims included girls as young as 10, three pregnant or lactating women, and one child with a psychosocial disability. The assaults documented were by army, community-based militias, and non-government armed groups.

A South Sudanese civil society organization reported that since Covid-19 restrictions were imposed in April, at least 1,535 girls were subjected to child mar-

HUMAN
RIGHTS
WATCH

"What Crime Was I Paying For?"
Abuses by South Sudan's National Security Service

riages, pregnancies, or forced prostitution in states of Western, Eastern, and Central Equatorial.

In May, UNMISS reported on the inadequate medical response for sexual and gender- based violence survivors in South Sudan, both because of underfunding by the government to the health sector (only 1.2 percent of the budget was allocated to the public health sector) and the inability of international organizations to meet needs because of other priorities and funding shortfalls.

Arbitrary Detentions, Freedom of Media

South Sudan's National Security Service detained journalists and activists critical of the government.

In January, NSS officers arrested Ijoo Bosco, a journalist working with a local radio station in Torit for six days, for airing news on United States government sanctions for human rights abuses against the first vice president, Taban Deng Gai.

In June, NSS officers detained Moses Monday, director of the Organization for Non-Violence, for erecting billboards demanding financial transparency in government spending. They released him without charge after two weeks.

On May 29, NSS detained political activist Kanybil Noon, and held him without charge for 117 days, releasing him on condition that he stop criticizing the government.

On June 22, access to the Sudans Post, a local news website, was blocked by the government following the publication of an article deemed defamatory by the NSS.

Sexual Orientation and Gender Identity

South Sudan punishes "carnal knowledge against the order of nature" with up to 10 years in prison and a fine, under section 248 of its 2008 Penal Code Act. The code also criminalizes forms of gender expression by condemning "any male person who dresses or is attired in the fashion of a woman in a public place" to up to one year in prison or a fine, or both.

Justice and Accountability

South Sudan made no progress establishing the Hybrid Court for South Sudan with the African Union Commission, to be staffed by South Sudanese and African judges, envisioned in the peace agreement, to try serious international crimes committed during the conflict. It has yet to sign a proposed memorandum of understanding with the AU or promulgate legislation on the court.

The Sudan People's Liberation Army Act provides that crimes against civilians should be tried by civilian courts. Yet in September, 26 soldiers were convicted by an army court martial for crimes, including rape, looting, killings, and harassment since the outbreak of the conflict in the Yei area in 2016.

In December 2019, the NSS announced the creation of a special tribunal to try officers for crimes against the state and abuses against civilians. To date, it is known to have tried only one officer for killing a fellow officer.

Key International Actors

In March, the UN Security Council renewed UNMISS for another year and in June the UN Human Rights Council renewed the Commission on Human Rights in South Sudan, which reported human rights abuses and impunity for widespread atrocities committed in the country's conflict, despite the 2018 peace agreement and formation of a unity government.

The UN Panel of Experts on South Sudan found evidence that South Sudan's neighbors violated a UN arms embargo imposed on South Sudan in 2018. Sudan delivered weapons three times between March and June 2019, and Ugandan troops entered the country without notifying the UN. Regional countries—as in previous years—also failed to report required cargo inspections.

In May, the UN Security Council renewed the UN arms embargo on the country and individual sanctions on eight South Sudanese nationals for their role in the conflict.

In January, the US Treasury sanctioned Vice President Deng Gai for serious human rights violations, including his role in the disappearance and reported killing of government critics Dong Samuel Luak and Aggrey Ezbon Idri who were kidnapped from Kenya in January 2017. In late December 2019, the US sanctioned five South Sudanese individuals for their role in the disappearance of the two men.

In July, local missions of the EU, France, Germany, Netherlands, Sweden, Canada and the UK, deplored the high levels of sexual and gender-based violence affecting children and women in South Sudan, and highlighted ongoing impunity for abuses.

South Sudan mediated peace talks between Sudan's transitional government and the Sudan Revolutionary Front, a coalition of rebel groups from the western region of Darfur and the southern states of South Kordofan and Blue Nile, leading to the signing of a peace deal in Juba on August 31.

On September 4, UNMISS announced the beginning of a plan to transform its protection of civilian sites, which host at least 180,000 displaced people under the protection of UN peacekeepers, into conventional displaced persons' camps with government police rather than UN force protection providing security, sparking fears in the camp populations of potential abuses by government forces and police.

Spain

Spain was hit hard by the public health and economic challenges of the Covid-19 pandemic. The government took steps to shore up social security support as unemployment and poverty rose. Violence against women rose during a nationwide lockdown imposed to manage the pandemic. Conditions in reception facilities for migrants and in informal settlements housing migrant agricultural workers were unsanitary. Prosecutions continued of pro-independence Catalan actors. Courts limited musicians' freedom of expression using overbroad criminal charges of glorifying terrorism and insulting the monarchy. In its October rule of law report, the European Commission flagged concerns about efficiency of the justice system and perceived lack of independence of the prosecutor general from the executive.

Covid-19

The World Health Organization estimated that 34,752 people had died from Covid-19 by October 28. Official national data showed excess deaths in people aged 65 and older as 18-24 percent higher than usual between March and October.

Organizations representing medical and care workers complained of ineffective, insufficient personal protective equipment in March and April, with many forced to rely on homemade masks and gowns during the early weeks of the pandemic. The Health Ministry confirmed that as of early June, 63 health workers had died from Covid-19.

The national government declared a state of emergency, with freedom of movement highly restricted during a lockdown across the country between March and June. Children across Spain were not allowed out of their homes at all for a six-week period between March 14 and April 26. Responding to increasing infection rates in late October, the national government declared a two-week state of emergency and sought parliamentary approval to impose a six-month state of emergency, ordering night curfews, and other measures at the discretion of regional authorities.

Schools nationwide closed for in-person learning in mid-March and reopened in September. Children's rights advocates raised concern that distance learning could increase gaps in educational attainment for children from migrant backgrounds and low-income families.

Poverty and Unemployment

The economic closures amid the pandemic led to widespread job losses. The government provided support through a nationwide furlough scheme through January 2021.

From March through September, the government decreed that utility providers could not cut off services to people on low incomes.

In May, the government announced a Minimum Vital Income scheme (IMV), as a form of financial support to people living in "very high" or "extreme" poverty on less than €4,350 (US$5,105) per year. The system, expected to reach 850,000 households, was soon overwhelmed with applications and the government extended its deadline for retrospective claims. The UN special rapporteur on extreme poverty and human rights called on the government to increase coverage and eligibility.

In July, the former UN special rapporteur on extreme poverty criticized the general social protection system for inadequate support to the country's poor, substandard housing conditions, and highlighted de facto segregation of Roma and migrant children in the education system.

Violence Against Women

In March, the Equality Ministry launched a plan to tackle gender-based violence during lockdown, including reinforcing staffing for telephone hotlines and setting up a new instant alert system to report domestic violence. Judicial authorities kept courts open to hear cases relating to domestic violence and child abuse during lockdown. Calls to the national gender-based violence helpline increased dramatically, with requests for assistance during April up 61.1 percent compared to the same period the previous year.

Migration and Asylum

According to the UN refugee agency UNHCR, by mid-October at least 20,499 people had arrived irregularly by sea to Spain's mainland, islands, and Ceuta and Melilla, the country's enclaves in Morocco, while 1,399 people entered the enclaves by land. As of August, at least 440 people had died or gone missing in the Western Mediterranean and the Atlantic Ocean en route to Spain. One man died scaling the Melilla border fence in August.

Asylum claims dropped by 13 percent during the year and fell to almost zero during the state of emergency during which all asylum interviews were canceled.

Between March and May, the Interior Ministry released all people detained in closed immigration detention centers on the Spanish mainland as border closures made deportations impossible. In September, the government announced it had reopened detention centers.

Overcrowding was a serious problem in the reception center in Melilla and a temporary shelter set up in the local bullring. Judges twice rejected attempts by authorities to put the open center under lockdown after Covid-19 cases were reported. UNHCR, the Council of Europe's Human Rights Commissioner, and NGOs urged authorities to find alternative accommodation and to transfer people to mainland Spain.

Spain failed to ensure adequate reception conditions or access to information on asylum amid a rapid increase in arrivals by sea to the Canary Islands starting in September. The autonomous community's chief prosecutor ordered authorities in November to stop separating children from their parents pending DNA verification.

In a ruling that threatened to weaken protection against refoulement, the Grand Chamber of the European Court of Human Rights ruled in February that the 2014 summary deportation of two sub-Saharan African men from Spain to Morocco did not violate their rights, because their action in scaling the Melilla border fence with other migrants had been unlawful.

The UN Committee on the Rights of the Child announced in October that Spain had violated the rights of unaccompanied migrant and asylum-seeking children in all 14 cases brought before it since 2019. The children, most of whom arrived by boat, did not receive age-appropriate protection and care as a result of a flawed age determination process and a lack of safeguards to ensure the best interests of the child.

Migrant agricultural workers, many from North and sub-Saharan Africa, continued to experience unsanitary living conditions and labor exploitation. In March, the government temporarily extended the validity of migrant workers' permits set to expire during the state of emergency to ensure harvesting was not affected. In May, the government announced a two-year agricultural work permit scheme for 18-21-year-old foreign nationals with regular status in Spain.

Seven UN special rapporteurs called on Spanish authorities in June to ensure safe living and working conditions and access to healthcare for seasonal agricultural workers. The use of masks and gloves, social distancing, and access to water and cleaning products, to prevent the spread of Covid-19, were not always ensured for seasonal agricultural workers. In July, Andalusia's regional human rights ombudsperson began investigating a series of fires that destroyed informal settlements housing migrant agricultural workers in Huelva.

Racism and Discrimination

Nongovernmental organizations (NGOs) and associations representing ethnic minorities documented what they considered to be a pattern of increased racism and discrimination against people of Chinese, African, Arab and gitano (Roma) origin during the state of emergency. People of Chinese, or perceived to be of Chinese, origin were victims of hate crimes. Police were accused of relying on ethnic profiling when carrying out identity document checks during lockdown and using heavy-handed tactics in neighborhoods with a high-proportion gitano population.

In October, the Council of Europe's Advisory Committee on the Framework Convention for Protection of National Minorities called on Spain to tackle anti-Roma prejudice and amend the criminal code to include "anti-Gypsyism" as an aggravating circumstance in hate crime.

Disability Rights

In September, the UN Committee on the Rights of Persons with Disabilities found that Spain had violated the right to inclusive education of a child with Down syndrome whom authorities sent to a special education center rather than provide reasonable accommodations to enable his inclusion in a mainstream school. The committee urged Spain to end educational segregation of children with disabilities, and not prosecute parents who claimed their children's right to inclusive education.

During the year advocates for the rights of children, people with disabilities and the gitano community launched a legislative campaign to end segregation in education and to create a domestic right to inclusive education.

Right to Housing

On March 31, the government announced six months of temporary mortgage and rent relief measures, and a halt on evictions of people it defined as "economically vulnerable." The government also approved temporary measures to provide increased housing support to victims of gender-based violence and homeless people during the state of emergency. Evictions resumed in June, with housing rights activists calling for an extension of the evictions ban through 2021. In September, the government ordered a further four-month extension of rent relief and allowed tenants with documented "economic vulnerability" who faced evictions to seek postponement until January.

Reproductive Rights

In February, the UN Committee on the Elimination of Discrimination against Women ruled that repeated invasive procedures, which a woman experienced without informed consent during pregnancy and childbirth in 2009, had violated her rights. The committee found that domestic courts had failed to take into account fully the evidence provided by the woman and subjected her to gender stereotypes and discrimination. In addition to reparations to the woman for physical and psychological damage, the committee recommended Spain provide more training about reproductive health and other rights to health workers and judicial and law enforcement personnel, and ensure access to justice in cases of obstetric violence.

Disputed 2017 Catalan Referendum

Spanish authorities continued to press charges against officials and pro-independence activists for their role in the disputed 2017 referendum on Catalan independence, deemed illegal by the Spanish courts. A Barcelona prosecutor filed criminal charges against 30 lower-level officials, civil servants, businesspeople, and journalists for their role in the disputed referendum.

In September, the Supreme Court upheld Catalonia President Quim Torra's 2019 conviction for disobedience for displaying a placard supporting imprisoned pro-independence activists on his office balcony during a pre-election period.

Freedom of Expression

Judicial authorities continued to prosecute musicians on overbroad offenses of glorifying of terrorism and lèse-majesté (injury to the crown), for lyrics or tweets that appeared to support banned armed groups or that criticized the monarchy.

In June, the Supreme Court sentenced rapper Pablo Hasel to nine months in prison after convicting him of glorification and insulting the king. That month, the Supreme Court also upheld an earlier High Court conviction and 6-month prison sentence of 12 members of the hip hop group La Insurgencia for glorifying terrorism. Spain continued to seek the extradition from Belgium of the rapper Valtònyc, convicted in 2018 of glorifying terrorism, lèse-majesté, and threats to a regional politician.

However, in February, the Constitutional Court overturned a 2017 Supreme Court conviction of musician César Strawberry for glorification and humiliating victims of terrorism in tweets he posted in 2013 and 2014, finding that the ruling violated his right to free expression.

In October, the trial began of a demonstrator for hate crimes and offending Catholic religious sentiment after carrying a giant plastic vulva through Seville's streets to mark International Women's Day in 2013.

Freedom of Assembly

In October, the European Court of Human Rights ruled that Spain had violated the free assembly rights of a woman left "permanently incapacitated" after being hit with a police truncheon during a peaceful 2014 anti-austerity protest in Valladolid.

Sri Lanka

Fundamental human rights protections in Sri Lanka came under serious jeopardy following Gotabaya Rajapaksa's election as president in November 2019. In February 2020, Sri Lanka withdrew its commitments to truth seeking, accountability, and reconciliation made at the United Nations Human Rights Council in 2015.

Human rights defenders, victims of past abuses, lawyers, and journalists, faced intimidation and surveillance from government security forces. Muslims and Tamils faced discrimination and threats.

President Rajapaksa transferred responsibility for large areas of civil administration to the Ministry of Defense, including the government's response to the Covid-19 pandemic. Following his party's victory in parliamentary elections on August 5, the government passed a constitutional amendment that removes constraints on presidential power.

After postponing parliamentary elections twice during the coronavirus pandemic, Sri Lanka in August, Sri Lanka successfully held polls with Covid-19 protection guidelines and reported a 71 percent turnout.

Accountability and Justice

On February 26, Sri Lanka announced at the UN Human Rights Council in Geneva that it was withdrawing from its commitments to provide justice and accountability for war crimes and other grave violations committed during and since the civil war between the government and the separatist Liberation Tigers of Tamil Eelam (LTTE), which ended in 2009.

Rajapaksa, who ran on a platform of protecting "war heroes" from prosecution, was defense secretary during the administration of his brother, then-President (now Prime Minister) Mahinda Rajapaksa, when the alleged abuses took place. Several senior members of his government, including the defense secretary, Kamal Gunaratne, and army chief Gen. Shavendra Silva, were also implicated. In February, the US State Department announced that General Silva was ineligible for entry into the United States due to his alleged involvement in extrajudicial killings.

On March 26, President Rajapaksa pardoned former Sgt. Sunil Ratnayake, who had been convicted of the massacre of eight Tamil civilians, including children, at Mirusuvil in 2000. He was one of very few members of the Sri Lankan armed forces ever held accountable for human rights violations.

The families of victims, including mothers of those forcibly disappeared, called on the UN Human Rights Council to adopt a new resolution establishing an international accountability mechanism to pursue justice for abuses.

Attacks on Human Rights Defenders

The Rajapaksa administration escalated surveillance and intimidation targeting victims' families and human rights defenders, as well as lawyers and journalists whose work was perceived as challenging the government. Those targeted included victims and activists who engaged with the Human Rights Council.

Families of the disappeared, who have been campaigning for years to know the fate of their relatives who were last seen in security forces custody, reported heightened surveillance and threats from the intelligence services. Human rights defenders received phone calls and visits from members of the security and intelligence agencies, who demanded to know the personal details of staff and inquired into their work on accountability for past abuses.

Authorities targeted funding that human rights groups receive from abroad, alleging that such money was used to support "terrorism." Human rights defenders reported that the banking system was preventing them from receiving international transfers. The nongovernmental organization secretariat, which regulates civil society organizations, was placed under the authority of the Ministry of Defense. The government proposed a new law to regulate foreign funding for Sri Lankan groups that raises free expression and association concerns.

On April 14, the police arrested Hejaaz Hizbullah, a lawyer who has represented victims of rights violations, under the draconian Prevention of Terrorism Act. He was held arbitrarily without charge and without being produced before a magistrate, and remained in custody. Kumaravadivel Guruparan, a lawyer representing the families of victims of enforced disappearance, was prevented from teaching law at Jaffna University following an intervention by the army. Other lawyers were also subjected to threats and arbitrary detention.

Nishantha Silva, a senior police investigator working on abuses committed under the previous Rajapaksa administration, fled the country shortly after the presidential election in November 2019. In July, the former head of the Criminal Investigation Department, Shani Abeysekera, who oversaw these cases, was arrested for allegedly concealing evidence, although a policeman testified that he had been pressured to falsely incriminate Abeysekera, who remained in detention.

Freedoms of Expression and Association

Several journalists reported receiving death threats or other intimidation, and some fled the country. Among them was Dharisha Bastians, a former editor of the *Sunday Observer* and contributor to the *New York Times*, whose laptop was seized and telephone records publicized by the government. A climate of self-censorship returned, reversing the relative openness that had prevailed under the previous administration.

On April 1, police announced that anyone "criticising" the government's response to the Covid-19 pandemic would be arrested. UN High Commissioner for Human Rights Michelle Bachelet criticised Sri Lanka for using the pandemic to stifle freedom of expression.

On April 9, Ramzy Razeek, a retired government official, received death threats after decrying religious discrimination in a social media post. When he complained to the authorities, he was arrested and released on bail over three months later.

Treatment of Minorities

For several years, Muslims in Sri Lanka have been the target of virulent hate speech in mainstream and social media, which worsened following the 2019 Easter Sunday bombings by Islamist militants that killed over 250 people. During the early months of the Covid-19 pandemic there were calls on social media to boycott Muslim businesses, and false allegations of Muslims spreading Covid-19 deliberately. After senior government figures made public comments implying—falsely—that the virus was particularly rife among Muslims, civil society organizations wrote to President Rajapaksa raising concerns that this had led to "outpourings of vitriol, and hate speech against Muslims."

In March, the government published guidelines requiring that the remains of all Covid-19 victims be cremated, which goes against Islamic tradition and was not required for public health. Four UN special rapporteurs criticized the requirement as a violation of religious freedom.

On June 2, President Rajapaksa established a Presidential Task Force for Archaeological Heritage Management in the Eastern Province, composed of security officials and Buddhist monks, raising fears that it would disadvantage the predominant Tamil and Muslim communities. Rajapaksa said the purpose of the task force was to "preserve our Buddhist heritage."

Sexual Orientation and Gender Identity

Same-sex relations are criminalized in Sri Lanka, and a law banning "impersonation" is used to target transgender people. Authorities use these powers to harass, detain, and extort gay, lesbian and transgender people, who also face societal discrimination.

Women's Rights

Reflecting a global pattern, the lockdown to contain the spread of Covid-19, saw a spike in gender-based violence in Sri Lanka. Women, particularly those working in garment factories, were initially stranded during the nationwide curfews, and later returned to their homes, but suffered due to wage loss. To minimize loss of workers' income, the Free Trade Zones and General Services Employees Union negotiated a tripartite agreement to ensure that all workers across different industries received at least 50 percent of their pay through September.

Militarization and Institutional Changes

The Rajapaksa government placed over 30 agencies, including the police, under the authority of the Ministry of Defense, and retired and serving military officers were appointed to numerous key posts previously held by civilians.

On June 2, President Rajapaksa established a Presidential Task Force to build a Secure Country, Disciplined, Virtuous and Lawful Society, composed entirely of military and security officials, with loosely defined powers and the authority to issue instructions to all government officials.

A 20th amendment to the constitution, passed on October 22, gives the president sweeping new powers, including to appoint senior judges, members of the Human Rights Commission and other independent institutions, such as anti-corruption bodies, to appoint and dismiss ministers including the prime minister, and to dissolve parliament at least two and a half years after elections. Revisions to the amendment diluted some provisions, while not significantly lessening the amendment's overall threat to human rights protections.

Key International Actors

In her update to the UN Human Rights Council on September 14, UN High Commissioner Michelle Bachelet warned of "a very negative trend," noted that Sri Lanka was "swiftly reneging on its commitments," and encouraged the council to "give renewed attention to Sri Lanka, in view of the need to prevent threats to peace, reconciliation and sustainable development."

The core group on Sri Lanka at the Human Rights Council (Canada, Germany, North Macedonia, Montenegro, and the United Kingdom) called for "an end to impunity for the violations and abuses of the past," but has not yet shown leadership in presenting a new resolution to advance international accountability.

Sri Lanka has military and security cooperation with the United States, India, Australia, and the United Kingdom, among others. Sri Lankan trade with the European Union under the GSP+ scheme links better market access to human rights and labor standards. However, the EU, like other foreign partners, has been muted in its response to Sri Lankan rights abuses. Sri Lanka is a participant in China's "Belt and Road" Initiative, although there are concerns about the debt burden this is creating.

Sudan

Sudan's first year of a three-year transition to democratic rule following the dramatic ouster of President Omar al-Bashir in 2019, was marked by a failing economy, political tensions and continuing popular protests for justice and reforms. These challenges were compounded by the Covid-19 pandemic.

The government introduced some reforms but has not yet implemented most of the institutional and law reforms called for in the August 2019 constitutional charter.

Authorities did not release the results of a national investigation into the violent crackdown on protesters in Khartoum on June 3, 2019, in which more than 120 people were killed. In June, the International Criminal Court (ICC) took into custody its first suspect of serious crimes committed in Darfur.

On August 31, the government and a coalition of rebel groups signed a peace deal in Juba that would end the country's internal armed conflicts and provide for cooperation with the ICC in its Darfur investigation, and establishing a national special court for Darfur crimes.

In Darfur and eastern Sudan, inter-communal violence surged. The United Nations/African Union Darfur peacekeeping mission (UNAMID) continued to draw down, while a new nationwide political mission began to deploy.

As the Covid-19 pandemic hit, about 6 million children were forced out of school due to school closures, and human rights groups reported a surge in domestic violence.

Donors pledged hundreds of millions of US dollars to support Sudan, while US President Donald Trump announced that the US would lift the state-sponsor of terrorism designation; Sudan and Israel officially agreed to normalize relations.

Reforms

Authorities repealed an abusive public order law, outlawed female genital mutilation, removed the death penalty and lashing as punishments for consensual same-sex conduct and many other offenses, and abolished apostasy as a crime.

However, many of the other reforms envisioned in the 2019 Constitutional Charter were not implemented.

The government has yet to set up a legislative council and key transitional commissions. It has not embarked on security sector reform beyond renaming the National Intelligence and Security Service (NISS) as the General Intelligence Service (GIS) and removing its arrest and detention powers.

Accountability

The committee to investigate the violent dispersal of protests in Khartoum on June 3, in which more than 120 were killed, has not released its findings. Victims' families and activists have strongly criticized its slow pace as well as its lack of witness protection and sexual and gender-based violence expertise.

The Attorney General's Office formed several committees to investigate past crimes and rights abuses including in Darfur, but no investigation has yet led to prosecutions. Authorities announced the discovery of two mass graves during the year they said contain the remains of military personnel killed during al-Bashir's rule.

On February 11, a member of the sovereign council, a collective presidency body composed of both civilians and military, publicly announced the government's commitment to cooperate with the ICC, which officials reaffirmed throughout the year.

On June 9, the ICC prosecutor announced that a Janjaweed militia leader, Ali Mohamed Ali ("Kosheib"), surrendered to the ICC in the Central African Republic and is currently facing charges at the Hague. ICC arrest warrants for al-Bashir, two former officials, and a rebel leader are outstanding. Al-Bashir and the two former officials are detained in Khartoum.

The ICC prosecutor visited Khartoum in October and discussed with Sudanese officials modalities of cooperation, including on the execution of outstanding arrest warrants.

Ex-President al-Bashir is currently standing trial alongside other former officials for undermining the constitutional order due their role in the 1989 coup against Sudan's last elected government.

Crackdowns on Protesters

Protesters continued calling for faster reforms and accountability. In some instances, government security forces dispersed them violently.

In Khartoum, on June 30, the one-year anniversary of a major protest following al-Bashir's ouster, police responded with violence, killing one protester and injuring several. On August 17, on the anniversary of the power-sharing deal, police used tear gas and whips against protesters gathered in front of the prime minister's office, arresting and injuring many.

In North Darfur, armed militia attacked a sit-in in Fata Borno, a displaced persons camp near Kutum, in North Darfur, on July 13, killing at least nine. The day before, government forces dispersed a protest in Kutum, arresting, beating and detaining dozens suspected of organizing the protests, witnesses told Human Rights Watch.

On October 15, security forces killed at least eight and injuring others in the eastern state of Kassala. Protests were called for by tribal leaders of Beni Amir after the dismissal of the state governor by the prime minister. A protester was also killed by security forces in Khartoum on October 21.

Arbitrary Detentions

Security officials continued to arbitrarily detain civilians. Throughout the year Rapid Support Forces (RSF) reportedly detained several members of the Mahamid Arab tribe due to their links to Musa Hilal, the former pro-government militia leader who is subject to UN sanctions for his role in Darfur atrocities.

RSF officials detained Abdulmalik Musa Saleh, a political activist and a relative of Hilal, several times during the year in Khartoum, and Osama Mohamed al-Hassan, 40, also an activist, from July 5 until September 17. At time of writing, while neither man is in custody, neither have they been charged with any offence and were never brought to court throughout their detention.

Hilal has been detained since November 2017 and is reportedly facing charges by a military court for crimes against government forces in Darfur.

On June 29, the former military governor of West Darfur ordered the imprisonment of 72 men and boys for six months under the emergency law, which allows authorities to detain people without judicial oversight. They were among a group of 122 arrested by the RSF in the preceding weeks during counter migration operations in Darfur.

Authorities charged them with crimes including looting, illegal migration, and illegal possession of firearms. They were never brought to trial.

Government security forces arrested and detained civilians in Kutum, North Darfur, and Kass, South Darfur, following protests in both locations. At least one of the released detainees from Kutum held by military officials told Human Rights Watch he was subjected to ill-treatment that could amount to torture while in detention.

Freedom of Expression and Assembly

In September, 11 artists were sentenced to two months in prison for being a "public nuisance" and "disturbing public peace," in part because of pro-democracy chants they shouted while in the police station.

In July, the transitional government amended the 2007 Cybercrimes Act, increasing its penalties rather than repealing vaguely worded offenses criminalizing the "spread of false news" and publication of "indecent materials." On July 18, the Sudanese army appointed a special commissioner to bring lawsuits against individuals who "insult" the military online, both inside and outside the country.

On January 7, the "dismantling committee," set up to tackle corruption and re-possess stolen assets and properties by the former ruling party, suspended *Al-ray al-am* and *al-Sudani* newspapers and two private TV channels for alleged financial links to al-Bashir's regime. The committee lacks judicial oversight and has faced criticism for being a political tool.

Conflict in Darfur and Eastern Sudan

Inter-communal violence intensified, exacerbated by the involvement of government security forces

In Al Geneina, West Darfur, fighting between Arab and Masalit communities flared in December 2019, six months after UNAMID forces had withdrawn from their base there. Armed militia groups, including members of the RSF, attacked a camp for displaced people and killed dozens of people, including children, raped women, and girls, destroyed schools, and burned homes, causing tens of thousands to flee.

On July 25, armed Arab militia attacked the town of Misteri, West Darfur. The attackers targeted ethnic Masalit, according to media. The UN said at least 60 were killed in the attack.

In eastern Sudan, at least 25 were killed after violent clashes between the Beni Amer and Nuba ethnic groups in Port Sudan. Scores were also killed after violent clashes in the city of Kassala in August, between tribal groups of Hadendawa and Beni Amer.

Key International Actors

In June, the European Union, Germany, the UAE, and Sudan co-hosted the Sudan Partnership Conference in Berlin. Donors pledged over $1.8 billion.

During the year, the EU encouraged and supported Sudan's ongoing peace efforts and democratic transition. The EU and its member states reiterated calls to the Sudanese authorities to secure justice for past atrocity crimes, including through full cooperation with the ICC, and to take concrete legislative and policy steps to advance protection of human rights. The EU welcomed Sudan's decision to ban female genital mutilation.

On June 3, the United Nations Security Council approved a new nationwide political mission, the UN Integrated Transition Assistance Mission (UNITAMS), to support Sudan's transition. The peacekeeping mission in Darfur, UNAMID, continued to downsize.

In February, the UN Security Council extended the mandate of the Panel of Experts on Sudan another year. In July, the UN Office of the High Commissioner for Human Rights indicated that its country office in Khartoum was operational. In October, the UN Human Rights Council terminated the mandate of the independent expert on the situation of human rights in Sudan but kept Sudan on its agenda through reporting by the High Commissioner for Human Rights.

On October 19, President Trump announced the intention of the US administration to remove Sudan from its state sponsor of terrorism designation. The US

Congress would need to approve this after being formally notified by the president. It followed months of negotiations in which Sudan agreed to pay US$335 million to victims of terrorist attacks that targeted US citizens abroad and led to Sudan's designation in 1993.

HUMAN
RIGHTS
WATCH

"Targeting Life in Idlib"
Syrian and Russian Strikes on Civilian Infrastructure

Syria

In 2020, civilians in Syria faced another year confronting stark challenges and abuses, first and foremost at the hands of the Syrian government and other authorities, despite a discernible decrease in violent conflict.

With the unprecedented depreciation of the national currency, the imposition of further international sanctions, and crises in neighboring countries, the Syrian economy went into freefall for much of 2020. For ordinary Syrians, this translated into an inability to procure food, essential drugs, and other basic necessities. As a result, more than 9.3 million Syrians have become food insecure and over 80 percent of Syrians live below the poverty line.

Meanwhile, human rights abuses in government-held territory continued unabated. Authorities brutally suppressed every sign of re-emerging dissent, including through arbitrary arrests and torture. Authorities also continued to unlawfully confiscate property and restrict access to areas of origin for returning Syrians.

The decade-long war has decimated the country's economy and healthcare system, significantly complicating efforts to respond to and mitigate the Covid-19 outbreak, even in areas where active fighting has receded. Despite official numbers being low, doctors and nurses in government-held areas cast doubt upon the accuracy of these official statistics and estimate that hundreds of thousands have been infected with coronavirus. Overwhelmed hospitals turned patients away, and severe shortages of personal protective equipment contributed to large numbers of deaths. The pandemic also exposed existing fissures in the country, including the discriminatory distribution of essential medical supplies.

Until March 2020, when a ceasefire was put in place, the Syrian-Russian military alliance continued its offensive on Idlib governorate, the last anti-government foothold in Syria. Since 2019, the alliance has targeted civilians and civilian infrastructure in the northwest in indiscriminate attacks, resulting in thousands of deaths and at least one million newly displaced people. The offensive also meant that the region was ill-prepared to deal with the pandemic. With over 50 percent of the health infrastructure destroyed, and hundreds of thousands without shelter and unable to practice social distancing, the region is increasingly at risk of a devastating outbreak.

The United Nations Security Council's closure of the sole authorized border crossing from Iraq to northeast Syria in January, due to a veto threat from Russia, and restrictions applied from government-held areas on the delivery of humanitarian aid, resulted in severe shortages of medical supplies and a dwindling number of hospitals capable of responding to the coronavirus pandemic in the region.

The difficulties with cross-border aid grew in July when the council closed one of two authorized crossings for UN aid deliveries from Turkey into northwest Syria. Now there is only one authorized crossing, resulting in bottlenecks and delays.

Meanwhile, the fate of thousands kidnapped by the Islamic State (ISIS), primarily in the northeast, remains uncertain. While the Kurdish-led Syrian Democratic Council (SDC), announced the creation of a civilian working group to trace and locate those who have been disappeared by ISIS, no significant progress has been made, and the US-led Global Coalition to Defeat ISIS remains largely absent on this issue.

Abuses by the Syrian-Russian Military Alliance, Use of Unlawful Weapons

The Syrian-Russian military alliance continued to deliberately and indiscriminately attack civilian objects—including schools, hospitals, markets, homes, and shelters—using what have become trademark tactics over the years, including the use of internationally banned weapons.

Human Rights Watch documented 18 unlawful attacks in Idlib between January and March 2020. The attacks killed at least 112 people and wounded at least another 359 and destroyed schools and healthcare facilities. Cluster munitions were used in two of the attacks on schools in Idlib City in February.

By March 2020, 84 medical facilities had suspended their operations in the governorates of Idlib and Aleppo according to the United Nations Office for the Coordination of Humanitarian Affairs (UNOCHA). Save the Children reported that 217 schools were abandoned or damaged due to the conflict in Idlib from December

2019 to March 2020.

Following the re-taking of specific areas, government ground forces—including the 25th Special Forces Division, a Russian-backed elite Syrian government force formerly known as the Tiger Forces—retaliated against civilians who chose not to leave the towns of Idlib and Aleppo governorates, shooting at them and despoiling the bodies of the dead. In February, disturbing video footage surfaced of government forces firing at older women in west Aleppo as civilians were packing their belongings to leave the area.

Obstacles to Humanitarian Aid and Reconstruction

While levels of violence have reduced significantly, over 11.1 million people in Syria still require humanitarian aid. A decade of war beset by violations, including crimes against humanity, has decimated the country's infrastructure, with homes and schools destroyed, lack of clean water and sanitation, and most of the population unable to make ends meet.

Despite this, the Syrian government continued to impose severe restrictions on the delivery of humanitarian aid in government-held areas of Syria and elsewhere in the country. Purporting to justify its acts according to its laws and policies, the government restricted humanitarian organizations' access to communities that needed aid, selectively approved aid projects to punish civilians in anti-government held areas, and required humanitarian groups to partner with security-vetted local actors. There is a continuing risk that aid and reconstruction funding in the future will be siphoned through the abusive state apparatus and used to underwrite human rights abuses.

In January, following the threat of a Russian veto, the United Nations Security Council (UNSC) ended its authorization for moving UN aid supplies from Iraq to northeast Syria. Non-UN aid groups that previously depended heavily on the UN for healthcare supplies have been unable to deliver enough aid from the Kurdistan Region of Iraq to northeast Syria to meet the population's needs. Meanwhile, Syrian authorities in Damascus maintained their longstanding restrictions on aid reaching Kurdish-held areas in northeast Syria. According to UNOCHA, only 30 percent of medical facilities that previously received supplies across the border were being reached from Damascus, resulting in severe shortages of medical

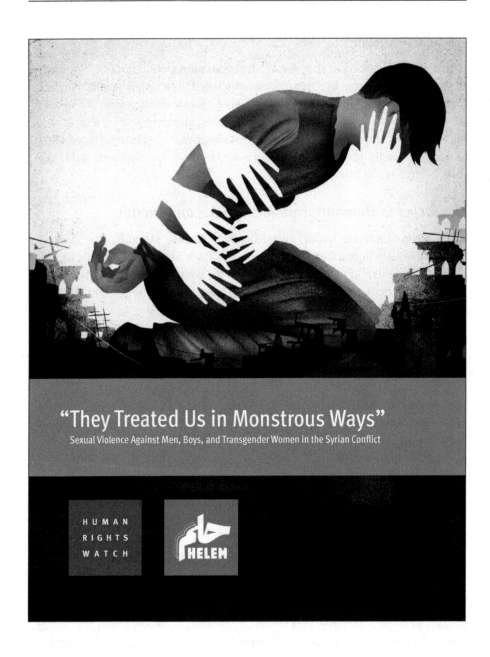

"They Treated Us in Monstrous Ways"
Sexual Violence Against Men, Boys, and Transgender Women in the Syrian Conflict

HUMAN RIGHTS WATCH

HELEM

supplies and closures of critical care centers, placing the right to health of over 2 million people at risk. In July 2020, the UN Security Council further gutted the cross-border mechanism by removing its authorization for one of the two border crossings to northwest Syria.

The Syrian government also continued to restrict access to residential buildings and to unlawfully demolish homes without adequate compensation. According to the UN Commission of Inquiry on Syria (COI), civilians were still being prevented from returning to their houses in Qaboun, Jawbar, Yarmouk camp, and parts of Darayya. The Syrian government is also using Decree 66 of 2012 and its overbroad counterterrorism law to confiscate the property of anti-government individuals and their families, without due process or adequate compensation.

Arbitrary Detentions, Torture, and Enforced Disappearances

Syrian security forces continue to arbitrarily detain, disappear, and mistreat people across the country, including returnees and individuals in retaken areas. According to the Syrian Network for Human Rights (SNHR), at least 100,000 Syrians remain forcibly disappeared. The network also estimates that nearly 15,000 have died due to torture since March 2011, the majority at the hands of Syrian government forces.

In February, a prominent human rights activist—Mazen al-Hummada—returned to Syria. According to his relatives and lawyer, he was detained upon return to Damascus airport. His whereabouts remain unknown. In June, Sweida residents began to organize mass gatherings to protest against the worsening economic conditions in the country. Syrian security forces and counter-protesters responded with brutal violence, quelling the protests, and arresting several anti-government activists. According to the COI, at least 34 men, one woman, and 10 children were disappeared in Daraa, Homs, Quneitra, Rif Damascus, and Sweida governorates by government security forces, including the Military Intelligence Directorate and the Military Police.

The spread of coronavirus has exacerbated concerns about detainees and the disappeared. Tens of thousands remain in government-detention facilities in horrific humanitarian conditions, where denial of access to healthcare is part of a state policy. On March 22, President Bashar al-Assad expanded the range of crimes included in an amnesty announced in September 2019, largely in response to the pandemic. However, only a few hundred people jailed for common crimes had been released so far, and the fate of thousands remains unknown.

The COI reported that women and girls faced sexual violence, including rape, in government detention facilities and areas under the control of armed groups. Both state and non-state actors continue to target men, boys, transgender women, gay and bisexual men, and nonbinary people, subjecting them to rape and other forms of sexual violence.

Violations by Anti-Government Groups

Hay'at Tahrir al-Sham (HTS), an Al-Qaeda affiliate rebranded into its own entity, remains predominantly in control of several regions in Idlib, where it continues a brutal pattern of repression against the civilian population. According to the COI, the group's abuses include arrests, torture of detainees, summary executions, lootings, blackmail, and monopolizing the electrical supply and internet services. The COI has documented four cases of executions of detainees and reviewed 10 additional reports of such cases between November 2019 and June 2020. According to the COI's report, HTS repeatedly interfered in the delivery of humanitarian aid and disrupted healthcare services.

Violations by Turkey and Turkish-Backed Factions

Turkey and the Turkish-backed Syrian National Army (SNA) have indiscriminately shelled civilian structures and systematically pillaged private property, arrested hundreds of individuals, and carried out at least seven summary executions in areas they occupy in northeast Syria. According to the COI, Turkish-backed forces have also committed sexual violence against women and men in territories under their control, including at least 30 incidents of rape.

Turkey and Turkish-backed factions have also failed to ensure adequate water supplies to Kurdish-held areas in northeast Syria. Around 460,000 individuals in Kurdish-held areas in northeast Syria depend on the supply of water from the Allouk water station near the town of Ras al-Ain (Serekaniye). The station's supply was interrupted 13 times following its takeover by Turkey and Turkish-backed forces in October 2019.

Violations by the Syrian Democratic Forces and the US-Led Coalition

The Syrian Democratic Forces, a Kurdish-led armed group, has arbitrarily detained at least eight activists in areas under its control on suspicion of affiliation with ISIS and refused to inform their families of their whereabouts. Kurdish-led authorities, with the support of the US-led military coalition against ISIS, continue to hold around 100,000 ISIS suspects and family members, most of them women and children. Tens of thousands of women and children affiliated with ISIS are held in locked desert camps in degrading and often life-threatening conditions, and at least 12,000 men and boys are in overcrowded prisons. Another 14,000 are from 60 other countries. None of the non-Iraqi foreigners has been brought before a judge to determine the necessity or legality of their detention.

In October, the Kurdish-led authorities announced two general amnesties. One for the 25,000 Syrians affiliated with ISIS in al-Hol camp, and another for low-level Syrian ISIS prisoners who were not charged with violent crimes. Until late October, close to 1,000 had been released.

Over the years, ISIS has kidnapped thousands of people, including journalists, activists, medical workers, community leaders, and human rights activists, whose fates continue to be unknown. In areas previously controlled by ISIS, more than 20 mass graves containing thousands of bodies have been discovered. In a positive step, on April 5, the Syrian Democratic Council (SDC), the de facto Kurdish authority currently in control of areas formerly held by ISIS, announced the creation of a new working group consisting of lawyers, activists, and relatives to help identify what happened to the people disappeared by ISIS. However, at time of writing, little progress had been made.

The global military coalition against ISIS has still not thoroughly investigated attacks by its members that killed civilians or created a program for compensation or other assistance for civilians harmed by coalition operations.

Displacement Crisis

Across the country, there are 6.1 million internally displaced. By mid-February, 900,000 people had been displaced due to hostilities in Idlib governorate, ac-

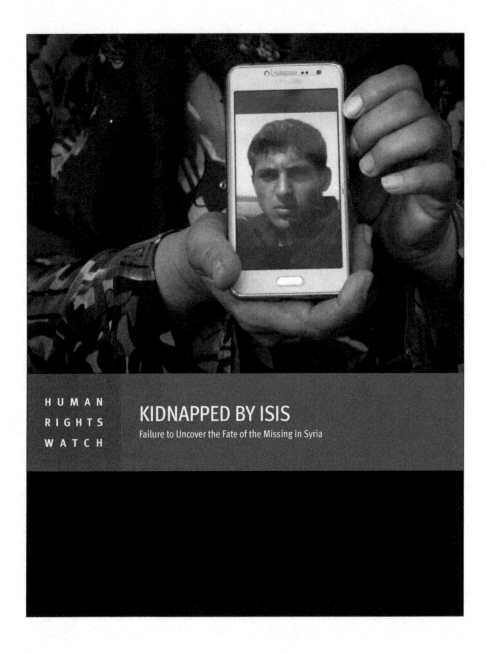

HUMAN
RIGHTS
WATCH

KIDNAPPED BY ISIS
Failure to Uncover the Fate of the Missing in Syria

cording to the UN Office for the Coordination of Humanitarian Affairs (UNOCHA). As of May, the UN High Commissioner for Refugees (UNHCR) records indicate that a total of 13,423 self-organized spontaneous returns had taken place from neighboring host countries. Turkey maintained a closed border.

On February 27, Turkey announced authorities would not intercept asylum seekers wishing to leave Turkey and head towards the European Union. Thousands of migrants and asylum seekers, including Syrian refugees, gathered at the Turkish-Greek border. Many of those that managed to cross into Greece were summarily pushed back. Greek security forces, along with unidentified armed men, detained, assaulted, sexually assaulted, robbed, and stripped asylum seekers and migrants, then forced them back to Turkey. Turkey continues to detain and summarily deport Syrians back to northern Syria in violation of its obligations under international law.

Syrian refugees in Lebanon bear the brunt of the deep economic and financial crisis in the country, in addition to widespread public and institutional discrimination.

Due to restrictive Lebanese residency policies, only 22 percent of an estimated 1.5 million Syrian refugees in Lebanon have the legal right to live in the country, leaving the majority to live under the radar, subject to arbitrary arrest, detention, harassment and summary deportation to Syria. At least 21 Lebanese municipalities have used the Covid-19 outbreak as a pretext to impose discriminatory restrictions on Syrian refugees that do not apply to Lebanese residents. The Covid-19 pandemic has exacerbated the already-difficult situation for refugees and internally displaced people with disabilities in Lebanon.

Even before pandemic-related school closures, more than 2 million children in Syria, and nearly a million refugee children, were out of school. Syrian refugee children face financial and bureaucratic obstacles to education beyond the primary level, with little support from host countries or international donors. Enrollment rates collapsed from as high as 95 percent in primary schools to less than 30 percent in upper-secondary schools in Turkey and in Jordan, and to less than 5 percent in Lebanon. Accommodations for refugee children with disabilities at schools were virtually non-existent in Lebanon and Jordan.

The Syrian government continues to bar humanitarian workers from accessing and providing aid to 12,000 refugees stranded at al-Rukban camp near the Jordanian border. Delivery of basic goods to the camp is sporadic and made through informal routes, according to UNOCHA.

In July, Danish Minister of Immigration and Integration Mattias Tesfaye announced that Denmark will be reviewing—and possibly revoking—residence permits for refugees whom it deems no longer need protection. The country has already revoked five permits for refugees from Damascus given that the situation there has "improved."

International Accountability Efforts

In April, the trial of two alleged former Syrian intelligence officials began in Koblenz, Germany, in a landmark case on torture in one of Syria's detention facilities. The same month, the first trial addressing genocide by an ISIS suspect against the Yazidi minority began in Frankfurt. Other countries, including France and Sweden, are pursuing similar cases under their universal jurisdiction laws.

The UN-mandated International, Impartial and Independent Mechanism (IIIM), established in 2016 to assist investigations and prosecutions of war crimes and other serious crimes in Syria, continued its work, including by engaging with national judicial authorities on their investigations.

The Investigation and Identification Team (ITT) at the Organisation for the Prohibition of Chemical Weapons continues to investigate chemical weapons attacks in Syria with the aim of identifying perpetrators. In April, the ITT confirmed that the Syrian air force carried out three chemical weapons attacks that targeted al-Lataminah in March 2017.

On June 17, the US Caesar Syria Civilian Protection Act came into force. While the stated purpose of the sanctions includes pursuing accountability for human rights violations, the act also allows US authorities to unilaterally impose sanctions—such as travel restrictions and asset freezing—on individuals, businesses, industries, and entities that provide material assistance to the Syrian government, its allies operating in Syria, and its paramilitary forces. Thirty-nine designations were initially made on June 17, followed by ten more on July 29. The full impact of these sanctions has yet to be assessed.

In September, the Netherlands notified Syria that it had invoked the United Nations Convention against Torture provision that provides for negotiations for disputes under the treaty and potential recourse to the International Court of Justice (ICJ).

Key International Actors

Despite the creation of a UN-facilitated constitutional committee, political negotiations remain at a virtual standstill. The committee, formed to bring Syrian parties together, was delayed in meeting, is not fully representative, and has failed to show concrete results thus far.

Russia, Turkey, and Iran continue to wield influence in Syria, with Russia spearheading efforts to politically legitimize the Syrian government, including through its use of the veto in the UN Security Council. Turkey's influence is seen in areas under its direct control in Syria, as well as indirectly in Idlib governorate, where in March it negotiated a ceasefire with Russia that remains intact.

The US maintains its support for the anti-ISIS coalition operating in Syria and provides financial and logistical support to the Syrian Democratic Forces, as well as stabilization aid in the region. In the UN Security Council, the US, and some European Council members have pushed for the reinstatement of the humanitarian cross-border mechanism and have supported accountability for violations in Syria. Russia has continued to use its veto power to eviscerate the cross-border aid mandate.

The European Union continued to condemn violations of human rights and international humanitarian law in Syria, and reiterated support for international accountability efforts. The EU hosted its fourth Brussels conference on Syria remotely, focusing on a political solution to the crisis and response to humanitarian needs.

Both the EU and the US renewed and expanded sanctions on the Syrian government.

Tajikistan

In 2020, Tajik authorities continued to jail government critics, including opposition activists and journalists, for lengthy prison terms on politically motivated grounds. They also intensified harassment of relatives of peaceful dissidents abroad and continued to forcibly return political opponents from abroad using politically motivated extradition requests. The government severely restricts freedom of expression, association, assembly, and religion, including through heavy censorship of the internet.

Until the end of April, the Tajik government denied the existence of the Covid-19 virus in the country and was late to introduce meaningful measures to slow its spread. Medical staff reported experiencing shortages of personal protective equipment.

Parliamentary and Presidential Elections

The Organization for Security and Co-operation in Europe's Office for Democratic Institutions and Human Rights (OSCE ODIHR) concluded that the March 2020 parliamentary elections "took place in a tightly controlled environment." Voters had no genuine political alternatives as fundamental political rights and freedoms had been curbed, and "genuine opposition had been removed."

Tajikistan held presidential elections on October 11. President Emomali Rahmon was reelected for a fifth term with 90.92 percent of the vote.

Prison Conditions, Treatment of Detainees

Conditions in Tajik prisons remain abysmal, activists regularly report on torture and ill-treatment.

In May, Radio Ozodi, the Tajik service of Radio Free Europe/Radio Liberty (RFE/RL), reported that the Dushanbe Prison No.1 authorities had not introduced any measures to limit the spread of Covid-19. Prisoners were "required to gather in a small space for counting, most of the prisoners did not wear masks or gloves, and conditions ... did not comply with sanitary standards."

In June, Rakhmatullo Radjab, a senior member of the Islamic Renaissance Party of Tajikistan (IRPT) jailed at the same prison, did not receive medical assistance when he showed Covid-19 symptoms, according to his son, Shukhrat. He and other prisoners were not tested for the coronavirus and relatives had to provide loved ones with medicines themselves. Each prisoner was also given one face mask; all inmates shared one thermometer. On July 13, Justice Minister Muzaffar Ashurion said in a press conference that 98 prisoners had been infected with pneumonia and 11 had died from it since the pandemic's start. He denied the existence of the virus in detention facilities in Tajikistan.

In August, prison authorities threatened prisoners to take them to a punishment cell if they communicated with jailed human rights lawyer Buzurgmehr Yorov, whose detention was deemed to be in violation of international law by the United Nations Working Group on Arbitrary Detention in 2019. Prison authorities had earlier attempted to make Yorov denounce IRPT in writing and its exiled leader Muhiddin Kabiri, but he refused.

Harassment of Dissidents Abroad

On December 5, 2019, pursuant to a Tajik extradition request, Russian authorities detained a Group 24 activist, Khursand Najmiddinov, at the Vnukovo airport in Moscow, after he arrived from Austria, where he has asylum. On December 9, 2019, a court in Russia ordered Najmiddinov's release. Following another Tajik extradition request, Group 24 supporter Jamshed Sharipov was detained by Russian authorities at the Moscow Sheremetyevo airport in February. He was released two days later.

In March, Austrian authorities extradited Hizbullo Shovalizoda to Tajikistan after denying him asylum. Shovalizoda was arrested upon arrival in Dushanbe, and accused of being an IRPT member and participating in an attempt to overthrow the government. The party reported that Shovalizoda had never been a member. In June, he was sentenced to 20 years in prison on vague charges of "organizing activity of an extremist organization" and "treason."

In Kaunas, Lithuania, in March, two men brutally beat and injured an exiled Tajik activist, Ilhomjon Yakubov, in a politically motivated attack. Yakubov had previously received dozens of threats over messaging apps and social media. The

Lithuanian police opened a criminal investigation into the attack and later that month detained one of the attackers.

Dissidents' Families

Authorities continued to harass Tajikistan-based relatives of peaceful dissidents, both in the country and abroad.

In June, Farzona Sayfullozoda, daughter of imprisoned Hikmatulloh Sayfullozoda, an editor of the now-banned party newspaper, Najot, denounced IRPT in a video. Sayfullozoda "urged people not to believe IRPT and its leadership" and said that IRPT is "a terrorist party and she regrets everything that happened to her family." According to Humayra Bakhtiyar, a Europe-based journalist and human rights defender, her statement was made under duress.

Also in June, the State Committee for National Security detained Asroriddin Rozikov, a son of an imprisoned senior member of IRPT, Zubaidullohi Rozik, on charges of "organizing activity of an extremist organization." According to Rozikov's brother Khisomiddin, Asroriddin was not involved in any political activity.

Thirteen family members of Jannatullohi Komil, an exiled IRPT member based in Germany, were harassed, detained, and questioned by Tajik authorities in June and July. Authorities also pressured them to testify on camera against the party. Three children were among the detained family members.

Freedom of Expression

The Tajik government continued to regularly block access to social media platforms, messaging apps and services, and news websites, including Radio Ozodi, Asia-Plus, and Akhbor.com.

There was a total of over 80 attacks of all kinds, physical and non-physical, including cyber-attacks and "attacks via judicial or economic means," on journalists in the country between 2017 to 2019, according to a report in April by the Justice for Journalists Foundation.

In February, the Supreme Court found an independent news outlet Akhbor.com, critical of the Tajik government, allegedly guilty of "serving terrorist and extremist organizations" and ruled to block the website.

The Dushanbe Shohmansur court in April sentenced a prominent independent journalist Daler Sharipov to one year in prison on charges of incitement of religious discord for printing copies of a dissertation.

On May 11, Asia-Plus journalist Abdullo Ghurbati, who had reported on Tajikistan's Covid-19 outbreak, was beaten near his home in Dushanbe and was beaten again on May 29 in the southern village Uyali while on assignment. The two assailants of the first attack were not identified. Three men involved in the second attack were sentenced to a fine on charges of petty hooliganism.

The Foreign Ministry refused to extend accreditation of Anushervon Aripov, a journalist with Current Time TV, a news outlet of RFE/RL and Voice of America, in August. Also in August, Radio Ozodi reported that eight longstanding accreditation requests for its journalists were still awaiting a decision by the Foreign Ministry, and several staff members received accreditation only for several months contrary to what is provided for in Tajik's legislation.

Freedom of Religion, Belief

On January 2, 2020, a Law on Countering Extremism came into force which allows authorities to further curb free expression. Since then, according to RFE/RL, at least 113 people, including university staff, students, entrepreneurs and public sector employees, have been arrested across Tajikistan, allegedly for being members of the Muslim Brotherhood movement, which the government has banned. Some accused were reportedly denied access to lawyers and their relatives.

In February, at least 30 Brotherhood suspects were released after they had spent 10 to 20 days in detention. In March, a court in Khatlon region sentenced Komil Tagoev, an alleged member, to a year in prison following his earlier arrest on charges of "organizing activity of an extremist organization" and "religious discord." In August, Sughd Regional Court in a closed trial sentenced another 20 people to between five and seven years in prison on extremism charges. One person was sentenced to a fine "for failing to report a crime."

Domestic Violence

Domestic violence remains a serious problem in Tajikistan. Women and girls who experience abuse lack adequate protection and support. Insufficient number of shelters and lack of specialized professional services, especially in rural areas, pose serious barriers for survivors' access to justice and refuge. Police often refuse to register complaints of domestic violence, fail to adequately investigate reports of abuse, or issue and enforce protection orders. Domestic violence and marital rape are not specifically criminalized in Tajikistan.

Dr. Pratibha Mehta, the UN Development Program Resident Representative in Tajikistan, in a speech at the meeting of the National Committee for Population Development in November 2019, stated that "24% of women aged 19-49 in Tajikistan" experienced physical or sexual violence and "97% of the perpetrators of violence [against] women [who are or have been married] are reported to be their current or former husbands."

In July, the head of the Committee on Women and Family Affairs, Hilolby Kurbonzoda, stated that in response to the increasing number of domestic violence complaints, the committee established a resource centre with a 24-hour hotline.

The head of "Nachoti Kudakon", a Tajikistan-based women's rights group, Kurbongul Kosimova, in June said there was a significant increase of domestic violence complaints in the first three months of the pandemic. She noted that laws concerning family violence are insufficient and domestic violence should be criminalized as a stand-alone offense.

Key International Actors

On June 29, 12 US senators in a letter to Rahmon called for the release of Yorov, the lawyer, and Sharipov, the journalist, on health and humanitarian grounds in the context of Covid-19.

In January, the United Nations Working Group on Arbitrary Detention released an opinion finding the detention and continued imprisonment of 11 senior IRPT members—Saidumar Husaini, Muhammadali Faiz-Muhammad, Rahmatulloi Rajab, Zubaidulloi Roziq, Vohidkhon Kosidinov, Kiyomiddin Avazov, Abduqahar Davlatov, Hikmatulloh Sayfulloza, Sadidin Rustamov, Sharif Nabiev and Abdusamat Ghayratov—in violation of Tajikistan's international human rights obligations and called for their immediate release.

The European Union raised a range of concerns during its annual human rights dialogue with Tajikistan in November 2019. It urged Tajikistan to "facilitate access to information for all journalists, and ensure free access to the Internet, news websites and social media for all citizens." The EU noted that "there is a shrinking space for human rights in Tajikistan, whereby political opponents are imprisoned, and members of their families and their lawyers harassed," and also called for criminalization of domestic violence.

In May, the EU, German, and French ambassadors to Tajikistan urged the government to ensure that freedom of expression and media freedom are allowed in the country without restrictions. In July, the EU encouraged Tajikistan to improve its human rights record in order to stand a better chance of being granted preferential access to the EU market through the EU's GSP+ scheme.

In February, Harlem Désir, then-OSCE representative for freedom of the media, called on the Tajik government to immediately release Daler Sharipov. In May, he appealed for the prosecution of the May 11 attackers on Ghurbati, and expressed his concern over the Tajik Supreme Court blocking access to Akhbor.com.

Thailand

Thailand faced a serious human rights crisis in 2020. Prime Minister Gen. Prayut Chan-ocha's government imposed restrictions on civil and political rights, particularly freedom of expression, arbitrarily arrested democracy activists, engineered the dissolution of a major opposition political party on politically motivated grounds, and enforced a nationwide state of emergency, using the Covid-19 pandemic as a pretext.

Dissolution of the Future Forward Party

Thailand's teetering efforts to restore civilian democratic rule were seriously undermined when the Constitutional Court dissolved the opposition Future Forward Party on February 21 on politically motivated allegations that the party took an illegal loan from its leader, Thanathorn Juangroongruangkit, and imposed 10-year political bans on 16 of its executive members.

In October, the Election Commission of Thailand, which brought a complaint in this case, announced that it would file criminal charges against Thanathorn and 15 other party executives for violating the prohibition of political donations exceeding 10 million baht (US$320,000) per person per year. If convicted, Thanathorn faces up to five years in prison, and other party executives face up to three years. In addition, the court ordered confiscation from the party of 181.3 million baht (US$5.8 million), the amount of the loan considered to exceed legal limits. The party's remaining members of parliament and members later formed the Move Forward Party in the opposition coalition.

Youth-Led Democracy Protests

Youth-led democracy protests started in universities and schools across Thailand after the Constitutional Court dissolved the opposition Future Forward Party in February. But the onset of the Covid-19 pandemic in March disrupted those protests.

As Thailand managed to control the spread of Covid-19, a second round of protests emerged. The Free Youth Movement organized a protest in Bangkok on July 18, calling for the dissolution of parliament, the drafting of a new constitution, and an end to government harassment and intimidation of people who exercise their right to freedom of expression. The protests continued to grow, with tens of thousands of participants regularly joining demonstrations. The agenda also broadened to include demands for reform of the monarchy.

The democracy movement quickly evolved to become the People's Movement by incorporating the demands and involvement of other groups, including children demanding greater freedoms on school grounds and in the classrooms; lesbian, gay, bisexual, and transgender (LGBT) groups demanding gender equality; labor groups demanding fair compensation for Covid-19 impacts and better employment conditions; ethnic Malay Muslims in the southern border provinces demanding an end to military control of their region; and people demanding accountability for state-sponsored rights violations.

State of Emergency, Restrictions on Freedom of Expression

The government enacted the draconian Emergency Decree on Public Administration in Emergency Situation nationwide on March 2 to control the spread of Covid-19, grant powers to impose curfews and other restrictions, and manage inter-agency response.

Despite Thailand's success in getting community transmission of Covid-19 under control, the Emergency Decree has been continually extended without justification, effectively using the coronavirus as a pretext to expand its repressive policies.

The government misused the Covid-19 emergency measures to clamp down on freedom of expression and of media, especially criticism about the government response to the pandemic. Whistleblowers in the public health sector were targeted by disciplinary actions and retaliatory lawsuits after they reported hoarding and black-market profiteering of surgical masks and medical supplies. Social distancing restrictions were enforced in a discriminatory manner, targeting activists. According to the Thai Lawyers for Human Rights, 73 activists who took part in anti-government protests and democracy protests were charged with violating social distancing measures intended to control the spread of Covid-19.

In August, the government dropped previous promises to listen to dissenting voices and adopted a more hostile stance toward democracy protests. On Octo-

ber 15, in response to the escalating protests, Prime Minister Prayut declared a "severe" state of emergency
in Bangkok. Shortly thereafter, riot police forcibly cleared protesters who had camped outside the Government House. On October 16, riot police used water cannons laced with blue dye and teargas chemicals to break up the protest in Bangkok's Pathumwan shopping district.

When Bangkok's severe emergency situation was lifted on October 22, at least 91 democracy activists faced charges of illegal assembly and violating the Emergency Decree for holding anti-government protests. Some protest leaders were also charged with sedition for making demands for reform of the monarchy. In addition, Ekachai Hongkangwan, Bunkueanun Paothong, and Suranat Paenprasert were charged with committing an act of violence against the queen, despite no violence taking place, and obstructing the royal motorcade.

On November 17, riot police used water cannons mixed with purple dye and teargas chemicals, as well as teargas grenades and pepper spray grenades to prevent a demonstration organized by the People's Movement from reaching the parliament, where a debate on constitutional amendments, including possible reforms to the monarchy, was underway. At least 55 people were injured, most from inhaling teargas. The injured included six democracy demonstrators who suffered gunshot wounds during a clash with pro-government ultra-royalist groups near the parliament.

In September, Thai Lawyers for Human Rights reported that police officers entered schools to intimidate students by taking photos and questioning children who participated in democracy protests. Officials also pressured students' families. School administrators punished students for wearing white ribbons on campus or showing the ubiquitous three-finger salute during the national anthem. At least four high school students in Bangkok and other provinces were charged with violating the Emergency Decree's ban on public gathering. A total of 103 harassment incidents were reported by Thai Lawyers for Human Rights in August.

Thai authorities were previously instructed by the king to avoid using the *lèse-majesté* (insulting the monarchy) provision under article 112 of the penal code. But on November 19, Prime Minister Prayut ordered Thai authorities to use "all laws and all articles" against pro-democracy protesters, bringing back *lèse-majesté* prosecution after a three-year hiatus. Since then, at least 14 activists have been charged under article 112 for making onstage speech or online commentary demanding reform of the monarchy.

In addition, making critical or offensive comments about the monarchy is also a serious criminal offense under the Computer-Related Crime Act. In September, the government filed computer crime cases against three democracy activists for posting commentaries about the monarchy on Facebook and other social media platforms.

In August, Facebook blocked access within Thailand to the Royalist Marketplace, a group that discusses the monarchy, after the company's local representative was served with a legal request from the Ministry of Digital Economy and Society. Facebook pledged to legally challenge the request, which it said "contravene[s] international human rights law."

In September, Digital Economy and Society Minister Buddhipongse Punnakanta filed a complaint with the Police Technology Crime Suppression Division accusing Facebook, Twitter, and YouTube of failing to fully cooperate with the court's takedown orders. It was the first time in Thailand that social media companies faced prosecution under the Computer-Related Crime Act.

On October 21, the Bangkok Criminal Court lifted a government order banning Voice TV, The Reporters, The Standard, and Prachatai. The court ruled that media freedom is guaranteed under the constitution and international human rights standards and that these media outlets' live broadcast reporting of the police dispersal of the democracy protest on October 16 was carried out in good faith.

Torture and Enforced Disappearance

Torture has long been a problem in Thailand, but torture is still not recognized as a criminal offense under the penal code. Despite public pledges by the military and the police, there has been no progress in the prosecution of soldiers responsible for the torture and murder of Yutthana Saisa—who was arrested in a drug raid—in an army camp in Nakhon Phanom province on April 17.

Thailand signed the International Convention for the Protection of All Persons from Enforced Disappearance in 2012 but has not ratified the treaty. The penal code does not recognize enforced disappearance as a criminal offense.

The United Nations Working Group on Enforced or Involuntary Disappearances has recorded 82 cases of enforced disappearance in Thailand between 1980 and 2015, including of prominent Muslim lawyer Somchai Neelapaijit. In recent years, nine dissidents who fled persecution in Thailand have been forcibly disappeared in neighboring countries. At least two of them, Chatchan Boonphawal and Kraidet Lueler, were found brutally murdered and dumped in the Mekong River after they were abducted in Laos in December 2018. On June 4, exiled democracy activist Wanchalearm Satsaksit was forcibly disappeared in Cambodia's capital city, Phnom Penh.

Thai authorities engage in practices that facilitate torture and enforced disappearances, such as the use of secret detention by anti-narcotics units, and secret military detention of national security suspects and suspected insurgents in the southern border provinces.

Lack of Accountability for State-Sponsored Rights Violations

Despite evidence showing that soldiers were responsible for most casualties during the 2010 political confrontations with the United Front for Democracy Against Dictatorship (the "Red Shirts") that left at least 99 dead and more than 2,000 injured, no military personnel or officials from the government of then-Prime Minister Abhisit Vejjajiva have been charged for killing or wounding demonstrators or bystanders.

The government has failed to pursue criminal investigations of extrajudicial killings related to anti-drug operations, especially the more than 2,800 killings that accompanied then-Prime Minister Thaksin Shinawatra's "war on drugs" in 2003.

Human Rights Defenders

The government failed to meet its obligation to ensure human rights defenders can carry out their work in a safe and enabling environment. There has been no progress in the police investigation of brutal attacks in 2019 targeting democracy activists Sirawith Seritiwat, Anurak Jeantawanich, and Ekachai Hongkangwan.

Cover-up actions and shoddy police work continued to hamper the efforts to prosecute soldiers who shot dead ethnic Lahu activist Chaiyaphum Pasae in March 2017 in Chiang Mai province and park officials involved in the murder of ethnic Karen activist Porlajee "Billy" Rakchongcharoen in April 2014 in Petchaburi province.

Despite the adoption of Thailand's National Action Plan on Business and Human Rights in October 2019, Thai authorities failed to protect human rights defenders from reprisals and end the abusive use of strategic lawsuits against public participation (SLAPP). An amendment to the Criminal Procedure Code to address this issue remain unused by prosecutors and courts.

In December 2019, Lop Buri Provincial Court sentenced journalist Suchanee Cloitre to two years in prison for a tweet she sent about the Thammakaset poultry farm that was accused of labor rights abuses. The Appeals Court acquitted her in October 2020. In March, a group of UN experts condemned the continued misuse of judicial processes by this company to harass and silence human rights defenders who spoke out against its abusive and exploitative labor practices. Former National Human Rights Commissioner and Magsaysay Award winner Angkhana Neelapaijit is one of the many activists hit with such retaliatory lawsuits.

The government took no steps to reform the National Human Rights Commission of Thailand, which was downgraded by the Global Alliance of National Human Rights Institutions in 2016 because of its substandard selection process for commissioners and its lack of political independence.

Violence and Abuses in the Southern Border Provinces

In January 2020, Barisan Revolusi Nasional (BRN) leaders signed the Deed of Commitment for the Protection of Children from the Effects of Armed Conflict, pledging their commitment to protect children and education in armed conflicts. This included a commitment not to recruit children or associate them with military operations. These pledges have yet to be implemented.

The armed conflict in Thailand's Pattani, Yala, Narathiwat, and Songkhla provinces, which has resulted in more than 7,000 deaths since January 2004, subsided partly due to BRN's unilateral ceasefire announcement on April 3 in response to the appeal made by the UN secretary-general for warring parties in conflicts around the world to observe ceasefires to help contain the Covid-19 pandemic. The ceasefire ended on April 30 when Thai security forces killed three BRN insurgents in a raid in Pattani province.

The government has not prosecuted members of its security forces responsible for torture and unlawful killings of ethnic Malay Muslims. In many cases, authorities provided financial compensation to the victims or their families in exchange for their agreement not to speak out against the security forces, and not file criminal cases against officials. Thailand has not endorsed the Safe Schools Declaration.

Refugees, Asylum Seekers, and Migrant Workers

Thailand is not a party to the 1951 Refugee Convention or its 1967 protocol. Thai authorities continued to treat asylum seekers, including those recognized as refugees by the UN High Commissioner for Refugees, as illegal migrants subject to arrest and deportation.

The government prevented the UN refugee agency from conducting status determination for Lao Hmong, ethnic Rohingya, and ethnic Uyghurs, as well as others from Myanmar and North Korea held in indefinite immigration detention.

Migrant workers—most of whom are from Myanmar, Cambodia, Laos, and Vietnam—were excluded or struggled to qualify for Covid-19 responsive government aid for unemployed workers. These workers are usually already indebted because of the recruitment fees they pay. Migrant workers find it difficult to report workplace abuses and seek redress, and reported instances of retaliation by employers, police, and other government officials when migrants publicize abuses.

Despite government-instituted reforms in the fishing industry, many migrant workers still face forced labor, remain in debt bondage to recruiters, cannot change employers, and receive sub-minimum wages that are paid months late. The US government listed the Thai fishing industry in its 2020 "List of Goods Produced by Child Labor or Forced Labor."

In April, the US suspended US$1.3 billion in trade preferences for Thailand because of its failure to adequately provide internationally recognized worker rights, such as protection for freedom of association and collective bargaining.

Gender Inequality

While Thailand enacted the Gender Equality Act in 2015, implementation remains problematic. There has been little progress in the parliamentary review of the Justice Ministry's Life Partnership Bill. If enacted, this draft law would be an important step towards recognizing the fundamental dignity of same-sex couples and providing them with important legal protections. The current draft, however, still needs improvements to comply with international standards on equality and non-discrimination. At time of writing, a gender recognition bill was poised to be brought before the parliament for consideration.

Domestic violence is a serious problem in Thailand. Despite the adoption of the Family Institute Protection Act in February 2019, which prescribes criminal action against perpetrators of domestic violence, gaps in the law and protections remain.

Key International Actors

After the March 2019 election, the US, Australia, Japan, and other countries normalized relations. These countries did not publicly speak out about the lack of significant human rights improvements.

The European Union has sought to broaden its engagement with Thailand since October 2019, and the commission has the mandate to take steps towards the resumption of negotiations for a bilateral free trade agreement with Thailand, which have been frozen since 2014. Renewed close military relations between the US and Thailand contributed to Washington's relative silence about the Thai military's continuing human rights violations.

In August, the UN Children's Fund issued a statement urging all actors, including schools and learning institutions, in Thailand to uphold children and young people's right to freedom of expression, and to protect them from all forms of violence and intimidation.

On November 18, the spokesperson for UN Secretary-General António Guterres expressed concern about the Thai government's use of force against peaceful protesters.

Tunisia

The 2019 legislative elections in Tunisia, the third to be held since massive street protests ousted previous president and autocrat Zine El Abidine Ben Ali in 2010, produced a fragmented parliament. The Islamist Ennahdha party came first, with 52 out of 217 seats, followed closely by Qalb Tounes Party, created in 2019 by media mogul Nabil Karoui.

In 2020, parliament made no progress in reforming laws that violate or threaten human rights. It also failed to agree on its allotted appointments of judges to the constitutional court, which could play a pivotal role in ensuring that laws conform with the rights provided by the 2014 constitution.

President Kais Saied, elected in 2019, renewed on May 30 a state of emergency that the government imposed following a 2015 attack in the capital Tunis that killed 12 members of the presidential guard.

Implementation of Constitution

The constitution of 2014 provided for a constitutional court to be put in place by 2015. However, because parliament has failed to agree on the four judges it is responsible for appointing, the court has not been able to start operating. The constitution endows the court with the power to void laws that are inconsistent with provisions of the constitution, including its human rights provisions.

Parliament also failed to create other authorities established by the constitution, such as the Human Rights Commission and the Commission on Corruption and Good Governance.

Freedom of Expression, Association and Assembly and Conscience

Authorities relied on repressive provisions of the penal code as well as other laws to punish speech, including criticism of public officials. Two social media activists, Anis Mabrouki, from Tebourba, and Hajer Awadi, from El Kef, were arrested in April in separate incidents and charged for criticizing on Facebook what they considered to be the government's inadequate or corrupt response to financial hardship caused by the Covid-19 pandemic. Prosecutors charged both with "creating a public disturbance." They also charged Mabrouki with "accusing public officials of crimes related to their jobs without furnishing proof of guilt" and Awadi with "insulting a civil servant." The courts acquitted Mabrouki and sentenced Awadi to two-and-a-half months in prison and a fine; she was free on appeal at time of writing.

On May 4, judicial police summoned Emna Chargui after she re-posted on Facebook a short text entitled "Sura Corona," written and formatted in the style of a Quranic verse (sura). The prosecutor charged Chargui with "inciting hatred between religions through hostile means or violence," under article 52 of the press freedom decree-law. On July 17, a Tunis First Instance Court sentenced Chargui to six months in prison and a fine. In the wake of controversy and prosecution, Chargui left Tunisia.

Transitional Justice

The government took a step for transitional justice by publishing in its Official Journal, on June 24, the final report of the Truth and Dignity Commission, a body tasked by a 2013 transitional justice law to investigate and expose serious human rights violations that took place in Tunisia from 1955 to 2013. The five-volume report includes recommendations for political, economic, administrative, and security sector reforms to safeguard against a return to repression.

Counterterrorism and Detention

The 1978 decree-law enacted by Tunisia's first president, Habib Bourguiba, governs declarations of a state of emergency. A draft law before parliament since 2018 would widen the powers of local and central authorities to restrict demonstrations and movement among other freedoms.

In November 2019, the counterterrorism prosecutor of the Tunis First Instance Court accused Mounir Baatour, a lawyer and president of Shams, a group that defends sexual minorities, of "incitement to hatred and to animosity between races, doctrines, and religions," under article 14 of Tunisia's overbroad 2015 counterterrorism law. The basis for the accusation was that he re-shared a post on his Facebook page that critics considered disparaging of the Prophet Muhammad. Baatour left Tunisia and obtained asylum in France.

Tunisian judges continued to pronounce death penalties but no one has been executed since a de facto moratorium took effect in 1991.

Tunisia allowed the return from Libya on January 23 of six orphaned children of Tunisian nationals who were suspected of being Islamic State members. At least 36 more children of suspected ISIS members remain stranded in Libya, as well as an estimated 160 Tunisian children believed to be held in camps in Syria or prisons in Iraq.

Women's Rights

Tunisian women continue to face discrimination in inheritance under the 1956 Personal Status Code, which provides that sons inherit double the share of daughters. A landmark bill, based on a recommendation made by a presidentially appointed Commission on Individual Freedoms and Equality in 2017, would make equal rights in inheritance the default. People would still be able to opt out of the default and choose instead to have their wealth distributed as the current legal framework provides. Parliament has yet to consider the bill. On August 13, National Women's Day, in Tunisia, President Kais Saied said he opposed equality in inheritance. On the same date two years earlier, the late President Beji Caid Essebsi had embraced recommendations for equality in inheritance.

The 1956 Personal Status Code—which was progressive for its time in the region, and also ahead of some European states—also discriminates against women by still referring to the husband as the "head of the family," giving him legal advantages in disputes over household management. The current draft law amendments are directed only at the inheritance section of the Personal Status Code.

In April, the Ministry of Women, Family, Childhood and Seniors opened a new shelter for female victims of domestic abuse. It also extended the hours of operation of the hotline for domestic violence complaints to 24 hours. The ministry said it received a significant increase in reports of domestic violence in late March during COVID-19 lockdown restrictions compared to the previous year. The ministry also introduced a mental health hotline to support families experiencing stress during the lockdown. Women reported difficulties in accessing protection orders (to prevent contact from their abusers), as per the 2017 Violence against Women law, due to court closures under lockdown.

Schools were closed in Tunisia in mid-March due to the Covid-19 pandemic and began re-opening in mid-September. Many children in public schools could not access education during the closures. In May, a National Statistical Institute survey of parents found that 66 percent of school-age children had engaged in no learning activities during the previous weeks, often due to a lack of remote learning options, study materials, or a lack of communication with teachers.

Sexual Orientation and Gender Identity

Authorities continued to prosecute and imprison presumed-gay men under article 230 of the penal code, which provides up to three years in prison for "sodomy."

On June 6, the Kef First Instance Tribunal sentenced two men charged with sodomy to two years in prison, reduced to one year on appeal. The men had refused police's demands to subject them to an anal exam, an invasive and discredited practice that Tunisian authorities routinely use to "prove" homosexual conduct. Despite accepting a recommendation during its Universal Periodic Review at the UN Human Rights Council in May 2017 to end anal testing, the government has not yet taken steps to carry out this pledge.

Turkey

The assault on human rights and the rule of law presided over by Turkey's President Recep Tayyip Erdoğan continued during the Covid-19 pandemic. The president's Justice and Development Party (AKP) and an allied far-right party enjoy a parliamentary majority enabling them to consolidate authoritarian rule by passing rushed legislation that contravenes international human rights obligations. Opposition parties remain sidelined under Turkey's presidential system and the government has reshaped public and state institutions to remove checks on power and to ensure benefits for its own supporters. The political opposition nevertheless controls the municipalities of Istanbul and Ankara.

Executive interference in the judiciary and in prosecutorial decisions are entrenched problems, reflected in the authorities' systematic practice of detaining, prosecuting, and convicting on bogus and overbroad terrorism and other charges, individuals the Erdoğan government regards as critics or political opponents. Among those targeted are journalists, opposition politicians, and activists—in particular members of the pro-Kurdish Peoples' Democratic Party (HDP). The largest targeted group consists of those alleged to have links with the movement headed by US-based Sunni cleric Fethullah Gülen which Turkey deems a terrorist organization and calls FETÖ and holds responsible for the July 2016 coup attempt.

Turkey's move to begin gas exploration in the East Mediterranean in the context of maritime boundaries contested with Greece and Cyprus almost spiraled into a naval clash with Greece in August. The European Union has made efforts to broker dialogue over conflicting claims in a dispute originally ignited by the discovery of gas reserves off Cyprus with its contested status.

Turkey provides military support to the United Nations-recognized Government of National Accord in Libya against a breakaway government in the east of the country. Turkey has expressed strong support for Azerbaijan in its conflict with Armenia over Nagorno-Karabakh. Turkey continues to exert effective control via Syrian non-state actors over areas of northern and northeast Syria where it has intervened militarily in the past four years, and where significant human rights abuses continue unabated. Turkey cites its aim as removing Kurdish forces formerly controlling the area closely linked to the armed Kurdistan Workers' Party

(PKK) with which Turkey has been engaged in a decades'-long conflict (see Syria chapter). Turkey played a key role in securing a March ceasefire in Syria's northwestern Idlib governorate, which has largely held.

Freedom of Expression, Association, and Assembly

Most TV and print media in Turkey are owned by companies close to the Erdoğan presidency or avoid reporting critical of the government. Critical online news and commentary websites persist, nevertheless. At the time of writing, an estimated 87 journalists and media workers were in pretrial detention or serving sentences for terrorism offenses because of their journalistic work.

Plans for strict regulation of social media companies in Turkey were made law in July after President Erdoğan used the example of insults against his family on social media to justify a need for stricter regulation. Under the new law, social media companies with over one million users a day will be required to have offices in Turkey and comply with government demands to block and remove content or else face very heavy fines. Companies that do not open an office will be fined and eventually have their bandwidth restricted, rendering the platform unusable. At time of writing, Facebook had indicated it would not comply with the law.

While Turkey in January lifted a blocking order on Wikipedia in place since April 2017, authorities continue to block thousands of websites, including critical news websites, and order the removal of online content.

Thousands of people face arrest and prosecution for their social media posts, typically charged with defamation, insulting the president, or spreading terrorist propaganda. In the context of Covid-19, the Interior Ministry announced that hundreds of people were under criminal investigation or detained by police for social media postings deemed to "create fear and panic" about the pandemic. Some of these postings included criticism of the government's response to the pandemic.

Turkey's official media regulation authority, the Radio and Television Supreme Board (RTÜK), ordered arbitrary fines and temporary suspensions of broadcasting of media outlets such as Halk TV, Tele 1 TV, and Fox TV, which include content critical of the government. Netflix complied with RTÜK's April demand that it remove an episode of TV drama series Designated Survivor on the grounds that it offered a negative portrayal of President Erdoğan, as well as in July canceling filming in Turkey of a new Turkish drama after RTÜK requested the removal of a gay character from the script.

Selectively using Covid-19 as a pretext, provincial governors banned peaceful protests of women's rights activists, healthcare workers, lawyers, and political opposition parties.

Terrorism charges continue to be widely misused to restrict the rights to free expression and association in the fourth year after the coup attempt. As of July 2020, Ministry of Justice and Interior figures stated that 58,409 were on trial and 132,954 still under criminal investigation on terrorism in cases linked to the Gülen movement. Of those 25,912 were held in prison on remand.

There are no published official numbers of prisoners held on remand or convicted for alleged links with the PKK, although on the basis of the previous years' figures the number is at least 8,500 and includes elected politicians and journalists. An April law on early prisoner release to reduce crowding in the context of the Covid-19 pandemic excluded remand prisoners and all prisoners detained or convicted of terrorism offenses. Covid-19 cases have been reported in prisons throughout Turkey, although authorities do not provide numbers of confirmed cases.

Human Rights Defenders, Lawyers

In February, an Istanbul court acquitted rights defender Osman Kavala and nine others of "attempting to overthrow the government by force and violence" in connection with the 2013 mass protests which began in Gezi Park. However, hours after his acquittal another court ordered Kavala's detention in the scope of an investigation into his alleged role in the July 2016 attempted coup. In October, the investigation culminated in another bogus indictment accusing Kavala and US academic Henri Barkey of attempting to overthrow the constitutional order and espionage. Kavala has been detained since November 2017, with Turkey flouting a European Court of Human Rights' judgment ordering his release on the grounds that his detention has been pursued for political aims.

In July, in a case against human rights defenders detained in 2017 while they attended a training workshop, an Istanbul court convicted Taner Kılıç, Amnesty International Turkey's honorary chair, on charges of membership of a terrorist organization to over six years in prison. İdil Eser, Amnesty Turkey's former director, and rights defenders Özlem Dalkıran and Günal Kurşun received sentences of 25 months on charges of aiding a terrorist organization, and 7 others, 2 of them foreign nationals, were acquitted. All are at liberty and the case is under appeal.

The government's restrictive approach to the public activities of lesbian, gay, bisexual, and transgender (LGBT) rights groups continued with the banning of events including Pride marches for a sixth year running and homophobic speeches by senior state officials.

The government in July passed a new law to reduce the institutional strength of Turkey's largest bar associations, which have strongly criticized Turkey's backsliding on human rights and the rule of law. Defense lawyers representing defendants in terrorism prosecutions have faced arrest and prosecution on the same charges as their clients. In September, the Court of Cassation upheld the conviction of 14 out of 18 lawyers for links with an outlawed leftist organization. One of the lawyers, Ebru Timtik, died on August 27 after a prolonged hunger strike in demand of a fair trial.

The first hearing against three police officers and a PKK militant accused of the fatal shooting of human rights lawyer Tahir Elçi on November 28, 2015, began in October with further hearings postponed until March 2021.

From May to July, at least 45 Kurdish women's rights activists were detained and face prosecution for links with the PKK. Femicide and domestic abuse are significant problems in Turkey. While official disaggregated data on numbers are not available, women's rights groups have reported that hundreds of women are killed annually as a result of domestic violence. Conservative groups and some government officials suggested Turkey may withdraw from the Council of Europe Convention on Preventing and Combatting Violence against Women and Domestic Violence (the Istanbul Convention), which Turkey was among the first to ratify in 2014.

669

Torture and Ill-Treatment in Custody, Enforced Disappearances

A rise in allegations of torture, ill-treatment, and cruel and inhuman or degrading treatment in police and military custody and prison over the past four years has set back Turkey's earlier progress in this area. Those targeted include people accused of political and common crimes. Prosecutors do not conduct meaningful investigations into such allegations and there is a pervasive culture of impunity for members of the security forces and public officials implicated.

There have been no effective investigations into the around two dozen reported cases of enforced disappearance over the past four years. In February and June 2020, two men out of six who resurfaced in police custody in Ankara months after disappearing in February 2019, stated in court hearings that they had been abducted, tortured, and forced to sign statements confessing to links with the Gülen movement.

In June, the government passed legislation to increase the numbers and powers of night watchmen who assist the police with community policing functions, granting them authority to stop and check IDs and to use lethal force. There have been reported instances of watchmen abusing their powers and ill-treating people.

The European Committee for the Prevention of Torture (CPT) has conducted three visits to Turkey since the July 2016 coup attempt. In August, the Turkish government granted permission for publication of two of the CPT reports from 2017 and 2019 visits identifying ill-treatment in police custody and degrading conditions and overcrowding in prisons.

Kurdish Conflict and Crackdown on Opposition

While sporadic armed clashes between the military and the armed Kurdistan Workers' Party (PKK) occur in Turkey's eastern and southeastern regions, the focus of the conflict is in the Kurdistan Region of Iraq, where Turkey conducts regular cross-border operations and airstrikes against PKK targets, in some cases killing and injuring civilians.

The Erdoğan government refuses to distinguish between the PKK and the democratically elected Peoples' Democratic Party (HDP) which won 11.7 percent of the national vote in the 2018 parliamentary elections and 65 local municipalities in the 2019 local elections. Former party co-chairs Selahattin Demirtaş and Figen Yüksekdağ have been in detention since November 2016. Turkey has refused to comply with a 2018 European Court of Human Rights ruling that Demirtaş should be immediately released.

Since August 2019, the Interior Ministry has justified the removal of 48 elected Peoples' Democratic Party (HDP) mayors on the basis that they face criminal investigations and prosecutions for links with the PKK. Repeating the approach taken in 2016-17, the government has replaced mayors in the southeast with Ankara-appointed provincial governors and deputy governor "trustees."

At time of writing, 19 mayors remain in pretrial detention. In March, a Diyarbakır court sentenced Adnan Selçuk Mızraklı, the dismissed mayor of Diyarbakır Metropolitan Municipality, to over nine years in prison based on a witness statement accusing him of links with the PKK. The case is under appeal. In October, an Ankara court ruled for the pretrial detention of Kars mayor, Ayhan Bilgen, and 16 other HDP officials, in connection with an investigation into their alleged role in 2014 protests.

In June, the Turkish parliament revoked the parliamentary seats of two HDP deputies, Leyla Güven and Musa Farisoğulları, on the grounds that the Court of Cassation had upheld convictions against them for membership in a terrorist organization, and Enis Berberoğlu, a deputy from the main opposition Republican People's Party, for revealing state secrets by sharing video footage of trucks of weapons being transferred to Syria with Cumhuriyet newspaper.

In June, an Istanbul appeal court upheld the conviction of Canan Kaftancıoğlu, Istanbul chair of People's Republican Party (CHP), to nearly 10 years in prison for tweets she made years ago. A further appeal is underway.

Refugees and Migrants

Turkey continues to host the world's largest number of refugees, around 3.6 million from Syria, and over 400,000 refugees and migrants from Afghanistan, Iraq, and other countries. On February 27, 2020, Turkey announced that authorities would not intercept asylum seekers wishing to leave Turkey through its borders with the European Union.

As a result, thousands of migrants and asylum seekers gathered at the Turkish-Greek border. Many of those that managed to cross the Evros River into Greece were summarily and violently pushed back by Greek security forces. The onset of the Covid-19 pandemic prompted Turkey to close the border again, but attempted crossings by migrants of land and sea borders and pushbacks from Greece continued.

At least 60 Afghans and others died after entering Turkey from Iran and crossing Lake Van in the eastern part of the country in a fishing boat. The border with Syria has been closed to new asylum seekers since 2016; Turkish border guards have killed or injured some of those attempting to cross and carried out mass summary pushbacks.

Key International Actors

Turkey's relationship with the European Union was strained by tensions in the East Mediterranean over contested maritime borders and access to gas reserves, as well as by Turkey's willingness to use migration as a political bargaining tool by briefly opening its border to Greece in February-March. Turkey formally remains a candidate for EU accession without expectation on either side of progress towards its membership.

In its Turkey report in the context of the accession process, the EU Commission stressed the "continued deterioration of democracy, the rule of law, fundamental rights and the independence of the judiciary … with further backsliding in many areas." The EU made a number of statements on negative developments, criticizing in February the re-arrest of Osman Kavala, and in July, the conviction of rights defenders including Taner Kılıç.

Turkish-US relations remain strained for multiple reasons, including the presence on US soil of Fethullah Gülen, US support for Kurdish-led forces in Syria, Turkey's acquisition of Russian S-400 missiles, and the forthcoming New York trial of a state-owned Turkish bank for Iran sanctions-busting and money laundering.

In June and October, Istanbul courts convicted two local employees of the US consulate in Istanbul on terrorism charges, imposing prison sentences ranging from five to nearly nine years because the employees had prior professional contact, years earlier, with police officers later accused of being Gülenists.

In a February report, the Council of Europe Commissioner for Human Rights focused on measures by authorities that have had "devastating consequences" for judicial independence and "unprecedented levels of disregard for the most basic principles of law" in terrorism prosecutions. Following the review of Turkey's human rights record by UN member-states in the context of the Universal Periodic Review, Turkey rejected core recommendations regarding its human rights record or claimed that it had already implemented them.

Turkmenistan

In 2020, Turkmenistan experienced cascading social and economic crises as the government recklessly denied and mismanaged the Covid-19 epidemic within the country.

The government's failure to address the ongoing economic crisis further aggravated the plight of the population. Severe shortages of affordable food and cash deepened social tension, resulting in unprecedented country protests.

The Turkmen government imposes punitive restrictions on media and religious freedoms, and tightly controls access to information. Independent activists, including in exile, face constant threat of government reprisal. Dozens of persons who have been forcibly disappeared, are believed to be languishing in Turkmen prisons. Arbitrary travel bans are routine.

Covid-19

As of October 2020, authorities claimed Turkmenistan had no Covid-19 cases. But media outlets have reported that numerous people died with Covid-19-like symptoms. In July, Radio Azatlyk, the Turkmen-language service of the US government-funded Radio Liberty, reported that there was a shortage of plastic bags and vehicles for transportation of corpses, and that health facilities in Ashgabat and Turkmenabat were overwhelmed with patients with Covid-19 symptoms.

Authorities coerced health workers into silence about the spread of Covid-19. Rights and Freedoms of Turkmen Citizens, a Prague-based independent group, reported that health workers are not provided with sufficient personal protective equipment (PPE), endangering their lives and health. Starting in June, the group received reports that authorities threatened doctors and nurses with criminal prosecution and that they would not be allowed to practice their profession if they refused to serve in facilities where people with suspected Covid-19 are isolated and treated. The group also reported that in July, authorities arrested on bogus hooliganism and other charges seven doctors in one region who had refused to follow orders to force patients with Covid-19 symptoms to pay for treatment. By October, the cases against them were dropped and they were released.

Turkmen Initiative for Human Rights (TIHR), an exile group, reported in July that authorities in Turkmenabat province threatened 120 health workers with prosecution, in response to their written plea to the regional administration to provide PPE and adequate equipment to treat what was described as a pneumonia outbreak there.

According to Rights and Freedoms, most medical workers were barred from bringing their mobile phones to work. An Ashgabat clinic forced doctors and nurses to sign nondisclosure statements, obliging them not to speak about conditions. TIHR reported in April that security officers detained a doctor working in a quarantine facility for two days for bringing his cell phone inside.

Food Insecurity

Turkmenistan's government denies the existence of poverty in the country and failed to ensure an adequate standard of living and the right to food for economically vulnerable groups. Shortages of subsidized food, the rise of market prices, and a drastic reduction in the amount of remittances from abroad force people to stand in lines for hours hoping to purchase minimal amounts of staple foods. They often leave empty-handed. Food rationing did not ensure access to subsidized food. People experienced restrictions on purchases arbitrarily imposed at the state stores. There are no publicly available official data on the population's food needs.

Constitutional Reform

On September 25, President Gurbanguly Berdymukhamedov approved amendments to the constitution that propose the creation of a bicameral legislature, and guarantee ex-presidents a seat in the upper chamber. The amended constitution does not guarantee freedom to travel abroad or ban censorship.

Civil Society

No independent local organizations can openly operate in Turkmenistan. Unregistered nongovernmental organization (NGO) activity is prohibited. The registration requirements are onerous. International human rights NGOs are not allowed to enter Turkmenistan.

In August, a police officer threatened to arrest Soltan Achilova, a correspondent for TIHR, for photographing a school bazaar in Ashgabat. In June, Natalia Shabunts, one of the country's very few openly active human rights defenders, told TIHR that for two weeks she was under surveillance by security agents.

Throughout the summer, Turkmen migrant workers in Turkey, Northern Cyprus, and the US held demonstrations to protest the government's failure to address the Covid-19 pandemic, ensure food security, and provide assistance to residents whose homes were destroyed by a devastating hurricane.

On July 19, Turkish police, following a complaint of the Consulate of Turkmenistan, detained Dursoltan Taganova, a protest participant and activist with the émigré opposition movement "Democratic Choice of Turkmenistan." In October, Taganova was released from detention in a deportation center in Istanbul and received a one-year international protection status in Turkey.

The Turkmenistan Helsinki Foundation (THF), a human rights organization in exile, and the Memorial Human Rights Center, an independent Russian group, and other sources reported detentions in Turkmenistan of people suspected of having links to the opposition abroad, and intimidation of these activists' relatives in Turkmenistan. In some cases, authorities summoned relatives for questioning, threatened them with dismissal from their jobs, and even beat some.

In June, Murad Dushemov was detained in Ashgabat and placed under house arrest, following his YouTube appeal for the exiled opposition to unite. In August, Reimberdy Kurbanov was released, having served a sanction of 15 days' detention for online communication with government critics abroad. In September, Pygambergeldy Allaberdyev was sentenced to six years on bogus charges under article 108 (intentional harm to health of moderate severity) and 279 (hooliganism) of the penal code for alleged connections with activists abroad. Authorities have denied Allaberdyev family visits and food and clothing parcels.

In July, an exile-run news website, Turkmen.news, reported that security officers in Turkmenistan repeatedly summoned the boyfriend of a woman who organized one of the protests in Turkey, beat, and ill-treated him.

In summer, unknown individuals broke into the Ashgabat apartment belonging to the Kyarizov-Serebryannik family, who had left Turkmenistan in 2015 and founded Rights and Freedoms. They smashed several windows and parts of the kitchen. The destruction took place shortly after the group gave an interview to Al-Jazeera in which they criticized the government's response to Covid-19.

Freedom of Assembly

Authorities prohibit any public expression of discontent. Despite risks of prosecution, people held several spontaneous peaceful gatherings to protest the economic crisis and shortages of subsidized food.

In May, TIHR reported that police briefly detained and questioned women after they surrounded a local official to express their frustrations over flour shortages.

Radio Azatlyk in April reported that nearly 100 women in Lebap province were threatened with 15 days' detention for gathering outside the city administration building to demand flour. Dozens of people protested in Mary province in early April against shortages of government-subsidized flour and vegetable oil.

Memorial reported that in September, Ashgabat's schools' administration threatened to expel students for participation in unsanctioned mass gatherings.

Freedom of Media and Information

There is no media freedom in Turkmenistan. All print and electronic media is state-controlled. Foreign media can very rarely access Turkmenistan. Authorities suppress independent voices and retaliate against local stringers for foreign outlets.

Internet access in Turkmenistan remains heavily state-controlled. Many websites, including social media and messengers, are blocked. The government monitors all means of communications.

Following April's severe hurricane in Lebap and Mary provinces, which caused serious damage and casualties, authorities detained dozens of people, accusing them of sending videos of the aftermath "abroad." In May, TIHR and Rights and Freedoms reported that police in Turkmenabat detained about 66 people for several days, after discovering images and videos of the aftermath of the hurricane on their phones. Two women were charged with criminal offences.

Turkmen.news reported in September that access to IMO messenger was jammed and that many Virtual Private Networks (VPN)s services were blocked. In late August – early September, in-country calls and calls from abroad using Internet Protocols (IPs) were blocked. In October, access to Yandex and Google browsers were blocked for two days.

According to Radio Azatlyk, in July about 30 mobile phone repairmen in Ashgabat were arrested, fined, and sentenced to 15 days' detention on unknown charges for providing VPN services to clients. In September, several sources reported 31 other persons in various cities were fined and sentenced to 15 days detention for similar reasons.

Freedom of Movement

The Turkmen government enforces arbitrary bans on foreign travel on various groups of people. In August, TIHR reported that 213 Turkmen citizens (mostly women and children), holders of Turkish residence permits, were arbitrarily barred from leaving Turkmenistan. Another source reported that the authorities maintain a blacklist of 5,000 people barred from foreign travel, including civil servants and their families, and relatives of emigres, including protest activists.

According to Turkmen.news, in February, migration officers arbitrary removed about 20 people from a flight to Turkey, including two persons traveling for medical treatment.

The Turkmen government has not responded to a United Nations Human Rights Committee (HRC) request for information, communicated to the authorities in 2019 regarding the case of the Ruzimatov family, relatives of a former official who has emigrated. Authorities have banned Rashid Ruzimatov and his wife, Irina Kakabaeva, from traveling abroad since 2003, and his son Rakhim since 2014.

Freedom of Religion

In Turkmenistan, activity by unregistered religious organizations is banned and registration requirements are hard to meet. There is no alternative military service and conscientious objectors face prosecution. Some conscientious objectors are convicted twice on the same charges.

Forum 18, an independent religious freedom group, reported five men jailed for conscientious objection this year, bringing the number of imprisoned objectors to 11. All are Jehovah's Witnesses. Two other objectors were released after completing their sentences.

In January, a court in Lebap province fined a homeowner for holding a Christmas celebration. In February, police raided two Protestants' gatherings in Dashogus, fining some congregants.

Political Prisoners, Enforced Disappearances, and Torture

The fate and whereabouts of many people, who disappeared in Turkmen prisons following convictions on what appear to be politically motivated charges, remain unknown. The exact number of political prisoners is impossible to determine because the justice system is untransparent and trials are closed in sensitive cases. Torture and ill-treatment continue to be endemic within the prison system.

Political dissident Gulgeldy Annaniazov, who should have been released in March 2019 after serving his full 11-year sentence, was subject to an additional five-year term of forced internal exile.

Dozens of prisoners remained victims of enforced disappearance or are held incommunicado, some for almost 18 years. The government has denied them access to families or lawyers. According to "Prove They Are Alive," an international campaign, which seeks to end enforced disappearances in Turkmenistan, at least 10 forcibly disappeared have served the full terms of sentences handed down to them, but have not been released and their whereabouts are unknown.

Sexual Orientation and Gender Identity

Homosexual conduct is criminalized under national legislation and is punishable by up to two years' imprisonment. In May, a Turkmen court sentenced a popular entertainer and several others to two years' imprisonment on sodomy charges.

In October 2019, Kasymberdy Garayev, a cardiologist from Ashgabat went missing for nearly one month after he came out, then briefly reappeared in the media to deny he was gay, before going silent again.

TIHR reported that in October 2019, regional health departments convened meetings with the heads of healthcare facilities in their areas. At one such meeting, officials pressured staff to identify gay people and implied that failure to report people suspected of being gay would result in criminal charges.

Key International Actors

After its July mission to Turkmenistan, the World Health Organization (WHO) stated that Turkmenistan had no "confirmed Covid-19 cases reported to the WHO," but expressed concern about "an increased number of cases of acute respiratory infection and pneumonia," and urged the government to "... send samples to WHO reference laboratories for confirmatory testing."

The US State Department's Trafficking in Persons (TIP) report 2020 maintained Turkmenistan's lowest possible ranking for failure to meet minimum standards to prevent human trafficking. The US State Department redesignated Turkmenistan as "a country of particular concern," citing "systematic ... violations of religious freedom."

In a June letter to President Berdimuhamedov, 12 US senators called for the release of Gulgeldy Annaniyazov, Mansur Mingelov, and Omriuzak Omarkulyev.

During its annual human rights dialogue with Turkmenistan in June, the European Union conveyed strong concerns on individual cases, called for cooperation with United Nations special procedures, and noted that Turkmenistan was "considering" a visit by the UN Working Group on Enforced Disappearances. The EU urged authorities to update the National Human Rights Action Plan in line with recommendations made during the Universal Periodic Review before the UN Human Rights Council (UNHRC) and underlined that the ombudsperson's office should engage on "all human rights issues, including enforced disappearances".

Turkmenistan has failed to respond positively to any visit inquiry by UN special procedures since 2008, despite 15 pending requests for access.

A June statement by the US mission to the Organization for Security and Co-operation in Europe (OSCE) expressed concern about "many prisoners of conscience," and requested an update on Annaniyazov and Omarkuliev.

United Arab Emirates

In 2020, United Arab Emirates (UAE) authorities continued to invest in a "soft power" strategy aimed at painting the country as a progressive, tolerant, and rights-respecting nation, yet its fierce intolerance of criticism was on full display with the continued unjust imprisonment of leading human rights activist Ahmed Mansoor, academic Nasser bin Ghaith, and other many activists and dissidents, some of whom had completed their sentences as long as three years ago and remain detained without a clear legal basis.

Prisons across the UAE held detainees in dismal and unhygienic conditions, where overcrowding and lack of adequate medical care is widespread. With the onset of the Covid-19 pandemic, detainees and prison staff were at heightened risk of contracting the virus.

In Libya, the UAE provided weapons and conducted air and drone strikes to support the Libyan Arab Armed Forces (LAAF) armed group, some of which killed and wounded civilians. In Yemen, UAE-backed Yemeni troops and armed groups committed abuses.

The UAE blocked representatives of international human rights organizations and UN experts from conducting in-country research and visiting prisons and detention facilities.

Freedom of Expression

Hundreds of activists, academics, and lawyers are serving lengthy sentences in UAE prisons, in many cases following unfair trials on vague and broad charges that violate their rights to free expression and association.

Ahmed Mansoor, a leading Emirati human rights defender, remained imprisoned in an isolation cell for a third year, leaving him in precarious health. The UAE in 2017 detained Mansoor on speech-related charges that included using social media to "publish false information that harms national unity." Authorities held him in an unknown location for more than a year with no access to a lawyer before sentencing him in May 2018 to 10 years in prison. On December 31, 2018, the UAE's Federal Supreme Court upheld Mansoor's sentence. Prominent academic Nasser bin-Ghaith, serving 10 years on charges stemming from criticism of UAE and Egyptian authorities, and university professor and human rights lawyer Mohammed al Roken, serving 10 years alongside 68 other people in the grossly unfair "UAE 94" trial, also remained in prison.

As of September 2020, UAE authorities continued to hold Khalifa al-Rabea and Ahmed al Mulla, two Emiratis who completed their sentences on state security charges two years and three years ago respectively. They were convicted in 2014 and 2016 on the basis of their ties to al-Islah, a legally-registered Islamist political movement that the UAE banned in 2014 as "terrorist." Authorities arbitrarily kept them behind bars for "counselling," according to Emirati activists.

Detainee Abuse and Dismal Prison Conditions

Especially in cases purportedly related to state security, detainees were at serious risk of arbitrary and incommunicado detention, torture and ill-treatment, prolonged solitary confinement, and denial of access to legal assistance. Forced confessions were used as evidence in trial proceedings, and prisoners complained of overcrowded and unhygienic conditions and inadequate medical care.

In March, a 21-year old Emirati woman imprisoned on state security charges reportedly attempted suicide after prison authorities subjected her and a second prisoner to prolonged solitary confinement and denied them adequate medical care. UAE authorities did not carry out an independent investigation into the incident.

In May, a UAE court sentenced a 21-year-old Omani man to life in prison following what appears to have been a grossly unfair trial. Following his arrest, authorities subjected him to incommunicado detention, prolonged solitary confinement and ill-treatment. As of September, according to a family member, UAE authorities had denied him contact with the outside world for six months, raising serious concerns for his health and well-being, especially amid a reported Covid-19 outbreak in al-Wathba prison.

Covid-19 outbreaks occurred in at least three UAE detention facilities, worsening already- dismal prison conditions, including inadequate access to medical care and treatment and communication with the outside world.

Throughout 2020, UAE prison authorities denied non-national detainees living with HIV uninterrupted access to lifesaving antiretroviral treatment, in flagrant violation of their right to health. In at least two UAE prisons, detainees living with HIV were segregated from the rest of the prison population and faced stigma and systemic discrimination. Prisoners living with HIV in the UAE who have been denied adequate medical care are at risk of experiencing serious complications if infected with the Covid-19 virus.

On March 17, United Nations human rights experts called on UAE authorities to urgently reform "degrading conditions of detention" in UAE prisons. Despite international calls to do so, the UAE refused to allow independent international monitors to enter the country and visit prison and detention facilities.

Unlawful Attacks and Detainee Abuse Abroad

Despite announcing the withdrawal of most of its ground troops from Yemen in 2019, the UAE remained part of the Saudi-led military operations, continued to maintain a presence in Aden and southern governorates, and continued to provide support for certain Yemeni forces who have committed grave abuses over the past several years.

In Libya, the UAE conducted air and drone strikes to support the Libyan Arab Armed Forces (LAAF), the eastern-based armed group under the command of General Khalifa Hiftar and one of two major Libyan parties to the armed conflict that began in April 2019, some of which killed and wounded civilians. One apparently unlawful UAE attack on a biscuit factory in the south of Tripoli in November 2019 killed eight civilians and wounded 27. According to media, UN, and other reports, the UAE carried out at least five other strikes that resulted in civilian casualties since April 2019. In addition to drones, the UAE supplied the LAAF with other weapons, ammunition, and combat vehicles, in violation of a 2011 UN Security Council arms embargo that prohibits such transfers, according to the UN Panel of Experts on Libya.

Migrant Workers

Foreign nationals accounted for more than 80 percent of the UAE's population, according to 2015 International Labour Organization figures.

The kafala (sponsorship) system tied migrant workers visas to their employers, whereby migrant workers are not allowed to change or leave employers without their permission. Those who leave their employers without permission faced punishment for "absconding," including fines, prison, and deportation. Many low-paid migrant workers were acutely vulnerable to forced labor.

The UAE's labor law excluded from its protections domestic workers, who faced a range of abuses, from unpaid wages, confinement to the house and workdays up to 21 hours to physical and sexual assault by employers. Domestic workers faced legal and practical obstacles to redress. While a 2017 law on domestic workers does guarantee some labor rights, it is weaker than the labor law and falls short of international standards.

The Covid-19 pandemic has further exposed and amplified the ways in which migrant workers' rights are violated. Tens of thousands of migrant workers lost their jobs and were trapped in the country in dire conditions. Many lived through strict lockdowns in crowded and unhygienic housing. While thousands left the UAE after facing summary dismissals, many struggled to return to their home countries because of travel restrictions and expensive plane tickets, and were left unable to pay rent or buy food.

Many migrant workers also faced unpaid wages for work they had done before being dismissed. Authorities imposed stricter Covid-19 lockdown conditions on domestic workers, banning them from seeing anyone outside of their employer's households and warning employers not to allow their domestic workers to meet anyone outside. Given that many employers already confine domestic workers to the household and overwork them, such conditions left them even more at risk of abuse, including increased working hours, no rest days, and physical and verbal abuse.

In March and April, Human Rights Watch and other international human rights organizations called on governments to take several steps to adequately protect migrant workers from the spread of the virus, including in immigration detention and labor accommodations.

Women's Rights

Discrimination on the basis of sex and gender is not included in the definition of discrimination in the UAE's 2015 anti-discrimination law.

Some provisions of the law regulating personal status matters discriminate against women. For a woman to marry, her male guardian must conclude her marriage contract. Men can unilaterally divorce their wives, whereas a woman must apply for a court order to obtain a divorce. A woman can lose her right to maintenance if, for example, she refuses to have sexual relations with her husband without a lawful excuse.

In 2019, the authorities introduced amendments to the personal status law that revoked a provision that had obliged women to "obey" their husbands. In August, they introduced other minor amendments tweaking the language of the 2019 amendments on obligations to appear more gender neutral. However, such changes merely remove discrimination in law but essentially still allow for judges to discriminate against women in practice.

Following amendments in 2016, the UAE's penal code no longer explicitly permits domestic violence. On December 31, authorities passed a law on protections from domestic violence, which came into effect in March. While the law has some positive provisions, including protection orders for the first time (restraining orders against abusers), it contains problematic provisions.

It defines domestic violence as "any abuse, violence or threat committed by a family member against any other family member or individual exceeding his guardianship, jurisdiction, authority or responsibility, and resulting in physical or psychological harm," suggesting that authorities can decide at what point male guardians have gone beyond their authority in disciplining their wives, female relatives, and children. It also requires that the public prosecution propose "conciliation" between the victim and the abuser before any criminal action is pursued.

In November, the UAE announced a series of legal reforms, including decriminalizing drinking or possessing alcohol and attempted suicide, allowing unmarried couples to cohabitate, and meaning men could no longer benefit from lighter sentences for assaulting a female relative for so-called honor crimes. The reforms, as announced, would also allow couples who married outside the UAE to follow the laws of their home country or the country in which they married in matters of divorce and inheritance.

Sexual Orientation and Gender Identity

Article 356 of the federal penal code criminalizes (but does not define) "indecent assault" and provides for a minimum sentence of one year in prison. UAE courts use this article to convict people for same-sex relations as well as consensual heterosexual relations outside marriage. Women are disproportionately impacted, as pregnancy serves as evidence of extramarital sex and women who report rape can find themselves prosecuted for consensual sex. The UAE's penal code punishes "any male disguised in a female apparel and enters in this disguise a place reserved for women" with one year's imprisonment, a fine of up to 10,000 dirhams (US$2,723), or both. Transgender women have been arrested under this law even in mixed-gender spaces.

Different emirates in the UAE have laws that criminalize same-sex sexual relations. In Abu Dhabi, "unnatural sex with another person" can be punished with up to 14 years in prison. Article 177 of Dubai's penal code punishes consensual sodomy by imprisonment up to 10 years.

Key International Actors

On August 13, the UAE and Israel announced that they had agreed to the full normalization of relations, paving the way for enhanced cooperation on cybersecurity and surveillance technology and sparking concerns it could lead to increased repression domestically and regionally.

The peace agreement, which was brokered by the United States, was accompanied by reports of a US sale of F-35 stealth fighter jets to the UAE. Israel is the only other country in the Middle East to have received F-35 jets.

Uganda

Authorities in Uganda stepped up restrictions on freedoms of expression and assembly ahead of general elections in February 2021. Authorities broke up opposition rallies, arrested government critics and opposition members, and placed restrictions on media. Security forces used Covid-19 restrictions as a pretext to beat, extort, and arbitrarily detain people.

Freedom of Expression and Assembly

The government introduced new requirements that restrict freedom of expression online. On September 7, the Uganda Communications Commission issued a public notice requiring "providers of online data and communication," including bloggers and online TV providers, to seek authorization from the body by October 5, 2020, and pay a fee of 100,000 Uganda shillings (US$26.82).

On July 24, Ugandan police arrested four comedians, part of a group called *Bizonto*, for a satirical video they posted online calling on people to pray for top Ugandan government officials. The video highlighted that the leaders are all from the western region of the country, implying that power is concentrated in a group of men from one region. The group was released after four days in detention.

On July 27, plainclothes police arrested television host Bassajja Mivule. Police said videos of him circulating on social media "promote hatred." Mivule told media that when he was questioned, the police played video clips of him speaking about Minister of Information and Communications Technology Judith Nabakooba, which they said was offensive toward her, and another in which Mivule rallied Baganda people "to rise up," for which police accused him of promoting sectarianism.

On March 26, the Constitutional Court nullified section 8 of the Public Order Management Act (POMA), which has been used by police to block, restrict, and disperse peaceful assemblies and demonstrations by opposition groups, often with excessive force. The move came after the court ruled on a 2013 petition by civil society organizations challenging the law as being unconstitutional.

On January 6, police blocked public meetings by presidential candidate Robert Kyagulanyi, also known as Bobi Wine, in Gayaza, just outside the capital Kampala, saying Kyagulanyi had not met all the requirements of POMA. As Kyagulanyi and his group were gathering to meet, police arrested them and fired teargas to disperse people from the area.

Sexual Orientation and Gender Identity

On March 29, community residents and police raided a Children of the Sun Foundation (COSF), a shelter for homeless lesbian, gay, bisexual, and transgender youth in Wakiso, outside Kampala. Police beat and arrested 23 adults, including shelter residents, and charged them with "a negligent act likely to spread infection of disease" and "disobedience of lawful orders." Twenty residents of the shelter were detained by police for over six weeks without access to lawyers for allegedly disobeying Covid-19 restrictions.

In May, the Office of the Director of Public Prosecutions withdrew the charges, and on May 18, the Nsangi Magistrate's Court ordered the release of the 20 detainees. On June 15, a court ruled that the prison system's refusal to allow the 20 people access to counsel violated their rights to a fair hearing and to liberty.

Uganda's penal code punishes "carnal knowledge" among people of the same sex with up to life in prison.

Arrest and Harassment of Opposition Members and Supporters

Authorities have on several occasions blocked meetings of opposition members as they sought to consult their constituents.

On January 7, police blocked parliamentarian Robert Kyagulanyi's pressure group People Power from accessing a venue where they were to hold a consultative meeting with the public, and the next day blocked another event planned by the group in Lira in northern Uganda. This time police detained Kyagulanyi, but released him shortly after. Police also arrested journalists covering the events in Gayaza, outside Kampala, and Lira, and reportedly ordered at least one reporter to delete his footage of the events.

Prosecutions for Serious Crimes

In 2020, the case of Dominic Ongwen, alleged former Lord's Resistance Army (LRA) commander charged with 70 counts of war crimes and crimes against humanity, concluded at the International Criminal Court (ICC). Closing statements took place from March 10 to 12. A verdict was pending at time of writing. Two ICC warrants remain outstanding for the arrest of LRA leaders Joseph Kony and Vincent Otti, who is presumed dead.

The International Crimes Division (ICD) of Uganda's High Court continued the trial of alleged former LRA commander Thomas Kwoyelo—in custody since his capture in the Democratic Republic of Congo in 2009—on charges of war crimes and crimes against humanity. The trial has had numerous delays, and proceedings also were suspended due to Covid-19.

Covid-19

In March, President Yoweri Museveni announced a series of measures to prevent the spread of Covid-19, including a ban on private and public transport, as well as the suspension of non-essential services, and the closure of bars, restaurants and non-food markets, schools and places of worship, the airport, and the country's borders.

On March 30, he directed the police to arrest politicians who distributed food. The government said that food donations had to go through a government-organized task force. On April 4, the government began to provide food assistance targeting 1.5 million people in Kampala and Wakiso, and eventually other parts of the country.

Abuses by Security Forces

Security forces in Uganda beat, extorted, shot, and arrested people for allegedly failing to comply with the government's Covid-19 restrictions.

On March 23, media reported that soldiers beat locals in Mityana district, outside Kampala, claiming they were not respecting the order to close bars. On March 24, Agnes Linda Auma, resident district commissioner in charge of security in Amuru district, Northern Uganda, threatened during a radio interview to beat people who congregated in public spaces.

On March 26, media reported that police shot and injured two construction workers, Alex Oryem and Kassim Ssebudde, who were riding a motorcycle taxi in Mukono, outside Kampala, in violation of the ban on motorcycle transport with multiple passengers. The same day, members of the Local Defense Unit (LDU), an armed paramilitary group affiliated with the army, used wires and sticks to beat several people, including vendors selling fruit and vegetables and motorcycle riders, in downtown Kampala in an apparent attempt to punish non-compliance with the measures to close non-food markets. On March 30, Army Chief of Defense Forces David Muhoozi publicly apologized to Hadijah Aloyo, Christine Awori, and Safia Achaya, three victims of the LDU attacks, and announced that the military would hold the individual members responsible, without specifying how. He also announced that there would be a new commander for the units in Kampala.

On March 28, six police officers shot at a group of people in Bududa, in the eastern region of Uganda, injuring one, ostensibly to enforce the ban on public gatherings. Media reported that the police subsequently arrested David Agaba, the policeman in command.

On March 30, stick wielding LDU members attacked Alfred Ssembajjwe, a journalist and motorcycle taxi driver in Makindye, in Kampala, purportedly claiming to implement the government's Covid-19 curfew and ban on public transport. The LDU members demanded a bribe from him then let him go. The Committee to Protect Journalists reported that security forces, purportedly enforcing these measures, have harassed or assaulted at least six journalists between March 19 and April 22.

In July, the military withdrew LDU forces from their operations, reportedly to undergo training on human rights, in response to criticisms of the group's enforcement of Covid-19 restrictions.

On April 19, police arrested and later beat parliamentarian Francis Zaake for distributing food to the public as part of Covid-19 relief assistance in Mityana. Police held him for several days at the Special Investigations Unit (SIU) in Kireka, Kampala, but released him on bond on April 27. Zaake accused police and military officers of torturing him while he was in detention. Previously in 2018, soldiers had beaten Zaake and 32 others; on that occasion, Zaake was brought unconscious by "men in military uniform" to a hospital in Kampala.

On June 9, a military tribunal dropped charges against UPDF soldiers accused of brutalizing students protesting fee increases during a raid on Makerere university in Kampala in October 2019. During the raid, police and soldiers fired teargas into student residences, raided dormitories, and beat and arrested students, detaining dozens for days without charge. The Military Police spokesperson said none of the students who were allegedly brutalized showed up to testify.

On February 5, 2020, Parliament's human rights committee released findings from an August 2019 investigation into allegations that the country's security agencies were detaining people in several unacknowledged and ungazetted places of detention across the country often referred to as "safe houses," and subjecting detainees to torture. The committee found that authorities continue to operate safehouses and to subject detainees to torture and abuse, with near total impunity.

Ukraine

The armed conflict in eastern Ukraine continued to take a high toll on civilians during 2020, from threatening their physical safety to limiting access to food, medicines, adequate housing, and schools.

The Covid-19 pandemic worsened these trends. Travel restrictions imposed by Russia-backed armed groups in parts of eastern Ukraine and by Ukrainian authorities in response to the pandemic had a devastating impact on economic and social rights, exacerbating hardship for civilians and driving them deeper into poverty. Older people, women, children, and people with disabilities were hit the hardest.

Armed groups controlling parts of Donetska and Luhanska regions continued to carry out arbitrary and incommunicado detentions and use ill-treatment and torture in conflict-related cases, including to extract confessions. Justice for conflict-related abuses by government forces, including arbitrary detentions, torture or ill-treatment remained elusive.

Members of groups advocating hate and discrimination continued putting ethnic minorities, lesbian, gay, bisexual, and transgender (LGBT) people and rights activists at risk, subjecting them to physical attacks and hate speech.

The government proposed legislative amendments that threaten freedom of expression and media. Journalists and media workers faced harassment and threats connected to their reporting.

Armed Conflict

Flare-ups in hostilities, notably in March and May, led to civilian casualties. According to data by the United Nations human rights monitoring mission, in the first seven months of 2020, 18 civilians were killed and 89 injured by shelling, small arms weapons fire, mine-related incidents and unmanned aerial vehicles (UAV) strikes. Schools and educational facilities continued to be damaged by shelling, small arms and light weapons fire. Most of incidents occurred in the nongovernment-controlled areas.

Armed groups in Donetsk and Luhansk regions carried out incommunicado detention, torture and ill-treatment, including beatings, asphyxiation, electric shocks, and sexual violence.

Draft legislation is pending in parliament that would provide reparations to civilians for loss of life, health, and property during the conflict.

In the first half of 2020, government policies linking pension eligibility with displaced persons' status continued to discriminate against and create hardship for older people living in nongovernment-controlled areas by forcing them to regularly travel across the line of contact to access their pensions. In February, parliament failed to pass legislation that would have addressed this linkage on the premise that the state budget could not cover the cost of arrears owed to these pensioners.

As a result of harsh Covid-19 restrictions imposed by armed groups in parts of Donetska and Luhanska regions and by Ukrainian authorities at least 1.2 million people living in conflict-affected areas have been unable to get their pensions or re-unite with family since March.

Ukraine authorities required people entering from nongovernment-controlled areas to install a smartphone app to monitor compliance with restrictions, even though many people do not own a smartphone. They also require people to self-isolate for 14 days, which is prohibitively expensive for older people living in these areas. In a welcome move, authorities temporarily lifted the requirement for internally displaced pensioners to undergo regular identification checks for the duration of the quarantine. Restricted access to pensions pushed older people deeper into poverty, forcing them to cut back on food, hygiene products, and vital medications.

Armed groups in Donetska region introduced severe travel restrictions in response to Covid-19, effectively prohibiting residents with local residence permits from leaving during the pandemic. Those with residency permits in government-controlled areas who wanted to leave Donetsk were required to sign a document undertaking not return until the end of the pandemic. When one of the four entry-exit checkpoints in Donetsk region reopened, armed groups only admitted people based on pre-approved lists, and required a 14-day quarantine in medical facilities for those entering the area under their control. Armed groups in

Luhanska region only admitted people who have local residence registration but imposed no restrictions on leaving.

Rule of Law, Administration of Justice

The trial of four defendants over the 2014 downing of Malaysia Airlines flight MH17, which began in the Netherlands in March, continued, with interruptions due to coronavirus restrictions. All four suspects were being tried in absentia.

No progress was made in the investigation and trials in cases related to 2014 clashes in Odesa, which claimed the lives of 48 people.

In December 2019, an appeals court released five former officers of the Berkut riot police, under investigation in the case of the killing of 48 protesters and attempted killing of 80 during the Maidan protests in Kyiv in February 2014. They were subsequently transferred to Donetsk and Luhansk as part of a prisoner exchange.

In February, authorities placed a law enforcement official under house arrest on charges of killing a Maidan protester in February 2014. Two months later, he was released on bail. In March, investigators detained two men for the abduction and torture of two Maidan protesters in January 2014, one of whom died as a result. At least two other investigations continued into the killings of protesters. One of these was against former president Viktor Yanukovich.

In April, authorities placed a Maidan activist under house arrest in connection with the February 2014 arson of the Party of Regions office, which led to the death of one man.

In August, Ukrainian groups expressed concerns about a smear campaign against the deputy prosecutor general, tasked with overseeing the work of the department for investigations of crimes committed during the armed conflict.

In September, parliament passed in first reading a draft law that would incorporate into domestic legislation provisions concerning the investigation and prosecution of genocide, crimes against humanity and war crimes.

Women's Rights

The Covid-19 pandemic disproportionately affected women, who account for over 80 percent of Ukraine's healthcare and social workers. The pandemic-related restrictions led to a surge in domestic violence, with reported cases increasing by 30 percent. According to service providers, victims were often unable to escape abuse during the pandemic due to lack of shelter space and inadequate police response.

In February, President Volodymyr Zelensky pledged to submit the Council of Europe (CoE) Convention on the Prevention of Violence against Women and Domestic Violence (Istanbul Convention) to parliament for ratification, pending additional instructions by relevant ministries. The government signed the convention in 2011.

Freedom of Expression

In December 2019, police apprehended three suspects in the ongoing investigation into the 2016 killing of journalist Pavel Sheremet.

In the same month, journalists Stanislav Aseyev and Oleh Halaziuk were released as part of a prisoner exchange, after having been captured and held by Russia-backed militants since 2017.

In January, the government introduced a legislative proposal against dissemination of "disinformation" that would have jeopardized freedom of expression and media independence. The proposal did not advance in parliament.

In June, a court in Kherson arrested a high-level municipal official for ordering the acid attack on the anti-corruption activist Katerina Handziuk in 2018, which resulted in her death.

In July, a journalist's private information was hacked and published online after a media outlet she co-founded published investigative reports alleging ties between far-right groups and Ukraine's media outlets. She fled Ukraine after receiving threats of death and other violence. In September, authorities opened a criminal case, but qualified the incident as "invasion of privacy" rather than "interference in journalistic activities."

Hate Crimes

Throughout the year, far-right groups and individuals carried out hate attacks against ethnic minorities and LGBT people. Authorities often failed to investigate hate crimes.

In June, a parliamentary committee declined to advance for further consideration draft legislation increasing accountability for hate crimes, including those based on gender identity and sexual orientation.

In August, a group of local residents attacked the home of a Roma family in Kharkiv region, following calls for anti-Roma violence in social media.

Also in August, a group of counter-protesters advocating "traditional values" attacked participants celebrating LGBT rights in Odesa Pride, threw objects at them, sprayed teargas and injured two policemen. The police arrested 16 people on hooliganism charges, but did not charge them with hate crimes.

In April, a group of men robbed, severely beat, and sexually assaulted a 19-year-old transgender person in Zhytomyr. The police initially registered the incident as a robbery, but in July, under pressure from human rights defenders, opened additional investigations into rape and a hate-motivated crime.

In September, police successfully thwarted attempts by far-right groups to disrupt Pride events in Zapirozhie and Kharkiv.

Crimea

Russian authorities continued persecuting Crimean Tatars activists in occupied Crimea by bringing unfounded terrorism charges against them.

In September, a Russian military court sentenced seven activists with Crimean Solidarity, a group that provides financial and legal assistance to Crimean Tatar families, to prison terms ranging from 13 to 19 years for alleged association with Hizb-ut Tahrir, banned in Russia as a "terrorist" organization but legal in Ukraine. One man was acquitted.

Russian authorities continued to conscript males in occupied Crimea to serve in Russia's armed forces, in violation of international humanitarian law. The authorities imposed criminal penalties against those who refused to comply with the draft. Russian authorities also conduct enlistment advertising campaigns in Crimea and provide military propaganda for schoolchildren there.

In January, Russian authorities denied entry to Crimea to Taras Ibragimov, a Ukrainian journalist, and banned him from entering Russia until 2054. Authorities did not provide a meaningful explanation, instead citing general concerns for national security and public order.

Key International Actors

In April, the United Nations Committee on Economic, Social and Cultural Rights expressed concern in its concluding observations about human rights implications of the draft amendments to Ukraine's trade union laws. It encouraged Ukraine to review the draft law, with a view to ensuring the effectiveness of collective bargaining and of the right to union representation.

In June, several UN agencies welcomed the adoption of a resolution that affirmed the voting rights of internally displaced persons. According to the UN High Commissioner for Refugees, the procedure affirmed "the rights of internally displaced persons to non-discrimination and equal participation in government affairs."

In June, during their annual human rights dialogue, the European Union and Ukraine agreed on the need to facilitate the payment of pensions to residents of non-government controlled areas, to de-link pension payments from IDP status, and to demonstrate progress in the investigations into crimes committed in 2014 and into the killings of Kateryna Handziuk and Pavlo Sheremet.

In July, the UN High Commissioner for Human Rights noted at the UN Human Rights Council that "human rights violations involving torture and other ill-treatment perpetrated by law enforcement agencies continued in Crimea." The High Commissioner reminded Ukraine of its obligation "to use all available means to ensure respect for the enjoyment of human rights in Crimea as well as of Crimean residents" outside of the area.

In September, the UN Children's Fund (UNICEF) called for Ukraine to "strengthen protection of schools" in the east, by accelerating the implementation of the Safe School Declaration. It stated that children and teachers in 3,500 educational facilities are "currently affected by the ongoing violence [in eastern Ukraine] and remain at risk."

Although Ukraine is not a member of the International Criminal Court (ICC), it accepted the court's jurisdiction over alleged crimes committed on its territory since November 2013. The ICC prosecutor's preliminary examination as to whether it should open an investigation into abuses committed during the armed conflict remained ongoing.

United Kingdom

The United Kingdom exited the European Union in January, and then faced the public health and economic challenges of the Covid-19 pandemic. The government's response to both highlighted its willingness to set aside human rights for the sake of political expediency and a worrying disdain for the rule of law. Black and Asian people were disproportionately impacted by Covid-19, while growing numbers depended on food banks to get by. Survivors of the Grenfell Tower fire and Black British citizens from the Windrush generation harmed by UK immigration policy awaited justice. The UK took positive steps to strengthen international human rights protection, and showed leadership on Belarus and Hong Kong, yet with no clear strategy on human rights in foreign policy equivocated in the face of abuses by Saudi Arabia and other states.

The Rule of Law and Human Rights

During the course of the year, the UK government showed a willingness to weaken the rule of law and democratic institutions that constrained its authority, in ways that put human rights at risk.

The government sought in February, to restrict media access to the Prime Minister' office and in August banned a media outlet from Ministry of Defense press conferences, raising concerns about media freedom.

In July, the government announced a panel of experts to review the power of courts to hold the executive to account, a move motivated by a desire to curb court powers.

In September, the government introduced legislation that would breach the Brexit treaty agreed with the EU the previous October, which a minister admitted in parliament "does break international law in a very specific and limited way." The move prompted widespread criticism in the UK and abroad, including concerns about the negative impact on human rights in Northern Ireland.

The possibility that the UK might end the year without a deal with the EU on future relations raised concerns about a negative impact on food and medicine

HUMAN
RIGHTS
WATCH

AUTOMATED HARDSHIP
How the Tech-Driven Overhaul of the UK's Social Security System
Worsens Poverty

supplies, on human rights in Northern Ireland and that the UK might seek to water down employment and other rights derived from EU law in future.

Covid-19

The Covid-19 pandemic had a widespread impact on life in the UK. WHO data showed that as of October 28, the UK had the most Covid-19 deaths in Europe with 45,365 dying of complications from the disease, many of them in facilities for older people. Specific concerns arose around as to whether the UK government had acted swiftly enough to protect the rights to life and health of people in these facilities.

In June, health authorities set out recommendations to reduce the health inequalities highlighted by the pandemic's disproportionate impact on the UK's Black and Minority Ethnic (BAME) population and on BAME healthcare workers in particular. At time of writing the government had failed to implement the recommendations.

Legal experts criticized the government's rushed emergency legislation in response to the pandemic for being uneven in its approach and unclear in its implementation. The UK parliament's human rights committee raised concerns that Covid-19 laws affecting fundamental rights were being passed without effective legislative scrutiny.

The emergency legislation's increased time limits for detention of people with mental health conditions and relaxation of rules and standards for social care services and assessments raised specific concerns for the rights of people with disabilities and older people during the pandemic.

Despite a record surge in claims for social security support, the government reinstated some of its draconian social security rules, including sanctions on and debt recovery from people's benefit payments, despite having relaxed restrictions between March and June and temporarily raised benefit levels. Longstanding flaws in the automated calculation of people's benefits remained a concern.

The UK government used emergency law to relax requirements on local authorities to make adjustments to ensure education delivery for children with disabilities after schools closed in March, raising serious concerns about discrimination and exclusion. Children from families living in poverty were disproportionately affected by disrupted schooling because many lacked the devices or internet access required for distance learning.

The economic downturn triggered by Covid-19 prompted a range of temporary emergency measures to mitigate the human impact, including employment support and a ban on evictions for private tenants. The evictions ban expired in September, with fears that up to 55,000 households in privately rented accommodation could face eviction in coming months.

Right to Food

The country's two main food bank networks published statistics showing that reliance on emergency food aid rose markedly after the Covid-19 pandemic, with food parcel distribution close to double the previous year's levels by May. One network, the Trussell Trust, reported in September that half of its users since the pandemic had never used a food bank before.

The decision by governments across the UK to close schools to contain the pandemic left local authorities struggling to ensure that children from families living in poverty, who often rely on free school meals as their main nutrition, received sufficient food. A flawed electronic system used in England to issue £15 (US$19) per week of supermarket vouchers to replace school meals caused severe problems for schools and families for two months before the system was improved. The government temporarily extended free school meal coverage for the duration of the pandemic to children living in poverty whose immigration status previously left them ineligible.

Migration and Asylum

In May, following a lawsuit brought in March by the nongovernmental organization (NGO) Detention Action, authorities released almost 1,000 immigration detainees who could not be returned to their home countries because of Covid-19 travel restrictions.

As approximately 5,000 migrants and asylum-seekers arrived irregularly by boat from France in the first 9 months of the year, the government threatened to opt out of the human rights law and use offshore detention and processing to facilitate the deportation of those arriving.

The UK continued to detain asylum-seeking children and migrant children facing deportation.

In March, an independent government-ordered review into the authorities' treatment of a group of British citizens, primarily from the Caribbean, wrongly threatened with deportation or deported from the UK with widespread consequences for their rights and wellbeing, published its findings. The report said the treatment of the group, known as the "Windrush generation," by the government as a result of its "hostile environment" migration policy demonstrated an "institutional ignorance and thoughtlessness ... consistent with some elements of the definition of institutional racism."

Campaigners and parliamentarians criticized the compensation scheme established in 2019 for not working fast enough, as members of the Windrush generation with claims pending died during the year, and only a small fraction of claims were settled.

Accountability for the Grenfell Tower Fire

Accountability remained elusive more than 3 years after the Grenfell Tower fire in London that killed 71 people. A statutory public inquiry was ongoing into the fire which destroyed an apartment block of primarily social housing, and its second phase began in September. At time of writing the government had yet to implement the first set of recommendations of the inquiry published in January or find a solution for owners of private apartments in buildings with similar dangerous cladding.

In February, the Attorney General agreed to grant immunity from future prosecution to a number of building contractors and architects concerned about self-incrimination, angering fire survivors and relatives of those killed.

Reproductive Rights

UK parliament regulations providing legal abortion in Northern Ireland in any circumstances up to the twelfth week of gestation, entered into force in March.

However, reproductive rights advocates reported that women seeking abortions in Northern Ireland continued to face obstacles from some healthcare professionals unwilling to carry out the procedure.

In March and April, in response to rising need for safe abortion services during the Covid-19 pandemic, authorities in Scotland, Wales, and England, temporarily eased restrictions to allow for self-management of medical abortions at home, a safe and effective method that avoids unnecessary surgical procedures and complies with public health guidance on self-isolation.

After serious delays, in September, the Department for Education introduced compulsory age-appropriate comprehensive sexuality education for primary and secondary students in England.

Violence Against Women and Girls

The UK fell within the global trend of escalating reports of violence against women during the Covid-19 pandemic. Groups providing assistance to victims of domestic violence, reported a surge in requests for help from women and girls and noted that remote services and English-only government campaigns disadvantaged BAME women in particular from accessing services. Anti-domestic violence groups raised concerns about the end of a £37 million ($48m) emergency fund to support services to women and girls experiencing violence. A draft law intended to help women who experience domestic violence fails to adequately protect migrant women.

In July, following a legal challenge and pressure from the UK's information oversight body, police scrapped the controversial "digital strip search" approach, which required rape victims to disclose their full mobile phone data to investigators.

Government data showed that prosecutions and convictions for rape hit a record low for the year ending March 2020. The Crown Prosecution Service launched a new five-year strategy for prosecuting rape and other serious sexual offences.

Sexual Orientation and Gender Identity

In March, the Court of Appeal ruled that human rights law did not require British passport authorities to provide a non-binary X gender marker on identity documents. In September, the government walked back plans to amend the Gender Recognition Act that would have allowed for legal gender recognition based on self-declaration.

Military Abuses and Impunity

In March, the government introduced legislation in the Overseas Operations Bill creating a "presumption against prosecution" for members of the armed forces accused of crimes, including torture, committed overseas more than five years ago. It remained pending in Parliament at time of writing.

Counterterrorism

About 100 UK nationals, including 60 children, remain held without judicial review in squalid camps and prisons for ISIS suspects and family members in northeast Syria. In July, the Court of Appeal in London ruled that Shamima Begum, an Islamic State (ISIS) suspect stripped of her UK citizenship in 2019 after travelling to Syria as a teenager, should be able to return from detention in northeast Syria to the UK to challenge the deprivation of her nationality.

In September, the government shared intelligence with US authorities about Alexanda Kotey and El Shafee Elsheikh allowing US prosecutions of the two high-profile ISIS suspects to proceed. The Supreme Court authorized the intelligence transfer following an assurance by the US government that the two men, stripped of their UK citizenship in 2018, would not face the death penalty.

Foreign Policy

The UK government's global human rights sanctions mechanism launched in July, allowing asset freezes and travel bans for those implicated in killings, torture, and forced labor. The mechanism underscored the need for a human rights strategy to ensure a more consistent approach to rights in UK foreign policy.

The welcome initial designation of officials from Saudi Arabia over the state killing of journalist Jamal Khashoggi was overshadowed by a decision to resume arms sales to the Saudi-led coalition the following day, despite clear evidence of the coalition's responsibility for war crimes in Yemen.

The UK strengthened its response to the human rights crackdown in Hong Kong, working to marshal international condemnation of China's actions, offering safe haven to Hong Kongers with UK ties, and suspending extradition to Hong Kong. At time of writing, the UK had yet to impose human rights sanctions on officials from China over abuses in Xinjiang or Hong Kong.

The UK played a largely positive role at the United Nations Human Rights Council, including leading a joint statement on China, and supporting a joint statement on Saudi Arabia, creation of a mechanism on Libya, and an urgent debate on Belarus (the UK also showed leadership on Belarus at the Organization for Security and Co-operation in Europe).

However, it was hesitant to support specific attention at the Human Rights Council to racism in the US or to use its influence to press for stronger action this year at the Human Rights Council on Sri Lanka and at the Security Council on Myanmar and Yemen. Since leaving the EU, the UK has refrained from speaking up against the decline of the rule of law in other European countries, including Hungary and Poland.

United States

Important human rights failings of the United States were laid bare in 2020.

The grossly disproportionate impact of Covid-19 on Black, brown, and Native people, connected to longstanding disparities in health, education, and economic status, revealed the enduring effects of past overtly racist laws and policies and continuing impediments to equality. The police killing of George Floyd in May, and a series of other police killings of Black people, sparked massive and largely peaceful protests, which in many instances were met with brutality by local and federal law enforcement agents.

The administration of President Donald Trump continued to dismantle the United States asylum system, limit access to women's health care, undermine consumer protections against predatory lenders and abusive debt collectors, and weaken regulations that reduce pollution and address climate change. After election officials across the US tallied the votes for the presidential election, determining that Joe Biden was the president-elect, Trump made baseless allegations of voter fraud.

In its foreign policy, the United States worked on several fronts to undermine multilateral institutions, including through the use of sanctions to attack the International Criminal Court. It flouted international human rights law as it partnered with abusive governments—though it did sanction a number of individuals and governments for committing human rights abuses.

Racial Justice

The Covid-19 pandemic has had a disproportionate impact on racial and ethnic minorities, primarily Black, Latinx, and Native communities, which faced increased risk for infection, serious illness, and death from the disease, as well as severe economic impacts. These disparities are linked to longstanding inequities in health outcomes and access to care, education, employment, and economic status.

Some localities and the state of California recognized that these disparities are connected to the legacy of slavery and considered various forms of reparations

HUMAN
RIGHTS
WATCH

THE CASE FOR REPARATIONS IN TULSA, OKLAHOMA
A Human Rights Argument
May 2020

to address them. At the federal level, HR 40, a bill in Congress proposing the establishment of a commission to investigate slavery's legacy and create reparations proposals, gained unprecedented momentum, with 170 co-sponsors in the House of Representatives and 20 co-sponsors in the Senate as of November.

In May, Human Rights Watch urged state and local authorities in Tulsa, Oklahoma, to provide reparations to descendants and the remaining survivors of the 1921 Tulsa Race Massacre, in which a white mob killed several hundred Black people and destroyed an affluent Black neighborhood.

Thousands of people of Asian descent reported incidents of attacks and racial discrimination after the outbreak of the Covid-19 pandemic. President Donald Trump repeatedly described the virus using racist language.

Poverty and Inequality

The Covid-19 pandemic exacerbated poverty and inequality in the United States, and disproportionately affected Black, Latinx, and Native communities. The pandemic and public health measures necessary to slow its spread resulted in lost wages or jobs, reduced health coverage, and reduced access to other essential goods and services. People of color—particularly women and immigrants—continued to be over-represented in low-wage service jobs, putting them at greater risk. Many, particularly in agriculture and food production, faced unsafe working conditions leading to outbreaks.

Increased unemployment protection and direct payments in relief packages that Congress passed significantly stemmed poverty rate growth. However, many protections expired in July and August. The relief bills lacked protections for those unable to pay bills or medical care costs, and excluded certain workers, including immigrants.

The administration continued to undermine consumer protections against predatory lenders and abusive debt collectors. The Consumer Financial Protection Bureau gutted a rule seeking to prevent small lenders—including so-called payday lenders—from charging exorbitant interest rates.

California voters passed a ballot initiative sponsored by app-based companies stripping app-based rideshare and delivery drivers of the minimum wage, paid sick leave, and other critical labor protections provided by a state law passed in 2019, setting a dangerous precedent for workers' rights in the US and globally.

Criminal Legal System

Police killings of George Floyd and Breonna Taylor and the shooting of Jacob Blake provoked massive protests calling for police accountability, reduction in the scope and power of police, elimination of extortionate court fines and fees, and investment in Black communities.

Rather than address problems of poverty or health that contribute to crime, many US jurisdictions focus on aggressive policing in poor and minority communities, fueling a vicious cycle of incarceration and police violence.

While no governmental agency tracks police killings, the Washington Post database has documented about 1,000 killings by shootings each of the past five years, revealing significant racial disparities.

Black people report being subjected to many forms of police abuse, including non-lethal force, arbitrary arrests and detentions, and harassment, at higher levels than white people. Police subjected Native American people to similar abuse, and killed them at even higher rates than they killed Black people.

The US continues to lead the world in reported incarceration rates. Approximately 2.3 million people were locked up on any given day in 2020. There are about 10 million admissions into jails each year. Based on 2017-18 data, about 4.4 percent of the US adult population were on probation or parole. In August, Human Rights Watch reported that violations of probation and parole are adding to jail and prison populations. Many people in the criminal legal system continue to face extortionate fines and fees, as well as bars to accessing public assistance, public housing, and the right to vote.

While their relative incarceration rates have declined steadily over the past decade, Black people, and to a lesser extent Latinx people, are still more likely to be imprisoned than white people.

Some of the nation's worst outbreaks of Covid-19 occurred in jails and prisons, with over 169,286 people in prison testing positive and at least 1,363 deaths by November. Some prisons lacked adequate safety and health measures. Some ju-

REVOKED
How Probation and Parole Feed Mass
Incarceration in the United States

HUMAN
RIGHTS
WATCH

"It Wasn't Really Safety, It Was Shame"

Young People, Sexual Health Education, and HPV in Alabama

risdictions took steps to release people or to limit the influx of new people, but few institutions made reductions sufficient to limit the spread of Covid-19.

Five US states had executed a total of seven men in 2020 at time of writing; the federal government had executed an additional eight, the first death sentences carried out by the federal government since 2003. Colorado joined 21 other states in abolishing the death penalty. Three other states have imposed moratoriums in recent years.

The US Congress has not passed further reform legislation since the 2018 First Step Act. Its implementation has had mixed results. While several thousand people's sentences were reduced, the government frequently opposed reductions for crack cocaine sentences. Advocates criticized programs for earning credits toward release as inadequate. A risk assessment tool used for release eligibility may create racial disparities and can be manipulated to prevent early release.

Nearly half-a-million people are held in local jails pretrial in the United States on any given day. Pretrial incarceration pressures many people to plead guilty regardless of actual guilt or to take on debt to pay money bail. Many jurisdictions have replaced or supplemented money bail with algorithm-based risk assessment tools, which do not necessarily reduce incarceration rates and entrench racial bias.

California voters rejected a law that abolished money bail but required courts to use risk assessment tools in pretrial incarceration decisions. New York implemented pretrial reform without these tools, resulting in substantial reductions in pretrial jail populations.

Children in the Criminal and Juvenile Justice Systems

Arrests of children under 18 for violent crimes have dropped by more than 50 percent over the last 20 years, and the number of incarcerated children has dropped by 60 percent since 2000. However, stark racial and ethnic disparities continue. Youth of color make up approximately one-third of teenagers under 18 but two-thirds of incarcerated youth in the United States.

A movement to utilize alternatives to incarceration for youth who commit certain offenses is reducing incarceration in California, Hawaii, Kentucky, Georgia, Florida, Mississippi, and Texas.

Vermont, Michigan, and New York also increased the age at which people can be tried in juvenile court. Even so, all US states have laws that permit or require children accused of serious offenses to be prosecuted as adults. Since 2009, 22 states have narrowed their adult transfer provisions.

Over 200,000 people were on sex offender registries for offenses committed when they were children, a Juvenile Law Center report found. Many were required to register, sometimes for life, for acts such as streaking, sexting, or consensual sexual activity between teenagers.

Drug Policy

Voters approved the country's first ballot initiative to expand access to evidence-based drug treatment and support and decriminalize the possession of all drugs for personal use in Oregon. Ballot initiatives legalizing marijuana for adult or medical use passed in Arizona, Mississippi, Montana, New Jersey, and South Dakota, bringing the total states legalizing adult-use marijuana to 15 and medical marijuana to 36. The US House of Representatives passed the Marijuana Opportunity Reinvestment and Expungement Act, a bill that, if enacted into law, would end federal marijuana prohibition.

However, drug possession for personal use remains by far the single most arrested offense in the United States. Arrests are marked by stark racial disparities, even though people report similar rates of use across racial groups; according to a 2020 report by the American Civil Liberties Union, in 2018, Black people were 3.64 times more likely to be arrested for marijuana possession than white people.

In the months following the declaration of a national public health emergency in response to Covid-19, the US experienced a surge in already high drug overdoses, roughly 17 percent higher than in 2019, according to one study. Access to the overdose-reversal drug naloxone has increased in recent years, but drug laws are an obstacle to life-saving harm reduction services in many states, and evidence-based treatment for substance use disorder is not available to many people who need it.

Rights of Non-Citizens

The administration continued to attack the rights of migrants and asylum seekers. Returns of non-Mexican asylum seekers to Mexico to wait for US asylum adjudications under the "Migrant Protection Protocols" continued with a substantial decrease from April to July, exposing tens of thousands, including many children, to precarious, dangerous conditions and denying fair hearings.

Human Rights Watch identified 138 cases of Salvadorans who were killed after being deported to El Salvador from the United States since 2013, illustrating the toll of inadequate US protection processes. The Trump administration expanded fast-track deportation procedures for families at the border and sent Honduran and Salvadoran asylum seekers to Guatemala under the problematic Asylum Cooperation Agreement. Human Rights Watch reported on how US restrictions on access to asylum harms LGBT people fleeing persecution, including sexual violence, in El Salvador, Guatemala, and Honduras.

As Covid-19 cases increased in March, the Centers for Disease Control and Prevention (CDC) issued an order closing the land borders, over-ruling career-CDC public health officials' opinions it was not warranted. This led to the expulsion of more than 400,000 people along the US-Mexico border, including children, without screening for eligibility for asylum or other protections.

Throughout the year, the administration proposed a series of regulations to severely restrict eligibility for asylum and other forms of protection.

US officials suspended some forms of immigration enforcement during the pandemic but continued deportations of migrants detained in the United States, risking spreading the virus globally.

Deaths in US immigration detention spiked to a 15-year high with at least eight fatalities related to Covid-19. In April, Human Rights Watch reported on the detention system's expansion since 2017 in privately run facilities where noncitizens are subjected to threats and use of force, due process violations, and unsanitary and crowded conditions. Though some were released in response to

HUMAN
RIGHTS
WATCH

WHAT DEMOCRACY LOOKS LIKE
Protecting Voting Rights in the US during the Covid-19 Pandemic

the pandemic, by November, more than 7,000 people had contracted Covid-19 while in detention.

A federal judge ruled in June that the US government was not in compliance with a settlement agreement limiting the detention of children in prison-like conditions to 20 days. In September, a whistleblower brought allegations of medical neglect and abuse by a doctor working with an immigration detention facility in the state of Georgia; subsequent reporting uncovered accounts of hysterectomies and other gynecological procedures performed without informed consent. Lawmakers called for a full investigation.

Health and Human Rights

At time of writing, the United States led the world in coronavirus cases and deaths. Trump and other government officials spread disinformation about the coronavirus.

The US has made coronavirus testing largely free, but states have struggled to increase testing capacity. Millions of people are uninsured and unable to access affordable health care. Costs of treatment may have forced many to forgo care or face financial ruin.

Rates of people without health insurance in the US were rising before the pandemic, including nearly 10 million women without coverage. Pandemic-related job loss likely increased this number dramatically, with a disproportionate impact on women.

Healthcare workers faced serious shortages of protective equipment.

Voting Rights

Election officials' responses to the Covid-19 pandemic seriously impaired some people's access to voting in primary elections, but access improved by the general election in November. A federal appeals court ruled people with criminal convictions in Florida had to pay fines imposed before being able to vote. As media organizations projected Biden had won the presidential election, President Trump made baseless allegations of voter fraud and filed lawsuits challenging certain states' electoral processes.

Right to Education

Schools were closed at some point in all 50 states in response to the pandemic. While closed, many schools switched to online learning, but one in five school-aged US children do not have access to a computer or high-speed internet at home. Various studies warned school closures would widen racial and economic inequalities in education, with a particularly significant impact on children with disabilities.

Environment and Human Rights

The Trump administration weakened car emission and air quality standards, and suspended many requirements for environmental monitoring.

United States farms continue to use more than 70 pesticides that are banned or in the process of complete phase out in the European Union, Brazil, or China, putting the health of farmworkers and nearby communities at risk.

Air pollution from industry, transportation, and wildfires, which are increasing due to climate change, continued to impact people in the US, particularly communities of color. A Harvard University study suggested people with Covid-19 are more likely to die if they are exposed to high levels of air pollution.

Some communities, especially Native Americans living on reservations, faced the Covid-19 pandemic without adequate access to water. Detroit failed to reconnect households, mostly minority, whose water had been shut off before the pandemic. We the People of Detroit, an organization committed to community research, found in July that zip codes with more water shutoffs correlated with more Covid-19 cases.

The United States is the world's second largest emitter of greenhouse gases. Trump withdrew the US from the Paris Agreement, which took effect on November 4. Biden vowed to rejoin the agreement on his first day in office.

Extreme weather events increased in frequency and intensity in part due to climate change and had a disproportionate impact on already marginalized communities. The summer of 2020 was one of the warmest documented. Some local governments warned about heat-related illness and mortality but most plans excluded pregnant people, who are more vulnerable to heat stress. Premature birth is also linked with heat. Black women, who already suffer higher rates of giving birth prematurely, are especially vulnerable.

Women's and Girls' Rights

Lack of access to health care contributes to higher rates of maternal and cervical cancer deaths than in comparable countries. Human Rights Watch documented in 2020 how Alabama is failing to provide young people with necessary information on sexual and reproductive health and failing to persuade the public to take the human papillomavirus (HPV) vaccine, which prevents several types of cancer, including cervical cancer. Vaccination rates throughout Alabama remain low in a state with one of the highest rates of preventable cervical cancer deaths in the country, with Black women more likely to die.

The Trump administration continued to limit access to women's health care. Since the "gag" rule went into effect in 2019, barring doctors receiving federal family planning (Title X) funds from giving women information on the full range of pregnancy options available to them, the patient capacity of the Title X network has been reduced by half. In July, the Supreme Court upheld rules permitting employers to opt out of contraceptive coverage in employee health insurance plans by claiming religious or moral objections.

Some states, like Ohio and Texas, used the pandemic as an excuse to further restrict access to abortion. In July, a law took effect in Florida requiring anyone under 18 to obtain consent from a parent or legal guardian before an abortion.

Older People's Rights

More than 40 percent of state-reported Covid-19 deaths in the US, but just 8 percent of total cases, were among people living in long-term care institutions. Nursing home operators pushed state and federal governments to give them broad legal immunity. Nursing facilities' longstanding infection control problems and reduced public oversight of nursing homes during the Covid-19 crisis put already vulnerable older residents at greater risk.

The Centers for Medicare and Medicaid Services (CMS) announced a "no visitors" policy for all nursing facilities in response to the pandemic, with limited ex-

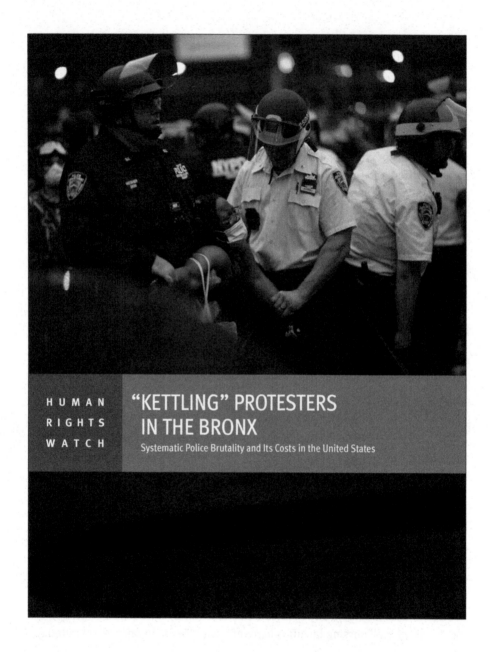

H U M A N
R I G H T S
W A T C H

"KETTLING" PROTESTERS
IN THE BRONX
Systematic Police Brutality and Its Costs in the United States

ceptions for end-of-life visits, cutting off over 1.5 million older residents from families and friends. Such visitors supplement care by staff, advocate on residents' behalf, and provide essential emotional support. CMS updated guidance in September to allow for visitation in some circumstances, though protocols varied widely across states.

Sexual Orientation and Gender Identity

In June, the Supreme Court ruled a federal law prohibiting sex discrimination in employment prohibits discrimination based on sexual orientation and gender identity.

Despite the ruling, the Trump administration attempted to roll back health and housing protections for transgender people. More than a dozen states also considered bills restricting gender-affirming care for children, putting their health and rights at risk. At least 28 transgender people were killed in the United States in 2020.

Congress failed to reauthorize the Violence Against Women Act, which includes provisions for LGBT survivors of violence, or pass the Equality Act, which would prohibit discrimination based on sexual orientation and gender identity.

Freedom of Expression and Assembly

President Trump continued to attack news outlets that questioned his administration's policies. After Twitter placed a fact-check label on Trump's tweets, the president issued an executive order that attempts to remove legal protections for social media platforms, an attack against online freedom of expression globally.

Local law enforcement agencies in several jurisdictions reacted with excessive force toward people protesting police violence.

President Trump took aggressive action against protesters demanding racial justice. He had federal police remove peaceful protesters from a park next to the White House to facilitate his appearance for photographs at a nearby church. Against the wishes of local officials, his administration sent federal officers to Portland, despite questions about their authority to take enforcement actions. Reports of excessive force and other misconduct followed.

National Security

In October, state and federal authorities charged 14 men linked to extreme-right movements with plotting to kidnap the governor of Michigan and overthrow the state government because of Covid-19 related restrictions. The men discussed "taking" the governor of Virginia for the same reason, the FBI said. That same month, the Department of Homeland Security identified white supremacists, along with cyber and other forms of election interference by China, Iran, and Russia, among top threats facing the US.

Also in October, a federal court charged two Islamic State (ISIS) suspects with involvement in the torture and killings of US journalists and aid workers. The UK shared key intelligence on the pair after the US agreed not to seek the death penalty.

The US reported completing repatriations of all citizens held as ISIS suspects and family members in Syria and Iraq, placing the total at 27.

In January, psychologists James Mitchell and John Bruce Jessen, architects of the Central Intelligence Agency's post-September 11, 2001 "enhanced interrogation" techniques, defended their use of torture on dozens of detainees in their first public testimony on the illegal program. The pair testified at the Guantanamo Bay Naval Base pre-trial military commission hearings for five men charged as co-conspirators in the September 11 attacks. Further proceedings were postponed to at least 2021 due to Covid-19 and the consecutive resignations of two presiding judges. Concerns persist regarding prison conditions and access to counsel for the 40 detainees still held at Guantanamo, most without charge.

Foreign Policy

The United States continued to disengage from multilateral institutions.

The administration took unprecedented action in June in issuing an executive order authorizing asset freezes and family entry bans against International Criminal Court (ICC) officials and others assisting them; in September it designated two ICC officials for sanctions. In July, the US took steps to withdraw from the World Health Organization.

This followed its previous withdrawal from the UN Human Rights Council and decision to end US funding for the UN Population Fund (UNFPA) and Palestinian refugee agency, United Nations Relief and Works Agency for Palestine Refugees in the Near East (UNRWA).

The US Department of State's Commission on Unalienable Rights, a body established in 2019 to "reexamine" US commitments to international human rights, released a report in August advocating a hierarchical approach to human rights and relegating abortion and marriage equality to "divisive social and political controversies."

In January, the Trump administration cancelled a policy to eliminate all antipersonnel landmines. The administration continued to entrench and expand implementation of its dangerous iteration of the "Global Gag Rule," and omitted gender identity and sexual orientation from a draft policy on gender by the US Agency for International Development.

The United States admitted 11,814 refugees in fiscal year 2020, an 85 percent decrease from the 85,000 admitted in 2016. In October, the Trump administration set the lowest US refugee resettlement cap on record—15,000—for fiscal year 2021.

President Trump continued to praise authoritarian leaders, and his administration continued to provide military assistance and approve arms sales to states with poor human rights records. The administration also continued to support the Saudi-led coalition's war in Yemen despite numerous laws-of-war violations and pursued a $478 million arms sale to Saudi Arabia despite two bipartisan votes in Congress to restrict weapons sales.

The United States imposed sanctions on perpetrators of grave human rights violations and corruption, including officials in Equatorial Guinea, Uganda, and South Sudan; Chinese and Hong Kong government officials, state agencies, and companies; and 39 Syrians, including Bashar Al-Assad.

Congress passed legislation highlighting human rights concerns in China and Hong Kong, yet some administration responses—including restricting visas for Chinese journalists, increasing scrutiny of students from China, and efforts to ban applications by Chinese tech companies—raised human rights concerns. The US signed an agreement with the Taliban on terms for a US troop withdrawal from Afghanistan. The agreement did not address human rights concerns, but the US did press for greater inclusion of women and civil society in the Afghan government's delegation for negotiations with the Taliban that began in September. The US did not publicly press the Afghan government on its abuses.

In Latin America, the administration focused on serious human rights abuses in Venezuela, Cuba, and Nicaragua but failed to scrutinize abuses in allied countries, such as Brazil, Colombia, El Salvador, and Mexico.

In the Middle East, the administration presented in January a plan to formalize Israeli annexation of large parts of the occupied West Bank, and helped broker agreements to normalize Israel's relations with the United Arab Emirates and Bahrain in September.

Meanwhile, the US took an increasingly hostile approach to Iran. In January, the US killed Qassem Soleimani, commander of Iran's Islamic Revolutionary Guard Corps Quds Force in a drone strike in Iraq; afterwards, President Trump tweeted that retaliation from Iran would be met by targeting Iranian cultural sites, which would constitute a war crime.

In September, following the UN Security Council's refusal to renew an arms embargo that expired in October as part of the Joint Comprehensive Plan of Action (JCPOA), the US argued it could reimpose UN sanctions. Other permanent members of the council and parties to the JCPOA, as well as the UN secretary-general, refused to accept the US position, since the US had withdrawn from the agreement.

In Africa, the US focused on normalizing relations with Sudan's transitional government and removed Sudan from the State Sponsors of Terrorism list; Sudan began a process of normalizing relations with Israel, reportedly in exchange. The US continued its military activity in Somalia, conducting dozens of airstrikes, some of which resulted in apparent civilian casualties that were not adequately investigated or acknowledged.

In May, the Department of Defense released its third annual report on civilian casualties, documenting civilian harm from certain US military activity and estimating 132 civilian deaths or injuries in 2019, a significantly lower estimate than those by nongovernmental organizations. The report also listed the number of allegations of civilian harm that had been received, concluding that only a fraction of the allegations were "credible."

Uzbekistan

Since Uzbekistan's President Shavkat Mirziyoyev assumed the presidency in 2016, the government has taken some concrete steps to improve the country's human rights record.

Nevertheless, Uzbekistan's political system remains largely authoritarian. Many reform promises remain unfulfilled. Thousands of people, mainly peaceful religious believers, remain in prison on false charges. The National Security Service still holds strong powers to detain perceived critics, and there is no genuine political pluralism.

During 2020, there were reports of torture and ill-treatment in prisons, most former prisoners were not rehabilitated, journalists and activists were persecuted, independent rights groups were denied registration, and forced labor was not eliminated.

Parliamentary Elections

On December 22, 2019, Uzbekistan held parliamentary elections. The Organization for Security and Co-operation in Europe's Office for Democratic Institutions and Human Rights (OSCE ODIHR) noted that the elections "took place under improved legislation and with greater tolerance of independent voices but did not yet demonstrate genuine competition and full respect of election day procedures."

Five registered political parties, all seen as loyal to the current administration, were allowed to run candidates in the elections, but no opposition parties or independent candidates were permitted to run for office.

Political Prisoners and Lack of Rehabilitation

More than 50 people imprisoned on politically motivated charges have been released since September 2016, including rights activists, journalists, and opposition activists. Uzbekistan has also reportedly released hundreds of independent Muslims, who practice Islam outside strict state controls, but this is impossible to verify. Many former prisoners have not been legally rehabilitated, meaning among other things that their unjust convictions have yet to be quashed and they have not received adequate medical treatment, despite being in poor health due to their imprisonment.

In August, President Mirziyoyev pardoned scholars Akrom Malikov and Rustam Abdummanapov, independent religious believer and former cleric, Ruhiddin Fahriddinov, and independent rights activist Iskandar Khudaiberganov. In February, Uzbek authorities released Aramis Avakyan, a farmer.

In March, Kashkadarya Regional Criminal Court of Uzbekistan fully acquitted rights defender Chuyan Mamatkulov, who in 2013 was sentenced to 10 years in prison on false charges and then released in 2018.

Criminal Justice, Torture

Uzbekistan's security services continued to retain enormous power, which they can use to harass and detain perceived critics, despite a 2018 decree that reduced their powers. They continued to detain so-called enemies of the state, invoking charges such as treason.

In January, a military court in a closed session sentenced a former diplomat, Kadyr Yusupov, to five years and six months in prison for treason. At the end of May, Yusupov was placed in solitary confinement for 16 days after he complained of non-adherence to standard rules of prisoners' treatment. His relatives said that in retaliation he was physically and psychologically tortured when he went on a hunger strike. Yusupov was repeatedly not allowed to contact his lawyer securely. Uzbek authorities denied appeals by Yusupov's relatives to change his prison sentence to house arrest during the Covid-19 pandemic due to his pre-existing medical conditions.

In another closed session, in March, a military court sentenced Vladimir Kaloshin, a former journalist of a Defense Ministry newspaper, to 12 years in prison on treason charges. Kaloshin was reportedly subjected to psychological torture consisting of threats of violence against his children, grandchildren, and wife. His trial was marred by procedural violations.

Thousands of others, most of them peaceful religious believers, remain in jail on overly broad "extremism" and other politically motivated charges. They include

Mirsobir Hamidkariev, a film producer, and Ravshan Kosimov and Alisher Achildiev, who are soldiers.

In November 2019, Uzbekistan established a National Preventive Mechanism on torture, but did not ratify the Optional Protocol to the United Nations Convention Against Torture. The Uzbek government also announced in May its plans to establish a Committee to Prevent Torture that will oversee, among other functions, the investigation of allegations of torture and legal rehabilitation to victims.

Civil Society, Freedom of Assembly

In January 2020, the government announced that it was working on a new non-governmental organization (NGO) code with the aim of streamlining legislation on civil society. However, the draft code fails to reform the existing restrictions. The government said the code would be revised, but Human Rights Watch is not aware of further steps that have been taken.

After three rejections from the Ministry of Justice, a local group focusing on criminal justice reform, Huquqi Tayanch ("Legal Support" in Uzbek), was granted registration on March 9, 2020. Mercy Corps, a US-based humanitarian organization, was granted registration on the same day.

Azimbay Ataniyazov, human rights activist and founder of Chiroq, an NGO that focuses on monitoring forced labor in the cotton sector, received at least two rejections from the Ministry of Justice in response to applications to register his group. Two founding members stepped back from the group after being harassed and threatened by Uzbek authorities in February 2020. The ministry also has rejected four applications by released rights defender Agzam Turgunov to register an NGO called "Human Rights House" that would focus on human rights issues, including rehabilitation.

In August, the government published the Draft Law on Public Assemblies. The draft law requires organizers to apply for permission at least 15 working days before the planned date of a mass event, despite promises by Uzbek officials to bring the law in line with international rights standards.

Covid-19

In March, Uzbekistan introduced new charges in the criminal code for disseminating false information about the spread of Covid-19 and other dangerous infectious diseases, with hefty fines or up to three years in prison for violations. The government also significantly increased existing criminal punishments for offenses such as violating medical quarantine or refusing to submit to medical examinations or treatment, including up to seven years in prison if such actions are deemed to lead to the death of another person, and up to 10 years for multiple deaths.

In March, Uzbekistan closed schools due to the pandemic, which affected more than 8 million children. During the lockdown, the government set up distance learning for students, but reportedly faced difficulties in offering high quality public education services. As of September 2020, a quarter of schools reopened. UN agencies called on the government to improve access to water and basic sanitation facilities in schools to ensure a safe return to school, and reduce school-related infections.

Human Rights Watch noted in April that authorities were seizing electronic devices, including mobile phones and bank cards of people in quarantine who were diagnosed with Covid-19 or were suspected to have the coronavirus. Even though personal items can be easily disinfected and contacts for tracing of the virus given voluntarily, the country's deputy justice minister, Khudayor Meliev, claimed that these items may have been contaminated and were needed to track others who had had contact with the quarantined person.

Freedom of Media

There has been an increase in media activity, but media outlets have to operate within clear boundaries set by the government. Much of media is controlled by the state, self-censorship is common, and journalists face harassment and sometimes detention.

In December 2019, the Uzbek government reportedly unblocked access to some websites that were previously restricted, including the news outlet Buzzfeed, the music platform SoundCloud, and the internet archive Wayback Machine. However, in the same month, websites of rights groups, including the Association for

Human Rights in Central Asia, International Partnership for Human Rights, Norwegian Helsinki Committee, and Uzbek Forum for Human Rights, were reportedly inaccessible for periods of time. Radio Ozodlik, the Uzbek service of Radio Free Europe/Radio Liberty, remains inaccessible.

The Uzbek government announced in January its plans to decriminalize defamation (article 138 of the criminal code) and insult (article 139). Activists and journalists in Uzbekistan told Human Rights Watch that Uzbek authorities continue to use these two offenses to silence critical voices.

Uzbek authorities started in August a preliminary investigation against independent journalist Bobomurod Abdullaev, reportedly on charges of "offenses against the president of the Republic of Uzbekistan" and "conspiracy to overthrow the constitutional regime," after he had been detained and unlawfully returned to Uzbekistan by Kyrgyz authorities on an Uzbek extradition request. Abdullaev was not allowed to travel within Uzbekistan without permission or to leave the country. On October 23, the State Security Service (SGB) informed Abdullaev that a criminal case opened against him on June 29 had been closed and travel restrictions imposed on him lifted.

In July 2020, the Uzbek government published draft amendments to the Law on Mass Media. According to one report, the amendments would ease registration requirements for media outlets.

Sexual Orientation and Gender Identity

Consensual same-sex relations between men continue to be criminalized in Uzbekistan, carrying a prison sentence of one to three years. The country's lesbian, gay, bisexual, and transgender (LGBT) population suffers deep-seated homophobia, persecution, and discrimination.

Women's Rights

The United Nations Human Rights Committee noted in April during its review of the situation in Uzbekistan persistent inequality between men and women, including through perpetuation of gender stereotypes and limited representation of women in legislative and judicial bodies.

The committee also raised concerns about forced and early marriage, polygamy, and domestic violence, and lack of protection, services, and access to justice for survivors. Lack of systematic data collection makes it difficult to know the scale of violence against women in Uzbekistan. Reports of domestic violence increased during a Covid-19 related lockdown according to media reports. At least one crisis center reported it could not accept survivors of violence for assistance during the lockdown. Neither domestic violence nor marital rape are explicitly criminalized.

Forced Labor

Uzbekistan has made significant efforts to address child and forced labor in its cotton sector, but forced labor remained widespread despite a public decree prohibiting forced mobilization. According to the International Labour Organization, in 2019, 102,000 cotton pickers "were subject to some form of coercion."

Positive steps included the criminalization in January of the use of forced labor, and the elimination in March of the production quota system.

In October, the Uzbek Forum for Human Rights found that the government forced employees of public institutions and enterprises to pick cotton or pay for replacement pickers during the 2020 harvest which started on September 15. The Uzbek Forum also found "more cases of child labor than in recent years, when only sporadic cases were identified." According the Uzbek Forum, it was "most likely due to the closure of schools because of the coronavirus pandemic, making children available to supplement their family's income."

Civil society groups fault the lack of fair recruitment and accountability systems for the continued reliance on forced labor.

Key International Actors

In November 2019, the United Nations Committee Against Torture found that in Uzbekistan, "torture and ill-treatment continue to be routinely committed by, at the instigation of, and with the consent of the State party's law enforcement, investigative and prison officials, principally for the purpose of extracting confessions or information to be used in criminal proceedings." The committee also expressed concern over continued reports that judges and prosecutors "tend to disregard and decline to investigate" allegations that confessions were obtained through torture.

In its April review, the UN Human Rights Committee (HRC) noted progress made in addressing human rights issues in Uzbekistan, but it expressed concerns about "torture and ill-treatment of people deprived of liberty, as well as restrictions on the freedom of conscience and religious belief, freedom of expression, freedom of association and peaceful assembly." The committee also concluded that the definition of torture in the criminal code does not meet the requirements of the convention. It criticized the overly broad and vague definition of extremism in the Counter-Extremism Act.

In July, the US State Department's Trafficking in Persons Report (TIP) kept Uzbekistan in its place on the "Tier II watch list" as the country does not "fully meet the minimum standards" to eliminate trafficking, but continues to make "significant efforts to do so."

In its statement following the annual Human Rights Dialogue with Uzbekistan, the European Union expressed concerns over existing challenges "related to the freedom of expression, registration of NGOs, the persistence of torture and ill-treatment in the penitentiary system, gender equality and women's rights, anti-discrimination." The EU also called on Uzbekistan to "take further commitments to eradicate torture, including by granting unhindered and independent monitoring to detention facilities," and "emphasized the need to rehabilitate former prisoners."

Venezuela

Venezuela is facing a severe humanitarian emergency, with millions unable to access basic healthcare and adequate nutrition. Limited access to safe water in homes and healthcare centers has contributed to the spread of Covid-19.

In September, a fact-finding mission appointed by the United Nations Human Rights Council (HRC) found high-level authorities responsible for atrocities that they believed amounted to crimes against humanity. The government of Nicolás Maduro and its security forces are responsible for extrajudicial executions and short-term forced disappearances and have jailed opponents, prosecuted civilians in military courts, tortured detainees, and cracked down on protesters. They used a state of emergency implemented in response to Covid-19 as an excuse to punish dissent and intensify their control over the population.

Venezuela remains at a political impasse since Juan Guaidó, the National Assembly president, claimed he was taking power as interim president of Venezuela in January 2019. Guaidó has the support of more than 50 governments globally, but Maduro still controls all institutions except for the legislative branch. In July, ahead of parliamentary elections scheduled for December 2020, the Supreme Court ordered the takeover of three leading political opposition parties by Maduro government supporters, and appointed government supporters to head the National Electoral Council (CNE). At time of writing, conditions were not met for free and fair elections.

The exodus of Venezuelans fleeing repression and shortages of food, medicine, and medical supplies represents the largest migration crisis in recent Latin American history. Difficulty accessing legal status in other countries and economic hardship as a result of measures to curb the spread of Covid-19 have led approximately 130,000 to return since March 2020. Returnees are subject to abuse upon arrival.

Persistent concerns include brutal policing practices, poor prison conditions, impunity for human rights violations, lack of judicial independence, and harassment of human rights defenders and independent media.

Refugee Crisis

Some 5.5 million of an estimated 32 million Venezuelans have fled their country since 2014, the United Nations High Commissioner for Refugees (UNHCR) reported in October. Many Venezuelans abroad remain uncounted. Causes of the exodus include political, economic, human rights, and humanitarian crises.

Many Venezuelans abroad remain in irregular status, undermining their ability to obtain work permits, send children to school, and access health care, while making them vulnerable to exploitation and abuse.

Government lockdowns to curb the spread of Covid-19 have caused migrants to lose their jobs in the informal sector and approximately 130,000 have made arduous journeys back to Venezuela, many on foot. In Venezuela, returnees have been held, often for weeks, in overcrowded, unsanitary quarantine centers that likely contribute to spreading Covid-19. Authorities and pro-government armed groups known as *colectivos* have threatened, verbally harassed, and mistreated returnees.

Persecution of Political Opponents, Arrests, and Torture

The government has jailed political opponents and disqualified them from running for office. As of September 30, prisons and intelligence headquarters held 348 political prisoners, according to the Penal Forum, a Venezuelan network of pro-bono criminal defense lawyers.

In August, Maduro announced pardons for 110 political prisoners, but fewer than half of them had been incarcerated for political motives, the Penal Forum reported, and some faced no charges. Many others remain in arbitrary detention or are subject to arbitrary arrest and prosecution. Some have been forced into exile, including opposition leader Leopoldo López, who fled in October. López had been sentenced to 13 years in prison on unsubstantiated charges of inciting violence during demonstrations against the government in 2014, and spent years in a military prison and under house arrest.

Intelligence and security forces have detained and tortured military personnel accused of plotting against the government. Authorities have tortured various detainees for information about alleged conspiracies. To determine the whereabouts of some suspects, authorities have detained and tortured family members.

During several crackdowns since 2014, Venezuelan security forces and *colectivos* have attacked demonstrations. Security forces have shot demonstrators at point-blank range with riot-control munitions, brutally beaten people who offered no resistance, and staged violent raids on apartment buildings.

Of more than 15,500 people arrested since 2014 in connection with protests—including demonstrators, bystanders, and people taken from their homes without warrants—some 9,255 had been conditionally released as of September 2020 but remained subject to prosecution. A total of 870 had been prosecuted by military courts.

The government has used the Covid-19 state of emergency as a pretext to repress dissent, arbitrarily detaining and prosecuting dozens of political opponents, including legislators, journalists, healthcare workers who criticize the government's handling of the pandemic, and lawyers who provide legal support to demonstrators protesting lack of access to water, gasoline, or medicines.

In July, the UN Office of the High Commissioner for Human Rights (OHCHR) reported 16 cases of alleged torture and ill-treatment from June 2019 to May 2020, saying the actual number could be "significantly higher." The cases include severe beatings with boards, suffocation with plastic bags and chemicals, waterboarding, electric shocks to eyelids and genitals, exposure to cold temperatures, and being handcuffed for extended periods of time. In some cases, doctors issued false or inaccurate medical certificates not disclosing signs of torture.

Alleged Extrajudicial Killings

Between 2016 and 2019, police and security forces killed more than 19,000 people, alleging "resistance to authority." OHCHR, analyzing open sources, found 2,000 individuals had been killed in security operations between January and August of 2020. Many of these deaths may constitute extrajudicial executions, according to OHCHR.

Agents of FAES, a special police force, and others have killed and tortured with impunity in low-income communities, instilling fear and maintaining social control. Previously, security force raids on low-income communities from 2015 through 2017, called Operations to Liberate the People, had resulted in widespread allegations of extrajudicial killings, mass arbitrary detentions, mistreatment of detainees, and forced evictions.

Armed Groups

Authorities have relied on *colectivos* to disperse demonstrations and crack down on protesters.

During the pandemic, these groups have also helped authorities engage in social control and attack and intimidate political opponents and journalists, sometimes to prevent coverage related to Covid-19. *Colectivos* have enforced the lockdown in neighborhoods with high levels of poverty, local groups report, beating and torturing those who allegedly fail to comply.

Illegal mining in Bolívar state is controlled by criminal groups—"syndicates"—which police citizens, impose abusive working conditions, and viciously treat those accused of theft and other offenses, sometimes dismembering and killing them in front of others. The syndicates operate with government acquiescence and sometimes involvement.

Armed groups—including the National Liberation Army, Patriotic Forces of National Liberation, and groups that emerged from the Revolutionary Armed Forces of Colombia—operate mostly in border states. In Apure state, they establish and brutally enforce curfews; prohibitions on rape, theft, and murder; and regulations governing everyday activities. They engage in murder, rape, forced labor, and child recruitment to establish social control. Impunity is the norm, and residents say security forces and local authorities often collude with the armed groups.

Impunity for Abuses

Between 2017 and the first trimester of 2020, the Attorney General's Office reported initiating 4,890 investigations into killings in the context of security operations, of which 13 had resulted in trials and one in a homicide conviction by March. It reported 517 state agents charged and 26 convicted for torture or ill-treatment, and 44 individuals charged and 10 detained while awaiting trial for human rights abuses during protests in 2014, 2017, and 2019.

Impunity for human rights abuses remains the norm. In July, OHCHR reported contributing factors include security forces tampering with crime scenes and withholding information; conflicts of interest; and security forces' intimidation, threats, and reprisals against victims and their families.

Judicial Independence

The judiciary stopped functioning as an independent branch of government when former President Hugo Chávez and supporters in the National Assembly took over the Supreme Court in 2004. Supreme Court justices have openly rejected the separation of powers and have consistently upheld abusive policies and practices.

Judge María Lourdes Afiuni has been the subject of an arbitrary prosecution since 2009, when she granted conditional release to a government critic, following a recommendation by the UN Working Group on Arbitrary Detention. She spent a year in prison and several under house arrest while charges were pending against her. The Supreme Court ruled in July 2019 that she no longer had to regularly present herself before the courts, but she was not allowed to leave the country, speak to media, or use social media. In July, SEBIN agents raided her home looking for evidence against her daughter, who worked with opposition leader Juan Guaidó in the United States.

Humanitarian Emergency and Covid-19

The government has not published epidemiological data since 2017, when the health minister released figures showing maternal mortality increasing by 65 percent in 2016, and infant mortality by 30 percent. Days later, the minister was fired.

Venezuela's health system is in collapse, leading to the resurgence of vaccine-preventable and infectious diseases. Shortages of medications and health supplies, interruptions of basic utilities at healthcare facilities, and the emigration of healthcare workers have led to a decline in operational capacity.

The World Food Program estimates that one out of three Venezuelans is food insecure and in need of assistance. Based on data collected prior to the pandemic, the 2020 National Survey of Life Conditions reported 8 percent of children under five acutely malnourished and 30 percent chronically malnourished, or stunted. In the most vulnerable neighborhoods, 14.4 percent of children under five are malnourished, Caritas, a nongovernmental organization, reported in July.

Many families are having difficulties feeding older children, in part due to the decline of school meal programs. School attendance, which had already decreased due to the humanitarian emergency, has declined further because of Covid-19 restrictions. In-person classes, suspended in March, remained suspended at time of writing.

As of November 2, Venezuela had confirmed 92,325 cases of Covid-19 and 801 deaths. Given the limited availability of reliable testing, lack of government transparency, and persecution of medical professionals and journalists who report on the pandemic, the actual numbers are likely much higher. Limited access to water in hospitals and homes, and overcrowding in low-income areas and prisons, likely contribute to rapid spread. Most healthcare centers face severe shortages of basic equipment such as gloves, face masks, alcohol gel, and soap. Lack of basic X-ray equipment, laboratory tests, intensive care beds, and respirators likely heightens the death rate.

Access to maternal health and sexual and reproductive services, which was already dire due to the humanitarian emergency, has further deteriorated due to the Covid-19 pandemic. UNOCHA estimates an 80 percent shortage of contraceptive methods and reported that 352 women died during pregnancy, childbirth, and postpartum in 2019. Maternal health centers have suspended pre- and postnatal services due to the pandemic, and NGOs report that pregnant women suspected of having Covid-19 have been denied prompt care.

National Assembly and Constituent Assembly

Despite repeated efforts to unseat it—and a spate of judicial rulings invalidating its decisions—the National Assembly remained Venezuela's only democratically elected institution in 2020. The opposition won more than two-thirds of seats in 2015.

At time of writing, a legislative election was scheduled for December 6. A coalition of 27 political parties led by Guaidó was planning to boycott it, protesting persecution of opposition politicians and lack of guarantees for a free and fair process, including the political takeover of opposition parties by the Supreme Court in mid2020.

In 2017, Maduro ignored the constitutional requirement of a public referendum to rewrite the Constitution and decreed a "Constituent Assembly" to do so. The assembly, consisting exclusively of government supporters, has effectively replaced the National Assembly. It has extended its mandate until December 2020 and lifted parliamentary immunity for several opposition legislators.

Freedom of Expression

For more than a decade, the government has expanded and abused its power to regulate media and close dissenting outlets. The government can suspend websites for vaguely defined "incitement," prosecute "disrespect" for high government officials, revoke media licenses if "convenient for the interests of the nation," and has blocked websites critical of the government. While a few newspapers, websites, and radio stations criticize authorities, fear of reprisals has made self-censorship a serious problem.

In 2017, the Constituent Assembly passed a vague Law Against Hatred, forbidding political parties that "promote fascism, hatred, and intolerance," and establishing prison sentences of up to 20 years for publishing "messages of intolerance and hatred." During the Covid-19 state of emergency, many people sharing or publishing information on social media questioning officials or policies have been charged with incitement to hatred or to commission of a crime.

Human Rights Defenders

Government measures to restrict international funding of NGOs—and unsubstantiated accusations that rights defenders undermine Venezuelan democracy—create a hostile environment limiting groups' ability to defend human rights.

In 2010, the Supreme Court ruled that individuals or organizations receiving foreign funding can be prosecuted for treason, and the National Assembly prohibited international assistance to organizations that "defend political rights" or "monitor the performance of public bodies."

On May 3, the NGO Provea called on authorities to respect the rights of 13 individuals, including two former US soldiers, detained during an alleged invasion attempt. Maduro accused Provea of receiving money from the CIA and of defending the rights of "terrorists" and "mercenaries."

Authorities have cracked down on human rights lawyers supporting demonstrators. In March, the National Guard detained lawyer Henderson Maldonado during a demonstration by renal and cancer patients. An agent hit him on the head and hand with a frozen water bottle, telling him he did not deserve to live. Charged with resisting authority and inciting criminal activity, Maldonado was released on condition that he report to court every 30 days.

Political Discrimination

Citizens and NGOs have credibly accused a government program that distributes food and basic goods at capped prices of discriminating against government critics. Previously, people supporting referenda that could have ended the Maduro or Chavez presidencies were fired from government jobs.

Prison Conditions

Corruption, weak security, deteriorating infrastructure, overcrowding, insufficient staffing, and poorly trained guards allow armed gangs effectively to control detainees. Excessive use of pretrial detention contributes to overcrowding. There have been reports of Covid-19 outbreaks and deaths due to health reasons in several Venezuelan prisons.

In May, an uprising at Los Llanos prison in Portuguesa state—protesting guards' withholding of food brought by families, which prisoners rely on—resulted in 47 deaths and 75 injuries, the NGO Venezuelan Observatory of Prisons reported.

Key International Actors

In September, the Independent International Fact-Finding Mission created by the UN Human Rights Council to investigate allegations of atrocities since 2014 concluded that there were reasonable grounds to believe that pro-government groups and high-level authorities, including Maduro, had committed violations amounting to crimes against humanity, including extrajudicial executions, politically motivated detention and torture, and abuses against protesters. The mission found the judiciary contributed to arbitrary arrests, impunity for egregious abuses, and denial of justice to victims.

In October, after the report release, the council adopted a new resolution extending the fact-finding mission's mandate for two years. The council also adopted a separate resolution presented by Iran to continue UN technical cooperation on human rights with Venezuelan authorities under Maduro.

OHCHR continues to monitor the situation in Venezuela. It maintains an in-country presence and has provided regular oral updates to the UN Human Rights Council in 2020 describing ongoing abuses, such as arbitrary arrests, torture, and forced disappearances, as well as on the dire humanitarian situation. In July, it reported on lack of judicial independence in Venezuela and abuses committed in the Orinoco Mining Arc, as mandated by the council.

In 2018, International Criminal Court (ICC) Prosecutor Fatou Bensouda announced a preliminary examination to analyze whether, since at least 2017, crimes occurring within the court's jurisdiction have taken place, including allegations of use of excessive force against demonstrators and detention of thousands of individuals, a number of whom are alleged to have suffered serious abuses in detention. Six countries—all ICC member states—subsequently requested an ICC investigation, and three other countries have since expressed support for the states' referral. In February, the Maduro government asked the Office of the Prosecutor to investigate possible crimes against humanity caused by "the application of unlawful coercive measures adopted unilaterally" by the US government.

In 2020, representatives from Latin American countries hosting most Venezuelans who have fled met as part of the Quito Process, created in 2018 to chart a common response to the Venezuelan exodus. In a meeting in October, participating foreign ministers committed themselves to strengthening international cooperation to address Venezuela's migration and humanitarian crises.

Several governments have imposed targeted sanctions on Venezuelan officials implicated in human rights abuses and corruption. The United States has sanctioned more that 150, and cancelled the visas of 1,000. In June, the European Union and Switzerland imposed sanctions on 11 officials for their role in acts undermining democracy and the rule of law, bringing the number of sanctioned Venezuelans to 36. Some Latin American governments have also prohibited Venezuelan officials from entering their countries.

Besides adopting targeted sanctions, the EU has consistently condemned abuses by the Venezuelan government and played a leading role in the International Contact Group to support ongoing efforts to find a political solution to the Venezuelan crisis and lay the groundwork for credible elections in December. In May, the EU and Spain co-hosted the International Donors' Conference, which raised over €2.5 billion (US$2.9 billion) to support Venezuelan refugees and migrants in the region. The European Parliament adopted two resolutions on Venezuela, focusing both on the political and on the humanitarian crisis.

Since 2017, the US has imposed financial sanctions, including a ban on dealings in new stocks and bonds issued by the Venezuelan government and its state oil company. Despite a humanitarian exception, these sanctions could exacerbate the already dire humanitarian situation in Venezuela, both due to the risk of overcompliance and because the sanctions reduce the resources available to the government to address the crisis. The extent to which the sanctions are in fact having this impact, and whether the government would have used any additional resources to help its people, is unclear.

An estimated 7 million people needed humanitarian assistance in 2020, the UN Humanitarian Response Plan for Venezuela noted. The plan calls for $762.5 million to assist 4.5 million of the most vulnerable Venezuelans, including $87.9 million to address the health and socio-economic impact of Covid-19. As of November 2, more than $132 million had been disbursed, and from January through May, 2.1 million people received assistance.

As a member of the UN Human Rights Council, Venezuela votes regularly to prevent scrutiny of human rights violations, including in Syria, Yemen, Myanmar, Belarus, Burundi, Eritrea, and Iran.

Venezuela withdrew from the American Convention on Human Rights in 2013, leaving citizens and residents unable to request intervention by the Inter-American Court of Human Rights when local remedies for abuses are ineffective or unavailable. The Inter-American Commission on Human Rights continues to monitor Venezuela, applying the American Declaration of the Rights and Duties of Man, which is not subject to states' ratification.

Vietnam

Vietnam continued to systematically violate basic civil and political rights in 2020. The government, under the one-party rule of the Communist Party of Vietnam, tightened restrictions on freedom of expression, association, peaceful assembly, movement, and religion. Prohibitions remained on the formation or operation of independent unions and any other organizations or groups considered to be a threat to the Communist Party's monopoly of power. Authorities blocked access to several websites and social media pages and pressured social media and telecommunications companies to remove or restrict content critical of the government or the ruling party.

Those who criticized the government or party faced police intimidation, harassment, restricted movement, physical assault, arbitrary arrest and detention, and imprisonment. Police detained political detainees for months without access to legal counsel and subjected them to abusive interrogations. Party-controlled courts sentenced bloggers and activists on fabricated national security charges.

Vietnamese authorities appeared to have had some successes in combating the Covid-19 pandemic. After adopting aggressive contact tracing, mass testing, public campaigns on hygiene, early border closures, social-distancing, and mandatory centralized quarantines, Vietnam by late 2020 reported only about 1,000 confirmed cases and 35 deaths. However, Vietnam's successes came at the cost of increasing violations of rights: restrictions on freedom of speech; failure to protect the right of privacy; and inequity in access to social services and government support.

Freedom of Expression, Opinion, and Speech

Online dissidents faced routine harassment and intimidation in 2020. Several were arrested and charged under Vietnam's penal code, which criminalizes speech critical of the government or which promotes "reactionary" ideas. The government prosecuted numerous dissidents throughout the year.

In April, June, and July, courts tried Phan Cong Hai, Nguyen Van Nghiem, Dinh Van Phu, and Nguyen Quoc Duc Vuong and sentenced them to between five and eight years each in prison for criticizing the party and the state.

Police arrested Nguyen Tuong Thuy in May and Le Huu Minh Tuan in June for involvement with the Independent Journalists Association of Vietnam (IJAVN) and charged them with anti-state propaganda under article 117 of the penal code. The organization's president, Dr. Pham Chi Dung, was arrested in November 2019, apparently in connection to his vocal opposition to the European Union-Vietnam free trade agreement. Between April and August, police arrested nine other people including independent blogger Pham Chi Thanh, land rights activists Nguyen Thi Tam, and former political prisoner Can Thi Theu and her sons Trinh Ba Phuong and Trinh Ba Tu. In October, police arrested prominent rights blogger Pham Doan Trang. All 10 were charged with anti-state propaganda under article 117 of the penal code.

Freedom of Media and Access to Information

The Vietnamese government continued to prohibit independent or privately owned media outlets and impose strict control over radio and television stations and printed publications. Authorities block access to websites, frequently shut blogs, and require internet service providers to remove content or social media accounts deemed politically unacceptable.

In April, the government throttled access to Facebook's local cache servers, demanding that the company remove pages controlled by dissidents. Facebook, bowing to pressure, agreed to restrict access to the pages within Vietnam, setting a worrying precedent. In early September, the Ministry of Information and Communications (MIC) praised Facebook and YouTube for their "positive change in collaborating with MIC to block information that violates Vietnam's law."

In April and May, a court sentenced two Facebook users, Chung Hoang Chuong and Ma Phung Ngoc Phu, to 18 months and 9 months' imprisonment respectively for posts on Facebook critical of the government under article 331 of the penal code. In June, authorities arrested Huynh Anh Khoa and Nguyen Dang Thuong for being the moderators of a Facebook group in which users discussed Vietnamese economic, social, and political issues, and charged them also under article 331.

Freedom of Association and Assembly

Prohibitions remained on independent labor unions, human rights organizations, and political parties. Organizers trying to establish unions or workers' groups face harassment, intimidation, and retaliation from employers and authorities. Authorities require approval for public gatherings, and systematically refuse permission for meetings, marches, or public gatherings they deem to be politically unacceptable.

In November 2019, the National Assembly passed a revised labor code effective in January 2021. The new code ostensibly will allow the formation of "Worker Representation Organizations" to represent workers, but such groups can only form with the permission of the government and are likely to be tightly controlled.

In April, the police arrested former political prisoner Tran Duc Thach for alleged association with a human rights group, the Brotherhood for Democracy. Authorities charged him with subversion under article 109 of the penal code.

As in previous years, the government confiscated land for various economic projects, typically without due process or adequate compensation. The term "dan oan," or "wronged people," as of 2020 has emerged as a common idiom in Vietnamese usage to describe people forced off their land by authorities.

In January, a violent incident occurred in Dong Tam, a commune in Hanoi, involving police and land rights activists involved in past protests against local land confiscations in the area. Details are unclear, but several deaths were reported, including three police officers and one villager. Authorities arrested 29 villagers and charged them with murder or resisting persons on public duty. In September, a court in Hanoi convicted and sentenced two of them to death. Another was sentenced to life in prison. The rest received either suspended sentences or various shorter terms, ranging up to 16 years. Defense lawyers said several defendants alleged they were tortured and forced to admit guilt.

Freedom of Religion

The government restricts religious practice through legislation, registration requirements, and surveillance. Religious groups are required to get approval

HUMAN
RIGHTS
WATCH

"My Teacher Said I Had a Disease"
Barriers to the Right to Education for LGBT Youth in Vietnam

from, and register with, the government and operate under government-con-trolled management boards. While authorities allow many government-affiliated churches and pagodas to hold worship services, they ban religious activities that they arbitrarily deem to be contrary to the "national interest," "public order," or "national unity," including many ordinary types of religious functions.

Police monitor, harass, and sometimes violently crack down on religious groups operating outside government-controlled institutions. Unrecognized religious groups, including Cao Dai, Hoa Hao, Christian, and Buddhist groups, face con-stant surveillance, harassment, and intimidation. Followers of independent reli-gious group are subject to public criticism, forced renunciation of faith, detention, interrogation, torture, and imprisonment.

Children's Rights

Violence against children, including sexual abuse, is pervasive in Vietnam, in-cluding in schools. Numerous media reports have described cases of teachers or government caregivers engaging in sexual abuse, beating children, or hitting them with sticks.

Vietnamese lesbian, gay, bisexual, and transgender youth face widespread dis-crimination and violence at home and at school. Pervasive myths about sexual orientation and gender identity, including the false belief that same-sex attrac-tion is a diagnosable and curable mental health condition, is common among Vietnamese school officials and the population at large.

Schools often fail to protect students from physical violence and school staff in-consistently respond to incidents of verbal and physical abuse and lessons often contain homophobic content. Authorities have not put in place adequate mecha-nisms to address cases of violence and discrimination.

Key International Actors

China remains the most influential outside actor in Vietnam. Maritime disputes continue to complicate the relationship.

In February, the EU and Vietnam held their ninth yearly human rights dialogue, an exercise that once again did not bring concrete results. In August, the EU-Vietnam Free Trade Agreement came into force, strengthening Vietnam's ties with the bloc. The deal includes vague, non-enforceable human rights provisions. Amid increasing repression of any form of dissent in the country, EU pressure focused solely on labor rights, triggering some reforms and commitments by Hanoi. Despite acknowledging major concerns over Vietnam's deteriorating human rights record, in February a majority in the European Parliament gave its consent to the deal.

2020 marked the 25th anniversary of the resumption of diplomatic relations between the United States and Vietnam. While the current US administration paid little attention to human rights situation in Vietnam, a number of US politicians continued to condemn the country's violations of rights and voice their supports for Vietnamese activists.

In April 2020, the United States Commission on International Religious Freedom published its report in which Vietnam is recommended for designation as a "Country of Particular Concern." In October 2020, the US and Vietnam held a human rights dialogue, virtually, during which US officials claim to have raised concerns about various human rights issues. However, the arrest of prominent dissident Pham Doan Trang, noted above, occurred less than 24 hours after the end of the dialogue, underscoring its lack of efficacy.

Australia's bilateral relationship with Vietnam continued to grow even as an Australian citizen, Chau Van Kham, remained in prison in Vietnam on a "terrorism" conviction for his alleged involvement in an overseas political party declared unlawful by the Vietnamese government.

Japan remained the most important bilateral donor to Vietnam. As in previous years, Japan has declined to use its economic leverage to publicly urge Vietnam to improve its human rights record.

Yemen

Six years into an armed conflict that has killed over 18,400 civilians, Yemen remains the largest humanitarian crisis in the world. Yemen is experiencing the world's worst food security crisis with 20.1 million people—nearly two-thirds of the population—requiring food assistance at the beginning of 2020.

Since March 2015, Saudi Arabia and the United Arab Emirates (UAE) have led a military coalition against Houthi-led forces that took over Yemen's capital, Sanaa, in September 2014. In 2020, fighting in northern Yemen increased sharply when the Houthis seized new areas held by the internationally recognized Yemeni government and advanced toward Marib governorate, where thousands of Yemenis were internally displaced and faced dire humanitarian conditions and increased risk of Covid-19.

In southern Yemen, the UAE continued its air operations and support for local Yemeni forces on the ground despite withdrawing most of its ground troops in mid-2019. The UAE-backed Southern Transitional Council (STC) continued to challenge the recognized Yemeni government in the south.

The protracted conflict has had a devastating impact on civilians across the country. Civilians suffer from destroyed critical infrastructure, lack of fuel, lack of basic services, abusive local security forces, a weak state, and fragmented governance. Unprecedented heavy rainfall in many parts of Yemen in 2020 killed scores of people and left others displaced. The floods destroyed and damaged houses and infrastructure, including buildings in Sanaa's old city, a UNESCO world heritage site.

Yemen's economy has been ravaged by years of conflict. Millions of people in Yemen have lost their income due to business closures and some working in the public sector have not received their full salaries regularly, leading to increased poverty. Millions of civilians in Yemen depend on humanitarian aid.

Houthi authorities did not allow United Nations experts to secure the Safer Oil Tanker off the coast of Hodeida, leaving Yemen at risk of environment disaster if the ship's 1.1 million barrels of oil leak into the Red Sea.

HUMAN
RIGHTS
WATCH

DEADLY CONSEQUENCES
Obstruction of Aid in Yemen During Covid-19

Covid-19

The country's first confirmed case of coronavirus was recorded on April 10, and by late September, the UN reported 2,034 confirmed cases and 588 deaths; however, the country's limited testing capacity means that the true number of cases is unknown. Houthi authorities in the north suppressed information about the spread and impact of Covid-19 in areas under their control.

In July, Human Rights Watch warned that detainees at the Bir Ahmed unofficial detention facility faced serious health risks from the rapidly spreading pandemic. In May, Human Rights Watch called for the protection of civilians in Marib as displaced people faced the double threat of renewed fighting and the uncontrolled spread of the virus.

Unlawful Attacks

All parties to the armed conflict in Yemen and have committed serious violations of the laws of war, many of which may amount to war crimes by responsible personnel. In 2020, Saudi-led coalition forces conducted airstrikes that indiscriminately killed and injured civilians. As of March, the Saudi-led coalition had conducted between 20,624 and 58,487 airstrikes since March 2015, according to the Yemen Data Project. Almost a third of all airstrikes carried out by the coalition hit civilian objects such as residential homes, hospitals, schools, weddings, farms, food stores, school buses, markets, mosques, bridges, civilian factories, detention centers, and water wells. The Saudi-led coalition and the Houthis have committed unlawful attacks against detention centers, killing and injuring detainees.

The Saudi-led coalition and Houthi forces continued to fire mortars, rockets, and other missiles indiscriminately into heavily populated areas including Marib, Taizz, and, *Hodeidah*. These weapons killed or wounded civilians and damaged critical infrastructure such schools and health facilities. In April, Houthi forces attacked the Taizz Central Prison complex, killing five female prisoners, two young girls, and a policewoman, and wounding nine others, according to Mwatana, a Yemeni human rights group. Houthi forces continued to fire ballistic missiles indiscriminately into Saudi Arabia.

Children and Armed Conflict

Roughly 80 percent of Yemen's population required humanitarian aid, including over 12 million children. UNICEF warned that the number of children under the age of 5 who suffer from acute malnutrition could rise to 2.4 million in 2020. The International Committee of the Red Cross (ICRC) reported in October 2019 that 50 percent of Yemeni children are experiencing irreversible stunted growth. UNICEF warned in June that that 7.8 million children had no access to education following Covid-19-related school closures and nearly 10 million did not have adequate access to water and sanitation.

The UN Group of Eminent International and Regional Experts on Yemen reported in 2020 that all warring parties have recruited children as soldiers. Some Yemeni boys were sent to Saudi Arabia for military training, then deployed back to Yemen to fight against Houthi forces. Houthi forces recruited children, including girls, at schools, and used boys for combat and girls "as spies, recruiters of other children, guards, medics and members of the Zainabiyat [female security forces]."

In June 2020, UN Secretary-General Antonio Guterres removed the Saudi-led coalition from his latest "list of shame" of parties responsible for grave violations against children during conflict, even though his report concluded that the coalition was responsible for 222 child casualties and four attacks on schools and hospitals in Yemen in 2019.

Landmines

Houthi forces used landmines, in particular anti-personnel landmines, in violation of international humanitarian law, causing civilian deaths and injuries. In 2019, landmines, improvised explosive devices (IEDs), and unexploded ordnance (UXO) have caused the deaths of 498 civilians, up 23 percent from 405 in 2018, according to the Civilian Impact Monitoring Project. The use of mines has exacerbated food insecurity and impeded aid workers from reaching vulnerable communities. The UN Group of Eminent International and Regional Experts on Yemen reported in September that Houthi forces have conducted indiscriminate attacks using anti-personnel landmines. The use of banned antipersonnel mines by any party in any circumstances violates the 1997 Mine Ban Treaty, to which Yemen is a party.

Arbitrary Detentions, Torture, and Enforced Disappearances

Houthi forces, the Yemeni government, the UAE, Saudi Arabia, and various UAE and Saudi-backed Yemeni armed groups have arbitrarily arrested, detained, abducted, or forcibly disappeared people, including children, and tortured or otherwise ill-treated detainees.

Human Rights Watch in March documented Saudi military forces and Saudi-backed Yemeni forces' grave abuses against civilians in al-Mahra governorate, in eastern Yemen, including torture, forced disappearances and arbitrary detention. Across Yemen, arbitrary detention by parties to the conflict remains pervasive. In June, Mwatana reported hundreds of cases of forced disappearances as well as torture and deaths of detainees in secret prisons by Houthi forces, Yemeni government-backed forces, and UAE-backed forces.

The UN Group of Eminent Experts on Yemen found that "parties to the conflict are continuing to engage in arbitrary detention, torture, including sexual violence, and other forms of ill-treatment, and enforced disappearance in violation of international human rights law and international humanitarian law. Such acts may amount to war crimes."

In September, the Yemeni government and the Houthis conducted a prisoner exchange of 1,083 prisoners brokered by the UN special envoy for Yemen, Martin Griffiths, and the ICRC.

Houthi forces continued to harass and prosecute dissidents, including academics, lawyers, students, religious minorities, and journalists. Houthi authorities prosecuted 35 parliamentarians in March, with Houthi-controlled courts sentencing them to death in absentia on charges of treason. Women human rights activists faced repression by parties to the conflict for their work on women's rights.

Blocking and Impeding Humanitarian Access

Human Rights Watch documented in September that Houthi authorities, Yemeni government and affiliated forces, and the UAE-backed STC were severely restricting the delivery of desperately needed humanitarian aid. Millions have been suffering in Yemen because the Houthis and other Yemeni authorities have denied the UN and other aid agencies unhindered access to people in need. International and local aid groups have faced a wide range of obstacles imposed by parties to the conflict on the ground, severely restricting their work.

The Houthi authorities have imposed hundreds of regulations and lengthy delays in approving aid projects. They block aid assessments required to identify people's needs, seek to control aid monitoring, and dictate or interfere with lists of aid recipients in order to divert aid to authority loyalists.

The coalition has forced the Sanaa International Airport to remain closed since August 2016.

Violence against Women

In 2020, the Yemeni government, the Houthi armed group, and the STC-affiliated Security Belt forces abused women and committed acts of gender-based violence, including sexual violence. The UN Group of Experts reported numerous allegations of rape by STC-affiliated forces in recent years, including the rape of an internally displaced woman in Aden in April. Violence against women increased during the Covid-19 crisis, according to UN Women in Yemen. Women migrants from Horn of Africa countries continue to face abuse, rape, and torture at the hands of smugglers and traffickers in Yemen while en route through the country to Saudi Arabia.

Women also continued to face severe discrimination in law and practice. They cannot marry without the permission of their male guardian and do not have equal rights to divorce, inheritance, or child custody. Lack of legal protection leaves them exposed to domestic and sexual violence. Child marriage also continued, and Yemen still has no minimum age of marriage.

Abuses against Migrants

The International Organization on Migration (IOM) reported that nearly 140,000 migrants entered Yemen in 2019. For those migrants stranded as a result of Covid-19, border closures, movement restrictions, and increasingly discriminatory attitudes in Yemen impacted migrants' access to essential services such as food, water, shelter and health assistance. Additionally, migrants stranded in Yemen have faced increased detention and have been subjected to forced transfers across front lines.

Using Covid-19 as a pretext, Houthi forces in April forcibly expelled thousands of Ethiopian migrants from northern Yemen, killing dozens and forcing them to the Saudi border. Saudi forces fired on the fleeing migrants, killing dozens more, while hundreds of survivors escaped to a mountainous border area until Saudi officials allowed hundreds to enter the country. After the Houthis forcibly expelled the migrants from Saada governorate in northern Yemen, Human Rights Watch reviewed satellite imagery that showed widespread destruction of over 300 tents and houses consistent with witness accounts in the migrant settlement area of al-Ghar.

Key International Actors

Arms sales to Saudi Arabia, the UAE, and other coalition members continued from Western countries including the US, France, Canada, and others. In July, the UK announced that it would resume arms sales to Saudi Arabia despite documented evidence of continuing laws of war violations by the coalition. News reports revealed that US State Department officials have warned that US officials could face prosecution for war crimes over arms sales to Saudi Arabia and coalition partners. Houthi forces continued to receive support from Iran.

In October, the UN Human Rights Council renewed and strengthened the mandate of the Group of Eminent International and Regional Experts on Yemen. In their third report, the group of experts urged the international community to address the longstanding impunity for serious crimes in Yemen, including by recommending the creation of a "criminally focused investigation body" and calling on the UN Security Council refer the situation to the International Criminal Court.

In June, 31 international donors pledged about US$1.35 billion in humanitarian aid for Yemen, far below the $2.4 billion the UN agencies required to keep all its programs running in the country. Lack of funding has led to the reduction or shutdown of more than one-third of the UN's humanitarian programs in Yemen.

UN Special Envoy for Yemen Martin Griffiths has been leading negotiations between the Houthi armed group and the Yemeni government with little progress. The UN Security Council continued to impose a sanctions regime against just one side, the Houthis, even though the Saudi-led coalition has committed numerous violations of the laws of war.

Zimbabwe

Zimbabwe's human rights situation continued to decline in 2020 under Emmerson Mnangagwa's presidency. Unidentified assailants, suspected to be state security agents, abducted and tortured more than 70 critics of the government during 2020. Security forces also continued to commit arbitrary arrests, violent assaults, abductions, torture and other abuses against opposition politicians, dissidents and activists. In July 2020, police arrested prominent journalist Hopewell Chin'ono and Transform Zimbabwe Party leader Jacob Ngarivhume after they called for nationwide anti-corruption protests. The police violently dispersed protests in July, wherein 16 protesters were injured and a further 60 were arrested.

Abuses, Ill-Treatment, and Torture

During 2020, unresolved cases of abductions and abuses, including torture, of government critics escalated without the abductors being brought to justice. In the last year, over 70 government critics were abducted and later released by unidentified men suspected to be state security agents.

On the eve of the July 30, anti-corruption protests, security forces raided the Bulawayo home of Mduduzi Mathuthu. Mathuthuisa prominent journalist and editor of the online newspaper Zimlive. Failing to find him, they arrested his family members, including his nephew, Tawanda Muchehiwa. The security agents allegedly tortured Muchehiwa. The torture resulted in serious injuries, including extensive bruises and an acute kidney injury.

On September 18, Zimbabwe National Students Union (ZINASU) leader Takudzwa Ngadziore was attacked, assaulted, and abducted by unidentified men while addressing a press conference to protest the torture of Muchehiwa. He was later arrested by police on charges of inciting public violence.

In May, three Movement for Democratic Change (MDC) Alliance activists, Cecilia Chambery, Netsai Marova, and member of parliament Joanna Mamombe, were abducted from police custody by suspected state agents after taking part in a peaceful protest in Harare. The protest was over the government's failure to support vulnerable communities under the Covid-19 pandemic lockdown. They were assaulted and sexually abused by their abductors. They were then dumped in Bindura, 80 kilometers from Harare. While receiving treatment for their injuries, the trio were arrested at the hospital and charged with making false reports about their abduction. At time of writing their trial was ongoing.

Lack of Accountability

During 2020, authorities still failed to do justice for cases of abductions and torture committed in 2019. Unresolved cases where there has been no accountability include the abduction by unidentified persons on September 14, 2019, of Dr. Peter Magombeyi. Dr. Magombeti was then-leader of the Zimbabwe Hospital Doctors Association (ZADHR) who had organized a series of protests to demand better salaries for public health workers. Released after four days, he fled the country a week after his release.

Other unresolved cases of abduction by masked and unidentified men in 2019 include those of Obert Masaraure, Samantha Kureya (known as "Gonyeti"), and Tatenda Mombeyarara. Masaraure, the national president of the Amalgamated Rural Teachers Union of Zimbabwe, was seized from his home in Harare on January 18, 2019, and beaten severely with leather whips. Kureya, a popular Zimbabwean comedian and government critic was abducted, severely beaten, and forced to drink raw sewage by six masked gunmen in August 2019. Finally, activist Mombeyarara was also abducted in August 2019 and beaten severely. He was left with a broken left leg and finger by men who accused him of organizing anti-government protests.

The Mnangagwa administration has so far failed to implement recommendations of the Motlanthe Commission of Inquiry, established to investigate widespread violence in the aftermath of the August 2018 elections. The commission presented its report to President Mnangagwa in December 2018, and found that 6 people had died and 35 others were injured as a result of actions by state security forces. It recommended that perpetrators be held accountable and that compensation be paid to families of the deceased and those who lost property.

Children's Rights

Among the Mnangagwa government's few positive steps on human rights in 2020 was the amendment of the Education Act. The amendment prohibits corporal punishment and the exclusion of pregnant girls from school in accordance with the Zimbabwe Constitution, which guarantees the right to education.

Prior to this amendment, a large number of students had suffered corporal punishment in Zimbabwe's schools. In a significant step for disability rights, the law mandates every school to provide suitable infrastructure for students with disabilities and requires authorities to ensure that schools protect the rights of students with disabilities.

Schools were closed at the end of March 2020, for at least six months as a public health measure during the pandemic. The closure affected about 4 million children across the country.

Covid-19

During 2020, the Zimbabwe government failed to provide continuous and affordable access to sufficient safe water to people across the country. The provision of safe water is an important measure to combat Covid-19.

Zimbabwe's long-standing severe water and sanitation crisis was worsened by the coronavirus pandemic and the government's imposition, on March 30, of a nationwide lockdown to slow the spread of the virus.

Over 2 million people in the capital, Harare, and the greater metropolitan area incorporating Chitungwiza, Epworth, Ruwa and Norton have no access to safe drinking water or adequate waste and wastewater disposal services. Thousands of women and school-age children spend long hours at crowded boreholes or narrow water wells to get safe, clean water.

The spread of Covid-19 in Zimbabwe posed major risks to the country's prisons and detention centers. These facilities remained unsanitary, overcrowded, and with no running water in cells for detainees to comply with recommended hygiene practices to stem the virus' spread. In March, the government acknowledged that Zimbabwe's prisons, with a capacity of 17,000, had a population of 22,000.

Between March and June, the government released 4,208 prisoners under a presidential amnesty order. Too many remained behind bars to allow for social distancing. Although masks are issued at prisons, many inmates and some wardens do not use them, partly due to insufficient understanding about protection against the virus.

Key International Actors

Following the police crackdown on anti-corruption protests in July, South Africa's governing African National Congress (ANC) dispatched a high-level delegation led by the party's Secretary-General Ace Magashule to Zimbabwe. The delegation was sent to help find a solution to the country's escalating economic and political crisis. The team raised serious concerns over Zimbabwe's deteriorating human rights situation. In August 2020, South African President Cyril Ramaphosa appointed two special envoys to help resolve the Zimbabwe crisis by identifying ways in which South Africa could assist.

On August 3, the chairperson of the African Commission on Human and Peoples' Rights, Solomon Dersso, responding to the arrests of protesters, warned in a Twitter post, "As we follow [the] situation in Zimbabwe, critical to reiterate the African Commission on Human Rights' view that actions of states even in fighting Covid-19 should comply with principles of legality, necessity, and proportionality, thus no basis for arbitrary deprivation of liberty or life, inhumane treatment or torture."

Chairperson of the African Union Commission (AUC) Moussa Faki Mahamat raised concerns about reports of disproportionate use of force by government security forces in enforcing Covid-19 emergency measures. Mahamat urged Zimbabwean authorities to exercise restraint in their response to peaceful protests.

In May, the European Union, United Kingdom and United States called for a "swift, thorough and credible investigation" into the abduction and torture of opposition Member of Parliament Joana Mamombe, along with Cecilia Chimbiri and Netsai Marova, as well an investigation into allegations of the assault on Nokuthula and Ntombizodwa Mpofu in Bulawayo.

In July, a spokesperson for the UN High Commissioner for Human Rights expressed concern about allegations that Zimbabwean authorities may be using the Covid-19 pandemic as a pretext to clamp down on freedom of expression and peaceful assembly and association. In June, UN human rights experts called on Zimbabwe to immediately end a reported pattern of enforced disappearances and torture that appear aimed at suppressing protests and dissent.